Library of
Davidson College

SHAKESPEARE: THE CRITICAL TRADITION

SHAKESPEARE: THE CRITICAL TRADITION

GENERAL EDITOR: BRIAN VICKERS
Centre for Renaissance Studies, ETH Zürich

King John Joseph Candido
Richard II Charles R. Forker
A Midsummer Night's Dream Judith and Richard Kennedy

SHAKESPEARE

THE CRITICAL TRADITION

KING JOHN

Edited by
JOSEPH CANDIDO

ATHLONE
London & Atlantic Highlands, N.J.

First published 1996 by
THE ATHLONE PRESS
1 Park Drive, London NW11 7SG
and 165 First Avenue,
Atlantic Highlands, NJ 07716

© Joseph Candido 1996
British Library Cataloguing in Publication Data
*A catalogue record for this book is available
from the British Library*

ISBN 0 485 81001 8

Library of Congress Cataloging in Publication Data
King John / edited by Joseph Candido.
     p.   cm. — (Shakespeare, the critical tradition)
   Includes bibliographical references and index.
   ISBN 0-485-81001-8
   1. Shakespeare, William, 1564-1616. King John. 2. John, King of England, 1167-1216—In literature. 3. Kings and rulers in literature. I. Candido, Joseph, 1945– . II. Series.
PR2818.K54 1996
822.3'3—dc20   96–1299
                                                                           CIP

All rights reserved. No part of this publication may be reproduced,
stored in a retrieval system, or transmitted in any form or
by any means, electronic, mechanical, photocopying or
otherwise, without prior permission in writing from the publisher.

Typeset by WestKey Limited, Falmouth, Cornwall
Printed and bound in Great Britain by
The University Press, Cambridge

FOR
MY MOTHER AND FATHER

General Editor's Preface

The aim of this series is to increase our knowledge of how Shakespeare's plays were received and understood by critics, editors, and general readers. His work, with its enormous range of represented situations, characters, styles, and moods, has always been a challenge, both to the capacity of readers and to their critical systems. Two main reactions may be expected: either the system is expanded to match the plays, or the plays are reduced to fit the system. If we study his reception in the neo-classic period, as I have done in my six-volume anthology of primary texts, *Shakespeare: The Critical Heritage, 1623–1801* (London and Boston, 1974–81), we see his plays being cropped – literally, cut, drastically adapted – to accommodate the prevailing notions of decorum and propriety. If not hacked about for the stage, they were evaluated by literary-critical criteria which seem to us self-evidently anachronistic and inappropriate, and found wanting. Yet despite this frequent mismatch between system and artefact, the focus of neo-classic critical theory on issues of characterization, structure and style did enable many writers to respond to the experience of reading or seeing his plays in a fresh and personal way.

Since most of the eighteenth-century material has been dealt with in the previously-mentioned collection, the main emphasis in this series will be on documenting the period 1790 to 1920. While the major Romantic critics (Coleridge, Hazlitt, Keats) have been often studied, and will need less representation here, there are many interesting and important writers of the early nineteenth century who have seldom attracted attention from modern historians. As one moves on chronologically, into the Victorian period, our knowledge becomes even more thin and patchy. But there was a continuous, indeed constantly increasing stream of publications in England, America, France, and Germany, hardly known today. (See my select bibliography of the 'History of Shakespeare Criticism' in the *Cambridge Bibliography of English Literature,* Third Edition, Volume 2: *1500–1700,* ed. Douglas Sedge, Cambridge University Press; forthcoming.) This period saw the founding of the Shakespeare Society by J.P. Collier in 1840, which produced a huge number of publications by 1853, when it unfortunately collapsed, following Collier's exposure as a forger. In 1873 the New Shakespere Society was founded by F.J. Furnivall, and over the following twenty years produced some eight series of publications, including its *Transactions,* which contain many important critical and scholarly essays, a group of reprints of early quartos, allusion books, bibliographies, and much else. This was also the period in which the first journals devoted exclusively to Shakespeare appeared, some short-lived, such as *Poet Lore* (Philadelphia 1889–97) and *Shakespeariana* (Philadelphia 1883), *Noctes Shakspearianae* (Winchester College,

1887), or *New Shakespeareana* (the organ of the Shakespeare Society of New York), but at least one still with us, the *Jahrbuch* of the *Deutsche Shakespeare Gesellschaft*, which appeared as such from 1865 to 1963, was divided into separate volumes for West and East Germany in 1964–65, but happily reunited in 1991.

Shakespeare's plays were constantly edited and reprinted in this period. Of the complete editions, the two great peaks are the 'third variorum' edition of James Boswell, Jr. in 21 volumes (1821), the apotheosis of the eighteenth-century editions by Johnson, Steevens, and Malone, and the Cambridge edition by William G. Clark, John Glover, and W. Aldis Wright in 9 volumes (1863–66), which in turn provided the text for the enormously long-lived one-volume 'Globe edition' (1864). The Cambridge edition, which presented Shakespeare's text with minimum annotation, broke with the eighteenth-century tradition of reprinting all the important footnotes from every earlier edition, an incremental process which burdened the page but certainly led to a great dissemination of knowledge about Shakespeare's plays. That service was recommenced on a new and more coherent plan in 1871 by Dr H. H. Furness with his *Variorum Edition* of separate plays, continued by his son H. H. Furness, Jr. (fifteen titles by 1908), and revived in our time as the *New Variorum Shakespeare*, currently under the aegis of the Modern Language Association of America. But in addition to these well-known scholarly editions, a vast number of competing sets of the plays were issued for and absorbed by an apparently insatiable public. Their popularity can be judged by the remarkable number of reprints and re-editions enjoyed, for instance, by Charles Knight's 'Pictorial edition' (8 vols., 1838–43), followed by his 'Library edition' (12 vols., 1842–44), re-christened in 1850–52 the 'National edition', not easily distinguishable from Knight's own 'Cabinet edition' (16 vols., 1847–48), not to mention his 'Imperial edition', 'Blackfriars edition', all of which being followed by a host of spin-offs of their constituent material; or those by J.P. Collier (8 vols., 1842–44, 6 vols., 1858, 8 vols., 1878, now described as having 'the Purest Text and the Briefest Notes'), or Alexander Dyce (6 vols., 1857; 9 vols., 1846–47; 10 vols., 1880–81, 1895–1901). Other notable editions came from J.O. Halliwell (16 vols., 1853–65); Howard Staunton (3 vols., 1856–60; 8 vols., 1872; 6 vols., 1860, 1873, 1894; 15 vols., 1881); John Dicks, whose 'shilling edition' (1861) had reputedly sold a million copies by 1868, but was undercut by the 'Shakespeare for Sixpence' edition (Cardiff, 1897); Nicolaus Delius (7 vols., 1854–61), the text of which was re-used by F.J. Furnivall for his one-volume 'Leopold edition' (1877, '100th Thousand' by 1910); Edward Dowden (12 vols., 1882–83); F.A. Marshall and Henry Irving in the 'Henry Irving edition' (8 vols., 1888–90); C.H. Herford's 'Eversley edition' (10 vols., 1899); the 'Stratford town edition' by A.H. Bullen and others (10 vols., 1904–7); the 'University Press' edition with notes by Sidney Lee and important introductions to the individual plays by over thirty critics (40 vols., 1906–9); and many, many more, as yet unchronicled by bibliographers.

America also launched a vigorous tradition of Shakespeare editing, starting with Gulian C. Verplanck's edition (3 vols., New York 1844–47), continuing with those by H.N. Hudson (11 vols., Boston 1851–56 and 20 vols., 1880–81); R.G. White (12 vols., Boston 1857–66, 1888), and the 'Riverside edition' (3 vols., Boston 1883); J.A. Morgan, the 'Bankside edition' (22 vols., New York, 1888–1906), with parallel texts of the plays from the quartos and folio; W.J. Rolfe, a larger edition (40 vols., New York 1871–96), and a smaller or 'Friendly edition' (20 vols., New York 1884); and two notable editions by women, Mary Cowden Clarke's (2 vols., 1860, 4 vols., 1864), and the 'First Folio edition' by Charlotte E. Porter and Helen A. Clarke (40 vols., New York 1903–13). These editions often included biographical material, illustrative notes, accounts of Shakespeare's sources, excerpts from contemporary ballads and plays, attempts to ascertain the chronology of his writings, and much else. The fortunate – largely middle-class – purchasers of these sets had access to a surprisingly wide range of material, much of it based on a sound historical knowledge. In addition to the complete works, there were countless editions of the individual plays and poems, many of them of a high scholarly standard, (the best-known being the original 'Arden edition', ed. W.J. Craig and R.H. Case in 39 vols., 1899–1924), not to mention numerous facsimiles of the folios and quartos.

The more we study the Victorian period, the less likely we shall be to indulge such facile dismissals of it as Lytton Strachey's *Eminent Victorians* (1918). Where Strachey could follow the common practice of rejecting the values of the preceding age, we now should have sufficient historical distance to place the scholarly and critical output of that period into a coherent perspective. Nineteenth-century scholars produced a number of studies that held their place as authorities for many years, and can still be used with profit. For Shakespeare's language there was E.A. Abbott, *A Shakespearian Grammar* (1869; many editions), Alexander Schmidt, *Shakespeare-Lexicon* (Berlin, 1874–5, 1886), revised and extended by Gregor Sarrazin (2 vols., Berlin, 1902), and Wilhelm Franz, *Shakespeare-Grammatik* (Halle, 1898–1900, 1909; Heidelberg, 1924). It is only very recently that modern works, such as Marvin Spevack, *A Shakespeare Thesaurus* (Hildesheim, 1993), have added anything new. On the fundamental issue of the authorship of Shakespeare's plays, such as his collaboration with John Fletcher in *Henry VIII*, the division of labour independently proposed for that play by Samuel Hickson and James Spedding in 1847 and 1850 has been largely confirmed by Jonathan Hope in *The Authorship of Shakespeare's Plays* (Cambridge, 1994). In other areas we now have more reliable tools to work with than the Victorians, but it was they who laid the basis for many of our scholarly approaches to Shakespeare.

As for their Shakespeare criticism, while a few authors are still known and read – A.C. Bradley for his *Shakespearean Tragedy* (1904), Walter Pater for his essay on 'Shakespeare's English Kings' in *Appreciations* (1889) – the majority are simply unknown. Among the English critics who clearly deserve to be revalued are Richard Simpson for his essays on Shakespeare's historical plays, R.G. Moulton, for his *Shakespeare as a Dramatic Artist* (1885; 3rd ed. 1906), Edward Dowden, and F.S. Boas. As for the many German critics whose work was eagerly translated into English – A.W. Schlegel, Hermann Ulrici, G.G. Gervinus, Karl Elze, Wilhelm Creizenach – who today can give any account of their writings?

Joseph Candido's full and detailed survey of *King John*, the first volume in this collection, has not only clarified the various critical traditions that emerged for this play in exemplary manner, but has also recovered three critics who seem to me outstanding, J. Lytelton Etty, Charlotte Porter, and John Munro. The fascination of this series will be not just the recovery of many forgotten writers but the unpredictable ways in which their work will redefine the history of Shakespeare's reception, and – paradoxical though it may seem – throw new light on the plays themselves.

Contents

	GENERAL EDITOR'S PREFACE	vi
	PREFACE	xiv
	ACKNOWLEDGEMENTS	xvi
	INTRODUCTION	1
1	EDMOND MALONE, commentary on *King John*, 1790	31
2	JOSEPH RITSON, response to Malone, 1792	42
3	GEORGE STEEVENS, response to Malone, 1793	45
4	GEORGE CHALMERS, on the date of *King John*, 1799	50
5	ELIZABETH INCHBALD, character and characterization, 1808	52
6	AUGUST WILHELM VON SCHLEGEL, personality and politics, 1815	54
7	NATHAN DRAKE, Shakespeare's art of characterization, 1817	56
8	WILLIAM HAZLITT, history and character, 1817	59
9	WILLIAM OXBERRY, prefatory remarks on *King John*, 1819	62
10	AUGUSTINE SKOTTOWE, *The Troublesome Raigne* and *King John*, 1824	64
11	SAMUEL WELLER SINGER, introduction to *King John*, 1826	68
12	GEORGE DANIEL, prefatory remarks on *King John*, 1826	70
13	JAMES BOADEN, Sarah Siddons as Constance, 1827	73
14	ANNA BROWNELL JAMESON, the character of Constance, 1832	75
15	THOMAS CAMPBELL, Sarah Siddons on Constance, 1834	82
16	THOMAS CAMPBELL, general remarks on *King John*, 1838	86
17	THOMAS PEREGRINE COURTENAY, *King John* and history, 1838	88
18	CHARLES KNIGHT, the Pictorial Edition of *King John*, 1838	97
19	GEORGE FLETCHER, the female roles in *King John*, 1843	111
20	JOSEPH HUNTER, editorial corrections in *King John*, 1845	124
21	HERMANN ULRICI, 'history', church, and state in *King John*, 1846	128
22	GULIAN CROMMELIN VERPLANCK, critical remarks on *King John*, 1847	136
23	HARTLEY COLERIDGE, critical notes on *King John*, 1851	140
24	FRANÇOIS PIERRE GUILLAUME GUIZOT, history, art, and character in *King John*, 1852	142
25	HENRY NORMAN HUDSON, introduction to *King John*, 1852	146
26	HENRY REED, history and character, 1855	152
27	WILLIAM WATKISS LLOYD, *King John* and nationalism, 1856	158
28	JOHN CHARLES BUCKNILL, the madness of Constance, 1859	168

CONTENTS

29	RICHARD GRANT WHITE, background and critical notes to *King John*, 1859	175
30	CHARLES COWDEN CLARKE, characterization, craft, and the philosophy of war, 1863	181
31	GEORG GOTTFRIED GERVINUS, politics, ethics, and character, 1863	189
32	JOHN ABRAHAM HERAUD, the politics of national interest, 1865	198
33	HENRY GILES, the transcendent sorrow of Constance, 1868	202
34	HENRY THOMAS HALL, national interest and personal loyalty, 1871	204
35	RICHARD SIMPSON, *King John* and contemporary politics, 1874	207
36	EDWARD DOWDEN, the baseness of John, 1875	212
37	ALGERNON CHARLES SWINBURNE, Shakespeare's art of characterization, 1875–6	215
38	JOHN WEISS, Constance and the nature of woman, 1876	220
39	FREDERICK JAMES FURNIVALL, *King John*, *Richard III*, and character, 1877	223
40	DENTON JAQUES SNIDER, the theme of nationality, 1877	225
41	GEORGE WILKES, *King John* and Roman Catholicism, 1877	233
42	FREDERICK GARD FLEAY, literary and historical background to *King John*, 1878	238
43	EDWARD ROSE, Shakespeare's adaptation of *The Troublesome Raigne*, 1878	242
44	GEORGE HENRY CALVERT, high praise for *King John*, 1879	249
45	HENRY JOHN HARDY, on Pandulph and history, 1887	255
46	HENRY MORLEY, on commodity, 1887	257
47	FRANCIS ALBERT MARSHALL, a balanced assessment of *King John*, 1888	261
48	HIRAM CORSON, on Constance and Arthur, 1889	265
49	WALTER HORATIO PATER, kingship, personality, and the human condition, 1889	270
50	OLIVER ELTON, the artistic excellence of *King John*, 1890	272
51	JAMES APPLETON MORGAN, *The Troublesome Raigne* and *King John*, 1892	275
52	LOUIS LEWES, on Constance, Elinor, and Blanch, 1894	280
53	BEVERLEY ELLISON WARNER, historical character and dramatic character, 1894	284
54	BARRETT WENDELL, the oddities of *King John*, 1894	287
55	FREDERICK SAMUEL BOAS, on the principal characters, 1896	290
56	GEORG MORRIS COHEN BRANDES, Shakespeare's uneven artistry, 1898	296
57	HENRY SEBASTIAN BOWDEN, Shakespeare's Roman Catholicism, 1899	301
58	CHARLES HAROLD HERFORD, Shakespeare's maturing artistry, 1899	307
59	HAMILTON WRIGHT MABIE, *King John* as a transitional play, 1900	311
60	GEORGE CHARLES MOORE SMITH, weaknesses and strengths of *King John*, 1900	313
61	J. LYTELTON ETTY, the character of John, 1901	318
62	FELIX EMANUEL SCHELLING, Shakespeare and Davenport, 1902	322
63	RICHARD GREEN MOULTON, the pendulum of history in *King John*, 1903	324
64	EDMUND KERCHEVER CHAMBERS, the formlessness of *King John*, 1906	329
65	GEORGE PIERCE BAKER, Shakespeare's dramatic development, 1907	332
66	HENRY CHARLES BEECHING, on the religion of Shakespeare, 1907	334

CONTENTS

67	RICHARD GARNETT, introduction to *King John*, 1907	336
68	IVOR BERTRAM JOHN, *King John* and *Richard II*, 1907	342
69	CHARLOTTE ENDYMION PORTER, the belittling of John, 1910	345
70	FRANK HARRIS, Constance and Shakespeare's shrewish wife, 1911	348
71	JOHN EDWARD MASEFIELD, on treachery and 'Englishness', 1911	351
72	STOPFORD AUGUSTUS BROOKE, on John, Faulconbridge, and Constance, 1913	355
73	JOHN JAMES MUNRO, Shakespeare's use of *The Troublesome Raigne*, 1913	362
74	JAMES BRANDER MATTHEWS, the artistic flaws of *King John*, 1913	367
75	HORACE HOWARD FURNESS, JR., on the Bastard, John, and the play, 1919	370
	NOTES	372
	A SELECT BIBLIOGRAPHY	387
	INDEX	391

Preface

The aim of the present volume is to extend the work of historical scholarship begun by Brian Vickers in his *Shakespeare: The Critical Heritage*, 6 vols (London, 1974–81) by providing a detailed examination of critical response to *King John* in the period 1790 to 1920. In accordance with the rubrics of the series, the emphasis is on the *English* rather than the continental tradition; hence included among the printed texts are only those volumes of continental criticism that, by virtue of being translated into English, have had a substantial influence upon scholarship written in English. Also in accordance with the rubrics of the series, scholarship dealing exclusively with theatrical history has been excluded, except when material of this sort raises issues about *King John* of a literary or interpretive nature, or when it seems in some way to reflect or direct the critical tradition.

The Introduction attempts to give a sense of the critical fortunes of *King John* from the earliest commentary about it to the most recent. It is hoped that this will both help to contextualize the scholarship excerpted here as well as point to important continuities and changes within the critical tradition. Those wishing to pursue some of the questions raised in the Introduction more fully may consult the over fifteen hundred items in Deborah T. Curren-Aquino's *'King John': An Annotated Bibliography* (New York, 1994), which concentrates predominantly on post-1940 scholarship on the play, but also includes many important items preceding that date.

The texts in this collection are taken from the first printed edition, unless otherwise noted; they reflect the following editorial changes: (1) the elimination of quotation marks in set-off quotations and at the beginning of each new line of prose; (2) the normalization of spelling and capitalization in the names of writers (including Shakespeare's), the names of Shakespearian characters, and the titles of plays, books, and articles; (3) the incorporation of some set-off quotations into the body of the text for ease of readability or to conserve space; (4) the alteration, in some instances, of punctuation, spelling, or italicization where older forms of typography or usage might create ambiguities for the modern reader, particularly in the case of book titles, play titles, or proper names. The emphasis throughout, however, has been to retain the character of the original if at all possible.

Footnotes in the original documents are retained, *except* when these designate act, scene, or line numbers, or consist of quoted material that modern usage normally dictates be placed in the text proper. Such footnotes have been silently omitted, and the designation or quotation placed in the appropriate place in the text. All footnotes, both those taken from the original documents and those included by the current editor, are designated by a single, consecutive numbering system. In order to differentiate these two separate types of documentation, however, the following method has been adopted: bracketed footnotes, i.e., [1], [2], etc., are those included by the current editor; unbracketed footnotes, 3, 4, etc., are those found in the original documents. Editorial notes within the text are also placed within square brackets, as are all other editorial additions. Omissions in the text are indicated by ellipsis dots (three at the beginning or in the middle of a sentence, four at the end), larger omissions by three asterisks.

All Shakespearian act, scene, and line references are to *The Riverside Shakespeare* (Boston, 1974), but passages in the documents are quoted as they appear in the documents themselves, not as they appear in the *Riverside* edition, for the obvious reason that a reading of any given passage is determined by the particular text used by an author and not a later version of it. All references to *The Troublesome Raigne* (by scene and line number) are to the edition of J. W. Sider (New York, 1979). Quotations from *The Troublesome Raigne* are treated in the same manner as those from *The Riverside Shakespeare*; that is, all quotations from the play are faithful to the text cited in the documents, with citations geared to the text of Sider's edition.

Dates of translations are those of the first *English* edition unless otherwise noted; classical translations are taken from those in the Loeb Classical Library.

Acknowledgements

It is a pleasure to acknowledge the gracious assistance of the librarians and staff of the Mullins Library of the University of Arkansas, the Sterling and Beinecke Libraries of Yale University, the University of Texas Library and the Harry Ransom Research Center at Austin, Texas, and the Indiana University Library and the Lilly Library at Bloomington, Indiana. I should like especially to thank Beth Juhl and Susanna Price of Mullins Library for their many resourceful and unfailing kindnesses. The completion of this project would have been greatly delayed if not for the generous financial assistance of Dean Bernard Madison of the Fulbright College of Arts and Sciences at the University of Arkansas, and Charles Adams, chairman of the English Department at the University of Arkansas. I am indebted also to many colleagues and friends for their wise counsel and support, among them Deborah T. Curren-Aquino, Charles R. Forker, Robert Turner, Richard Knowles, Virginia Haas, Thomas Berger, Rhonda Adams, and Lyna Lee Montgomery. To Brian Vickers, the general editor of this series, I owe a special debt of gratitude; his unfailing energy, meticulousness and sound advice, made me a better literary historian and this a better book. As usual, my wife Anne Marie read more of the manuscript than she should have and, in her accustomed manner, administered kind correction.

Introduction

I
Beginnings to 1790

The guarded and sometimes grudging appreciation so regularly accorded *King John* extends to its critical beginnings. The prominent group of seventeenth-century writers, commentators, adapters, and men of letters who did so much to shape the early critical response to Shakespeare – people such as Jonson, Pepys, D'Avenant, Dryden, Shadwell, Rymer, Ravenscroft, Otway, Tate, Dennis, Gould, Langbaine, Collier, et al. – have, literally, nothing of critical importance to say about the play. Looking to the major literary figures of the seventeenth century for early interpretive stirrings on *King John*, we bend our eyes on vacancy. It is not until nearly a century after the publication of the First Folio of 1623, which contains the first printed text of *King John*, that critical interest in the play appears in any concrete or recognizable form. Charles Gildon (1710), a devoted neo-classicist who had nevertheless assailed Thomas Rymer's *Short View of Tragedy* (1673) in an attempt to 'vindicate' Shakespeare from Rymer's zealously prescriptive outbursts, is the first to confer upon the play anything resembling serious critical attention.[1] In predictable fashion, he disparages its lack of Aristotelian 'tragic Imitation' and 'just Design' (339), and faults the behavior of Constance and the Bastard (whom he nonetheless praises as highly engaging dramatic characters) for being directed to no proper end. Yet despite such reservations, Gildon, like so many later critics of the play, extols the passion of Constance as 'just and masterly' (340), except of course at those moments when it descends to un-ladylike extravagance, as in the scolding-match with Elinor. Juliet Dusinberre has recently commented upon the 'embarrassment' this celebrated scene has produced for generations of actors and directors from the eighteenth century onward;[2] and it is interesting to see concerns over the propriety of the episode appearing in the very first critical comment on the play. Indeed, a similar suspicion regarding the decorousness of Constance's behavior is suggested in the editorial practice of Gildon's contemporary, Alexander Pope. In his idiosyncratic and controversial edition of Shakespeare (1723–5), Pope quite literally marginalized certain passages that he deemed unworthy of Shakespeare's genius; these he 'degraded' to the bottom of the page where they were clearly visible to the reader as banished lines. In *King John*, one of the most thoroughly degraded plays in Pope's edition, nearly one-quarter of Constance's role drops to the lower margin, the majority of her rejected lines coming during the 'embarrassing' episode with Elinor.[3]

King John, then, does not appear to have entered the critical lists as one of

Shakespeare's most respected or inviolate creations. Among the small but influential group of Shakespearian editors preceding Johnson (1765), only William Warburton appears to have sensed even the *potential* tragic powers of the play. Lewis Theobald, in the headnote to *King John* in his edition of 1733, credits Warburton with the following observation:

> Of all the *English* Princes, (as Mr. *Warburton* observ'd to me,) that *Shakespeare* has taken into Tragedy, King *John* was the fittest to have made a Hero for a Tragedy on the antient Plan. *Henry* IV, V, and VIII, had Qualities great enough for it, but were generally fortunate. *Richard* II, and *Henry* VI, (*sit Verbo Venia*) were, at times, little better than Poltrons: And *Richard* III. was so black a Villain, that the Antients would have thought him fitter for a Gibbet than a Stage. But *John* had that Turbulence and Grandeur of the Passions, that Inconstancy of Temper, that equal Mixture of Good and Ill, and that Series of Misfortunes consequent thereto, as might make him very fit for a Hero in a just Composition.[4]

Warburton's telling proviso, 'in a just Composition', turns his near-praise of the play into critical regret over its failure to observe strict neo-classical principles of tragedy. Even in expressing a certain elemental attraction to *King John*, Warburton finally aligns himself with those, like Gildon and Pope, who are troubled by what they perceive as serious inadequacies in the play's decorousness or design.

Colley Cibber's notorious adaptation, *Papal Tyranny in the Reign of King John* (1745),[5] however, is perhaps the most obvious expression of a certain eighteenth-century disregard for the artistic integrity of the work. Cibber mangled Shakespeare's original, excising, supplementing, or otherwise modifying long passages of dialogue, deleting Elinor, Austria, and the entire first act, significantly diminishing the role of Faulconbridge, and greatly expanding the roles of Constance and Pandulph, the latter of which he played himself. The Prologue, which Cibber spoke in performance, frankly dismisses *King John* as a play of inferior artistry:

> Yet Fame, nor Favour ever deign'd to say,
> *King John* was station'd as a first rate Play;
> Though strong and sound the Hulk, yet ev'ry Part
> Reach'd not the merit of his [Shakespeare's] usual art! (9–12)

But Cibber's crowning disparagement of *King John* comes in the Dedication of his play to Philip, Earl of Chesterfield, in which he claims that 'I have endeavour'd to make it more like a Play than what I found it in *Shakespeare*' (Sig.A4). What Cibber found considerably less of in Shakespeare is the strident anti-Catholicism with which he invests *Papal Tyranny*. This feature of the play, as critics have frequently noted, dovetailed conveniently with widespread fears at the time of an imminent Roman Catholic rebellion favoring the royal claim of Charles Edward Stuart. Far less frequently noted, however, is a statement in Cibber's Dedication that initiates a scholarly debate on the subject of religion that is to ripen some hundred years later. Anticipating what was to become a *cause célèbre* for a generation of nineteenth-century critics, Cibber addresses the question of Shakespeare's Roman Catholicism with particular reference to John's statement decrying the practice of buying and selling spiritual influence: 'Purchase corrupted pardon of a man / Who in that sale sells pardon from himself' (3.1.166ff.). Cibber argues that no Roman Catholic could possibly have written such an obvious affront to papal authority, and that the lines reflect Shakespeare's real feelings toward the old church. But despite whatever topical (or theological) importance Cibber tried to ascribe to *Papal Tyranny*, the play never achieved real dramatic success. It was incisively derided by an anonymous author who, as Gildon had done, praised Shakespeare's characterization of Faulconbridge and Constance even as he wryly belittled Cibber's attempt to make *King John* 'more like a Play' by reforming it along neo-classical lines: 'But of all *Shakespeare*'s Plays this is that which sins most against the three Grand Unities of the Stage, *Time, Place* and *Action*, and is on that Account the less reducible to *Rule*'.[6] Interestingly, this writer, whose essay bristles with urbane irony on questions such as Cibber's attempts to 'inspirit' John with Protestant zeal, is silent on the matter of religious bias. His remarks on the violation of the classical unities in *King John*, however, echo a widespread eighteenth-century attitude, initiated by Gildon and reinforced editorially by Pope and dramaturgically by Cibber, that the play somehow lacks form. So it is that John Upton (1748) can impugn *King John* as 'faulty' in structure and design, characterizing it as an uninspired 'mixture of incoherent and monstrous parts' pieced together 'without head or tail'.[7] Citing *King John* and *Henry VIII* in particular, Upton defends the Horatian principle that the life and actions of a single figure do not necessarily constitute a single dramatic action; in both plays, he alleges, Shakespeare sacrifices dramatic unity to mere chronicle writing, a point that is to surface in various ways and with far more critical elaboration throughout the nineteenth century.

The great editorial tradition of the neo-classical period (and the related practice of publishing scholarly 'notes', 'readings', or glosses on disputed or problematical Shakespearian passages) naturally played a vital role in establishing the early critical agenda for *King John*.[8] Pope, for example, created the play's most enduring critical red herring by attributing *The Troublesome Raigne* (with impressionistic conviction but without real evidence) jointly to Shakespeare and William Rowley, thus muddying the waters of scholarly debate on the sources of *King John* for generations to come.[9] Just how pervasive this surmise became in some quarters may be seen in the remarks of John Bowle (1764), who in his preface to a reprint of *The Troublesome Raigne* asserts that the play is not only Shakespeare's but also 'his earliest publication'.[10] Bowle finds the canonical *King John* 'curtailed', and praises *The Troublesome Raigne* for its 'singular humour . . . particularly in the ballad-metre-dialogue between [the Bastard] and the friar' (Sig.A3). Although Pope's claim of at least partly Shakespearian authorship of *The Troublesome Raigne* was based on his belief in the authenticity of the 1611 quarto (with the designation 'Written by W. Sh.' on the title page), he was apparently unaware of the existence of the earlier 1591 quarto in which no authorial attribution appeared. Richard Farmer (1767) exposed the basis of Pope's error, casting serious doubt upon Shakespeare's putative authorship and his supposed collaboration with Rowley.[11] Yet Pope's conjectures had staying power. Even Edward Capell (1779), who imperiously rejected Rowley's purported hand in *The Troublesome Raigne*, nonetheless agreed partially with Pope and entirely with Gerard Langbaine (1691) in asserting Shakespeare's authorship, and with Bowle in situating the play at the outset of Shakespeare's career:

> Shakespeare was the author alone of the 'John' in two parts, whose second begins at Arthur's attempt to escape and his consequent death: From evidence of their date [1591] and some other, we may pronounce them – his first undisputed excursion into the regions of drama; and, as such, they are but a feeble performance, sprinkled with some quotations from classicks, and, in the comedy part, with some monkish Latin: notwithstanding, they bear his marks in some places, and in the dying scene strongly. . . .[12]

Capell, whose pleasure in his own wise avoidance of the errors of various 'moderns' is unmistakably apparent in his notes,[13] ironically 'corrected' Pope by refining and then elaborating upon one of his maligned predecessor's most reckless statements of fact. In so doing he also managed to tinge his sagacity with the unsubstantiated speculations of Langbaine and Bowle.

Certainly one of the most critically influential editions of the eighteenth century was that of Dr. Johnson (1765).[14] In a series of terse but evidential explanatory notes to *King John*, Johnson addresses many of the important critical issues that had already gathered around the play even as he establishes the grounds for new areas of inquiry. He sides with Farmer in rejecting Pope's attribution of *The Troublesome Raigne* to Shakespeare and dismisses Rowley's hand in the play; praises Shakespeare's 'knowledge of the passions' as highly 'agreeable to nature' in his depiction of the sorrows of Constance (415); upholds Pope's insertion of twelve altered and rearranged lines of the Bastard's speech from *The Troublesome Raigne* (2.133–56) at 3.1.133, adding that 'there are many other passages in the old play, of great value' (417); defends the speech of Pandulph at 3.1.280ff., which Warburton had ridiculed as casuistical and nonsensical; and praises the episode in which John seeks to blame Hubert for Arthur's death (4.2.231ff.) as exhibiting 'many touches of nature' and 'an intimate knowledge of mankind' (425). Johnson's final assessment of *King John*, in its tone of cautiously restrained approbation, typifies the critical ambivalence about the play so characteristic of his age:

> The tragedy of *King John*, though not written with the utmost power of Shakespeare, is varied with a very pleasing interchange of incidents and characters. The Lady's grief is very affecting, and the character of the Bastard contains that mixture of greatness and levity which this authour delighted to exhibit. (428)

Perhaps Johnson's most revealing comments on *King John*, however, come in two passing references not included in either his explanatory notes to the play or his short critical afterword. In evaluating Shakespeare's histories as a group, he ranks *King John* (along with *Henry VIII* and *Richard III*) as belonging 'in the second class' of chronicle plays; and elsewhere, in defending Shakespeare's authorship of the *Henry VI* trilogy, he reinvigorates the issue of the formal inadequacies of *King John* raised previously by Gildon, Cibber, and Upton: 'These plays [the *Henry VI* plays], considered, without regard to characters and incidents, merely as narratives in verse, are more happily conceived and more accurately finished than those of *King John, Richard II*, or the tragick scenes of *Henry IV.* and *V.*'[15] By thus locating literary value in *King John* mainly in its parts (i.e., isolated 'characters' and 'incidents') rather than in the structural or artistic whole, Johnson gives further impetus to a developing critical response to the play: *King John* is an essentially flawed drama with some fine things in it.[16]

Nowhere is this attitude more apparent than in the remarks of Francis Gentleman (1770), the author of the first full-length critical essay on the play.[17] Gentleman praises many episodes in *King John* for their artistry and fidelity to nature, particularly the scene in which John tempts Hubert to murder Arthur, and the ensuing conversation between Hubert and Arthur in which the young prince begs successfully for mercy. In the latter episode Shakespeare has 'most happily traced nature, and . . . touched the tender feelings in a powerful manner, without straining them too much', even to the extent of moving an audience to tears of 'concern and satisfaction' (II, 162). Gentleman also praises the 'pathetic and forceable' grief of Constance (II, 171), but like others before him, draws a sharp distinction between her elevated sorrow over the demise of her son and her termagant-like scolding in the fight with Elinor.[18] In so doing he becomes the critical locus for a sort of bifurcated eighteenth-century perspective on the passion of Constance: her temperamental extravagance is noble as an expression of victimized sorrow, but offensive as fierce combativeness. The gross disregard 'for essential delicacy' (II, 157) that Gentleman sees in the scolding-match, however, is only one instance of the indecorousness that in his view pervades the play. To Gentleman's ears Austria and the Bastard sound more like 'coalheavers than men of rank and education' (II, 157); and the Bastard on the whole is too much given to licentiousness and rude expression, often reminding us, as he does in the scene with Lady Faulconbridge, of 'the bully of a brothel' (II, 156). The death of John is unseemly, the entire first act better omitted,[19] and the language in places obscure and ill-suited. Moreover, Gentleman's final assessment of the play could almost serve as a short abstract of neo-classical misgivings over its formal limitations:

> In writing this play, SHAKESPEARE disclaimed every idea of regularity, and has huddled such a series of historical events on the back of one another, as shame the utmost stretch of probability; his muse travels lightning winged, being here, there, and every where, in the space of a few minutes. (II, 167)

Pronouncing *King John*, 'shameful' in its 'irregularity of plot', Gentleman ends his critical remarks by asserting that the conceptual and dramatic limitations of the play render it 'a better reading than an acting piece' (II, 172).

In the wake of such observations it is not a little surprising to come upon the criticism of Elizabeth Griffith (1775).[20] Although Griffith epitomizes a widespread eighteenth-century preoccupation with the morality of art, she reprimands those critics of her day whose 'learned ignorance' causes them to judge Shakespeare by a set of 'antient' and narrowly prescriptive rules: 'Shakespeare is a *model*, not a *copy*; he looked into nature, not into books, both for men and works' (vi). In thus distancing herself from critics like Gildon, Upton, and Gentleman, and in aligning herself with Johnson whom she often cites with approval, Griffith typifies a prominent strain of eighteenth-century Shakespearian criticism: aesthetically her sensibilities draw her away from rigid neo-classicism, morally they reincline her to the ethical prescriptions of her age. She does not, for example, join the chorus of those who fault the structural inadequacies of *King John*; rather she ignores the issue in order to pursue two quite separate concerns: the moral and ethical truths represented in the play and, more importantly, the characterization of Constance. Griffith's stated critical purpose is to place Shakespeare's 'Ethic merits in a more conspicuous point of view' (ix).[21] This she does in her discussion of *King John* by citing numerous passages worthy of moral reflection, among them the Bastard's speech on Commodity, his later attempt to bolster the spirits of John (5.1.44ff.), John's recrimination of Hubert, and Salisbury's conversation with the Dauphin on rebellion and duty (5.2.9ff.). But it is in her treatment of the personality of Constance that she becomes most critically engaged. Griffith deals with the problem of the bifurcated view of Constance's passions, so sharply defined in Gentleman, by simply ignoring the scolding match with Elinor entirely and focusing instead on Constance's grief over the fate of Arthur. Following Johnson, she emphasizes Shakespeare's fidelity to nature in his depiction of Constance as a fearless woman buffeted by misfortune. Griffith somewhat embroiders the observations of her critical predecessors, however, by seeing Constance not only as an 'affecting' victim (177, 180) but also as a figure of considerable moral grandeur:

> In the same Scene [3.1], when Salisbury tells her that the two kings had sent for her, and that *he must not return* without her, the answer she makes is full of that dignity, which grief, mixed with resentment, is capable of conferring on illustrious unfortunates; and her whole demeanour upon that occasion is expressive of a great soul, rendered still braver by misfortunes. (178)

It is something of a critical commonplace to dismiss Griffith as a reflexive and ponderous moralist who reduces Shakespeare's plays to dramatic homilies;[22] the fact remains, however, that whatever her critical limitations, she is the first to see greatness as well as pathos in the sorrows of Constance.

Significant, too, is another aspect of Griffith's response to Constance that seems to indicate a subtle but important change in the critical perception of the character. Griffith alludes in some detail to the nature of Constance's language, using such words as 'shocking', 'wild', 'enthusiastic', and 'suffocating' to describe its effect upon others (179–81). She attributes particular importance to the lines 'never, never / Must I behold my pretty Arthur more' (3.4.88–9):

> There is something very tender and affecting in her making use of the epithet *pretty*, in the last line. It has a better effect there than *dearest*, *angel*, or even *lovely*, (though this last has a more comprehensive sense) would have had in that place. I must beg leave to refer to the Reader's own taste for the justness of this observation; for I own, I cannot explain why it strikes me in this manner myself. (180–1)

The idea that Constance is somehow a dexterous manipulator of language, and that in language lies a good deal of her 'affecting' power, also manifests itself in a comical Epilogue to *King John* written by George Keate to accompany a production of the play at Hackney in 1769 but first published in 1781.[23] In Keate's Epilogue Constance reappears, despite her terrible misfortunes in the play proper, as the rhetorically triumphant 'bully' of two kings, likening herself to such female subduers of men as Xantippe, Roxana, Cleopatra, Joan of Arc, and even Queen Elizabeth. Defending her declamatory speeches throughout the play (but not distinguishing between her scolding and her 'affecting' modes of speech), Constance explains that 'I had no Weapon left me but my Tongue'; she then suggests to all women in the audience that the only sure way to 'Dethrone usurping Man' is to out-talk him. Keate's Epilogue can of course be easily dismissed as a frivolous set-piece designed (in the manner of the genre) as a pleasantly urbane severing of dramatic illusion. This it most certainly is. But in its own way and on its own terms it touches a critical nerve that both hearkens back to Gildon's earliest misgivings over the propriety of Constance's language and reinforces Griffith's notions that the character somehow is grandly affective. To borrow Dusinberre's term once more, Constance could be seen as 'embarrassing' for both reasons: she offends not only because of her indecorousness, but perhaps also because her strength of passion may somehow subvert male power.

Certainly the most exhaustive eighteenth-century treatment of *King John* is that of Thomas Davies (1784).[24] Davies's remarks on the play are a curious and lively mixture of source study, character analysis, theatrical history of a decidedly anecdotal nature, occasional moral digressions, and textual readings at once pedantic, charming, and politely contentious. His importance as a critic, however, cannot be underestimated, for he is the earliest and most detailed defender of the merits of the play. Using Cibber as a sort of critical whipping-boy, Davies often magnifies the artistry of *King John* by comparing its excellencies with the 'cold crudities and prosaic offals' of *Papal Tyranny* (I, 52). Davies is important also in that he addresses, in one way or another, many of the scholarly concerns that were fast developing into an identifiable critical tradition. He affirms that Shakespeare had no hand in *The Troublesome Raigne*, admires the 'noble ardor' of the Bastard (I, 97), agrees tacitly with Cibber on the matter of Shakespeare's Roman Catholicism, and joins those who praise the conversation in Act III between John and Hubert and the interview in Act IV between Hubert and Arthur (despite what he sees in the latter as Shakespeare's unfortunate habit of playing on words). Moreover, Davies often pushes to the critical forefront issues for which he has seldom received full scholarly credit. In taking up the question of Shakespeare's erroneous conflation of Leopold, Duke of Austria and Widomar, Viscount of Limoges into the single character of the Duke of Austria,[25] he observes that 'Shakespeare oftener studies stage effect than he adheres to the truth of history; and, in treating of remote story, he is certainly justifiable for this deviation' (I, 19). The sentiment is one later critics would have done well to ponder, or at least to credit Davies with as they debated the question of Shakespeare's fidelity to historical truth. Likewise, Davies receives scant credit from his critical successors for raising the question of the omission of Magna Carta from *King John*, which he attributes to the popularity of Queen Elizabeth and a lingering attitude favoring royal prerogative. He is also the first critic actually to praise the structure of the play, citing Act IV in particular for its 'judicious' and 'artfully contrived' management of plot (I, 67–8). Davies's praise for the 'grief, anguish, and despair' of Constance is unstinting; even the trials of Clytemnestra, Hecuba, Andromache, Crëusa, and Merope do not compare to hers (I, 54–5). Yet despite this praise for the 'sublime pathos' of the Constance of Act III, Davies nonetheless rather docilely follows those who find her earlier behavior more like that of a 'scold or virago' than a lady of real nobility (I, 33). In his final assessment of the play, however, he strikes out in a critical direction all his own:

> To Cibber's vanity we owe the revival of this excellent tragedy, which had lain in obscurity above one hundred and twenty years.
> I think its worth has been rather underrated. . . . (I, 114)

Even if Davies had contributed nothing else to the early debate on *King John*, this lone note of critical independence should have been enough to spare his remarks on the play the misfortune of scholarly neglect.

II
Malone to Furness

No scholar of the eighteenth century did more to solidify and define the critical tradition of *King John* than Edmond Malone (No. 1). In an influential essay on the dating of Shakespeare's plays first published with the 1778 Johnson-Steevens edition and later reprinted in his own edition of 1790, Malone assigns *King John* to 1596.[26] In so doing he becomes the first to link the play with the death of Shakespeare's son Hamnet in August of that year (seeing the playwright's own grief reflected in the lamentations of Constance) and with the English expedition to Cadiz in June 1596, to which he finds an allusion at 2.1.66ff. Malone's notes to the play are an important scholarly testament in their own right, if for no other reason than that they engage and often challenge so much of the editorial and interpretive tradition informing *King John*, particularly the scholarly recklessness of Pope. In his edition Malone frequently omits, shortens, supplements, or otherwise corrects the notes of previous commentators and, of course, adds some new notes of his own. Malone's re-shaped commentary, as well as his remarks on the date of the play, helped reinvigorate the scholarly animus of old antagonists of his such as Joseph Ritson (No. 2) and George Steevens (No. 3), and later George Chalmers (No. 4), each of whom had already contributed importantly to the critical tradition of *King John* and continued to do so while challenging Malone.[27]

King John could hardly rival *Hamlet* as a literary and cultural icon for the generation of Romantic critics that followed Malone; nevertheless early nineteenth-century responses to the play were by no means sparse or insignificant. Although Coleridge wrote virtually nothing about *King John*, he occasionally referred to the play in his lectures and table talk, citing it, along with *Richard II* and *Henry VIII*, as an example of historical drama in its purest form.[28] He had special praise for the natural language of Constance's grief as well as the expressively subtle characterization of James Gurney, remarking in the latter case on Shakespeare's extraordinary 'power *in minimus*' to create a genuine character in a single line of dialogue.[29] Schlegel (No. 6) and Hazlitt (No. 8), however, were the two most influential Romantic critics of the play. The political uses to which the Romantics put literary criticism has, of course, been thoroughly documented, most recently by Jonathan Bate;[30] and in Schlegel this tendency is unmistakably apparent. Schlegel's belief in the public theatre as a kinetic locus for the fashioning of a national identity clearly appears in his remarks on *King John*, which he regards as a fitting prologue to Shakespeare's two great historical tetralogies. The dramatist's skill in combining a certain political cynicism with a sympathetic vision of frail humanity also appealed to the German critic, as did the topicality of the play in the current atmosphere of anti-French (and specifically anti-Napoleonic) political and cultural sentiment. In Hazlitt's criticism of *King John* the sympathetic strain in Romantic critical thought finds eloquent expression, particularly in Hazlitt's artfully contrived melancholy over the fact that the suffering depicted in the play had a real truth in history. Hazlitt follows the fast-developing practice of relegating the morally loathsome John to the critical background of the play, preferring instead to focus empathetically upon characters he either pities or admires, like Arthur, Constance, and the Bastard. Much of the remaining criticism of the first thirty years of the century, like that of Inchbald (No. 5), Drake (No. 6), Oxberry (No.9), Skottowe (No. 10), Singer (No. 11), and Daniel (No. 12), merely ratifies common critical assumptions: John is cruel and venal, his scene with Hubert (3.3) and Hubert's with Arthur (4.1) are superb,[31] Constance is the embodiment of lofty maternal suffering, Arthur is a figure of delicate and tender pity, and the Bastard a lively compound of wit and vibrant animal spirits. Here, we may say, response to *King John* seemed comfortably to be at rest, until a flurry of critical activity, primarily occurring in the decade of the thirties, worked some unsettling variations on settled critical themes.[32]

The first real watershed in the critical history of *King John* in the period after Malone comes, appropriately enough, by way of the theatre. On 10 December 1783 at Drury Lane Sarah Siddons gave her first performance in the role of Constance, a dramatic event repeated on various occasions until 8 June 1812, and one which in time acquired the status of a major critical interpretation. The powerful influence of Siddons's performance may be seen in the views of Inchbald (No. 5) and perhaps Daniel (No. 12); but it is through the work of Boaden (No. 13), Jameson (No. 14), and Campbell (No. 15), that Siddons's interpretation of the role gathers real critical force. As early as Gildon, critics had grappled with the perceived anomalies of Constance's character, a woman at once dignified and indecorous, engaging victim and offensive scold. Boaden only partially addresses these difficulties in his discussion of Siddons's performance, suggesting that even in Constance's frenzy there is an intellectual dimension that Siddons alone seems able to capture. Jameson and Campbell, however, take matters much further. Jameson was a friend and admirer of Siddons (as well as of her niece Fanny Kemble) and contemplated writing a biography about her, but was defeated in this purpose by Campbell, who refused to relinquish his rights to a project he had already begun.[33] Nevertheless, in Jameson's *Characteristics of Women* (1832) and Campbell's *Life of Mrs. Siddons* (1834), there emerges a rather striking interpretive consensus on the character of Constance, undoubtedly owing to Siddons's own detailed remarks on the acting of the role printed in Campbell's biography – remarks with which Jameson apparently was also familiar some two years earlier, since they seem so clearly to inform her own understanding of the character.[34]

Siddons thus affects the critical tradition of *King John* in two major ways: (1) through her performance of the role of Constance over a thirty-year period on the London stage, and (2) through her apparent influence over the critical response to her own performance in the work of both Jameson and Campbell. The Siddons-Jameson-Campbell school, despite whatever animus Jameson and Campbell may have retained over the question of biographical authority, speaks virtually with one voice on Constance: the character is one of 'pride' and 'majesty', but above all a 'mother' ('maternal' is the preferred adjective in all criticism on Constance), whose considerable imaginative and intellectual 'power' is selflessly spent in securing the interests of her son; she is ambitious only for him, never for herself. By emphasizing the motherly and essentially female aspects of Constance (both Jameson and Campbell refer to her as a mother eagle), but linking these qualities with an uncommon 'power' of imagination, intellect, and pride, the Siddons-Jameson-Campbell triumvirate place the so-called indecorousness of Constance in favorable light. She is contentious, but only to defend her son; ambitious, but only for his sake; and in this expression of maternal devotion her innate passion rises to a powerful and imaginative grandeur.[35]

As the decade of the thirties drew to a close, two studies appeared which did much to establish the scholarly agenda for *King John* for the rest of the century: Thomas Courtenay's essays on the historical accuracy of Shakespeare's histories (No. 17), and Charles Knight's extremely popular Pictorial Edition of the plays (No. 18). Although Courtenay concedes in his essay on *King John* that any historical dramatist must take liberties with history, his rather pedantic treatment of Shakespeare's departures from historical truth becomes a sort of critical lightning rod for those, like Knight, whose scholarly tastes include occasionally florid defenses of higher truth and imaginative prerogative. These arguments, of course, are not new (Knight can sound a bit like Sidney, and Davies had mildly addressed the issue over fifty years earlier); but they do invest the critical debate on *King John* with a certain renewed energy as a result of Courtenay's earnest pedantry (he worries about misrepresenting history to the young) and Knight's often witty and ironic response to it. Courtenay's attitudes, whether the critic is mentioned by name or not, soon become an object of almost universal scorn. Even those who value historical scholarship, like Hermann Ulrici (No. 21), Richard Grant White (No. 29), G. G. Gervinus (No. 31), and H. J. Hardy (No. 45), dismiss his reductively 'historical' approach out of hand.[36] Indeed, the spate of essayists and editors of the period cautioning that the dramatic artist has no obligation to adhere to the facts of history all clearly write with Courtenay's views in mind. His inoffensive and well-intentioned pedantry thus provides the ideological foundation for one of the largest (and most comfortable) critical bandwagons of the day.

Knight, however, does much more than just discredit Courtenay in his edition of *King John*; he mounts a serious attack on Malone's dating of the play, in the process questioning the traditional use of topical allusion for such purposes, and also provides a cogent defense of the play's much-maligned structure, seeing a formal unity in its repeated focus upon the fate of Arthur. But it is in his biography of Shakespeare (1843), comprising the final volume of the Pictorial Edition, that Knight resuscitates an issue that had essentially lain dormant since Cibber's *Papal Tyranny*: the question of Shakespeare's religious attitudes as reflected in *King John*. Shakespeare's religious orientation, of course, had been addressed at length by earlier biographers, usually without specific allusion to the play; but the question becomes a matter of critical importance for *King John* by virtue of the fact that Knight (without crediting Cibber) rather polemically cites John's statement against the selling of indulgences (3.1.166ff.) as strong evidence of Shakespeare's aversion to Roman Catholicism. Knight's statement occupies a mere three lines in his biography; it would spark one of the most prolonged scholarly debates of the century.[37]

Modifications to the view of Constance's character expressed by Siddons and Jameson in the 1830s appeared in the following decade from George Fletcher (No. 19). Fletcher was a great admirer of Helen Faucit, one of Siddons's notable successors in the role of Constance, and saw in Faucit's performance the basis for a necessary corrective to the Siddons-Jameson perception of the character. Faucit lacked Siddons's majestic stage presence (the 'power', 'pride', and imaginative energy that so attracted Jameson); but her own special gifts of 'tenderness' and 'feeling' allowed her to create a character whom Fletcher regards as more authentically Shakespearian in 'intellectual' and 'poetical' qualities than the grandly imperious but less graceful Constance of Siddons. Fletcher not only refuses to ascribe any trace of ambition to Constance, he further softens the notion of the character's majestic pride and passion by seeing her as highly composed – indeed perfectly rational – in her feminine poise and tenderness of spirit. In Fletcher we are as far from the termagant Constance as nineteenth-century criticism is capable of taking us; here is a figure, transported via Helen Faucit's eloquently modulated performance, straight from the Victorian drawing room into the pages of literary criticism.[38]

The ensuing critical debate on Constance, thus revivified and refined by two highly memorable performances of the role, was one of the most vigorous of the period. A mere five years after the appearance of Jameson's study Hermann Ulrici published the first German edition of *Shakespeare's Dramatic Art* (No. 21);[39] here, in his discussion of Constance, Ulrici conducts one of the most remarkable rear-guard actions in the whole critical tradition. Clearly at odds with the proto-feminist agenda of Jameson's book, Ulrici declares that women ought not to interfere in history since they lack the capacity to do so. He goes on to disparage the very qualities of power and imagination that Jameson had praised in Constance, arguing that the character is both precipitous *and* ambitious, a woman whose impetuosity and blind passion ruins herself and her innocent son. Ulrici's position has obvious affinities with the eighteenth-century view of Constance as an indecorous scold; and both attitudes appear, either independently or together, in a small group of critics whose voices are persistent on the subject well into the twentieth century, among them Hartley Coleridge (No. 23); Henry N. Hudson (No. 25); John Weiss (No. 38), who breezily makes distinctions between the female and male temper that could play into the hands of either Ulrici or Jameson; Barrett Wendell (No. 54), who sees Constance as overly declamatory; and Frank Harris (No. 70) and Brander Matthews (No. 74), both of whose rather extraordinary denunciations of Constance we shall consider later in some detail.

The Siddons-Jameson influence, however, was by far the more influential, reflected in one form or another over several decades in the remarks of dozens of critics. Many of these, like Henry Giles (No. 33); H. T. Hall (No. 34); Francis Marshall (No. 47);

Louis Lewes (No. 52); Georg Brandes (56); C. H. Herford (No. 58); and Richard Garnett (67) pay homage to Jameson by essentially appropriating her ideas with only slight variations; others, however, embroider her findings in critically interesting ways. John Bucknill (No. 28), for example, agrees with Jameson that Constance is a figure of passion and grandeur, but also one in whom ambition vies with maternal love. Drawing upon his considerable experience as a physician specializing in the treatment of the mentally ill, Bucknill proceeeds to examine Constance as if she were one of his patients. His analysis is memorable both in its anticipation of later Bradleian-style 'character criticism' as well as for its 'diagnosis' of the cause of Constance's repeated vituperative outbursts: she is insane, the unhappy victim of precisely those towering passions that Jameson praised as powerfully 'imaginative.'[40] Interesting, too, is Gervinus's incorporation of some of Jameson's ideas (but by no means all of them) as the basis for his revealing depiction of Constance – vain, poetical, and imaginative – as a female counterpart to Richard II (No. 31). We may also observe in the more docile acceptance of Jameson's views by Hiram Corson (No. 48), as well as in the critical refinements worked upon them many years later by Stopford Brooke (No. 72), just how canonical Jameson's arguments, and even her vocabulary, had become. By an irony somehow suited to the odd critical fortunes of *King John*, Siddons's eighteenth-century performance – the informing spirit behind a conception of character that, through Jameson, shaped critical opinion for decades – becomes perhaps the most influential nineteenth-century reading of the play.

From about the middle of the century forward we may discern several strains of criticism, each in its own way signalling important changes and developments in the ongoing interpretive tradition of *King John*. As far back as Schlegel, critics had emphasized the overtly nationalistic and patriotic qualities of the play; but with the appearance of Henry Reed's series of lectures on Shakespeare (No. 26) this attitude takes a subtle but significant change of direction. Reed is the first of a small but articulate group of critics to emphasize the nationalism of *King John*, locating heroism not in any particular character (as some previous critics had unsuccessfully tried to do) but in the English nation as a whole. The curious effect of this perspective is somewhat to soften (but not whitewash) the character of John, who becomes associated with English nationhood. In this context the Bastard is naturally singled out for special praise; and Reed, taking a hint from Coleridge, provides a disarmingly sensitive reading of Faulconbridge's scene with James Gurney as illustrating the highest ideals of English chivalry. A year later William Watkiss Lloyd (No. 27) took Reed's ideas even further, seeing John not merely as a representative of the national interest but, astonishingly, as an able and energetic leader. The rehabilitation of John's character continued with the arrestingly pragmatic reading of the play by John Heraud (No. 32), who sees a dedication to national interest as its guiding idea. Heraud argues that since 'the national interest receives its incarnation in the person of John', his individual goodness or venality is irrelevant; he is great because the nation is great, and as the 'impersonation' of national policy justly commands obedience. H. T. Hall (No. 34) merely echoes Heraud; but Denton J. Snider (No. 40), although annoyingly prolix, works some interesting variations on the theme of nationalism. From Snider's perspective John's fatal mistake is his abandonment of a viable (if illegal) authority based upon his opposition to foreign interference for the mere personal satisfaction of a legitimate title. Snider, like the other members of his critical coterie, sees *King John* as more of an ideological tract than a drama of human emotion or high moral design. This quality is perhaps best illustrated in Snider's treatment of Constance. The towering figure whom Jameson and her ilk had made the emotional centerpiece of the play functions in Snider's philosophical scheme as an example (along with Elinor) of the dangers of introducing domestic considerations into history. We are not very far from Ulrici here; but one always has the sense that Snider's gelid masculinization of history is more the result of his ideological 'system' than any Ulrici-style aversion to females or even the sort of 'embarrassment' identified by Dusinberre. But despite the obvious limitations Snider's interpretive scheme places on his sensitivity to Constance, it opens up some interesting perspectives on the Bastard, particularly regarding the question of legitimacy. In denying his familial sonship for that of Richard Cœur de Lion, the Bastard claims a national legitimacy rather than a personal one. He thus becomes a true child of the nation, an act which 'consecrate[s] him more exclusively to the State' and further legitimizes his status as the embodiment of English national ideals. Snider's criticism will never be confused with Hazlitt's or Jameson's for its empathetic insights into human nature; but it can, despite its ponderous over-reliance on a restrictive interpretive scheme, at times make shrewd observations on the structural dynamics of Shakespeare's plays.[41]

The long-standing interest in the morality of Shakespeare's dramas and in his art of characterization produced, from mid-century forward, a group of critics whose moral readings of *King John* situated them in clear opposition to the Reed-Lloyd-Heraud axis of ideological pragmatists. Chief among these is Ulrici, whose remarks on the play embody the highest principles of Victorian moral idealism. Ulrici sees the play as depicting a series of powerful moral dualities pitting individual freedom against hierarchical control (i.e., Church vs. State), a struggle that is reflected disturbingly in the character of John. The drama presents us with a pervasive sense of moral decay, in John himself, his government, and the Church; Faulconbridge alone stands apart as the great natural embodiment of true morality (what L. Dora Schmitz in her 1876 translation of Ulrici terms 'the moral ethico-religious spirit'). Unlike those critics who try to mitigate the venality of the play and its 'hero' by subjugating personal morality to the claims of national interest (a curious nineteenth-century version of eliding the character issue), Ulrici draws sharp and unmistakable moral conclusions: Church and State decay when they fail to be guided by true morality; the want of self-control is fatal to history; and women are hereditarily incapable of practicing self-control.

The most prominent among the group of 'moral' critics who follow Ulrici are Gervinus (No. 31), Charles Cowden Clarke (No. 30), and Edward Dowden (No. 36). Gervinus, whose explicitly moral and patriotic purpose is clear in his treatment of the Bastard, sees a great lesson for the German people in the behavior of Faulconbridge: namely, the wise abandonment of a narrow, literal morality for the higher good of the nation. There are, of course, strains of the morally pragmatic view here (and elsewhere) in Gervinus, whose argumentative subtlety on *King John* makes him a difficult figure to place in any single critical category. But his more conventionally moral view of the play is quite apparent in his treatment of the 'seductions' of Commodity, which he sees as the guiding principle of the action, and in light of which he makes his often sophisticated and complex judgements of character. The 'Commodity' that Gervinus disparages in *King John* Clarke terms 'craft', and for him John is its most glaring proponent, 'a hideous reptile-thing' from whom we shrink in moral revulsion; Arthur and Constance are profoundly affecting, and the Bastard a grand creation, particularly when he speaks in Shakespeare's own voice as a moral chorus to the play. Clarke's criticism, although roughly contemporaneous with that of Reed, Lloyd, and Heraud, could hardly be at a greater interpretive and emotional remove from theirs, particularly in its penchant for oratorical flourish (the essays originated as public lectures), moral ardor, and unabashedly encomiastic appreciation of Shakespeare's art. Aron Y. Stavisky has called this sort of thing 'the gush', tracing it from Coleridge through Bradley;[42] and it also appears to some extent in Dowden, though not perhaps as clearly in his criticism of *King John* as of some other plays. Yet even here the emphasis on delicacy of expression and moral sensitivity is unmistakable. For Dowden, John is no more than a hollow pretense of kingship; and Arthur, Constance, and the Bastard are 'the only presences of human virtue or beauty which are to be perceived in the degenerate world depicted by Shakespeare.'

By the time Henry Morley (No. 46) wrote his largely derivative essay (obviously indebted to Gervinus) on Commodity as the keynote of the play, the 'moral' approach to *King John* had pretty much run its ideological course.[43] Some attempt at its critical rejuvenation occured, however, around the turn of the century from two very different thinkers, Henry Sebastian Bowden (No. 57) and J. Lytelton Etty (No. 61). Bowden, an ardent Roman Catholic apologist strongly influenced by the historical scholarship of Richard Simpson (No. 35), represents the last scholarly gasp of the century on the question of Shakespeare's religious views initiated some fifty years earlier by Knight. Following Simpson, who had converted to Roman Catholicism in his twenties, Bowden cites numerous examples of topical allusions in *King John*, arguing that they turn the play into a sort of 'moral and political essay' on contemporary affairs, even going so far to suggest that Pandulph's advocacy of tyrannicide (3.1.174–9) may reflect Shakespeare's own feelings with regard to Elizabeth. But Bowden's moral interest in the play hardly stops here. He is determined to prove Shakespeare's innate sympathy with the old faith, and in so doing turns traditional moral readings of the play inside out. In Bowden's view Pandulph is a respected moral authority, far-sighted and full of sympathy for the afflicted (i.e., Constance and Arthur), and even the Pope is an honest broker, perceived by Shakespeare as a reasonable arbiter of international disputes. That Bowden's views failed to sway his contemporaries is hardly surprising; they are interesting, however, as an assault on certain entrenched moral responses to the play that, in the hands of Etty, receive far more revealing and sophisticated critical attention. Etty comes to the play unfettered by Bowden's theological bias (or indeed any ideological 'system'); and this allows him to make some of the most incisive and dispassionate moral observations about John in the whole critical tradition. Confronting squarely the distaste that so many critics express for the play, Etty locates this critical aversion in a moral-aesthetic paradox inherent in John's character: he is a striking figure in history but a poor one for a play because his evil is powerless to evoke hatred, interest, or pity. This friendless, dogged, and coldly remote creature becomes, in one of the supremely expressive phrases in all *King John* criticism, 'an incomplete hypocrite':

> He could plot, deceive, and beguile with the utmost subtlety; he could manufacture complicated schemes for out-witting his enemies with complete patience, – in fact in action his ingenuity was consummate. But of a merely passive hypocrisy he was incapable; his natural impatience had to find a vent in plots and deep designs; when his mind was not so occupied, he was unable to conceal his real nature.

In the modifications Etty works upon the moral character of John he typifies the best of late nineteenth-century character criticism as practiced by Boas (No. 55) and later by Bradley. Inexplicably consigned to critical oblivion by his scholarly successors (he is simply never cited), Etty remains the most perceptive of the abandoned commentators on *King John*.

The mention of Richard Simpson in the paragraph above suggests one of the most notable critical controversies of the Victorian period, by no means confined exclusively to commentary on *King John*, but clearly reflected in late nineteenth-century attitudes toward the play. In 1873 F. J. Furnivall (No. 39) founded The New Shakespeare Society[44] in the hopes that, among other things, its activities would provide some sort of scholarly rein on the growing body of floridly impressionistic criticism being produced by the likes of Swinburne (No. 37), Weiss (No. 38), Calvert (No. 44), and Pater (No. 49). In opposition to this kind of critical effusion Furnivall stood fast, by no means abandoning critical interpretation, but desiring it to be founded upon the hard factual evidence produced by such scholars as F. G. Fleay (No. 42) and Simpson. (We must recall that Simpson's influential essays on the topical allusions in Shakespeare's histories were first delivered before The New Shakespeare Society and published in their *Transactions*.) Both sides in what became a spirited dispute took delight in caricaturing the other, and Swinburne and Furnivall in particular feuded waspishly in print on questions of interpretive values over a period of years.[45] One need only consider the plain style of Furnivall's and Fleay's introductions to *King John*, the matter-of-fact pronouncements each makes on the play, and particularly Fleay's preoccupations with cast size, distribution of parts, sources, speech headings, and other 'factual' concerns (often with accompanying charts or graphs), to see the wide gap that separates their scholarly procedures from the orotund critical pronouncements of Swinburne, Pater, et al. Examples of these differences could be drawn from almost any two adversaries in the debate, but nowhere do we see the ideological distinctions between the two sets of attitudes more clearly than in Pater's and Furnivall's separate characterizations of John. Pater sees in John 'a kind of greatness, making the development of the play centre in the counteraction of his natural gifts – that something of heroic force about him – by a madness which takes the shape of reckless impiety'; Furnivall calls him a 'skunk'.

The last important development in Victorian criticism on *King John* hearkens back to the earliest aesthetic concerns about the play – the question of its form. Gildon's 1710 indictment that the piece lacks 'just Design' aptly sums up many of the mid-to late-century critical misgivings about the work, such as those found in Hartley Coleridge (No. 23) or François Guizot (No. 24). Even Swinburne can sound a bit like Cibber or Gentleman when he claims that in *King John* 'the best parts are discernible from the rest' and that the play falls short of the structural unity and polish of Shakespeare's later dramas. Only two years after the appearance of Swinburne's remarks, however, Edward Rose (No. 43) published his important article on Shakespeare's adaptation of *The Troublesome Raigne* (Rose, by the way, also occasionally delivered papers on dramatic structure before Furnivall's New Shakespeare Society). Rose, a playwright and adapter himself,[46] begins by demonstrating how, in many respects, Shakespeare improved upon his original; but he also points out troubling instances in which the later dramatist failed even to rise to the artistic level of *The Troublesome Raigne*. He then asks rhetorically what it is that has 'neutralised' Shakespeare's efforts to make *King John* as successful a stage play as, for instance, *Richard III*. The answer, according to Rose, lies in the inadequacy of John as the main subject for a play (the very point Etty was soon to make in a somewhat different context). If Shakespeare had thrust this inherently dramatic figure into the forefront of his play rather than largely re-tracing the outlines of *The Troublesome Raigne*, he could have forged a drama of real structural and thematic integrity. By instead creating a play with a different hero for each act and failing to develop the character of John, Shakespeare produced an occasionally appealing dramatic action but one deprived of a thematic center.

Rose's views soon acquired the status of something like critical orthodoxy. Even those who sometimes found little common ground on other interpretive matters, like Marshall (No.47), Wendell (No. 54), Brandes (No. 56), Smith and Bulthaupt (No. 60), Etty (No. 61), Schelling (No. 62), Chambers (No. 64), Baker (No. 65), and John (No. 68), speak in one voice (indeed often appropriating Rose's terminology) on the absence in *King John* of a strong central figure and the play's lack of artistic unity.[47] What makes this view different from eighteenth-century versions of the same idea, however, is the quietly developing notion that the absences in the drama – of hero, structural center, or guiding principle – are somehow thematically expressive. Barrett Wendell, writing in 1894, confronts this question obliquely in his discussion of the 'oddities' of the play. Wendell's debt to Rose is obvious, but unlike Rose he sees *King John* not so much as an artistic failure as a transitional piece, the apparent infelicities of which can be explained away as artistic growing pains on Shakespeare's part as he struggles to free himself from the restrictive conventionality of an earlier style. Wendell's failure to elaborate upon his suggestive conclusion – that the play's 'very excellencies emphasize its faults and its oddities' – is rectified in 1910 by Charlotte Porter in her critical introduction to *King John* (No. 69). Porter's neglected essay is one of the most important in the interpretive history of *King John* for the simple reason that it attempts a critical defense of the puzzling unimportance of John in his own play. Porter speaks interestingly of Shakespeare's 'scattering' attention away from John as a deliberate act of dramatic artistry, seeing this 'scattering quality' as the primary vehicle through which the playwright situates John and his reign in history. The systematic 'belittling' of John (the very point that since Rose had provided such a stumbling block to any appreciation of the play's structure) thus becomes the essential feature of a subtly virtuosic design:

> John is so much of a minor character stranded amid the persons and events of his wrecked life that Shakespeare has prompted everybody to talk less of him than several others. Yet it has scarcely been realized that this qualifying of us all to ignore John in his own History is of itself a descriptive master-stroke in this portrait of 'confounded royalty'.

In turning what so many of her critical predecessors see as a structural deficiency into an aesthetic *tour de force*, Porter becomes the first commentator to anticipate later twentieth-century strategies for dealing with the play's many puzzling or disturbing anomalies.[48]

Porter's essay in many ways marks the beginning of twentieth-century criticism on *King John*. In the decade between the appearance of her remarks and Furness's variorum edition (No. 75), however, there appeared a small cluster of studies that reflected the growing pains felt by the critical tradition as it moved from from Victorian to 'modern'. At first blush Frank Harris's astonishing attempt to prove Shakespeare's wife a shrew (No. 70) seems easy enough to dismiss as a *sui generis* act of critical whimsy, carried out in joyous defiance of all previous scholarship. Yet despite its quite deliberate iconoclasm, Harris's essay on Constance has deep roots in some of the most venerable aspects of the critical tradition. Harris unskeptically accepts Malone's surmise that the death of Shakespeare's son Hamnet in 1596 accounts for Constance's 'mother-grief'; and although he is the only critic who goes so far as to associate the vituperative queen with Anne Hathaway (they are both intolerable scolds), he sounds positively Augustan in his aversion to Constance's excessive displays of anger yet attraction to her grand maternal suffering. Harris, a self-styled radical who openly flouted Victorian conventions of behavior, would bristle at any comparison with Francis Gentleman; but on the matter of female ranting he is essentially an eighteenth-century critic in modern dress. In the wake of Harris's remarks, John Masefield's essay on the multiple 'treacheries' in the play (No. 71) seems almost reactionary. Indeed, in its emphasis upon treachery as an overarching principle of dramatic action it recalls Gervinus's or Morley's attempt to unify *King John* around the concept of 'Commodity'. But Masefield's remarks look forward as well as backward. Building on attitudes toward the king first suggested by Etty and Porter (but without citing either) Masefield also takes up the question of John's puzzling deficiencies, seeing him as 'that most subtle of all the images of treachery, a man who cannot conform to the standard of his own ideas':

> He has a bigger intellect than any one about him. His brain is full of gusts and flaws that blow him beyond his age, and then let him sink below it. Persistence in any one course of treachery would give him the greatness of all well-defined things. He remains a chaos shooting out occasional fire.

The ethical dispassionateness of this statement takes us back (tonally if not substantively) to the Reed-Heraud-Lloyd axis even as it anticipates judgements involving moral ambivalences, paradoxes, and anomalies that proliferate in later twentieth-century responses to the play.[49] We may also note the embryonic stirrings of such ideas in the remarks of Brooke (No. 72), who *does* turn substantively to Reed, Heraud, and Lloyd, emphasizing John's status as the representative of national interest and, almost in Lloyd's very words, calls the king 'an able politician, a wise war-leader, a bold and ready pursuer of his aim'. That the same critic who makes this statement could fully endorse Jameson's romantic notions of Constance (again, appropriating her critical vocabulary as his own) gives some indication of the ideological vortex in which early twentieth-century criticism on *King John* found itself.[50]

The last important voice before Furness's variorum was that of the noted theatre historian and dramaturge James Brander Matthews (No. 74), whose remarks on *King John* could have been published in 1770 along with Gentleman's. Here we learn that the play is un-Aristotelian in construction, powerful only in places, lacks a controlling motive or dominating figure, fails to integrate key episodes and characters sufficiently into the action, and, moreover, contains 'a couple of common scolds' who are 'unseemly', 'unqueenly', and 'unwomanly'. In Matthews, and again in the tepid remarks of Furness six years following (where the Bastard is reconstructed as a sort of hearty post-Great War soldier, tested and improved by adversity, and John seen as a moral coward whose life is a poor subject for a play), it almost seems as if criticism on *King John* is taking a last easeful and retrospective repose before contemplating the new directions to come.

III
1920 to the Present

The daunting task of summarizing the critical reception of *King John* in the period following the Furness variorum may perhaps best be appreciated by contemplating the 1,568 items in Deborah T. Curren-Aquino's impressive 1994 annotated bibliography, chiefly (but not exclusively) devoted to twentieth-century responses to the play.[51] To this full and meticulous work of scholarship I refer those interested in pursuing exhaustively the vagaries of *King John* criticism in the last seventy-five years. What follows is, of necessity, a highly selective attempt to capture something of the variety of this criticism in broad strokes, with a particular eye toward two related concerns: (1) how the scholarly issues raised in the pre-Furness period have fared in our own century and, (2) what departures from old critical orthodoxies have been forged by recent generations of scholars. Critical trends, of course, do not develop in discrete chronological segments, one idea gracefully expiring only to relinquish its ideological place to another. With the explosion of scholarly activity in the twentieth century (particularly in the period after World War II) there occurs quite naturally a sustained dialogue of voices and perspectives on a full range of scholarly issues. In treating some of the more important aspects of twentieth-century criticism on *King John* by topic, therefore, I do not intend to impose upon this vast body of work a false sense of orderliness or neat chronological succession. Each of the separate issues treated below develops hand-in-hand with other concerns and, obviously enough, both influences and is influenced by them. Nevertheless, even in the midst of this relative critical cacophony, prevailing voices do emerge that signal important new developments or changes of scholarly direction.

A curious feature of twentieth-century scholarship on *King John* is its tendency to revisit (furnished with its own theoretical wise saws and modern instances) the oldest critical questions about the play. One of the most enduring – and critically stable – of these questions was the relationship of *King John* to *The Troublesome Raigne*. Since Langbaine and Pope, of course, scholars had argued mildly over such matters as the probable author(s) of *The Troublesome Raigne*, Shakespeare's likely hand in it, and his relative success in adapting it, but never with the slightest doubt as to its chronological relationship to the 'later' *King John*. With the appearance in 1954 of E. A. J. Honigmann's edition of *King John*, however, the long-held orthodoxy that *The Troublesome Raigne* preceded Shakespeare's play received its most formidable challenge.[52] Andrew Cairncross (1936) and Peter Alexander (1939) had already suggested a rethinking of the chronology of the two plays some years earlier, but undertook no wholesale defense of the position.[53] Honigmann, however, fleshed out Cairncross's and Alexander's ideas in more detailed fashion, arguing not only that *King John* was the earlier play but also dating it sometime during the winter of 1590 or spring of 1591. As so often happens in the critical history of a work (*King John* being no exception), a notion that had previously been anathema, once it has been powerfully affirmed, suddenly acquires a critical following. (Note, for example, Malone's earlier attempt to link the death of Shakespeare's son Hamnet to the sorrows of Constance and to a probable 1596 date for the play.) At any rate, Honigmann's hypothesis, although sharply rebutted by most, did find acceptance among a respected group of scholars, among them William H. Matchett (1966) and L. A. Beaurline (1990).[54] Opposition to Honigmann's revamped chronology, however, continues to be formidable;[55] and although his opinion hardly appears to be acquiring anything like canonical status, it nonetheless occupies a secure niche in the critical debate on the sources of *King John*.

Another modern reworking of an old critical shibboleth occurs in twentieth-century treatments of Shakespeare's religious attitudes as reflected in the play. In the forties and fifties, particularly in the work of such Roman Catholic apologists as John Henry de Groot (1946) or H. Mutschmann and Karl Wentersdorf (1952),[56] discourse on the issue takes the form of erudite polemics of the Simpson-Bowden variety (even including an attempted rehabilitation of the character of Pandulph). For most of the century the debate is hardly distinguishable from its nineteenth-century prototype – that is, adherents on both sides demonstrating either Shakespeare's Protestant or Roman Catholic leanings, usually with reference to his adaptation of *The Troublesome Raigne*.[57] In a rather extraordinary decade from 1982 to 1992, however, the traditional lines of argument reconfigure themselves in startling ways. Roy Battenhouse (1982), for example, sees Shakespeare's play as not so much a partisan doctrinal statement as a reformulation of the religious issue entirely. In Battenhouse's scheme the dramatist advocates neither the Protestant nor Roman Catholic position; rather he depicts a bastardized and commoditized world in which genuine religious feeling (as seen in Arthur and Hubert) gets relegated to the margins of history by 'iron age opportunists'.[58] Despite Battenhouse's essentially providentialist view (Arthur and Hubert finally transcend their sorry world), there is a faint touch in his essay of the 'ambivalence' and 'contingency' that is our century's salient contribution to criticism on *King John*. But it is in the work of three critics of very different ideological stripe, Honigmann (1985), John Loftis (1987), and Donna B. Hamilton (1992), that the issue of Shakespeare's religious attitudes acquires a somewhat more 'modern' critical edge, arising (to a greater degree in Hamilton than in Honigmann and Loftis) from prevailing interpretive habits of mind.[59] Honigmann argues that although the dramatist belonged to a Roman Catholic family he nonetheless appealed in *King John* to an 'anti-papal fury' (121). Shakespeare's animus, however, is directed against Rome specifically (not *English* Roman Catholics), and thus has certain affinities with the ambivalence he expresses in the Sonnets toward the Dark Lady. By thus implying that Shakespeare's divisions (Roman Catholic in religion but English in nationality) are clearly reflected in *King John*, Honigmann considerably modifies the terms of the doctrinal debate on the play. Since in Honigmann's view *King John* precedes *The Troublesome Raigne*, it cannot be argued (as so many previous critics have tried to do) that in *King John* Shakespeare ameliorated the more stridently anti-Roman views of an 'earlier' play; instead what we have in *King John* is Shakespearian ambivalence, deriving from no earlier drama, but firmly rooted in his conflicting 'Roman' and 'English' identities.

In Loftis's study the question of ambivalence arises in quite another fashion. Building importantly upon the work of Simpson a century earlier, Loftis approaches the question of religion in the play from the perspective of European politics (specifically Anglo-Spanish relations), seeing the presence of Blanch in *King John* as representing contemporary Spanish claims to the English crown. In this context the play becomes unambiguously (but problematically) Protestant, a drama of moral paradoxes in which good and bad are subtly entangled. Hamilton's thesis, however, is the most revisionist on the question of the politico-religious significance of the play. She is far less concerned with simple doctrinal distinctions like Protestant and Roman Catholic; instead she approaches the play from a cultural-historicist viewpoint that emphasizes matters of power, church government, and religious conformity. Clearly embracing the dense ideological inventiveness of post-Greenblattian New Historicism, with its powerful bias for de-mystifying art by seeing it merely as one of many interrelated cultural transactions, Hamilton argues that Shakespeare, in *King John* as well as in other plays, repeatedly questions the hierarchical, absolutist, and conformist positions of the English Church. In what amounts to a radical reconstruction of Shakespeare as a religious thinker, Hamilton sees his adaptation of *The Troublesome Raigne* as reflecting the anti-Catholic rhetoric of nonconformist challenges to the established religion, particularly as regards matters of property, privacy, obedience, and authority. Although Hamilton, like so many others before her, uses *The Troublesome Raigne* as an ideological window into *King John*, she sees Shakespeare's play not so much as embodying his personal faith as his attitudes toward political power. Since Cibber's *Papal Tyranny*, of course, the matter of Shakespeare's religion has had unmistakably political overtones. In Hamilton, however, the old formulation undergoes a serious and deliberately reductive change in focus; she is interested in Shakespeare's play not so much for what it seems to affirm theologically, but what it seems to undermine politically.

The earliest critical issue concerning the play — the extent of its structural and artistic unity — also gives rise to some of the most provocative twentieth-century attempts to 'explain' its thematic, dramatic, or ideological complexities. The late Victorian critical orthodoxy that the play is an artistic failure, refined and given fresh impetus by Rose's 1878 essay, prevails until roughly mid-century.[60] With the appearance of Adrien Bonjour's article on the structure of *King John* (1951), however, a new set of attitudes regarding the coherence of the play, and particularly the 'form' of that coherence, reinvigorate the critical debate.[61] Bonjour, writing under the obvious influence of a New Critical aesthetic that affirmed structural unity and often found it in neglected strands of meaning, calls for a complete reassessment of the play. Positioning himself in clear opposition to the prevailing attitude of artistic negativism about *King John*, he argues that the play has an artfully balanced structure defined by the falling curve of John's fortunes and the rising curve of the Bastard's. The neatness of Bonjour's argument (John and the Bastard are 'complementary panels of a great diptych' and the 'organic unity' of the play is finely enhanced by 'dramatic irony' (273–4), one of the great rhetorical catch-alls of the New Criticism) appealed to a whole generation of like-minded critics. So it is that James Calderwood (1960) and William H. Matchett (1962) could echo Bonjour in another key, each locating structural unity in the conflict between two powerfully opposed principles of behavior, commodity and honor.[62]

It is also important to note during this period, however, the beginnings of what we might call, to use Charlotte Porter's phrase back in 1910, the 'scattering away' of traditionally formalist rhetoric in favor of a new critical vocabulary with which to speak of the structural tensions and 'meanings' of the play. Even as Calderwood and Matchett were treating the Bastard as a key element in defining the ethical and structural coherence of *King John*, Julia Van de Water (1960) was debunking the character, seeing no consistency in his development and dismissing him as a '"ficelle" playing a variety of roles'.[63] The strong implication here of political cynicism, moral deception, and ambiguous and self-interested theatricality, becomes cemented into the critical vocabulary on *King John* with John R. Elliott's important essay treating the divided personality of the king (1965).[64] Elliott finds conflicting 'ambiguities' in the sixteenth-century reconstruction of John's character, locating these in two opposed historical images of the monarch: (1) a negative medieval image dating back to Roger of Wendover and Matthew Paris, and (2) the revision of this image by many (but not all) Tudor historians to serve the political ends of the Reformation. This 'double image' of kingship is appropriated by Shakespeare to create a title character, and a play, of disturbing ambiguities and contradictions situated in a world of harsh political pragmatism. Elliott's emphasis upon a play divided, where moral decisions are shifting, contingent, or unclear, becomes the common perspective uniting virtually all criticism on *King John* for the duration of the century. What emerges in the wake of Elliott's article, curiously enough, is not so much an attempt to disparage the thematic or structural unity of *King John*, as an attempt to recast altogether the terms in which that unity is perceived. The 'unity' of the play, as implied by Elliott and affirmed by an army of critical successors, inheres paradoxically in its sustained contradictions, discontinuities, polarities, or unresolved shifts of focus or perspective. Falstaff merely turned diseases to commodity; the last generation of critics on *King John* (owing much more to Charlotte Porter than it acknowledges) has effectively turned the most opprobrious infelicities of the play into the essential features of a complex and meaningful artistic design.

A seminal essay in establishing this perspective is that of Sigurd Burckhardt (1966).[65] Burckhardt's celebrated observation that in *King John* Shakespeare becomes a 'modern' (134) could also be applied to the critical agenda his essay does so much to advance. The rapidly developing idea that a dense thematic logic is somehow embedded in the internal contradictions and polarities of *King John* finds its fullest expression in Burckhardt's radical de-mystification of the Tudor doctrine of order and obedience. Proceeding along the skeptical and disintegrationist lines that generally characterize his criticism of Shakespeare, and that have made his work a sort of critical rallying point for so many later readers of the play, Burckhardt argues that *King John* repeatedly unmasks the 'unresolvable contradiction' at the heart of the Tillyardian 'Tudor Myth' (143): i.e., that the system of belief is only workable when there is a single clear and ultimate authority. Since the play never gives us a circumstance in which this situation occurs, 'the whole beautiful cosmic structure' falls to pieces (143) with no viable construct to replace it. Like the Bastard, we remain hopelessly confused, 'beset by too many and too radical ambiguities' (150). Although Burckhardt's essay does not treat the structural problem specifically, its conclusions are clearly applicable to it. Precisely the sense of open-endedness or contingency that he sees pervading the moral atmosphere of the play is the single factor his critical successors seize upon as the governing principle – often indeed the implied structural center – of their revisionist readings of *King John*.

The clear line of descent leading from Burckhardt to the most current twentieth-century criticism is unmistakable. Typical of this movement is the article by Jonathan Reeve Price (1970), revealingly titled '*King John* and Problematic Art'[66], in which Price argues that Shakespeare's purpose in the play is to evoke shifting, contradictory, and uncertain responses in order to create 'provocative ambiguity' (26). This ambiguity, however, is hardly the sign of a poorly structured dramatic action; on the contrary, the play moves toward a genuine sense of closure, but a closure that leaves all contingencies open to interpretation and equally (and problematically) confirmed. In like manner, Douglas C. Wixson (1981) views the play as 'dialectical' in structure, simultaneously advocating a number of competing 'platforms' and points of view but refusing to arrange them in any order of moral ascendancy.[67] Wixson sees this dialectic, in the manner of Price, as a structural *tour de force* heretofore unappreciated by those who disparage the play for its lack of unity. *King John* is unified, but its unity inheres in a series of episodic and semi-autonomous scenes that illustrate the complexity of politics rather than clear moral lessons. In criticism of this sort the emphasis is frequently on audience response, particularly the way in which Shakespeare, reconstructed as a modern playwright, manipulates us in a sort of proto-absurdist manner, even to the extent of alienating, de-familiarizing, or otherwise 'making strange' whatever settled verities we bring with us to the theatre.[68]

In the last decade or two the emphasis has been not so much on the play as an artistic failure as on the deep *sense* of failure (moral, political, or personal) it so keenly expresses. Eamon Grennan (1978), clearly influenced by Burckhardt, emphasizes the ways in which Shakespeare manipulates audience response in *King John* to allow the play to function as an exposé of traditional humanist views of history.[69] Humanist *historia*, which formed the ideological basis of Shakespeare's first tetralogy, dissolves before our eyes in *King John*, a play that looks forward to the dramatist's far more sophisticated treatment of history in the sequence from *Richard II* to *Henry V*. Failure, collapse, disintegration, hollowness: these comprise the new vocabulary with which a whole generation of literary scholars speaks about the 'meaning' of the play. So it is that a cadre of latter day critics, each of whom ascribes some element of structural coherence and design to *King John*, can see that very design expressed in such problematical features as 'missed opportunities',[70] overt 'fictionality',[71] abrupt and disorienting reversals of expectation,[72] subversive, hollow, and false images of kingship,[73] or even the manipulative emptiness of modern television commercials, 'especially those that market a product to a plurality of audiences simultaneously by creating multiple subject positions'.[74] As Deborah T. Curren-Aquino has remarked, the major recovery effort regarding the play that Emrys Jones called for in 1977 has been heeded: 'Weaving in and out of the twentieth century, *King John* has finally "arrived," enjoying a special rapport with the critical, theatrical, and political temper of the last fifteen to twenty years.'[75] Indeed, with the proliferation of late twentieth-century skeptical readings of the play, the critical fortunes of *King John* seem to take a reflexive and lugubrious turn from sharply differentiated debate on the nature of its art or morality to a virtually univocal affirmation of its moral miasma.

Nowhere is the congeniality of the play with the 'political temper' to which Curren-Aquino alludes more obvious than in recent feminist criticism, where interest in questions of power and subversion have led to a complete rethinking of *King John* (particularly as regards the status of Constance) to suit the aims of a specific social, political, and interpretive agenda. As far back as Jameson, who defined Constance's 'power' in terms of imaginative, intellectual, or maternal energy, the nature and degree of the character's assertiveness have been an important critical concern. But whereas Jameson sees the power of Constance as essentially *personal*, praising her towering emotional, psychological, and intellectual attributes, recent feminist critics see her power in expressly *political* terms. (Interestingly, the heretofore *de rigueur* interest in Constance as a mother, what Jameson calls her 'maternal character', either disappears or becomes refracted by political and social concerns in late twentieth-century feminist discourse.) Dusinberre (1990), as we have seen, discusses male anxiety over the extent of female domination in the play, to which Constance clearly is a party.[76] Like the other females in *King John* Constance repeatedly challenges official language, embarrasses men, and subverts their most cherished values; and when she leaves the stage the play falls apart, deprived of the last remnants of female energy that sustains the action dramatically even as it undermines it politically. Phyllis Rackin (1989) speaks for a whole generation of feminist critics when she says that in *King John* 'before the masculine voice of history can be accepted as valid, it must come to terms with women and the subversive forces they represent'.[77] For Rackin, the females in the play, as sources and embodiments of conflict, figure importantly in determining the course of history. In this ideological context the shouting match between Elinor and Constance loses all traces of its former offensiveness, functioning rather as a moment of cultural breakthrough in which women blur traditional definitions of gender, thereby claiming their rightful place in a heretofore male-dominated historical narrative. And in a statement that both ideologically and semantically encapsulates criticism of the play in the last two decades, Rackin observes:

> In *King John*, Shakespeare leaves his audience, like the Bastard, 'amaz'd' and lost 'among the thorns and dangers' of an incomprehensible world (4.3.140–1), where every source of authority fails and legitimacy is reduced to legal fiction. For the characters within the play, there is no clear royal authority. For the audience watching it, there is no unblemished cause and no unquestioned authority to claim their allegiance. (84)

Rackin's study appears in the only volume of essays devoted entirely to *King John*, grouped with other readings of the play bearing titles like '*King John*: A Study in Subversion and Containment'; 'The King's One Body: Unceremonial Kingship in *King John*'; 'Blots, Stains, and Adulteries: The Impurities in *King John*'; 'The Four Voices of the Bastard'; and 'The "Un-End" of *King John*'.[78] It is by no means clear that the reassessment of the play begun nearly fifty years ago by Burckhardt has yet run its course, but it certainly has built to something like a critical consensus.

NOTES

1. Gildon's 'Remarks on the Plays of Shakespeare' (1710) first appeared in the spurious 'seventh' volume of the second edition of Nicholas Rowe's *Works of Mr. William Shakespeare*, 6 vols (London, 1709). Tonson published the two Rowe six-volume editions of 1709, and Curll the so-called seventh volume in 1710, which included Shakespeare's poems and two critical essays by Gildon. Page references to Gildon and all other authors cited in the Introduction (except those reprinted in this volume) are noted parenthetically. Later in *The Laws of Poetry Explain'd and Illustrated* (London, 1721), p. 233, Gildon also disparaged 'the long and tedious *soliloquy* of the bastard *Faulconbridge* in the play of *King John* [1.1.182ff.], just after his being receiv'd as the natural son of *Cœur de Lion*, [as] not only impertinent to the play but extremely ridiculous'. See *Shakespeare: The Critical Heritage*, edited by Brian Vickers, 6 vols (London, 1974–81), II, 371. On Gildon and Rymer see Vickers, II, 1–9; 25–59; and 63–85.
2. '*King John* and Embarrassing Women', *Shakespeare Survey*, 42 (1990), 37–52 (p. 40).
3. On Pope's editorial practice see A. D. J. Brown, 'The Little Fellow Has Done Wonders: Pope as Shakespeare Editor', *Cambridge Quarterly*, 21 (1992), 120–49; for a discussion of Pope's treatment of *King John* in particular see Joseph Candido '"Women and fooles, break off your conference": Pope's Degradations and the Form of *King John*', in *Shakespeare's Histories: A Quest for Form and Genre*, edited by John W. Velz (Binghamton, N.Y., 1996), pp. 91–109. Pope's degradations influenced acting versions (and even some editions) of *King John* for some time, particularly his shortening of the first three acts, which included the scolding match between Elinor and Constance. His twelve-line interpolation from *The Troublesome Raigne* (altered and rearranged from 2.133–56) at 3.1.133 of Shakespeare's play, where the Bastard explains that the basis for his hostility to Austria is revenge for his father's death, held the boards for some seventy years after its introduction in 1723. All references to *The Troublesome Raigne* are to the edition of J. W. Sider (New York, 1979).

4 *The Works of Shakespeare*, 7 vols (London, 1733), III, 167. There are, of course, some early commentators who respond positively to *King John*; most of these tend to praise individual scenes, characters, or dramatic moments rather than the artistic whole. Such a critic is Leonard Welsted, *The Works of Dionysius Longinus* (London, 1712), who sees in 3.3 (the episode in which John persuades Hubert to murder Arthur) analogies to the sublime in classical authors (pp. 166–8).

5 *Papal Tyranny*, although first performed in 1745, was written much earlier, perhaps in some version as early as 1703; it was also in rehearsal as early as 1723 and again later in 1736. See *Shakespeare: The Critical Heritage*, edited by Brian Vickers, 6 vols (London, 1974–81), III, 9.

6 *A Letter to Colley Cibber, Esq; on his Transformation of 'King John'* (London, 1745), p. 9. The letter is reprinted in full in H. H. Furness Jr.'s New Variorum Edition of *King John* (Philadelphia, 1919), pp. 540–55 and excerpted in Vickers, III, 155–62, who suggests that it may have been written by the author of 'The Occasional Prompter' series in *The Daily Journal*, 1736–7 (p. 155).

7 *Critical Observations on Shakespeare* (London, 1748), p. 54. Upton's study was first published in 1746; the second edition, 'with alterations and additions', is cited here.

8 The most comprehensive historical and biographical account of this tradition is Arthur Sherbo's *The Birth of Shakespeare Studies: Commentators from Rowe (1709) to Boswell-Malone (1821)* (East Lansing, Michigan, 1986). Two extremely interesting commentators in the 'notes' and 'readings' tradition are Zachary Grey and Richard Roderick. The former's *Critical, Historical, and Explanatory Notes on Shakespeare*, 2 vols (London, 1754) includes extensive commentary on *King John* in which Grey takes up such questions as the origins of cannon (I, 281), methods of Roman Catholic excommunication and cursing (I, 285–7), Shakespeare's ignorance of the circulation of the blood (I, 288–9), and Arthur's longing for the shepherd's life (4.1.16–18), which he glosses by quoting a Spenserian passage from *The Faerie Queene* (6.20–30) (I, 289–93). Roderick's observations appear in Thomas Edwards's *Canons of Criticism*, sixth edition (London, 1758); seventh edition (London, 1765). In his brief notes to *King John* (seventh edition, pp. 251–5), Roderick frequently disparages the play, speaking of Shakespeare's 'low and paltry' style (p. 252) and his 'licentious manner' (p. 253). Both statements, interestingly, refer to the 'embarrassing' scolding match between Elinor and Constance (2.1) that Pope degraded and the age generally found so offensive. See also Benjamin Heath, *A Revisal of Shakespeare's Text* (London, 1765), pp. 222–32, who engages every important editor preceding him and praises Roderick.

9 Pope, III, 115. The first published attribution of *The Troublesome Raigne* to Shakespeare (but with no mention of any collaboration with Rowley) was in Gerard Langbaine's *Account of the English Dramatic Poets* (Oxford, 1691), p. 467.

10 *Miscellaneous Pieces of Antient English Poesie* (London, 1764), Sig.A2^v.

11 *An Essay on the Learning of Shakespeare*, second edition (Cambridge, 1767), p. 76. Farmer rejects only Shakespeare's authorship, not Rowley's.

12 *Notes and Various Readings to Shakespeare*, 3 vols (London, 1779–83), I, part 2, 115–16. E. K. Chambers, *William Shakespeare*, 2 vols (Oxford, 1930), II, 289, says that 'the first part of [Capell's] commentary [was published] in 1774, but withdrawn, reprinted with a second part in 1779, and republished, with third and fourth parts printed in 1780, in *Notes and Various Readings to Shakespeare*, 3 vols. (1783)'. On the long delay between the publication of Capell's edition of Shakespeare (10 vols, London, 1767–8) and his *Notes and Various Readings* see Colin Franklin, *Shakespeare Domesticated: The Eighteenth-Century Editions* (Aldershot, 1991), pp. 112–16. See also Arthur Sherbo, *Shakespeare's Midwives: Some Neglected Shakespeareans* (Newark, De., 1992), p. 30.

13 Capell, for example, had nothing but contempt for Pope's inclusion of the Bastard's lines from *The Troublesome Raigne* at 3.1.133, claiming it could 'be justify'd by no reasons whatever' (I, part 2, 127).
14 *The Plays of William Shakespeare*, 8 vols (London, 1765); all citations of Johnson's commentary on *King John* are to Arthur Sherbo, *Johnson on Shakespeare*, 2 vols (New Haven, 1968), I, 405–28.
15 Sherbo, II, 658; 611–12.
16 Even William Kenrick, (*A Review of Doctor Johnson's New Edition of Shakespeare* (London, 1765), pp. 129–33), who treated only thirteen of the plays Johnson edited and made the notes to *King John* one of the focal points of his scathing denunciation of the whole edition, did not take Johnson to task for his critical assessment of the play. For Johnson's edition and response to it see *Shakespeare: The Critical Heritage*, edited by Brian Vickers, 6 vols (London, 1974–81), V, 55–249.
17 *The Dramatic Censor; or Critical Companion*, 2 vols (London, 1770), II, 155–73.
18 On only one occasion does Gentleman find fault with Constance's grief over Arthur's plight, when 'she speaks of the courtship of death' (II, 161).
19 In this respect Gentleman seems to agree with Cibber, who begins *Papal Tyranny* before Angiers, thus omitting all of Shakespeare's first act.
20 *The Morality of Shakespeare's Drama Illustrated* (London, 1775).
21 Here Griffith acknowledges a strong debt to Johnson, who in the Preface to his 1765 edition extols the 'system of civil and oeconomical prudence' reflected in Shakespeare's works, and goes on to say that 'From his writings indeed a system of social duty may be selected, for he that thinks reasonably must think morally' (Sherbo, pp. 62, 71).
22 See Augustus Ralli, *A History of Shakespearian Criticism*, 2 vols (London, 1932), I, 72–3; and Michael Dobson, *The Making of the National Poet: Shakespeare Adaptation and Authorship, 1660–1769* (Oxford, 1992), p. 214.
23 *The Poetical Works of George Keate, Esq.*, 2 vols (London, 1781), II, 147–9.
24 *Dramatic Miscellanies*, 3 vols (London, 1783–4), I, 1–114.
25 The mistake was first pointed out by George Steevens (based upon information he received from his friend Henry Blake) in the first Johnson-Steevens edition, *The Plays of William Shakespeare*, 10 vols (London, 1773), V, 47–8.
26 The most extensive treatment of Malone's importance in establishing the scholarly agenda for his age and for generations to come is Margreta de Grazia's *Shakespeare Verbatim: The Reproduction of Authenticity and the 1790 Apparatus* (Oxford, 1991).
27 Ritson and Malone first clashed after Ritson's *Remarks, Critical and Illustrative, on the Text and Notes of the Last Edition of Shakespeare* (London, 1783) challenged Malone's views on the status of Shakespeare's text; their mutual attacks continued until well after the appearance of Malone's 1790 edition (see headnote to No. 2). Malone's rift with Steevens was also long-standing (see headnote to No. 3); his controversy with Chalmers developed over the Ireland forgeries but touched upon issues relating to *King John* (see headnote to No. 4). See Vickers, *Shakespeare: The Critical Heritage*, VI, 334–48.
28 See *The Collected Works of Samuel Taylor Coleridge: Lectures 1808–1819: On Literature*, edited by R. A. Foakes, 2 vols (London and Princeton, 1987), II, 285.
29 Foakes, II, 466; *The Collected Works of Samuel Taylor Coleridge: Table Talk*, 2 vols, edited by Carl Woodring (London and Princeton, 1990), I, 67; II, 57.
30 *The Romantics on Shakespeare* (London, 1992), pp. 1–35. See also Bate's *Shakespearean Constitutions: Politics, Theatre, Criticism 1730–1830* (Oxford, 1989). Also of political importance was Richard Valpy's adaptation of *King John* (Reading, 1800; second edition 1803), designed for a country at war. Full of anti-French propaganda, the play was first acted by the boys at

Reading School and later at Covent Garden on 20 May 1803. Valpy owes a clear debt to Cibber's *Papal Tyranny*, but the anti-Papal vitriol of the earlier play is shifted here to contempt for Napoleonic ambitions and the hypocrisy of revolutionary France.
31 Oxberry is the lone dissenter, strongly dispraising the scene between Hubert and Arthur.
32 One cannot overlook the prevalence in this period of separate volumes of 'notes and readings' of the plays, dealing with textual, historical, or semantic cruces, as well as other interpretive problems. This practice, which continued into the twentieth century, comprises a sort of scholarly sub-genre in its own right. Limitations of space make it impossible to record in this volume the vast number of 'readings' of *King John* produced by this indefatigable group of scholars, but one can glean some sense of the tradition by consulting the detailed and scholarly notes of Joseph Hunter (No. 20) and Richard Grant White (No. 29). Each of these volumes intersected importantly with the ongoing editorial tradition as well; see, for example, the headnote to Hunter.
33 See Frances Anne Kemble, *Records of a Girlhood* (New York, 1883), p. 128; first edition, 3 vols (London, 1878). See also Jameson's Preface to the second edition of *Characteristics of Women* (London, 1835), I, vi.
34 That Siddons's remarks on Constance circulated in some form in Fanny Kemble's circle of friends is apparent from her *Records of a Girlhood*, p. 517.
35 Interesting in this regard are the comments of Fanny Kemble who disagrees with her aunt Siddons and Jameson. She sees Constance as a 'royally ambitious queen', indeed 'a queen more than anything else'. See *Records of A Girlhood*, pp. 517–18.
36 A notable exception is Beverly Ellison Warner (No. 53) who was reviving Courtenay's concerns as late as 1894.
37 See Knight, VIII, 38; Horace Howard Furness, Jr., in his variorum edition of *King John* (Philadelphia, 1919), devotes a separate section of his appendix on criticism to the issue (pp. 642–55). See also Hunter (No. 20); Hudson (No. 25); Gervinus (No. 31); Simpson (No. 35) and his disciple Bowden (No. 57); Wilkes (No. 41); Calvert (No. 44); Marshall (No. 47); Morgan (No. 51); and Beeching (No. 66). Noteworthy, too, is W. J. Birch *An Inquiry Into the Philosophy and Religion of Shakespeare* (London, 1848) who ransacks the plays for any references to religion (*King John*, pp. 33–4; 253–261), finding Shakespeare 'no Roman Catholic' (254); S. W. Fullom, *History of William Shakespeare, Player and Poet* (London, 1864), who declares Shakespeare a Protestant (pp. 61ff.); and Ebenezer Forsyth, *Shakespeare: Some Notes on His Character and Writings* (Edinburgh, 1867), who echoes Knight's remarks on *King John* (p. 14).
38 See Carol J. Carlisle, 'Constance: A Theatrical Trinity', in *'King John': New Perspectives*, edited by Deborah T. Curren-Aquino (Newark, De., 1989), pp. 144–64; and *William Charles Macready's 'King John'*, edited by Charles Shattuck (Urbana, 1962), pp. 49–51.
39 First translated into English in 1846 (see headnote to No. 21).
40 Bucknill's book was one of a remarkable series of volumes of its type, approaching Shakespeare's work from the perspective of either the legal or medical profession. See also Bucknill's *The Medical Knowledge of Shakespeare* (London, 1860); John Lord Campbell's *Shakespeare's Legal Acquirements Considered* (New York, 1859), and the response to it by Robert Cartwright, *The Footsteps of Shakespeare* (London, 1862); C. K. Davis's *The Law in Shakespeare* (Washington, 1883); J. Portman Chesney's *Shakespeare as a Physician* (Chicago, 1884); and Edward J. White's *Commentaries on the Law in Shakespeare* (St. Louis, 1911). All of these volumes include references to *King John*, but none of critical importance.
41 Worthy of mention, too, is Snider's treatment of Philip and Lewis. He draws a revealing moral distinction between father and son: Philip is guided throughout the play by a spiritually informed and principled conscience, whereas Lewis merely follows his own

designs unscrupulously, occasionally using his plighted faith as a means of deception.
42 *Shakespeare and The Victorians* (Norman, Ok., 1969), p. 22 and passim.
43 The degree to which some opinions had become entrenched may be seen in the critical remarks of Henry Hudson (No. 25), more a synthesizer of others' views than an independent critical thinker. He is strongly indebted to Knight, Schlegel, Hazlitt, and Ulrici, drawing heavily for ideas and terminology from the latter.
44 Furnivall, of course, would have disapproved of this spelling. The organization he founded was 'The New Shakspere Society', the spelling of the author's name being dictated, in Furnivall's view, by the most scientific (hence reliable) research of the day.
45 See Stavisky, pp. 89–100.
46 See the headnote to his article (No. 43)
47 There are exceptions, of course, even to critical orthodoxy. The staunch group who retain praise for the structure of the play after Rose's essay is best represented by Morley (No. 46) and Morgan (No. 51).
48 See Deborah T. Curren-Aquino, *'King John': An Annotated Bibliography* (New York, 1994), pp. xxii–xxiii.
49 In Masefield's revision of *William Shakespeare* (New York, 1954), the passage cited above appears as follows:

> On the stage [King John] seems usually to be played as a truculent butcher not quite sober: but a little thought in the player should make him much more than that, and give him great qualities, at great moments. One might say of him, as here shown, that he is an opportunist with successful moments, which lift above his age, and evil moments that disgrace him: he is a somewhat smoky chaos, shooting out occasional fire, and, at instants, light. His defiance scene with the Legate is superb. (p. 55)

In Masefield's revised essay he completely abandons the idea of 'treachery' (not even mentioning the word) and clearly heightens the 'greatness' of John.
50 See also F. S. Boas (No. 55) who cites Jameson by name as late as 1896.
51 *'King John': An Annotated Bibliography* (New York, 1994).
52 *King John* (London, 1954).
53 See Cairncross's *The Problem of 'Hamlet': A Solution* (London, 1936), pp. 136–43; and Alexander's *Shakespeare's Life and Art* (London, 1939), pp. 85–6.
54 See Matchett (ed.) *The Life and Death of King John* (New York, 1966), pp. 153–99; and Beaurline (ed.) *King John* (Cambridge, 1990), pp. 194–210. Beaurline suggests a date no later than 1590 for the composition of the play.
55 See R. L. Smallwood (ed.) *King John* (Harmondsworth, 1974), pp. 365–74, who explicitly addresses the ideas of Honigmann and Matchett in defending the majority position; and also, A. R. Braunmuller (ed.) *The Life and Death of King John* (Oxford, 1989), pp. 2–19.
56 de Groot, *The Shakespeares and 'The Old Faith'* (New York, 1946), pp. 182–223; Mutschmann and Wentersdorf, *Shakespeare and Catholicism* (New York, 1952), pp. 309–19.
57 The most intriguing example of this phenomenon espousing the Protestant (and specifically Anglican) position is Roland Mushat Frye's *Shakespeare and Christian Doctrine* (Princeton, 1963), pp. 282–8. Frye discusses a copy of F2 (1632) with expurgations by the English Jesuit William Sankey, seeing the deletions as 'clearly doctrinal in character' (p. 288). Support for Frye's position can also be found in James C. Bryant's *Tudor Drama and Religious Controversy* (Macon, Ga., 1984), pp. 129–49.
58 'King John: Shakespeare's Perspective and Others', *Notre Dame English Journal*, 14 (1982), 191–215 (pp. 201–3). See also Battenhouse's later essay, 'Religion in *King John*: Shakespeare's View', *Connotations*, 1 (1991), 140–9.

59 Honigmann, *Shakespeare: The 'Lost Years'* (Manchester, 1985), pp. 119–22; Loftis, *Renaissance Drama in England and Spain* (Princeton, 1987), pp. 72–82; Hamilton, *Shakespeare and the Politics of Protestant England* (Lexington, Ky., 1992), pp. 30–58.
60 See, for example, the remarks on the artistic integrity of the play by Logan Pearsall Smith, *On Reading Shakespeare* (London, 1933), pp. 143–5; M. R. Ridley, *Shakespeare's Plays: A Commentary* (London: 1937), pp. 85–9; Mark Van Doren, *Shakespeare* (New York, 1939), p. 106; E. M. W. Tillyard, *Shakespeare's History Plays* (London, 1944), pp. 232–3; John Palmer, *Political Characters of Shakespeare* (London, 1945), pp. 321–3; H. B. Charlton, *Shakespearian Tragedy* (Cambridge, 1948), pp. 63–9; F. M. Salter, 'The Problem of *King John*', *Proceedings and Transactions of the Royal Society of Canada*, third series, 43, Section 2 (June 1949), 115–36 (especially pp. 134–6); and Donald A. Stauffer, *Shakespeare's World of Images* (New York, 1949), pp. 84–8.
61 Adrien Bonjour, 'The Road to Swinstead Abbey: A Study of the Sense and Structure of *King John*', *ELH*, 18 (1951), 253–74.
62 Calderwood, 'Commodity and Honour in *King John*', *University of Toronto Quarterly*, 29 (1960), 341–56; and Matchett, 'Richard's Divided Heritage in *King John*', *Essays in Criticism*, 12 (1962), 231–53. The question of Commodity as a governing structural concern in the play goes as far back as Gervinus (No. 31).
63 'The Bastard in *King John*', *Shakespeare Quarterly*, 11 (1960), 137–46 (p. 146).
64 'Shakespeare and the Double Image of King John', *Shakespeare Studies*, 1 (1965), 64–84.
65 '*King John*: The Ordering of This Present Time', *ELH*, 33 (1966), 133–53.
66 *Shakespeare Quarterly*, 21 (1970), 25–8.
67 '"Calm Words Folded Up in Smoke": Propaganda and Spectator Response in Shakespeare's *King John*', *Shakespeare Studies*, 14 (1981), 111–27. See also Charles Stubblefield's 'Some Thoughts About *King John*' *CEA Critic*, 35, No. 3 (1973), 25–8, which compares Shakespeare's world with that of Kafka's. The world of *King John*, although confused and insecure, is nonetheless internally unified.
68 For important treatments of audience response in *King John* see Alexander Leggatt, 'Dramatic Perspective in *King John*', *English Studies in Canada* (Toronto), 3 (1977), 1–17; and Larry S. Champion, '"Confound Their Skill in Covetousness": The Ambivalent Perspective of Shakespeare's *King John*', *Tennessee Studies in Literature*, 24 (1979), 36–55 and *Perspective in Shakespeare's English Histories* (Athens, Ga., 1980), pp. 92–110.
69 'Shakespeare's Satirical History: A Reading of *King John*', *Shakespeare Studies*, 11 (1978), 21–37.
70 Jay L. Halio, 'Alternative Action: The Tragedy of Missed Opportunities in *King John*', *Hebrew University Studies in Literature and the Arts*, 11, No. 2 (Spring 1983), 254–69.
71 David Scott Kastan, '"To Set a Form Upon that Indigest": Shakespeare's Fictions of History', *Comparative Drama*, 17 (1983), 1–16.
72 Virginia Mason Vaughan, 'Between Tetralogies: *King John* as Transition', *Shakespeare Quarterly*, 35 (1984), 407–20.
73 Sandra Billington, *Mock Kings in Medieval Society and Renaissance Drama* (Oxford, 1991), pp. 123–34, especially pp. 128–9.
74 Barbara Hodgdon, *The End Crowns All: Closure and Contradiction in Shakespeare's History* (Princeton, 1991), p. 28.
75 '*King John*': *An Annotated Bibliography* (New York, 1994), p. xviii; and Jones, *The Origins of Shakespeare* (Oxford, 1977), p. 235.
76 '*King John* and Embarrassing Women', *Shakespeare Survey*, 42 (1990), 37–52.
77 'Patriarchal History and Female Subversion in *King John*' in '*King John*': *New Perspectives*, edited by Deborah T. Curren-Aquino, (Newark, De., 1989), p. 77. See also Margaret

Loftus Ranald, 'Women and Political Power in Shakespeare's English Histories', *Topic*, 36, (1982), 54–65.
78 Curren-Aquino, *'King John': New Perspectives*; the essays, in order, are by Virginia M. Vaughan (pp. 62–75); Barbara H. Traister (pp. 91–8); Joseph Candido (pp. 114–25); Michael Manheim (pp. 126–35); and Larry S. Champion (pp. 173–85).

1 Edmond Malone, commentary on *King John*

1790

From *The Plays and Poems of William Shakespeare, in Ten Volumes; Collated* Verbatim *with the Most Authentick Copies, and Revised: with the Corrections and Illustrations of Various Commentators; to Which are Added, An Essay on the Chronological Order of His Plays; An Essay Relative to Shakespeare and Jonson; A Dissertation on the Three Parts of King Henry VI.; An Historical Account of the English Stage; and Notes; by Edmond Malone* (11 vols, London, 1790).

Edmond Malone (1741–1812), critic and editor, was a friend of Johnson, Boswell, and numerous other luminaries in the literary and political worlds. He played a significant role, both inspirational and editorial, in assisting Boswell with the *Life of Johnson* (London, 1791), and also edited the work through several reissues. Malone came to London from Ireland in 1777, and in short order produced an influential list of Shakespearian studies, most notably *An Attempt to Ascertain the Order in Which the Plays Attributed to Shakespeare Were Written*, published with the Johnson-Steevens edition of 1778, and reprinted as part of the introductory apparatus to Malone's 1790 *Plays and Poems*. His other important scholarly contributions include a *Supplement* to the Johnson-Steevens edition (2 vols, London, 1780), a *Second Appendix* to the *Supplement* (London, 1783), and *A Dissertation on the Three Parts of King Henry VI, Tending to Shew That Those Plays Were Not Written Originally by Shakespeare* (London, 1787). The preparation of a new multi-volume edition of Shakespeare occupied Malone's energies considerably after 1790, but numerous other projects (among them his detailed exposé of William Henry Ireland's forged Shakespeare papers in 1796 and an edition of Dryden's prose works in 1800) caused delays, and he died before the enterprise could be completed. The materials for this new project were entrusted to James Boswell the younger, who brought Malone's plans to fruition in his twenty-one volume edition of 1821.

[From *An Attempt to Ascertain the Order in Which the Plays of Shakespeare Were Written*[1]]

King John, 1596

This historical play was founded on a former drama, entitled *The Troublesome Raigne of John King of England, with the Discoverie of King Richard Cordelion's base Son, vulgarly named the Bastard Fawconbridge: also the Death of King John at Swinstead Abbey. As it was (sundry times) publickely acted by the Queenes Majesties Players in the honourable Citie of London.* This piece, which is in two parts, and was printed at London for Sampson Clarke, 1591, has no author's name in the title-page. On its republication in 1611, the bookseller for whom it was printed, inserted the letters *W. Sh.* in the title-page; and in order to conceal his fraud, omitted the words – *publikely* – *in the honourable Citie of London*, which he was aware would proclaim this play not to be Shakespeare's *King John*; the company to which he belonged, having no *publick* theatre in London: that in Blackfriars being a private play-house, and the Globe, which was a publick theatre, being situated in Southwark. He also, probably with the same view, omitted the following lines addressed *to the Gentlemen Readers*, which are prefixed to the first edition of the old play:

> You that with friendly grace of smoothed brow
> Have entertain'd *the Scythian Tamburlaine*,
> And given applause unto an infidel;
> Vouchsafe to welcome, with like curtesie,
> A warlike Christian and your countryman.
> For Christ's true faith indur'd he many a storme,
> And set himselfe against the man of *Rome*,
> Until base treason by a damned wight
> Did all his former triumphs put to flight.
> Accept of it, sweete gentles, in good sort,
> And thinke it was prepar'd for your disport. [IA2, 1ff.]

Shakespeare's play being then probably often acted, and the other wholly laid aside, the word *lately* was substituted for the word *publickly*: ' – as they were sundry times lately acted,' &c.

Thomas Dewe, for whom a third edition of this old play was printed in 1622, was more daring. The two parts were then published, '*as they were sundry times lately acted;*' and the name of *William Shakespeare* inserted at length. *By the Queenes Majesties players* was wisely omitted, as not being very consistent with the word *lately*, Elizabeth being then dead nineteen years.

King John is the only one of our poet's uncontested plays that is not entered in the books of the Stationers' company. It was not printed till 1623, but is mentioned by Meres in 1598, unless he mistook the old play in two parts, printed in 1591, for the composition of Shakespeare.

It is observable that our author's son, Hamnet, died in August, 1596. That a man of such sensibility, and of so amiable a disposition, should have lost his only son, who had attained the age of twelve years, without being greatly affected by it, will not be easily credited. The pathetick lamentations which he has written for Lady Constance on the death of Arthur, may perhaps add some probability to the supposition that this tragedy was written at or soon after that period.

In the first scene of the second act the following lines are spoken by Chatillion, the French ambassador, on his return from England to King Philip:

> And all the unsettled humours of the land –
> Rash, inconsiderate, firy voluntaries,
> With ladies' faces and fierce dragons' spleens, –
> Have sold their fortunes at their native homes,
> Bearing their birth-rights proudly on their backs,
> To make a hazard of new fortunes here.
> In brief, a braver choice of dauntless spirits
> Than now the English bottoms have waft o'er,
> Did never float upon the swelling tide,
> To do offence and scathe to Christendom. [2.1.66ff.]

    Dr. Johnson has justly observed in a note on this play, that many passages in our poet's works evidently shew that 'he often took advantage of the facts then recent and the passions then in motion.'[2] Perhaps the description contained in the last six lines was immediately suggested to Shakespeare by the grand fleet which was sent against Spain in 1596. It consisted of eighteen of the largest of the Queen's ships, three of the Lord Admiral's, and above one hundred and twenty merchant ships and victuallers, under the command of the earls of Nottingham and Essex. The regular land-forces on board amounted to ten thousand; and there was also a large body of *voluntaries* (as they were then called) under the command of Sir Edward Winkfield. Many of the nobility went on this expedition, which was destined against Cadiz. The fleet sailed from Plymouth on the third of June 1596; before the end of that month the great Spanish armada was destroyed, and the town of Cadiz was sacked and burned. Here Lord Essex found 1200 pieces of ordnance, and an immense quantity of treasure, stores, ammunition, &c. valued at twenty million of ducats. The victorious commanders of this successful expedition returned to Plymouth, August 8, 1596, four days before the death of our poet's son. Many of our old historians speak of the splendor and magnificence displayed by the noble and gallant adventurers who served in this expedition; and Ben Jonson has particularly alluded to it in his *Silent Woman*, written a few years afterwards.[3] To this I suspect two lines already quoted particularly refer:

> Have sold their fortunes at their native homes,
> *Bearing their birth-rights proudly on their backs.*

Dr. Johnson conceived that the following lines in this play –

> And meritorious shall that hand be call'd,
> Canoniz'd, and worshipp'd as a saint,
> That takes away by any secret course
> Thy hateful life. [3.1.176ff.]

might either refer to the bull published against Queen Elizabeth, or to the canonization of [Henry] Garnet, [Guy] Faux [i.e., Fawkes], and their accomplices, who in a Spanish book which he had seen, are registered as saints.[4] If the latter allusion had been intended, then this play, or at least this part of it, must have been written after 1605. But the passage in question is founded on a similar one in the old play, printed in

1591, and therefore no allusion to the gunpowder-plot could have been intended.

A line of *The Spanish Tragedy* [1.2.170–2] is quoted in *King John*. That tragedy, I believe, had appeared in or before 1590.

In the first act of *King John* [1.1.244], an ancient tragedy, entitled *Solyman and Perseda*, is alluded to. The earliest edition of that play, now extant, is that of 1599, but it was written, and probably acted, many years before; for it was entered on the Stationers' books, by Edward Whyte, Nov. 20, 1592.

Marston's *Insatiate Countess*, which, according to Langbaine, was printed in 1603, contains a passage, which, if it should be considered as an imitation of a similar one in *King John*, will ascertain this historical drama to have been written at least before that year:

> Then how much more in me, whose youthful veins,
> Like a proud river, overflow their bounds. [3.4.72ff.][5]

So, in *King John*:

> Why holds thine eye that lamentable rheum,
> Like a proud river peering o'er his bounds. [3.1.22ff.]

Marston has in many other places imitated Shakespeare.

A speech spoken by the bastard in the second act of this tragedy [2.1.455–67: 'Here's a stay. . . .'] seems to have been formed on one in an old play entitled *The Famous History of Captain Thomas Stukely*. Captain Stukely was killed in 1578. The drama of which he is the subject, was not printed till 1605, but it is in the black letter, and, I believe, had been exhibited at least fifteen years before.

Of the only other note of time which I have observed in this tragedy, beside those already mentioned, I am unable to make any use. 'When I was in *France*', says young Arthur, 'Young gentlemen would be as sad as night / Only for wantonness' [4.1.14ff.]. I have not been able to ascertain when the fashion of being *sad and gentlemanlike* commenced among our gayer neighbours on the continent. A similar fashion prevailed in England, and is often alluded to by our poet, and his contemporaries. Perhaps he has in this instance attributed to the French a species of affectation then only found in England. It is noticed by Lyly in 1592, and by Ben Jonson in 1598. (I, part 1, 310–15)

[From the explanatory and commentary notes to *King John*]

[1] [Headnote]
A play entitled *ThE Troublesome Raigne of John King of England*, in two parts, was printed in 1591, without the writer's name. It was written, I believe, either by Robert Greene, or George Peele; and certainly preceded this of our author. Mr. Pope, who is very inaccurate in matters of this kind, says that the former was printed in 1611, as written by W. Shakespeare and W. Rowley. But this is not true.[6] In the *second* edition of this old play in 1611, the letters W. Sh. were put into the title-page, to deceive the purchaser, and to lead him to suppose the piece was Shakespeare's play, which at that time was not published. – See a more minute account of this fraud in

An Attempt to Ascertain the Order of Shakespeare's Plays, Vol. I. [310–15]. Our author's *King John* was written, I imagine, in 1596. The reasons on which this opinion is founded, may be found in that Essay [see above]. This drama was evidently formed on the old anonymous play. Probably, however, Shakespeare also perused Holinshed's account of this reign, he being undoubtedly his guide in all his historical plays. . . . (IV, 445)

[2] [On 1.1.27ff.: 'Be thou the trumpet of our wrath, / And sullen presage of your own decay', where Johnson objects to 'sullen']
I do not see why the epithet *sullen* may not be applied to a *trumpet*, with as much propriety as to a *bell*. In our author's *King Henry IV*. P. II. [1.1.102] we find – 'Sounds ever after as a *sullen bell* – .' (IV, 447; *Supp*. I, 164)[7]

[3] [On 1.1.85: 'He hath a trick of Cœur-de-lion's face', where Steevens argues that 'trick' refers to the tracing of a drawing or forming an outline][8]
Our author often uses this phrase, and generally in the sense of a peculiar air or cast of countenance or feature. So, in *K. Henry IV*. P. I [2.4.402ff.]: 'That thou art my son, I have partly thy mother's word, partly my own opinion; but chiefly a villainous *trick* of thine eye, – '. . . . In *K. Lear*, as Mr. Mason has observed, the word is applied to the voice: 'The *trick* of that voice I do well remember' [4.6.106].[9] (IV, 450)

[4] [On 1.1.143: 'Look, where three-farthings goes', where Theobald contends that the reference is to a coin picturing Elizabeth with a rose behind her][10]
Mr. Theobald has not mentioned a material circumstance relative to these three-farthing pieces, on which the propriety of the allusion in some measure depends; viz. that they were made of silver, and consequently extremely *thin*. From their thinness they were very liable to be cracked. . . . (IV, 452–3; *Supp*. I, 164)

[5] [On 1.1.162: 'Arise sir Richard, and Plantagenet']
It is a common opinion, that *Plantagenet* was the surname of the royal house of England, from the time of king Henry II.; but it is, as Camden observes in his *Remains*, 1614, a popular mistake.[11] Plantagenet was not a family name, but a nick-name, by which a grandson of Geffrey, the first earl of Anjou, was distinguished, from his wearing a *broom-stalk* in his bonnet. But this name was never borne either by the first earl of Anjou, or by king Henry II. the son of that earl by the Empress Maude; he being always called Henry *Fitz-Empress*; his son, Richard *Cœur-de-lion*; and the prince who is exhibited in the play before us, John *sans-terre*, or *lack-land*. (IV, 454)

[6] [On 1.1.207: 'For he is but a bastard to the time. . . .']
He is accounted but a mean man in the present age, who does not shew by his dress, his deportment, and his talk, that he has travelled, and made observations in foreign countries. (IV, 458)

[7] [On 2.1.144: 'As great Alcides' shoes upon an ass']
i.e. upon the *hoofs* of an ass. Mr. Theobald thought the *shoes* must be placed on the

back of the ass; and, therefore, to avoid this incongruity, reads – Alcides *shows*.[12] This endeavour to make our author's similes correspond exactly on both sides, is, as has been more than once observed, the source of many errours. (IV, 468)

[8] [On 2.1.149: '*K. Phi*. Lewis, determine what we shall do straight']
In the old copy [the First Folio] this line stands thus: King Lewis, determine what we shall do straight.

To the first three speeches spoken in this scene by King Philip, the word *King* only is prefixed. I have therefore given this line to him. The transcriber or compositor having, I imagine, forgotten to distinguish the word *King* by Italicks, and to put a full point after it, these words have been printed as part of Austria's speech: 'King Lewis,' &c. but such an arrangement must be erroneous, for Lewis was not king. Some of our author's editors have left Austria in possession of the line, and corrected the error by reading here, 'King *Philip*, determine,' &c. and giving the next speech to him, instead of Lewis.

I once thought that the line before us might stand as part of Austria's speech, and that he might have addressed *Philip* and *the Dauphin* by the words, King, – Lewis, &c. but the addressing Philip by the title of King, without any addition, seems too familiar, and I therefore think it more probable that the error happened in the way above stated. (IV, 468)

[9] [On 2.1.335: 'Say, shall the current of our right roam on?']
Thus the old copy. The editor of the second folio substituted *run*, which has been adopted in the subsequent editions. I do not perceive any need of change. In the *Tempest* we have – 'the *wandering* brooks' [4.1.128]. (IV, 476; *Supp.* I, 165)

[10] [On 2.1.354: 'mousing the flesh of men']
Mousing, like many other ancient and now uncouth expressions, was expelled from our author's text by Mr. Pope; and *mouthing*, which he substituted in its room, has been adopted in the subsequent editions, without any sufficient reason, in my apprehension.[13] *Mousing* is, I suppose, mamocking, and devouring eagerly, as a cat devours a mouse. So, in *A Midsummer Night's Dream*: 'Well *mous'd*, Lion!' [5.1.269]. . . . (IV, 477; *Supp.* I, 165)

[11] [On 2.1.371: 'King'd of our fears', in support of Thomas Tyrwhitt's emendation of the First Folio's 'Kings' to 'King'd'][14]
i.e. Our fears being our kings, or rulers. The old copy reads – *Kings*. . . . It is manifest that the passage in the old copy is corrupt, and that it must have been so worded, that their *fears* should be styled their *kings* or masters, and not they, kings or masters of their fears; because in the next line mention is made of these *fears* being *deposed*. Mr. Tyrwhitt's emendation produces this meaning by a very slight alteration, and is therefore, I think, entitled to a place in the text. . . .

This passage in the folio is given to King Philip, and in a subsequent part of this scene, all the speeches of the citizens are given to Hubert; which I mention, because these, and innumerable other instances, where the same error has been committed in that edition, justify some licence in transferring speeches from one person to another. (IV, 478; *Supp.* I, 165–6)

[12] [On 2.1.455ff.: 'Here's a stay / That shakes. . . .']
Stay, I apprehend, here signifies a *supporter of a cause*. Here's an extraordinary partizan, that shakes, &c. [Quotes the following Shakespearean examples of the usage in support: *King John*: 5.7.68–9; *3 Henry VI*: 2.1.69; *Richard III*: 2.2.74]. . . .

It is observable that *partizan* in like manner, though now generally used to signify an *adherent* to a party, originally meant a pike or halberd.

Perhaps, however, our author meant by the words, Here's a *stay*, 'Here's a fellow, who whilst he makes a proposition as a *stay* or *obstacle*, to prevent the effusion of blood, shakes,' &c. . . . It is, I conceive, no objection to this interpretation, that an *impediment* or *obstacle* could not shake death, &c. though the *person* who endeavoured to *stay* or prevent the attack of the two kings, might. Shakespeare seldom attends to such *minutiae*. – But the first explanation appears to me more probable. . . . (IV, 483; *Supp.* I, 166–7)

[13] [On 2.1.477ff.: 'Lest zeal, now melted, by the windy breath / Of soft petitions, pity, and remorse, / Cool and congeal again to what it was', where Steevens sees Shakespeare comparing zeal to metal in a state of fusion, and not to dissolving ice][15]
The allusion, I apprehend, is to dissolving ice; and if this passage be compared with others in our author's plays, it will not, I think, appear liable to Dr. Johnson's objection [that zeal is more properly represented as conveying its utmost power in a flame, and not 'congealed', as Shakespeare represents it].[16] The sense, I conceive, is, *Lest the now* zealous *and to you well-affected* heart *of Philip, which but lately was cold and hard as ice, and has* newly *been* melted and softened, *should by the soft petitions* of Constance, *and pity* for Arthur, *again* become congealed *and frozen*. I once thought that 'the windy breath of soft petitions,' &c. should be coupled with the preceding words, and related to the proposal made by the citizen of Angiers; but I now believe that they were intended to be connected, in construction, with the following line. – In a subsequent scene we find a similar thought couched in nearly the same expressions:

> This act, so evilly born, shall *cool the hearts*
> Of all his people, and *freeze* up their *zeal*. [3.4.149ff.]

Here Shakespeare does not say that *zeal*, when '*congealed*, exerts its utmost power,' but, on the contrary, that when it is congealed or frozen, it *ceases* to exert itself at all; it is no longer zeal.

We again meet with the same allusion in *King Henry VIII*:

> ——This makes bold mouths;
> Tongues spit their duties out, and *cold hearts freeze*
> *Allegiance* in them. [1.2.59ff.]

Both zeal and allegiance therefore, we see, in the language of Shakespeare, are in their highest state of exertion, when *melted*; and repressed or diminished, when *frozen*.

The word *freeze* in the passages just quoted, shews that the allusion is not, as has been suggested [by Steevens], to *metals*, but to *ice*.

The obscurity of the present passage arises from our author's use of the word *zeal*, which is, as it were, personified. *Zeal*, if it be understood strictly, cannot 'cool and congeal again to what it *was*,' (for when it cools, it ceases to be *zeal*,) though a *person* who is become warm and zealous in a cause, may afterwards become cool and indifferent, *as he was*, before he was warmed. – 'To what it was,' however, in our author's licentious language, may mean, 'to what it was, *before it was zeal*.' (IV, 484–5; *Supp*. I, 167)

[14] [On 3.1.69: 'For grief is proud, and makes his owner stoop']
Our author has rendered this passage obscure, by indulging himself in one of those conceits in which he too much delights, and by bounding rapidly, with his usual licence, from one idea to another. This obscurity induced Sir T. Hanmer for *stoop* to substitute *stout*;[17] a reading that appears to me to have been too hastily adopted in the subsequent editions.

The confusion arises from the poet's having personified grief in the first part of the passage, and supposing the afflicted person to be *bowed* to the earth by that pride or haughtiness which Grief is said to possess; and by making the afflicted person, in the latter part of the passage, actuated by this very pride, and exacting the same kind of obeisance from others, that Grief has exacted from her. – 'I will not go (says Constance) to these kings; I will teach my sorrows to be proud; for Grief is proud, and makes the afflicted *stoop*; therefore here I throw myself, and let them come to me.' Here, had she stopped, and thrown herself on the ground, and had nothing more being added, however we might have disapproved of the conceit, we should have had no temptation to disturb the text. But the idea of throwing herself on the ground suggests a new image; and because her *stately* grief is so great that nothing but the huge earth can support it, she considers the ground as her *throne*; and having thus invested herself with regal dignity, she as queen in *misery*, as possessing (like Imogen) 'the supreme *crown* of grief' [*Cymbeline*: 1.6.4], calls on the princes of the world to bow down before her, as she has herself been *bowed down* by affliction.

Such, I think, was the process that passed in the poet's mind; which appears to me so clearly to explain the text, that I see no reason for departing from it. (IV, 492–3)

[15] [On 3.3.39: 'Sound one unto the drowsy race of night']
The word *one* is here, as in many other passages in these plays, written *on* in the old copy. Mr. Theobald made the correction.[18] He likewise substituted *unto* for *into*, the reading of the original copy; a change that requires no support. In Chaucer and other old writers *one* is usually written *on*. . . .

The instances that are found in the original editions of our author's plays, in which *on* is printed instead of *one*, are so numerous, that there cannot, in my apprehension, be the smallest doubt that *one* is the true reading in the line before us. [Quotes *Coriolanus*: 3.1.142–4; *Cymbeline*: 2.5.15–16; *Romeo and Juliet*: 3.2.60; *The Comedy of Errors*: 4.2.34; *All's Well That Ends Well*: 2.5.28–9; *Love's Labor's Lost*: 1.1.166 and 4.3.140]. . . .

I should not have produced so many passages to prove a fact of which no one can be ignorant, who has the *slightest knowledge* of the early editions of these plays, or of our old writers, had not the author of *Remarks, &c. on the Last Edition of Shakespeare* [Joseph Ritson], asserted, with that *modesty and accuracy* by which his pamphlet is distinguished, that the observation contained in the former part of this note was made by one totally unacquainted with the old copies, and that 'it would be difficult to find a *single instance*' in which *on* and *one* are confounded in those copies. . . .[19] (IV, 511–12; *Supp.* I, 169)

[16] [On 3.3.52: 'Then, in despight of brooded watchful day']
Brooded, I apprehend, is here used, with our author's usual licence, for *brooding*; i.e. day, who is as vigilant, as ready with open eye to mark what is done in his presence, as an animal at brood. For the hint of this interpretation I am indebted to Mr. Steevens.[20] Shakespeare appears to have been so fond of domestick and familiar images, that one cannot help being surprized that Mr. Pope in revising these plays should have gained so little knowledge of his manner, as to suppose any corruption here in the text. He, however, instead of *brooded*, substituted *broad-ey'd*, a more poetical epithet perhaps, but certainly an unnecessary emendation; though it has been adopted in all the subsequent editions.[21] Had this alteration been made by Theobald, and had Pope been better acquainted with our author's manner and the language of his time, such a change would have afforded him an abundant topick for merriment; for it is very similar to many of those which he has introduced, by way of ridicule on all *restorers* and annotators, in his VIRGILIUS RESTAURATUS. . . . (IV, 512–13)

[17] [On 3.4.2: 'convicted sail']
Overpowered, baffled, destroyed. To *convict* and to *convince* were in our author's time synonymous. . . . Mr. Pope, who ejected from the text almost every word that he did not understand, reads – *collected* sail;[22] and the change was too hastily adopted by the subsequent editors. (IV, 514; *Supp.* I, 169–70)

[18] [On 3.4.110: 'the sweet word's taste']
The *sweet word* is *life*; which, says the speaker, is no longer sweet, yielding now nothing but shame and bitterness. Mr. Pope, with some plausibility, but certainly without necessity, reads – the sweet *world's* taste.[23] (IV, 519)

[19] [On 3.4.182: 'Strong reasons make strange actions']
Thus the old copy. The editor of the second folio for *strange* substituted *strong*; and the two words so nearly resemble each other that they might certainly have been easily confounded. But in the present instance I see no reason for departing from the reading of the original copy; which is perfectly intelligible. (IV, 522)

[20] [On 5.1.19: 'a gentle convertite']
A *convertite* (a word often used by our old writers, where we should now use *convert,*) signified either, one converted *to the faith*, or one reclaimed from worldly pursuits, and devoted to penitence and religion.

Mr. Mason says, a *convertite* cannot mean a *convert*, because the latter word 'in the language of the present times means a person that changes from one religion to another.'[24] But the question is, not what is the language of the present time, but what was the language of Shakespeare's age. Marlowe uses the word *convertite* exactly in the sense now affixed to *convert*. John, who had in the former part of this play asserted in very strong terms the supremacy of the king of England in all ecclesiastical matters, and told Pandulph that he had no reverence for 'the Pope or his *usurp'd* authority' [3.1.159ff.], having now made his peace with 'holy church,' and resigned his crown to the Pope's representative, is considered by the legate as one newly converted to the true faith, and very properly styled by him a *convertite*. The same term, in the second sense above mentioned, is applied to the *usurper*, Duke Frederick, in *As You Like It*, on his having 'put on a religious life, and thrown into neglect the pompous court' [5.4.181ff.]: '——out of these *convertites* / There is much matter to be heard and learn'd' [5.4.184ff.]. (IV, 547)

[21] [On 5.4.11: 'Unthread the rude eye of rebellion']
Some one, observing on this passage, has been idle enough to suppose that the *eye of rebellion* was used like the *eye* of the *mind*, &c. Shakespeare's metaphor is of a much humbler kind. He was evidently thinking of the *eye of a needle*. Undo (says Melun to the English nobles) what you have done; desert the rebellious project in which you have engaged. In *Coriolanus* we have a kindred expression: 'They would not *thread the gates*' [3.1.124].

Our author is not always careful that the epithet which he applies to a figurative term should answer on both sides. *Rude* is applicable to *rebellion*, but not to *eye*. He means in fact, – the eye of rude rebellion. (IV, 558–9)

[22] [On 5.7.15ff.: 'Death, having prey'd upon the outward parts, / Leaves them invisible; and his siege is now / Against the mind. . . .']
Invisible is here used adverbially. Death, having glutted himself with the ravage of the almost wasted body, and knowing that the disease with which he has assailed it is mortal, before its dissolution, proceeds, from mere satiety, to attack the mind, leaving the body *invisibly*; that is, in such a secret manner that the eye cannot *precisely* mark his progress, or see when his attack on the vital powers has ended, and that on the mind begins; or in other words, at what particular moment reason ceases to perform its function, and the understanding, *in consequence of a corroding and mortal malady*, begins to be disturbed.

Henry is here only pursuing the same train of thought which we find in his first speech in the present scene [5.7.1–5]. . . .

Mr Rowe reads – *her* siege –,[25] an errour derived from the corruption of the second folio. I suspect, that this strange mistake was Mr. Gray's authority for making *Death* a female; in which, I believe, he has neither been preceded or followed by any poet [Quotes 'Ode on a Distant Prospect of Eton College', ll. 83ff.]: 'The painful family of *Death*, / More hideous than their *queen*'.

The old copy, in the passage before us, reads – Against the *wind*; an evident errour of the press, which was corrected by Mr. Pope, and which I should scarcely have mentioned, but that it justifies an emendation made in *Measure for Measure* [2.3.11], where by a similar mistake the word *flawes* appears in the old copy instead of *flames*. (IV, 565–6)

2 Joseph Ritson, response to Malone

1792

From *Cursory Criticisms on the Edition of Shakespeare Published by Edmond Malone* (London, 1792).

Joseph Ritson (1752–1803) was a contentious, pedantic, and highly productive antiquary and literary scholar. Reputed for his eccentricity, combativeness, and fierce attention to detail, Ritson created his first scholarly disturbance in the Shakespearian world with his *Remarks, Critical and Illustrative, on the Text and Notes of the Last Edition of Shakespeare* (London, 1783). Herein he roundly castigated the Johnson-Steevens edition of 1778 for sloppiness and pretension, singling out Malone in particular for making the excessive claim, in his 1780 *Supplement* to the edition, that the text of Shakespeare's plays seemed finally to have been settled. Ritson later scornfully attacked Isaac Reed's editorial work for the 1785 revision of the Johnson-Steevens edition in *The Quip Modest* (London, 1788), but saved his most truculent and personal venom for Malone's 1790 edition. Malone, clearly stung by the intensity and occasional acuity of Ritson's criticisms, responded in *A Letter to the Rev. Richard Farmer* (London, 1792), acknowledging only a mere eight of the many errors Ritson claimed to have found in his edition. Perhaps the most notable outcome of the whole controversy was Malone's assault on the reliability of the second folio (1632), the textual authority of which he justly discounted, even in the face of Ritson's intemperate objections.

[From the Preface]

. . . By a *judicious restoration of ancient readings*, Mr. Malone seems to understand the replacing of all the gross and palpable blunders of the first folio, from which it has been the labour of such critics as Rowe, Pope, Theobald, Warburton, and Hanmer to purge the text. Mr Malone is a critic of a very different description.

I have thought proper, in the following pages, to make a few observations on some of Mr. Malone's notes. Now Mr. Malone will take this exceedingly ill; for Mr. Malone has a very high opinion of himself, and a very mean one of every body else. But I confess I do not seek to please Mr. Malone: I wish to rescue the language and sense of an admirable author from the barbarism and corruption they have acquired in passing through the hands of this incompetent and unworthy editor. In a word, I mean to convict and not to convince him.

The total want of *ear* and *judgement*, under which Mr. Malone will be found to labour, is undoubtedly a natural defect, for which he would be an object rather of pity than of reprehension, if he had not forced himself into an employment for which ear and judgement were essential, and nature, of course, in depriving him of those indispensable requisites, had utterly disqualified him. Want of courage, in a common man, may be considered as mere weakness of nerves; in a commander, it is punished with death.

But it is not the want of ear and judgement only of which I have to accuse Mr. Malone: he stands charged with divers other high crimes and misdemeanors against the divine majesty of our sovereign lord of the drama; with deforming his text, and degrading his margin, by intentional corruption, flagrant misrepresentation, malignant hypercriticism, and unexampled scurrility. These charges shall be proved – not, as Mr. Malone proves things, by groundless opinion and confident assertion, but – by fact, argument, and demonstration. How sayest thou, culprit? Guilty or not guilty? . . . . (viii–x)

★ ★ ★

[After his general prefatory remarks, Ritson mounts a specific defense of the textual authority of the second folio.]

. . . I shall now proceed to make the editor of the second folio some amends for the injustice, malevolence, and personal abuse of his Hibernian adversary, by displaying a few instances not only of his actual superiority to his predecessor (if, in fact, either edition had any other editor than the compositor of the press), but also where that superiority is admitted by Mr. Malone's own adoption. The latter case is distinguished by an asterisk. It was once my intention to have given, what Mr. Malone ought to have done, a fair and faithful collation of the various readings of the two editions; but the space and press-work required even by the following specimen and the necessity I should have thought myself under of going through them a second time, which no one needs to be told is a work of time and patience, will be a sufficient apology for not having carried it into effect at present. However, as Mr. Malone has preserved all the *errors* of the second folio, and I shall exhibit a considerable number, at least, of its *emendations*, the reader will, between us, have a tolerably complete view of the controversy. The first reading is that of the folio 1623, the other that of the folio 1632. . . . (9–10)

> K. JOHN.
> *It* would not be sir Nob in any case.
> *I* would not be sir Nob in any case. [1.1.147]
>
> Say, shall the current of our right *roam* on.
> Say shall the current of our right *run* on.[*] [2.1.335]
>
> Strong reasons make *strange* actions.
> Strong reasons make *strong* actions.[1] [3.4.182]
>
> 'Tis true to hurt his master, no *mans* else.
> 'Tis true to hurt his master, no *man* else.[*] [4.3.33] (22)

KING JOHN. P. 454 [1.1.161]
Kneel thou down, Philip, but rise more great.

'*More* is here used as a *dissyllable*.' [Malone's note]
To be sure it is: and this Mr. Tyrwhitt might have thought an additional proof that our poet 'had not forgotten his Chaucer:'

Kneel thou down, Philip, but rise *moré* great.

What an admirable thing is it to have a delicate ear! A plain hobbling fellow unblessed with that advantage would have only thought the little word *up* wanting, and spoiled, of course, a most excellent mono-dissyllable.

P. 468 [2.1.144]
It lies as sightly on the back of him
As great Alcides' *shoes* upon an ass:

'i.e. upon the hoofs of an ass.' [Malone's note]
This comment is at least in unison with the text. The idea of Hercules's *shoes* (N.B. Hercules wore no shoes) *lying* upon the *hoofs* of an *ass* is every way worthy of the ingenious Hibernian, from whom alone it could proceed. (60–1)

3 George Steevens, response to Malone

1793

From *The Plays of William Shakespeare. In Fifteen Volumes. With the Corrections and Illustrations of Various Commentators. To Which are Added, Notes by Samuel Johnson and George Steevens. The Fourth Edition. Revised and Augmented (with a Glossarial Index) by the Editor of Dodsley's Collection of Old Plays* (15 vols, London, 1793).

George Steevens (1736–1800) was one of the most active, influential, and fractious Shakespearians of his day. His involvement in major editions of Shakespeare in 1773, 1778, 1785, and 1793 drew him into frequent literary and personal squabbles, not the least of which was his celebrated rift with Edmond Malone. Malone had contributed a few notes for the Steevens-Reed edition of 1785 in which he disagreed with Steevens, leading Steevens to demand (unsuccessfully) that Malone reprint Steevens's notes unaltered in the new edition Malone eventually published in 1790 (No. 1 above). But according to William C. Woodson (see below), the friction between the two may have had its roots even earlier, during the preparation of the 1785 edition, at which time Malone appears to have discovered that Steevens was planning his own new edition, presumably to subvert Malone's, even as Malone was sharing his commentary notes with Steevens and Reed. The appearance of Steevens's edition in 1793 represented a personal and scholarly triumph of sorts, for his text soon supplanted Malone's as the standard version of the plays, enjoying frequent reprintings well into the nineteenth century. See Woodson, 'The 1785 Variorum Shakespeare', *Studies in Bibliography*, 28 (1975), 318–20; and 'The Printer's Copy for the 1785 Variorum Shakespeare', *Studies in Bibliography*, 31 (1978), 208–10. But also see Arthur Sherbo, 'George Steevens's 1785 Variorum Shakespeare', *Studies in Bibliography*, 32 (1979), 241–6, who argues that the breach between Steevens and Malone was rather less acrimonious than Woodson contends. Brian Vickers, however, *Shakespeare: The Critical Heritage*, 6 vols (London, 1974–81), VI, *passim* reprints numerous instances of the two editors feuding, at times rather hotly, in print.

[From the explanatory and commentary notes to *King John*]

[1] [On 1.1.27ff.: 'Be thou the trumpet of our wrath, / And sullen presage of your own decay', where Johnson objects that 'sullen' may not be applied to a trumpet but Malone argues that the metaphor is appropriate]

That here are two ideas, is evident; but the second of them has not been luckily explained. *The sullen presage of your own decay*, means, *the dismal passing bell, that announces your own approaching dissolution*. (VIII, 8)

[2] [On 1.1.161: 'but arise more great']
The old copy reads only – *rise*. Mr. Malone conceives this to be the true reading, and that '*more* is here used as a dissyllable.' I do not suppress this opinion, though I cannot concur in it. (VIII, 17)

[3] [On 2.1.65: 'With them a bastard of the king deceas'd', where Steevens sees the Folio reading 'king's' as erroneous, while Malone contends that there is no corruption since the same phrase occurs elsewhere in Shakespeare]
It may as justly be said, that the same error has been elsewhere repeated by the same illiterate compositors. (VIII, 32)

[4] [On 2.1.149: '*K. Phi.* Lewis, determine what we shall do straight']
Thus Mr. Malone, and perhaps rightly; for the next speech is given in the old copy (as it stands in the present text) to *Lewis* the dauphin, who was afterwards Lewis VIII. The speech itself, however, seems sufficiently appropriated to the King; and nothing can be inferred from the folio with any certainty, but that the editors of it were careless and ignorant. (VIII, 38)

[5] [On 2.1.335: 'Say, shall the current of our right run on?', where Malone follows F1's 'roam']
I prefer the reading of the second folio. So in *K. Henry V*: 'As many streams *run* into one self sea' [1.2.209]. The King would rather describe his right as *running on* in a *direct* than in an *irregular* course, such as would be implied by the word *roam*. (VIII, 50)

[6] [On 2.1.354: 'mouthing the flesh of men', where Malone, following F1, reads 'mousing' rather than Pope's 'mouthing']
I retain Mr. Pope's emendation,[1] which is supported by the following passage in *Hamlet*: ' – first *mouth'd* to be last swallowed' [4.2.18ff.]. Shakespeare designed no ridicule in this speech; and therefore did not write, (as when he was writing the burlesque interlude of *Pyramus and Thisbe*,) – *mousing* [5.1.269]. (VIII, 51)

[7] [On 2.1.477ff.: 'Lest zeal, now melted, by the windy breath / Of soft petitions, pity, and remorse, / Cool and congeal again to what it was', where Steevens sees Shakespeare comparing zeal to metal in a state of fusion rather than to dissolving ice, and Malone elaborately disagrees]
The *windy breath* that will *cool metals in a state of fusion*, produces not the effects of *frost*. I am therefore yet to learn, how 'the *soft petitions of Constance*, and *pity* for Arthur,' (two gentle agents) were competent to the act of *freezing*. – There is surely somewhat of impropriety, in employing *Favonius* to do the work of *Boreas*. (VIII, 61)

[8] [On 3.4.110: 'the sweet world's taste', where Malone, following F1, reads 'word's' rather than Pope's 'world's']
I prefer Mr. Pope's reading,[2] which is sufficiently justified by the following passage in *Hamlet*:

> How weary, *stale, flat* and unprofitable
> Seem to me all the uses of this *world*! [1.2.133ff.]

Our present rage for *restoration* from ancient copies, may induce some of our readers to exclaim, with Othello, – 'Chaos is *come again*' [3.3.92]. (VIII, 113)

[9] [On 3.4.182: 'Strong reasons make strong actions', where Malone upholds F1's 'strange actions']
The repetition in the second folio is perfectly in our author's manner, and is countenanced by the following passage in *King Henry V*:

> Think we King Harry *strong*,
> And, princes, look, you *strongly* arm to meet him. [2.4.48ff.]

[10] [On 5.7.15ff.: 'Death, having prey'd upon the outward parts, / Leaves them insensible; and his siege is now / Against the mind. . . .', where Malone reads 'invisible']
. . . As often as I am induced to differ from the opinions of a gentleman whose laborious diligence in the cause of Shakespeare is without example, I subject myself to the most unwelcome part of editorial duty. Success, however, is not in every instance proportionable to zeal and effort; and he who shrinks from controversy, should also have avoided the *vestibulum ipsum, primasque fauces*[3] of the school of Shakespeare.

Sir Thomas Hanmer gives us – *insensible*, which affords a meaning sufficiently commodious.[4] But as *invisible* and *insensible* are not words of exactest consonance, the legitimacy of this emendation has been disputed. It yet remains in the text, for the sake of those who discover no light through the ancient reading.

Perhaps (I speak without confidence) our author wrote – *invincible*, which, in sound, so nearly resembles *invisible*, that an inattentive compositor might have substituted the one for the other. – All our modern editors (Mr. Malone excepted) agree that *invincible* in *King Henry IV. P. II* [3.2.313] was a misprint for *invisible*; and so (*vice versa*) *invisible* may here have usurped the place of *invincible*.

If my supposition be admitted, the Prince must design to say, that Death had battered the royal outworks, but, seeing they were *invincible*, quitted them, and directed his force against the mind. In the present instance, the King of Terrors is described as a besieger, who, failing in his attempt to storm the bulwark, proceeded to undermine the citadel. Why else did he change his mode and object of attack? – The Spanish ordnance sufficiently *preyed* on the ramparts of Gibraltar, but still left them *impregnable*. – The same metaphor, though not continued so far, occurs again in *Timon of Athens*:

> ——————————Nature,
> To whom all sores lay *siege*. [4.3.6ff.]

Again, in *All's Well That Ends Well*:

>   —and yet my heart
> Will not confess he owes the malady
> That does my life *besiege*. [2.1.8ff.]

Mr. Malone, however, gives a different turn to the passage before us; and leaving the word *siege* out of his account, appears to represent Death as a gourmand, who had satiated himself with the King's body, and took his intellectual part by way of change of provision.

Neither can a complete acquiescence in the same gentleman's examples of adjectives used adverbially, be well expected; as they chiefly occur in light and familiar dialogue, or where the regular full-grown adverb was unfavourable to rhyme or metre. Nor indeed are these docked adverbs (which perform their office, like the witch's rat, 'without a tail,') discoverable in any solemn narrative like that before us. A portion of them also might be no other than typographical imperfections; for this part of speech, shorn of its termination, will necessarily take the form of an adjective. – I may subjoin, that in the beginning of the present scene [5.7.2], the adjective *corruptible* is not offered as a *locum tenens*[5] for the adverb *corruptibly*, though they were alike adapted to our author's measure.

It must, notwithstanding, be allowed that adjectives employed adverbially are sometimes met with in the language of Shakespeare. Yet, surely, we ought not (as Polonius says) to 'crack the wind of the poor phrase' [*Hamlet*, 1.3.108], by supposing its existence where it must operate equivocally, and provoke a smile, as on the present occasion.

That Death, therefore, 'left the outward parts of the King *invisible*,' could not, in my judgement, have been an expression hazarded by our poet in his most careless moment of composition. . . . Besides, if the outward part (i.e. the body) of the expiring monarch was, in plain, familiar, and unqualified terms, pronounced to be *invisible*, how could those who pretended to have just *seen* it, expect to be believed? And would not an audience, uninitiated in the mystery of adverbial adjectives, on hearing such an account of the royal carcase, have exclaimed, like the Governor of Tilbury Fort in the *Critic*:

>   —thou canst not *see* it,
> Because 'tis *not in sight*.[6]

But I ought not to dismiss the present subject, without a few words in defence of Mr. Gray, who had authority somewhat more decisive than that of the persecuted second folio of Shakespeare, for representing *Death* as a *Woman*.[7] The writer of the *Ode on a Distant Prospect of Eton College*, was sufficiently intimate with Lucretius, Horace, Ovid, Phaedrus, Statius, Petronius, Seneca the dramatist, &c. to know that they *all* concurred in exhibiting *Mors* as a *Goddess*. Mr. Spence in his *Polymetis*, p. 261,[8] (I refer to a book of easy access,) has produced abundant examples in proof of my assertion, and others may be readily supplied. One comprehensive instance, indeed, will answer my present purpose. Statius, in his eighth Thebaid, describing a troop of ghastly females who surrounded the throne of Pluto, has the following lines:

> *Stant Furiæ circum,* variæque *ex ordine* Mortes,
> *Sævaque multisonas exercet Pœna catenas.*[9]

From this group of personification, &c. it is evident, that not merely *Death*, as the source or principle of mortality, but each particular kind of Death was represented under a feminine shape. For want, therefore, of a corresponding masculine term, Dobson, in his Latin version of the second *Paradise Lost*, was obliged to render the terrific offspring of Satan, by the name of *Hades*; a luckless necessity, because *Hades*, in the 964th line of the same book, exhibits a character completely discriminated from that of *Death*.[10]

Were I inclined to be sportive, (a disposition which commentators should studiously repress,) might I not maintain on the strength of the foregoing circumstances, that the editor of the folio 1632 (far from being an ignorant blunderer,) was well instructed in the niceties of Roman mythology? And might not my ingenious fellow-labourer, on the score of his meditated triumph over Mr. Gray, be saluted with such a remark as reached the ear of Cadmus? –

> ——Quid, *Agenore nate, peremptum*
> *Serpentem spectas? et* tu *spectabere serpens.*[11]

Fashionable as it is to cavil at the productions of our Cambridge Poet, it has not yet been discovered that throughout the fields of classic literature, even in a single instance, he had mistook his way. (VIII, 177–80)

[11] [On 5.7.35: 'Poison'd, – ill-fare']
Mr. Malone supposes *fare* to be here used as a dissyllable, like *fire, hour*, &c. But as this word has not concurring vowels in it, like h*ou*r, or f*ai*r, nor was ever dissyllabically spelt (like fi*er*) fa*er*; I had rather suppose the present line imperfect, than complete it by such unprecedented means. (VIII, 181)

4 George Chalmers, on the date of *King John*

1799

From *A Supplemental Apology for the Believers in the Shakespeare-Papers: Being a Reply to Mr. Malone's Answer, Which Was Early Announced, but Never Published: with a Dedication to George Steevens, F.R.S. S.A. and a Postscript to T. J. Mathias, F.R.S. S.A. the Author of The Pursuits of Literature*, by George Chalmers, F.R.S. S.A. (London, 1799).

George Chalmers (1742–1825), Scottish antiquary and scholar, author of *Caledonia, or an Account Historical and Topographical, of North Britain* (3 vols, London, 1807, 1810, 1824), etched a small but permanent place for himself in literary history by being one of the most prominent literati deceived by William Henry Ireland's Shakespeare forgeries. Malone's *Inquiry into the Authenticity of Certain Miscellaneous Papers and Legal Instruments* (London, 1796), meticulously exposed the amateurism of Ireland's ruse and derided the scholarly capacities of those who had been duped by it. Chalmers retaliated, not so much to defend his now untenable position, but rather to vindicate the scholarly methods Malone had so imperiously dismissed in the *Inquiry*. To this end he published *An Apology for the Believers in the Shakespeare-Papers, Which Were Exhibited in Norfolk Street* (London, 1797), followed two years later by the *Supplemental Apology*. The latter work virtually abandons the question of the Ireland forgeries, but is nevertheless a striking example of Chalmers's scholarly values, particularly as they apply to matters of historical investigation.

... This tragedy [*King John*] exhibits, to the discerning eye, another example of Shakespeare's custom, of borrowing, continually, from preceding writers, *plots*, sentiments, speeches, and language.[1] As early as 1591, there had been a play, entitled, *The Troublesome Raigne of John King of England*. Shakespeare's tragedy was known to Meres, in 1598; as he names it in his *Wit's Treasury*, among our poet's other tragedies. It was, soon after, still better known to Marston, who plainly copied, as his custom was, when it suited him, a line of Shakespeare's drama into his *Insatiate Countess*, which was published, in 1603.

> Shak.   Why holds thine eye that lamentable rheum,
> Like a proud river peering o'er his bounds? [3.1.22ff.]

> Mars.   Then, how much more in me, whose youthful veins,
> Like a proud river, overflow their bounds.[2] [3.4.72ff.][3]

Such are the proofs, which show pretty certainly, that Shakespeare's *King John*, was written, between 1591, and 1598. In order to draw these extreme points closer together, Mr. Malone [No. 1 above] says, that Shakespeare having lost his only son, in 1596, was brought, by this misfortune, into a proper temper, for writing the pathetic lamentations of Constance, on her Arthur's death. But, at what time of his life, was Shakespeare unfit for drawing similar scenes of deeper distress? Johnson has observed, in a note, on this play, what applies more pertinently to the purpose, 'that many passages, in our poet's works, evidently show, how *often he took advantage of the facts then recent, and the passions, then in motion.*'[4] The fact is, that there are many allusions, in Shakespeare's *King John*, to the events of 1596, and to some, in 1597; though the commentators have not been very diligent, to collect them. The Pope published a Bull, against Elizabeth, in 1596; and the Pope's Nuntio made some offers to Henry IV, against Queen Elizabeth.[5] The scene with Pandulph, the papal legate, which alludes to those offers, must, as Johnson remarks, have been at the time it was written, during our struggles with popery, a very captivating scene.[6] The contradictory, shifting, policy of England, and France, as represented in *King John*, forms an admirable parody on the *adverse*, friendly, conduct of Elizabeth, and Henry the IV.[7] Let the siege of Angiers, in *King John*, be compared with the loss, and recapture of Amiens, in 1597, chiefly by the valour of the English reinforcements, under the gallant Baskerville. The altercations between the bastard, Faulconbridge, and Austria, while the conduct of the Archduke Albert was so unpopular in England, must have afforded a rich repast to an English audience. There is a strong allusion, particularly, in the last act, to the quarrel between Essex, and Raleigh, which began at Calais, in 1596, and rose to a more remarkable height, in 1597.[8] Owing to the many piques among the great, occasioned by the selfish ambition of Essex, the concluding remark of Faulconbridge must have been felt, and applauded, by the auditory:

———————Nought shall make us rue,
If England to itself do rest but true. [5.7.117ff.]

If to all those intimations, we add the remark of Johnson, how much advantage Shakespeare, constantly, derived from facts *then recent*, and the *passions then in motion*, there can no doubt remain, but that our poet's *King John* must be fixed to the spring time of 1598; as the true epoch of its original production. (356–9)

5 Elizabeth Inchbald, character and characterization

1808

From *King John; A Historical Play, in Five Acts; By William Shakespeare. As Performed at the Theatre Royal, Covent Garden. Printed Under the Authority of the Managers from the Prompt Book. With Remarks by Mrs. Inchbald* (London, 1808).

Elizabeth Inchbald (1753–1821) parlayed her celebrated beauty and natural charm into a modestly successful acting career, which she began shortly after her marriage to Joseph Inchbald, painter and actor, in 1772. Upon the sudden death of her husband in 1779 she turned to playwriting, producing on average a play a year from 1782 to 1799, many of which met with critical success. Her most important work, however, was the prose romance *A Simple Story* (4 vols, London, 1791), which attained immediate popularity, enhancing both her financial status and literary reputation. From 1806–9 she edited the twenty-five volume *British Theatre*, supplying brief prefatory 'remarks' to each acting copy.

[From the Prefatory 'Remarks']

This tragedy is one amongst Shakespeare's dramas, which requires, in representation, such eminent powers of acting, that it is scarcely ever brought upon the stage, but when a theatre has to boast of performers highly gifted in their art.

The part of King John is held most difficult to perform. John is no hero, and yet he is a murderer – his best actions are debased by meanness, deceit, or cowardice, and yet he is a king. Here is then to be portrayed, thirst of blood, without thirst of fame; and dignity of person, with a groveling mind.

Garrick was so little satisfied with his own performance of this character, that, after playing it with cold approbation from the audience, he changed it for the illegitimate Faulconbridge; where nature forced him to oppose the author's meaning by a diminutive person, though art did all its wonders in his favour.

The genius of Kemble gleams terrific through the gloomy John. No auditor can hear him call for his

> Kingdom's rivers to take their course
> Through his burn'd bosom, [5.7.38ff.]

and not feel for that moment parched with a scorching fever....

Though Hubert sinks in importance by not being of the blood royal in this play, his character is illustrious from his virtue. Cooke, in the habit of performing characters far superior, elevates Hubert so much above the level where performers in general place him, that he displays, in this single instance, abating every other, abilities of the very first class.

Constance is the favourite part both of the poet and the audience; and she has been highly fortunate under the protection of the actress. It was the part in which that idol of the public, Mrs. Cibber, was most of all adored; and the following lines, uttered by Mrs. Siddons in Constance,

> ————Here I and sorrow sit:
> This is my throne, bid kings come bow to it, [3.1.73ff.]

seem like a triumphant reference to her own potent skill in the delineation of woe, as well as to the agonizing sufferings of the mother of young Arthur.

Faulconbridge, one of the brightest testimonies of Shakespeare's comic power, is excellent relief to that part of the tragedy which may be styled more dull than pathetic. Mr C. Kemble personates this child of love, as Shakespeare himself could wish. – If those who remember Garrick in the part complain of C. Kemble's inferior gaiety and spirit, the inferiority is granted. Still, he would be something nearer an equality with this great archtype of actors, could but those critics recall *their* gaiety and spirit, which, in their juvenile days, inspired them with the ardour to admire.

Prince Arthur is of more importance than either manager or actors generally conceive. They seldom care whether a princely or plebeian child is to perform the part; whether from feature, or from voice, Arthur shall belie his royal birth, and take away all sympathy in his own and his mother's sufferings.

Though Shakespeare's *King John* is inferior to many of his plays, yet it contains some poetic passages, and some whole scenes, written with his hand, beyond all power of forgery. . . . (3–5)

6 August Wilhelm von Schlegel, personality and politics

1815

From *A Course of Lectures on Dramatic Art and Literature, by Augustus William Schlegel: Translated from the Original German by John Black. In Two Volumes* (2 vols, London, 1815). Revised [in one volume] by The Reverend A. J. W. Morrison, M.A. (London, 1846).

August Wilhelm von Schlegel (1767–1845), German poet, translator, and critic, was one of the leading figures of European Romanticism, a position he only solidified with a controversial attack on French classicism, *Comparaison entre la Phèdre de Racine et celle d'Euripide* (Paris, 1807). His poetical translation of Shakespeare's plays, which first appeared in unfinished form (9 vols, Berlin, 1797–1810) and was eventually completed under the superintendence of Ludwig Tieck by Tieck's daughter Dorothea and Graf W. H. Baudissin (9 vols, Berlin, 1825–33), is still widely regarded as a major scholarly and artistic achievement. Schlegel's most important critical observations on Shakespeare, however, occur in his lectures on dramatic art and literature, delivered at Vienna in the spring of 1808, and first published in German under the title *Über dramatische Kunst und Literatur* (2 vols, Heidelberg, 1809–11). The text reprinted here is that of Morrison, whose slight stylistic changes of Black's version are based on the last German edition of Schlegel's work. For ease of reference page numbers are given for both editions.

[From Lecture XXVI: 'Criticisms on Shakespeare's Historical Dramas']

[After a brief discussion of the relationship among the plays of the first and second tetralogies, Schlegel turns to *King John* and *Henry VIII.*]
... The two other historical plays taken from the English history are chronologically separate from this series: King John reigned nearly two centuries before Richard II., and between Richard III. and Henry VIII. comes the long reign of Henry VII., which Shakespeare justly passed over as unsusceptible of dramatic interest. However, these two plays may in some measure be considered as the Prologue and the Epilogue to the other eight. In *King John*, all the political and national motives which play so great a part in the following pieces are already indicated: wars and treaties with France; a usurpation, and the tyrannical actions which it draws after it; the influence of the clergy, the factions of the nobles. *Henry the Eighth* again shows us the transition to another age; the policy of modern Europe, a refined court-life under a voluptuous

monarch, the dangerous situation of favourites, who, after having assisted in effecting the fall of others, are themselves precipitated from power; in a word, despotism under a milder form, but not less unjust and cruel. By the prophecies on the birth of Elizabeth, Shakespeare has in some degree brought his great poem on English history down to his own time, as far at least as such recent events could yet be handled with security. He composed probably the two plays of *King John*[1] and *Henry the Eighth* at a later period, as an addition to the others.

In *King John* the political and warlike events are dressed out with solemn pomp, for the very reason that they possess but little of true grandeur. The falsehood and selfishness of the monarch speak in the style of a manifesto. Conventional dignity is most indispensable where personal dignity is wanting. The bastard Faulconbridge is the witty interpreter of this language: he ridicules the secret springs of politics, without disapproving of them, for he owns that he is endeavouring to make his fortune by similar means, and wishes rather to belong to the deceivers than the deceived, for in his view of the world there is no other choice. His litigation with his brother respecting the succession of his pretended father, by which he effects his acknowledgement at court as natural son of the most chivalrous king of England, Richard Cœur de Lion, forms a very entertaining and original prelude in the play itself. When, amidst so many disguises of real sentiments, and so much insincerity of expression, the poet shows us human nature without a veil, and allows us to take deep views of the inmost recesses of the mind, the impression produced is only the more deep and powerful. The short scene in which John urges Hubert to put out of the way Arthur, his young rival for the possession of the throne, is superlatively masterly: the cautious criminal hardly ventures to say to himself what he wishes the other to do. The young and amiable prince becomes a sacrifice of unprincipled ambition: his fate excites the warmest sympathy. When Hubert, about to put out his eyes with the hot iron, is softened by his prayers, our compassion would be almost overwhelming, were it not sweetened by the winning innocence of Arthur's childish speeches. Constance's maternal despair on her son's imprisonment is also of the highest beauty; and even the last moments of John – an unjust and feeble prince, whom we can neither respect nor admire – are yet so portrayed as to extinguish our displeasure with him, and fill us with serious considerations on the arbitrary deeds and the inevitable fate of mortals. (Morrison, 422–4; Black, II, 222–4)

7 Nathan Drake, Shakespeare's art of characterization

1817

From *Shakespeare and His Times: Including the Biography of the Poet; Criticisms on His Genius and Writings; A New Chronology of His Plays; A Disquisition on the Object of His Sonnets; and a History of the Manners, Customs, and Amusements, Superstitions, Poetry, and Elegant Literature of His Age. By Nathan Drake, M.D. Author of 'Literary Hours,' and of 'Essays on Periodical Literature'* (2 vols, London, 1817).

Nathan Drake (1766–1836) was able to strike a harmonious balance between his vocation as a physician and a lifelong interest in literature and literary studies. He was an active writer whose miscellaneous essays were highly regarded in his own time, but his major contribution to scholarship was his ambitious examination of Shakespeare's life and times, the unusual breadth and comprehensiveness of which set it apart from most earlier works on the subject. Some measure of Drake's influence may be gleaned from the appearance of two foreign reprints of his book: a one-volume French edition in English (Paris, 1838; reprinted 1843) and a German edition under the title *Shakespeare-almanach* (Berlin, 1836).

[From Chapter XI]

We are well aware, that, to many of our readers, the chronological discussion incident to a new arrangement [for the dating of Shakespeare's plays], will be lamented as tedious and uninteresting; the more so, as nothing absolutely certain can be expected as the result. That this part of our subject, therefore, may be as compressed as possible, we shall, in future, be very brief in offering a determination between the decisions of the two previous chronologers, reserving a somewhat larger space for the few instances in which it may be thought necessary to deviate from both.

Of the plays enumerated by Meres, in September, 1598, only two remain to be noticed in this portion of our work, namely, *King John* and *Love's Labour's Wonne*: –

16. KING JOHN: 1598.[1] Mr. Chalmers having detected some allusions in this play to the events of 1597, in addition to those which Mr. Malone had accurately referred to the preceding year, it becomes necessary, with the former of these gentlemen, to assign its production to the spring of 1598.[2]

If *King John*, as a whole, be not entitled to class among the very first rate compositions of our author, it can yet exhibit some scenes of superlative beauty and effect, and two characters supported with unfailing energy and consistency.

The bastard Faulconbridge, though not perhaps a very amiable personage, being somewhat too interested and worldly-minded in his conduct to excite much of our esteem, has, notwithstanding, so large a portion of *the very spirit of Plantagenet* in him, so much heroism, gaiety, and fire in his constitution, and, in spite of his vowed accommodation to the times,[3] such an open and undaunted turn of mind, that we cannot refuse him our admiration, nor, on account of his fidelity to John, however ill-deserved, our occasional sympathy and attachment. The alacrity and intrepidity of his daring spirit are nobly supported to the very last, where we find him exerting every nerve to rouse and animate the conscience-stricken soul of the tyrant.

In the person of Lady Constance, *Maternal Grief*, the most interesting passion of the play, is developed in all its strength; the picture penetrates to the inmost heart, and seared must those feelings be, which can withstand so powerful an appeal; for all the emotions of the fondest affection, and the wildest despair, all the rapid transitions of anguish, and approximating phrenzy, are wrought up into the scene with a truth of conception which rivals that of nature herself.

The innocent and beauteous Arthur, rendered doubly attractive by the sweetness of his disposition and the severity of his fate, is thus described by his doating mother: –

> But thou art fair, and at thy birth, dear boy!
> Nature and fortune join'd to make thee great;
> Of Nature's gifts thou may'st with lillies boast,
> And with the half-blown rose. [3.1.51ff.][4]

When he is captured, therefore, and imprisoned by John, and, consequently, sealed for destruction, who but Shakespeare could have done justice to the agonising sorrows of the parent? Her invocation to death, and her address to Pandulph, paint maternal despair with a force which no imagination can augment, and of which the tenderness and pathos have never been exceeded: [Quotes generously and haphazardly from 3.4.25ff., citing the text of Reed's 1803 variorum edition].

Independent of the scenes which unfold the striking characters of Constance and Faulconbridge, there are two others in this play which may vie with any thing that Shakespeare has produced; namely, the scene between John and Hubert, and that between Hubert and Arthur. The former, where the usurper obscurely intimates to Hubert his bloody wishes, is conducted in so masterly a manner, that we behold the dark and turbulent soul of John lying naked before us in all its deformity, and shrinking with fear even from the enunciation of its own vile purpose; 'it is one of the scenes,' as Mr. Steevens has well observed, 'to which may be promised a lasting commendation. Art could add little to its perfection; and time itself can take nothing from its beauties.'[5]

The scene with Hubert and the executioners, where the hapless Arthur supplicates for mercy, almost lacerates the heart itself; and is only rendered supportable by the tender and alleviating impression which the sweet innocence and artless eloquence of the poor child fix with indelible influence on the mind. Well may it be said, in the language of our poet, that he who can behold this scene without the gushing tribute of a tear,

> Is fit for treasons, stratagems, and spoils; –
> Let no such man be trusted. [*The Merchant of Venice*: 5.1.85ff.]

As for the character of John, which, from its meanness and imbecillity, seems not well calculated for dramatic representation, Shakespeare has contrived, towards the close of the drama, to excite in his behalf some degree of interest and commiseration; especially in the dying scene, where the fallen monarch, in answer to the enquiry of his son as to the state of his feelings, mournfully exclaims, –

> Poison'd, – ill fare; – dead, forsook, cast off. [5.7.35] (II, 419–22)

8 William Hazlitt, history and character

1817

From *Characters of Shakespeare's Plays* (London, 1817).

William Hazlitt (1778–1830), essayist and critic, owed (and acknowledged) a substantial intellectual debt to Schlegel (No. 6 above); but it was the long critical shadow of Dr. Johnson that provided the real impetus for Hazlitt's gathering of essays on Shakespeare. Hazlitt regarded Johnson's Shakespearian criticism as reductively insistent upon artistic rules, conventional propriety, and the dull tyranny of common sense, all of which, in Hazlitt's view, joined unhappily to obscure Johnson's perception of what was most fanciful or passionate in Shakespeare. In opposition to Johnson's tendencies toward over-generalization and didacticism, Hazlitt undertook his corrective study, with its strong emphasis upon delicate and highly particularized shades of character, fineness of feeling, and imaginative intensity. The result was a landmark of romantic criticism, that, in its often eloquent and at times extravagant resistance to Augustan principles of art, cast a long critical shadow of its own.

King John is the last of the historical plays we shall have to speak of; and we are not sorry that it is. If we are to indulge our imaginations, we had rather do it upon an imaginary theme; if we are to find subjects for the exercise of our pity and terror, we prefer seeking them in fictitious danger and fictitious distress. It gives a *soreness* to our feelings of indignation or sympathy, when we know that in tracing the progress of sufferings and crimes, we are treading upon real ground, and recollect that the poet's 'dream' *denoted a foregone conclusion* – irrevocable ills, not conjured up by fancy, but placed beyond the reach of poetical justice. That the treachery of King John, the death of Arthur, the grief of Constance, had a real truth in history, sharpens the sense of pain, while it hangs a leaden weight on the heart and the imagination. Something whispers us that we have no right to make a mock of calamities like these, or to turn the truth of things into the puppet and play-thing of our fancies. 'To consider thus' may be 'to consider too curiously' [*Hamlet*, 5.1.205ff.]; but still we think that the actual truth of the particular events, in proportion as we are conscious of it, is a drawback on the pleasure as well as the dignity of tragedy.

King John has all the beauties of language and all the richness of the imagination to relieve the painfulness of the subject. The character of King John himself is kept pretty much in the back-ground; it is only marked in by comparatively slight indications. The crimes he is tempted to commit are such as are thrust upon him rather by circumstances and opportunity than of his own seeking: he is here represented as more cowardly than cruel, and as more contemptible than odious. The play embraces only a part of his history. There are however few characters on the stage that excite more disgust and loathing. He has no intellectual grandeur or strength of character to shield him from the indignation which his immediate conduct provokes: he stands naked and defenceless, in that respect, to the worst we can think of him: and besides, we are impelled to put the very worst construction on his meanness and cruelty by the tender picture of the beauty and helplessness of the object of it, as well as by the frantic and heart-rending pleadings of maternal despair. We do not forgive him the death of Arthur because he had too late revoked his doom and tried to prevent it, and perhaps because he has himself repented of his black design, our *moral sense* gains courage to hate him the more for it. We take him at his word, and think his purposes must be odious indeed, when he himself shrinks back from them. The scene in which King John suggests to Hubert the design of murdering his nephew is a master-piece of dramatic skill, but it is still inferior, very inferior to the scene between Hubert and Arthur, when the latter learns the orders to put out his eyes. If any thing ever was penned, heart-piercing, mixing the extremes of terror and pity, of that which shocks and that which soothes the mind, it is this scene. We will give it entire, though perhaps it is tasking the reader's sympathy too much. [Quotes 4.1].

His [Arthur's] death afterwards, when he throws himself from his prison-walls, excites the utmost pity for his innocence and friendless situation, and well justifies the exaggerated denunciations of Faulconbridge to Hubert whom he suspects wrongfully of the deed. [Quotes 4.3.123–33: 'There is not yet so ugly a fiend of hell. . . .'].

The excess of maternal tenderness, rendered desperate by the fickleness of friends and the injustice of fortune, and made stronger in will, in proportion to the want of all other power, was never more finely expressed than in Constance. The dignity of her answer to King Philip, when she refuses to accompany his messenger, 'To me and to the state of my great grief, let kings assemble' [3.1.70ff.], her indignant reproach to Austria for deserting her cause, her invocation to death, 'that love of misery' [3.4.35], however fine and spirited, all yield to the beauty of the passage, where, her passion subsiding into tenderness, she addresses the Cardinal in these words: – [Quotes 3.4.76–98: 'Oh father Cardinal, I have heard you say. . . .']. The contrast between the mild resignation of Queen Katherine [in *Henry VIII*] to her own wrongs, and the wild, uncontrollable affliction of Constance for the wrongs which she sustains as a mother, is no less naturally conceived than it is ably sustained throughout these two wonderful characters.

The accompaniment of the comic character of the Bastard was well chosen to relieve the poignant agony of suffering, and the cold, cowardly policy of behaviour in the principal characters of this play. Its spirit, invention, volubility of tongue, and forwardness in action, are unbounded. *Aliquando sufflaminandus erat*, says Ben Jonson of Shakespeare.[1] But we should be sorry if Ben Jonson had been his licenser. We prefer the heedless magnanimity of his wit infinitely to all Jonson's laborious caution. The character of the Bastard's comic humour is the same in essence as that of other comic characters in Shakespeare; they always run on with good things and are never exhausted; they are always daring and successful. They have words at will and a flow of wit, like a flow of animal spirits. The difference between Faulconbridge and the others is that he is a soldier, and brings his wit to bear upon action, is courageous with his sword as well as tongue, and stimulates his gallantry by his jokes, his enemies feeling the sharpness of his blows and the sting of his sarcasms at the same time. Among his happiest sallies are his descanting on the composition of his own person, his invective against 'commodity, tickling commodity' [2.1.573ff.], and his expression of contempt for the Archduke of Austria, who had killed his father, which begins in jest but ends in serious earnest. His conduct at the siege of Angiers shews that his resources were not confined to verbal retorts. – The same exposure of the policy of courts and camps, of kings, nobles, priests, and cardinals, takes place here as in the other plays we have gone through, and we shall not go into a disgusting repetition.

This, like the other plays taken from English history, is written in a remarkably smooth and flowing style, very different from some of the tragedies, *Macbeth*, for instance. The passages consist of a series of single lines, not running into one another. This peculiarity in the versification, which is most common in the three parts of *Henry VI.* has been assigned as a reason why those plays were not written by Shakespeare. But the same structure of verse occurs in his other undoubted plays, as in *Richard II.* and in *King John*. The following are instances: – [Quotes 2.1.423–45: 'That daughter there of Spain, the lady Blanch. . . .'].

Another instance, which is certainly very happy as an example of the simple enumeration of a number of particulars, is Salisbury's remonstrance against the second crowning of the king. [Quotes 4.2.9–16: 'Therefore to be possessed with double pomp. . . .']. (243–54)

9 William Oxberry, prefatory remarks on *King John*

1819

From *King John. A Historical Play; by William Shakespeare. With Prefatory Remarks. The Only Edition Existing Which is Faithfully Marked with the Stage Business, and Stage Directions, as it is Performed at the Theatres Royal. By W. Oxberry, Comedian* (London, 1819).

William Oxberry (1784–1824) was an actor of modest but hardly negligible reputation and accomplishment who distinguished himself chiefly as a performer of minor comic roles. His acting career was both extensive and varied, and his association with the theatre virtually lifelong. His *King John* forms part of *The New English Drama*, a series of one-hundred and thirteen plays, each preceded by Oxberry's terse yet often pithy critical remarks, which appeared regularly from 1818 to 1825.

[From the Prefatory 'Remarks']

King John, though certainly not the best, is amongst the best, of Shakespeare's Tragic Dramas; there is in it, a great variety of characters and all distinguished with most wonderful precision. The great defect is, that the interest does not sufficiently centre in any one individual of the play, and the death of King John, the ultimate object, is not obviously connected with the minor incidents; yet, even this last censure must be admitted within certain limits, for a connexion does exist between the general events and the catastrophe, though not perhaps very strongly marked; the quarrel with France, respecting Arthur, leads to the invasion of that country, the invasion to a treaty; and from the breaking of this treaty, by the papal ban, arises the violent seizure of the property of the Church, and this again induces the poisoning of the monarch, by a revengeful monk. In all this, there seems to be no want of context; not a link in the chain is broken; the fact seems to be, that the beginning and the end are too remote from each other; there are too many connecting links between the first and the last object, that when we have attained the one, we lose sight of the other.

The character of John, though drawn with great accuracy and vigour is not precisely one of those which affect our sympathy or excite our admiration; vice, when accompanied by any splendid quality, whether it be wit, or mind, or courage, is sure to obtain our reluctant approbation; in the scale of depravity, Richard [III] is infinitely above King John, yet the giant iniquities of the former always delight; while the cold, weak, suspicious John lives without our pleasure and dies without our regret. Not that we would infer that the character of John is less true to nature; far from it, but there are some virtues as well as vices, which are too quiet to excite our sympathy.

Faulconbridge, is one of those characters which Shakespeare apparently delighted to draw, and in which he has never found a rival. In Congreve, and in the French Comedies, all the witty characters seem to be wits by profession; their aim is, ever to say, smart pointed things; and certainly, these efforts are successful; – but Shakespeare's Faulconbridge has no effort; he is humorous from the overflowing abundance of his fancy, and from animal spirits[1] that are incapable of restraint; with him wit is a part of his nature, a quality which he can no more change than the height of his stature; – with the French, wit is an assumption; a thing of education, or rather of habit.

The grief of Constance, on the loss of her darling child, is another proof of Shakespeare's admirable knowledge of the human heart; it is not only true to nature, but true to character; it is indeed royal grief.

The scene between Hubert and the child, though it has been much praised, has little deserved it; the wretched conceits put into the mouth of young Arthur, are fatal to it; and, neither on the stage, [n]or in the closet, does it produce the least effect.

As a whole, though the plot is far from excellent, and the language with few exceptions is not of the first order, yet the variety and exquisite truth of the characters, place it high on the scale of dramatic composition. (i–ii)

10 Augustine Skottowe, *The Troublesome Raigne* and *King John*

1824

From *The Life of Shakespeare; Enquiries into the Originality of His Dramatic Plots and Characters; and Essays on the Ancient Theatres and Theatrical Usages*. By Augustine Skottowe (2 vols, London, 1824).

The scant facts available regarding the life and personality of Augustine Skottowe may perhaps be inferred from his *Memoir of the Life and Writings of Charles Mills* (London, 1828). This short biography, anonymously published and relentlessly encomiastic, includes a good deal of undocumented correspondence between Mills and certain anonymous 'friends', one of whom may very probably be Skottowe. A shorter version of Skottowe's *Life of Shakespeare*, revised by Adolph Wagner, appeared as part of the forty-three volume edition of Shakespeare's dramatic works by A. W. Schlegel, et al. (Vienna, 1825–7).

[Skottowe, following Malone (No.1 above), dates *King John* 1596.]

In the composition of his English historical plays, Shakespeare usually referred to the Chronicles of Holinshed for the facts necessary for his purpose. On the present occasion, however, he rested satisfied with the authority of an anonymous play, in two parts, printed in 1591. Its title is, *The Troublesome Raigne of John King of England, with the Discoverie of King Richard Cordelion's base Sonne (vulgarly named the Bastard Faulconbridge): also, the Death of King John at Swinstead Abbey.*

The various events of John's confused reign are ill calculated for dramatic representation, in which the want of a leading interest is imperfectly supplied by a mere collection of incidents. The great fault of the old play is, that it gives a very inadequate idea of what it professes to represent. If the reader be not previously acquainted with the history, he will in vain seek a knowledge of it from the progress of the scene. It is scarcely ever clear, for instance, whether the barons are in arms against the king in defence of their own liberties, or as the tools of Philip and partisans of Lewis, and thus the supporters of the cause of the pope. Throughout the play, indeed, John's disagreement with his nobility, and their extensive confederacy against him, for the protection of their independence, are kept too much out of sight; and of an event so important as the signature of Magna Charta, there is a total neglect. With almost implicit fidelity, Shakespeare copied the old play in its story and scenic arrangement of circumstances. He seldom corrects his author, but with him attributes the death of Richard the First to the Duke of Austria, and names that duke 'Lymoges' [3.1.114]. Richard was, indeed, imprisoned on his return from Palestine, by Leopold Duke of Austria; but he met his death, several years afterwards, from the hand of Bertrand de Gourdon, while besieging Vidomar, vicount of Limoges, in the castle of Chalus. Holinshed relates that Arthur was imprisoned in Falais, and afterwards at Rouen, and in this latter place he was supposed to be murdered: in the old play, Arthur is confined somewhere in England, and there Shakespeare also confines him.

Shakespeare has forcibly displayed the art, sophistry, insincerity, and ambition of the court of Rome; but it is singular that he has not, like the author of the old play, exhibited the depravity of the monastic orders, and the horrid tendency of papistical principles.

The same view is taken of John's character by Shakespeare, and by the anonymous author. In prosperity he is bold and insolent, and overbearing; in adversity, an abject coward; – weak in judgment, precipitate in action. With no views beyond the exigency of the moment, he eagerly attempts the accomplishing of his desires, unrestrained by religious awe, and unchecked by moral principle. Devoid of talent, he reaps not the benefit of his villainy: superior ability overreaches him; he succumbs to the power he insolently defies, and affectedly despises, and he is at once the object of hatred and contempt.

The old play makes John an usurper, and not, as represented by Holinshed, the legal possessor of the throne under the dying testament of his predecessor, and brother, Richard. It was the object of both the dramatists to excite pity in favour of Arthur, and they, therefore, judiciously suppressed the facts recorded by Holinshed, that the nobility 'willingly took their oaths of obedience' to John, and that the pretensions of his nephew were at one time so little insisted upon, that 'a peace was concluded upon betwixt King John and Duke Arthur.'[1]

The most celebrated, and, indeed, the best scene in Shakespeare's play, is that in which the tyrant insinuates to Hubert his wishes for the death of Arthur: its whole merit is Shakespeare's, the bare hint for such an interview in the original play being comprised in the following lines: [Quotes *The Troublesome Raigne*: 4.30–5].

The sequel to this scene, Hubert's explanation to John that Arthur had not been sacrificed, is generally illustrative of Shakespeare's method of treating his predecessor's composition [4.2]. The beautiful passage descriptive of the general and deep sensation excited by the report of the death of Arthur is entirely Shakespeare's, as are, also, John's ungrateful reflections on Hubert's supposed obedience to his command. [Quotes 4.2.208ff.: 'It is the curse of kings to be attended / By slaves. . . .'].

The remainder of the scene is inimitably amplified from the following passage of the old play: [Quotes *The Troublesome Raigne*: 8.261–71].

Shakespeare's representation of John suffering under poison, and desiring winter and the bleak winds of the north to cool his internal heat, is a circumstance borrowed from the old play: how eloquently he has amplified the idea of his predecessor, requires not to be pointed out:

> Philip, some drink; oh! for the frozen Alps,

> To tumble on and cool this inward heat
> That rageth as the furnace seven-fold hot. [15.53ff.]

Few scenes of deeper pathos occur in Shakespeare than the triumph of humanity over sternness in the breast of Hubert, and the glory is due to Shakespeare only.

The pleadings of Arthur, in the old play, are the reasonings of an adult, harsh, quaint, and cold. Shakespeare has converted the young man into a child, and artfully invested his supplications with the beautiful simplicity of infantine innocence. One specimen of the style of the old play will be sufficient. [Quotes *The Troublesome Raigne*: 7.103–33].

From Arthur we naturally turn to his mother, the Lady Constance, who makes a far less prominent and alluring figure in history than on the stage. The tragic muse has not described her as the widow of Geffrey, the divorced wife of the earl of Chester, and the actual consort of a third husband, Guie de Tours, but has represented the only beautiful feature in her character — maternal tenderness, — and super-added the '*widow's* plaint, that issues from a wounded soul' [*The Troublesome Raigne*: 2.457ff.]. In Shakespeare, also, she is

> ——————————— sick and capable of fears,
> Oppress'd with wrongs, and therefore full of fears;
> A *widow, husbandless*, subject to fears. [3.1.12ff.]

The maternal distress of Constance, in the old play, is clamorous and passionate, vindictive and contumelious. The hand of Shakespeare tempered her rage into vehemence, attuned her clamour to eloquence, and (for the most part) modulated her coarse vindictiveness into a deep sense of gross injuries and undeserved misfortunes. For those passages in her character most worthy of admiration, Shakespeare drew chiefly from his own resources. Of her eloquent rejoinder to the prayer of Arthur that she would be 'content' [3.1.42], not a trace is to be met with in the original, nor of that noble burst of passion [Quotes 3.1.68–74: 'I will instruct my sorrows to be proud. . . .'].

Equally free from obligation, also, in the same scene, is Constance's designation of the nuptial day of Blanch and Lewis, and her animated exposure of the perfidy of Philip and Austria.

The entrance of Constance, in the fourth scene of the third act, is prefaced, in the old play, by Philip's observation:

> To aggravate the measure of our grief,
> All malcontent comes Constance for her son.
> Be brief, good madam, for your face imports
> A tragick tale behind that's yet untold.
> Her passions stop the organ of her voice,
> Deep sorrow throbeth mis-befall'n events;
> Out with it lady, that our act may end
> A full catastrophe of sad laments. [5.16ff.]

Shakespeare substituted the following vivid picture:

> Look, who comes here! a grave unto a soul;
> Holding the eternal spirit, against her will,
> In the vile prison of afflicted breath: – [3.4.17ff.]

The whole of the part is Shakespeare's from the striking apostrophe to death [Quotes 3.4.25ff.: 'Death, death: – O amiable, lovely death. . . .'], to Constance's beautiful detail of her inducements for doating upon grief [Quotes 3.4.93ff.: 'Grief fills the room up of my absent child. . . .']. This is the last scene of her appearance.

The bold admixture of broad humour, sarcastic bitterness, and playful levity, in a plain, blunt, and unpretending Englishman [i.e., the Bastard], was first sketched in the *Troublesome Raigne*. The character is not wrought with the care, nor pointed with the emphasis, that mark the Faulconbridge of Shakespeare, yet it is delineated with much discrimination and vigour. . . . (I, 127–35)

Faulconbridge's keen reflections on the universal sway of interest in every transaction of life [2.1.561ff.: 'Mad world, mad kings. . . .'], is entirely Shakespeare's, as is the fine strain of humour with which Austria is taunted through the first scene of the third act. Shakespeare has nobly elevated the Bastard by his feeling and manly conduct when Hubert is accused of the murder of Arthur [4.3], and by assigning him some of the most animated sentences in the play. Of his appeal to the courage, pride, and glory of John [Quotes 5.1.44ff.: 'But wherefore do you droop. . . .']; his bold defiance of Lewis [Quotes 5.2.128ff.: 'Now hear our English king. . . .']; and his affectionate lament over the dead body of the king, there are no traces in the original play.

The singular inattention of Shakespeare to a highly poetic passage in the old *King John*, demands its quotation here. It is the imprecation of the Bastard on Austria, whom he had in vain pursued in the field of battle.

> And art thou gone! misfortune haunt thy steps,
> And chill cold fear assail thy times of rest.
> Morpheus, leave here thy silent ebon cave;
> Besiege his thoughts with dismal fantasies,
> And ghastly objects of pale threatening maws.
> Affright him every minute with stern looks,
> Let shadow temper terror in his thoughts,
> And let the terror make the coward mad,
> And in his madness let him fear pursuit,
> And so in frenzy let the peasant die. [2.236ff.]

Shakespeare is the author of the best passages in John, Arthur, Constance and Faulconbridge, though the stamp of each character remains unaltered from what he found it. He did not act fairly by himself: he adopted the plot of his predecessor in all its details, and his characters in their several groupings, and thus circumscribed his own power of improvement. (I, 137–8)

11 Samuel Weller Singer, introduction to *King John*

1826

From *The Dramatic Works of William Shakespeare. With Notes, Original and Selected,* by Samuel Weller Singer, F.S.A. and a *Life of the Poet,* by Charles Symmons, D.D. (10 vols, Chiswick, 1826).

Samuel Weller Singer (1783–1858), editor and translator, devoted much of his active scholarly life to the study of sixteenth- and seventeenth-century literature. He is best known among Shakespearians for his 1826 edition of the plays, reissued in 1856 with a series of critical essays by his friend William Watkiss Lloyd (No. 27 below); but he also contributed an important (and early) attack on the authenticity of John Payne Collier's manuscript corrections in the so-called Perkins Folio, *The Text of Shakespeare Vindicated* (London, 1853). His scholarly interests ranged widely, embracing the history of playing cards, Anglo-Saxon linguistics, and the editing of historical documents, most notably the correspondence of Henry Hyde, Earl of Clarendon and his brother Lawrence Hyde, Earl of Rochester (London, 1828). Even in his so-called 'retirement' he produced editions of Herrick (2 vols, London, 1846), Bacon's essays (London, 1856), and a translation of Luther's *The Way to Prayer* (London, 1846).

[From the 'Preliminary Remarks']

... Shakespeare has followed the old play [i.e., *The Troublesome Raigne*] in the conduct of its plot, and has even adopted some of its lines. The number of quotations from Horace, and similar scraps of learning scattered over this motley piece, ascertain it to have been the work of a scholar. It contains likewise a quantity of rhyming Latin and ballad metre; and, in a scene where the Bastard is represented as plundering a monastery, there are strokes of humour which, from their particular turn, were most evidently produced by another hand than that of Shakespeare. Pope attributes the old play to Shakespeare and Rowley conjointly; but we know not on what foundation.[1] Dr. Farmer thinks there is no doubt that Rowley wrote the old play; and when Shakespeare's play was called for, and could not be procured from the players, a piratical bookseller reprinted the old one under his name.[2]

Though, as Johnson observes, *King John* is not 'written with the utmost power of Shakespeare,'[3] yet it has parts of preeminent pathos and beauty, and characters highly interesting, drawn with great force and truth. The scene between John and Hubert is perhaps one of the most masterly and striking which our poet ever penned. The secret workings of the dark and turbulent soul of the usurper, ever shrinking from the full developement of his own bloody purpose, the artful expressions of grateful attachment by which he wins Hubert to do the deed, and the sententious brevity of the close, manifest that consummate skill and wonderful knowledge of human character which are to be found in Shakespeare alone. But what shall we say of that heart-rending scene between Hubert and Arthur, a scene so deeply affecting the soul with terror and pity, that even the sternest bosom must melt into tears; it would perhaps be too overpowering for the feelings, were it not for the 'alleviating influence of the innocent and artless eloquence of the poor child.'[4] His death afterwards, when he throws himself from the prison walls, excites the deepest commiseration for his hapless fate. The maternal grief of Constance, moving the haughty unbending soul of a proud queen and affectionate mother to the very confines of the most hopeless despair, bordering on madness, is no less finely conceived than sustained by language of the most impassioned and vehement eloquence. How exquisitely beautiful are the following lines: [Quotes 3.4.93–8: 'Grief fills the room up of my absent child. . . .'].

Shakespeare has judiciously preserved the character of the Bastard Faulconbridge, which was furnished him by the old play, to alleviate by his comic humour the poignant grief excited by the too painful events of the tragic part of the play. Faulconbridge is a favourite with every one: he is not only a man of wit, but an heroic soldier; and we lean toward him from the first for the good humour he displays in his litigation with his brother respecting the succession to his supposed father: –

> He hath a trick of Cœur de Lion's face,
> The very spirit of Plantagenet! [1.1.85; 1.1.167]

This bespeaks our favour toward him: his courage, his wit, and his frankness secure it. . . .

. . . Our commiseration is a little excited for the fallen and degraded monarch toward the close of the play. The death of the king and his previous suffering are not among the least impressive parts; they carry a pointed moral. . . . (IV, 327–9).

12 George Daniel, prefatory remarks on *King John*

1826

From *King John: A Tragedy, in Five Acts, By William Shakespeare. Printed from the Acting Copy, with Remarks, Biographical and Critical, to Which are Added, a Description of the Costume, – Cast of the Characters, Entrances and Exits, – Relative Positions of the Performers on the Stage, – and the Whole of the Stage Business. As Now Performed at the Theatres Royal, London. Embellished with a Portrait of Mr. Macready, as King John* (London, 1826).

George Daniel (1789–1864) spent a good deal of his early literary life writing topical satires and theatrical comedies and farces. From 1823 to 1831, however, he undertook the ambitious task of editing *Cumberland's British Theatre, with Remarks, Biographical and Critical. Printed from the Acting Copies, as Performed at the Theatres-Royal, London*. Writing under the initials 'D——G', Daniel produced brief and eclectic prefatory 'remarks' to the nearly three hundred plays in the series, which, in addition to their critical acumen, often provided valuable insights into the theatrical practices and tastes of the day. In his later years Daniel became a serious collector of books and literary artifacts, establishing himself as a noted authority on Elizabethan ballads, Shakespearian quartos and folios, and various other theatrical curiosities.

[From the prefatory 'Remarks']

... The plot of *King John* is from the English historians: on this foundation Shakespeare has raised a superstructure of great variety and beauty. If the towering majesty that distinguishes some of his grander productions be not always discernible in this, there are certain parts that bear full evidence of the master's hand: and terror and pity, two of the most powerful attributes of tragedy, are excited in no ordinary degree by the unrelenting cruelty of John, and the maternal sorrows of Lady Constance.

The portrait of King John is maintained with historical truth. He has all the ferocity of Richard [III], without any of his bravery – cruel, fickle, and treacherous – irresolute, save in the commission of evil – and then pursuing his dark purposes without pity or remorse; for, in the scene with Hubert, where he reproaches his minion with the death of young Arthur, and impatiently exclaims –

> It is the curse of kings, to be attended

> By slaves, that take their humours for a warrant
> To break within the bloody house of life – [4.2.208ff.]

it is not compunction for the deed, but dread of the consequences, that wring from him those passionate expressions. The incursions of France, with a powerful army into his dominions – the unexpected death of his mother – the desertion of his most attached courtiers – have broken down his spirit: added to these disasters, his superstitious fears are awakened by signs and wonders equally mysterious and alarming: [Quotes 4.2.182–6: 'My lord, they say *five moons* were seen to-night. . . .']. In the vain hope of appeasing the wrath of man – and the still vainer one, of heaven – he becomes reconciled with the Romish church; and, if the authority of history may be relied on, falls by the treachery of one of that communion, into whose arms he had thrown himself for pardon and protection.

There is no character in the writings of Shakespeare that bears stronger evidence of his peculiar manner than the Bastard Faulconbridge. He is a singular compound of heroism, levity, and – if his accommodating himself to the spirit of the times deserve so harsh a term – servility. He is, in truth, a soldier of fortune; acknowledging no law but that of honour, which, in a military sense, has somewhat of an equivocal signification. He compromises his own interest, and his mother's fame, for the proud distinction of being esteemed the base-born son of the Lion-hearted Richard; and enlists himself under the banners of a tyrannical usurper, for the vaunted display of personal prowess against the injured and unprotected. Yet, with all these blemishes, Shakespeare has painted him in such bewitching colours – he has given him such nobleness of spirit – so much candour and frankness – such exquisite powers of wit and raillery – that his very errors are turned to good account, and, like the irregularities of Falstaff, form the most seductive parts of his character. To reconcile such seeming incongruities, is one of the many triumphs of Shakespeare. He knew that character consists not of *one*, but of *various* humours; and to blend them skillfully, without violating nature or probability, was an art that he left for the study and emulation of all future dramatists.

But the great charm of this play, is the Lady Constance: a character conceived with Shakespeare's profoundest art, and finished with his utmost skill. Every feeling of her bosom – every emotion of joy or sorrow – have their origin in *maternal tenderness*. In that all-powerful passion every thing is centered: her anxious solicitude – her bitter reproaches – her phrenzy – her despair. Can indignation and contempt borrow stronger terms than her reply to Austria: [Quotes 3.1.114–29: 'O Lymoges! O Austria! thou dost shame / That bloody spoil. . . .']. Where is sorrow depicted with greater pathos, than her distraction for the death of Arthur; and grief unutterable and past consolation, never produced an image more solemn and majestic than the following: –

> To me, and to the state of my great grief,
> Let kings assemble ―――――
> ―――――――――――Here I and sorrow sit
> Here is my throne – bid kings come bow to it. [3.1.70ff.]

The belief that those whom we have loved, and have been beloved by, on earth, shall meet, and recognise each other in a happier state of existence – a belief, glorious for the consolation that it affords, and perfectly consistent with our ideas of immortality – is thus pathetically alluded to by Lady Constance, in her reply to Cardinal Pandulph: [Quotes 3.4.76–8: 'O, father cardinal, I have heard you say. . . .'].

There are two scenes of superlative excellence in this play: the one, where John discloses his dark purpose to Hubert; the other, where the horrible imaginings of Hubert are defeated by the artless innocence and pathetic entreaties of the unhappy Arthur. Indeed, the latter is almost too powerful a trial for our sensibility: the effects are so truly distressing, that to render them bearable is the strongest test of dramatic skill.

The language of this play is for the most part dignified and impressive. All that belongs to Lady Constance is of the highest mood of sentiment and poetry. The gaiety of Faulconbridge, though occasionally running into freedom and extravagance, is bold and characteristic, and might be allowable in an age when thoughts and words bore less palpable constructions. The incidents are deficient in connexion and continuity, and embrace a considerable portion of time: the scene is alternately laid in England and France. . . . (5–7)

[Daniel concludes his introductory essay with anecdotal comments on celebrated actors who played the major roles in *King John*, noting that although Eliza O'Neill as Constance displayed 'grace, dignity, and true feeling', her performance lacked the 'electric fire' Sarah Siddons brought to the role. Very brief and impressionistic comments on male actors who played in *King John* follow (7–8).]

13 James Boaden, Sarah Siddons as Constance

1827

From *Memoirs of Mrs. Siddons. Interspersed with Anecdotes of Authors and Actors. By James Boaden, Esq.* (2 vols, London, 1827).

James Boaden (1762–1839) was a noted journalist, serving as the first editor of *The Oracle*, and the author of a number of popular plays from 1793 to 1803. He was an early believer in the Ireland forgeries, but publicly recanted his views in *A Letter to George Steevens* (London, 1796); years later he entered the scholarly lists more credibly with a series of articles in *The Gentleman's Magazine* for 1832 in which he identified the mysterious 'Mr. W. H.' to whom the sonnets are dedicated as William Herbert, afterwards Earl of Pembroke. These articles were to become the basis for a later book, *On the Sonnets of Shakespeare* (London, 1837). Boaden spent the last years of his life writing biographies of famous stage personalities, including Kemble (1825), Mrs. Siddons (1827), Mrs. Jordan (1831), and Mrs. Inchbald (1833). His *Memoirs of the Life of John Philip Kemble, Esq.* (2 vols, London, 1825) also includes some brief and impressionistic remarks on the performance of Mrs. Siddons as Constance.

[After briefly describing Kemble as King John, Boaden praises the 'assumed *irony* and *majestic* sorrow' of Siddons as Constance; he then offers some critical observations on *King John* suggested by Siddons's performance.]

... The only other scene, the fourth of the third act, is too well known to the readers of Shakespeare, to make it necessary that I should quote from it. Constance is too impassioned for *hope*; she sees the future in the instant: Arthur in the power of her enemy is already dead to her; and it is in *another* world that, worn down with early [earthly?] sorrow, she fears she shall not know him. Her prophetic soul has disposed of him in *this*. She, therefore, does not linger in expectation, but expires of frenzy, before his own rashness, rather than his uncle's violence, has ended her pretty Arthur. In the exit of Constance, the sharp shrillness of the organ itself will do something for an actress not highly intellectual: – however vehement in her exclamations, Constance has meaning in her language; this was truly given by Mrs. Siddons, and not an inarticulate *yell*, the grief of merely savage nature.

I preserve the dresses of Mrs. Siddons, where I find a note of them in my papers: in Constance she wore a *black* body and train of satin, and a petticoat of white, disposed in certainly the most tasteful forms of that day. The true actress is in every thing an artist; the genius before us dishevelled even her hair with graceful wildness.

By whatever power of *writing* adorned, the frank bravery of Faulconbridge, the quick succession of opposite tidings, and the fate of John, it was dangerous to shew such a meteor as Constance, and linger two acts further, after she has disappeared. Such is the inconvenience of chronicle plays; passion demands one termination and history another: – You call on individual interest as your aid and are ruined by your auxiliary. It is the *Æneid* after the fate of Dido.

That the theatre should teach history is little extraordinary. A most ingenious writer, William Godwin, was now publishing *Sketches of History*, in six *sermons* [London, 1784]!

But whatever might be the motive for acting John at the theatre, it was not then so popular as it was expected to be. Two scenes of Siddons, however exquisite, were not enough for those who had been accustomed to see her occupy every act, of plays more essentially female. (II, 61–3)

14 Anna Brownell Jameson, the character of Constance

1832

From *Characteristics of Women, Moral, Poetical, and Historical. With Fifty Vignette Etchings. By Mrs. Jameson, Author of 'The Diary of an Ennuyée,' 'Memoirs of Female Sovereigns,'* &c. (2 vols, London, 1832).

Anna Brownell Jameson (1794–1860) was a remarkably productive author who wrote indefatigibly on a variety of subjects, most notably travel, art, literature, and church history. She maintained throughout her life a large circle of devoted friends, many of whom came to her financial aid when her husband, Robert Jameson, a noted barrister to whom she was unhappily married, left no maintenance for her after his death. Other than *Characteristics of Women*, which was her first real scholarly accomplishment, Jameson is best remembered for her massive *Sacred and Legendary Art*, a pictorial and prose history of the church from Roman times to the seventeenth century, which appeared in four separate installments from 1848 to 1864, the last segment 'continued and completed by Lady Eastlake' four years after Jameson's death. The extract from *Characteristics of Women* below is taken from the third edition, corrected and enlarged (2 vols, London, 1835, 1836).

. . . We have seen that in the mother of Coriolanus, the principal qualities are exceeding pride, self-will, strong maternal affection, great power of imagination, and energy of temper. Precisely the same qualities enter into the mind of Constance of Bretagne: but in her these qualities are so differently modified by circumstances and education, that not even in fancy do we think of instituting a comparison between the gothic grandeur of Constance, and the more severe and classical dignity of the Roman matron.

The scenes and circumstances with which Shakespeare has surrounded Constance are strictly faithful to the old chronicles, and are as vividly as they are accurately represented. On the other hand, the hints on which the character has been constructed are few and vague; but the portrait harmonizes so wonderfully with its historic background, and with all that later researches have discovered relative to the personal adventures of Constance, that I have not the slightest doubt of its individual truth. The result of a life of strange vicissitude; the picture of a tameless will, and high passions, for ever struggling in vain against a superior power: and the real situation of women in those chivalrous times, are placed before us in a few noble scenes. The manner in which Shakespeare has applied the scattered hints of history to the formation of the character, reminds us of that magician who collected the mangled limbs which had been dispersed up and down, re-united them into the human form, and re-animated them with the breathing and conscious spirit of life. . . . (II, 191–3)

[Jameson now devotes several pages to the historical Constance of Bretagne, detailing the political situation at the time of her birth in 1164, her crowning as Duchess of Bretagne in 1169, her ensuing marriage to Geoffrey Plantagenet and early widowhood, the birth of Arthur, her enforced second marriage to Randal de Blondeville, Earl of Chester and his ignominious removal from Bretagne, her subsequent imprisonment at his hands with the approval of Richard I, the wasting of Bretagne by Richard, her divorce from the Earl of Chester and ensuing marriage to Guy, Count de Thouars, the placing of Arthur into the protective hand of the King of France, and finally, a brief summation of her character that forms the basis for the literary analysis that follows.]

. . . In considering the real history of Constance, three things must strike us as chiefly remarkable.

First, that she is not accused of any vice, or any act of injustice or violence; and this praise, though poor and negative, should have its due weight considering the scanty records that remain of her troubled life, and the period at which she lived – a period in which crimes of the darkest dye were familiar occurrences. Her father, Conan, was considered as a gentle and amiable prince – 'gentle even to feebleness;' yet we are told that on one occasion he acted over again the tragedy of Ugolino and Ruggiero, when he shut up the Count de Dol, with his two sons and his nephew, in a dungeon, and deliberately starved them to death; an event recorded without any particular comment by the old chroniclers of Bretagne. It also appears that, during those intervals when Constance administered the government of her states with some degree of independence, the country prospered under her sway; and that she possessed at all times the love of her people and the respect of her nobles.

Secondly, no imputation whatever has been cast on the honour of Constance as a wife and as a woman. The old historians, who have treated in a very unceremonious style the levities of her great-grandmother Matilda, her grandmother Bertha, her godmother Constance, and her mother-in-law Elinor, treat the name and memory of *our* Lady Constance with uniform respect.

Her third marriage, with Guy de Thouars, has been censured as impolitic, but has also been defended: it can hardly, considering her age, and the circumstances in which she was placed, be a just subject of reproach. During her hated union with Randal de Blondeville, and the years passed in a species of widowhood, she conducted herself with propriety: at least I can find no reason to judge otherwise.

Lastly, we are struck by the fearless, determined spirit, amounting at times to rashness, which Constance displayed on several occasions, when left to the free exercise of her own power and will; yet we see how frequently, with all this resolution and pride of temper, she became a mere instrument in the hands of others, and a victim to the superior craft or power of her enemies. The inference is unavoidable; there must have existed in the mind of Constance, with all her noble and amiable qualities, a deficiency somewhere, – a want of firmness, a want of judgement or wariness, and a total want of self-control.

In the play of *King John*, the three principal characters are the King, Faulconbridge, and Lady Constance. The first is drawn forcibly and accurately from history: it reminds us of Titian's portrait of Cæsar Borgia, in which the hatefulness of the subject is redeemed by the masterly skill of the artist, – the truth, and power, and wonderful beauty of the execution. Faulconbridge is the spirited creation of the poet.[1] Constance is certainly an historical personage; but the form which, when we meet it on the record of history, appears like a pale indistinct shadow, half melted into its obscure back-ground, starts before us into a strange relief and palpable breathing reality upon the page of Shakespeare.

Whenever we think of Constance, it is in her maternal character. All the interest which she excites in the drama turns upon her situation as the mother of Arthur. Every circumstance in which she is placed, every sentiment she utters, has a reference to him; and she is represented through the whole of the scenes in which she is engaged, as alternately pleading for the rights, and trembling for the existence of her son.

The same may be said of the Merope. In the four tragedies of which her story forms the subject,[2] we see her but in one point of view, namely, as a mere impersonation of the maternal feeling. The poetry of the situation is every thing, the character nothing. Interesting as she is, take Merope out of the circumstances in which she is placed, – take away her son, for whom she trembles from the first scene to the last, and Merope in herself is nothing; she melts away into a name, to which we can fix no other characteristic by which to distinguish her. We recognise her no longer. Her position is that of an agonized mother; and we can no more fancy her under a different aspect, than we can imagine the statue of Niobe in a different attitude.

But while we contemplate the character of Constance, she assumes before us an individuality perfectly distinct from the circumstances around her. The action calls forth her maternal feelings, and places them in the most prominent point of view: but with Constance as with a real human being, the maternal affections are a powerful instinct, modified by other faculties, sentiments, and impulses, making up the individual character. We think of her as a mother, because, as a mother distracted for the loss of her son, she is immediately presented before us, and calls forth our sympathy and our tears; but we infer the rest of her character from what we see, as certainly and as completely as if we had known her whole course of life.

That which strikes us as the principal attribute of Constance is *power* – power of imagination, of will, of passion, of affection, of pride: the moral energy, that faculty which is principally exercised in self-control, and gives consistency to the rest, is deficient; or rather, to speak more correctly, the extraordinary development of sensibility and imagination, which lends to the character its rich poetical colouring, leaves the other qualities comparatively subordinate. Hence it is that the whole complexion of the character, notwithstanding its amazing grandeur, is so exquisitely feminine. The weakness of the woman, who by the very consciousness of that weakness is worked up to desperation and defiance, the fluctuations of temper and the bursts of sublime passion, the terrors, the impatience, and the tears, are all most true to feminine nature. The energy of Constance not being based upon strength of character, rises and falls with the tide of passion. Her haughty spirit swells against resistance, and is excited into frenzy by sorrow and disappointment; while neither from her towering pride, nor her strength of intellect, can she borrow patience to submit, or fortitude to endure. It is, therefore, with perfect truth of nature, that Constance is first introduced as pleading for peace. [Quotes 2.1.44–9: 'Stay for an answer to your embassy, / Lest unadvised you stain your swords with blood. . . .'].

And that the same woman, when all her passions are roused by the sense of injury, should afterwards exclaim,

> War, war! No peace! peace is to me a war! [3.1.113]

That she should be ambitious for her son, proud of his high birth and royal rights, and violent in defending them, is most natural; but I cannot agree with those who think that in the mind of Constance, *ambition* – that is, the love of dominion for its own sake – is either a strong motive or a strong feeling: it could hardly be so where the natural impulses and the ideal power predominate in so high a degree. The vehemence with which she asserts the just and legal rights of her son is that of a fond mother and a proud-spirited woman, stung with the sense of injury, and herself a reigning sovereign, – by birth and right, if not in fact: yet when bereaved of her son, grief not only 'fills the room up of her absent child' [3.4.93], but seems to absorb every other faculty and feeling – even pride and anger. It is true that she exults over him as one whom nature and fortune had destined to be *great*, but in her distraction for his loss, she thinks of him only as her 'Pretty Arthur.' [Quotes 3.4.103–5: 'O lord! my boy, my Arthur, my fair son! . . .'].

No other feeling can be traced through the whole of her frantic scene: it is grief only, a mother's heart-rending, soul-absorbing grief, and nothing else. Not even indignation, or the desire of revenge, interfere with its soleness and intensity. An ambitious woman would hardly have thus addressed the cold, wily Cardinal: [Quotes 3.4.76–89: 'And, Father Cardinal, I have heard you say. . . .'].

The bewildered pathos and poetry of this address could be natural in no woman, who did not unite, like Constance, the most passionate sensibility with the most vivid imagination.

It is true that Queen Elinor calls her on one occasion, 'ambitious Constance' [1.1.32]; but the epithet is rather the natural expression of Elinor's own fear and hatred than really applicable.[3] Elinor, in whom age had subdued all passions but ambition, dreaded the mother of Arthur as her rival in power, and for that reason only opposed the claims of the son: but I conceive, that in a woman yet in the prime of life, and endued with the peculiar disposition of Constance, the mere love of power would be too much modified by fancy and feeling to be called a *passion*.

In fact, it is not pride, nor temper, nor ambition, nor even maternal affection, which in Constance gives the prevailing tone to the whole character: it is the predominance of imagination. I do not mean in the conception of the dramatic portrait, but in the temperament of the woman herself. In the poetical, fanciful, excitable cast of her mind, in the *excess* of the ideal power, tinging all her affections, exalting all her sentiments and thoughts, and animating the expression of both, Constance can only be compared to Juliet.

In the first place, it is through the power of imagination that, when under the influence of excited temper, Constance is not a mere incensed woman; nor does she, in the style of Volumnia, 'lament in anger, Juno like' [*Coriolanus*, 4.2.52–3], but rather like a sybil in a fury. Her sarcasms come down like thunderbolts. In her famous aside to Austria –

> O Lymoges! O Austria! thou dost shame
> That bloody spoil! thou slave! thou wretch! thou coward! &c.
> [3.1.114ff.]

it is as if she had concentrated the burning spirit of scorn, and dashed it in his face: every word seems to blister where it falls. In the scolding scene between her and queen Elinor, the laconic insolence of the latter is completely overborne by the torrent of bitter contumely which bursts from the lips of Constance, clothed in the most energetic, and often in the most figurative expressions. [Quotes 2.1.120–33; 159–78; 191–5].

And in a very opposite mood, when struggling with the consciousness of her own helpless situation, the same susceptible and excitable fancy still predominates: [Quotes 3.1.11–37: 'Thou shalt be punish'd for thus frighting me . . . .'].

It is the power of imagination which gives so peculiar a tinge to the maternal tenderness of Constance; she not only loves her son with the fond instinct of a mother's affection, but she loves him with her poetical imagination, exults in his beauty and his royal birth, hangs over him with idolatry, and sees his infant brow already encircled with the diadem. Her proud spirit, her ardent enthusiastic fancy, and her energetic self-will, all combine with her maternal love to give it that tone and character which belongs to her only: hence that most beautiful address to her son, which coming from the lips of Constance, is as full of nature and truth as of pathos and poetry, and which we could hardly sympathize with in any other: – [Quotes 3.1.42–58: Arthur's 'I do beseech you, madam, be content', and Constance's reply, 'If thou, that bid'st me be content, wert grim. . . .'].

It is this exceeding vivacity of imagination which in the end turns sorrow to frenzy. Constance is not only a bereaved and doating mother, but a generous woman, betrayed by her own rash confidence; in whose mind the sense of injury mingling with the sense of grief, and her impetuous temper conflicting with her pride, combine to overset her reason; yet she is not mad: and how admirably, how forcibly she herself draws the distinction between the frantic violence of uncontrolled feeling and actual madness! – [Quotes 3.4.44–50: 'Thou art not holy to belie me so; / I am not mad. . . .'].

Not only has Constance words at will, and fast as the passionate feelings rise in her mind they are poured forth with vivid, overpowering eloquence; but, like Juliet, she may be said to speak in pictures. For instance –

> Why holds thine eye that lamentable rheum?
> Like a proud river peering o'er its bounds. [3.1.22ff.]

And throughout the whole dialogue there is the same overflow of eloquence, the same splendour of diction, the same luxuriance of imagery; yet with an added grandeur, arising from habits of command, from the age, the rank, and the matronly character of Constance. Thus Juliet pours forth her love like a muse in a rapture: Constance raves in her sorrow like a Pythoness possessed with the spirit of pain. The love of Juliet is deep and infinite as the boundless sea: and the grief of Constance is so great, that nothing but the round world itself is able to sustain it.

> I will instruct my sorrows to be proud;
> For grief is proud and makes his owner stout.
> To me, and to the state of my great grief
> Let kings assemble, for my grief's so great,
> That no supporter but the huge firm earth
> Can hold it up. Here I and sorrow sit;
> Here is my throne, – bid kings come bow to it! [3.1.68ff.]

An image more majestic, more wonderfully sublime, was never presented to the fancy; yet almost equal as a flight of poetry is her apostrophe to the heavens;

> Arm, arm, ye heavens, against these perjured kings,
> A widow calls! – be husband to me, heavens! [3.1.107ff.]

And again –

> O that my tongue were in the thunder's mouth,
> Then with a passion would I shake the world! [3.4.38ff.]

Not only do her thoughts start into images, but her feelings become persons: grief haunts her as a living presence: [Quotes 3.4.93–8: 'Grief fills the room up of my absent child. . . .'].

And death is welcomed as a bridegroom; she sees the visionary monster as Juliet *saw* 'the bloody Tybalt festering in his shroud' [*Romeo and Juliet*, 4.3.42ff.], and heaps one ghastly image upon another with all the wild luxuriance of a distempered fancy: [Quotes 3.4.25–36: 'O amiable, lovely death . . . .'].

Constance, who is a majestic being, is majestic in her very frenzy. Majesty is also the characteristic of Hermione: but what a difference between *her* silent, lofty, uncomplaining despair, and the eloquent grief of Constance, whose wild lamentations, which come bursting forth clothed in the grandest, the most poetical imagery, not only melt, but absolutely electrify us!

On the whole, it may be said that pride and maternal affection form the basis of the character of Constance, as it is exhibited to us; but that these passions, in an equal degree common to many human beings, assume their peculiar and individual tinge from an extraordinary development of intellect and fancy. It is the energy of passion which lends the character its concentrated power, as it is the prevalence of imagination throughout which dilates it into magnificence.

Some of the most splendid poetry to be met with in Shakespeare, may be found in the parts of Juliet and Constance; the most splendid, perhaps, excepting only the parts of Lear and Othello; and for the same reason, – that Lear and Othello as men, and Juliet and Constance as women, are distinguished by the predominance of the same faculties, – passion and imagination.

The sole deviation from history which may be considered as essentially interfering with the truth of the situation, is the entire omission of the character of Guy de Thouars, so that Constance is incorrectly represented as in a state of widowhood, at a period when, in point of fact, she was married. It may be observed, that her marriage took place just at the period of the opening of the drama; that Guy de Thouars played no conspicuous part in the affairs of Bretagne till after the death of Constance, and that the mere presence of this personage, altogether superfluous in the action, would have completely destroyed the dramatic interest of the situation; – and what a situation! One more magnificent was never placed before the mind's eye than that of Constance, when, deserted and betrayed, she stands alone in her despair, amid her false friends and her ruthless enemies! [3.1]. The image of the mother-eagle, wounded and bleeding to death, yet stretched over her young in an attitude of defiance, while all the baser birds of prey are clamouring around her eirie, gives but a faint idea of the moral sublimity of this scene. Considered merely as a poetical or dramatic picture, the grouping is wonderfully fine; on one side, the vulture ambition of that mean-souled tyrant, John; on the other, the selfish, calculating policy of Philip: between them, balancing their passions in his hand, the cold, subtle, heartless Legate: the fiery, reckless Faulconbridge; the princely Lewis; the still unconquered spirit of that wrangling queen, old Elinor; the bridal loveliness and modesty of Blanch; the boyish grace and innocence of young Arthur; and Constance in the midst of them, in all the state of her great grief, a grand impersonation of pride and passion, helpless at once and desperate, – form an assemblage of figures, each perfect in its kind, and, taken all together, not surpassed for the variety, force, and splendour of the dramatic and picturesque effect. (II, 191–232)

[Jameson's treatment of the women in *King John* concludes with short biographical sketches of the historical Queen Elinor and Blanch of Castile.]

15 Thomas Campbell, Sarah Siddons on Constance

1834

From *Life of Mrs. Siddons. By Thomas Campbell* (2 vols, London, 1834).

Thomas Campbell (1777–1844), poet and critic, first attracted the serious attention of the literary world with *The Pleasures of Hope* (London, 1799), a long poem in heroic couplets expressing an optimistic faith that the hard injustices of life could improve, and a sincere (if often naïve) belief in ideal love, the abolition of slavery, and the liberation of Poland. A trip to Germany in 1800 further excited both Campbell's romantic temperament and his English patriotism, providing the creative impetus for the three poems by which he is perhaps best known, 'Ye Mariners of England' (1801), 'Hohenlinden' (1802), and 'The Battle of the Baltic' (1809). His uneven *Specimens of the British Poets* (7 vols, London, 1819), was followed by a long but only modestly successful tenure as editor of *The New Monthly Magazine* (1820–30), and a brief editorship of the ill-fated *Metropolitan Magazine* (1831–2). Campbell's most important published remarks on Shakespeare appear in his *Life of Mrs. Siddons* and in the brief critical biography prefixed to *The Dramatic Works of William Shakespeare* (London, 1838; No. 16 below).

... It does credit to the taste of George the Third, that his wish to see the Siddons and the Kemble together, in the tragedy of *King John*, was the immediate cause of her coming out this season [at Drury Lane, 10 December 1783] in the new character of Constance.[1] I find, to my surprise, the cotemporary daily newspapers exceedingly truculent in their remarks on her performance of this part; and, if their testimony were to be solely relied upon, we must believe that she was at first an infinitely less popular Constance than she ultimately proved to be. Attaching as I do a certain consequence to the newspaper criticism of that period,[2] I should nevertheless be sorry to give it my arbitrary credence only when it speaks in favour of my heroine. It was her boast, that she gradually improved in all her characters, and that she never repeated her performance of any part without studying it anew to the utmost of her power and leisure. Thus I can believe it possible, that she was not at this period the same perfect Lady Constance, such as I saw her some ten years afterwards [at Drury Lane in 1792]. Besides, the entire tragedy of *King John*, from conforming to history more than to our wishes, disappoints us by Constance belonging to it only in two acts, and disappearing before its catastrophe. This circumstance is a disadvantage to any actress, however great she may be in the part; or, at least, a difficulty not likely to be overcome, till, by repeated impressions, she has won the public to feel the tragedy worth seeing, for the sake of Constance alone. . . . (I, 206–8)

. . . [Mrs. Siddons] was ere long regarded as so consummate in the part of Constance, that it was not unusual for spectators to leave the house when her part in the tragedy of *King John* was over, as if they could no longer enjoy Shakespeare himself when she ceased to be his interpreter. I could speak as a wonderstruck witness to her power in the character, with almost as many circumstantial recollections of her as there are speeches in the part. I see her in my mind's eye, the embodied image of maternal love and intrepidity; of wronged and righteous feeling; of proud grief and majestic desolation. With what unutterable tenderness was her brow bent over her pretty Arthur at one moment, and in the next how nobly drawn back, in a look at her enemies that dignified her vituperation. When she patted Lewis on the breast, with the words 'Thine honour! – oh, thine honour!' [3.1.316] there was a sublimity in the laugh of her sarcasm. I could point out the passages where her vicissitudes of hurried and deliberate gesture would have made you imagine that her very body seemed to think. Her elocution varied its tones from the height of vehemence to the lowest despondency, with an eagle-like power of stooping and soaring, and with the rapidity of thought.[3] But there is a drawback in the pleasure of these recollections, from their being so little communicable to others; and, besides, in attempting to do them justice, I am detaining the reader from more interesting matter which Mrs. Siddons has left me in her Memoranda, namely, her own remarks on the character of Constance.

'My idea of Constance,' she says, 'is that of a lofty and proud spirit, associated with the most exquisite feelings of maternal tenderness, which is, in truth, the predominant feature of this interesting personage. The sentiments which she expresses, in the dialogue between herself, the King of France, and the Duke of Austria, at the commencement of the second Act of this tragedy, very strongly evince the amiable traits of a humane disposition, and of a grateful heart. [Quotes 2.1.32–4: 'Oh! take his mother's thanks. . . .'].

Again, in reply to the King's bloody determination of subjugating the city of Angiers to the sovereignty of her son, she says [Quotes 2.1.44–9: 'Stay for an answer to your embassy. . . .'].

The idea one naturally adopts of her qualities and appearance are, that she is noble in mind, and commanding in person and demeanour; that her countenance was capable of all the varieties of grand and tender expression, often agonized, though never distorted by the vehemence of her agitations. Her voice, too, must have been 'propertied like the tuned spheres' [*Antony and Cleopatra*, 5.2.83ff.], obedient to all the softest inflections of maternal love, and all the pathos of the most exquisite sensibility, to the sudden burst of heart-rending sorrow, and to the terrifying imprecations of indignant majesty, when writhing under the miseries inflicted on her by her dastardly oppressors and treacherous allies. The actress, whose lot it is to personate this great character, should be richly endowed by nature for its various requirements: yet, even when thus fortunately gifted, much, very much remains to be effected by herself; for in the performance of the part of Constance great difficulties, both mental and physical, present themselves. And perhaps the greatest of the former class is that of imperiously holding the mind reined-in to the immediate perception of those calamitous circumstances which take place during the course of her sadly eventful history. The necessity for this severe abstraction will sufficiently appear, when we remember that all those calamitous events occur whilst she herself is absent from the stage; so that this power is indispensable for that reason alone, were there no other to be assigned for it. Because, if the representative of Constance shall ever forget, even behind the scenes, those disastrous events which impel her to break forth into the overwhelming effusions of wounded friendship, disappointed ambition, and maternal tenderness, upon the first movement of her appearance in the third Act, when stunned with terrible surprise she exclaims, –

> Gone to be married – gone to swear a peace!
> False blood to false blood joined – gone to be friends! [3.1.1ff.]

– if, I say, the mind of the actress for one moment wanders from these distressing events, she must inevitably fall short of that high and glorious colouring which is indispensable to the painting of this magnificent portrait.

The quality of abstraction has always appeared to me so necessary in the art of acting, that I shall probably, in the course of these remarks, be thought too frequently and pertinaciously to advert to it. I am now, however, going to give a proof of its usefulness in the character under our consideration; and I wish my opinion were of sufficient weight to impress the importance of this power on the minds of all candidates for dramatic fame. Here then is one example among many others which I could adduce. Whenever I was called upon to personate the character of Constance, I never, from the beginning of the play to the end of my part in it, once suffered my dressing-room door to be closed, in order that my attention might be constantly fixed on those distressing events which, by this means, I could plainly hear going on upon the stage, the terrible effects of which progress were to be represented by me. Moreover, I never omitted to place myself, with Arthur in my hand, to hear the march, when, upon the reconciliation of England and France, they enter the gates of Angiers to ratify the contract of marriage between the Dauphin and the Lady Blanch; because the sickening sounds of that march would usually cause the bitter tears of rage, disappointment, betrayed confidence, baffled ambition, and, above all, the agonizing feelings of maternal affection to gush into my eyes. In short, the spirit of the whole drama took possession of my mind and frame, by my attention being incessantly riveted to the passing scenes. Thus did I avail myself of every possible assistance, for there was need of all in this most arduous effort; and I have no doubt that the observance of such circumstances, however irrelevant they may appear upon a cursory view, were powerfully aidant in the representations of those expressions of passion in the remainder of this scene, which have been only in part considered, and to the conclusion of which I now proceed.

Goaded and stung by the treachery of her faithless friends, and almost maddened by the injuries they have heaped upon her, she becomes desperate and ferocious as a hunted tigress in defence of her young, and it seems that existence itself must nearly issue forth with the utterance of that frantic and appalling exclamation – [Quotes

3.1.83–95: 'A wicked day, and not a holy day. . . .' and Philip's response at 3.1.96–8: 'By heaven! Lady, you shall have no cause. . . .'].

What countenance, what voice, what gesture, shall realize the scorn and indignation of her reply to the heartless king of France? [Quotes 3.1.99–103: 'You have beguil'd me with a counterfeit. . . .'].

And then the awful, trembling solemnity, and utter helplessness of that soul-subduing, scriptural, and prophetic invocation – [Quotes 3.1.107–11: 'Arm, arm, ye heavens! against these perjur'd kings. . . .'].

If it ever were, or ever shall be, portrayed with its appropriate and solemn energy, it must be then, and then only, when the power I have so much insisted on, cooperating also with a high degree of enthusiasm, shall have transfused the mind of the actress into the person and situation of the august and afflicted Constance. The difficulty, too, of representing with tempered rage and dignified contempt the biting sarcasm of the following speeches to Austria, may be more easily imagined than explained: [Quotes 3.1.113–29: 'War! war! no peace – peace is to me a war. . . .'].

But, in truth, to beget, in these whirlwinds of the soul, such temperance as, according to the lesson of our inspired master, shall give them smoothness, is a difficulty which those only can appreciate who have made the effort.

I cannot indeed conceive, in the whole range of dramatic character, a greater difficulty than that of representing this grand creature. Brought before the audience in the plenitude of her afflictions; oppression and falsehood having effected their destructive mark; the full storm of adversity, in short, having fallen upon her in the interval of their absence from her sight, the effort of pouring properly forth so much passion as past events have excited in her, without any visible previous progress towards her climax of desperation, seems almost to exceed the powers of imitation. Hers is an affliction of so 'sudden floodgate and o'erbearing nature'[*Othello*, 1.3.56], that art despairs of realizing it, and the effort is almost life-exhausting. Therefore, whether the majestic, the passionate, the tender Constance, has ever yet been, or ever will be, personated to the entire satisfaction of sound judgement and fine taste, I believe to be doubtful; for I believe it to be nearly impossible.

I now come to the concluding scene [3.4]; and I believe I shall not be thought singular, when I assert, that though she has been designated the ambitious Constance, she has been ambitious only for her son. It was for him, and him alone, that she aspired to, and struggled for, hereditary sovereignty. For example, you find that from that fatal moment when he is separated from her, not one regret for lost regal power or splendour ever escapes from her lips; no, not one idea does she from that instant utter which does not unanswerably prove that all other considerations are annihilated in the grievous recollections of motherly love. The following scene, I think, must determine that maternal tenderness is the predominant feature of her character. [Quotes 3.4.17–105: the episode in which Constance extravagantly expresses her grief in the presence of Philip and Pandulph].

Her gorgeous affliction, if such an expression is allowable, is of so sublime and so intense a character, that the personation of its grandeur, with the utterance of its rapid and astonishing eloquence, almost overwhelms the mind that meditates its realization, and utterly exhausts the frame which endeavours to express its agitations.' (I, 206–26)

16 Thomas Campbell, general remarks on *King John*

1838

From *The Dramatic Works of William Shakespeare. With Remarks on His Life and Writings*, by Thomas Campbell (London, 1838).

On Campbell see the head-note to No. 15. A brief assessment of Campbell's edition and its generally unfavorable reception appears in Mary Ruth Miller's *Thomas Campbell* (Boston, 1978), pp. 137–9. The selection below is taken from the 'new edition' of *The Dramatic Works* (London, 1844).

[From the prefatory 'Remarks on the Life and Writings of William Shakespeare']

[Campbell cites *The Troublesome Raigne* as a source for *King John*, then proceeds to his critical remarks.]

... Thus there was an older English historical play than that of Shakespeare on the subject of King John, and it is curious to find that the former was almost an exact forerunner of the latter, in point of incidents and personages. I say personages and not characters, for Shakespeare has thrown more vivacity into the part of Faulconbridge than can be found in the prototype; more dignity into that of Constance, and more pathos into that of Arthur. In the old piece there was no anticipation of Shakespeare's high painting. I am not sure, however, in his almost, though not entirely, copying the incidents of the old play, that Shakespeare has not omitted some which he could have turned from golden dross into pure gold. I mean particularly that scene in the old play where Faulconbridge, in fulfilling King John's injunction to plunder the religious houses, finds a young smooth-skinned nun in a chest where the abbot's treasures were supposed to be deposited. If ever romantic tragedy needed comic relief it was Shakespeare's *King John*, and this scene under his comic touches would have relieved it.

It is remarkable that the Poet of England, and the most eloquent Poet who ever summed up the virtues of Brutus, should have dramatised the reign of King John without the most distant allusion to Magna Charta. Was he afraid of offending Elizabeth? I think not; for he brought out *Julius Caesar* in the reign of King James, whose petty mind was more jealous of popular principles than that of Elizabeth. His main object was probably to recast, with all dispatch, an old piece into a new one for the stage.

I regret further that his mighty genius did not turn to poetical account another event in King John's reign, still more adapted to poetry, namely, the superstitious desolation of the English mind, which immediately followed the papal excommunication that was issued from Rome against England and her King. The shutting up of the churches, the nation's sudden deprivation of all the exterior exercise of its religion, the altars despoiled of their ornaments, the cessation of Sabbath bells, and the celebration of mass with doors shut against the laity; all these circumstances have been wrought up by Hume into an historic picture that is worthy of Livy,[1] and what would they not have been as materials for a poetical picture in the hands of Shakespeare?

But let us be thankful for our Poet's *King John*, such as it is. No doubt it sets the seal as to the question about the probability of good historical tragedies proceeding from the pen of the best poets, and a negative seal; for after Constance leaves the stage, Shakespeare's *King John* is rather the execution of a criminal than an interesting tragedy.

There are scenes and passages, however, in our Poet's *King John* which may never be forgotten. The pathos of Arthur's conference with Hubert is entirely Shakespeare's, and so is the whole of the part of Constance, his mother, as well as that most appallingly interesting of dialogues between King John and Hubert, touching the murder of young Arthur. In the old play, Constance has a good deal of the virago in her portraiture; in Shakespeare she is the most interesting character in nature – a doating and a bereaved mother. Those who find themselves, as I do, older than they could wish to be, may derive some consolation for their age, in recollecting that they were born early enough to have seen Mrs. Siddons perform the part of Constance. (xl–xli)

17 Thomas Peregrine Courtenay, *King John* and history

1838

From 'Shakespeare's Historical Plays, Considered Historically', *The New Monthly Magazine*, 53, No. 210 (June 1838), 250–65. Reprinted with revisions in *Commentaries on the Historical Plays of Shakespeare* (2 vols, London, 1840).

Thomas Peregrine Courtenay (1782–1841) spent a lifetime in public service as MP for Totnes and in a number of appointed governmental positions. In addition to his writings on affairs of state, he also published *Memoirs of the Life, Works, and Correspondence of Sir William Temple, Bart.* (2 vols, London, 1836). Courtenay's essays on the history plays were first published in *The New Monthly Magazine* from June 1838 to March 1839, and reprinted in book form in 1840, with slight corrections and alterations, as *Commentaries on the Historical Plays of Shakespeare*. The extract below is taken from the 1840 book. For ease of reference page numbers are provided for both versions of Courtenay's remarks on *King John*; the first citation is to the revised essay of 1840, the second to the original of 1838.

[In the brief preface to his book Courtenay addresses such questions as the historical accuracy of history plays, Shakespeare's patriotism, his use of sources and tolerance for anachronism, etc. He readily acknowledges that 'to make a good play, it is necessary to take great liberties' with source material (I, ix; 252), and concludes with a statement outlining the scholarly aims of his study.]

. . . But, whatever opinion may be formed upon any of these topics, I cannot think that, after all that has been said of Shakespeare as a teacher of history, as well as a poet, the inquiry upon which I now purpose to enter will be altogether uninteresting, namely, *what were Shakespeare's authorities for his history, and how far has he departed from them? And whether the plays may be given to our youth, as 'properly historical?'* The inquiry has not been anticipated by any of the commentators. Steevens and Malone have each a few historical notes; but the range of their historical criticism is extremely small, and the former is sometimes careless. . . . (I, xi–xii; 252)

. . . [*King John*] is the first in chronological order of the historical plays. Steevens[1] mentions it with others as closely following Hall, Holinshed, Stow, and other chroniclers; but he mentions also an old play, (*The Troublesome Raigne of King John*)[2] of which the author is not exactly known. I cannot concur with Steevens in thinking it possible that Shakespeare himself wrote this play; but he certainly took from it the outline of his plot, and some of his scenes. We shall judge, in going through his play, whether he went any further for his history.

That old play is itself supposed,[3] upon the slightest possible evidence, to have been taken from a still older performance, which had for its author John Bale, the first Protestant Bishop of Ossory, whose object was to expose, by a reference to the history of the reign of John, the abuses of the Romish church.[4] But it is very doubtful whether this play was seen by the author of the other.

The first impression conveyed by Shakespeare's play is, that the young Prince Arthur had a legitimate claim to the crown of England, that the crown was usurped by his uncle John, and that the King of France, having summoned John, by his ambassador Chatillion, to surrender the crown, forthwith declared war against him, in order to put Arthur in possession of his right.

'The succession of John,' says Hallam,[5] 'has certainly passed in modern times for an usurpation. I do not find that it was considered as such by his own contemporaries on this side the Channel;'[6] and the same well-informed author shows, that the preference of a nephew to a brother, in the line of succession, was by no means an established rule of the law of England. Shakespeare himself is mainly responsible for the prevalency of this belief of usurpation. I do not say he created it, because he found it in the old play.

Our poet places King John at Northampton, where he is thus addressed by Chatillion, the ambassador of France: – [Quotes 1.1.7–14].

Now, I do not find, either in Holinshed, or in any other history, English or French, that Chatillion, or any other diplomatic agent, was sent by Philip Augustus to John; or that the crown of *England* was demanded by the French King on the part of Arthur. Philip apparently, and with reason, disclaimed an interest in the disposal of that crown; whereas, of the transmarine possessions of the Kings of England, as well as of Brittany, he claimed to be lord paramount.

Commentators have already shewn that the introduction of the Archduke of Austria is a mistake borrowed from the old play. Leopold, the Duke of Austria, by whom Richard was thrown into prison, died in 1195; the Limoges, who in a subsequent scene is confounded with him, was the owner of the castle of Chaluz, before which Richard was slain. . . .'[7] (I, 1–3; 252–3)

[Courtenay now addresses other historical facts behind the play, such as John's being abroad upon the death of his brother Richard, the timing of French hostilities against England, John's return to England and his reception there, the symbolic importance of Arthur's name to some of his adherents, and the actual neutrality of Angiers; he then turns to the 'unlady-like scolding' of Elinor and Constance, citing Holinshed as the source for this 'well-known feature in the play'.] (I, 7; 255)

Of the character of Elinor we know something: Malone takes for granted, without sufficient authority, her infidelity to her first husband, Lewis the Seventh of France;[8] but that she was an ambitious and high-spirited person is sufficiently proved by her conduct to her second husband, against whom she joined her sons in rebellion. Of Constance we know little, for certainly Holinshed's account of Elinor's opinion of her is of no authority. Nor does it appear that these two princesses ever met. According to Shakespeare, Elinor was conscious of the weakness of her son's title.

[Quotes 1.1.39–43]. But when arguing in public, she cited a will of Richard Cœur de Lion: [Quotes 2.1.191–2]. There is contemporary authority for the dying declaration of Richard in favour of John,[9] though he had formerly declared Arthur his heir. . . . (I, 7–8; 255)

The dramatist has passed over some vicissitudes in the life of Arthur, previous to the marriage of Blanch, which might perhaps have produced interesting scenes. Although Philip, in his fruitless negotiation with John, had demanded Anjou and other provinces for Arthur, he made use of his auxiliary force in a way more conducive to his own interests than to those of the young prince. Having taken one of Arthur's towns, he razed the fortifications; this so offended Arthur's general, La Roches, that he advised the prince to make a peace with his uncle, to whom he fled from Paris,[10] 'though the same served but to small purpose.' Some towns were, in consequence of this treaty, given up to John. [Quotes Holinshed, III, 160: the account of Arthur's flight to Angiers and Constance's ensuing marriage to Guy de Thouars].[11] John went to England; and it was now that Arthur and his mother had, in truth, quarrelled, as well with Philip as with John, that the two kings came to the agreement which excited, according to Shakespeare, the indignation of Constance, so forcibly in the play. [Quotes Holinshed, III, 161: the account of the marriage agreement between Lewis and Blanch].

In the play John gives a very liberal dowry to the Princess Blanch, whom by a poetical licence he brings into France. She was, in fact, in her own country when betrothed, and the queen-mother went to fetch her. [Quotes 2.1.527–30]. Both kings were aware that this arrangement would not be acceptable to Constance.

>K. Philip. And, by my faith, this league that we have made
>Will give her sadness very little cure.
>Brother of England, how may we content
>This widow lady? In her right we came:
>Which we, God knows, have turn'd another way,
>To our own vantage.
>K. John.   We will heal up all,
>For we'll create young Arthur Duke of Bretagne
>And Earl of Richmond; and this rich fair town
>We make him lord of. [2.1.545ff.]

This representation of the marriage settlements is not borne out by history; John did not give up the five provinces, but only 'the city of Evreux, and some other towns, being those (according to Holinshed) which the King of France had taken from him in the war. The King of England likewise did homage to the French King for Brittany, and again received homage for the same country, and for the county of Richmond, of his nephew Arthur.'[12] Holinshed says that this peace was displeasing to many, and especially to the Earl of Flanders;[13] but says nothing of any protest on the part of Constance. I need not say that the grief and indignation of Constance furnish some of Shakespeare's finest scenes. Arthur he represents as endeavouring to pacify his mother: –

> *Arth.* I do beseech you, madam, be content. [3.1.42]

The young prince, however, as we shall afterwards hear, was not by any means of the unambitious disposition which would be inferred from this attempt to moderate the anger of his mother.

From this time the confusion of facts and dates is almost insurmountable. But I would here observe, that no ancient chronicle, or modern writer, is entirely to be depended upon. What we call the Chronicles (such as Holinshed's) were, for the most part, written long after the events related, and are less to be depended upon than even modern historians. And the same remark applies to the more ancient histories not contemporaneous with the events – as, in the present case, that of Matthew Paris; though it may perhaps be averred that such histories are founded upon contemporary annals kept in the monasteries. Contemporary historians we have for only a part of King John's time.[14]

Immediately after the conclusion of these preliminaries of peace and marriage contract, Shakespeare brings Pandulph, the Pope's legate, reproving John for refusing to admit Stephen Langton as Archbishop of Canterbury. Now, the election of Langton did not take place till five years afterwards, and the interdict and excommunication were still later.

However, Shakespeare is correct in making John stand out stoutly against the Pope, and assert boldly his independence. He contended, in fact, for *domestic nomination*; and told the Pope plainly, as we learn from monkish authority –

> that he would not admit a man who had been brought up in France among his enemies; he reminded the Pope of the value of England to the papal see as a fruitful source of revenue, and declared that, as there was an abundance of learned men within his dominions, he would not go to any foreigner for justice or judgment.[15]

This was going very far in rebellion against the head of the Roman Catholic church. It is possible that Shakespeare, in the speech which he has put into John's mouth, had in his mind the king's supremacy, asserted afterwards more effectually by Henry the Eighth and Elizabeth: – [Quotes 3.1.147–60: 'What earthly name to interrogatories. . . .']. . . . (I, 9–14; 255–7)

[After demonstrating that John's speech also derives from a passage in *The Troublesome Raigne*: 3.73–82, Courtenay moves on to the character of the historical Arthur.]

. . . we are told that this young prince, whom Mr. Schlegel, with poetical licence, styles *the amiable Arthur* [No. 6 above], did not make himself more acceptable than his uncle himself to the people whom he desired as his subjects. Queen Elinor, the regent, got into Mirabeau, in Anjou, which was besieged by Arthur, and, according to some, she was taken there. But John displayed the activity of which he boasted when he said, '*Whatever the King of France may take I will recover in one day.*'[16] He attacked Arthur, took him prisoner, and confined him at Falais. Here, according to our histories, [Quotes Holinshed, III, 165: where John asks Arthur 'to forsake his friendship and alliance with the French King', and Arthur, out of his own 'wilful opinion, made a presumptuous answer', denying John's request and demanding the restoration of his rightful crown].

The King hereupon confined him closely, and a rumour of his death was spread through France. The Breton and Poictevin lords in vain solicited his liberty; and

> it was now reported that King John, *through persuasion of his counsellors*, appointed certain persons to go into Falais, where Arthur was kept in Prison under the charge of Hubert de Burgh, and there to put out the young gentlemen's eyes. [Holinshed, III, 165]

I continue the quotation, because it is the foundation of one of the most beautiful of Shakespeare's scenes ; –

> But through such resistance as he made against one of the tormenters that came to execute the King's commandment (for the other rather forsook their prince and country than they would consent to obey the King's authority herein), and *such lamentable words as he uttered*, Hubert de Burgh did preserve him from that injury, not doubting but rather to have thanks than displeasure at the King's hands, for delivering him of such infamy as would have redounded to his highness if the young gentleman had been so cruelly dealt withal. For *he considered that King John had resolved upon this point only in his heat and fury* (which moveth men to undertake many an inconvenient enterprise, unbeseeming the person of a common man, much more reproachful to a prince, all men in that mood being more foolish and furious, and prone to accomplish the perverse conceits of their ill-possessed hearts), *and that afterwards, upon better advisement, he would both repent himself so to have commanded and give them small thank that would see it put in execution*. Howbeit, to satisfy his mind for the time, and to stay the rage of the Bretons, he caused it to be bruited through the country that the King's commandment was fulfilled, and that Arthur also, through sorrow and grief, was departed out of this life. For the space of fifteen days *this rumour ran incessantly through both the realms of England and France*, and there was ringing for him through towns and villages as it had been for his funeral. It was also bruited that his body was buried in the monastery of St. Andrews of the Cisteaux order. But when the Bretons were nothing pacified, but rather kindled more vehemently to work all the mischief they could devise, in revenge of their sovereign's death, there was no remedy but to signify abroad again that Arthur was as yet living and in health. [Holinshed, III, 165]

Upon a few expressions of this Chronicle Shakespeare has built the first scene of his fourth act, in which Arthur dissuades Hubert from putting out his eyes. The prince was now about fifteen years old – an age at which we generally cease to speak of a 'pretty child' and his 'innocent prate.' Shakespeare has done quite right, for dramatic interest, in giving this character to the prince and his talk; but it is not quite consistent with that in which he appears in the late revolt.

The fine scene [3.3] between John and Hubert, in which Hubert undertakes that

Arthur shall be put to death, is a creation of the poet, and one for which we are infinitely indebted to him. But surely there is an inconsistency between this scene and that (which is taken from the Chronicles) in which Hubert, without any indication of an intention to murder the prince, proceeds to put out his eyes. For *this* he had, according to Shakespeare, a written authority (which the old play gives at length) yet, in the subsequent interview with the King, he is made to produce a warrant *for the murder.*

The scene [4.2] in which the King reproaches his minister for complying too readily with his commands, was apparently suggested by the passage which I have quoted from Holinshed; and this is perhaps the only passage which leads me to believe that Shakespeare did not *entirely* rely upon the old play. That piece describes John as repenting vehemently; but there is nothing upon which these fine touches in Shakespeare can have been founded. [Quotes 4.2.208–14: 'It is the curse of kings to be attended. . . .'].

What follows is full of poetry and dramatic art; where John imputes his own crime to the suggestion of Hubert's 'abhorred aspect,' and his too ready acquiescence in what was only darkly hinted. [Quotes 4.2.231–41].

Warburton and Malone[17] consider Shakespeare as paying his court to Elizabeth by a covert attempt to throw upon poor secretary Davison the death of Mary Queen of Scots.

As Holinshed affords a sufficient foundation for both these fine passages, it is doubtless unnecessary to have recourse to any courtier-like or political motive in the poet. But from the unbounded love of flattery and personal attention which characterized our celebrated Queen, I attribute much probability to this opinion of the critics.

The circulation of the report of Arthur's death, and the contradiction of it, are taken from the Chronicle; as is also the Prince's loss of life in an attempt to escape, though this is only stated doubtfully as one of many rumours.[18] Other reports made John the murderer of his nephew with his own hand. Considering how essential to the plot is John's cruel treatment of Arthur, I am surprised that Shakespeare did not rather adopt one of these. He has, however, followed the old play. I do not offer any decided opinion upon the manner of Arthur's death.[19]

I do not find that about the time of the battle of Mirabeau (August 1202), the French fleet suffered any damage to justify the commencement of the fourth scene of this act – [Quotes 3.4.1–3].

The remainder of this scene [3.4] is occupied with the grief of Constance for the capture of her son. The hint upon which Shakespeare has wrought one of the finest scenes in the acted play was afforded by some very bad lines in the old play. I should be well contented to believe that the Princess answered to the Pope's legate, when attempting to console her –

> He talks to me who never had a son! [3.4.91]

But I am afraid that the balance of testimony goes to show that Constance, whom the play keeps alive until the year in which John submitted to the Pope [4.2], did in fact die *before* the battle of Mirabeau. . . . (I, 15–22; 258–61)

[Courtenay now discusses the historical accuracy of Shakespeare's depiction of the English lords, finding no historical truth in their objection to John's second coronation, and pointing out other minor inaccuracies in their dramatic representation in *King John*.]

Though Shakespeare appears to have incorrectly dated the disaffection of some of the barons, it is true that at this time discontents prevailed among them. The peers were summoned to attend the King at Portsmouth, in order to a fresh expedition into France; but, meeting at Leicester, they resolved that they would not go with him beyond sea, *unless he would restore to them their rights*.[20]

It is remarkable that Shakespeare assigns no cause for the revolt of the barons, excepting that for which he had the least authority, the imprisonment and death of Arthur, whom the poet assumes to have been the rightful heir to the crown. Historians mention his profligacy, effeminacy, neglect of business, and pecuniary exactions. To these no allusion is made by Shakespeare, otherwise than in the following speech of Faulconbridge: –

> How I have sped among the clergymen,[21]
> The sum I have collected shall express.
> But, as I travelled hither through the land,
> I find the people strangely fantasied,
> Possess'd with rumours, full of idle dreams,
> Not knowing what they fear, but full of fear. [4.2.141ff.]

Of his exactions from the church, Faulconbridge here speaks boastfully. The complaints of the people, which we are taught [from Holinshed and Matthew Paris] to believe well founded, he treats as 'idle dreams.'

I have already said, that all the events connected with Arthur and Constance occurred before the quarrel with the Pope about Stephen Langton, the excommunication of John, and the confederacy against him between his barons and the Dauphin.

Shakespeare places the first excommunication with Lewis immediately after the death of Arthur, involves Salisbury in it, and refers to a meeting of malcontents at St. Edmund's Bury. The next act [5] he opens with the preparations of the King of France to invade England, in conspiracy with the discontented barons, and John's surrender of his crown to the Pope, which did not occur until 1213, more than ten years after the death of Arthur.

Shakespeare commences the act with the legate's *restoration* of the crown, which he is said to have retained in his hands for five days; but he makes no use of the speech published in the Chronicle, as 'The saucy speech of Cardinal Pandulph, the Pope's lewd legate, to King John, in the presumptuous Pope's behalf.'[22] The plot now makes a start, from the reconciliation of John with the Pope, to the landing of Lewis the Dauphin in England, of which he claimed the crown in right of his wife, the daughter of John's sister. I would here observe, that, if Shakespeare intended to represent the barons as the protectors of the hereditary succession to the crown, interrupted only by the forfeiture of John, he and they passed over fair Elinor, 'the damsel of Bretagne,' who succeeded to all the rights of her brother Arthur, and was kept in prison by John, without remonstrance, so far as I know, from English or Bretons.[23] Lewis landed in 1216. In the interval, the foreign[24] and civil wars had raged with varied success; but *one* event had happened, of which, although it is that by which we now chiefly remember King John, Shakespeare takes no notice whatever. This event is no other than the signature of MAGNA CHARTA.

How shall we account for Shakespeare's omission of an incident so essential in 'the life and reign of King John,' and so good for stage effect? It had occurred to me, especially when considering the omission of all reference to popular topics, that, as Shakespeare was a decided courtier, he might not wish to remind Queen Elizabeth, *who set Magna Charta at nought, in its most interesting particular,* of the solemn undertakings of her ancestors. But perhaps the omission of it in the old play is sufficient.

I suspect that for some ages before the commencement, in the reign of James the First, of the great struggle between the crown and the people, Magna Charta was not much thought of among Englishmen. Even by those who may be deemed constitutional writers, no stress was laid upon it; at least I do not find it in Fortescue, nor does Sir Thomas Smith advert to it in his Popular View of the English Commonwealth.[25] By Holinshed it is mentioned [III, 185–6], but not as of great or permanent interest to Englishmen, or in a way to attract the particular attention of the poet. In our days, it is prominent even among English histories intended for the nursery; and I well remember that, when an attempt was made to versify and set to music the multiplication-table, and other rudiments of education,

> Magna Charta we gain'd from John,
> Which Harry the Third put his seal upon,

were two lines of 'the Chapter of Kings.' Surely, upon Coleridge's principle,[26] Magna Charta ought to have been the prominent feature of the play.[27]

In the remainder of the play the history is pretty closely followed, except as to persons and places. Edmundsbury, I believe, is an interpolation by the editors, on the authority of the old play; that town is not mentioned in the Chronicles. It does not appear *where* Shakespeare meant to place the engagements to which he refers; nor, indeed, are the histories at all precise.

The death and confessions of Count Melun are mentioned by Holinshed [III, 193; from Matthew Paris]; as is also the story of John's death being occasioned by poison, administered by a monk of Swinestead Abbey in Lincolnshire. I find nothing of the loss of a French flotilla on Goodwin Sands [5.5], but the loss of a part of John's army in the washes of Lincolnshire [5.6] is warranted by the Chronicles. Not so the operations of Hubert in that part of the country; his service consisted in a gallant and successful defence of Dover.

The last scene of the play brings the revolted lords again to the King; it is said, and indeed is quite natural, that Melun's information made them think seriously of returning to their allegiance; but John's death came upon them too suddenly. . . .(I, 27–32; 262–4)

The lamentations of Constance, when represented by a powerful actress, form a very attractive part of this play; but her language is not uniformly admirable: and, surely, the scenes between John and Hubert are those which, coldly read in the closet, are the most striking of all. And I must do Johnson the justice to say, that, though he omits it in his recapitulation, he has commended the second of these conferences [4.2] as exhibiting 'many touches of nature.'[28] And this is the better of the two – the former being somewhat disfigured by conceits and obscurities.

The character of Constance, though founded upon reality, is not the less poetical. Mrs Jameson[29] is a little too enthusiastic about the historical princess; but her highly-wrought notice of Shakespeare's Constance is exceedingly attractive. Notwithstanding the command to put Arthur to death, the character of John is not brought out by the dramatist in the singularly odious light in which all modern historians have taught us to view it; still there is nothing inconsistent either with nature or with history. Possibly, a tradition from the revolting barons, and the writings of ecclesiastics, who have the great advantage of recording the deeds of their enemy, may have exaggerated the faults of this unfortunate king.

The merits of this play consist chiefly in the scenes, as distinguished from the plot, and the discrimination of character. In some of these scenes there is admirable force and beauty; and I should indeed be sorry that the doubts which I have raised of their historical accuracy should lessen the pleasure of any one in reading them. (I, 32–3; 263)

18 Charles Knight, The Pictorial Edition of *King John*

1838

From *The Pictorial Edition of the Works of Shakespeare* (8 vols, London, 1838–43). Volume III. *King John; King Richard II; King Henry IV, Part I; King Henry IV, Part II; King Henry V* (1838).

Charles Knight (1791–1873) devoted much of his life to the dissemination of information and ideas for popular audiences, serving tirelessly either as author, editor, or publisher for numerous periodicals, pamphlets, and books on a wide variety of subjects. The great scholarly achievement of his life, however, was *The Pictorial Shakespeare*, originally issued in fifty-five parts from 1838 to 1843, and later gathered into eight volumes. Knight's edition was both popular and intellectually serious, providing valuable information on the historical, textual, and theatrical backgrounds of the plays. The apparatus is extensive, containing an 'Introductory Notice' to each play, 'Illustrations' and 'Historical Illustrations' following each act, and a concluding 'Supplementary Notice'. In these sections one may find detailed information relating to text, sources, criticism, performance, costume, dating, historical accuracy, and other relevant concerns. The scholarly influence of *The Pictorial Shakespeare* was further enhanced in 1843 by the publication of Knight's biography of the poet, which comprised the final volume of the edition. Knight's edition was often reprinted; and selected portions of it also appeared in his *Studies in Shakespeare* (London, 1849).

[From the 'Introductory Notice' to *King John*: 'State of the Text and Chronology']

. . . *King John* is one of the plays of Shakespeare enumerated by Francis Meres, in 1598.[1] We have carefully considered the reasons which have led Malone to fix the date of its composition as 1596, and Chalmers as 1598; and we cannot avoid regarding them as far from satisfactory.

There can be no doubt, as we shall have to shew in detail, that Shakespeare's *King John* is founded on a former play. That play, which consists of two parts, is entitled *The Troublesome Raigne of John, King of England, with the Discoverie of King Richard Cordelion's base son, vulgarly named the Bastard Faulconbridge; also the Death of King John at Swinstead Abbey.* – This play was first printed in 1591. The first edition has no author's name in the title-page; – the second, of 1611, has, 'Written by W. Sh.'; – and the third, of 1622, gives the name of 'William Shakespeare.' We think there can be little hesitation in affirming that the attempt to fix this play upon Shakespeare was fraudulent; yet Steevens, in his valuable collection of *Twenty of the Plays* that were printed in quarto, says, 'the author (meaning Shakespeare) seems to have been so thoroughly dissatisfied with this play as to have written it almost entirely anew.'[2] Steevens afterwards receded from this opinion. Coleridge, too, in the classification which he attempted in 1802, speaks of the old *King John* as one of Shakespeare's 'transition-works – not his, yet of him.'[3] We cannot understand how Coleridge, at any rate, should have supposed it possible that the two works could be produced by the same pen. We must, for our own parts, hold to the opinion that the old *King John* was not either 'his, or of him.' The date, then, of this older play of *King John*, 1591, and the mention of Shakespeare's play, by Meres, in 1598, allow us a range of seven years for the period of the production of this, the first *in the order of History* of Shakespeare's historical plays.

Shakespeare's son, Hamnet, died in August, 1596, at the age of twelve. Hence the inspiration, according to Malone, of the deep pathos of the grief of Constance on the probable death of Arthur. We doubt this. The dramatic poetry of Shakespeare was built upon deeper and broader foundations than his own personal feelings and experiences. In the Sonnets, indeed, which are professedly a reflection of himself, we have, as far as we can judge, a key to as much of the character as he chose to disclose of the one man, Shakespeare; but in the plays his sense of individuality is entirely swallowed up in the perfectly distinct individuality of the manifold characters which he has painted. From the first to the last of his plays, as far as we can discover, we have no 'moods of his own mind,' – nothing of that quality which gives so deep an interest to the poetry of Wordsworth and Byron, – and which Byron, with all his genius, could not throw aside in dramatic composition. We are, for this reason, not disposed to regard the opinion of Malone upon this point as of much importance. The conjecture is, however, recommended by its accordance with our sympathies; and it stands, therefore, upon a different ground from that absurd notion that Shakespeare drew Lear's 'dog-hearted daughters' with such irresistible truth, because he himself had felt the sharp sting of 'filial ingratitude' [*King Lear*, 4.3.45; 3.4.14].

If the domestic history of the poet will help us little in fixing a precise date for the composition of *King John*, we apprehend that the public history of his times will not assist us in attaining this object much more conclusively. A great armament was sent against Spain in 1596, under the command of Essex and Lord Howard. 'The fleet,' says Southey,[4] 'consisted of one hundred and fifty sail; seventeen of these were of the navy royal, eighteen men of war, and six store-ships, supplied by the state; the rest were pinnaces, victuallers, and transports: the force was, 1000 *gentlemen volunteers*, 6368 troops, and 6772 seamen, exclusive of the Dutch. There were no hired troops in any of the queen's ships; all were gentleman volunteers, chosen by the commanders' [39–40]. Essex, in a letter to Bacon, speaking of the difficulty of his command, with reference to the nature of his force, describes his followers as 'the most *tyrones*, and almost all *voluntaries*' [43]. 'In numbers and strength,' continues Southey, 'the armament was superior to any that this country had sent forth since the introduction of cannon.' This expedition was directed, as the reader of English history knows, against Cadiz. It left Plymouth on the 3rd of June, 1596; and returned on the 8th of August; having effected its principal object, the destruction of the Spanish fleet. It is to this great armament that Malone thinks Shakespeare alludes, in the following lines in the second Act, where Chatillion describes to King Philip the expected approach of King John: –

> . . . all the unsettled humours of the land –
> Rash, inconsiderate, fiery, voluntaries,
> With ladies' faces, and fierce dragons' spleens, –
> Have sold their fortunes at their native homes,
> Bearing their birthrights proudly on their backs,
> To make a hazard of new fortunes here.
> In brief, a braver choice of dauntless spirits,
> Than now the English bottoms have waft o'er,
> Did never float upon the swelling tide,
> To do offence and scath in Christendom. [2.1.66ff.]

The supposed coincidence is, a great armament, principally composed of *voluntaries*. But does Shakespeare speak of these voluntaries in a manner that would have been agreeable to an English audience; or that, however just it might be, was in accordance with the public recognition of the conduct of the army of Cadiz? The 'unsettled humours of the land' – the 'rash, inconsiderate, fiery, voluntaries' – the 'birth-rights on their backs' – the 'offence and scath to Christendom,' – are somewhat opposed to the sentiment expressed in the public prayer of thanksgiving, written by Burleigh, in which the moderation of the troops in the hour of victory was solemnly recognised. 'War in those days,' says Southey, 'was conducted in such a spirit, that for the troops not to have committed, and with the sanction of their leaders, any outrage upon humanity, was deemed a point of special honour to the commanders, and calling for an especial expression of gratitude to the Almighty' [72–3]. But the narrative of this expedition, given in *Hakluyt's Voyages*, by Dr. Marbeck, who attended the Lord High Admiral, is not equally honourable to the 'voluntaries,' as regards their respect for property. He speaks of the 'great pillage of the common soldiers' – 'the goodly furniture that was debased by the baser people' – and 'the intemperate disorder of some of the rasher sort.'[5] Shakespeare might have known of this, – but would he go out of his way to reprobate it? If he had written this play a few years later than 1596, he might have kept the expedition in his eye, and have described its 'voluntaries,' without offence to the popular or the courtly feeling. If he had written it earlier than 1596, he might have described 'voluntaries' in general, from the many narratives of reckless military adventure with which he would be familiar.

There is another allusion, according to Johnson,[6] which fixes this date to 1596, or to the later date of 1605, which sets aside the evidence of Meres altogether, unless it be supposed that he assigned the old *King John* to Shakespeare. Pandulph thus denounces John: –

> And meritorious shall that hand be call'd,
> Canonized, and worshipp'd as a saint,
> That takes away by any secret course
> Thy hateful life. [3.1.176ff.]

The pope published a bull against Elizabeth in 1596; – and in 1605, the perpetrators of the Gunpowder treason were canonized. We have, fortunately, a proof that Shakespeare, in this case, abstained from any allusion to the history of his own times. In the old play of *King John* he found the following passage: –

'I, Pandulph,' &c. 'pronounce thee accursed, discharging every of thy subjects of all duty and fealty that they do owe to thee, and pardon and forgiveness of sin to those or them whatsoever, which shall carry arms against thee, or murder thee.' [3.92ff.]

Chalmers carries the passion of mixing up Shakespeare's incidents and expressions with passing events, to a greater extent than Malone or Johnson. According to him, the siege of Angiers is a type of the loss and recapture of Amiens, in 1597; the altercations between the Bastard and Austria were to conduce to the unpopularity of the Archduke Albert; and the concluding exhortation, – 'Nought shall make us rue, / If England to itself do rest but true' [5.7.117ff.], had allusion to the differences amongst the leading men of the Court of Elizabeth, arising out of the ambition of Essex.[7]

For the purpose of fixing an exact date for the composition of this play, we apprehend that our readers will agree with us, that evidence such as this is not to be received with an implicit belief. Indeed, looking broadly at all which has been written upon the chronology of Shakespeare's plays, with reference to this particular species of evidence, namely, the allusion to passing events, we fear that, at the best, a great deal of labour has been bestowed for a very unsatisfactory result. The attempt, however, has been praiseworthy; and it has had the incidental good of evolving many curious points connected with our history and manners, that present themselves more forcibly to the mind in an isolated shape, than when forming a portion of any large historical narration. Yet we are anxious to guard against one misapprehension which may have presented itself to the minds of some of our readers, as it did to our own minds, when we first bestowed attention upon the large collection of facts, or conjectures, that have regard to the chronological order of our poet's plays. Properly to understand the principle upon which Shakespeare worked, we must never for a moment suffer ourselves to believe that he was of that class of vulgar artists who are perpetually on the look-out for some temporary allusion (utterly worthless except in its relation to the excitement which is produced by passing events), for the mean purpose of endeavouring to 'split the ears of the groundlings' [*Hamlet*, 3.2.10–11]. If we should take literally what has been told us as regards to this play, without examining the passages upon which such opinions are founded, – that it had allusions, for instance, to the expedition to Cadiz, to the bull of the pope against Elizabeth, and to the factions of Essex, – we might believe that the great poet, who, in his 'Histories,' sought

> To raise our ancient sovereigns from their hearse,
> Make kings his subjects, by exchanging verse;
> Enlive their pale trunks, that the present age
> Joys in their joys, and trembles at their rage,[8]

was one of those waiters upon events who seized upon a fleeting popularity, by presenting a mirror of the *past* in which a distorted *present* might be seen. But, rightly considered, the allusions of Shakespeare to the passages of his own times are so few and so obscure, that they are utterly insufficient to abate one jot of his great merit, that 'he was for all time.' He was, indeed, in dealing with the spirit of the past, delighted, as Wordsworth has beautifully said in delineating his character of the poet, 'to contemplate similar volitions and passions as manifested in the goings on of the universe, and habitually impelled to create them where he does not find them.'[9] His past was, therefore, wherever it could be interfused with the permanent and universal, a reflex of the present. Thus, in the age of Elizabeth, and in the age of Victoria, his patriotism is an abiding and unchanging feeling; and has as little to do with the mutations of the world as any other of the great elements of human thought with which he deals. When the Bastard exclaims, – [Quotes 5.7.112–7: 'This England never did, nor never shall. . . .'] we feel such lines had a peculiar propriety when they were uttered before an audience that might have been trembling at the present threats of a Spanish invasion, had they not been roused to defiance by the 'lion-port' of their queen, and by the mightier power of that spirit of intellectual superiority which directed her councils, and, what was even more important, had entered into the spirit of her people's literature. But these noble lines were just as appropriate, dramatically, four hundred years before they were written, as they are appropriate in their influence upon the spirit two hundred and fifty years after they were written. Frederick Schlegel has said of Shakespeare, 'the feeling by which he seems to have been most connected with ordinary men is that of nationality.'[10] It is true that the nationality of Shakespeare is always hearty and genial; and even in the nationality of prejudice there are to be found very many of the qualities that make up the nationality of reflection. For this reason, therefore, the nationality of Shakespeare may constitute a link between him and 'ordinary men,' who have not yet come to understand, for example, his large toleration, which would seem, upon the surface, to be the antagonist principle of nationality. The time may arrive when true toleration and true nationality may shake hands. Coleridge has, in a few words, traced the real course which the nationality of Shakespeare may assist in working out, by the reconciliation of these seeming opposites: – 'Patriotism is equal to the sense of individuality reflected from every other individual. There may come a higher virtue in both – just cosmopolitism. But this latter is not possible but by antecedence of the former.'[11]

There is one other point connected with Shakespeare's supposed subservience to passing events, which we cannot dismiss without an expression of something more than a simple dissent. In reading the grand scene of the fourth Act, between John and Hubert, where John says, –

> It is the curse of kings to be attended
> By slaves, that take their humours for a warrant
> To break within the bloody house of life, – [4.2.208ff.]

had we not a commentator at our elbow, we should see nothing but the exquisite skill of the poet, in exhibiting the cowardly meanness of John in shrinking from his own 'warrant' when its execution had proved to be dangerous. This, forsooth, according to Warburton, 'plainly hints at Davison's case, in the affair of Mary Queen of Scots;'[12] and Malone thinks 'it is extremely probable that our author meant to pay his court to Elizabeth by this covert apology for her conduct to Mary.'[13]

Apology? If Shakespeare had been the idiot that these critics would represent him to have been, Elizabeth would very soon have told him to keep to his stage, and not meddle with matters out of his sphere; – for, unquestionably, the excuse which John attempts to make, could it have been interpreted into an excuse for Elizabeth, would have had precisely the same effect with regard to Elizabeth which it produces with regard to John, – it would have made men despise as well as hate the one as the other. As an example of the utter worthlessness of this sort of conjecture, we may add, that Douce says, 'may it not rather allude to the death of Essex?'[14] Mr. Courtenay, in his 'Shakespeare's Historical Plays considered historically' [No. 17 above], – which we have noticed in the Illustrations to Act I., – agrees with Warburton and Malone in their construction of this passage. Mr Courtenay is not, however, a blind follower of the opinions of other critics, but has theories of his own upon such matters. One of these conjectures upon Shakespeare's omission of the event of the signature of Magna Charta, is at least amusing: 'How shall we account for Shakespeare's omission of an incident so essential in "the life and reign of King John?" It had occurred to me, especially when considering the omission of all reference to popular topics, that as Shakespeare was a *decided courtier*, he might not wish to remind Queen Elizabeth, who set Magne Charta at nought in its most interesting particular, of the solemn undertakings of her ancestors.' Mr Courtenay subsequently says, that no great stress was laid upon Magna Charta, even by constitutional writers, before the days of Coke; but that, nevertheless, 'Magna Charta ought to have been the prominent feature of the play.' He says this, upon Coleridge's definition of a historical play, which is, at the best, not to understand Coleridge. Colley Cibber, in 1744, altered *King John* [*Papal Tyranny in the Reign of King John*, first performed in 1745], and he says, in his dedication, that he endeavoured 'to make his play more like one than what he found it in Shakespeare.' He gave us some magnificent scenes between John and the pope's nuncio, full of the most orthodox denunciations of Rome and the Pretender. He obtained room for these by the slight sacrifice of Constance and the Bastard. We have no doubt that upon the same principle, an ingenious adapter, into whom the true spirit of 'Historical Plays considered historically' should be infused, might give us a new *King John*, founded upon Shakespeare's, with Magna Charta at full length, – and if Arthur and Hubert were sacrificed for this end, as well as Constance and Faulconbridge, the lovers of poetry might still turn to the obsolete old dramatist, – but the student of history would be satisfied, by dramatic evidence, as well as by the authority of his primer, that

> Magna Charta we gain'd from John,
> Which Harry the Third put his seal upon.

The end and object of the drama, and of the Shakespearian drama especially, is to maintain that 'law of unity, which has its foundations, not in the factitious necessity of custom, but in Nature itself, the unity of feeling.'[15] In Shakespeare's *King John* this object is attained as completely as in *Macbeth*. The history at once directs and subserves the plot. We have shewn this fully in our Supplementary Notice; and we think, therefore, that the omission of Magna Charta in *King John* may find another solution than that which Mr. Courtenay's theory supplies. . . . (III, 1–5)

KING JOHN

[From the 'Introductory Notice' to *King John*: 'Sources of the "History" of *King John*']

. . . It is upon the conventional 'history' of the stage that Shakespeare built his play. It is impossible now, except on very general principles, to determine why a poet, who had the authentic materials of history before him, and possessed beyond all men the power of moulding those materials, with reference to a dramatic action, into the most complete and beautiful forms, should have subjected himself, in the full vigour and maturity of his intellect, to a general adherence to the course of that conventional dramatic history. But so it is. The King John of Shakespeare is not the King John of the historians which Shakespeare had unquestionably studied; it is not the King John of his own imagination, casting off the trammels which a rigid adoption of the facts of those historians would have imposed upon him; but it is the King John, in the conduct of the story, in the juxtaposition of the characters, and in the catastrophe, – in the historical truth, and in the historical error, – of the play which preceded him some few years [*The Troublesome Raigne*]. This, unquestionably, was not an accident. It was not what, in the vulgar sense of the word, is called a plagiarism. It was a submission of his own original powers of seizing upon the feelings and understanding of his audience, to the stronger power of *habit* in the same audience. The history of John had been familiar to them for almost half a century. The familiarity had grown out of the rudest days of the drama, and had been established in the period of its comparative refinement, which immediately preceded Shakespeare. The old play of *King John* was, in all likelihood, a vigorous graft upon the trunk of an older play, which 'occupies an intermediate place between moralities and historical plays,' – that of *Kynge Johan*, by John Bale, written probably in the reign of Edward VI. Shakespeare, then, had to choose between forty years of stage tradition, and the employment of new materials. He took, upon principle, what he found ready to his hand. But none of the transformations of classical or oriental fable, in which a new life is transfused into an old body, can equal this astonishing example of the life-conferring power of a genius such as Shakespeare's. Whoever really wishes thoroughly to understand the resources which Shakespeare possessed, in the creation of characters, in the conduct of a story, and the employment of language, will do well, again and again, to compare the old play of *King John*, and the *King John* of our dramatist. . . . (III, 5–6)

[Here Knight quotes extensively from John Payne Collier's introduction to *Kynge Johan* (London, 1838) in order to illustrate Collier's statement (quoted above) that Bale's play 'occupies an intermediate place between moralities and historical plays'. He then concludes his discussion of the literary genealogy of Shakespeare's play by demonstrating how *The Troublesome Raigne* improves upon *Kynge Johan*, and how *King John* in turn improves 'with surpassing grace and tenderness' upon *The Troublesome Raigne*, particularly in its realization of the Bastard and in the episode involving Arthur and Constance (3.1.42–74).]

[From the 'Historical Illustration' to Act I]

It would appear scarcely necessary to entreat the reader to bear in mind, – before we place in apposition the events which these scenes bring before us, and the facts of history, properly so called, – that the 'Histories' of Shakespeare are Dramatic Poems. And yet, unless this circumstance be watchfully regarded, we shall fall into the error of setting up one form of truth in contradiction to, and not in illustration of, another form of truth. It appears to us a worse than useless employment to be running parallels between the poet and the chronicler, for the purpose of shewing that for the literal facts of history the poet is not so safe a teacher as the chronicler; and yet, at the present time, we have offered to us a series of laborious essays, that undertake to solve these two problems, – 'What were Shakespeare's authorities for his history, and how far has he departed from them? And whether the plays may be given to our youth as properly historical.'[16] The writer of these essays decides the latter question in the negative, and maintains that these pieces are 'quite unsuitable as a medium of instruction to the English youth;' – and his great object is, therefore, to contradict, by a body of minute proofs, the assertion of A. W. Schlegel, with regard to these plays, that 'the principal traits in every event are given with so much correctness, their apparent causes and their secret motives are given with so much penetration, that we may therein study history, so to speak, after nature, without fearing that such lively images should ever be effaced from our minds.' Schlegel appears to us to have hit the true cause why the youth of England have been said to take their history from Shakespeare. The 'lively images' of the poet present a general truth much more completely than the tedious narratives of the annalist. The ten English 'histories' of Shakespeare – 'the magnificent dramatic *Epopée*, of which the separate pieces are different cantos' – stand in the same relation to the contemporary historians of the events they deal with, as a landscape does to a map. Mr. Courtenay says, 'Let it be well understood that if in any case I derogate from Shakespeare as an historian, it is as an historian only.' Now, in the sense in which Mr. Courtenay uses the word 'historian,' – by which he means one who describes past events with the most accurate observances of time and place, and with the most diligent balancing of conflicting testimony – Shakespeare has no pretensions to be regarded. The principle, therefore, of viewing Shakespeare's history through another medium than that of his art, and pronouncing, upon this view, that his historical plays cannot be given to our youth as '*properly* historical,' is nearly as absurd as it would be to derogate from the merits of Mr. Turner's beautiful drawings of coast scenery, by maintaining and proving that the draughtsman had not accurately laid down the relative positions of each bay and promontory.[17] It would not be, to our minds, a greater mistake to confound the respective labours of the landscape painter and the hydrographer, than to subject the poet to the same laws which should govern the chronicler. There may be, in the poet, a higher truth than the literal, evolved in spite of, or rather in combination with, his minute violations of accuracy; we may in the poet better study history, 'so to speak, after nature,' than in the annalist, – because the poet masses and generalizes his facts, subjecting them, in the order in which he presents them to the mind, as well as in the elaboration which he bestows upon them, to the laws of his art, which has a clearer sense of fitness and proportion than the laws of a dry chronology. But, at any rate, the structure of an historical drama and of an historical narrative are so essentially different, that the offices of the poet and the historian must never be confounded. It is not to derogate from the poet to say that he is not an historian; –

it will be to elevate Shakespeare when we compare his poetical truth with the truth of history. We have no wish that he had been more exact and literal. . . . (III, 21–2)

[From the 'Supplementary Notice' to *King John*]

. . . The great connecting link that binds together all the series of actions in the *King John* of Shakespeare, – which refuses to hold any actions, or series of actions, which arise out of other causes, – is *the fate of Arthur*. From the first to the last scene, the hard struggles, and the cruel end of the young Duke of Brittany, either lead to the action, or form a portion of it, or are the direct causes of an ulterior consequence. We must entreat the indulgence of our readers whilst we endeavour to establish this principle somewhat in detail.

In the whole range of the Shakespearian drama there is no opening scene which more perfectly exhibits the effect which is produced by coming at once, and without the slightest preparation, to the main business of the piece:-'Now say, Chatillion, what would France with us?' [1.1.1].

In three more lines the phrase 'borrowed majesty,' at once explains the position of John; and immediately afterwards we come to the formal assertion by France of the 'most lawful claim' of 'Arthur Plantagenet,' – 'To this fair island, and the territories; / To Ireland, Poictiers, Anjou, Touraine, Maine' [1.1.4, 9, 10ff.]. As rapid as the lightning of which John speaks is a defiance given and returned. The ambassador is commanded to 'depart in peace;' the king's mother makes an important reference to the 'ambitious Constance;' and John takes up the position for which he struggles to the end, – 'Our strong possession, and our right, for us' [1.1.23, 32, 39]. The scene of the Bastard is not an episode entirely cut off from the main action of the piece; his loss of 'lands,' and his 'new-made honour' [1.1.187], were necessary to attach him to the cause of John. The Bastard is the one partisan who never deserts him.

The second act brings us into the very heart of the conflict on the claim of Arthur. What a Gothic grandeur runs through the whole of these scenes! We see the men of six centuries ago, as they played the game of their personal ambition – now swearing hollow friendships, now breathing stern denunciations; – now affecting compassion for the weak and suffering, now breaking faith with the orphan and the mother; – now 'Gone to be married, gone to swear a peace' [3.1.1], now keeping the feast 'with slaughtered men' [3.1.302]; – now trembling at, and now braving the denunciations of spiritual power; – and agreeing in nothing, but to bend 'their sharpest deeds of malice' [2.1.380] on unoffending and peaceful citizens, unless the citizens have some 'commodity' to offer which shall draw them 'To a most base and vile-concluded peace' [2.1.586]. With what skill has Shakespeare, whilst he thus painted the spirit of the chivalrous times, – lofty in words, but sordid in acts, – given us a running commentary which interprets the whole, in the sarcasms of the Bastard! But amidst all the clatter of conventional dignity which we find in the speeches of John, and Philip, and Lewis, and Austria, the real dignity of strong natural affections rises over the pomp and circumstance of regal ambition, with a force of contrast which is little less than sublime. In the second Act, Constance is almost too much mixed up with the dispute to let us quite feel that she is something very much higher than the 'ambitious Constance' [1.1.32]. Yet even here, how sweetly does the *nature* of Arthur rise up amongst these fierce broils, – conducted at the sword's point with words that are as sharp as swords, – to assert the supremacy of gentleness and moderation: – [Quotes 2.1.163–5: 'Good my mother peace. . . .']. This is the key note to the great scene of Arthur and Hubert in the fourth Act. But in the mean time the maternal terror and anguish of Constance become the prominent objects; and the rival kings, the haughty prelate, the fierce knights, the yielding citizens, appear but as puppets moved by destiny to force on the most bitter sorrows of that broken-hearted mother. We have here the true characteristic of the drama, as described by the philosophical critic, – 'fate and will in opposition to each other.' Mrs Jameson, in her very delightful work, *The Characteristics of Women*, [No. 14 above] has formed a most just and beautiful conception of the character of Constance: – [Quotes extensively here from Jameson's argument that Constance is a sublime combination of 'power' with the 'exquisitely feminine', a creature of 'passion', 'towering pride', and 'strength of intellect' whose 'extraordinary development of sensibility and imagination' gives her a 'rich poetical colouring' that is the hallmark of her character].

How exquisitely is this feminine nature exhibited when Constance affects to disbelieve the tale of Salisbury that the kings are 'gone to swear a peace' [3.1.1]; or rather makes her words struggle with her half belief, in very weakness and desperation: – [Quotes 3.1.11–18]. Here is the timid, helpless woman, sick even at the shadows of coming events; but when the shadows become realities, the haughty will 'Like a proud river peering o'er his bounds' [3.1.23], asserts its supremacy in little matters which are yet within its control: – [Quotes 3.1.65–75: Constance's insistence that kings 'bow' to her sorrow]. The pride of grief for a while triumphs over the grief itself: – 'Arm, arm, you heavens, against these perjur'd kings!' [3.1.107]. She casts away all fear of consequences, and defies her false friends with words that appear as irrepressible as her tears. When Pandulph arrives upon the scene, she sees the change which his mission is to work, only through the medium of her own personal wrongs: –

> Good father cardinal, cry thou, amen,
> To my keen curses: for, without my wrong,
> There is no tongue hath power to curse him right. [3.1.181ff.]

Reckless of what may follow, she, who formerly exhorted Philip, 'Stay for an answer to your embassy, / Lest unadvis'd you stain your swords with blood' [2.1.44ff.], is now ready to encounter all the perilous chances of another war, and to exhort France to fall off from England, even upon her knee 'made hard with kneeling' [3.1.310]. This would appear like the intensity of selfishness, did we not see the passion of the mother in every act and word. It is thus that the very weakness of Constance, – the impotent rage, the deceiving hope, – become clothed with the dignity that in ordinary cases belongs to patient suffering and reasonable expectations. Soon, however, this conflict of feeling, – almost as terrible as the 'hysterica passio' of Lear [*King Lear*, 2.4.57], – is swallowed up in the mother's sense of her final bereavement: – [Quotes 3.4.93–105: 'Grief fills the room up. . . .'].

Matchless as is the art of the poet in these scenes; – matchless as an exhibition of maternal sorrow only, apart from the whirlwind of conflicting passions that are mixed up with that sorrow; – matchless in this single point of view, when compared with the 'Hecuba' which antiquity has left us,[18] and of the 'Merope' which the imitators of the Greek drama have attempted to revive; – are we to believe that Shakespeare intended that our hearts should sustain this laceration, and that the effects should pass away when Constance quits the stage? Are we to believe that he was satisfied that his 'incidents should be various and affecting,' but 'independent of each other, and without any tendency to produce and regulate the conclusion?' Was there to be no 'unity of feeling' to sustain and elevate the action to the end?[19] Was his tragedy to be a mere dance of Fantoccini [i.e., little puppets]? No, no. The remembrance of Constance can never be separated from the after-scenes in which Arthur appears; and at the very last, when the poison has done its work upon the guilty king, we can scarcely help believing that the spirit of Constance hovers over him, and that the echo of the mother's cries is even more insupportable than the 'burn'd bosom' and the 'parched lips' which neither his 'kingdom's rivers,' nor the 'bleak winds' of the north can 'comfort with cold' [5.7.38–41].

Up to the concluding scene of the third Act we have not learnt from Shakespeare to hate John. We may think him an usurper. Our best sympathies may be with Arthur and his mother. But he is bold and confident, and some remnant of the indomitable spirit of the Plantagenets gives him a lofty and gallant bearing. We are not even sure, from the first, that he had not something of justice in his quarrel, even though his mother confidentially repudiates 'his right' [1.1.40]. In the scene with Pandulph we completely go with him. We have yet to know that he would one day crouch at the feet of the power that he now defies; and he has therefore all our voices when he tells the wily and sophistical cardinal, 'That no Italian priest / Shall tithe or toll in our dominions' [3.1.153ff.]. But the expression of *one thought* that had long been lurking in the breast of John, sweeps away every feeling but that of hatred, and worse than hatred; and we see nothing, hereafter, in the king, but the creeping, cowardly assassin, prompting the deed which he is afraid almost to name to himself, with the lowest flattery of his instrument, and shewing us, as it were, the sting which wounds, and the slaver which pollutes, of the venomous and loathsome reptile. The 'Come hither, Hubert – O, my gentle Hubert, / We owe thee much' [3.3.19ff.] – the 'By heaven, Hubert, I am almost asham'd / To say what good respect I have of thee' [3.3.27ff.] – make our flesh creep. The warrior and the king vanish. If Shakespeare had not exercised his consummate art in making John move thus stealthily to his purpose of blood – if he had made the suggestion of Arthur's death what John afterwards pretended it was – 'the winking of authority' – the 'humour' 'Of dangerous majesty, when, perchance, it frowns' [4.2.211ff.], – we might have seen him hemmed in with revolted subjects and foreign invaders, with something like compassion. But this exhibition of low craft and desperate violence we can never forgive.

At the end of the third Act, when Pandulph instigates the Dauphin to the invasion of England, the poet overleaps the historical succession of events by many years, and makes the expected death of Arthur the motive of policy for the invasion. [Quotes 3.4.164–8]. Here is the link which holds together the dramatic action still entire; and it wonderfully binds up all the succeeding events of the play.

In the fourth Act the poet has put forth all his power of the pathetic in the same ultimate direction as in the grief of Constance. The theme is not now the affection of a mother driven to frenzy by the circumstances of treacherous friends and victorious foes; but it is the irresistible power of the very helplessness of her orphan boy, triumphing in its truth and artlessness over the evil nature of the man whom John had selected to destroy his victim, as one 'Fit for bloody villany, / Apt, liable, to be employed in danger' [4.2.225ff.]. It would be worse than idle to attempt any lengthened comment on that most beautiful scene between Arthur and Hubert, which carries on the main action of this play. Hazlitt has truly said [No. 8 above], 'if anything ever was penned, heart-piercing, mixing the extremes of terror and pity, of that which shocks and that which soothes the mind, it is this scene.' When Hubert gives up his purpose, we do not feel the less that 'The bloody fingers' ends of John' [3.4.168] have not been washed of their taint: − 'Your uncle must not know but you are dead' [4.1.127], tells us, at once, that no relenting of John's purpose had prompted the compassion of Hubert. Pleased, therefore, are we, to see the retribution beginning. The murmurs of the peers at the 'once again crown'd' [4.2.1], − the lectures which Pembroke and Salisbury read to their sovereign, − are but the preludes to the demand for 'the enfranchisement of Arthur' [4.2.52]. Then comes the dissembling of John, 'We cannot hold mortality's strong hand' [4.2.82], − and the bitter sarcasms of Salisbury of Pembroke: − [Quotes 4.2.86–8]. 'This must be answer'd' [4.2.89] is as a knell in John's ears. Throughout this scene the king is prostrate before his nobles; − it is the prostration of guilt without the energy which too often accompanies it. Contrast the scene with the unconquerable intellectual activity of Richard III., who never winces at reproach, seeing only the success of his crimes and not the crimes themselves. . . . [John] turns upon Hubert in the extremity of his fears, and attempts to put upon his instrument all the guilt of that deed. Never was a more striking display of the equivocations of conscience in a weak and guilty mind. Shakespeare is here the true interpreter of the secret excuses of many a criminal, who would shift upon accessories the responsibility of the deviser of a wicked act, and make the attendant circumstances more powerful for evil than the internal suggestions. When the truth is avowed by Hubert, John does not rejoice that he has been spared the perpetration of a crime, but he is prompt enough to avail himself of his altered position: − 'O haste thee to the peers' [4.2.260]. Again he crawls before Hubert. But the storm rolls on.

The catastrophe of Arthur's death follows instantly upon the rejoicing of him who exclaimed, 'Doth Arthur live?' [4.2.260] in the hope to find a safety in his preservation upon the same selfish principle upon which he had formerly sought a security in his destruction. In a few simple lines we have the sad dramatic story of Arthur's end: − [Quotes 4.3.1–5]. How marvellously does Shakespeare subject all his characters and situations to the empire of common sense! The Arthur of the old play, after receiving his mortal hurt, makes a long oration about his mother. The great dramatist carries on the now prevailing feeling of the audience by one pointed line: − 'O me! my uncle's spirit is in these stones' [4.3.9]. If any other recollection were wanting, these simple words would make us feel, that John was as surely the murderer of Arthur, when the terrors of the boy drove him to an inconsiderate attempt to escape from his prison, as if the assassin, as some have represented, rode with him in the dim twilight by the side of a cliff that overhung the sea, and suddenly hurled the victim from his horse into the engulphing wave: – or as if the king tempted him to descend from his prison at Rouen at the midnight hour, and, instead of giving him freedom, stifled his prayers for pity in the waters of the Seine. It is thus that we know the anger of 'the distempered lords' [4.3.21] is a just anger, when, finding Arthur's body, they kneel before that 'ruin of sweet life,' and vow to it the 'worship of revenge' [4.3.65, 72]. The short scene between Salisbury, Pembroke, the Bastard, and Hubert, which immediately succeeds, is as spirited and characteristic as anything in the play. Here we see 'the invincible knights of old,' in their most elevated character – fiery, implacable, arrogant, but still drawing their swords in the cause of right, when that cause was intelligible and undoubted. The character of Faulconbridge here rises far above that we might have expected from the animal courage, and the exuberant spirits of the Faulconbridge of the former Acts. The courage indeed is here, beyond all doubt: – [Quotes 4.3.95–8]. But we were scarcely prepared for the rush of tenderness and humanity that accompany the courage, as in the speech to Hubert: – [Quotes 4.3.125–33]. It is this instinctive justice in Faulconbridge, – this readiness to uplift the strong hand in what he thinks a just quarrel, – this abandonment of consequences in the expression of his opinions, – that commands our sympathies for him whenever he appears upon the scene. The motives upon which he acts are entirely the antagonist motives by which John is moved. We have, indeed, in Shakespeare none of the essay-writing contrasts of smaller authors. We have no asserters of adverse principles made to play at see-saw, with reverence be it spoken, like the Moloch and Belial of Milton. But, after some reflection upon what we have read, we feel that he who leapt into Cœur de Lion's throne, and he who hath 'a trick of Cœur de Lion's face' [1.1.85], are as opposite as if they were the *formal* personifications of subtlety and candour, cowardice and courage, cruelty and kindliness. The fox and the lion are not more strongly contrasted than John and Faulconbridge; and the poet did not make the contrast by accident. And yet with what incomparable management are John and the Bastard held together as allies throughout these scenes. In the onset the Bastard receives honour from the hands of John, – and he is grateful. In the conclusion he sees his old patron, weak indeed and guilty, but surrounded with enemies, – and he will not be faithless. When John quails before the power of a spiritual tyrant, the Bastard stands by him in the place of a higher and a better nature. He knows the dangers that surround his king: – [Quotes 5.1.30–4]. But no dangers can daunt his resolution: – [Quotes 5.1.46–53]. The very necessity for these stirring words would shew us that from henceforth John is but a puppet without a will. The blight of Arthur's death is upon him; and he moves on to his own destiny, whilst Faulconbridge defies or fights with his enemies; and his revolted lords, even while they swear 'A voluntary zeal, and an unurg'd faith' to the invader [5.2.10], bewail their revolt, and lament 'That, for the health and physic of our right, / We cannot deal but with the very hand / Of stern injustice and confused wrong' [5.2.21ff.]. But the great retribution still moves onward. The cause of England is triumphant; 'the lords are all come back' [5.6.33]; – but the king is 'poisoned by a monk' [5.6.23]. . . . It is the poet's office to preserve a unity of action; it is the historian's to shew a consistency of progress. In the chroniclers we have manifold changes of fortune in the life of John after Arthur of Brittany has fallen. In Shakespeare Arthur of Brittany is at once revenged. The heart-broken mother and her boy are not the only sufferers from double courses. The spirit of Constance is appeased by the fall of John. The Niobe of a Gothic age, who vainly sought to shield her child from as stern a destiny as that with which Apollo and Artemis pursued the daughter of Tantalus, may rest in peace! (III, 72–8)

19 George Fletcher, the female roles in *King John*

1843

From *Studies of Shakespeare in the Plays of* King John, Cymbeline, Macbeth, As You Like It, Much Ado About Nothing, Romeo and Juliet: *With Observations on the Criticism and the Acting of Those Plays. By George Fletcher, Author of Historical and Critical Essays, Entitled 'Heloise and Abelard,' 'Robin Hood,' 'Hampton Court,' &c.* (London, 1847).

George Fletcher's critical and theatrical essays on Shakespeare appeared regularly in *The Athenæum* and *The Westminster Review* from February 1843 to September 1845. They were later reprinted, arranged in the chronological order in which they were originally written and published, in Fletcher's *Studies of Shakespeare*. Here they were accompanied by a prefatory essay defending Fletcher's theatrical and dramatic approach to Shakespearian texts, and calling for a new critical understanding of the plays that would lead to their full artistic realization in the theatre.

1. CHARACTER OF THE LADY CONSTANCE.
February 11th, 1843[1]

In her elaborate consideration of the character of The Lady Constance, Mrs. Jameson [No. 14 above] falls somewhat into the error which has constantly, more or less, been committed in treating of Shakespeare's historical plays – that of failing to consider, not only the composition of each drama on the whole, but the conception and development of every character in it, primarily and independently with relation to dramatic art, and without any regard whatever to real or alleged departures from the literal or even the substantial truth of history. Unless this point of view be steadily maintained by the critic in forming his *dramatic* judgment, his opinions will, at every moment, be liable to fall into inconsistency and injustice. A very little reflection should have sufficed to shew any commentator the preposterousness of dragging Shakespeare, the dramatist – the dramatist transcendently and exclusively – to the bar of historical criticism – a kind of procedure which, in the following observations, we shall studiously avoid.

The subject of the piece before us, then, is not so much 'The Life and Death of King John,' as it is the triumph of right, and justice, and feeling, and beauty, and poetry, for all time, in the universal heart of mankind, over the very meanness, selfishness, and crime, which oppress and crush them for the hour. Whatever doubts might exist at the historic period in question, as to the validity of young Arthur's title to the crown of *England*, any such doubtful title would have been little to the purpose of the dramatist; and accordingly we find, in the play, that Arthur's claim and John's usurpation are regarded by all parties as clear and indisputable. In the very opening of the piece, 'Your strong possession, much more than your right, / Or else it must go wrong with you and me' [1.1.40ff.], says John's mother, Queen Elinor, assuredly his warmest and staunchest partisan. This clearness of Arthur's title cannot be overlooked for a moment, without essentially perverting and weakening the interest which the poet has attached to the position as well as character of the widowed mother, Constance of Bretagne. Nor is it Shakespeare's fault if the reader or spectator fail to be forcibly reminded of this fact, at numerous intervals throughout the play. Among the most remarkable of these instances are the passages to that effect in those ruminating speeches of Faulconbridge (the most intelligent as well as devoted and spirited of John's adherents) which form, as it were, the chorus of the tragedy. Thus, when moralising on the peace patched up between the two kings by the marriage of Blanch to the Dauphin, he speaks of the French monarch as one 'whose armour conscience buckled on, / Whom zeal and charity brought to the field, / As God's own soldier' [2.1.564ff.]; and adds that this 'commodity,' this self-interest, against which the speaker is railing, 'Hath drawn him from his own determin'd aid, / From a resolv'd and honourable war, / To a most base and vile-concluded peace' [2.1.584ff.]. Again, at the close of the fourth act, over the dead body of Arthur, addressing Hubert, he says – [Quotes 4.3.139–45: 'Go bear him in thy arms. . . .']. It is in tracing the course of the retribution upon John, political and personal, as a usurper and a murderer, brought upon him by those unscrupulous means which he had taken to prevent it, that the interest of the concluding act resides, and the satisfaction which it affords to the feelings of the auditor.

So far, then, from representing either Arthur or his mother as ambitious, the poet, in legitimate pursuit of his *dramatic* object, has studiously excluded from view every historical circumstance that could countenance the smallest impression of that nature. He has not only reduced the prince's age to such tender years as would hardly admit of his harbouring a political sentiment; but, in direct opposition to the recorded facts, represents the boy as one of a peculiarly mild and quiet temper, devoid of all princely airs and all appetite for command – simple-hearted, meek, and affectionate. . . . Is it not plain that this very inoffensiveness is designed by the dramatist to place in the stronger light the clearness of Arthur's title, as the *exclusive* reason for his uncle's hostility, at the same time that it deepens so wonderfully the pathos of the scene wherein he pleads for the preservation of his eyes? Another element of this pathos is, the exceeding beauty which the poet has ascribed to the princely boy, which is made to affect the hearts of all who approach him, even the rudest of his uncle's creatures, and gives to this only orphan child the crowning endearment to his widowed mother's heart.

That mother herself, it is most important to observe and to bear in mind, whatever she was in history, is *not* represented by the poet as courting power for its own sake. Had he so represented her, it would have defeated one of those fine contrasts of character in which Shakespeare so much delighted – that between Constance and

Elinor, which is perfect in every way. The whole conduct and language of Constance in the piece, shew that her excessive fondness for her son, and that alone, makes her so eagerly desire the restitution of his lawful inheritance. She longs to see this one sole, and beautiful, and gracious object of her maternal idolatry, placed on the pedestal of grandeur which is his birthright, that she may idolize it more fondly still – 'Thou and thine usurp / The domination, royalties and rights / Of this oppressed boy' [2.1.175ff.]. Such is her defiance to Elinor. Still more strikingly unfolded is the entire subordination, in the breast of Constance, of all ambitious view, to the concentrated feelings of the doting mother, in the well-known address to Arthur, when her sworn friends have betrayed her: – [Quotes 3.1.43–56: 'If thou, that bidst me be content, wert grim. . . .'].

If we could still doubt the absolute and all-absorbing predominance of the maternal affection, it is disclosed to us in all its awful and beautiful depth, in those bursts of sublimest poetry that gush from her heart when informed of Arthur's capture. In all these she never once thinks of him as a prince, who ought to be a king – far less of the station to which she is herself entitled. It is the thought of never more beholding her 'absent child,' her 'pretty Arthur,' her 'fair son,' that is driving her to distraction – [Quotes 3.4.101–5].

We come now to consider the most important point of all that should guide us in judging of the histrionic expression of this character – namely, the indications afforded by the whole tenour of the incident and dialogue, as to the individuality of Constance's person and disposition as a *woman* – independently even of that maternal relation in which the drama constantly places her before us.

That Constance, in the poet's conception, is of graceful as well as noble person, we are not left to infer merely from the graces of her vigorous mind, nor from the rare loveliness of her child, and her extreme sensibility to it. We hear of her beauty more explicitly from the impression which it makes upon those around her – especially from the exclamations of King Philip on beholding her distress for Arthur's loss, the greater part of which we regret to find omitted in the present acting of the play – [Quotes 3.4.37; and 3.4.61–2: where the adjective 'fair' is twice applied to Constance].

But it is the moral and intellectual beauty, the logic and the poetry of the character, that it is most essential to consider. And here we are called upon to dissent materially from the view of this matter which Mrs. Jameson has exhibited at some length. In commencing her essay on this character, she numbers among the qualities which the Lady Constance of Shakespeare has in common with the mother of Coriolanus, 'self-will and exceeding pride.' In a following page, she speaks again of 'her haughty spirit' and 'her towering pride.' Again, of 'her proud spirit' and 'her energetic self-will;' and 'her impetuous temper conflicting with her pride.' Once more – 'On the whole it may be said, that pride and maternal affection form the basis of the character of Constance;' and 'in all the state of her great grief, a grand impersonation of pride and passion.' But the contrary of all this inherent pride and self-will which the critic alleges, appears in the poet's delineation. It is the mild language of gratitude and patience that we first hear from Constance, in the scene where she thanks the French king and the Austrian duke for their espousal of her dear son's cause, but entreats them to wait for John's answer to the French ambassador before they proceed to bloodshed. In the scene where she encounters Elinor, all the 'pride and self-will' are on the side of her enemies; the outraged right and feeling, on her own. To Elinor's 'Who is it thou dost call usurper, France?' [2.1.120] it is but natural that she should say, 'Let me make answer – thy usurping son' [2.1.121]. And Elinor's atrocious imputation upon her, of adultery and of guilty ambition – 'Out insolent! – thy bastard shall be king, / That thou mayst be a queen, and check the world! [2.1.122ff.] – more than justifies all the keenness of retort that follows. That she resents the insults thus added to the injuries of her foes, infers but little *pride*. To have remained silent under them, would have been nothing less than meanness in any woman – most of all in a sovereign princess on so public an occasion. Again, in all her exclamations on the betrayal of her cause by her selfish allies, we find, indeed, all the sensitive and intellectual widow and mother, 'Oppress'd with wrongs, and therefore full of fears' [3.1.13]; but where is the proud self-will? It seems extraordinary that Mrs. Jameson and others should not have reflected that, had a particle of it been represented as belonging originally and inherently to the character of Constance, it would utterly have marred the grand, the sublime effect of her concluding words in this majestic scene. It is simply because there is no pride in her nature – nothing but the indispensable self-respect of the woman, the mother, and the princess, – and more especially because the whole previous tenour of this scene itself exhibits her as anything but 'an impersonation of *pride*' – [Quotes 3.1.12–16] – that the passage in question is so wonderfully impressive. It is not the proud, fierce, haughty woman, but the sensitive and apprehensive woman alone, lashed out of all her usual habits of mind and temper, by direst injury and basest treachery, into intense resistance and resentment, to whom it can ever occur to say, –

> I will *instruct* my sorrows to be proud;
> For grief is proud, and *makes* his owner stout.
> To me, and to the state of my great *grief*,
> Let kings assemble; for my *grief's* so great,
> That no supporter but the huge firm earth
> Can hold it up. Here I and *Sorrow* sit;
> Here is my throne – bid kings come bow to it! [3.1.68ff.]

Here is pride indeed! wrung, for the first time, from a noble tender nature, by the awful climax of indignant sorrow, and placing the 'gentle Constance' on that towering eminence from whence, in the desolate majesty of afflicted right, she hurls the keen lightnings of her eloquence upon the mean-souled great ones around her. Theirs, indeed, is the gain, but hers is the triumph!

So much have we deemed it necessary to say in vindication of the moral qualities wherewith Shakespeare has endowed his heroine. We must now say something, for the guidance, it may be, both of the reader and the performer, in correction of some erroneous views, as we esteem them, to which the authoress above-cited, and others, have given circulation, respecting the intellectual powers developed in this character. The substance of Mrs. Jameson's observations on this head is contained in the following sentence: – 'The moral energy, that faculty which is principally exercised in self-control, and gives consistency to the rest, is deficient; or rather, to speak more correctly, the extraordinary development of sensibility and imagination, which lends to the character its rich poetical colouring, leaves the other qualities comparatively subordinate.'

Following out this view of the matter, Mrs. Jameson speaks of the dramatic Constance as 'a generous woman, betrayed by her own rash confidence.' Generous she is; but where is the rashness of her confidence? What better resource have she and her son, than to trust in the solemn protestations which the potentates best able to assist them are made to deliver at the opening of the second act? What weakness of intellect is here implied? It is clearly her best policy to confide in them. Again, Mrs Jameson desires us to observe, that the heroine cannot, from her intellectual resources, 'borrow patience to submit, or fortitude to endure.' But, all feeling apart, what, we would ask, betrayed on every hand, and friendless as she is, has she to gain by submitting and enduring? Constance herself understands her own position as clearly, as she feels it keenly; and states it, too, with her own ever forcible and coherent logic. In answer to the legate's observation, respecting the excommunication of King John – 'There's law and warrant, lady, for my curse' [3.1.184] – most justly does she reply, – [Quotes 3.1.185–90: 'And for mine too. . . .'].[2]

Equally logical – more strikingly and terribly consequential than the cool reasonings of the Cardinal himself – are these sentences addressed to him in her despairing scene: – [Quotes 3.4.76–89: 'And, father cardinal, I have heard you say. . . .']. Here, indeed, her heart may be said to stimulate her intellect to a sort of preternatural activity; but she does not rave, she reasons herself into the climax of despair. Yet Mrs. Jameson speaks of 'the bewildered pathos and poetry of this address;' and in a subsequent page proceeds in the same strain – 'It is this exceeding vivacity of imagination which in the end turns sorrow to frenzy,' – and calls the sublime effusions of her despair 'the frantic violence of uncontrolled feeling.' This is nothing less than using to the afflicted mother the language addressed to her by the cold-blooded papal diplomatist, 'Lady, you utter madness, and not sorrow' [3.4.43]: and Constance's own answer to the Cardinal is a triumphant refutation of all such criticism: – [Quotes 3.4.44–60: 'Thou art not holy, to belie me so. . . .'].[3]

But in spite of this convincing protest, Mrs. Jameson sees only, in the lady's invocation to Death, that 'she heaps one ghastly image upon another with all the wild luxuriance of a distempered fancy': – [Quotes 3.4.25–36: 'O amiable, lovely death. . . .']. For our own part, we can only exclaim upon this, oh! tremendous and resistless logic of high and true passion! oh, 'lion sinews' lent to the intellect by the fearful pressure of despair upon the heart!

We deem it requisite to dwell a little longer upon Mrs. Jameson's general view of this matter, because the error into which she seems to us to fall respecting it, is an essential one, and pervades her criticism of Shakespeare's more poetical characters. . . . [Fletcher now quotes extensively from Jameson's essay where the earlier critic contends that Constance, like Juliet, Lear, and Othello, utters 'some of the most splendid poetry to be met with in Shakespeare', attributing this trait to the 'predominance' in these characters of 'passion and imagination'.]

Here seems to us to lie a radical error, that of regarding the '*excess* of the ideal power,' the *predominance* of passion and imagination, as productive of 'the most splendid poetry.' For the very reason that Lear and Othello, Juliet and Constance, are sublime poets, that is, possess the creative mental power in the highest degree, neither fancy nor passion, however vigorous in them, can be predominant, but must exist in due proportion to the strength of the reasoning faculty. Otherwise, the result would be, not poetry, but mere wild, incoherent raving, such as Mrs. Jameson has mistakenly attributed to the most impassioned speeches of Constance herself. But, as she herself protests, she is not mad; and not being mad, her most impassioned are also her most logical passages; as is ever the case with a being like her, in whom a noble nature has unfolded itself in harmonious vigour. Her glowing heart, indeed, stirred by the deepest of all passions, a widowed mother's boundless and idolatrous love, puts her rich and lively fancy into most active play; but only her bright strong intellect could mould and elevate those crowding images into glorious and deathless imaginings. Whatever the actual princess might be, *Shakespeare's* Constance is a poetess of the first order: and so, in one sense, must the actress be who undertakes to personate her. Feeling, fancy, and reason, in her soul, must each be strong, and all harmoniously blended.

This brings us to the histrionic part of our observations; and as, in the course of Mrs. Siddons's theatrical career, the Lady Constance became one of her great parts, we turn, of necessity, to the record which Mr. Campbell's Life of that great performer [No. 15 above] affords us, of what were her conception and execution of this arduous character.

The remarks, then, extracted from Mrs. Siddons's memoranda on the character of Constance, whom she designates as 'the majestic, the passionate, the tender,' show that she felt and appreciated the essential tenderness of the character more fully and justly than the literary critic of her own sex, from whom we have been quoting. Still we find, from a careful perusal of the great actress's observations, that the ideals of pride and majesty and command unduly predominate in her conception of the 'gentle Constance.' One source of this error it is important to point out. The first mention of Constance in the play speaks of her as 'that ambitious Constance' [1.1.32]; and we affirm most confidently, that there is not another syllable in the piece from which it is possible to infer ambition on her part. It is quite plain, that the indolence or carelessness of most readers – a carelessness or indolence of which we might cite many similar examples – has caused this description of Constance to pass with them as the *dramatist's own* view of the character. But what is the fact? That these words come from the lips of Constance's deadly enemy and rival, Queen Elinor, who almost in the same breath confesses to us the fact of her and her son John's usurpation. This same essential fact, attested by their own words, leaves not the smallest scope for ambition in Constance, even supposing that the poet had, which he has not, represented her as loving power for its own sake. Surely it is no more a proof of ambition, that she desires to see her son possessed of a crown which is his birthright, than it is of covetousness for a man to desire the payment of a debt which is justly due to him. Yet we find even the acute perception of Mrs. Siddons to have been misled by the prevailing prepossession, – though, abandoning the most absurd form of it, she says, 'I believe I shall not be thought singular when I assert, that though she has been designated the ambitious Constance, she has been ambitious only for her son. It was for him, and him alone, that she aspired to, and struggled for hereditary sovereignty.' The same mistaken impression leads the great performer to speak repeatedly of 'disappointed ambition,' 'baffled ambition,' as among the indignant feelings of Constance at the treachery of her allies. To the same source it must surely be attributed, that this interesting critic tells us at the very outset of her observations – 'My idea of Constance is that of a lofty and proud spirit, associated with the most exquisite feelings of maternal tenderness.'

This mistake, on which we have already had occasion to descant, of regarding her in the grand scene with her treacherous protectors as possessed by a pride *inherent* and *personal*, instead of seeing that her sublime scorn and indignation spring *exclusively* from her deep, keen sense of violated friendship, now added with lightning suddenness to outraged right and feeling and affection, lent, we suspect, a colouring not quite appropriate, a too predominant bitterness and asperity of tone, to Mrs. Siddons's acting of this scene, majestic and wonderful as it must have been. The sarcasms, we fear, were uttered too much in the manner of a woman *habitually* sarcastic; and she seems to have fallen somewhat into the same error which we have pointed out in Mrs. Jameson's criticism, of confounding with mere frenzy the awful poetry that bursts from the tortured heart of the heroine. 'Goaded and stung,' she says, 'by the treachery of her faithless friends, and almost maddened by the injuries they have heaped upon her, she becomes desperate and ferocious as a hunted *tigress* in defence of her young, and it seems that existence itself must surely issue forth with the utterance of that *frantic* and appalling exclamation, "A wicked day, and not a holy day!" [3.1.83] &c.' Yet Constance might more justly be likened to a hunted hind than a hunted tigress; nor should her exclamations on this occasion, however appalling, be termed frantic. In all this, the poet, ever true to nature, has observed a due gradation. Here, indeed, is grief in its utmost, its proudest intensity; but here is no despair – she is not even on the way to frenzy, as we find her to be in the scene which follows the capture of her son [3.4].

Mr. Campbell, who, in speaking of Mrs. Siddons's performance of this character, professes to have 'almost as many circumstantial recollections of her as there are speeches in the part,' and who saw her enact it when ten years of practice and improvement in it must have brought her performance to its greatest perfection, relates one particular of it which seems to us to exemplify very strikingly the erroneous bias which we have indicated as warping her judgment respecting the essential qualities of the character. 'When,' says her biographer, 'she patted Lewis on the breast with the words, "Thine honour! oh, thine honour!" [3.1.316] *there was a sublimity in the laugh of her sarcasm.*' Now, we must affirm, that anything like sarcastic expression of this passage is quite inconsistent with the essential character of Constance, and most inappropriate to the occasion upon which it is delivered. Here we must again insist upon the strict consequentiality and the sterling policy of the heroine's behaviour throughout this agitated scene. Her expressions of indignation and her appeals to heaven, are not only natural in themselves, but the inspiring instinct of maternal solicitude teaches her, that friendless and powerless as she is otherwise left, they are the only instruments, the only weapons, remaining to her. Her one sole chance of redress now lies in the effect which her indignant logic may yet work upon the sensibility to shame and guilt that lingers in the breasts of some at least of her selfish allies, and which, it is barely possible, may move them to recede from their last disgraceful compact. Her invocation, in itself so sublimely fervent and impressive – [Quotes 3.1.107–12: 'Arm, arm, you heavens. . . .'] – takes the awful character of prophecy from the almost immediate appearance of the legate, in whose mission there comes to her aid an accidental indeed, and indifferent, but a most powerful ally. She is now encouraged to strain every nerve of her intellect and her eloquence in enforcing the cardinal's denunciation against her principal oppressor, and his menace to the most potent of her treacherous friends. The dauphin, whose sense of honour, throughout the piece, is represented as more susceptible than his father's, is the first to shew signs of retracting their late political engagements. Upon this relenting emotion she eagerly lays hold; and in opposition to the entreaty of his bride, the Lady Blanch, who kneels to beg that he will not turn his arms against her uncle, makes the fervant religious adjuration –

> Oh, upon *my* knee,
> Made hard with kneeling, I do pray to thee,
> Thou virtuous dauphin, alter not the doom
> Forethought by heaven! [3.1.309ff.]

And to Blanch's last appeal – 'Now shall I see thy love. What motive may / Be stronger with thee than the name of wife?' [3.1.313ff.] – she rejoins by urging triumphantly the noble moral sentiment – '*That which upholdeth him that thee upholds, / His honour: oh, thine honour, Lewis, thine honour!*' [3.1.314ff.]. And on Philip's consenting to break the treaty, she concludes with the grateful exclamation – 'Oh, fair return of banish'd majesty!' [3.1.321].

Where, we would ask, is the tone of *sarcasm* in all this? The slightest touch of it might have defeated the very object, dearest to her on earth, for which she was pleading, by checking and offending those 'compunctious visitings'[*Macbeth*, 1.5.45] the first symptoms of which she was alert to observe and to nourish in the breasts of her unfaithful friends. *Sarcasm* from her lips, at such a moment! No, indeed – Constance, and Shakespeare, know too well what they are about. (11–26)

2. ACTING OF THE LADY CONSTANCE, QUEEN ELINOR, THE LADY BLANCH, AND LADY FAULCONBRIDGE; BY MISS HELEN FAUCIT, MISS ELLIS, MISS FAIRBROTHER, AND MRS. SELBY.
February 18th, 1843[4]

[The production alluded to in Fletcher's essay is William Charles Macready's *King John* at Drury Lane Theatre, performed twenty-six times from October 1842 to May 1843.]

. . . What strikes us first of all in Miss Helen Faucit's personation [of Constance], is, her clear and perfect conception that *feeling*, not *pride*, is the mainspring of the character; that the dignity of bearing natural to and inseparable from it, and which the advantage of a tall, graceful figure enables this actress to maintain with little effort, is at the same time an easy, unconscious dignity, quite different from that air of self-importance, that acting of majesty, which has been mistakenly ascribed to it by those who have attributed to the heroine an ambitious nature. She makes us feel throughout, not only the depth, the tenderness, and the poetry of the maternal affection, dwelling in a vivid fancy and a glowing heart; but is ever true to that 'constant, loving, noble nature' [*Othello*, 2.1.289], which is not more sensitive to insult from her foes and falsehood from her friends, than it is ever ready to welcome with fresh gratitude and confidence the return of better feelings in any who have injured her.

That intimate association, in short, of gracefulness with force, and of tenderness with dignity, which this lady has so happily displayed in other leading characters of Shakespeare, is her especial qualification for this arduous part – the most arduous, we believe, of all the Shakespearian female characters – for this plain reason, that while it is one of those exhibiting the highest order of powers, the range of emotions included in it is the widest, and the alternations, the fluctuations, between the height of virtuous indignation and contempt, and the softest depth of tenderness, are the most sudden and the most extreme. The principle of contrast, in fact – that great element of the romantic drama, as of all romantic art – which Shakespeare delighted to employ, not only in opposing one character to another, but in developing each character individually, is carried to the highest pitch by the trials to which the course of the dramatic incident subjects the sensitive, passionate, and poetic – the noble and vigorous nature of Constance.

Here, again, we turn, for an illustration, to Mrs. Siddons's performance of the part. It seems well established, by the concurring testimony of all who preserve distinct recollections of her acting, that on a general estimate of her tragic powers, it was in gracefully commanding *force* that she so wonderfully excelled, and in the expression of *tenderness* that she was often felt to be deficient, – a defect which must have been especially apparent in her personation of those Shakespearian characters wherein exquisite feeling is combined with extraordinary vigour. It has not surprised us, therefore, in conversing with persons on whose judgment and candour we can rely, and who have repeatedly witnessed the great actress's representation of the Lady Constance, to find that in the passages of melting tenderness which abound in the part, a want of adequate expression was very sensibly felt. Majestic and terrible, then, as her performance of the indignant scenes undoubtedly was, yet it must have failed, for want of sufficient contrast, to derive all that startling boldness of relief which the dramatist himself has given to those electric passages.

Labouring, too, under the misconception already pointed out, as to the essential qualities of the character, it would be but natural that, in the scenes where Constance and her son stand alone, deserted and betrayed, amid their treacherous friends and their triumphant enemies, Mrs. Siddons, properly making the impulse of resentful scorn the immediate spring of her vituperation, should have failed to clear its expression wholly from her brow in those passages wherein the action requires her to turn it upon her child. We think it one of the most notable merits in the representation of the part by the lady who now personates it, that so far from letting the indignant excitement cast for one moment the slightest shade upon her brow or harshness into her tone when turning to the boy, she follows undeviatingly the poet's indication; and, in like manner as he has made the first effusion poured out by Constance on hearing her abandonment, one of maternal grief and tenderness only, so amidst her subsequent bursts of indignant reproach and fiery denunciation, in every look and word which the present actress addresses to Arthur, the afflicted mother seems to find relief from those effusions of bitterness, as repugnant to her nature as they are withering in their power, by melting into double tenderness over the beauties and misfortunes of her child. . . .

We must speak rather more at large of Miss Faucit's acting in the following scene [3.1], the most difficult of all in so difficult a part. Undoubtedly, the dramatist conceived of his heroine as of one endowed with the most vigorous as well as exquisite physical powers. Only such a person could rise to the adequate expression of that towering sublimity of virtuous invective and religious invocation which was indispensable to this part of his dramatic purpose. Equally certain it seems to be, that these solemnly appealing and witheringly scornful passages, demanding, above all things, the display of what is commonly meant by *tragic force*, were the most successful parts of Mrs. Siddons's personation of The Lady Constance. Not having had the advantage of witnessing those majestic efforts of the great actress, we are not enabled to compare the force of delivery shown in those particular sentences by Mrs. Siddons and by the present actress respectively. But we *have* the means of comparing the force of execution in the present performer with what we conceive that the part itself demands, and in that view we find her personation adequate. The force which Shakespeare exhibits in the eloquence of Constance, is not the hard force of an arrogant, imperious termagant, such as we see in his Queen Elinor, but the *elastic* force that springs from a mind and person having all the vigour of a character at once so intellectual, so poetical, and so essentially feminine as that of Constance. To the expression of this highest and most genuine *tragic force* we repeat that Miss Faucit shows her powers to be not only fully equal, but peculiarly adapted. She has that truest histrionic strength, which consists in an ample share of physical power in the ordinary sense, combined with exquisite modulation of tone and flexibility of feature – by turns the firm and the varying expressiveness of figure, voice, and eye. . . .

[Fletcher concludes this portion of his essay with a detailed and encomiastic description of Helen Faucit's performance of Constance; he then turns to the other female roles in the play.]

Small a space as Queen Elinor occupies in the dialogue of this piece, it is important to mark the clear indications which every line of it assigned to her affords us, of the character as conceived by the dramatist. Here, indeed, we have arrogance and unscrupulous love of power personified; and accordingly, her vehemence in repelling the charge of usurpation against herself and John, is proportioned to the clear consciousness which she betrays of the justice of the imputation. In her violent altercation with Constance [2.1], she makes up for the inferiority of her eloquence to that of her rival, by boldness of assertion and fierceness of reproach. Her sentences are brief, but each one of them speaks a volume respecting her own predominant qualities; and her vituperation, it must be owned, is truly imperial. 'Thou monstrous slanderer of heaven and earth! [2.1.173] is her answer to the beautiful words of Constance on the weeping of her son – 'His grandam's wrongs, and not his mother's shames, / Draw those heaven-moving pearls from his poor eyes' [2.1.168ff.]. But more thoroughly are the whole heart and conscience of the speaker betrayed in the exclamation – 'Out, insolent! – thy bastard shall be king, / That thou mayst be a queen, and check the world!' [2.1.122ff.] – a speech most forcibly characteristic of the woman whose own youthful gallantries had given such public scandal, divorcing her from her first royal husband, and who in age had shown, that her chief solicitude to have John a king rather than Arthur, was, that she herself, ruling his political councils, might really 'be a queen and check the world.'

And here let us point out the art which the dramatist has used, to cast the greatest possible improbability upon the charge of conjugal infidelity brought against The Lady Constance by her insolent oppressor, no less than upon that of unlawful ambition. The striking resemblance of her son to her deceased husband is placed repeatedly before us. King Philip, especially, in his address to John upon their first meeting, says, pointing to Arthur: –

> Look here upon thy brother Geffrey's face:
> These eyes, these brows, were moulded out of his;
> This little abstract doth contain that large
> Which died in Geffrey; and the hand of time
> Shall draw this brief into as huge a volume. [2.1.99ff.]

Here, then, is strong countenance for Constance's own allegation in answer to Elinor: –

> My bed was ever to thy son as true
> As thine was to thy husband; and this boy
> Liker in feature to his father Geffrey,
> Than thou and John, in manners being as like
> As rain to water, or devil to his dam. [2.1.124ff.]

Nor, considering the established character of Elinor as a wife, and the bitterness of her slander, can we help holding Constance excusable for retorting: – 'My boy a bastard! – by my soul, I think / His father never was so true begot; / It cannot be, an if thou wert his mother' [2.1.129ff.].

We find it the more necessary to cite these sentences of Constance, because they are not heard upon the stage. The constant omission, in modern acting, of the most characteristic passages in this dialogue between her and 'the mother queen' [2.1.62], cramps exceedingly the development which the dramatist, in this place, has clearly, though rapidly, made of the respective moral character and position of the two personages; and has contributed to establish the prevalent notion of this scene, as a mere piece of *scolding* between two angry rivals.

The nature of the moral tie between Elinor and John – a bond much more of common interest than affection – contrasts finely, throughout the piece, with the mutual tenderness between Constance and her son. The 'little prince' [4.1.9] desires not greatness at all; and his mother desires it only for his sake. Elinor and John love power equally for its own sake: but as for personal affection, the mother-queen loves the greatness of her son chiefly for the sway which it secures to herself; while John betrays no spark of filial, any more than he does of any other attachment. He loves everybody, even his royal mother, just after the fashion that he so vehemently protests he *loves* Hubert – that is, exactly so far as he can *use* them. Thus, in his exclamation upon hearing of Elinor's death – 'My mother dead! / How wildly then walks my estate in France! [4.2.127ff.] – we find the language, not of affection, but of sheer self-interest. Elinor, indeed, is shown here, as in history, to have been John's political genius, infusing such spirit and sagacity as had found their way into his councils; and accordingly, in the course of righteous retribution which forms the sequel of the play, the death of Elinor by the hand of heaven is made by the dramatist to follow immediately upon that brought upon Constance by maternal anguish and despair – 'The Lady Constance in a frenzy died / Three days before' [4.2.122ff.]. 'My mother dead!' [4.2.181] is the exclamation we find John still repeating. Feeling the sole stay of his mean and cowardly spirit to be thus struck from him at the moment when he needed it the most, we find his resolutions thenceforward utterly paralysed; we see him staggering on from one personal and political meanness to another; abandoning wholly to his 'valiant kinsman Faulconbridge' [5.3.5] 'the ordering of this present time' [5.1.77]; and dying at last, in spite of all that kinsman's eloquent exhortations, not like a brother of Cœur-de-lion, with harness on his back, but like a craven plunderer of monastic treasuries, with poison in his stomach.

Although, from the limited space which this character occupies in the drama, we are aware that it can seldom fall into the hands of a first-rate performer, yet it is plain, that the actress who undertakes to personate Queen Elinor should be as *imperial-looking* as possible. Heiress to a sovereign duchy, married successively to the two most powerful monarchs of the age – Louis the Seventh of France, and Henry the Second of England, – and now brought before us in the drama as directing the councils of her royal son, – the habit no less than the love of command should be expressed in her every look and tone, as well as in all the rest of her demeanour. No approach to tenderness should be heard in her accent or read upon her brow. She should present to us that very impersonation of pride and love of sway – that *conscious* self-importance – somewhat of that 'acting of majesty,' as we have said before – which both critic and performer have too frequently attributed to Constance herself; although they should have seen, that the most palpable dramatic propriety requires the natural dignity of person and rank in the mother of Arthur to stand out very clearly distinguished from the arrogant dignity of her intriguing and ambitious rival.

The lady (Miss Ellis) who now enacts this part at Drury-Lane, though manifestly very young to represent a character so decidedly aged, sustains it respectably. One error which she commits as regards the business of the stage, we will point out, because it seems to us to be at once evident and easy of correction. In the scene immediately following Arthur's capture, the dramatist, it will be remembered, makes Elinor take Arthur aside, as if to leave John at liberty to confer with Hubert about the disposal of the young prince's person. And from John's words to Hubert – 'Throw thine eyes on *yon'* young boy' [3.3.59ff.] – it is plain that the boy is meant to be taken aside to some distance on the stage. The glance of the king's eye towards him, even at the farthest corner of the stage, Shakespeare evidently and naturally thought would be regarded as intelligible enough to so confidential a servant as Hubert, even though John's desire of getting Arthur into his power had not been pretty notorious. But in the present acting, the queen-mother does not really go *aside* at all. She remains in the front of the stage, almost in the middle of it, and so near to John and Hubert, that it is difficult to conceive of their talking together in ever so low a whisper without their being overheard by Arthur himself. To this palpable improbability is added one yet more painful to the eye and mind of the auditor. Instead of alternately bending and raising her figure, as if diverting the child's attention with some light and varied conversation, Elinor's representative remains stooping over him, and he looking up to her, in one unvaried posture, during the very considerable time occupied by the conference between Hubert and his master. There are some matters relative to arrangement and grouping on the stage, respecting which, perhaps, the auditor is better situated for judging than the manager himself. The case before us seems to be one of these, and deserving attention, since the defective arrangement here complained of can so easily be remedied, and, while it is continued, mars one of the most effective scenes of his own acting.

The Lady Blanch, occupying still less space in the piece than Queen Elinor, is one of those subordinate characters, as they are commonly called, which nevertheless demand very graceful and judicious acting. The part is in itself so slight, and yet so elegant, that we cannot help regretting to see such interest as the poet has given to it abridged by omissions in acting. The leaving out, indeed, of the beautifully descriptive lines – [Quotes 2.1.426–31: 'If lusty love should go in quest of beauty. . . .'] – is one of those curtailments which, we suppose, the necessities of the stage, as regards time, now render indispensable: but we can hardly admit any such plea as an excuse for omitting the short pathetic speech of Blanch herself, when her heart is torn asunder, as it were, by the fresh rupture which takes place between her husband's party and her uncle's, even on her bridal day: – [Quotes 3.1.326–38: 'The sun's o'ercast with blood. . . .']. To suppress this passage, is to destroy the chief point of tragic interest about the character of Blanch, which consists in vividly showing her as the victim, in her torn feelings, of the triumph of political over domestic considerations.

Miss Fairbrother is playing what is left of this part *prettily*; that is, she *looks* pretty in it, for she cannot look otherwise. It would be well, however, if she could so far imagine herself to be the high-blooded 'daughter of Spain' [2.1.423], as to throw more dignity into her air and her delivery – that same graceful majesty in *carrying the head* is so very, very hard to acquire.

As for the few sentences that have to be spoken in 'Lady Faulconbridge,' they are delivered, perhaps, as adequately by Mrs. Selby as they would be by any other lady. We will only venture to suggest, that, in any case, the dramatist's conception of Philip Faulconbridge's mother, must have been of a lady whose personal charms might at some time have done honour to the choice of Richard Cœur-de-lion. We say this, be it well observed, without at all presuming to raise the delicate question as to how far the present Lady Faulconbridge fulfills this condition. It is just one of those points whereupon each auditor must be left to judge for himself. (26–41)

20 Joseph Hunter, editorial corrections in *King John*

1845

From *New Illustrations of the Life, Studies, and Writings of Shakespeare. Supplementary to All the Editions. By Joseph Hunter, a Fellow of the Society of Antiquaries, and an Assistant Keeper of the Public Records* (2 vols, London, 1845).

Joseph Hunter (1783–1861), antiquary and Presbyterian minister, was the author of over thirty books and pamphlets of which two were devoted to Shakespeare: *A Disquisition* on *The Tempest* (London, 1839), attempting to reassign the play to the early phase of Shakespeare's career, and the *New Illustrations*. The latter comprised part of an ongoing critical and editorial debate on the status of Shakespeare's text, dating back to the earliest editions, which was rekindled around the middle of the century by the many reprintings of Knight's edition (1838–43; 1842–44; 1867 [No. 18 above]) and that of John Payne Collier (8 vols, London, 1842–4). The year before the appearance of Hunter's *Illustrations*, Alexander Dyce published his *Remarks on Mr. J. P. Collier's and Mr. C. Knight's Editions of Shakespeare* (London, 1844) in which he took issue with hundreds of readings in both texts. Hunter's comments are in no way a direct response to Dyce, but they are very much in Dyce's mode. Moreover, in their concern to reassess the editorial tradition of Shakespeare and in their strongly critical orientation, they can sometimes contribute interpretive vigor to an old scholarly debate.

KING JOHN

If anything were wanting to shew how much a new edition of the dramatic writings of Shakespeare is wanted, in which we should have a text the result of deep consideration of the various texts presented by the old editions, with occasional emendations, carefully and judiciously made, or borrowed from preceding editors, and in which the passages where the meaning is obscure to nine-tenths of the readers or spectators were elucidated, so that their full force and meaning were accurately exhibited, one of the most striking passages in the play now before us would be sufficient. No one who ever witnessed the performance of this play, or who ever entered on the serious study of it at home, can have forgotten the scene in which King John seeks to induce Hubert to put Prince Arthur to death, without actually committing himself to give the hateful command: and no one will ever forget that particular portion of the dialogue in which King John addresses Hubert thus: –

> I had a thing to say; – but let it go:
> The sun is in the heaven, and the proud day,
> Attended with the pleasure of the world,
> Is all too wanton, and too full of gauds,
> To give me audience: – If the midnight bell
> Did with his iron tongue and brazen mouth
> Sound on into the drowsy race of night;
> If this same were a churchyard where we stand,
> And thou possessed with a thousand wrongs:
> Or if the surly spirit Melancholy
> Had baked thy blood, and made it heavy, thick,
> Which else runs tickling up and down the veins,
> Making that idiot Laughter keep men's eyes
> And strain their cheeks to idle merriment,
> A passion hateful to my purposes. [3.3.33ff.]

Such is the passage nearly as it stands in the original copies. Turn now to the Variorum [the Boswell-Malone edition of 1821], and one of the lines will be found printed thus:

> Sound *one* into the drowsy race of night;

and this is generally understood to be the true reading, both at the theatres and elsewhere, and the Poet is supposed to speak of a clock-bell on which the hour of *one* is struck.

For this substitution of *one* for *on*, and for the idea that the Poet meant to speak of the bell of a clock or a bell sounding the hour, we are indebted, it seems, to Theobald. 'Mr. Theobald made the correction,' says Mr. Malone [No. 1 above], and he overwhelms some unfortunate person [Joseph Ritson; No. 2 above] who had expressed a doubt of the correctness of the new reading with numerous instances in our old writers in which the numeral *one* is printed *on*. There can be no doubt that *one* is sometimes found printed without the final *e*, but there also can be no doubt that *on* much more frequently is neither more nor less than the particle which we so write at present. The utmost, therefore, that is proved by Mr. Malone's heap of authorities is, that *one* was sometimes printed *on*, so that if the exigencies of a passage really required that *on* should be understood to be equivalent to *one*, it might be so taken.

The slight incongruity of the bell on which the hour of *one* is struck being spoken of as the *midnight* bell has not been held sufficient to disprove the correctness of the new reading. But it was soon discovered that this change required another, and that for *into* we must read *unto* –

> Sound one unto the drowsy race of night –

that is, strike one so as to be heard of the sleepers at that dead time of night. This second change is made in some of the editions, and would have been found in the last Variorum, had not Mr. Malone discovered that *into* and *unto* are sometimes written indifferently, so that he kept *into* in the text, directing that it should be understood as if it were *unto*.

Thus the passage was left in 1821; where we have the incongruity (1) of the midnight bell striking the hour of one in the morning; (2) of the hammer of a clock striking on the outside of a bell being presented to the mind by the 'iron tongue and brazen mouth,' in which, on a little reflection, we cannot but perceive that it was the pendulous clapper, not the hammer striking on the outside of the bell, that must have been in the Poet's mind; and (3) of men steeped in sleep being described by such a poet as Shakespeare by the phrase 'the drowsy race of night.' Any one of these, if due attention were given to the passage, would have been sufficient to shew that there was something rotten in the state of Denmark.

Let us now see how the latest editor has dealt with the passage.[1]

> We prefer the old reading – 'Sound on into the drowsy race of night' – on all accounts. Many of the commentators would read *one* instead of 'on,' which is contradicted by the 'midnight bell' in a line just preceding. There is more probability in reading *ear* instead of 'race,' recollecting that of old *ear* was spelt *eare*, and the word might possibly be mistaken by the printer: but still 'race' in the sense of *course* or *passage* conveys a fine meaning; the midnight bell with its twelve times repeated strokes may be very poetically said to 'sound on into the drowsy race of night,' one sound produced by the 'iron tongue' driving the other 'on' or *forward*, until the whole number was complete, and the prolonged vibration of the last blow on the bell only left to fill the empty space of darkness.

Such is the state in 1844.[2]

Now the Poet certainly had not in his thoughts the striking of a clock at all; and the intervention of this idea has the effect of marring in a very extraordinary degree the beauty and grandeur of the conception.

The King has a horrid purpose to unfold, or rather to stimulate his victim to conceive for himself the horrible design. It happens that their conversation takes place in the open day and in broad sunshine. Such a time is favourable to gay and cheerful thoughts: the night is for the thoughts and deeds of darkness. He seeks therefore to withdraw the mind of Hubert out of the influence of the actual circumstances, and to place him where the influences from external things would be suitable to his purposes. This is not a fit scene, says he, for audience of the thing I was about to say: 'the sun is in the heaven.' Transfer yourself to a scene of the night and darkness, a place where you hear the great bell of a church tolling in the depth of midnight, and imagine that you are pacing the churchyard in the dark midnight amidst the graves of the many dead, and where spirits are sometimes said to wander. Think of yourself as a man much injured by the world, and as given up to an habitual melancholy.

The mere striking of the church clock, whether once, or with twelve times repeated strokes, is a weak, puerile, incongruous conception: but the continuous tolling of the bell at midnight, which was what Shakespeare meant, adds greatly to the impressiveness of a night scene; and this especially when we recollect on what occasions it was that the church bell would be heard 'sounding on' in the darkness of midnight. It might be as a passing bell, a soul just then taking its flight; but it is more probable that the poet had in his mind the tolling at a midnight funeral, and that the full conception of the passage is this: that Hubert is to be transported in thought to the grave-ground at the foot of some lonely tower, from which is heard the heavy tones of the bell tolling through the darkness of night, while, in the distance, are occasionally discerned the torches about the hearse of some eminent person, who is being borne along to be laid in the vault of his ancestors. In such a scene there was everything to feed melancholy, and put the mind of Hubert into a frame favourable to the King's purposes; – everything to stir up in his mind thoughts which the sun should not look upon.

This then, I conceive, to be the true explanation of the passage. 'Sound on' is the common phrase in Shakespeare for continuous or repeated blasts of a trumpet, just as here it is for the continuous or repeated strokes of the bell-clapper. 'Into the drowsy race of night,' if it required any justification, as meaning the step or course of night, would receive it by comparison with the . . . following passages from other plays, – [Here Hunter quotes *Henry V*, 4.Chorus.20–3; *A Midsummer Night's Dream*, 5.1.367–8; *1 Henry IV*, 1.1.101–3; and Sonnet 71, 1–6, in support].

We have suffered a great deal of the poetry of life and manners to slip away from us; and few, in these times, had ever the opportunity of being placed in such a scene as that which the King conjured up before the mind of Hubert.

There is so much in this Play which shews that the mind of the Poet was intent, when he wrote it, on affairs connected with the church, that it may be submitted as a probability not at once to be rejected, that in thus placing Hubert in imagination in a scene of horror, the Poet had in his mind what was alleged to be a practice of the Jesuits of the time. They had their 'Chamber of Meditation,' as they called it, in which they placed men who were 'to undertake some great business of moment, as to kill a King, or the like.' 'It was a melancholy dark chamber, where [one] had no light for many days together, no company, little meat, ghastly pictures of devils all about him,' and 'by this strange usage they made him quite mad, and beside himself.'[3]

The word 'Convertite,' which occurs in this Play [5.1.19], is an ecclesiastical term, with a peculiar and express meaning, distinct from 'Convert.' It denotes a person who, having relapsed, has been recovered, and this, it will be perceived, is the sense in which Shakespeare uses it. . . .

[Hunter concludes by quoting Pandulph's speech at 3.1.174–9: 'And blessed shall he be. . . .' to illustrate that Shakespeare could not possibly have been a member of the Roman Catholic Church.] (II, 8–14)

21 Hermann Ulrici, 'history', church, and state in *King John*

1846

From *Shakespeare's Dramatic Art: And His Relation to Calderon and Goethe. Translated from the German of Dr. Hermann Ulrici* [by A. J. W. Morrison] (London, 1846). Second English edition. *Shakespeare's Dramatic Art. History and Character of Shakespeare's Plays. By Dr. Hermann Ulrici. Translated from the Third Edition of the German, with Additions and Corrections by the Author, By L. Dora Schmitz* (2 vols, London, 1876).

Hermann Ulrici (1806–84), German philosopher and literary critic, was trained in the law, but abandoned that profession upon the death of his father in 1829, turning instead to the study of literature, philosophy, and science. A severe critic of Hegelian philosophy, Ulrici devoted much of his career as a philosopher to proving the existence of God and the soul in opposition to the materialistic strain of contemporary German thought. *Shakespeare's Dramatic Art* belongs to Ulrici's early phase as a writer and thinker; it first appeared under the title *Über Shakespeares Dramatische Kunst und sein Verhältnis zu Calderon und Goethe* (Halle, 1839) and soon afterwards entered the English critical tradition with Morrison's translation of 1846, which was in turn superseded by Schmitz's version in 1876. Although the two translations are substantially the same, Schmitz's is based on a revised and somewhat enlarged version of Ulrici's work, and hence is the one reprinted here. For ease of reference page numbers are provided for both translations.

[In a short chapter entitled 'Introductory Remarks to the English Histories' (Schmitz, II, 209–13), not included in Morrison's 1846 translation, Ulrici addresses the question of historical accuracy in the plays. He criticizes what he sees as Courtenay's excessive emphasis on the details of history (No. 17 above), preferring instead to follow Gervinus (No. 31 below) in stressing Shakespeare's adherence to a 'higher and universal truth' that does not depend on 'external historical facts'.]

... The most frequent and most striking deviations from history are therefore to be found in the three parts of *Henry VI.*, in *Richard III.*, and in *King John*. In regard to the latter piece – which I place at the head of my discussions, because, in Schlegel's words [No. 6 above], it forms the prologue to the other English histories – this is in the first place explained by the fact that Shakespeare had to follow an older and, as it seems, an exceedingly popular drama of the same name and subject, and which, to some extent deserved the great applause it received [i.e., *The Troublesome Raigne*]. But in addition to this, the historical subject itself, as we shall see, demanded, comparatively speaking, more abbreviations, condensations and violations of chronology, etc., than elsewhere. And yet even in *King John* all the principal facts and characters are portrayed with historical fidelity; the deviations from history are only that Arthur (at least according to the Chronicle of Math. Paris) at the time of his imprisonment was not so young, so innocent, or so sensitive a child, as to have taken no part in politics;[1] that the interval between his death and that of John was far greater (almost fourteen years); that the archduke of Austria, who kept Richard Cœur de Lion a prisoner for some time, is dragged into the history of King John, and confounded with the Duke of Limoges in front of whose castle it was that Richard fell; that Faulconbridge, the bastard, is not the historical character which he here appears, but is merely believed, by popular tradition, to be a natural son of Richard Cœur de Lion, Philip by name (who, according to Holinshed, is said to have, in 1199, murdered the Duke of Limoges to avenge his father's death); and lastly that it was not John's bad government and despotic violation of the rights of the nobility and of the people, but Arthur's death – of which he is accused – that is represented as the principal motive of the revolt of the barons; for which reason there is no mention of the granting of the Magna Charta. The omission of so important a historical fact is the chief thing censured in the poet by modern historians and critics, and is regarded as a want of historical appreciation. Courtenay thinks that 'as Shakespeare was a decided courtier, he might not wish to remind Queen Elizabeth – who set Magna Charta at nought in its most interesting particular – of the solemn undertakings of her ancestors.' But Kreyssig[2] justly reminds us that even the historians of the sixteenth century entered but very superficially and cursorily into the history of that famous privilege, and that the whole constitutional question did not receive its actual significance till the struggles between the Stuarts and the House of Commons. Shakespeare's public probably knew little or nothing about the Magna Charta, and still less about its historical importance. This importance it, in fact, did not possess directly at the time of its origin, but acquired it only at a subsequent period. The Barons and burgesses of the day regarded it, and had demanded it, only as a means of protecting themselves against John's arbitrary rule, and of strengthening the promise he had given of a better government. The poet upon whom it devolved to give a representation of the internal truth of the reign of King John, and thereby a reflex of the spirit and character of the Middle Ages in general – not indeed merely its political motives and principles, but its ethical motives and principles as well – could, accordingly, not admit into his play an external and at the same time an unimportant fact which referred only to John's personal conduct, without burdening it with superfluous ballast and detracting from the historico-poetical interest of his work. It was for similar reasons and with equal justice, that he made the other deviations in the historical data, or rather retained them from the older play of *Kynge Johan*.[3] For the historical dramatist is the court-poet, not the court-servant of history; he can frequently be true to history only by being untrue in other things. And this infidelity is justified by history itself, according to which every great event, like every great man, is surrounded by a number of satellites, attendants and servants, the selection of whom appears more or less accidental, and who, accordingly might have been different without this doing injury to the significance contained in the principal incidents of the historical development. All that which serves clearly to exhibit this importance of the facts the poet must take into consideration, even though it were apparently ever so trivial and insignificant; everything else can be left to the free disposal of his artistic genius. The greater the poet, the less he will have to alter, and the more will his free creation be an historical poem. Only in this manner can history and historical truth, in the limitation imposed upon the poet by the artistic form, be a work of art. This is the reason why history cannot be learned even from Shakespeare's dramas – there are schoolmasters and historical books enough in the world for this – and therefore Courtenay's inquiry, as to whether Shakespeare's histories are adapted for teaching history, that is, for taking the place of a schoolmaster, is very superfluous.... (Schmitz, II, 211–13)

After these introductory remarks, which apply to all Shakespeare's English histories, I begin my discussion with *King John*, because, in more than one respect, the piece is not only the prologue, but the basis of the whole cycle. As in *Coriolanus* the nature of the ancient state is depicted in the relation most important to its foundation, the family bond, so, in the present case, we first of all obtain an insight into the essentially different conception of the mediæval state. The ancient state, inasmuch as it had proceeded from the natural bond of family life, was itself but the extended, legally established and organised family bond, and would have fulfilled its idea, if that which the family represented in a limited sphere, and in a loose, undeveloped and personal form, had, in its extended shape, assumed a general, legally-established and organised form. And in this case there would never have existed any conflicts between the rights of the family and those of the state. In other words, the natural order of human life – which in the family bond was given in a direct personal manner, and thus existed still as a mere germ – ought, when the family extended into a tribe and nation, to have been reflected in the state with conscious clearness and definiteness, and to have developed into a just and legally fixed organism. This was the idea of the ancient state and the aim of its development, which accordingly tended towards the republican form, and approached its aim most closely during the short, palmy days of the Roman republic.

The mediæval state was very different. It developed partly out of the deeply-rooted tendency of the Germanic mind towards unlimited personal freedom, partly upon the basis of ethical ideas and of the general view of life entertained by Christianity as conceived by the spirit of the age. The interaction, the alternate struggle and peace between these two principles constituted the mediæval state: the first principle gave the form, i.e., the feudal system of the state; the second, the ideal, ethical substance, i.e., the idea of the state as the earthly reflex of the Kingdom of God, which was represented by the church – a reflex naturally supported and conditioned by its prototype. Just as the mind, in alternate harmony and discord, possesses the body as its organ, so the church, in a similar degree of correlation, ought to be the higher and guiding spirit of the state. Its foundation, accordingly, was no longer the natural existence of man with his natural institutions; what was naturally-human was rather to be done away with, and to be replaced by the divinely-human, and the natural order of things, therefore, to be replaced by the divine order, that is, by the hierarchy and its head, the representative of Christ. This, at least, was the aim of the Pope and the clergy, and they managed throughout the Middle Ages to obtain universal acceptance for their view. It may, therefore, be said: the family bond was represented, during the Middle Ages, by two essentially ethical communities, as the foundation of its structure and the principle of its development; first by the feudal community which was founded upon free devotion and personal fidelity, secondly, by the religious community, the church. The latter was the universal, the necessary and indissoluble union of all men into a many-membered whole directed by the Holy Spirit, that is, a whole governed by Pope and clergy; the feudal community, on the other hand, was the special union of individuals with an individual, which had ever to be renewed, and accordingly, was dissoluble. In the latter community, the greatest possible scope was granted to personal freedom, and the feudal chief, as well as the vassal, was valued only in so far as he could maintain his authority by his own power and personal energy. This bond was as loose and weak as the former was firm and strong; and as both principles stood opposed to one another in inward contradiction – inasmuch as the desire for personal freedom which scorned all restraints, necessarily came into conflict with the hierarchical endeavour to obtain absolute power – they could not but come into hostile collision, wherever they came into contact at all. In this conflict the church was necessarily victorious as long as this idea of the state and of the feudal system continued to exist. For, according to this idea, the state when coming into conflict with the church, was, at the same time, at strife with itself, and, therefore, it was quite natural that, in such a contest, the feudal community was always in a state of dissolution, because the church – as the ruler of consciences – could deprive it of its foundation, the binding power of the oath, and hence of its obligation to fulfil its promise of fidelity. On the other hand, the feudal system, of itself, was a perpetual temptation to every great vassal to play the part of the chief himself, and, in the same way, as he had helped the king to the throne and was a prop of the throne, would endeavour to overthrow it when it suited his purpose. The feudal system itself, therefore, was in a continual state of change, between decay and reconstruction, and hence, ever the ready tool for the arrogances of the church.

This nature, this condition, of the mediæval state forms, so to say, the general ground on which move the ten great dramas headed by *King John*. For, as in *Coriolanus*, we have the antique state in conflict with its foundation, the family bond and its rights, so in *King John*, the centre of the action lies in the struggle between the mediæval state and its one basis, the church. As the latter was or pretended to be the ideal side of political life, and thus, as it were, the ethos, that is, the conscience of the state, this struggle is first of all reflected in John's own life and character; we have it exhibited in the perpetual conflict between his better self, which was naturally disposed to manly dignity, independence, and quick and resolute action, and his tendency to arbitrary proceedings, love of dominion and pretension, to caprice and passionate recklessness. Being in conflict with himself, his naturally discordant disposition degenerates into complete inconsistency and want of character. Hence, although he has even resorted to murder, he cannot maintain his tottering throne, either against

Arthur's legitimate claims, or against the interferences of France and of the church. His own unjust title to the crown, his violence, and his inconsistent and arbitrary actions, his dispute with the church, and the intrigues of the latter, become the motives of France's breach of faith, of the ever-recurring contests from without, as well as of the internal dissensions of the kingdom. The relation between Church and State is the pulse of the whole historical action; John's dilemmas, his degradation and his death are its work, and the only means that it employs are that it contrives cleverly to make use of the illegitimacy attached to his crown, the weakness of his own character, and the want of strength in the feudal community, which again was the result of John's despotic rule.

However, this state of decay is manifested not only externally, in John's kingdom and his relation to the barons and people, but also internally, and again not only in the State, for the Church itself is rotten to its inmost core; the policy of both is immoral, selfish and pretentious, and therefore loosened from its true foundation. The church, too, is desirous only of outward splendour, authority and power; it has entirely mistaken its own nature and its true vocation, and has fallen as low as the secular power, owing to its disloyal, intriguing actions, and its sophistic perversion of the fundamental laws of all morality. Cardinal Pandulph is the truest picture ever painted by [any] poet of an arrogant hierarchy, wholly absorbed in love of dominion and selfishness. This is why, in the end, neither the church nor the royal power conquer in the struggle; it is rather the people and the barons that reap the advantage; they are, comparatively speaking, soundest both morally and politically. Their representative is Faulconbridge, the natural son of Richard Cœur de Lion. Of all the characters in the play, he is the most independent, the most vigorous; a man bound by no prejudice, or by any consideration of the past. This advantage he owes to his very birth which connects him with the reigning dynasty, but also with the people. His motives are of the purest, or, at least, gradually become motives of pure, devoted patriotism and kingly honour; hence he alone can, with impunity, speak the truth to all, and he says it with that overflowing wealth of humour, which, according to Shakespeare's psychology, is generally at the command of minds in a truly vigorous and healthy state. This humour – which does not proceed from subtle reflection, but which springs forth from the genuine, energetic and straightforward naturalness of his disposition, as from a clear mountain spring, whose source lies high above the abodes of corrupt civilization – he applies, with bold and pertinent epithets, to ridicule the selfishness, the cowardliness and pretentiousness, the fickleness and untruthfulness of the leading characters of the action, as well as the low selfishness of the policy both of Church and State; in the mirror of his cutting irony, he shows us the rotten condition of both. As he alone bears within his breast the enduring, restoring and saving power of morality, so it is mainly through him that England is saved from the misery of civil strife, from the claws of France and of the papacy. Accordingly, the power of the mightiest potentates is surpassed by the externally-subordinate power of knighthood and citizenship, because the latter are supported by moral energy and manliness. This is the lesson history is ever repeating, and, at the same time, is the meaning of the Magna Charta.

The result of the disturbances and struggles is the freedom of the English people;

it is established inwardly by the overthrow of John's despotic government, outwardly by the victory over France and over the pretensions of the church. John dies, but his death is the beginning of the restoration of the state; not only do the English barons return to their obedience, whereby France, at the same time, is defeated, but the poison which the hands of a priest had mixed for the king, also proves the ruin of the advantage gained by the church, for the feudal supremacy of Rome over England, which had been acknowledged by John, is buried with him. The rivalry of the Church against the State, and its endeavour to obtain external power and dominion proves its own ruin.

Hence the theme of the drama, the representation of modern history in its peculiar and essential relation to Church and State, is worked out in many variations, and the play shows that this relation is in truth not external, no imaginary ideal as conceived by the Middle Ages, but an internal, real-ethical relation, and that the organism of the state necessarily becomes unsound and decays, wherever it has lost its ethical power, and consequently its equilibrium. It shows that history is not dependent either upon royalty or upon the papacy, or upon this or that form of Church or State, or, in fact, upon Church or State at all; that both are rather but forms of the moral ethico-religious spirit, and that, therefore, neither Church nor State can accomplish anything without, much less against, the moral force, let the latter appear ever so powerless. It may, accordingly, be said that the leading thought of the play is intimated in the closing words, when Faulconbridge says: [Quotes 5.7.112–18: 'This England never did, nor never shall. . . .']. For the State cannot be true to itself unless it is animated by an ecclesiastical spirit, the Church by a political spirit, that is, unless both are inspired by the spirit of true morality.

The fortunes, the doings and the sufferings of all the secondary figures are, of course, determined and conditioned by the course of the main action, as the latter is determined by the leading thought of the whole; accordingly, it will also be reflected in all the secondary parts. The plans of the King of France, of the Dauphin, and of the Archduke of Austria are frustrated by their own selfish, arrogant, and faithless policy, which is equally opposed to the nature of the state; consequently it also proves the ruin of Blanch's hopes. The conduct of the English barons is explained from their feudal position to the royal power and from John's usurped sovereignty, the unjustness of which is manifest from its very weakness, uncertainty, and violence. Where the inmost nature of the body is unsound, the separate members cannot be perfectly healthy. The fortunes of Constance and Arthur are a kind of episode in John's own life, but yet appear significantly interwoven with the history of the state. Their story may be said to form a pendant to the fundamental moral of the play: that nothing is more disavowed by history than passionateness and want of self-control, the hereditary failings of woman's nature. Women ought not to interfere with history, as history demands action, for which they are usually unfit. The pathos of maternal love which rules the soul of Constance is indeed a motive as noble as it is just, considering the circumstances. But, on the one hand, this love is not quite pure and disinterested, it is manifestly mixed with a goodly amount of ambition and love of dominion; on the other hand, owing to Constance's impetuous nature, it becomes immoderate passion, which blindly and heedlessly follows its own object, and in trying in vain to force the iron course of history from its path, rises to a height where it turns into suicidal rage. In fact, Constance and her son are ruined by the very vehemence of the passion with which she endeavours to obtain his rights, although Arthur, not being of age, could not have ascended the throne. The boy, because dependent, as the child of his mother, had therefore to forfeit his life, although he was himself innocent, and had already once been saved from John's murderous designs by the compassion of Hubert. Had Constance possessed more prudence, and waited till he himself, of his own manly strength, could have asserted his right – that which belonged to them would have fallen into their hands of its own accord.

Moreover, the historical subject-matter offered by the reign of King John – the perpetually conflicting interests, the disorganised state of the body politic, the many fluctuations of fortune, and the vacillation of a selfish policy, the alternate advance and retrogression of the course of history before it arrived at its proper result – in short, the great variety of events and characters imperatively demanded that this multiplicity should be reduced and concentrated in definite and prominent individuals. Shakespeare, therefore, required representatives: above all a person in whom to exhibit John's injustice, his violence, and recklessly despotic government, a person in John's treatment of whom these fundamental features of his character (which were pre-eminently the cause of his own ruin) could be set forth in the sharpest and most distinct form; in other words a character such as Arthur, who, notwithstanding his childish innocence, gracefulness and amiability, John pursues to the very death, merely because he stands in the way of his love of dominion, and whose fate, therefore, gives us a clear and pregnant illustration of the ethical element here interwoven with state policy. But Shakespeare also required a representative of the generally heroic and chivalrous spirit of the age, such as Faulconbridge, a contrast to whom we have in the hollow, boastful Archduke of Austria; both, at the same time, are the representatives of the history of the immediate past under Richard Cœur de Lion; the poet further required, a representative of the papacy, such as Cardinal Pandulph; representatives of the English aristocracy, such as the earls of Pembroke and Salisbury; a representative of the loyalty that still prevailed among the people, of the ready obedience to the royal power, which, however, as a sign of its healthy mind, recoils with horror from an unequivocal crime, such as we have in Hubert de Burgh; he even required a representative of mediæval superstition (a caricature of the powerful ecclesiastical faith), such as the prophet Peter of Pomfret. History does not everywhere, and at every period, offer such representative men; where they do not exist, the poet has to create them, not, however, according to his own fancy, he has, as it were, to form them out of given historical features. Only as such, as likenesses of the spirit of the age, can they claim historical authority, and it is only the greatest masters in historico-dramatic composition that will succeed in drawing such likenesses. (Schmitz, II, 213–21; Morrison, 359–65)

[The following remarks on the date of *King John* appear only in the 1876 translation of Ulrici's work, immediately following the passage above.]

As regards the question as to when *King John* first appeared on the stage, our only external evidence is the fact that the play is mentioned by Meres. If, as Tieck thinks,[4] Meres did not refer to the older play of *Kynge Johan* [i.e., *The Troublesome Raigne*], which appeared in print in 1591, because, as I think, the piece was not written by Shakespeare, then all that is certain is that Shakespeare's play must have appeared before 1597. Most critics do not place it earlier than 1596–97. I, for my part, believe that it may have appeared some years earlier. It is true that it contains but few passages in rhyme (as the subject offered no occasion either for lyrical effusions or for the expression of calm contemplative reflection), but these rhymes are often just those very alternate rhymes which are always less frequently met with in Shakespeare's later works. The drama is also written wholly in verse, to the exclusion of all prose; but this circumstance, to which Gervinus draws attention [No. 31 below], I do not consider of any great importance, for in Shakespeare's tragedies and historical dramas (except in the comic scenes introduced) it is invariably only persons from the lower ranks who speak in prose, and such persons and such scenes do not occur in *King John*. Of greater weight, in my opinion, is the generally clear and regular flow of the language, which is still free from complicated similes and constructions, and also the regular, almost monotonous versification with its usually masculine endings. . . . I am therefore inclined to assume that *King John* may have appeared in 1593–94, that is, in the interval after the completion of the earlier tetralogy of English histories. . . . (Schmitz, II, 221–2)

22 Gulian Crommelin Verplanck, critical remarks on *King John*

1847

From *Shakespeare's Plays: With His Life. Illustrated with Many Hundred Wood-Cuts, Executed by H. W. Hewet, after Designs by Kenny Meadows, Harvey, and Others. Edited by Gulian C. Verplanck, LL.D. With Critical Introductions, Notes, etc., Original and Selected. In Three Volumes* (3 vols, New York, 1847).

Gulian Crommelin Verplanck (1786–1870) was a lawyer and legislator who served several terms in the New York State Assembly and in the New York Senate; he was also elected to the United States Congress in 1824, eventually serving as the chairman of the Ways and Means Committee from 1831 to 1833. A productive essayist and satirist, Verplanck founded (with Charles King) *The New York American*, in which he published a series of satires aimed at De Witt Clinton, mayor of New York from 1803 to 1815; these later appeared under the title *The State Triumvirate, a Political Tale, and the Epistles of Brevet-Major Pindar Puff* (New York, 1819). He also published *Essays on the Nature and Uses of the Various Evidences of Revealed Religion* (New York, 1824), a work strongly indebted to the Scottish school of common-sense philosophy and conservatively deistic in nature. One of Verplanck's most celebrated legislative achievements was his key role, as a congressman in 1831, in passing a law improving the copywrights of authors. His edition of Shakespeare, strongly indebted to Collier's text of 1842–4, was initially issued in separate parts from 1844 to 1847, then in three volumes in 1847 as 'The Illustrated Shakespeare'.

[From the 'Introductory Remarks']

. . . Meres mentions *King John*, in his list of Shakespeare's works, before 1593; but, indeed, that weighty evidence is hardly needed to authorize our assigning its production to that second, or – if we admit *Pericles* and *Andronicus* to be the juvenile essays of his muse – to that third period of his literary progress, when, after the success of his first comedies, his style and versification gained a larger freedom, his characters a deeper stamp of truth and individuality, as well as a richer variety, and his exhibitions of emotion, passion, and suffering, more minuteness and accuracy, as well as more vividness of painting; while the flowing lines, with a certain regularity of pause – the somewhat diffuse and perspicuous diction – still distinguish his manner quite as much from that of *Othello* and *Lear*, as it otherwise varies from that of the *Two Gentlemen of Verona*. In these respects, the contrast between the English historical plays and the Roman tragedies is worthy of notice – the former being more assimilated, in their general poetic tone, to the *Merchant of Venice*, as the latter are to the great tragic master-pieces of the author's zenith of power. Yet in both classes alike – the English and the Roman histories – in *King John* as in *Coriolanus*, we can trace the same overflowing creative mind, which crowded *Hamlet*, and *Macbeth*, and *Lear*, with character, passion, allusion, reason, poetry, until the language bent under the weight of thought and sentiment. In *King John* and its companions, these characteristics of style are seen but occasionally, appearing as in their very rudiments; while in the later works they appear in a calmer and moderated exercise, rather as the effect of habit than of effort. . . .

[Verplanck now discusses the relationship of *King John* to *The Troublesome Raigne*, dispraising the latter's unity, noting its silence on Magna Carta, and assigning it on stylistic grounds to Rowley rather than to Shakespeare.]

. . . [Shakespeare's] entire and thorough re-writing of the chronicle drama affords a strong indication that [he] had no claim to its dialogue or poetry, for this is a process which no author would unnecessarily apply to his own work, and it is one which we know with certainty, that he was not in the habit of using in his enlargements and improvements, from those of *Love's Labor's Lost*, to the more thorough re-writing of much of *Romeo and Juliet* and of *Hamlet*. This argument is the stronger from the consideration that there is much of the ordinary dialogue of the older play, necessary for the conduct of the plot, unmarked by any special excellence or defect, which had it been written by him, he would of course have preferred retaining, with such modifications only as might be required to adapt it to the new matter, instead of actually re-writing the whole as he appears to have done. I must add that there are some words of touching tenderness in the dying speech of Arthur in the old play, (see note, act iv., scene 3),[1] which, had the thought been originally his own, I cannot but think that he would have expanded and improved instead of throwing them aside, as the poetical property of another which he did not care to use; whilst the historical incidents and personages drawn from the old chronicles or from prior plays, he might justly regard as the common property of every dramatist who might choose to employ them. My own impressions are therefore strongly in accordance with the opinions of the best English authorities, (Farmer, Steevens, Knight, Collier, etc.),[2] that Shakespeare had no hand whatever in the two parts of *The Troublesome Raigne* – which two parts, by the way, have themselves a contrast of manner that give reason to think that more than one author was employed in their preparation. Still, it is within the bounds of possibility that these may have been among Shakespeare's earlier essays in historic tragedy, and it is just to add, that if such were the case it would not be at all discreditable to his genius, though the contemptuous remarks of some of the editors would give their readers a different impression. It does not furnish choice extracts such as those by which the taste of Charles Lamb has made some second rate Elizabethan dramatists familiar to modern readers, but as a whole it compares advantageously enough with the dramas of its time; less extravagant in diction and imagery than many of them, it puts the historical personages and their actions as related by the more popular English chroniclers on the scene with spirit and distinctness; whilst the Bastard, whether drawn from tradition or from the author's invention, is strongly marked as a courageous, active, ambitious soldier, and though a little 'robustious,' noisy, and ranting, yet not more so than the other dramatic military heroes of his time, who were generally expected to 'split the ears of the groundlings' [*Hamlet*, 3.2.10ff.]. . . .

. . . The two parts of the chronicle dramatic story are compressed into one dramatic action, retaining all the incidents and circumstances, but often compressing the dialogue in some of the scenes, throwing others, like that of the preaching of the Prophet of Pomfret, or the Bastard's plunder of the Abbeys, into brief narrative, and again giving bolder prominence to the points on which the tragic interest of the remodelled tragedy was designed to rest. For this last purpose, the Poet has elevated the character of Constance from the fond and wronged mother, somewhat quick-tempered and sharp-tongued, of the old play, to a majesty of maternal grief rivalling the high conceptions of Grecian poetry and art. The reverence due to a mother's sorrows is heightened and saddened by the lofty bearing and noble eloquence of one fitted to be the mother of a royal race. Every thing that can touch the natural sympathies in the youth, the innocence, the winning affection of Arthur, is beautifully and touchingly elaborated, – not a little at the expense of historical accuracy as to the Prince, who was no longer a child when his uncle's prisoner, and also beyond the representation or conception of the older dramatist. Thus his fate, his mother's sorrows, his uncle's guilt, and the retributive justice that closes the drama become the central points of interest, and give to the narrative the depth and continuous unity of interest that mere dramatic history could not attain. Subservient to the general effect, and powerfully contributing to it, yet in itself a master-piece of tragic art, is the whole of the dialogue in which we see John – 'sound the depths of Hubert's soul, / Whilst in his own contending passions roll.' (Churchill, *Rosciad* [1021ff.]).[3]

These scenes owe nothing to the older play, being entirely original, except so far as they may have been suggested by some very slight or transient expressions in Hollingshed's narrative. They are worthy of being placed by the side of corresponding scenes in *Richard* [*III*], in *Othello*, and in *Macbeth*, all exhibiting varied forms of temptation to the worst crimes, differently modified by the fears, the remorse, the craft, the hardened conscience or the determined will of the several tempters. . . .

Whilst the dramatic chronicle was thus condensed into a dark tragedy of the sorrows of Constance, the harrowing wrongs of her engaging child, and the guilt of John, a false and selfish tyrant, whose sins are unredeemed by any of the nobler qualities of talent and courage or wit that gild the crimes of Iago and Richard – the author also saw that this sad tale would receive deeper truth, and a more living reality, from frequent contrast and gay relief. This contrast he supplies from the constant flashes of high spirits and gay courage, which his own genius strikes out so abundantly from the original hard and rough character of Cœur-de-lion's son. He is made the comic relief to the purely tragic portion of the action, and yet, being himself the secondary hero upon whom the audience's sympathy is to repose, he is in himself a tragi-comedy of the higher order, a compound of Hotspur and Mercutio, a character of which we sometimes meet the resemblance amongst young soldiers and sailors, and, if it had been drawn at a later period, I should say more Irish than English. But Shakespeare drew him from his own countrymen, and he belongs to a class rather than a nation. If the Poet had any other model in his eye than living nature, it was the historical and legendary character of Richard himself, whose son hath 'the very spirit of Plantagenet' [1.1.167].

Thus Shakespeare's *King John*, in one sense the least original of its author's works, – for there is not a single incident or character, scarcely a whole scene, not substantially to be found in the older play, – is in another and higher respect, that of feeling, poetry, dramatic skill, and ethical truth, one of his most original productions.

It resembles one of those extensive but commonplace landscapes, such as may be travelled over a hundred times without fixing its features upon the memory, but which at once acquires a unity and depth of expression and sentiment, combining or recalling swarms of joyous or solemn associations, when presented to the mind in a single point of view, under the lights of Ruysdael, or the colouring of Cole....[4] (I, 5–8)

23 Hartley Coleridge, critical notes on *King John*

1851

From *Essays and Marginalia. By Hartley Coleridge. Edited by His Brother. In Two Volumes* (2 vols, London, 1851).

Hartley Coleridge (1796–1849), eldest son of Samuel Taylor Coleridge, was himself a poet, essayist, and biographer of modest but hardly negligible accomplishment. Sensitive, shy, and mercurial by nature, he experienced more than common difficulty in adapting to the practicalities of life, often giving himself over to long periods of isolation and reverie. His most notable scholarly accomplishment was an edition of *The Dramatic Works of Massinger and Ford* (London, 1840), accompanied by useful biographies, but without the projected critical apparatus that he never found time to complete. The *Essays and Marginalia* were edited by Coleridge's younger brother Derwent, the first volume consisting of reprints of selected periodical essays, and the second of notes transcribed from the margins of Hartley Coleridge's books.

KING JOHN.
ON THE HISTORICAL PLAYS.

Shakespeare's historical plays certainly include a considerable space of time, but their duration should not be computed by the chronicle dates. However distant the events might be in actual occurrence, if the drama makes them interdependently consecutive, they have all the connection which just criticism requires. If the ideal unity be preserved, if the continuity be uninterrupted, it is little matter whether the period be long or short in which the incidents are supposed to occur. It must be recollected that the Dramatic History is a distinct species of composition, inferior, perhaps, to the regular tragedy as a panorama is inferior to a true tragic or epic picture; but, at any rate, different, and not amenable to the same rules.

ELINOR AND CONSTANCE.
ACT II., SCENE I. [the scolding match]

I should be glad to find that this altercation was transferred from the old '*troublesome reign*' for it is very troublesome to think it Shakespeare. I do not exactly know how great ladies scold, and there are reasons for supposing that Queen Elizabeth herself was not always quite queenlike in her wrath; but there is so little of humour, propriety, or seemliness in the discourse of the two princesses, and Constance is at last so confused and unintelligible, if not corrupt, that the whole might well be spared. Massinger, in the *Duke of Milan* [2.1], has a yet grosser dialogue of vituperation between Mariana, Isabella, and Marcelia; but it is not so utterly out of place; and, besides, Massinger's ladies are seldom gentlewomen.

CHARACTER OF KING JOHN.
ACT III., SCENE III.

In the old play of *King John*, 1591 [i.e., *The Troublesome Raigne*], Faulconbridge's execution of this order [to 'shake the bags / Of hoarding abbots' (7ff.)] is exhibited on the stage, and he finds a young smooth-skinned nun in a chest where the abbot's treasures were supposed to be deposited. It showed the good taste and boldness of Shakespeare that he did not retain this incident, so well calculated to make vulgar spectators laugh. He makes no reflection on the doctrine or discipline of Rome, far less does he calumniate the purity of her devoted virgins. He makes a king speak the sentiments of every king who did not need the Pope's countenance. John, when he found this need, crouched as vilely to the Pope as the most grovelling of Papists, and Shakespeare does not conceal the circumstance. How different from the absurdity of Bishop Bale, who makes the murderous, lustful, impious infidel John, a Protestant hero.

LATER SCENES OF THE PLAY.

These latter scenes of *King John* are very *serious*. After the death of Arthur all interest is at an end, and Faulconbridge himself proves bad enough to be the legitimate son of a speech-making peer. Fine lines, fine sentences, fine orations may be quoted, but all lies dead; neither for John nor his opponents do we longer care. This protraction of the business, after the interest has ceased, is a crying sin, and, in fact, the worst that Shakespeare is ever guilty of. Some other plays have it in a less degree, *e.g. Henry VIII.*, where it is impossible to care about any body after Wolsey and Queen Catherine are gone. Of the dying scene, where John begs for cold comfort, I could never make up my judgment. It is either admirable or execrable; but, at any rate, it does not result from the foregoing passages of the play. Of the historic dramas, *King John* is perhaps the worst constructed, and *King Richard II.*, which wants little to be a regular tragedy, is certainly the best. . . . (II, 150–3)

24 François Pierre Guillaume Guizot, history, art, and character in *King John*

1852

From *Shakespeare and His Times. By M. Guizot* (London, 1852).

François Pierre Guillaume Guizot (1787–1874) was a brilliant scholar, statesman, and orator, and one of the most influential personalities of his age. Born into a Huguenot family, Guizot began his political career as a liberal respected for his tact and diplomacy, but gradually adopted more conservative views, finally becoming a dedicated supporter of the monarchy in the face of ever-growing republican sentiment. Among the highlights of his wide and varied career in public life were his important role in furthering educational reform in France during his tenure as minister of the Department of Public Instruction from 1832 to 1836, and his successful diplomatic efforts as minister of foreign affairs during the 1840s to avoid war with England. His most bitter disappointment was the failure of French constitutional monarchy, an event that brought his political life to a close. *Shakespeare and His Times* was first published in Paris in 1852; in the same year English translations appeared in Britain and America. Guizot's remarks on the life and work of Shakespeare first appeared as an introduction to the French edition of Shakespeare's complete works (13 vols, Paris, 1821), edited jointly by Guizot and Amédée Pichot, and later in book form as *De Shakespeare et de la Poésie Dramatique* (Paris, 1822). *Shakespeare and His Times* is a revised and expanded version of these earlier studies of Shakespeare.

In choosing the reign of John Lackland as the subject of a tragedy, Shakespeare imposed upon himself the necessity of not scrupulously respecting history. A reign in which, as Hume says, 'England was baffled and affronted in every enterprise,'[1] could not be represented in its true colours before an English public and an English Court; and the only recollection of King John to which the nation could attach any value – I refer to Magna Charta – was not a topic likely to interest, in any great degree, such a Queen as Elizabeth. Shakespeare's play accordingly presents only a summary of the last years of this disgraceful reign; and the skill of the poet is employed to conceal the character of his principal personage without disfiguring it, and to dissemble the colour of events without altogether changing it. The only fact concerning which Shakespeare has distinctly adopted a resolution to substitute invention for truth, is the relation of King John to France; and assuredly, all the illusions of national vanity were necessary to enable Shakespeare to describe, and the English to witness, Philip Augustus succumbing beneath the ascendancy of John Lackland. Such a picture might indeed have been presented to John himself when – living in total inactivity at Rouen, whilst Philip was regaining all his possessions in France – he vauntingly said, 'Let the French go on: I will retake in a day what it has cost them years to acquire.'[2] All that which, in Shakespeare's play, is relative to the war with France, seems to have been invented in justification of this gasconade of the most cowardly and insolent of princes.

In the rest of the drama, the action itself, and the indication of facts which it was impossible to dissemble, are sufficient to give us a glimpse of a character, into the inmost recesses of which the poet did not venture to penetrate, and into which he could not have penetrated without disgust. But such a personage, and so constrained a manner of description, were not capable of producing a great dramatic effect; and Shakespeare has therefore concentrated the interest of his drama upon the fate of young Arthur, and has devolved upon Faulconbridge that original and brilliant part in which we feel that he takes delight, and which he never refuses to introduce into any of his works.

Shakespeare has presented the young Duke of Bretagne to us at that age at which it first became necessary to assert his rights after the death of King Richard – that is, at about twelve years old. We know that at the period to which Shakespeare's tragedy refers, Arthur was about twenty-five or twenty-six, and that he was already married, and an object of interest from his amiable and brilliant qualities, when he was taken prisoner by his uncle; but the poet felt how much more interesting the exhibition of weakness in conflict with cruelty became when exemplified in a child. And besides, if Arthur had not been a child, it would not have been allowable to put forward his mother in his place; and by suppressing Constance, Shakespeare would, perhaps, have deprived us of the most pathetic picture that he ever drew of maternal love – one of the feelings of which he evinced the profoundest appreciation.

But, at the same time that he rendered the fact more touching, he lessened the horror which it inspires by diminishing the atrocity of the crime. The most generally received opinion is, that Hubert de Bourg, who had promised to put Arthur to death only that he might save him, had, in fact, deceived the cruelty of his uncle by false reports and a pretended burial; but that John, on being informed of the truth, first withdrew Arthur from the Castle of Falaise, in which he was confined under Hubert's guardianship, and transferred him to the Castle of Rouen, whither he proceeded at night, and by water, had his nephew conveyed into his boat, stabbed him with his own hand, tied a stone to his body, and threw him into the river. Such an image would naturally be rejected by a true poet. Independently of the necessity of absolving his principal personage of so odious a crime, Shakespeare perceived how much more dramatic and conformable to the general nature of man, the cowardly remorse of John, when he perceived the danger in which he was plunged by the report of his nephew's death, would be, than this excess of brutal ferocity; and certainly, the fine scene between John and Hubert, after the withdrawal of the lords [4.2], is amply sufficient to justify his choice. Besides, the picture which Shakespeare presents had too strong a hold upon his imagination, and had acquired too much reality in his eyes, for him not to be conscious that, after the incomparable scene in which Arthur obtains his safety from Hubert [4.1], it would be impossible to endure the idea of any human being laying hands on this poor child, and forcing him again to undergo the agony from which he has just escaped. The poet also knew that the sight of Arthur's death, although less cruel, would be intolerable if accompanied, in the minds of the spectators, by the anguish which the thought of Constance would add to it; and he is therefore careful to inform us of the death of the mother before making us witness the death of the child; just as if, when his genius had conceived, to a certain degree, the painfulness of any particular feeling or passion, his tender heart became alarmed at it, and sought to modify it for its own sake. Whatever misfortune Shakespeare may depict, he almost invariably leads us to anticipate a still greater misfortune, before which his mind recoils, and which he spares us the unhappiness of beholding. . . .

[Guizot now mentions Shakespeare's indebtedness to *The Troublesome Raigne*, particularly for the character of Faulconbridge, and assigns the authorship of the play to Rowley rather than to Shakespeare.]

According to his custom, while borrowing whatever he pleased from Rowley, Shakespeare has added great beauties to his original, and has retained nearly all its errors. Thus, Rowley supposed that it was the Duke of Austria who killed Richard Cœur-de-Lion, and at the same time he makes the Duke of Austria perish by the hand of Faulconbridge, an historical personage whom Matthew Paris[3] mentions under the name of Falcasius de Breaute, the natural son of King Richard, and who, according to Holinshed, slew the Viscount of Limoges, in revenge for the death of his father, who, it is well known, was killed at the seige of Chaluz, a fortress belonging to that nobleman. In order to reconcile Holinshed's version with his own, Rowley has made Limoges the family name of the Duke of Austria, whom he designates [in the *dramatis personae*] as 'Limoges, Duke of Austria.' Shakespeare has copied him exactly in this part of his story. He also attributes the murder of Richard to the Duke of Austria; in his play also, the Duke of Austria falls by the hand of Faulconbridge; and, as regards the confusion of the two personages, it would appear that Shakespeare was as unscrupulous about it as Rowley, if we may judge from Constance's speech to the Duke of Austria in the first scene of the third act, in which she addresses him as 'O Lymoges! O Austria!' [3.1.114]. The character of Faulconbridge is one of those creations of Shakespeare's genius in which we discover the nature of all times and of all countries. Faulconbridge is the true soldier, the soldier of fortune, personally recognising no inflexible duty but that which he owes to the chief to whom he has devoted his life, and from whom he has received the rewards of his valour; and yet a stranger to none of those feelings upon which other duties are founded, and even obeying the instincts of natural rectitude whenever they do not come into contradiction with the vow of implicit fidelity and submission to which his existence, and even his conscience, is devoted. He will be humane, generous, and just, whenever this vow does not ordain him to practise inhumanity, injustice, and bad faith; he forms a correct judgment of the things to which he is subject, and is in error only regarding the necessity of subjecting himself to them. He is as skilful as he is brave, and does not alienate his judgment while renouncing its guidance: he is a man of powerful nature, whom circumstances and the necessity of employing his activity in some way or other, have reduced to a moral inferiority, from which a calmer disposition, and profounder reflections upon the true destination of man, would most probably have preserved him. But, with the fault of not having sought the objects of his fidelity and devotion in a sufficiently lofty sphere, Faulconbridge possesses the eminent merit of unchangeable fidelity and devotion, two singularly lofty virtues, both as regards the feeling from which they emanate, and the great actions of which they may be the source. His language is, like his conduct, the result of a mixture of good sense and ardour of imagination, which frequently involves his reason in a jumble of words very natural to men of Faulconbridge's profession and character; being incessantly exposed to the shock of the most violent scenes and actions, they cannot find in ordinary language the means of conveying the impressions which compose the habit of their life.

The general style of the play is less firm and decided in colour than that of several other tragedies by the same poet; the contexture of the work is also rather vague and feeble, but this is the result of the absence of one leading idea, which should continually direct all the parts of the drama towards the same centre. The only idea of this kind which can be discerned in *King John,* is the hatred of foreign dominion gaining the victory over the hatred of tyrannical usurpation. In order for this idea to be salient, and constantly to occupy the mind of the spectator, it would be necessary for it to be reproduced in every direction, and for everything to contribute to give conspicuity to the misfortune of a conflict between the two feelings. But this plan, which would be rather vast for a dramatic work, was, moreover, irreconcilable with the reserve which Shakespeare had imposed upon himself with regard to the character of the King; and thus a great part of the play is passed in discussions of but little interest, and in the remainder, the events are not well arranged; the lords change sides too lightly, first on account of the death of Arthur, and afterwards from motives of personal alarm, which does not present their return to the cause of England under a sufficiently honourable point of view. The poisoning of King John, moreover, is not prepared with that care which Shakespeare usually bestows upon the foundation and justification of the slightest circumstances in his dramas; and there is nothing to indicate the motive which could have led the monk to commit so desperate an action, as at that moment, John was reconciled to Rome. The tradition from which Shakespeare has borrowed this apocryphal anecdote, ascribes the monk's conduct to a desire to revenge an offensive epithet which the King had used regarding him. We cannot tell what could have induced Shakespeare to adopt this story, which he has turned to so little account; perhaps he desired to mingle with John's last moments something of infernal suffering, without having recourse to remorse, which, in fact, would not have been in more accordance with the real character of this contemptible prince, than with the modified delineation of it which the poet has supplied. (349–57)

25 Henry Norman Hudson, introduction to *King John*

1852

From *The Works of Shakespeare: The Text Carefully Restored According to the First Editions; with Introductions, Notes Original and Selected, and a Life of the Poet; by the Rev. H. N. Hudson, A.M. In Eleven Volumes* (11 vols, Boston and Cambridge, 1851–6). Volume IV. *The Winter's Tale; The Comedy of Errors; Macbeth; King John* (1852).

Henry Norman Hudson (1814–86) launched his career as a Shakespearian with an extremely popular series of lectures on the plays, which became the basis for his first book, *Lectures on Shakespeare* (2 vols, New York, 1848). He was ordained an Episcopal priest in 1849, and while serving in this capacity, and as editor for *The Churchman*, completed his first edition of Shakespeare. After an eventful tour of duty as a Union army chaplain during the American Civil War, at which time he was placed under arrest for hostile criticism of the military policies of his departmental commander, he turned again to literary pursuits. His *Shakespeare, His Life, Art, and Characters* (2 vols, Boston, 1872) essentially reprints, with some stylistic variations and additions, the introductions to his 1851–6 edition of the plays. The so-called 'Harvard Edition' (20 vols, Boston, 1880–1), and the many subsequent editions of Shakespeare that appeared under Hudson's name, contain essentially verbatim reprints of the 1872 essays, which are in turn intimately derived from his 1851–6 introductions.

[From the Introduction]

. . . As a work of art, [*King John*] has indeed considerable, though by no means the highest merit; but as a piece of historical portraiture, its claims may easily be overstated. In such a work diplomatic or documentary exactness is not altogether possible, nor is it even desirable any further than may well consist with the laws of art, or with the conditions of the poetic and dramatic form. For to be truly an historical *drama*, a work should not adhere to the literal truth of history in such sort as to hinder the dramatic life, or to cramp, or fetter, or arrest its proper freedom of movement and spirit. In a word, the laws of the drama are here paramount to the facts of history; which of course infers that where the two cannot stand together, the latter are to give way. Yet, when and so far as they are clearly compatible, neither of them ought to be sacrificed: historical accuracy, so far forth as it can be made to combine freely with the principles and methods of dramatic life, seems essential to the *perfection* of the work. And perhaps Shakespeare's mastery of his art is in nothing more forcibly approved than in the *degree* to which he has reconciled them. And the inferiority of *King John*, as an historical drama, lies in that, taking his other works in the same line as the standard, the facts of history are disregarded much beyond what the laws of art seem to require. For it need scarce be urged that in an historical drama literal truth is fairly entitled to give law, whenever dramatic truth does not overrule it. . . .

[Hudson now provides an extensive treatment of the departures from historical truth in *King John*, followed by a short examination of the relationship of the play to *The Troublesome Raigne* and a description of Bale's *Kynge Johan*; the ideas here essentially reiterate the findings of earlier critics. He then takes up Shakespeare's treatment of Roman Catholicism.]

. . . In both the old plays . . . an intense hatred of Popery runs as a special purpose through the drama. Which matter is reformed altogether in Shakespeare; who, no doubt, understood well enough that any such *special* purpose would not consist with the just proportions of art; that to make the drama a vehicle for any such particular invective or sarcasm was quite 'from the purpose of playing, whose end, both at the first, and now, was, and is, to hold, as 'twere, the mirror up to nature' [*Hamlet*, 3.2.20ff.]. He therefore betrays no repugnance to popery save in the form of a just and genuine patriotism; has no particular symptoms of a Protestant spirit, but only the natural beatings of a sound, honest English heart, resolute to withstand alike all foreign encroachments, whether from kings, or emperors, or popes. Thus his feeling against Rome is wisely tempered in that proportion which is equally required by the laws of morality and of art, issuing in a firm, manly national sentiment with which all men may justly sympathize, be their creed what it may. And, surely, no English mouth can refuse the words, – 'We must be free or die, who speak the tongue that Shakespeare spake'.[1] So that the Poet's *King John*, viewed thus in connection with the model after which it was framed, yields a most forcible instance and proof of his universality. He follows his guide in those things which appeal to the feelings of man as man; but forsakes him in whatever flatters the prejudices and antipathies of men as belonging to this or that party or sect. And as aversion to Rome is chastised down from the prominence of a special purpose in the play, the parts of Arthur and Constance and Faulconbridge proportionally rise; parts that spontaneously knit in and combine with the common sympathies and sentiments of humanity, – such a language as may always dwell together with the spirit of a man, and be twisted about his heart forever.

Still the question recurs, why did Shakespeare, with the authentic materials of history at hand, and with his own matchless power of shaping those materials into beautiful and impressive forms of dramatic life, – why did he in the single instance of *King John* depart from his usual course, preferring a fabulous history to the true, and that, too, even though, for aught now appears, the true would have answered his purpose as well.[2] It is with the view of suggesting a probable answer to this question that we have dwelt so much at length on the two plays that preceded his. We thus see that for special causes the subject of *King John* was early brought upon the stage. The same causes long operated to keep it there. The *King John* of the stage, striking in with the passions and interests of the time, had become familiar to the people, and twined itself closely with their feelings and thoughts. A faithful version would have worked at great disadvantage in competition with the theatrical one already thus established. This strong prepossession of the popular mind Shakespeare probably did not think it wise to offend or disturb. We agree therefore with Mr. Knight [No. 18 above], that 'it was a submission of his own original powers of seizing upon the feelings and understanding of his audience, to the stronger power of *habit* in the same audience.' In other words, the current of popular association being so strong already, he chose to fall in with it, rather than undertake to stem it. We may regret that he did so; but we can scarce doubt that he did it knowingly and upon principle; nor should we so much blame him for not turning that stream, as thank him for thus purifying it.

The only extant or discovered notice of Shakespeare's *King John*, till it appeared in the folio of 1623, is by Meres in his *Wit's Commonwealth*. So that all we can say with any certainty is, that the play was written some time before 1598. Blount and Jaggard made an entry in the Stationers' Register, November 8, 1623, of the plays 'not formerly entered to other men;' and *King John* is not among them. From which we might naturally infer that the play had been 'entered to other men,' and perhaps already published; but nothing of the sort has been heard of in our day. In the folio it stands the fifteenth in the volume, and the first in the division of the Histories; printed so clearly and carefully in the main, as to leave little room for question concerning the text.

Divers attempts have been made to argue the date of the writing from allusions to contemporary matters; respecting which attempts we cannot stop, nor is it worth the while, to say more than that they do not really amount to any thing at all. Some of the German critics, on the other hand, seem altogether out, when, arguing from the internal evidence of style, structure of the verse, tone of thought, and peculiarity of dramatic logic, they refer *King John* to the same period of the author's life with *The Tempest*, *Cymbeline*, and *The Winter's Tale*.[3] In all these respects it strikes us rather as having something of an intermediate cast between *The Two Gentlemen of Verona* and *The Merchant of Venice*. We are persuaded, though we should be troubled to tell why, that it was written some time before the two parts of *King Henry IV*. The play, especially in the first three acts, has a certain smoothness and fluency of diction, an uniformity of pause, and a regularity of cadence; therewithal, the persons deliver themselves somewhat in the style of set speeches, rather as authors striving for effect, than as men and women stirred by the real passions and interests of life; there is something of a bookish grandiloquent tang in the dialogue: all which smacks as if the Poet had here written more from what he had read in books, or heard at the theatre, than from what his most prying, quick, and apprehensive ear had overheard of the hitherto unwritten drama of actual and possible men. These peculiarities, to be sure, have been partly justified by Schlegel [No. 6 above], as growing naturally out of the subject: still we must think them to have proceeded mainly from the undergraduate state, so to speak, of the author's genius. 'In *King John*,' says that accomplished scholar and critic, 'the political and warlike events are dressed out with solemn pomp, for the very reason that they have little of true grandeur. The falsehood and selfishness of the monarch speak in the style of a manifesto. Conventional dignity is most indispensable where personal dignity is wanting. Faulconbridge is the witty interpreter of this language; he ridicules the secret springs of politics, without disapproving of them; for he owns that he is endeavouring to make his fortune by similar means, and would rather be of the deceivers than the deceived, there being in his view of the world no other choice.' In the last two acts, however, we have much more of the full-grown Shakespeare, sure-footed and self-supporting: the hidden elements of character, and the secret subtle shapings and turnings of guilty thought, shining out in clear transparence, or flashing forth amidst the very stress of action and the exigencies of passion; with frequent kindlings of poetic and dramatic inspiration, such as might befit his wealthiest years. . . .

[Hudson here devotes several paragraphs to the 'actual history' behind the play, then proceeds to his closing critical remarks.]

The characterization of this play in the degree of excellence corresponds very well with the period to which we have on other grounds assigned the writing. The king, as he stands in authentic history, was such a piece of irredeemable depravity, so thoroughly rotten-hearted, weak-headed, and bloody-handed, that to set him forth truly without seeming to be dealing in caricature or lampoon, required no little art. The Poet was under the necessity in some sort of leaving his qualities to be inferred, instead of directly expressing them: the point was to disguise his meannesses, and yet so to order that disguise as to suggest that it covered something too vile to be seen. And what could better infer his cringing, cowardly, slinking, yet malignant spirit, than his two scenes with Hubert de Burgh, where he durst not look his purpose in the face; and his base mind dodges and skulks and backs out from fathering its own issues; and he tries by hints and fawning innuendoes to secure the passage of his thought into effect, without committing himself to any responsibility for it; and wants another should be the agent of his will, and yet bear the blame as if acting of his own accord; and then, when the consequences begin to threaten and press upon him, he accuses the aptness of the instrument as the cause of his suggestion; and the only sagacity he shows is in shirking and shifting the responsibility of his own guilty purpose; his sneaking selfish fear inspiring him with a quickness and fertility of thought, such as he could never exert in any good cause.

The genius and art of Mrs. Siddons, to which the part of Constance was no doubt peculiarly fitted, have apparently caused the critics of her time, and their immediate followers, to set a higher estimate upon the character than seems fully borne out by the work itself. The abatement, however, that we would make refers not so much to the idea of the character, as to the style of the execution, wherein we cannot but think her far from exemplifying the Poet's full strength and inwardness with nature. The idea is well stated by Hazlitt [No. 8 above] as 'the excess of maternal tenderness, rendered desperate by the fickleness of friends and the injustice of fortune, and made stronger in will, in proportion to the want of all other power.' The character, though drawn in the best of situations for its amiability to appear, is not a very amiable one, and therein is perhaps the truer to history, as the chroniclers make her out rather selfish and weak; not so religious in motherhood, but that she betrayed a rather unhandsome impatience of widowhood. Nevertheless, it must be owned that the voice of maternal grief and affection speaks from her lips with not a little majesty of pathos, and occasionally flows in strains of the most melting tenderness: though in general the effect of her sorrow is marred by too great an infusion of anger; in her grief she has too much pride, self-will, and volubility of scorn, to have the full touch of our sympathies; her speech being stinging and spiteful, and sounding quite as much of the intemperate scold, as of the broken-hearted and disconsolate mother. As to the execution of the part, there is in many of her speeches too much of what we have already referred to as smacking more of the author than of the woman; a redundancy of rhetoric and verbal ingenuity giving them something of a theatrical relish, as though they were spoken rather for effect than from true feeling.

As Shakespeare used the allowable license of art in stretching the life of Constance beyond its actual date, that he might enrich his work with the eloquence of a mother's love; so he took a like freedom in making Arthur younger than he really was, that he might in larger measure pour in the sweetness of childish innocence and wit. At all events, we cannot in either case blame the fault, if it be one, the issue of it being so proper[4]. And in Arthur he gained thereby the further advantage, that the sparing of his eyes is owing to his potency of tongue and the awful might of unresisting gentleness; whereas in actual history he is indebted for this to his strength of arm. The Arthur of the plays is an artless, gentle, natural-hearted, but high-spirited and eloquent boy, in whom we have the voice of nature pleading for nature's rights, unrestrained by pride of character or of place; who at first braves his uncle, because set on to do so by his mother, and afterwards fears him, yet knows not why, because his heart is too full of the holiness of youth to conceive how any thing so treacherous and unnatural can be, as that which he fears. In his dying speech, – 'O me! my uncle's spirit is in these stones' [4.3.9], – our impression against John is most artfully heightened, all his foregoing inhumanity being, as it were, gathered and concentrated into an echo. Of the scene between him and Hubert, when he learns the order to put out his eyes, Hazlitt justly says [No. 8 above], – 'If any thing ever were penned, heart-piercing, mixing the extremes of terror and pity, of that which shocks and that which soothes the mind, it is this scene.' Yet even here the tender pathos of the loving and lovely boy is marred by some artificial conceits and prettinesses which we cannot believe Shakespeare would have let fall in his best days. The Poet has several times thrown the sweet witchery of his genius into pictures of nursery life, bringing children upon the scene, and delighting us with their innocent archness and sweet-witted prattle, as in the case of Hermione and Mamillius in *The Winter's Tale*, and of Lady Macduff and her son in *Macbeth*; but the part of Arthur is by far his most charming and powerful thing in that line. That his glorious, manly heart loved to make childhood its playmate, cannot be doubted.

The reign of King John furnished no characters fully answerable to the demands of dramatic interest. To meet this want, therefore, there was need of one or more *representative* characters, – men in whom should be centralized and consolidated various elements of national character, which were in fact dispersed through a multitude of individuals.[5] And such is Faulconbridge, with his fiery flood of Norman vigour bounding through his veins, his irrepressible gush of animal spirits, his athletic and frolicsome wit, his big, brave, manly heart, his biting sword, and his tongue equally biting, afraid of nothing but to do what were dishonourable or wrong. And with all his laughing roughness of speech, and iron sternness of act, so blunt, bold, and downright, he is full of humane and gentle feeling. With what burning eloquence of indignation does he denounce the supposed murder of Arthur though he has no thought of abetting his claim to the throne against the present occupant. The Poet has managed with great art that he may be held to John throughout the play, by ties which he is too clear of head and too upright of heart to think of renouncing. 'In the outset he receives honour from the hands of John, – and he is grateful: in the conclusion he sees his old patron, weak indeed and guilty, but surrounded with enemies, – and he will not be faithless.'[6] In his clear-sighted and comprehensive patriotism the diverse interests that split others into factions, and plunge them into deadly strife, are smoothly reconciled; and he is ready with tongue and sword to beat down whatsoever any where obstructs the reign of a broad and generous nationality. Verily, he stands next to Falstaff as an ideal representative of actual men. Thoroughly Gothic in features and proportions, and as thoroughly English in temper and spirit, his presence rays life and true manliness into every part of the drama, where they would else be wanting. Is it strange that a nation which could grow such originals should have beaten all the rest of the world in every thing useful, or beautiful, or great? (IV, 350–61)

26 Henry Reed, history and character

1855

From *Lectures on English History and Tragic Poetry, as Illustrated by Shakespeare* (Philadelphia, 1855).

Henry Reed (1808–54) abandoned a career in the law for a professorship of rhetoric and English literature at the University of Pennsylvania, a position he held from 1835 until his death. Reed's major contribution to literary studies in America was his unwavering (and at times undiscriminating) advocacy of the poetry of Wordsworth. He produced influential editions of the poet in 1837 and 1851, the *Memoirs of William Wordsworth* (Boston, 1851), and also gave frequent essays and public lectures on Wordsworth throughout his career. *Lectures on English History* comprises one of numerous volumes published by Reed that had their origin in public oratory, a form which provided him abundant opportunity for the discursive and appreciative style of criticism for which he was so highly regarded.

[From Lecture IV: 'The Reign of King John']

[After a brief historical overview from the time just before the Norman conquest to the onset of John's reign, and an admission that the 'historic poet' must impose some order on historical events, Reed turns to *King John*.]

. . . The first scene of the tragedy of *King John* has that significancy which distinguishes the openings of Shakespeare's plays – an intimation of the whole plot, the full meaning of which is regularly developed in the progress of the drama. In almost the first words, King John's royalty is spoken of as 'borrowed majesty' [1.1.4], and he is summoned by the embassy of his great contemporary, Philip Augustus of France, to yield his kingdom up to the rightful heir, Arthur Plantagenet, the son of his dead brother, Geoffrey. The succession of John was usurpation, beginning in fraud and violence, and continued in crime; but of the previous Norman reigns, four out of six of the kings had possessed themselves of the sceptre by the law of the strong hand. The rule of succession could, therefore, as yet be scarcely considered as established; but, instead of it, there seems to have been, in that unsettled political condition, little more than what Rob Roy calls – 'The good old rule, the simple plan, / That they should take who have the power, / And they should keep who can.'[1]

When this is considered, and when we remember, too, that the absence of Richard on the Crusade gave peculiar opportunities to his brother John to pave the way to the succession, it is not surprising that John became the king, especially as the rightful heir was in his youth, and the government had not yet attained that period when, under constitutional forms, a minority reign becomes practicable. Accordingly, at the opening of the drama, Shakespeare does not at once awaken indignation at the injustice of the usurpation, and, indeed, rather leads us to admire the calm royal bearing with which the king answers the threat of war; as if, unconscious of wrong to his nephew, he relies upon his 'strong possession and his right' [1.1.39], and confidently hurls back defiance to the King of France. We see, therefore, from the very beginning, how differently, and in how much finer a spirit, Shakespeare treats the character of King John, than that coarse and common mode, by which it has been represented in such black and unrelieved colours that no humanity can be found in him, and he is looked on with unmitigated horror and contempt. It has been said with reference to the 'vivid speaking characters' in which Shakespeare has placed so many of the English kings in imperishable individuality before us, – 'Only look at his King John, look at any historian's. Which gives you the liveliest, faithfullest representation of that prince and of his age, the poet's or the historian's? Which most powerfully exposes his vices and awakens the greatest horror at them? Yet in Shakespeare he is still a man, and, as such, comes within the range of our sympathy: we can pity, even while we shudder at him; and our horror moves us to look inward into the awful depths of the nature which we share with him, instead of curdling into dead hatred and disgust. In the historian's he is a sheer monster, the object of contemptuous loathing, a poisonous reptile whom we could crush to death with as little remorse as a viper.'[2]

The tragedy begins with the voice of state, of diplomacy, of policy, and of the rivalry of England and France; and we shall see how, in the various characters, all the elements of mediæval life are present – the papacy and the priesthood – the monarchy and the nobility – the commonality and the soldiery – all are there. It has, however, been ingeniously said by a German critic that – 'The hero of this piece stands not in the list of personages, and could not stand with them, for the idea should be clear without personification. The hero is England.'[3] This means, as I understand it, that Shakespeare has made England the great and ever-present idea of the play; that, without any artifice of national vanity, he has so written the history of the reign of King John as to inspire a deep and fervid spirit of nationality. It is comparatively an easy thing to animate the hearts of a people with such a spirit by presenting the *glorious* parts of their country's annals; the mere touch of the memory of victories won by their ancestors will kindle enthusiasm and pride in the breasts of posterity. . . .

But it was Shakespeare's arduous achievement to fire the sentiment of patriotism with the story of a reign that was tyrannical, oppressive, cowardly, – a period of usurpation and national degradation. He has accomplished this chiefly by means of one character, which is almost altogether a creation of his mind from very slight historical materials. The fertile imagination of the poet, and his genial exuberance of happy and gentle feelings, seem to have craved something more than the poverty of the history supplies; he wanted somebody better than a king, better than a worldly ecclesiastic, and better than the bold but fickle barons. It is in the highest order of dramatic art, and especially in the historic drama, that Shakespeare, on no other historical basis than the mere existence of a natural son of Richard, has created the splendid and most attractive character of Philip Faulconbridge. Besides playing an important part himself, he fulfils something like the function of the chorus of the ancient drama; for he seems to illustrate the purposes of the history, and to make the real personages more intelligible. He is the embodiment, too, of the most genuine national feeling, and is truer to his country than king or noble. With an abounding and overflowing humour, a dauntless courage, and a gentleness of spirit that characterizes true heroism, Faulconbridge carries a generous strength and a rude morality of his own, amid the craft and the cruelties and the feebleness of those who surround him. The character, imaginary as it is, has an historical value also in this, that it represents the bright side of feudal loyalty. Honoured by the king, Faulconbridge never deserts him in his hour of need and peril, when the nobles are flying off from their allegiance and a foreign enemy is at hand. It is no servile fidelity, but such genuine and generous loyalty that we look upon it as faithfulness to his country rather than adherence to the fortunes of the king. He is, as it were, the man of the people in the play, and we hear him prompting brave actions and a generous policy – encouraging the feeble king to a truer kingly career; we see him withstanding the haughty barons, and still more indignant at papal aggression. He dwells in an atmosphere of heartlessness and villany, but it pollutes him not; rather does his presence partially purify it. It is remarkable that we do not and cannot, I think, associate him injuriously with the character of King John, with whose fortunes he is identified, but from whose vices he is wholly aloof; and I am almost tempted to apply to him what has been said of a very different character: 'His soul was like a star and dwelt apart.'[4]

The character and position of Faulconbridge in the play, seem to me finely to illustrate the workings of the principle of chivalry during this early feudal period of history, – that principle of which Mr. Burke wisely said that – 'Without confounding rank, it produced a noble equality, and handed it down through all the gradations of social life. It was this opinion,' said that philosophic statesman, 'which mitigated kings into companions, and raised private men to be fellows with kings.'[5] The effects of the principle of chivalry, as manifested in the intercourse of King John and Faulconbridge, cannot escape observation; but the reader of the drama may probably overlook a very short passage which seems to me to illustrate the workings of it as it passes down, to use Mr. Burke's phrase, through all the gradations of life and touches the humbler range of society. It is a passage which struck the fancy of Coleridge, who was in the habit of quoting it as an instance of Shakespeare's power *in minimis*; and it certainly does show how comprehensively careful a poet's genius is of minute as well as of great things. In the list of the persons of the play, you may notice the name of 'James Gurney, servant to Lady Faulconbridge.' He makes his appearance once, – but once, – then only for a very little while; he does not speak till spoken to, says four words, – scarce more than four monosyllables, – then '*Exit James Gurney*' [1.1.232 s.d.], and that is all. Yet Coleridge speaks of the *character* of this person, and finds it in these very few words – that single touch of Shakespeare's pen portraying the affectionate respectfulness of an aged domestic.[6] When Faulconbridge is about to extort from his mother the secret of his parentage, a sense of delicacy leads him to desire a conference with her alone, and he requests the attendant to withdraw, saying, – 'James Gurney, wilt thou give us leave awhile?' [1.1.230], and the meek answer, which pleased Coleridge's fancy, is simply – 'Good leave, good Philip' [1.1.231]. I refer to the passage for a reason different from Coleridge's, and to notice the spirit of Faulconbridge's playful reply, as he says – 'James, / There's toys abroad. Anon I'll tell thee more' [1.1.231ff.]. Now, I beg you to notice the familiar and affectionate tone of this intercourse, as they address each other by their Christian names, 'Philip' and 'James;' and then the fine, gentlemanly, and considerate feeling which prompts Faulconbridge to promise the old servant – his old domestic friend – to tell him more after awhile, as a kind of indirect apology for even asking him to withdraw. Minute as the instance is, it is an historical illustration of the gentleness with which the genuine principles of chivalry looked down to the humble, as well as upward to the high born.

The alliances of France and Austria, which are, at the beginning, proclaimed in support of Arthur's claim to the throne of England against King John, are soon dissolved. A new wind of policy blows over them, and the friendship of king and duke, which a little before had been proffered to the helpless and injured Arthur with so much of pomp and declamatory assurance, all passes away; his cause is abandoned: new friendships and a different policy are formed on the instant. The hollowness and heartlessness of this conduct are more deeply felt when we behold the wild anguish of Constance, in desperate disappointment, clamouring for the lost rights of her child; and, as if the huge firm earth could alone support a grief so great as hers, seating herself on the ground for kings to come and bow to her loneliness and desolation.

The contrast between the beauty, the strength, and grandeur of natural feeling, and the ugliness and the instability of the politic zeal of ambitious kings and princes, is felt, not only when we are listening to the voluble utterances of maternal passion, but when we turn to the gentle exclamations of the innocent Arthur, as he would fain escape the turmoil of an ambitious destiny:

> Good my mother, peace!
> I would that I were low laid in my grave:
> I am not worth this coil that is made for me. [2.1.163ff.]

The peace of the grave was speedily to be the portion of this unhappy prince, – a youth whose character history has not especially deigned to record; but we can believe that he was, in truth, the thoughtful and gentle-hearted being that Shakespeare has shown to us, not only in his own actions and speech, but as he was endeared to the agitated affections of Constance. In his brief life we behold the sacrificial beauty and purity, which seem to mark him for the victim of the selfish and wicked passions that are raging around him.

The treaty between John and Philip Augustus, built on the sandy foundation of a broken faith and foresworn promises, proved an unstable and hollow armistice, as if the wild prayer of Constance, in her hour of desolation, had a speedy answer, when, deserted by earthly alliances, she cried – [Quotes 3.1.107–11: 'Arm, arm, you heavens, against these perjured kings. . . .'].

In that renewed war the destiny of Arthur was sealed: he fell into the power of his victorious uncle, – the young and rightful claimant of the English crown was in the perilous possession of the wicked usurper. Two words more – a prison – death – close the story of the career of Arthur of Brittany. Impenetrable mystery hangs over his death, and all that can be discerned in the darkness of it is the guilt of King John. How he died is not known; but history, tradition, poetry, all have laid the guilt of that death upon the conscience of King John, whose cowardice and cruelty were someway the agents of the murder. The essential guilt lies there, and it does not matter greatly, whether Arthur pined away in prison to an early death, or whether he perished in an attempt to escape, or whether John perpetrated the deed of horror with his own hand, in mid-river loneliness and midnight silence, by plunging his dagger into the bosom of his helpless kinsman, and then casting the poor child's bleeding body into the deep waters of the river Seine.

It does not belong to my subject to comment on the matchless dramatic skill of those two great scenes, – that appalling one in which the king commits Arthur to the deadly keeping of Hubert, and that other piteous one between Hubert and Arthur. In the consummate poetic art of those scenes, there is, at the same time, a no less admirable historic charity; for, in the obscurity of the history, Shakespeare has impressed the mind with a deep sense of the guilt of the king without aggravating it with needless horrors or more than human atrocity. Arthur, in the play, perishes in his attempt at escape; but to the perilous leap that caused his death he was driven by the dread of John's power; and he had already, by John's cruel purpose, endured the terror and anguish at the presence of the executioner and the sight of the instruments of torture.

When Arthur fell by the fortune of war into the hands of King John, the possession of his young rival brought security to the usurper, but it brought also temptation to make assurance double sure by converting the custody of a prison into the inviolable custody of the grave. The moral view, and, I believe, a most just historic view, which Shakespeare gives us, is this – that, however the events are separated in time, all the after-misery of the reign of King John was the penal retribution for the murder of Arthur. In consequence of it, his continental dominions passed away from him, to make up the splendid French monarchy of the Capets, and at home he struggled through a distracted reign, amid disloyal nobles and a discontented people. The sequel of the reign, after Arthur is taken prisoner, is finely told in the play, when the deep political sagacity of Cardinal Pandulph foretells the course of things. Exciting the Dauphin to claim the English throne, he bids him mark – [Quotes 3.4.131–40: 'John hath seized Arthur. . . .', where Pandulph argues that the 'fall' of Arthur is inevitable]. When the Dauphin questions what he is to gain by Arthur's fall, and doubts his success, the wily Cardinal replies – [Quotes 3.4.145–68: 'How green you are, and fresh in this old world. . . .'].

It is just before these cold-hearted and crafty speculations respecting Arthur's death, that Constance addressed the Cardinal with that beautiful and pathetic utterance of her first grief at her son's captivity: [Quotes 3.4.76–89: 'Father Cardinal, I have heard you say. . . .']. The words fall ineffectual on Pandulph's ear; and he who, with his sacred function, might have poured consolation into the aching void of a mother's heart, answers with a rebuke. He was busy with intrigues of state, weaving meshes to catch or entangle kings; and what audience could maternal grief find with the crafty and corrupt priest, burdened with worldly policy, like such other cardinals as Wolsey and Richelieu and Mazarin and Portocarrero, the politician-ecclesiastics of modern Europe?[7] When, with like coldness, King Philip – he who had selfishly advocated and selfishly abandoned the cause of Constance and her son – tells her she is 'As fond of grief as of her child' [3.4.92], she gives the last justification of her impassioned sorrow: [Quotes 3.4.93–8: 'Grief fills the room up of my absent child. . . .'].

The appearance of Cardinal Pandulph in this play introduces another of the great contests of this distracted reign, – the struggle between King John and the papal power during that splendid period of it, the papacy of Innocent the Third. The controversy turned on the election of the Primate of England, and John's refusal to admit Stephen Langton to the see of Canterbury. When the papal claim is asserted by Cardinal Pandulph, as the legate of the pope, it is answered by King John in a high strain of defiance, which arrays the independence of his realm and sovereignty in bold antagonism against papal aggression: [Quotes 3.1.147–71: the dialogue between John and Philip, where John defies both the pope and the French king]. This resistance brought upon John the penalty of excommunication, and upon the realm, in punishment of the sovereign, that more dreadful and extraordinary infliction, the papal *interdict*. This penalty – the general effect of which was to stop all religious services – was a form of ecclesiastical punishment which, according to the authority of Roman Catholic historians, was unknown in the early ages of the church, and did not come distinctly into use before the eleventh century. It is accounted for as an expedient resorted to for the purpose of counteracting and controlling feudal tyranny. In this case the sentence of a general interdict over the whole of England was proclaimed. . . .

After a reign of conflict and confusion and disgrace, John dies a miserable and a suffering death; and the last words that fall upon his dying ear are the evil tidings of continued disaster. The spirit of Arthur is avenged.[8]

At the close of the tragedy, Shakespeare, with some disregard of chronological accuracy, brings back the nobles to their allegiance; and then, with the voice of Faulconbridge – the very embodiment of patriotism and loyalty – he raises the mind from the weakness and degradation of the reign to a sense of England's power and independence. It is in a high strain of that national self-confidence which, though it may degenerate into national vanity or swell into intolerable national pride, is part of the power which makes a people unconquerable, – it is in such a spirit that Faulconbridge tells the young prince and the nobles – [Quotes 5.7.112–18: 'This England never did, nor never shall. . . .'].

Let me add that these lines were composed by Shakespeare not long after that year in which the formidable invasion by the Spanish Armada was driven back in ruin from the shores of England. The poet's heart beat high as he beheld the banners of the ships of Spain hung out as trophies from the battlements of the Cathedral of St. Paul's, when queen Elizabeth, in the midst of a rejoicing people, went up to that metropolitan temple to give thanks to God for the safety of her realm. (129–46)

27 William Watkiss Lloyd, *King John* and nationalism

1856

From *The Dramatic Works of William Shakespeare. The Text Carefully Revised with Notes by Samuel Weller Singer F.S.A. The Life of the Poet and Critical Essays on the Plays by William Watkiss Lloyd M.R.S.L., etc. etc.* (10 vols, London, 1856).

William Watkiss Lloyd (1813–93), although never formally trained for the scholarly life, became a noted man of letters through sheer industry and unwavering devotion to literary studies, particularly the classics and Shakespeare. His best known work is the extremely learned but stylistically dense *Age of Pericles* (2 vols, London, 1875), a history of the politics and art of Greece from the Persian to the Peloponnesian War. Precisely that quality of incisive learning fused with occasional abstruseness which typifies Lloyd's work in classical studies also appears in his critical and biographical essays on Shakespeare; these were written for Samuel Weller Singer's second edition of the dramatist, and later reprinted by Lloyd as *Essays on the Life and Plays of Shakespeare* (London, 1858).

[From 'Critical Essay on *King John*']

. . . It is an observation of Schlegel's [No. 6 above] that these two terminal plays, *King John* and *Henry the Eighth*, are in the position of prologue and epilogue to the other eight, and thus in the first we are introduced to all the political and national motives which play so great a part in the succeeding pieces. Regarding then the series as a connected whole – not composed, it is true, in the order of the history, but each later work carefully adjusted to each earlier performance, we must look for a governing idea which in the whole and even in each play is dominant over that which is indicated by its separate title. The true hero of the series, heroic either in access of suffering, or height of action, or scope of aspiration, is a nationality; is the conception of the poet, which in the case of a true poet falls into identity with the natural essence, of the honour and dignity, the truest worth and interest of the English nation, – of his native land.

The play of *King John* then embodies the fortunes and destinies of England as affected by the character and position of this special monarch, and of like scope is each succeeding history bearing the title of the several kings. The poet fixes and realizes monarchical England, and all the accidents and liabilities, so far as developed to his time, of such a combination. It will prove accordingly that the personal element of the play owes its chief interest to its bearing on the national, of which it becomes the direct or indirect exponent. However the pomp of the swelling scene may appear to illustrate an individual, however our attention may be riveted by a picture of suffering or passion, the action is ever so conducted that the idea continues ever present, of the mightier interest that is behind. A national historical play necessarily excites, and therefore wisely considers and appeals to, the sentiment of patriotism, of nationality. Thus the main effectiveness of the play results from the fact that the spectators are animated with, or for the nonce assume, the spirit and instincts of Englishmen, and watch with concern the unfolding how the fortunes and fate of the country are affected for good, or ill, or uncertainty, by the character and position of the occupant of the throne, the prime influence on the country's resources and energies. . . .

Apparently the most frequent and pregnant theme is the unhappy consequence of disputed succession to the throne, but we trace without difficulty the origin of the troubles and disasters that fill the chronicle, still deeper to the unsettled and semi-barbarous state of society. Custom, and indeed the very necessities of the case, gave in those days authority to a king that no human being can be trusted with and remain uncorrupted, and which in any case it required first-rate qualifications and intellect, resource and vigour to exercise. The lack of these, not unaided by some loose impressions of the law of succession, infallibly led to depositions and transferment of allegiance, and thence in the same generation, or the next, various lines of rival claimants to the crown, with all the aids of factions and parties; and now the prestige of tradition and legitimacy sustained the pretensions of one every way incapable, while the stigma, and still more unfortunately the consciousness of usurpation, was attached to the administration of the accomplished and efficient prince. Hence the fierce passions, and hence the frightful crimes of which it would never have been suspected that human nature was capable, but for its exposure to a combination of exciting and corrupting influences which hamper the better nature, and give license and stimulus to all that is inferior and faulty in man's constitution. The defective legal title of the able, the weakness of the imbecile, and the enormities of the vicious, are alike disasterous and damaging to the nation in honour and happiness, and if ever a happy coincidence of admitted title, of vigour and ability, and of adequate self-control does once come round, it briefly passes away, and when a single happy element is wanting the rest are neutralized – are nullities.

The monarchical, however, is not the only though the most conspicuous power that is out of joint for the well-being of the country; all the other political influences, whether of the turbulent military barons, of the accused and perhaps envied clergy, of the impetuous and ignorant commonality, are alike undefined and irregular; and it is in the midst of such a chaos that some hope and promise of ultimate order is found in a manifestation of that spirit which the nation has always proudly asserted as its own.

The drama of *King John* prepares for the full development of all these complications, and at the same time expresses an epoch by marking them in one particular phase. A certain power of independence is the first condition whether in a man or a people for individuality as a self and for self-respect; and the exhibition of the concern of English honour, in regard to invasion or interference from abroad, is properly the leading point in the first of the English series. The dramatized reign of John excites and disciplines in every form of excitement, the repugnance to foreign intermeddling whether civil or ecclesiastical, in internal affairs. The shamefulness and mischievousness of admitting it whether with the best or worst of motives, is set before us most livelily, and the moral is even authorized in set words at the conclusion, that for glory and safety equally our own concerns must be in our own hands, and that the condition of this, indispensable and all-sufficient, is internal union, – that England to itself should rest but true. . . .

There is a degree of uncertainty allowed to rest in the play, on the true claim of John or Arthur to the crown, which expresses, not so much the hesitations of historians with which a poet has nothing to do, but an actual condition of things. John is found in strong possession, strong in itself in his personal qualities and in national support; beyond this, Queen Elinor, it is true, hints at a will in his favour barring the claim of Arthur of Brittany the representative of the elder branch, but she scarcely cares to insist on it. Although, however, Elinor whispers a protest of conscience when John appeals to his right; though even Faulconbridge over the dead body of Arthur recognizes some sacred sanction of his prior claim, while it is assumed by the allies of Constance as self-evident; still there is in the abstract such superior fitness of John for his position, and backed by willing English barons, he appears to such advantage in opposition to the allies of Arthur, that we are left with the impression that with such allegiance he had in truth a better claim, had he understood the just principles of sovereign claim, than even he himself supposes.

Such however is the sickness of the immature time; his conscience is touched and defiant, and hence he is disposed to means of force rather than those arguments of peaceful negotiation in which even his mother saw a possible settlement of all. His enemies and those of England again are prompt to take advantage of the reputed flaw, and thus the action commences. The disputed title to the crown gives opportunity to the French king to intermeddle in the domestic affairs of England, by acceding to the solicitations of one claimant for support; then John in the interest of his usurpation sacrifices the national interest which he otherwise represents, by easily surrendering the provinces to conciliate peace. His surrender goes for nothing from the interference at this moment of the Pope on a quarrel of his own; the provinces have been given up, yet his right to the rest still impugned, his rival still supported. He grapples however with his difficulties manfully, and with equal courage, alertness and conduct conquers the French king and defies the denunciations of the Pope. But again mistrust of his title and consciousness of his own motive confound him; he is tempted to the brutal crime of destroying Arthur, and brings upon himself by the suspected fact a domestic rebellion, which allies itself unadvisedly but dangerously with French power, and to escape from the difficulty thus brought on he submits himself without reserve to Papal dictation. By this time his failing energies would make wreck of the whole fortune of the state, but that better powers are at hand in the true nationality and sound spirit and energies of a subject. The fair front and bold bearing of Faulconbridge despite disaster, and the returning allegiance of the barons whose better tendencies are recovered by accidental discovery of the treachery of their unnatural allies, bring all into position to take fresh and more promising commencement. . . .

The title of national interests and national honour to over-ride inferior considerations of personal sympathy, devotion to an individual and class interests, – the dignity, that is, of the historical or national motive, is set forth by exhibiting its preponderance when the opposite scale is weighed with the antagonist impulses in their most effective form. We are drawn towards John, that is, towards England and Faulconbridge, notwithstanding our personal sympathy is engaged so strongly for Constance and her hapless son. John and Elinor are selfish-guilty, but their fortunes, whether by accident or no, are those of nationality, and receive some consecration from the alliance. Usurpation, however, in availing itself of the indulgence accepts the bond to have like measure meted to it when it transfers itself to the false position of its now prostrate enemies, nor can legitimacy escape the law. In Richard III. we find again a murderous usurper, as later history furnishes an hereditary tyrant, opposed to pretenders invading with foreign aid; but in both instances the foreign power or interest is decidedly in subjection to the domestic, and gains neither immediate nor implicit ascendancy.

John therefore, however he attained his position, is able, energetic, and the spirit of nationality sides with him against a claimant under the tutelage of France and gaining aid by condonation to a treacherous poltroon of the death of Cœur de Lion. Still, it is not the less revolted at his cold blooded cruelty to his nephew, and indignant at his concessions to France and cringing to Rome, and casts about with anxiety for some way out of the labyrinth – losing its way like Faulconbridge in a moment of dejection, amazed among the thorns and dangers of the world [4.3.140ff.].

In the future historical plays, as in this, we shall find the weakening of the royal power that results from informal title, gives the aiding or accomplice barons inordinate power and presumption dangerous to the peace and to the united power of the state. Pembroke and Essex and Salisbury are antecedents of those who made and unmade kings, of the Warwicks, Northumberlands and Hotspurs, who rid the country of one tyrant only to endeavour to tyrannize over or virtually dismember it in the name of a puppet, and when he is contumacious, to tear society to pieces by rebellion.

Hence the expedients of the kings recorded in other plays to employ the rash spirits of the nobility in crusades or wars with France, always disastrous in the end with whatever glory accompanied; or to decimate and destroy, at least to weaken the order to a degree not more injurious to its dignity than to its proper usefulness which will not be prematurely spared.

This however is for future development; in the present piece, as we have seen, the evil set forth is that unpatriotic concession to foreign powers from motives personal to the king, that reached its height under the later Stuarts, not till long after Shakespeare had exposed it for reprobation; but that was abundantly rife in our earlier chronicled history, and contrasted most strongly with the genius of the government of Elizabeth. Before and after the time of Shakespeare, the contested titles of the English kings, deriving from the dethronements caused or even necessitated by their vices and tyranny or by their general incapacity, induced the betrayal of the national interest or glory for the sake of protection against subjects, or to escape from contests which such weakness disabled them from carrying through.

The source of a remedy for these difficulties in the working of a monarchy, and they are as salient in our century as ever, is adumbrated in *King John* where the Bastard of Faulconbridge is an impersonation at once of loyalty to his sovereign and of truth to the national honour; and having committed to him, by the failing John, the delegated government 'Take thou the order of the present time' [5.1.77], is at the head of that scheme of administration that becomes possible when a nation at large or the efficient majority of it, is as sound at heart as Faulconbridge. This is the promise of that happier form of constitutional government, barbarous and bewildering though it may be in its fictions and anomalies, that relieves monarchy from the cares and consequences of undue responsibility, and allows the conduct of national affairs to proceed, if not entirely at least to a very great extent, uninfluenced by the defects of age, of ability, of disposition and caprice, that are incident to the convenience of hereditary succession; which gives an arm of youth unchanging, because ever changing to wield the vigour of the nation, and has ever the opportunity to mark the man that expresses the clear sense of the nation when its mind is resolved, or that it is prepared to follow with most confidence when doubtful and at a loss, or when action must respond to exigent emergency.

The character of the Bastard and its progress are most effectively realized, and contrast with the successive phases of the spirit of John. From the beginning to the end he is uniformly bluff and outspoken, but at first with a certain affectation of bluffness that smacks of the country and wears off without in any degree impairing his hearty sincerity, when he has seen more of the world, but never could be mistaken for bluster. Though not embarrassed by delicacy he preserves a principle of conscientiousness; and when, transferred to court, here cognizes the genius of the place, it is in self-defence alone that he proposes to cope with it. Interest and influence and power are the stakes on the board, the gamesters are unscrupulous, and he will cultivate the wit he does not lack to make sure he is not cheated.

In the scenes in France he is the brave soldier and little more; a looker-on in scenes of general treaty, and blurting out indignation with no cautious regard to his relative diplomatic position. Only when a course is to be adopted in active management he frames a plan that, in his own words, 'smacks somewhat of the policy' [2.1.396]. After the unprincipled convention of the kings indeed he professes allegiance to gain in his personal capacity, but he does not graduate far; his ransacking the abbey chests is not noted as affected by private peculation and he rises by nobler means.

What we call in compliment to ourselves an English spirit, – a spirit of independence, of fair play in hard fighting and of directness in negotiation, hatred of cruelty and meanness, and disgust at the pursuit of secular purposes under a religious pretext, especially in a foreign interest, – this is the spirit that animates the other English barons, but especially the Bastard, expressed casually and intermittently at first, but when the heart and health of John decline together he rises at once in consistency, dignity and force. He gains in elevation and composure, without relaxing one whit in energy; and sparing no exertion to keep the country together and place the quarrel on an open and healthy footing, he entertains the shrewd and only safe conviction that preparation for hard knocks will best support negotiation if unhappily too late to supersede it. He presents a prototype of the loyalty of which our history furnishes so many examples, loyalty to the ideal qualities that would best become the throne, and that it persists in assuming, – such is the assistance of personal association, to sustain its enthusiasm and for the encouragement of the cause that should be in itself motive and stimulant enough. Thus there is still nothing slavish in his loyalty: the older dramatist [i.e., the author of *The Troublesome Raigne*], to whose work we must presently advert, allows him to appeal to the divine right: –

> I say 'tis shame and worthy all reproof
> To wrest such petty wrongs in terms of right
> Against a king anointed by the Lord.
> Why, Salisbury admit the wrongs are true,
> Yet subjects may not take in hand revenge
> And rob the heavens of their proper powers,
> Where sitteth he to whom revenge belongs. [11.114ff.]

But the Faulconbridge of Shakespeare directs his eye to a different point of right entirely, and loyalty is enjoined because patriotic, not patriotism on the ground of loyalty: –

> And you degenerate, you ingrate revolts,
> You bloody Neroes ripping up the womb
> Of your dear mother England, blush for shame. [5.2.151ff.]

The introduction of Peter of Pomfret, and the indication of the popular agitation and uneasiness with which he is connected, could not be spared in a play that is to be introductory to the histories in several of which popular commotion was to play so large a part. We may recognize in these delusions the seed-bed of the wild and foolish sects, as in the indicated position of the clergy, the confiscation and plunder, that came on with the better consequences of the reformation. In this earliest play and remotest action it was easy to indicate without offence the necessity for harmonizing the influences of Church and State, so far at least that they might work if not together not in opposition.

For the rest of the play presents a picture of almost chaotic turbulence; England and its body politic rocks and tumbles in disruptions, return and subsidence. In the first part in the war with France we have war and peaceful treaty and war again, in a sequence of scenes divided by no extended interval; in the second portion of the play allegiance, rebellion and reunited fealty succeed and alternate with like rapidity, and the relations with Rome change as quickly from open defiance to cringing submission, and from covert to declared antipathy, rendering altogether a wonderfully true impression of the history as recorded.

The picture of Popish interference and power makes the play peculiarly the picture of an epoch. The kingdoms of modern Europe are still in the gristle, and the remains of ancient Roman civilization is potent among the irregular communities which are yet unprepared to make terms of compromise or boldly to assert independence. The degraded position of both John and Lewis successively, – degrading and disastrous, provokes appeal to a national spirit which the centuries ripen. Thus is stated the problem that is scarcely solved at present, the harmony and identity of national sympathies with the true as distinguished from the counterfeit, cosmopolitan.

Pandulph, the legate, stands in a group with the feudal princes like the representative of the adult fraud and heartlessness of priestcraft; the inheritor of high faculties cultivated to refined ill purposes from the old Roman pontifices; the root of evil living among the ashes of the empire and springing up amongst and poisoning the better and unsophisticated tendencies of the northern nations, apprentices in civilization it is true but also novices in deceit. In his elaborate explaining away of perjury, his authorization by religious sanction of secret, treacherous murder and revolt, and in his cold-blooded complacency as he speculates on the certain murder of Arthur if dexterously provoked and the advantages to result to Holy Church therefrom, we have most striking contrast to the spirit of honour, of hatred of cruelty, and of compassion for the weak and afflicted, that characterizes the English Barons. The power of the natural affections over a rude nature is expressed most glowingly in the relenting of Hubert, but scarcely more touchingly than by the tears of Salisbury at the distress of Constance, or in his bitterness of heart at his false position as an enemy: − [Quotes 5.2.18–19], and by the generous indignation of the barons his companions, and of Faulconbridge no less, at the jeopardy and murder of Arthur. Formal religion is arrayed in the person of its official minister against the religion of humanity and sympathy; and the corruption of an artfully organized administration offends the spectator by assuming the honours and prerogatives of devotion and piety, when at war with all the feelings that by their essential qualities and in their own right are properly devout, moral and pious; and hence neither in falling off from their allegiance nor in returning to it do the barons admit the slightest weight, or even refer to the authority of Pandulph, a sign of the future which is quite as significant as the hankering of the kings and nobles after ecclesiastical hoards, which seconded the popular movement so efficiently at last.

Magna Charta is omitted in the play, and the obtaining of it from the reluctant and speedily recusant John was, in fact, as regards the leading movement of the reign, an episode, and omitted of necessity. The struggle that Magna Charta symbolizes awaited still its grandest manifestation when Shakespeare lived and wrote; and it was on the very day that he breathed his last at Stratford-upon-Avon, that a chief person in the action which is still undramatized, Oliver Cromwell, at the threshold of manhood was entering his name as a student at Sidney Sussex College, Cambridge. Still the genius of Magna Charta is infused into the play, and in the concession which John is forced to make to the barons in the interest of humanity and conciliation of his subjects, we recognize the seal of the cause of justice against arbitrary administration.

It is observable that after the legate, the excess of unscrupulousness and cruelty is the patrimony of the kings, − to some extent of Philip of France, though he is not utterly incapable of compunction, but chiefly of King John and his rival the Dauphin. The atmosphere of high place and isolated dignity hardens their hearts and deadens their nature so far as to render them entirely different to the nobles who otherwise are stern enough.

For the rest it is of course natural enough that a national poet should give a national advantage, and accordingly Shakespeare is not guilty of unduly ennobling the French. Their interested desertion of Constance and Arthur, after holy and conscientious professions, is placed in contrast to the pity of Salisbury; and not even John himself, suborning Hubert not without conscious shame and agitation, is so hateful as Lewis entertaining and seconding the Machiavellian prophecy of the Cardinal; even more degraded is the nature that appears in his misconception and mean consolation of the noble emotion of Salisbury: – [Quotes 5.2.54–62: 'Lift up thy brow, renowned Salisbury. . . .'].

Shakespeare's play of *King John* is immediately founded upon and follows an earlier play in two parts of the same subject and title [i.e., *The Troublesome Raigne*]. There is so much of sterling gold in the old, or rather say the earlier, *King John* in language and versification, in poetical ideas and expression, in humour, in power of dramatization, so to express the digesting of desultory narrative into an orderly series of scenes, and in adumbration of character, that the author has good claim for some trouble to be taken to identify him. . . .

[Lloyd now takes up the relationship between *The Troublesome Raigne* and *King John*, suggesting either Greene, Marlowe, Peele, or Lodge as possible authors of the former. He briefly treats the many parallels between the two plays and the expansion or deletion of material from the earlier drama, particularly as these bear upon the characters of John, Arthur, and the Bastard. He then takes up other possible sources of Shakespeare's play.]

. . . Of the still more remote sources of the character of Faulconbridge there is more to be said; but in illustration of the reference of the contest of the brothers to the political play, it may be noted that Robert and Philip Faulconbridge are like John and Arthur, rival kinsmen claiming an inheritance on grounds where right and equity, possession and personal qualifications, are strangely contrasted and complicated; and the tendencies of lucre and ambition as interfering with the delicacies of natural affection or domestic sympathy, are prepared for by one brother's cool exposition of the lapse of his mother, and the off-hand appeal of the other to the lady herself.

I cannot satisfy myself that there is positive proof that Shakespeare applied to Holinshed's Chronicle, or any other, for assistance or suggestion. But even if he did, the merit will still remain with the earlier writer, of inventing the main scheme of the dramatic digest of a disorderly period. He it was who recognized the effectiveness of making the murder of Arthur the very hinge and turning-point between the high-spirited success of the commencement of the reign, and the disgrace and dejection that ensued; and he it was who gave such heightening emphasis to the indignation excited by the death of Arthur, as to place the selfish and heartless policy of the princes and legate in the most obvious and odious light; and who, lastly, had the clearness of sight to fix upon the assertion of national independence against invading Frenchmen and encroaching ecclesiastics, as the true principle of dramatic action of the time. Time and the hour do not allow me to follow out all his footsteps, but I have seen enough to convince me that he diligently consulted not only Holinshed but the more varied and remote authorities.

Confining, however, our attention to Holinshed, there might be some reason to suspect that he had been read carelessly in one chief matter, were not the artistic motive for the interpretation adopted so evident. The sympathy for Arthur was chiefly among his own subjects or allies in Poictou or Brittany, the Britains, as they are called by the Chronicler, and the term may have been applied too extensively. John, after the capture of Arthur, caused himself to be re-crowned and then returned to Normandy, where 'true it is great suit was made to him to have Arthur set at liberty, as well as by the French King as by William de Riches, a valiant Baron of Poictou, and divers other noblemen of the Britains, who, when they could not prevail in their suit, they banded themselves together and joining in confederacy,' and so forth [III, 165].[1] Presently after follows the account of the relenting of Hubert de Burgh, and the reluctance of the meaner instruments; and lower down the murmurs of John's own knights, not however in the pure disinterestedness of the play, but in apprehension that, if taken by the King of France, they would be 'made to taste of the like cup' [III, 165]. The nearest approach to this motive in the old play is in the words of Essex: – 'What hope in us for mercy on a fault, / When kinsman dies without impeach of cause' [8.224ff.]. But this, perhaps, may be enough to assure us that it was in deliberate preference that the dramatist invented the nobler motive, or rather its unusual and exclusive force, and thus brought another group into happy composition with that supplied to him by the historian, of the lamenting and supplicant Arthur.

I think we must note it also as a happy error or equally happy thought of the first dramatist, to unite Austria and Lymoges into a single character, and thus concentrate the odium both of the imprisonment and death of Cœur-de-Lion on the antagonist of Faulconbridge. The research into the materials and hints that suggested the creation of the stalwart Englishman is interesting, but I can give the results of only a cursory examination. Holinshed has this passage which is usually cited, and, as far as it goes, is to the point: – 'The same year also (the first of John) Philip, bastard son to King Richard, to whom his father had given the castle and honour of Coynack, killed the Viscount of Lymoges, in revenge of his father's death, who was slain as ye have heard in besieging the castle of Chalus Cheverell' [III, 160]. The meagreness of this notice was remedied by the dramatist with fair dramatic skill, by combining the characteristics of another contemporary bastard who makes great figure for good or ill, but ever for energy as servant of King John. This is Foukes de Brent, or in the Latin of Matthew Paris, Falcasius, or Falco de Brenta, easily modified to Faulconbridge. At his first introduction he is mentioned as a knight who had been placed by King John in charge of the march of Wales, and then summoned to assist against the barons, A.D. 1212, and this is added – 'Erat autem *ruptarius nequissimus*, Neuster natione et *spurius*; sed et ipse multo crudelius quam ei jussum fuit in ipsos desævit sicut dicetur inferius.'[2] The promised notice recounts his taking various castles, especially that of Bedford which was given him by the king with a housekeeper to boot, the noble lady Margareta de Ripariis, or Margaret de Rivers, for a wife, together with all her possessions and the lands of many of the Barons. Hence in the old play Faulconbridge appeals to a half promise that he should wed the Lady Blanch and have a fair dowry of lands; and Shakespeare retains at least a hint of his sense of the aid that knighthood gives the match and money seekers, 'Well now I can make any Joan a lady' [1.1.184]. Less questionable activities are recorded of the worthy in the operations under Henry III. which resulted in the expulsion of Lewis from the country. A considerable detachment of the French party were in possession of Lincoln city and pressed the siege of the castle, which was held against them valiantly by a noble lady Nichola. The Earl of Pembroke invested the city and assaulted the gates and was opposed from the walls. In the meantime Foukes de Brent entered the castle at the back by a postern gate with considerable force, and rushing thence into the city took the defendants in the rear. On this diversion the gates were presently forced, and after a severe battle within the walls the French party was defeated with great slaughter, and the day, which was Saturday in Whitsun-week, was called thereafter in derision, Lewis's fair. I am quite prepared to expect that the scheme of Faulconbridge to attack Angiers simultaneously on opposite sides, which is indicated in the earlier play, was in fact borrowed from this exploit. . . . (379–95)

28 John Charles Bucknill, the madness of Constance

1859

From *The Psychology of Shakespeare* (London, 1859).

Sir John Charles Bucknill (1817–97) was a successful physician, specializing in the treatment of the mentally ill, who from 1862 to 1876 served as the Lord Chancellor's medical visitor of lunatics. A member of the Royal College of Physicians, he delivered a series of lectures to that body in 1878 on 'Insanity and its Legal Relations'. Bucknill was noted for his enlightened attitudes toward those suffering from mental illness; and his chapters on the diagnosis, pathology, and treatment of psychological disorders in *A Manual of Psychological Medicine* (London, 1858), which he co-authored with Daniel H. Tuke, served for many years as the standard treatment of these subjects. He also wrote an extensive and detailed study on *The Medical Knowledge of Shakespeare* (London, 1860), which is largely a compendium of all the passages in Shakespeare that allude in any way to disease, illness, or medical practice. *The Psychology of Shakespeare* was reprinted, with very slight revisions, under the title *The Mad Folk of Shakespeare* (London, 1867).

CONSTANCE.

Constance is delineated with Greek simplicity. The grandeur of one great passion is weakened by no subordinate parts of character on which the mind can rest and feel relief. All is simple and clear, like the one thrilling note of a trumpet, rising higher or falling lower, but never altering its tone. The wondrous eloquence in which the passion clothes itself does but display its force. Its unity and direction of purpose remain unchanging and unchangeable. Passion is not seen except when transformed into action. Like a great wind, it would be voiceless except for opposition; it would be viewless except for its effects. There may be a few tossed leaves, or a whirling cloud-rack, or the crash of forests. The invisible force remains the same, measured most imperfectly by the casualties of resistance.

But this passion itself, single in its onward force, is not altogether so in its nature and origin. It wears the garb of maternal affection, of the strong love a widowed mother bears to her only child; but as in Queen Margaret [in the *Henry VI* plays], the fury of ambition is added: ambition for herself, as much as for her son, which Elinor perceives, and with wounding truth expresses: 'Out insolent! thy bastard shall be king, / That thou may'st be a queen and check the world' [2.1.122ff.]. This fierce desire of power and place, which is but coldly expressed in the word ambition, is as undeniable in Constance as her mother's love. Had she no child she would be ambitious for herself. Having one, she is more vehemently ambitious for him, and indirectly for herself. The tenderness of love alone would have led her to shun contention and to withdraw her child from danger; as Andromache sought to withhold her husband from the field of honour with unalloyed womanly apprehension. But love influenced by ambition, and ambition stimulated by love, produced that compound passion which incurred all risks, braved all dangers. Combined passions are weak or strong, according to their perfection of union, and singleness of purpose. If concurrent desires are but half of one mind, they pull diverse ways, and give rise to the weakness of inconsistency; but if they are thoroughly of one accord, chemically combined as it were, the product acquires new and irresistible strength. This force of compound emotion is finely developed in Constance, in contrast with the other female characters of the drama. Ambitious without love, she would have possessed the hard vigour of Elinor; loving without ambition, she would have been tenderly devoted like Blanch. Under the lash of the combined passion she is a fury, whom her boundless love and her deep woe barely suffice to redeem from our horror.

The first words of Constance are those of prudent advice, the suggestion of a strong vehement nature against the first move in the dread game of war. They contrast well with the ready boasts of a coward Austria and feeble France: 'Stay for an answer to your embassy, / Lest unadvis'd you stain your swords with blood' [2.1.44ff.]. It is the only tranquil speech which the poor woman is permitted to utter. The scolding match into which she immediately precipitates herself with Queen Elinor develops the irritability and vehemence of her temper. To Elinor's taunt of unchastity she replies with acrid *tu quoque*[1] invective. She fairly overwhelms the queen-mother with vituperation, and does her best to merit the contemptuous entreaty of John, 'Bedlam, have done!' [2.1.183] and at length the expostulations of her own friend: [Quotes 2.1.191–7: the interchange involving Elinor, Constance, and Philip]. She has already incurred the remonstrance of her gentle son: [Quotes 2.1.163–5: 'Good my mother, peace. . . .'].

Her very tenderness to her child is fierce, like that of some she-beast of prey. Had there been no motive in the mother's heart but that of love, this appeal might well have checked not only the unbridled use of speech, but the dangerous course of action into which Constance throws herself. But at this period, ambition is stronger than love, and it would be hard to say to what extent ambition for herself was not mixed up with that for her son. The scene affords clear insight into the natural character of Constance, as a proud ambitious woman, of irritable and ungoverned temper. The flight of her imagination, like that of her passion, is yet comparatively low. She well scolds her opponents indeed, but not until later is her unrivalled power of invective fully developed.

In nothing is Shakespeare's master-hand more evident than in the manner in which he lays a true and consistent foundation for his characters. To have built such an one as that of Constance, on the basis of the common female virtues, would have been monstrous. Constance, in whom fierce passion is not the result, but the cause of madness, could only have been from the beginning, what she is plainly shewn to have been, a haughty, irascible woman, whose tongue and temper were dreaded by friend and foe.

Although accurate history has little to do with dramatic representation of character, it is worthy of remark, that the imperious claim of Constance to the crown of England for her son, was not founded upon that indefeasible right which would have been recognized at a later period. . . .

When the alliance between John and Philip has been determined, the latter enquires for her, and the Dauphin replies, 'She is sad and passionate in your highness' tent' [2.1.544]. Philip thinks the peace 'will give her sadness very little cure,' and in real apprehension asks his brother of England, 'how may we content this widow lady?' [2.1.546ff.]. John proposes to give up Bretagne and other dignities and powers to Arthur, and trusts in this manner to appease if not to satisfy her ambition, and avert her vituperation: [Quotes 2.1.555–8]. John, however, had reckoned without his host; the lady's will was not to be so readily satisfied, nor her passionate exclamation so easily stopped. When Salisbury bears to her the message of the kings, and the information of their new compact, her rage knows no bounds, and the expression of it is as vehemently eloquent as that of her passionate grief when she has really lost all. Those, who in deference to the sacred virtues of womanhood attribute all the language and conduct of Constance to the all-sanctifying motive of maternal love, will do well to remark that this passionate scene takes place while her son is with her and free from danger, except that which her own ambition prepares for him. Her rage arises from the thought that Blanch shall have those provinces instead of her son: [Quotes 3.1.1–18, 29–37]. In this violent language the spirit of disappointed ambition is paramount: ambition not only for Arthur but for herself, 'What becomes of me?' [3.1.35]. The attack on Salisbury, the innocent messenger, so unworthy of a lady and a princess, can only be excused on the supposition that she is beside herself with fruitless rage, and vents it on any one within reach. It wants but little that she should turn her tongue or her hands even upon Arthur. When, alarmed by her fury, he interposes, 'I do beseech you, madam, be content' [3.1.42], she replies with a strange sophistry, which a true mother's heart would never employ, that if he were 'grim, ugly, and sland'rous to his mother's womb,' &c.:

> I would not care, I then would be content;
> For then I should not love thee; no, nor thou
> Become thy great birth, and deserve a crown. [3.1.43ff.]

When was true mother's love ever measured by the beauty of her child? When did it not rather increase with the child's imperfections? Sacred miracle of nature, a mother's love hangs not on such casual gifts as form and beauty. The crétin idiot, hideous and half-human, claims and receives more than its share. Even moral deformities cannot exhaust this unselfish all-enduring fount of love; as the reprobate son, the outcast of the family, knows full well, feeling that there is a bond holding him to one pure heart which can never loosen. But the love of Constance is alloyed with pride, and ambition, and selfishness. Not simply because Arthur is her son is he dear to her, but also because he is rightful heir to a crown, and because his beauty flatters her pride: 'Of nature's gifts thou may'st with lilies boast, / And with the half-blown rose' [3.1.53ff.]. With the true selfishness of intense pride, she attributes the sufferance of all Arthur's injuries to herself. She alone feels and must under-bear the woes of disappointed ambition. She calls upon the peer whom she has so insolently and causelessly abused, to assist in her vituperations: [Quotes 3.1.62–5: 'Tell me, thou fellow. . . .']. She will not go with Salisbury to the kings. Did they know her truly they would never send for her. She is in an ecstasy of passion, which she miscalls grief and sorrow. The idea that she will make the huge firm earth the throne of this great emotion carries one beyond the earth in its grandeur. The intensity of her passion is almost Satanic. Her humanity is alone vindicated by her subjection to its powers. Such passion in a questionable cause, moving a strong nature, would excite only fear and abhorrence; endured by a weak one it excites our extremest pity. Insanity alone redeems such passion to the kindred of womanhood, and is already foreshadowed in that culminating point where the extremes of pride and grief meet in the dust: [Quotes 3.1.68–74: 'I will instruct my sorrows to be proud. . . .'].

There is one word in the above quotations which must not pass without comment. Constance avows herself in ill health: 'For I am *sick*' [3.1.12]. This point of physical disturbance is rarely omitted by Shakespeare, in the development of insanity. It may be referred to in this instance in the most casual and careless manner, for the drama can take little cognizance of the physical imperfections of our nature. Still, however skillfully and imperceptible, the point is made. In a sick frame, passion like that of Constance would have fuller sway. The irritable nerves would act and re-act on the irritated mind. Emotion would obtain more complete and disastrous empire.

When Constance, unobserved before, rises from the ground amidst the congratulating court, with the dignified and solemn denunciation of kingly treachery, one of the finest possible dramatic effects is produced with the simplest means. Her eloquence throughout this scene is magnificent. The interests even of kingdoms seem below its lofty aim. The truth of kings, and, as a minor term, the truth of all other men, is counterfeit. The invocation to the Heavens, that they should arm for her, and be husband to her, and set discord betwixt these perjured kings, is the climax of eloquence. To Austria's entreaty, 'Lady Constance, peace' [3.1.112]; she replies in utter forgetfulness of all miseries except her own: 'War! War! War! peace is to me a war' [3.1.113]. No idea of the Pythoness, or of any woman inspired by good or evil influences, ever represented a more extatic state of eloquent emotion. The poet's own representation of inspired insanity, Cassandra in *Troilus and Cressida*, is tame and indistinct, in comparison: [Quotes *Troilus and Cressida*, 2.2.100–1]. Constance descends from this exalted strain, to wither Austria with her unmatched powers of vituperation, in which she does not even disdain a ridiculous image: 'Thou wear a lion's hide! doff it, for shame, / And hang a calf-skin on those recreant limbs' [3.1.128ff.]. The war she invokes is near at hand in the 'holy errand' [3.1.137] of the Legate. When this clerical despot pours the vials of the church's wrath on the head of John, who 'blasphemes' [3.1.161] in terms of English patriotism and protestantism, Constance must vie with the curses of authority, for which there's 'law and warrant' [3.1.184]: [Quotes 3.1.179–83: 'O, lawful let it be. . . .']. Afterwards she only contributes short sentences to the dialogue, so pregnant with mighty interest; but they are artfully conceived to incline the wavering mind of King Philip and Lewis to the warlike decision she so ardently desires, and they are expressed with fierce unity of purpose. As she has imprecated from heaven the bloody arbitrament of battle, she invokes hell itself, to alarm the timid soul of Philip: 'Look to that devil! lest that France repent, / And by disjoining hands, hell lose a soul' [3.1.196ff.]. Lewis she taunts with his unfledged bride, and the coyness of his honour. Her passion stimulates her lofty intellect, and enables her to suggest in the strongest possible manner to each person, the motive likely to weigh most.

She gains her purpose, and the issue of war is to decide her rights. Blanch, with true woman's heart, laments for the sake of those she loves simply and for themselves. To her, 'The sun's o'ercast with blood' [3.1.326]. But Constance, to whom peace is war, war is of all things most welcome, as the means to the end of her ambition, her fiendish ambition. May those who seek for war ever bear its heaviest penalties. May the general murderer feel the truth of Pandulph's assertion of the particular one: 'For he that steeps his safety in true blood, / Shall find but bloody safety and untrue' [3.4.147ff.]. So it is with Constance. She loses her cause and her son, and the passion of ambitious love now appears in the form of grief, perhaps of remorse.

When all purpose of ambition is at an end, and even the chief object of it lost, its instigations are no longer predominant in the poor woman's heart; in the prostrating grief she now endures there is no thought of the lost kingdom; one monster grief, like Aaron's rod, devours all smaller ones; there is from henceforth only one thought, one feeling, one mental object, one fixed idea, – that her son is for ever lost. King Philip recognizes in her one already dead to the world: [Quotes 3.4.17–19]. Constance taunts him with his and her own calamities as the result of his peace, whereas they were in reality the issue of her war. This is the only point on which her quick intellect ever trips. She shews no signs of bending, though her spirit is wounded unto death. Her invincible pride rejects all comfort, all solace. The charnel-house ideas of her invocation to death is poetic delirium, the frenzy of imagination. Juliet's imagination, embracing the same ideas, is feeble and prosaic compared with this horror: [Quotes 3.4.23–36: 'No, I defy all counsel. . . .']. In her fierce, unconquerable pride, she would make death itself obey her as a vassal, and would shake the world even in leaving it: [Quotes 3.4.38–40: 'O that my tongue were in the thunder's mouth. . . .'].

Pandulph tells her plainly that she is mad, and rouses that eloquent defence of her reason, in which she repeats the test of madness which Lear applies to himself, the recognition of personal identity, and in which she expresses the same idea of madness as a refuge from sorrow, which Gloucester does:

> *Pand.*   Lady, you utter madness, and not sorrow.
> *Const.*   Thou art not holy to belie me so;
>   I am not mad: this hair I tear, is mine;
>   My name is Constance; I was Geffrey's wife:
>   Young Arthur is my son, and he is lost:
>   I am not mad: – I would to heaven, I were!
>   For then, 'tis like, I should forget myself:
>   O, if I could, what grief should I forget! –
>   Preach some philosophy to make me mad,

> And thou shalt be canoniz'd cardinal;
> For, being not mad, but sensible of grief,
> My reasonable part produces reason,
> How I may be deliver'd of these woes,
> And teaches me to kill or hang myself:
> If I were mad, I should forget my son;
> Or madly think, a babe of clouts were he:
> I am not mad: too well, too well I feel
> The different plague of each calamity. [3.4.43ff.]

. . . Angrily as Constance rejects the idea of madness, yet she is mad; the very type of acute reasoning mania. In real life the intellect would scarcely be so consistent and consecutive in its operations; but in real life neither sane nor insane people talk blank verse, and express even their deepest emotions in the magnificent imagery which great poets use. The raving of maniacal frenzy, in which the emotions are exclusively involved, would be represented by short and broken sentences, in which every link in the idea-chain would not be expressed, and which would therefore represent, more or less the features of incoherence. The poet fills up these chasms in the sense, and clothes the whole in the glowing language of excited intellectual power; and thus we have in Constance the representation of a frenzied woman, speaking with more arrangement of ideas, than frenzy really permits. King Philip bids her bind up her tresses, which she has been madly tearing with her own hands to prove herself not mad. These tresses, 'Where but by chance a silver drop hath fallen' [3.4.63], she will bind up as she is bid; she will even do this in fanciful reference to the one subject of all thought, her son's imprisonment: [Quotes 3.4.70–5].

The despairing cry of overwhelming misery, which can apprehend no hope even in heaven, expresses itself in the fancy that she can never again see her son even beyond the grave, for canker sorrow will change him:

> And so he'll die; and, rising so again,
> When I shall meet him in the court of heaven
> I shall not know him: therefore never, never
> Must I behold my pretty Arthur more. [3.4.86ff.]

Her last words indicate a state of hallucination. Grief represents her son's voice and figure to her senses. Or if this be not taken literally, it at least represents one manner in which hallucination is produced. An absorbing emotion constantly directs the attention to one idea-image. This creation of the mind at length becomes accepted by the sense, and the hallucination of insanity exists. This differs in its origin, and its significance, from hallucination arising from some abnormal state of the nerves of sense merely, which may exist, as it did in Ben Jonson and Nicolai,[2] without any deviation from a sound state of mental health. If the lively representation of Arthur's presence be not intended to convey the idea of actual hallucination, it at least expresses the complete dominion which an absorbing emotion attains over the attention and mental conception: [Quotes 3.4.92–106: Constance's conversation with Philip, during which Constance claims that Grief takes the place of her child, and exits tearing her hair].

The frightful spectacle, of acute mania pursuing its course to a fatal end, was no attractive subject for dramatic representation. Shakespeare exhibited the growing horror to the extreme limit which decent regard to human weakness permitted, and then mercifully drew the veil. The spectacle of sleepless nights and restless days, of fierce raving and desperate outrage until exhausted nature sinks, this he could not and would not exhibit to the public gaze. In one short line alone he tells the end, 'The Lady Constance in a frenzy died' [4.2.122]. . . .

Constance even more than Lear establishes the fact that Shakespeare held the origin and nature of insanity to be emotional. Until the last there is no delusion, scarcely a deviation from reason, and yet she is conducted through a tempest of emotional disturbance into the very midst of maniacal excitement. All the causes of disease are purely emotional. The predisposing cause is her fiercely passionate disposition. The exciting cause is grief. The symptoms are the same as the causes, transformed into abnormal conditions of degree. Disorder in the wit is felt, but scarcely exhibited. Loss of control over the operation of the intellect is manifested in the last speech only [3.4.93–105], or perhaps also in the disconnected expression preceding, 'To England if you will' [3.4.68]. Nature is above art, as Lear says [*King Lear*, 4.6.86] and a truth now appreciated by science needs not the support of opinion even from so great an artist as Shakespeare. But perfect art is founded upon science, the science of exact observation at least, and to such a test there can be little doubt that this character was submitted in the crucible of the poet's great brain, before it was moulded into that form of fierce power and beauty, in which it excites our admiration and awe. The wondrous eloquence of Constance is second to that of no other character except Lear. It would seem that Shakespeare revels in the free swing of fancy, in the repudiation of all mental restraint which half madness justifies. He uses these characters as the motley favourites of old courts were often used, to speak bitter truth without fear or favour, without hesitation or retention, without prudential subtraction or self-seeking after thought. The madmen of Shakespeare are his broadest exponents of humanity.

In the development of the insanity of Constance, the power of passion finds a potent ally in that of imagination. Imagination, that creative faculty which paints in the mind's eye those images which in health may be dismissed at will, but which in disease haunt the oppressed brain with their importunate presence. The faculty of forming sensational ideas without the intervention of the external senses, is one which, if not kept in subjection to a sober judgment, is more perilous to mental health than ought else except unbridled passion. In actual insanity this function runs riot, and the world of reality is supplanted by that of fancy. . . . (213–28)

29 Richard Grant White, background and critical notes to *King John*

1859

From *The Works of William Shakespeare. The Plays Edited from the Folio of MDCXXIII, with Various Readings from All the Editions and All the Commentators, Notes, Introductory Remarks, a Historical Sketch of the Text, an Account of the Rise and Progress of the English Drama, a Memoir of the Poet, and an Essay upon his Genius* (12 vols, Boston, 1857–66). Volume VI. *King John; Richard II; 1 Henry IV; 2 Henry IV* (1859).

Richard Grant White (1821–85) was a lawyer by training, but by temperament far more suited to the study of art, music, and literature. His many articles on politics, criticism, and the arts appeared regularly in such periodicals as *Putnam's Magazine*, *Atlantic Monthly*, *The Galaxy* and the London *Spectator*. White's reputation as a Shakespearian today rests largely upon his neat and erudite exposure of John Payne Collier's forgeries in *Shakespeare's Scholar* (New York, 1854); his edition of the plays had the bad fortune to appear while Clark, Glover, and Wright were publishing the most influential text of the century, the so-called 'Globe' edition (London, 1864), derived from their 'Cambridge Shakespeare' (9 vols, Cambridge, 1863–66), consequently obscuring the importance of White's achievement and that of most other editors of the day. White's text, however, was republished as *The Riverside Shakespeare* (3 vols, Boston, 1883), and also served as the basis of a later edition called *The New Grant White Shakespeare*, newly edited and annotated by William P. Trent, Benjamin W. Wells, and John B. Henneman (18 vols, Boston, 1912).

[From the Introduction to *King John*]

Shakespeare's Historical Plays are often discoursed about as if they were a projected series of interdependent works, written in pursuance of a plan, the purpose of which was to illustrate English History. That they illustrate history, and in a certain sense were meant to do so, is manifest upon their very face; but that they do this in conformity with a systematic design, there is neither external nor internal evidence to show. The origin of a contrary opinion must be traced to a tradition first mentioned by Gildon, according to which Shakespeare told Ben Jonson, that 'finding the nation generally very ignorant of history, he wrote plays in order to instruct the people in that particular.'[1] But of all the unfounded stories told of Shakespeare, this is the most difficult of belief. Such a declaration could not have been made by one of those men to the other with a grave face, actors though they were. For Historical Plays, or Histories, as they were called, were in vogue with our ancestors before Shakespeare began to write for the stage; and so far was he from seeking to impart historical knowledge to the audiences at the Blackfriars, that he did not even attempt to correct the grossest violations of historical truth in the older play upon which he founded one of his Histories – this very *King John*; and in other instances, in which he went for his story directly to the Chronicles, he did not hesitate to bring together events really separated by years, (though connected as cause and effect, or means to a common end), when, by so grouping them, he could produce a vivid and impressive dramatic picture of the period which he undertook to represent.

In writing the Histories he had the same purpose as in writing the Comedies and Tragedies; that purpose always being, to make a good play: and with him a good play was one which would fill the theatre whenever it was performed, and at the same time give utterance to his teeming brain, and satisfy his dramatic intuition. He wrote Histories because they suited the taste of the day; and in their composition, – no less, and no more, than in that of Comedies and Tragedies, – he used, as the basis of his work, the materials nearest at hand and best suited to his purpose. He would have written a play upon the life and death of King Lud, had any incidents in the reign of that monarch susceptible of dramatic treatment been known to him; and, above all, had some dramatist of the preceding generation produced a successful play founded upon them which he could have used as foundation or as scaffolding. . . .

Two of Shakespeare's Histories – *King John* and *Henry VIII.* – are entirely isolated. The latter was written as a show piece; the former because its main incidents appealed to the patriotic and protestant feeling of the Elizabethan era, and because the subject was one already familiar to the public and there was an old play at hand to work upon. The events of King John's reign had twice been made the subject of dramatic treatment before Shakespeare produced his History: once by Bishop Bale, the zealous reformer, whose *Kynge Johan*[2] is a singular cross between the Moral play with its allegorical characters, and the Historical play with its real personages, and distinctly marks a transition period in our early drama; and again by certain unknown authors who produced *The Troublesome Raigne of John, King of England*,[3] the play on which Shakespeare founded his *Life and Death of King John*.

Of the prelate's play, Shakespeare probably knew nothing; yet it is certain that his own was in some measure affected by it. *Kynge Johan* was written to make proselytes to the reformed church; and the events of that monarch's reign which the author selected as the basis of his work were those only which could be used to the prejudice of the Church of Rome; – the dictatorial assumption of the Pope, the King's resistance, the consequent interdict and the suffering caused by it, the final submission of John, and his alleged death by poison administered by a fanatical monk of Swinstead Abbey. The play is without interest of any kind: no ray of poetry or wit, no gleam even of keen malice, lights up the uncouth structure of its antiquated verse; its allegorical and historical personages are alike in their tameness and want of character; story or plan it has none; and the ribaldry and grossness of its language are entirely at variance with our notions of decency, not to say of clerical dignity. Yet it determined, in a measure, the form of Shakespeare's *King John*, because it created a precedent which was followed by the intermediate play, which Shakespeare followed in his turn. The great dramatist modified the structure of a play which itself was but a modification of another; and thus, like some abbey or minster, the noble fabric rose from additions to and alterations of an original mean and rude, yet not without an inherent strength and vitality of purpose.

As Bishop Bale's play was quite surely written after the accession of Edward VI., and could not have been produced after Mary had ascended the throne with any hope that it would be performed, the year 1550 may safely be assumed as about the date of its appearance. It seems more than probable that after the five years' gloom of Mary's bloody and bigoted despotism had passed away, *Kynge Johan* emerged again into genial light, to be welcomed with enthusiasm; and that it was to take advantage of the favor which its subject had acquired, that *The Troublesome Raigne of King John* was written about thirty years afterward. In the rapidly advancing state of our drama at that time, *Kynge Johan* had become obsolete in its very form and elements ere the generation that first received it as a novelty had passed away. The play which took its place was entirely different from its predecessor in motive as well as in structure. In *The Troublesome Raigne* no allegorical personages appear; and ecclesiastical protestantism is not taught in dull didactics or scurrilous polemics. The characters are all copied from real life or taken from history; and they appear upon the stage only in connection with the incidents upon which the interest of the play depends. It is in spirit and form absolutely dramatic, though not highly so, and is as purely a historical play as that which succeeded and eclipsed it. It only fails to be as good, because among all its authors there was not a ray of the genius which blazed, sun-like, in the all-illuminating mind of Shakespeare. Yet it is interesting to observe in *The Troublesome Raigne* the introduction of Faulconbridge as a compensation for the loss of Sedition, an allegorical character that supplied the comic element of the elder piece. He is no more like Shakespeare's Faulconbridge than a practical joke is like wit; but in his scenes with the monks he fulfilled the jester's function, and made the sport needful for the people.[4] For in *The Troublesome Raigne* the attacks upon the church of Rome take the form of acted satire, and the Bastard, when sent by King John to extort money from an abbey, after a scene of ludicrous expostulation on the part of a friar, finds a nun hidden in the abbot's chest where he expected to find 'a thousand pound in silver and in gold' [6.38]. It need hardly be said that Shakespeare could have retained this laughable incident with advantage, had he chosen to do so; but patriotism, not fanaticism, animated his play; and he avoided here, as, indeed, he always did, the offence of holding one body of Christians up to the malicious ridicule of another. He continued the Bastard, however, in his office of mirth provider, by his masterly development of the braggart of the old play, (who is only Pistol without his cowardice and his ridiculous absurdity,) into a matchless embodiment of that kind of manhood whose fullness of animal life and boundless good humor, joined to a sturdy common sense and a downrightness of disposition which often becomes impudence, always turn the momentary laugh against the feeble propriety of men like 'old Sir Robert's son' [1.1.224] and the noisy assumption of pompous pretenders like the Archduke of Austria.

Though there is no likeness between the characters or the poetry of the old play, and those of Shakespeare's, the dramatis personæ and the course of events are nearly the same in both. In both we have King John, Queen Elinor, Constance, Arthur, Hubert, the Faulconbridges, Philip of France, Louis [i.e., Lewis], Blanch, Chatillion, Pandulph, Melun, and the other minor characters; – even Peter of Pomfret is not forgotten. In both the action opens with the threatening interview between Chatillion and King John, which is succeeded by the introduction of the Faulconbridges: in both the action is next transferred to France before Angiers, where the same contention with the same hymeneal termination takes place, the rejoicing being in both interrupted by the entrance of Pandulph to break the new-knit bonds asunder and provoke the battle which costs Austria his head. In both Arthur is committed to the care of Hubert, who undertakes to kill him, or put out his eyes, but relents; Arthur being killed in his attempt to escape, and his death precipitating the revolt of the nobles: in both the King yields to Rome, receives his crown from the Pope's legate, and is poisoned by a monk. The changes which Shakespeare made in the composition of the play are the result of omission and condensation. He compressed all the essential action of a long, tedious dramatic story in two parts into an ordinary five act piece, in which, although there is less of bustle and incident than is crowded into *Richard III.*, events of importance and scenes of interest succeed each other so rapidly that the attention is kept constantly awake.

Although not even the germ of any thought, or scene, or character, (except, perhaps, Queen Elinor) that gives Shakespeare's *King John* its value, is to be found in *The Troublesome Raigne*, that play is not without some poetical and dramatic merit, which, indeed, is considerable for a drama produced in its period of the Elizabethan era; and, what is far more important to the subject in hand, there is evidence in the former that the language of the latter was much in Shakespeare's mind, even if its text were not constantly before his eyes, while he was writing the new play. Numerous instances of parallel passages in which the thought is similar and the words sometimes the same are cited in the Notes,[5] and will show the reader that Shakespeare worked with the old play in his head if not in his hand; nevertheless in no degree diminishing our admiration of the greatness and fecundity of the genius, which, having conceived by such a play as that, could bring forth such a play as this. . . . (VI, 7–14)

[From the Notes to *King John*]

[On 3.1.1: 'Gone to be married? Gone to swear a peace. . . .', the place at which Theobald begins Act III, relocating it from 3.1.74, where it begins in the First Folio][6]

Here Theobald began Act III. which in the folio, as in this edition, begins with the entrance of the two Kings, Louis [i.e., Lewis], Blanch, and the rest after the marriage; and now for a century and a quarter his arrangement has been accepted by all editors, either without remark, or with commendation, as being in the words of Johnson 'judicious,' in those of Malone 'certainly right,' in those of Mr. Collier the correction of 'a decided error.'[7] But an examination of the text, and of Theobald's reasons for the change made by him, leads to a directly opposite conclusion. Theobald justified himself on the ground that "tis evident Lady Constance in her Despair seats herself on the Floor: and She must be supposed as I formerly observ'd immediately to rise again, only to go off & end the Act decently; or the flat Scene must shut her in from the Sight of the Audience, an Absurdity,' he says, 'I cannot wish to accuse Shakespeare of.' From the suspicion of such an 'absurdity,' he relieves Shakespeare by making the third Act begin with this Scene, and for these reasons: – 'The Match being concluded, in the Scene before That, betwixt the Dauphin & Blanch, a Messenger is sent for Lady Constance to K. Philip's Tent for Her to come to St. Mary's Church to the Solemnity, The Princes all go out: as to the Marriage; and the Bastard staying a little behind, to descant on Interest and Commodity, very properly ends the Act. The next Scene then in the French King's Tent brings us Salisbury delivering his Message to Constance, who refusing to go to the Solemnity, sets herself down on the Floor. The whole Train returning from the Church to the French King's Pavilion, Philip expresses such Satisfaction on Occasion of the happy Solemnity of that Day, that Constance rises from the Floor & joins in the Scene by entering her Protest against their Joy, & cursing the Business of the Day. Thus, I conceive, the Scenes are fairly continued, and there is no Chasm in the Action, but a proper Interval made both for Salisbury's coming to Lady Constance, and for the Solemnization of the Marriage. Besides, as Faulconbridge is evidently the Poet's favourite character, 'twas very well judged to close the Act with his Soliloquy.'

Theobald's notion, that to end the Act decently Constance must rise and go off the stage, is as little worth attention as his remark about the 'flat Scene.' In Shakespeare's days there were no flat scenes; and that the curtain should fall upon Constance as, drawing her boy to her breast, she seats herself upon the ground, will certainly be considered by stage managers and dramatic critics not only a 'decent,' but a very impressive manner of using the situation and closing the Scene. In the phraseology of the modern stage, it presents a very fine tableau. With regard to the 'chasm in the action,' and the 'proper interval for Salisbury's coming to Lady Constance,' Theobald and his followers seem to have forgotten, first, the relative situation of places and personages, and next, that when a King sends an Earl to bid a Princess to a royal marriage, at least time enough is to be allowed for the messenger to perform his office and return. The Kings, just at the gate of Angiers, are about to go, in such 'unprepared pomp' 'as haste will suffer' to Saint Mary's Chapel, to celebrate the marriage: a 'speedy messenger' is required to summon Constance to the ceremony, and the Earl of Salisbury undertakes the office [2.1.554ff.]. He has only to go to the French King's tent, just outside the walls of the town; and he leaves the gates at the same time that the royal parties enter them. The Bastard's soliloquy gives him time to reach the French King's tent; and there, at the opening of the next Scene, we find him, having, as we learn from Constance's exclamation, just delivered his message. She refuses to be present at the marriage, and sits enthroned in sorrow upon the ground. Salisbury returns with her answer; the preparation for the marriage and the ceremony itself take place between the Acts, without her presence; and the third Act opens with the entrance of the newly allied Kings and the newly married pair, – Philip naturally being host in his own land, and introducing his daughter-in-law to his pavilion, where of course the moody Constance is found with Arthur.

But according to Theobald's disarrangement of the order of the original copy, at the very time when Salisbury delivers his message to Constance, summoning her to the solemnization of the marriage, the ceremony has already taken place; and she has hardly refused to be present at it, when the royal trains enter the tent, which Salisbury has little more than reached, although since he left them they have made some hasty preparation for the marriage, gone to Saint Mary's Chapel in the town, had the ceremony performed, and come thence to the very place whither their 'hasty messenger' was sent! Theobald might know no better than this, but Salisbury did; for his last speech, when Constance tells him to return without her, and before she sits upon the ground, is, 'Pardon me, madam; I may not go without you to the Kings' [3.1.65ff.]; which shows his consciousness that the ceremony awaited his return, and which is made ridiculous by the immediate entrance of Philip with Blanch as his daughter-in-law. The interval between the Acts is necessary, as Theobald remarks, for the solemnization of the marriage, but clearly not for Salisbury's coming to Constance; and the marriage takes place between the Acts according to either arrangement.

It is noteworthy that although the exits at the ends of Acts andScenes are marked with particular care in the folio, none is directed after Constance's last speech in this Scene; which supports the belief that on Shakespeare's stage the curtain fell as she sat upon the ground. With the Third Act, too, according to the original division, comes in a new element of dramatic interest: the power of Rome in the person of Pandulph appears upon the scene, which hitherto has been entirely occupied by the conflicting interests of England and France, John and Arthur. A break in the action is therefore required by the unity of dramatic interest which seems to have been the great principle upon which Shakespeare constructed his dramas. . . . Theobald's arrangement, which has so long obtained, would not have been disturbed in this edition, had not the change seemed imperatively necessary. The reader was entitled to the reasons for the return to the original division; and for the convenience of those who refer to the play for quotations, the beginning of Theobald's Act III. is indicated in the text.

Neither history nor the old *King John* aids us in determining this question. For no such events as those which occupy the second Act of this play and the first Scene of the third, took place; Blanch having been espoused in England and brought solemnly over to France to be married, and Pandulph not having been appointed legate until five years after the espousals. In the old play Constance and Arthur are present when the Citizen of Angiers proposes the marriage; and they remain on the stage during its solemnization. This noble Scene, unsurpassed in dramatic literature, is in its action no less than its poetry entirely Shakespeare's. (VI, 117–19)

30 Charles Cowden Clarke, characterization, craft, and the philosophy of war

1863

From *Shakespeare-Characters; Chiefly Those Subordinate* (London, 1863).

Charles Cowden Clarke (1787–1877), author, editor, and lecturer, spent a fruitful and happy life devoted to art, music, and literature. While still in his teens, he served as a tutor to John Keats at the Middlesex school kept by his father, John Clarke, and remained on warm terms throughout his life with many of the leading figures of English romanticism. His marriage to Mary Victoria Novello, the daughter of a long-time friend, was happy in all respects, not the least of which being the opportunity it afforded the Clarkes to collaborate on a number of important literary studies. Among these were *The Shakespeare Key* (London, 1879) and *Recollections of Writers* (London, 1878), which included many pleasant letters and memoirs of Keats, Leigh Hunt, the Lambs, and other well-known literary figures of the nineteenth century. Perhaps the greatest accomplishment of Clarke's scholarly life, however, was his enormously popular series of lectures on Shakespeare and other dramatists and poets, many of which were later published. The lectures included in *Shakespeare-Characters* were among Clarke's most famous; even in these 'revised and remodelled' versions, one can glean something of the rhetorical clarity, dramatic polish, and earnest appreciation of the morality of Shakespeare's art that made Clarke's lectures so appealing to nineteenth-century audiences.

[From Chapter XIII]

... The prevailing characteristic both of the plot and of the chief personages in the play of *King John* is that of 'craft.' The poet, it is true, has taken – as he found it in the monkish record – the *historical* character of the king; but he has, with his own supreme genius, worked it out from the first scene to the last with undeviating consistency, and a revolting determination of purpose. He has shown him to us, seizing with unscrupulous hand the birthright and throne belonging to another, and that other his own orphan nephew. He has shown him to us preparing to pour forth the blood, and peril the lives of his subjects in support of this bad, unjust cause, in a war with France, when it disputes his usurping claim. He has shown him to us revolving in his selfish expediency how extortion and oppression at home shall supply the expenses thus incurred abroad. ...

We next see him paltering and sophisticating with the truth in the matter of Robert Faulconbridge's heritage, preparing to wrest the estate from the legitimate son, and to bestow it on the illegitimate one – contrary to the will of the bequeather – on a plea false in spirit, though plausible in letter.

His next appearance is on the shores of France, making wheedling speeches to his nephew, Arthur, specious ones to the citizens of Angiers, patching up hollow compacts with the French king, followed by sudden breach of faith, and reckless plunge into the carnage of the battle-field.

Then comes his dark purpose against his young kinsman distilled into Hubert's ear: and then his return to his own kingdom, where we find him employed in warily seeking to ingratiate himself with his nobles, in striving to avert their but too-well-founded suspicions of his blood-guiltiness, and in sneakingly proffering them all sorts of rotten promises and lying declarations.

Next, we behold him shrinking with craven, selfish forebodings from the consequences of his own craft and cruelty, watching with coward eye the increasing disaffection at home and approaching danger from abroad, and studying how, by new guile, he may ward off the inevitable issue of old untruths and misdeeds. The picture of his base and dastard soul trembling in all the alarm of awakened, conscious guilt, with its dreaded results, is a revelation terrible in its bare and naked deformity. We turn, as from a hideous reptile-thing, from the spectacle of this despicable royal murderer, liar, and villain, alone with his own conscience and its fears; and we find him next trying, with loathsomest subterfuge, to fasten upon the factor of his monster-crime its responsibility and retribution. The shuffling sophistry and meanness of reproach with which he turns upon Hubert in this scene [4.2.], throwing upon him the whole blame of a deed which he himself originally conceived, and had instigated Hubert to perpetrate, is the very flagrance and crassitude of baseness. It is scoundrelism – not dreading to *be* scoundrel, but to be *proved* scoundrel, and to meet scoundrel's due. . . . And yet, in this 'lowest deep,' there is still a 'lower deep' in the character and conduct of this pitiful king; most of all does he appear vile and ignoble in the act of truckling and stooping to priestly tyranny. Here he not only degrades himself, but his whole people in his own person. By servilely seeking to fawn and cringe into the good graces of the Vatican, he compromises the honour of his throne and nation; and in lifting the golden symbol of sovereignty from his own head, he shamefully places the crown of England beneath the foot of Rome, to be spurned or foreborne by Papal toe. But, to sum the conduct of this hateful king, he is hideous in his crimes, hideous in his hypocrisy, and hideous even in his remorse, because that arises from fear, and not from repentance of his foul deeds. A bold bad man, like Richard III., rises into an object of absolute admiration, compared with the crawling, abject wickedness of such a being as John. . . .

[Clarke now gives further instances of 'craft' in the play, citing other aspects of John's character, but also the guile of Elinor during her argument with Constance (2.1.122–94), and her sly advice to John regarding the match between Lewis and Blanch (2.1.468–73). After citing the citizens of Angiers and Pandulph as further examples of craft, Clarke discusses Constance.]

Constance is a sublime personification of the maternal character, lashed into frenzy by the potency of will, but impotence of power to right herself of the injustice with which she is surrounded. She is a lioness at bay, her resources failed, and her retreat cut off. In the blind desire to secure her child's birthright, and in her wrath at his oppression, she fatally loses sight of the great privilege of his existence. How true to nature all this, and how accurately do we trace the gradual subsiding of her spirit of fury and resentment into an outpouring of tenderness and deprecation, as all her hopes and prospects of success fade away. What majesty in her reply to the French king when she refuses to attend his summons and accompany his messenger: – [Quotes 3.1.65–74: Constance's reply to Salisbury].

Magnificent as this is, it is even surpassed in beauty by the tearful passion of tenderness in that passage where she addresses the cardinal, when the little prince is taken from her: – [Quotes 3.4.76–105: Constance's response to Pandulph and Philip regarding the extravagance of her grief].

I know of nothing in dramatic contrast surpassing in grandeur that of Constance with the other characters in this tragedy – open, direct, vehement action, with bravery, but without judgment; opposed to cunning, treachery, and cruelty, without courage – moral or physical. . . .
[Clarke concludes this portion of his essay by citing 'the bully, Austria' and the naïve Dauphin as contrasts to the crafty John and Pandulph.]

There are few of Shakespeare's or of any other poet's dramas that exhibit more strikingly the philosophy of war, than this of *King John*. What can be more palpable and more touching than the comment upon the utter worthlessness – even the folly of all strife and contention, than is comprised in that one affecting appeal of the little Arthur to his mother, Constance, in the midst of the tumult of the bad passions? Could anything tend more effectually to rebuke the worldly ambition of the mother, the aged spite of Elinor, the wily villany of John, the interested vacillation of France, 'whose armour conscience buckled on – whom zeal and charity brought to the field as God's own soldier' [2.1.564ff.], than this morsel of instinctive wisdom from the mouth of an innocent child? 'Out of the mouth of babes and sucklings hast thou ordained praise' [Psalms 8.2]; and here is a babe preaching, in spirit, the gospel of Christianity to the callous and case-hardened of the old world – the professing viceregent of that Being who pronounced that 'All they that use the sword shall perish by the sword' [Matthew 26.52]; the intriguing and strife-fomenting cardinal shows foully by the Christian humility of the royal child: [Quotes 2.1.163–5: 'Good, my mother, peace. . . .'].

Do we not feel deeply in our hearts, too, the instinctive yearning for sympathy and affection – a blessing so priceless, so far above worldly honour and conventional rank and distinction – which prompts the little prince to say to Hubert – [Quotes 4.1.22–4: 'Is it my fault that I was Geffrey's son. . . .']. The childlike sweetness and simple beauty of that appeal surely never were exceeded. The gentle nature and innate perception of the folly of ambition – the *'low* ambition,'[1] as Pope finely calls it – of dominion, again appears in that simple speech – [Quotes 4.1.12–18: 'Mercy on me. . . .'].

Afterwards, he uses his rank as a plea, when reminding Hubert of his tender care of him, when he (Hubert) had an illness: – [Quotes 4.1.50–6].

This honest disclaiming of cunning, as being the basest of injurious imputations, comes with artistical contrast and relief to the main spirit of the play – the spirit of 'craft' and treachery.

But the grandest carrying out of the author's intention in displaying the 'philosophy of war,' is to be found in the character of Faulconbridge. It forms throughout, as it were, a *moral chorus* to the tragedy, embodying Shakespeare's own sentiments as to the worthlessness of strife and contention, and proving the medium of forcing this conviction upon his audience. The way in which the character is first introduced is in correct costume and keeping throughout. We behold a young and fiery spirit grasping at the earliest chance of what he deems honour, even at the expense of the honour of his mother, wherein he eagerly seeks to derive his descent from Cœur-de-Lion – not so much as being *King* Richard, but as the *war*-like monarch, the renowned military leader, the byword and terror of the East, the plume in the helmet of Christian chivalry. He pants for distinction, come it how it may; and perceiving the cant of 'craft' to be the court-fashion, he immediately announces his intention of adopting that course; adding – [Quotes 1.1.207–16: 'For he is but a bastard to the time. . . .'].

And this lesson he instantly puts in practice by his sophistical speech to his mother, in allusion to her amour with Cœur-de-Lion, whereby he himself was descended: – [Quotes 1.1.261–9: 'Some sins do bear. . . .'].

On his first battle-field his tornado spirit hurries him at once into a quarrel with the Duke of Austria, against whom (with the instinctive dislike that men of courage entertain towards a blusterer and a bully) he at first sight conceives an antipathy. His disgust, moreover, is hereditary; for in Austria he hates the traitor to his own father, Cœur-de-Lion, whom he had kidnapped and imprisoned. . . .
[Clarke now quotes generously from 2.1 to show that the Bastard is a 'young and eager soldier, whose sole thought is glory and military ambition' (331).]

But then comes the soliloquy on 'commodity,' ('interestedness'), and how finely the better nature of the man revolts against the hollowness and want of good faith which he detects in the French king; yet Shakespeare, ever watchful, ever consistent, causes his eyes to open only by degrees; and Faulconbridge concludes this very speech with adhering to his former resolution of pursuing his fortunes, keeping 'commodity' as his lode-star. the soliloquy is remarkable for its vigorous worldly sense, as well as for the felicity with which the poet sustains his metaphor, in comparing self-interest, or 'commodity,' to the bias in the ball used by the player at bowls. When the assembly have gone out, having patched up the hollow compact between the French and English sovereigns, Faulconbridge, being left alone, he breaks forth: – [Quotes 2.1.561–98].

But the important and decided change that takes place in the character of Faulconbridge is when he first hears of the death of little Arthur, and at the same time hears it ascribed to John, to whom he himself is deeply indebted. His speeches after this event are still those of the courageous, high-spirited man, but they are distinctly those of the man of *moral* courage as contrasted with his previous *physical* courage. Like one of truly noble nature, he scorns to fall off from the patron to whom he owes so much; but the discovery of that patron's baseness and treachery acts like a talisman to unseal his eyes to the vain-glory and wickedness of 'vaulting ambition' [*Macbeth*: 1.7.27] and low cupidity. He still cleaves to the cause of the king, and endeavours to screen him from the indignation of his revolting nobles; but he now discourses with a calm dignity totally unlike the rash impetuosity of Faulconbridge in the opening of the play. And when Pembroke says, in justification of their revolt from King John, 'Sir, sir, impatience hath his privilege' [4.3.32], Faulconbridge sedately and finely answers, ''Tis true: to hurt his master, no man else' [4.3.33]. And to Salisbury, who openly proclaims the blood-guiltiness of the king, he calmly replies, 'Whate'er you *think*, good words, I think, were best' [4.3.28]. And Salisbury's rejoinder to this dignified rebuke does not quicken his pulse – 'Our griefs, and not our manners, reason now' [4.3.29]; he retorts, 'But there is little reason in your grief; therefore 'twere reason you had manners now' [4.3.30ff.]. All this is very different from his former bearing; and how the genius of the poet is displayed in quelling the fiery spirit of the man only by the chilling mist of suspicion and misplaced confidence. This is a beautiful tribute to the character of Faulconbridge. The only time after this that his old impetuosity returns is when Salisbury threatens him – 'Stand by, or I shall gall you, Faulconbridge!' [4.3.94]. Then he flares out: – [Quotes 4.3.95–100: 'Thou wert better gall the devil, Salisbury. . . .'].

The staring fact of the death of the little Prince Arthur is before him, he cannot blink that; he is pushed to a corner and hedged in, and yet he evades the charge, with the object pointed at. How natural all this; and how like a thorough and determined partisan. He is compelled to acknowledge thus much; he does confess – 'It is a damned and a bloody work; / The graceless action of a heavy hand, / *If* that it be the work of any hand' [4.3.57ff.].

He makes no farther concession to the rebel lords. When, however, they have left the scene, and he is alone with Hubert, he turns round upon him in a strain of sublime vituperation – [Quotes 4.3.116–134: the Bastard's conversation with Hubert over the latter's responsibility for Arthur's death].

With the exception of the explosion with the nobles (and this arose only from his valour being chafed) throughout the whole scene [4.3], we discover working in him that divine maturer insight into the rottenness of contest and strife, which gradually takes the place of his young ambition, and which finds words at length in that grand and solemn soliloquy – closing the scene – where he bids Hubert bear away the little dead prince: – [Quotes 4.3.140–54: 'I am amaz'd, methinks, and lose my way. . . .'].

After this scene we find him bravely fighting for John, showing a valiant front to his enemies, and supporting him in his death-agony; but the moral perfectioning of his own character is wound to a climax in the closing words of the play: – [Quotes 5.7.112–18: 'This England never did. . . .'].

Was I not correct in saying that the character of Faulconbridge forms a 'moral chorus' to the play to reveal to us the hidden skeleton beneath the veil and roses of war and ambition?

I have frequently recurred to Shakespeare's ingenuity in contrasting his characters in his dramas; great as this is, however, both this talent and effect are surpassed by the wonderful skill and ease with which he *contrasts characters with themselves*, as in this one of Faulconbridge. The graduated manner in which he contrives to make one master-passion supersede another, and each in turn to become the dominant, still retaining the integrity, and even plausibility of the original construction, is in itself a profound metaphysical study.

One more remark upon this grand personation. Upon the question that the reign of King John was deficient in characters fully answering the demand for the *dramatic* interest in the play, and that in consequence the instinct of our poet perceiving the necessity for a supply of *representative* characters to meet that demand, the fine character just dismissed, – certainly one of the very finest in the whole gallery of Shakespearian *inventive* portraits, – is precisely the 'representative' character required.[2] Thoroughly Gothic in features and proportions, and as thoroughly English in temper and spirit, his presence rays life and manliness into every part of the drama, where they would else be wanting. 'Is it strange,' says well the Boston editor of our poet, 'that a nation which could grow such originals, should have surpassed the rest of the world in all that is vigorous, and useful, and great?'[3]

Beautifully conceived, too, is the career of Hubert. It would seem that no circumstance in his deportment, up to the period of his temptation by the king, could harmonise with his fulfilling the horrid mission he had undertaken; nevertheless, his being a court-retainer, and a pliant and assiduous one, justifies his being selected by John as the tool for his cruel purpose. In the last Act, Hubert nobly clears himself from suspicion of having murdered the child; and his scene in the prison, with the little prince pleading for his eyes, can barely receive the due estimation of its tenderness and genuine pathos [4.1].

As an instance of the caution with which Shakespeare conducts and fills up the design in his dramas, and contrives to make even the most subordinate parts accord with the main outline, and constitute a portion and necessary adjunct to the consummated plot, may be noticed the introduction on the scene of the dying French lord, Melun, – with the sublime lesson put into the mouth of a man, 'right in whose eyes are seen the cruel pangs of death' [5.4.59ff.]. At that solemnest moment of all the junctures in a man's life, it was especially fine in the poet to place truth, and honour, and fidelity in contrast with dissimulation, fraud, and treachery. The revolted English nobles have gone over to the French king, and Melun warns them to fly; for that his sovereign, if victorious, means to recompense their services to him by cutting off their heads. Well might Salisbury exclaim, 'I'm stifled with this smell of sin!' [4.3.113]. The dying speech of this French lord – one of the least important agents, be it observed, in the history – is scarcely to be exceeded in effect by any other in the play. He says: – [Quotes 5.4.22–39].

These revolted nobles, too, are sketched with the same propriety and distinctness that mark all the poet's characters, however slight the portion of words they have to deliver. Thus, we have the Lord Salisbury, generous and gentle, sympathising with the Lady Constance in her sorrows, – the text to his character being traceable in her words, as is frequently the case in Shakespeare: thus, it is imperative upon all actors studying their parts, to study likewise all the other characters in the piece, for hints as to their own characters and by-play; so artfully, and, withal, so naturally do they dove-tail, and carry out and explain each other. Thus Constance, in her address to Salisbury, upon hearing that her professing ally, the French king, had joined issue with John against the claim of her son Arthur: – [Quotes 3.1.19–24: 'What dost thou mean by shaking of thy head. . . .']. . . .

In the scenes at the court of King John, he [Salisbury] is distinguished by a graceful flow of courtier-like eloquence; for his is the oft-quoted speech that he utters upon the *second* coronation of the king, which he says is, – [Quotes 4.2.11–15: 'To gild refined gold, to paint the lily. . . .'].

This eloquence is ingeniously contrasted with Pembroke's more blunt and straightforward utterance; and the characteristic diversity between these two lords is consistently maintained throughout the play. . . .

[Clarke now turns to William Charles Macready's *King John*, performed at Drury Lane in 1842, which he finds interesting for its mimetic heightening of subtle yet revealing features of the play.]

. . . [W]hat I would principally distinguish as the crowning talent displayed in that very fine revival, was the conception of the character of King John himself. It was the more artistical, inasmuch as the peculiar moral features of that bad king are rather to be suggested to the imagination than palpably and broadly developed. The stealthy watchfulness, the crafty caution, and the want of faith in human goodness, are all features that demand acute discrimination to perceive, and refined and delicate touches to embody.

It requires subdued deportment, self-mistrust, or rather the want of self-confidence – nice points of character to study, and all which few actors dare to personate with fidelity, because, unless they be understood and appreciated by an audience, it is frequently thought to be tame or under acting.

The whole character and bearing of John, in the version of Shakespeare, form a striking contrast to those of Henry V.[4] The one is ardent, brave, confident in the love and support of his people – the true English king; the other, wily, artful, making every movement by a stratagem, and feeling that he holds his subjects by no other tenure than the right of might, and an appeal to the baser passions of their nature.

They who call to mind those two brilliant and impetuous speeches – those rousing appeals to the zeal of his people in *Henry V.* – beginning, 'Once more unto the breach, dear friends' [3.1.1]; and, 'What's he that wishes so? my cousin Westmoreland?' [4.3.18ff.], the celebrated speech upon the eve of the Agincourt fight; and then draw a parallel between them and the speech that King John makes to the citizens of Angiers, 'These flags of France that are advanced here, / Before the eye and prospect of your town' [2.1.207ff.], sneaking his way, as it were, and feeling the pulse, as he proceeds, of those whom he is addressing, – they, I repeat, who institute a comparison between these speeches in the two plays, will perceive my meaning. These words may be taken as keys to the two characters. In John we have no confiding appeals, no 'dear friends;' but the extortionate tyrant to his people appears in such phrases as – [Quotes 3.3.7–11: 'Ere our coming, see thou shake the bags / of hoarding abbots. . . .'].

Compare this with Harry Monmouth's courageous and magnanimous reflection: – [Quotes *Henry V*, 4.1.4–12: 'There is some soul of goodness in things evil. . . .']. And then note his playful intercourse with his soldiers, and those sprightly exclamations to his faithful old adherent, Sir Thomas Erpingham, 'God 'a mercy, old heart, thou speakest cheerfully' [4.1.34]. Compare his confident reliance on his English bosoms, with John's misgivings and doubts, as of a man conscious and feeling that he has no right to the love of his subjects in the scene of his recoronation: 'And looked upon, I hope, with cheerful eyes' [4.2.2]. And again, 'I have a way to win their loves again' [4.2.168]; as well as his storm of reproach and remorse, and base endeavour to shift the ponderous load of his guilt on to the shoulders of his instrument, Hubert.

After this comparison, they who fortunately witnessed the two performances, will not forget the manner in which Mr Macready impersonated the two kings, and the artistical way in which he demonstrated the unhappiness of wickedness throughout his *King John*; the gradual and constant declension of his spirit, its tide being always at the ebb; his small amount of confidence, his suggested consciousness of meanness, guilt, and the loss of all respect; his bearing latterly as that of a man who felt that indignant eyes were flashing on him, and his gait as if surrounded by pitfalls; in short, the general substratum of wretchedness which pervades the whole character, and yet is only known and felt, not blazoned; all this unprotruded demeanour, and which the million do not appreciate, greatly surpassed in merit the conception, even of his dying scene, terrifically real as that was. . . . (319–342)

31 Georg Gottfried Gervinus, politics, ethics, and chararacter

1863

From *Shakespeare Commentaries by Dr. G. G. Gervinus, Professor at Heidelberg. Translated under the Author's Superintendence by F. E. Bunnett, Author of 'Louise Juliane, Electress Palatine and Her Times', etc.* (2 vols, London, 1863).

Georg Gottfried Gervinus (1805–71) was an influential German literary and political thinker who produced the first comprehensive and scholarly history of German literature, *Geschichte der Poetischen Nationalliteratur der Deutschen* (5 vols, Leipzig, 1835–42). His career as a university professor at Göttingen and Heidelberg was both distinguished and controversial, often punctuated by his active involvement in German political affairs. As a staunch constitutionalist, dedicated to national expansion and unification, he helped found the *Deutsche Zeitung*, one of the most important political journals of the century, and also served as deputy for the Prussian province of Saxony to the National Assembly in 1848. Gervinus's interest in Shakespeare had a distinctly moral and political dimension; for he saw in the works of the English dramatist evidence of that healthy and practical morality he tried so assiduously to cultivate in the German people. His lifelong attraction to both English and German culture is clearly evidenced in his *Händel und Shakespeare* (Leipzig, 1868), in which he argues for intellectual and personal affinites between the composer and the poet attributable to their common Teutonic origins. *Shakespeare Commentaries* first appeared in German as *Shakespeare* (4 vols, Leipzig, 1849–50); Bunnett's translation was reprinted in a one-volume version (London, 1875), with only slight stylistic changes.

[From the chapter entitled 'Historical Pieces']

[Gervinus discusses Shakespeare's histories as a great expression of English patriotism and nationalism, then addresses Courtenay's observations (No. 17 above) regarding their faithfulness to historical truth.]

. . . Shakespeare has had but one law in the using of each and all of his sources, a law which he applied equally to the driest historical chronicle as to the most fantastic novel: he sought after nature and inner truth; and this he took possession of as his property wherever he found it, and the opposite he rejected whatever authority might hold it out to him. . . . (I, 350)

... But this truth is throughout, as we discover, not to be taken in the prosaic sense of the historian, who seeks it in the historical material in the smallest particulars and according to its most different sides; but it is only one higher and universal truth, which is gathered by the poet from a series of historical facts, yet which from this very circumstance, that it springs from historical, true, and actual facts, and is supported and upheld by them, acquires, it must be admitted, a double authority, that of poetry and of history at the same time. The historical drama, formed of these two component parts, will be therefore most agreeable to the imaginative friend of history and to the realistic friend of poetry.... (I, 352)

[From the chapter entitled '*King John*']

... Little place, [in *King John*], as in *Richard II.*, is given to the prose, and in one passage rhyme has maintained its ground; play upon words and conceits in unsuitable places are even more frequent here than in *Richard II.*, a piece to which *King John* appears to be almost contemporary, if it were only on account of the great family-resemblance between the character of Constance and that of Richard II. . . . (I, 492)

... Shakespeare delineates his Faulconbridge (and himself in him) rigidly and bitterly enough as a good Protestant in the base treatment of popish arrogance. In suitable passages he gives full play to the indignation of the English at popish rule and intrigue, encroachment and oppression, which at that time was readily listened to in London. But he did not go so far as to make a farce of Faulconbridge's extortions from the clergy; the old piece [i.e., *The Troublesome Raigne*] offered him here a scene [6.1–121], in which merry nuns and brothers burst forth from the opened coffers of the 'hoarding abbots' [*King John*, 3.3.8], a scene certainly very amusing to the fresh Protestant feelings of the time, – but to our poet with his impartial mind, the dignity of the clergy, nay indeed the contemplativeness of cloister-life, was something too sacred for him to introduce it in a ridiculous form into the seriousness of history. . . . (I, 493–4)

King John has outwardly no reference to the two historical tetralogies which we have previously discussed; but with regard to the thought it contains, we shall see the poet in this piece also, working with the same political views, which distinguish the circle of ideas in the histories from that of the exact dramas. If we turn away from the historical subject, we might pronounce this piece to be a tragedy of the purest water, simply representing the idea of so many of the ancient tragedies: that 'there is no sure foundation set in blood; no certain life achieved by others' death' [4.2.104ff.]. But to this general idea the purport of the whole piece does not pervadingly refer. A rich web of political actions aiming at one central point, circles round Arthur's death, which forms indeed the main turning-point of John's fortune, but it is in no wise the sole cause of this reverse of fortune, any more than the guilt of the king alone is so; but from these political actions is developed, as in *Richard II.*, an idea at once political and ethical, of the more special character of the leading thoughts of all Shakespeare's real and strict histories. . . . (I, 495)

Throughout this piece Shakespeare has softened for the better the traits of the principal political characters, and has much obliterated the bad; his John, his

Constance, his Arthur, his Philip Augustus, even his Elinor, are better people, than they are found in history. The ground of this treatment, which is commonly not peculiar to him, is not merely this, that in this instance he did not draw directly from the sources of the chronicle; there is also the design in it, which will be explained in what follows, that the vehicles of the political story should be merely men of ordinary stamp, who derive the motives for their actions from no deep-lying passions, men neither of a very noble nor of a very ignoble sort, but, as it is wont to be in the political world, men who act from selfishness and common interest. The base previous history of Elinor and Constance is touched upon partly only in cursory insinuations, and partly not at all; the older, active Arthur of history is transformed into an inactive innocent boy; King John himself is kept much in the back-ground, even *his* historical character is softened and refined by Shakespeare. As he appears at the commencement, he is like a vigorous man prepared for everything, resolved with a strong hand to defend his possession of the throne against every assault. He is, as Faulconbridge subsequently, referring to this early period, reminds him, 'great in thought' [5.1.45]; in the thought, he means, of maintaining with all his power against every pretension the English land, which actually is on his side and has sworn allegiance to him, and of identifying the kingdom with his fatherland, as the straight-forward Bastard ever does. He is not the image of a brutal tyrant, but only the type of the hard manly nature, without any of the enamel of finer feelings, without any other motives for action than those of the instinct of this same inflexible nature and of personal interest. Severe and earnest, an enemy to cheerfulness and merry laughter, conversant with dark thoughts, of a restless, excited spirit, he quickly rises to daring resolves; he is uncommunicative to his best advisers, laconic and reserved; he did not agree to the good design of his evil mother, that he should satisfy Constance and her claims by an accommodation; better does it please his warlike manly pride to bear arms against the threatened arms; in his campaigns against Constance and her allies, the enemy himself feels that the hot haste, managed with so much foresight, and the wise order in so wild a cause, are unexampled. Thus lord of his presence, and allied to the great interest of the country, he appears feared, but not loved and in favour, and he presents in truth no amiable side. No child-like reverence draws him to his mother, but her political wisdom; no vein of kindred to Faulconbridge, but his usefulness; to Hubert he speaks love, when he needs him, and of abhorrence, after his services have proved injurious; the property of the church loses its sanctity for him in necessity; – but this manner of consulting only his immediate advantage in all circumstances, leads him by degrees so far as to betray the great possession of the state in another time of need to this same despised and crushed church, whose arrogant interference he had before withstood with scornful defiance. A higher principle sustains not the man and his energetic designs in time of danger, the great idea at his outset leaves him during the progress and at the end of his career. After his power, as he displays it against France, has risen even to the defiance of the Pope and the church, and to the inconsiderate design upon the life of a child, whose temper was not to be feared and by him had not been even tried, it sinks down, struck by conscience, by curses, and by prophecies, by dangers without and within; he becomes anxious, mistrustful, superstitious, fearful to absolute weakness and to a degree of faint-heartedness, in which he sells his fatherland as cheaply, as once in his self-confidence, he had held it dearly and had defended it boldly.

In contrast to the entirely political relation between the usurper and his mother, is the entirely maternal relation of Constance to her son Arthur, on whose side is the legitimate claim. The suspicious Elinor sees in him a bloom which may ripen into mighty fruit; Shakespeare too has given a profound mental capacity to the pure and spotless mind of the tender boy; in that scene with Hubert which affects the soul of the spectator with such agitating emotions of fear and pity, it is not alone his loving nature which disarms cruelty, it is also a persuasive spirit full of wise, even of cunning precaution, which terror at once ripens into a saving power. Yet at the time no pretender would have been less to be feared than he. He would that he were low laid in his grave, when he hears the contention over his right. He would gladly be a shepherd, so that he might be merry, and be free from the unmerited fault of being his father's son and heir. But all the more firmly does his ambitious mother cling to the legitimate claim of the child, who knows of no ambition. She has called France to arms for her fair son, whom she loves with all the intensity of maternal pride; she would be less ambitious for herself and him, if nature had not made him so worthy of command. She herself is yet beautiful as a matron, she pleases herself, it appears, not a little in the beauty of her child, and to argue from the impression, which she makes on the bystanders, her charms must even in her extreme and utterly unfeigned sorrow enhance the spectacle of her grief. Ambition spurred by maternal love, maternal love goaded by ambition and womanly vanity, these form the distinguishing features of this character, features out of which from the adversity of fate, that raging passion is developed, which at last shatters the soul and body of the frail woman. She is a woman, not to say *the* woman, whose weakness amounts to grandeur, and whose virtues sink into weakness; she is, like John in his masculine sphere, without those mental and moral resources, which could make her moderate in prosperity or calm in adversity. To the daring man, misfortune is the stone against which he stumbles, to the passionate woman, it would have been success. From the transporting violence of her love and of her grief we may conclude, how violent she could have been in hatred and arrogance. Her coarse outbursts against Elinor, her contemptuous and sarcastic outbreaks against the Duke of Austria, when she stands on the doubtful ground between success and misfortune, testify to the sanguine, womanly, even womanish, want of self-command, which makes her irritable at fear, and would make her irritable at haughtiness. Her biting speech is even too bitter for her child, and too immoderate for her friends. Shakespeare has depicted in her the female counterpart to Richard II., who imperious in prosperity, was speedily lost in adversity. Powerless to forward their own cause, the one from early self-abandonment, the other from the outward grounds of her position and sex, both alike powerless in active defence and revenge, they both sink into the exaggeration of a passion, which rages within the man in smouldering heat, within the woman in a brightly blazing fire, an exaggeration of the mind and the fancy, which manifests itself in the most brilliant outpourings of eloquence and reflection, in the invectives of rage as well as in the outbursts of sorrow. Just as in Richard, there gushes forth in Constance a deeply poetic vein in all her misery, and like him her imagination revels in her grief, which she calls so great, that 'no supporter but the huge firm earth can hold it up' [3.1.72ff.]. Like Richard, she delights in picturing to herself dark images of death and its desired horrors, like him she plays with her sorrow in witty words and similes. Like him, her pride and majesty rise with misfortune. On the throne and state of her grief, she feels herself more exalted than her false royal friends; and in the extreme of hopelessness she is seized with the frenzy, which only threatened Richard. As the end, the ruin, the agony of King John has ever been regarded as one of the most satisfactory themes for English actors, such as Garrick, so from Mrs. Cibber to Mrs. Siddons and later, the part of Constance has been esteemed as one of the most acceptable tasks. The change of mood and the oscillations from the highest pitch of excited bitterness to the softest depth of maternal tenderness, offer infinite scope to the artist. In the third act we must compare the Shakespearian play with the similar scenes in the older *King John* [i.e., *The Troublesome Raigne*], to estimate thoroughly, what he has here accomplished. How the whole frail, trembling frame of the woman is agitated at the first tidings of her forlorn condition! What variety of feeling is expressed and felt in those twenty lines, in which she enquires anxiously after the truth of that which shocks her to hear! [3.1.1–20]. How her grief as long as she is alone, restrains itself in calmer anguish, in the vestibule of despair! How her sorrow first bursts forth in the presence of others in powerless revenge, rising even to a curse which brings no blessing to herself, and how atoningly behind all this unwomanly rage lies the foil of maternal love! How justly measured throughout is the light and the shade! We should be moved with too violent a pity for this love, leaning as it does on the one dear object, which is snatched away from it, if it did not weaken our interest by its want of moderation; we should turn away from the violence of the woman, if the strength of her maternal affection did not irresistibly enchain us.

These two opponents, unstable and unprincipled as we find them, the one without judgment, dependent on doubtful allies, the other on the wisdom of his relatives, entangle themselves in conformity with this their nature amid the alternations of fortune in a series of unnatural confederacies, where weakness and mistrust in a cause not wholly pure, seek support, and interest strives to counteract interest. . . .

[Gervinus next mentions a number of these 'unnatural confederacies', citing Constance's alliance with France and Austria, the settlement at Angiers, John's ensuing league with France, France's 'unhallowed league' with Rome, the English lords' defection to the French, John's 'shameful treaty of subjection' to Rome, etc., noting how each reverts to 'natural enmity' (I, 502–6).]

Amid these errors and intricacies, these inclinations and aversions, these alliances and quarrels, self-interest and advantage, the ruler of all political affairs, bears sway. Faulconbridge solemnly rebukes this, in the first league between John and France, in Philip's breach of faith to Constance, as the author of this double godless course of action, as 'that broker, that still breaks the pate of faith'; as 'that daily break-vow; he that wins of all' [2.1.568ff.]; that cheats all: [Quotes 2.1.574–80: from the speech on Commodity].

To this power, to this lever in every commotion, high and low abandon themselves more or less readily. King John and Constance are urged by the force of direct nature, by want of principle, by lack of moral and patriotic sense, to grasp at its offers; the

French princes follow its dictates with a deliberation, which overcomes the counter-balance of honour; the Duke of Austria stands ever cowardly close to the strong and marches with them; the papal legate is the master, who thinks to take this moving-power in his hand and to guide after his own intention. In what relation to the errors and seductions of this power and to its confused world of policy, do those men stand, in whom the fire of morality and of genuine patriotism is not quite extinguished? Shakespeare has placed this contrast of a better humanity in opposition to those slaves of interest, in four gradations.

The young Arthur is in his unspotted innocence quite a stranger to this world of guilt and selfishness. In this strife of hostile powers, only the discord of quarrel meets his ear, and even that is intolerable to the saintly creature. The superiority of a nature angelic, untried, and uninjured, drives the tender being early from the noisy world, for which he has neither understanding nor heart; it is as if he would remove from his keeper Hubert the temptation to an evil deed, while in full consciousness he incurs the danger of the suicide, which proves fatal. It happens repeatedly in Shakespeare's plays, that childlike innocence meets in this manner with a tragic fate: it is so with the sons of Edward in *Richard III.*, with Macduff's bold and heroic boy, with Mamillius in *The Winter's Tale*, and here with Arthur. Shakespeare has always painted this innocence in the most charming colours; he has not cast the lightest mote across the moral spotlessness of these characters, he has indeed on each occasion added the interest of intellectual endowments to them; all these youthful beings are premature in their development and precocious in their minds. How is the pitiable destruction of these creatures consistent with the demands of that poetic justice, which lay so near to the heart of the poet? They could not perish in moral justice; how could we impute guilt to childlike innocence and make retribution, when no deeds are committed? Nevertheless, in the historical piece of *Richard III.*, for example, the death of Edward's sons was imposed upon the poet in his subject; he could not evade it. What did he do, to reconcile feeling and fancy with the cruel destiny? He yielded to the pious popular belief, which says, that God takes to himself most early the sweetest children, and to that other, so often expressly repeated in Richard, that children 'so wise so young, do ne'er live long' [*Richard III*, 3.1.79]. He delineated these guiltless souls in such angelic perfection, that they appear too good for this lower world, so that with sorrow and pity for their end, a feeling of happiness is mingled, at seeing them withdrawn from the rough contingencies of life. And this poet appeared to Voltaire an intoxicated savage![1]

It is best for the pure innocent nature to be withdrawn from the confusion of the political world, – this is a doctrine, which even the master of policy, Machiavelli, has taught. But not everyone is in the position to be withdrawn from it by the force of destiny, or to be able voluntarily to avoid it. A moral nature and a duty national and political are at variance in the noble Salisbury, and create for him a struggle of soul, which leads to false steps, if such they can be considered; the right line of action in such political perplexities is expressly represented as one so delicate, as not even to be always accurately discovered by the most just sense of morality. . . .

The great Vassal sees himself from his mere social position obliged to act from *political* consideration, – the smaller servant of the king, Hubert, appears only in a *personal* relation to the king; Salisbury sees himself in a bitter struggle between duty to his country, and the impulse of a deeply excited abhorrence resting on moral principles; Hubert's struggle only consists between habitual service and a half-wakened sense of conscience, which never before had been called forth. The unthinking man true to his feudal oath, instigated by his king in a spoken hint to the murder, and in written command to the blinding of Arthur, this man follows the course of habit in blind obedience, till the sight of Arthur and his supplications awaken in him his slumbering better nature. He seeks to approach the dull but not wholly inaccessible conscience of the king, that he may effect the rescinding of the command, or find excuse for his disobedience. He feels not the sharp goad of moral consciousness, which at once separated Salisbury, on account of this murder, from his fidelity to the king. He revolts not from the king, as the other did, from the higher impulse of obedience to the divine law; he preserves himself from a breach with his country, but the stain of the suspicion cleaves to him, for which the revolted vassals threaten him with death. It is very skilful, how afterwards the Count Melun betrays the treacherous designs of the Dauphin against these English Vassals, partly on account of his English descent, partly, and this touch Shakespeare added to the older piece, *for love of Hubert*. This reflects a respect for the man, whom they had too readily condemned, who now becomes their preserver on the side of his nobler nature, in the same measure as before, from the plot against Arthur which the king, building upon his rough exterior, committed to him, he had become an accessory to his death.

The gentle Arthur perished in the political struggles, in which he was placed; the manly Salisbury was misled in his political path by the delicacy of his moral feeling, the rougher Hubert erred in his higher moral duty from his faithful zeal; the Bastard Faulconbridge is carried through all these disturbances by his upright patriotic spirit, his sound understanding, and an acute moral instinct of not too tender a texture. The poet makes him not only look steadily at the pole-star, which can alone lead in these intricacies of political life, but he has also designed in his character that kind of nature, which is the most qualified for this unerring steering through a stormy and dangerous sea. The Bastard Faulconbridge among Shakespeare's humorous characters, is one in which the poet does not separate the spirit of seriousness and mirth as in most of the others, giving to the latter usually the preponderance, but he exhibits them both in a close and well-balanced combination. His mode of expression throughout even in the most elevated, most solemn passages, bears the manner of the uncommon, striking expression of a sceptic, habituated to wit and bitter sarcasm. But as he is placed by fate at the very outset in the busy political world, occupation and work leave him no time to indulge this merry vein, and his deep seriousness in action counterbalances his idle inclination to trifle and to jest. His course through the tragic events, offering so little food to comic humour, is the very reverse to that of King John. The latter begins with power and kingly thoughts and ends in weakness, the Bastard bounds light of heart into the wider sphere that opens before him, and advances continually in seriousness and strength even to a tragic greatness. In his first soliloquy [1.1.182–219] he looks jestingly upon his new dignity; his merriment is changed to bitter irony in the second soliloquy [2.1.561–89] after the sad experience of the French breach of faith with Constance; in the third soliloquy [4.3.139–59?], from the gloomy course of events, he rises to most serious reflection; and at last, ever increasing in power and personal importance, he wholly assumes the direction of the great concerns of the state, and concludes with the tragic resolve, which Shakespeare, in an antique grandeur of sentiment, has imputed to all his faithful servants, to Horatio and to Kent, as well as here to Philip, to follow his deceased king. The metal, out of which this character is moulded, is of a similar masculine character, as in John. The older piece furnished the die for the character, Shakespeare fashioned it into a true work of art. Even there he is depicted as a bold madcap, rude and daring; he is a wild intrepid warrior, whose defiance amounts to proud boasting, he has a straight-forward, hearty sense for nature, he is coarse-grained in understanding, and in morals, a contrast to the crafty, considerate diplomatist, to the faithless wrangler, to all custom and conventionality, a bastard to the time which is regulated by such arts, as he is a bastard by birth. Shakespeare in this character also, is occupied with the idea of show and reality, of genuine nature, propriety, and prejudice. Faulconbridge is in the rare position of being permitted, as it were, to choose between a legitimate birth from an indifferent father, or an illegitimate one from the famous Cœur-de-Lion. This first introduction at once develops his character, which clings rather to substantial honour than to conventional form. He is more proud of a descent shameful in the eyes of the world, from a great and famous father, than of an honourable legitimate descent from an insignificant father; he prefers a full-face from the mighty hero, than a 'half-face' [1.1.92] like his brother from lawful birth. His domestic position bears a resemblance to the historical circumstances of King John. He is the eldest son and heir of his alleged father, but the younger brother charges him with illegitimacy, and thus threatens his inheritance. The Bastard would fain preserve his property and the honour of his mother, he would also fain have so glorious a king for his father. His sound feeling decides in favour of devotion towards so noble a father and such an hereditary honour, which promises to call him to still higher honour, and he *rejects* legitimacy of birth, his mother's honour, inheritance, possession, and interest. He flatters himself that he is, what John also calls himself, 'lord of his presence' [1.1.137; 2.1.367], and that he may thank his merits for his success, as John might have done, had he continued as noble-minded in his kingly calling as at the outset. The coarse moral of the Bastard, which he utters like a catechism, suits both equally: [Quotes 1.1.169–175: 'What though? / Something about, a little from the right. . . .']. It is suitable to this worldly, unamiable, but respect-compelling man, so far removed from a subtle morality, but still more inaccessible to all dishonour, that the poet only makes him occasionally think of being religious; that he imputes an excessive reverence for the church to him as little as to John, that he twice gladly and successfully executes the king's command to lay the clergy under contribution, and to shake their bags; that he upholds the defiance of his prince towards the Pope, only with a more contemptuous opposition, in a time of misfortune and danger, while John only ventures upon it in prosperity. If we would personify the English national character, if we would sketch the idea of John Bull according to the then existing condition of the popular civilization and life, we should say that in the plain, blunt, unpretending Faulconbridge, in this simple straight-forwardness of sound common sense, of hearty ability and natural cheerfulness and wit, the traits of the national English character are gathered together as we should expect in a tragedy of this purport, in which this representative of the people is assigned the task of deciding for the popular welfare in the critical political transactions, in which the bad are ruined and the good confounded. . . .

[Gervinus now traces the activities of the Bastard throughout the play, seeing him as genuinely and unpretentiously patriotic, a man who places dedication to justice and love of country above self-interest.]

. . . The feeling for his country binds him to the king, when the sense of law and morality loosens Salisbury from him; each of them knows that he is only halfway on the right path; the Bastard execrates the murder and curses the subjection to Rome, Salisbury weeps manly tears over the necessity for a state-crime, by which he would save his country. The moral finer-feeling man commits the greater political error, the greater politician takes the side less morally pure, but in perfect firmness of conviction that in such conflicts, the country and its independence and preservation, is the only way-mark to follow, that for patriots the foundation of all virtue is persistent steadfastness, which in the service of the fatherland can invest even moral transgression with a nobility. He discovered selfishness, interest, and advantage, to be the star which governs the political world; if it be so, then as a last resort, the advantage of the country should be that before which all others are to be silent. Therefore in the opinion of the poet as well as of Faulconbridge, no foreign policy and no hostile sword should heal domestic wounds. Hearty unity with a natural enemy is of no value to him, and the national discontent at the league with foreign propaganda, whether it be even against tyranny and arbitrariness at home, is to him a sight full of ignominy and dishonour. A lesson grandly inculcated upon us Germans, for whom there will be no state, politics, common nationality, and public welfare, until, endeavouring to act up to it, we understand how to apply to ourselves, the conclusion of this piece, which is at the same time the soul of it: [Quotes 5.7.112–18: 'This England never did, nor never shall. . . .']. (I, 497–518)

32 John Abraham Heraud, the politics of national interest

1865

From *Shakespeare: His Inner Life, as Intimated in His Works* (London, 1865).

John Abraham Heraud (1799–1887), poet, dramatist, and essayist, had a wide circle of literary acquaintances, including Coleridge, Wordsworth, Southey, Lockhart, and Carlyle. A frequent contributor to periodicals and reviews, Heraud became the dramatic critic for *The Athenæum* from 1843 to 1868, in which capacity he established himself as one of the most prominent theatrical critics of his time. He was also a dramatist of solid reputation, two of his most successful plays being the tragedies *The Roman Brother* (1840) and *Videna* (1854). His other published work was varied and extensive, including two attempts at epic poetry, 'The Descent Into Hell' (1830) and 'The Judgment of the Flood' (1834), as well as a number of essays and poetic treatises on philosophical, moral, or historical subjects.

[From 'Part II: Fantastic and Historical Period – 1591–1598'. 'Chapter I']

[Heraud begins his treatment of *King John* by discussing its indebtedness to *The Troublesome Raigne*, but also noting the relative absence in Shakespeare's play of the anti-Catholic virulence of its predecessor.]

... It is evident that [Shakespeare] was inclined to treat the clergy with respect; and that his aim in refashioning the tragedy was exclusively political. This aim has become the central idea of the subject, and in his hands regulates its treatment. The dispute between the brother and the late king and the nephew of the latter to the throne, originates the action of the play. Shakespeare, however, does not touch on the fact that in the thirteenth century hereditary right was not uniformly regarded, or that without the consent of parliament no king could reign, and that, in fact, parliament did confer the crown on John, preferring him to the young Arthur, then only eleven years of age. On the other hand, history records that, notwithstanding the said fact, John was jealous of his nephew's pretensions, and having succeeded in securing him as a prisoner, took care that nothing more should be heard of him. Young Arthur was imprisoned, according to Holinshed, first in Falais and subsequently at Rouen, where he was supposed to have been murdered. The old play confines him somewhere in England; and, as it was convenient to the conduct of the plot, Shakespeare unhesitatingly adopted the suggestion. Indeed, in its story and stage-arrangements he copies almost implicitly the old play; portraying John as an usurper, and Arthur as the rightful heir, – a view which lends a pathos to the story not intrinsically belonging to it, but fitting it better for a dramatic purpose.

In other respects, Shakespeare has done more justice to John than history. The latter describes this monarch as weak and cowardly, taking the circumstances in which the man was placed for his character. Shakespeare regards him more properly as the representative of the country, and the exponent of her policy. Those epithets belong as much to England as to him. In truth, they are strictly inapplicable to either, but are crude substitutes for terms more philosophical descriptive of the time and people. John's troubles are England's troubles, and both have to meet them with what means they can extemporise. The state is internally unsettled and externally endangered. We have to wait for the inter-action of the inward and outward forces, which in the end conducts by a painful process to their reconciliation. Only by being faithful to herself can England withstand a foreign foe; and this fidelity of all parties to a common national interest may only be secured by a series of trials showing the bitter evils of civil contention. This notion of interest, then, is the idea embodied in the tragedy and in its characters. The national interest receives its incarnation in the person of John, who stands accordingly for the Policy of England. It is not either as a good or bad man individually that John is painted; but simply as a politician. Even to the end of the tragedy, notwithstanding his crimes, John is spoken of with respect. Thus says the noble Salisbury, returning to his allegiance: [Quotes 5.4.49–57: the speech that ends with Salisbury referring to 'our ocean. . . our great King John']. Yes; 'great,' just as England was then; no greater, but no less. England's Policy was impersonated in John; in Salisbury no policy at all. In the latter, we have merely the natural man, noble of mind, strong in love, an excellent friend and neighbour, but no politician. His good feelings lead him into political errors, and so much at last he practically acknowledges. The poet shows in this, that, in his idea and mode of treating the historical transactions, he transcended the pettier moralities of private life, and fixed his attention exclusively on their political and national issues.

Salisbury attracts no attention until the fourth act, and then contributes rather to the poetry than the action of the drama. He is recusant against the second coronation of John, for which he cannot appreciate the subtle reason that led to the monarch's submission to it as a desirable expediency: [Quotes 4.2.9–16]. He takes the most obvious, not a recondite, view of affairs; he stands also on the ancient ways, and dislikes novelties. Understanding that Arthur is dead, he affects no reticence, puts no restraint on his feelings, but goes all lengths in disaffection: [Quotes 4.2.93–5: 'It is apparent foul-play. . . .']. Faulconbridge tells him and Pembroke plainly afterwards that 'there is little reason in his grief,' and that 'impatience has only privilege to hurt his master, no man else' [4.3.30ff.]. But there is no chance of his listening to reason or argument; for the sight of the mangled body of the prince, fallen from the castle-walls, transports him into an ecstasy of passion. He will accept no explanation, but gives his fancy free wing, and allows his 'hasty spleen' [4.3.97] to follow suggestion into the wildest suspicions.

We next meet with Salisbury at the French court. He is still the same man. His feelings outrun his reason. He has combined with the stranger against his country, upon what he considers good grounds, yet he cannot restrain his patriotic lamentations: [Quotes 5.2.20–3: 'such is the infection of the time. . . .']. Most remarkable is Lewis's reply to this manifestation of an insupportable sorrow – an irrepressible remorse: [Quotes 5.2.40–59]. But Lewis himself anon has to yield to passionate impulse, when Pandulph enters with the news that John has reconciled himself to the Pontiff. France, as little as England, will be 'propertied' [5.2.79], or consent merely to underplay the game of crafty Rome. The name of 'holy Church' [5.2.71] sinks before that of the dearer State, nor will Lewis sacrifice the latter to the policy of the former. To Pandulph's remark that 'you look but on the outside of this work' [5.2.109], Lewis replies: 'Outside or inside, I will not return / Till my attempt so much be glorified, / As to my ample hope was promised' [5.2.110ff.]. Shockingly must Salisbury's confidence have been shaken by this scene. The legate whom Lewis had invoked 'to give a warrant from the hand of heaven, and on his actions set the name of right with holy breath' [5.2.66ff.], had already sanctioned the cause of John instead. The revolted baron, indeed, says nothing; but when we next meet with him, he is in a state of surprise at the promising prospects of the English monarch: 'I did not think the king so stored with friends' [5.4.1]. With these words he opens the scene; and when Count Melun is led in wounded, to disclose the intended treachery of the French court against 'the revolts of England' [5.4.7], he is prepared to believe the warning, and hesitates not for a second to return to his allegiance. From that moment England is safe. When her princes shall have come home again, then will the Bastard proclaim the national conviction that, 'Come the three quarters of the world in arms, / And we shall shock them. Nought shall make us rue, / If England to itself but rest as true' [5.7.116ff.].

Shakespeare found the character of Faulconbridge in the elder play, but he so remodelled the character as to make it the exponent of the ruling idea of his own. Faulconbridge serves the poet as a kind of chorus; and thus at the end of the second act delivers a lecture on Commodity (or Interest), which Shakespeare was careful to add in this place as a soliloquy, not to be found in the old play. It was to this idea, thus in his usual manner introduced, that he trusted, as the principle of internal unity, by which all the characters and details of the action should be linked together. Such was Shakespeare's sublime notion of dramatic unity, and which he so wisely substituted for the empirical unities of the Greek drama, which grew merely out of the conveniences of its limited stage. By it he elevated the English drama above the sphere of the accidental, and gave to it a philosophical life, which will permanently secure its status at the highest attainable level of poetical endeavour, and invested it with an epic character that will be eternal; a life independent of the stage and its conditions, and which will continue to interest the human race, as a written register of human thought and feeling, long after it shall have ceased to be acted.

Shakespeare here views the character of the Bastard on the best side. Faulconbridge owes his good fortune to his irregular birth, and therefore is not tempted to resentment on that account, like Edmund in *Lear*. Of a rough humour in the beginning, but rising soon to the dignity of his new position, he finds in his occupation a motive to seriousness, and enters on his work with the earnestness of a busy man, who has his way in the world to make. Examples teem around him of self-interestedness, and therefore he is not ashamed, but rather encouraged, to regard

Gain as his deity. His experience of kings and worldly policies begets in him a spirit of irony, which he is not slow to indulge. Nevertheless, he is through all faithful to his sovereign and the land, and steadily wins his way upward by force of his fidelity and independence. He is a partisan who is never even tempted to forsake his cause, either by internal motive or external circumstance, but fits into his place as exactly as it fits him. His courage and daring enable him to encounter all dangers, and carry him successfully through all enterprises. To King John he is an invaluable servant, and is esteemed by all for his boldness and honesty, as well as feared for his straightforward and precipitate valour. . . .

[Heraud now discusses the history behind *King John*, following this with a good deal of plot summary and a digression on Shakespeare's reputation in his own time; he then returns to the play.]

    The tragedy of *King John* is admirable in structure, and capable of being placed on the stage without alteration. It is, indeed, almost as classical for its regularity, as it is for the genius displayed in it. We may judge from it not only the merits of Shakespeare, but those of the playwrights capable of assisting him. The art of historical tragedy, when that of *The Troublesome Raigne* was published, had far advanced. Shakespeare found the skeleton complete; he clothed it with flesh and blood, and added to it beauty. He quickened the body with a soul, and inspired it with an idea; but its mechanism had already been mastered by inferior minds. Our poet was an artist among artists. He could measure himself by others. If among the giants of that elder time he seems a giant, we may judge more accurately of his actual stature than if we measured him by himself alone. But not only may he be compared with his predecessors and contemporaries advantageously, but in many points he presents a perfect contrast to them. It is, for instance, as a politician and philosopher that Shakespeare shines in this magnificent tragedy; as the latter, manifesting an equality with Bacon – in certain aspects, indeed, a superiority. In the transcendental elements of metaphysical science he was far in advance of the learned chancellor, and anticipated the most important discoveries of modern thinkers. And he was all this without ostentation: bearing, in the garden of his mind, philosophy and poetry as naturally as the tree bears fruit; and improving as gradually in power and abundance, as, in more earthly gardens, the most excellent fruit-trees may be made to do, by the aid of cultivation, and the application of diligence and skill. (143–160)

33 Henry Giles, the transcendent sorrow of Constance

1868

From *Human Life in Shakespeare* (Boston, 1868).

Henry Giles (1809–82) was born in Ireland and educated for the Roman Catholic priesthood, but later became a Unitarian, the denomination from which he received a license to preach. Giles's skills in oratory were legendary, and it was primarily as an orator and essayist that he made his reputation. In addition to his many lectures on morals and doctrine (which were frequently published), he also produced a number of books on literary and aesthetic subjects. Among these are his *Illustrations of Genius* (Boston, 1854), which included essays on Cervantes, Hawthorne, Burns, Wordsworth, and De Quincey, as well as on philanthropy, conversation, and music; and the much-admired *Lectures and Essays* (Boston, 1850), which Mary Russell Mitford singled out for special praise in her *Recollections of a Literary Life* (New York, 1852) as an eloquent example of American oratory (515–6). The same could also be said for the lectures printed in *Human Life in Shakespeare*, which were first delivered at the Lowell Institute in Boston to admiring audiences regularly exceeding the house capacity of twelve hundred.

[From Chapter IV: 'Woman in Shakespeare']

. . . In his tragic plays it is that Shakespeare does the sublimest justice to the power which the affections hold in womanly nature. This appears in connection with the two great elements of tragedy – the *pathetic* and the *terrible*. Two or three instances I will adduce in the pathetic. There is a motherly feeling in Constance. And truly in motherly feeling is room for all the depths of tragedy; that feeling – brave and beautiful it is – which, with a passion of desire, welcomes the feeble into light, which watches them through every stage to maturity, nor quits them even then, but still exults or grieves in their success or their misfortunes; and *that* heart which, in the freshness of maternity, the infant's smile could gladden more than could the praise of nations, bounds elastic from the chill of age at any good tidings from the man or woman that once was folded to its beatings; ay, and as it once had bled at the infant's slightest hurt, it can still bleed for that man or woman's misery or sin. This most womanly instinct becomes in Constance the medium of a grief which shakes the entire soul; and Constance – who would otherwise be commonplace – raises herself by her anguish above thrones and worlds. This sorrow of hers in the majesty of motherhood helps us to understand the profound Scripture of 'Rachel weeping for her children,' and refusing to be comforted [Matthew 2.18]. In the daring grandeur of affliction her words speak the divinity of nature; like the words of a death-bed, they spurn dignities and they scorn power. Maternal fear and grief carry her above orators and kings; trouble stirs within her the holiest principles of life: it gives her an authority which conquers sophistry and humbles pomp. Most augustly does she say, – [Quotes 3.1.68–74: 'I will instruct my sorrows to be proud. . . .']. (149–50)

34 Henry Thomas Hall, national interest and personal loyalty

1871

From *Shakespearian Fly-Leaves and Jottings, A New and Enlarged Edition, By H. T. Hall, Author of Shakespearian Statistics, Dramatic Album, The May-Queen, The Latest Edition of the Rye-House Plot, &c.* (London, 1871).

Henry Thomas Hall produced one major study of Shakespeare, *Shakespearian Fly Leaves*, originally published in 1864, and later enlarged with additions that included a chapter on *King John*. Hall's remarks are strongly indebted to those of Heraud (No. 32 above), particularly in his assessment of John and Salisbury; but his essay, despite its occasionally derivative quality, does manage some pointed critical statements of its own. Hall's only other scholarship on Shakespeare consists of two pamphlets: *Shakespearian Statistics* (Cambridge, 1865, 1874), and *Shakespeare's Plays: the Separate Editions of, with the Alterations Done by Various Hands* (Cambridge, 1873, 1880).

. . . [*King John*] is one of the most interesting of the great series of historic plays, for it is full of variety, force and splendour, and the poetic side of the principal characters, so necessary to dramatic fitness; is most excellently preserved. The darker shades in the character of King John are partially lightened up by Shakespeare, for he makes the king to be the representative of the country and the exponent of her policy.[1] The cares and troubles of John are not alone his personal cares and troubles, but they are the cares and troubles of the English nation. In the king we see the nation and his deeds are made to represent the national will. The king is an incarnation of the national interest, and it is as an incarnation of that feeling, that he is always treated with respect, even by his opponents, despite the follies and crimes of which he has been guilty.

The closing scene of John's life is most masterly drawn and it fails not to win our pity for the dying king, whose 'heart is cracked and burned' [5.7.52], and whose life is 'turned to one thread, one little hair' [5.7.54], which breaks when he learns from the lips of his cousin, that the power on which he had trusted for the defence of his kingdom, was with his treasures, 'in the night,' 'all unwarily devoured by the unexpected sea' [5.7.61ff.].

It is a great advantage to this play, a strong element in its success, that its chief interest should be of a national character. Its appeals are thus of a higher character than when appealing to motives of a personal nature, for they affect the spectator and the reader nationally, animating and developing their patriotic feelings and causing them to watch its course with much concern and interest, for the fortunes of their country are involved, either for evil or for good, in the fortunes of the king, who thus becomes the representative of the national policy. . . .

[A completely derivative treatment of Constance follows, in which Hall echoes Jameson (No. 14 above) regarding Constance's maternal love, pride, and power of imagination. After briefly mentioning Arthur as a suffering innocent, Hall moves on to other characters in the play.]

The character of Hubert in his relation to the king is most consistently drawn, for he is a complete courtier, desirous of obeying his sovereign's behests, and he thereby becomes a ready instrument in carrying out the king's will. He is loyal to the king, because in doing so, he is loyal to the state. He is loyal in obedience to his feudal oath and from habitual service, till it hath become with him a necessity. Owing to this latter reason, he, does not like Salisbury and some others of the barons' revolt against the king, and it also prevents him from committing a breach against his country, and preserves his nationality. He is fully cognizant of the craft and subtlety of John, being thoroughly versed in the sinuous policy of his master, and he readily understands the insinuations and murderous intent of the king towards young Arthur, Constance's 'fair son' [3.4.103]. . . . The violence of the times, for it was a barbarous age, have given to Hubert that external roughness and harshness, which he himself thinks prevails within, in this he is however mistaken, for the better part of his nature is not altogether dead, there is a leaven of humanity left, and though he resolves to commit the murder, when he attempts its committal, he is deterred therefrom by the pleadings of the young prince. His latent power of goodness is awakened, he is not proof to the earnest appeals of the fair boy, his resolution is broken down, and though he knows he must undergo 'much danger' [4.1.133] for not perpetrating the deed he 'will not do it for all the treasure that thine uncle owns' [4.1.122]. This is probably one of the greatest dramatic scenes ever penned by Shakespeare, for the two extremes of pity and terror are most wonderfully pourtrayed. It must be ranked among the finest productions of the 'Swan of Avon,' stamping him as a master that completely understood the nature of humanity and the development thereof.

The character of cardinal Pandulph is not only essentially true in its relation to humanity, but it is also true to history. The Annals of the monastery of Burton, recently published, show how thoroughly correct Shakespeare is in his delineation of this papal prelate.[2] Haughty and arrogant, the result of his vanity and the office which he held, Shakespeare fails not to pourtray these features of his character, and he justly puts in his mouth, language by which the desires of the dictatorial priest are fully developed; language which cannot fail to awaken in a discerning and patriotic audience, an intense disgust and hatred of papal pride and papal intolerance. . . .

[Faulconbridge is now briefly treated as an example of the English national character, rough, cheerful, brave, witty, and full of devotion to country.]

Salisbury is a purely natural man, strong in love, a true friend, an excellent neighbour, but no politician.[3] Lacking politics, Salisbury does not attract much attention until the close of the history. He is a man of feeling, not of reasoning powers, and by his feelings he is mostly actuated and directed. When leagued with France against his native land, and having good grounds for such alliance, his feelings will crop up, and he cannot withhold his lamentations, which are strongly imbued with patriotic feeling. He says, [Quotes 5.2.20–6: 'Such is the infection of the time. . . .'].

Salisbury is somewhat surprised at the prospects of his sovereign, his inattention to politics prevented him from forming anything approaching a correct idea of the king's strength, for he says, 'I did not think the king so stored with friends' [5.4.1]. When he is made aware of the intended treachery of France, in the words of the dying Melun, his private wrongs become entirely subservient to the love of his native land. He fails not to take warning, reverting back to his former allegiance, and the honor and safety of England is affirmed.

Both Philip of France and he of Austria, are true representatives of their class. They are selfish and calculating, caring not whether their actions are right or wrong, so long as they will be benefitted by the course of action which they resolve on. In the nature of their kingliness they take oaths, make promises and then as readily break them. They think only of themselves, and their immediate class. They do not seek to advance the interest of the whole, but only their own self-interest, which they consider to be the state. Within the circle of their crowns is concentrated every thing that has a tendency for the promotion of their own advancement, at the same time they are quite oblivious to the advantage of the people. They are firm believers in the divinity that doth hedge a king, though their frequent oath-breakings and acts of rapacity completely demonstrate the fallacy of their belief.

The grouping of the characters is most exquisitely managed, the picture is in every way complete. No other hand but Shakespeare's could have drawn it, and no other brain but his could have pourtrayed with such dramatic power the varied characters of this history, which teaches us a most important lesson, a lesson that should be remembered by all those who are desirous of promoting the welfare of a nation, that no hostile sword, no appeal to a foreign power can ever heal the domestic wounds of a state. The cure must come from within, it lies not in outward intervention. What Faulconbridge exultingly says of his native land, admits of general application: [Quotes 5.7.112–18: 'This England never did, nor never shall. . . .']. (175–83)

35 Richard Simpson, *King John* and contemporary politics

1874

From 'The Politics of Shakespeare's Historical Plays', *The New Shakespeare Society's Transactions*, Part 2 (1874), 396–441.

Richard Simpson (1820–76) became vicar of Mitcham, Surrey in 1844, a position he resigned the following year by virtue of his conversion to Roman Catholicism. As a Catholic of liberal tendencies (and as co-editor of the *Home and Foreign Review* and later as contributor to the *North British Review*), he occasionally ran afoul of church authorities, particularly Cardinal Wiseman. It was in Shakespearian studies, however, that Simpson found a most congenial intellectual home. Fluent in French, German, Italian, Spanish, and Flemish, and meticulous by nature, he became an authority on the holdings at the State Paper Office, finding there just the sort of factual information it pleased him to incorporate into his work on Shakespeare and the Elizabethans. His biography of the adventurer Sir Thomas Stukeley, for example, printed in Simpson's *The School of Shakespeare* (2 vols, London, 1878), is respected to this day.

I. *KING JOHN*.

The alterations from the Chronicles in *King John* are many and considerable, and almost all taken from the old play (*The Troublesome Raigne*, 1591). But though the plot is borrowed, the political tendency of the old play is entirely suppressed. The clearly expressed design of the old play is to show the precursorship of John to the reforming Messiahship of Henry VIII. John was like David, unworthy to build the temple because his 'hands with murder were attaint' [1 Chronicles 22.8]. But a Solomon should succeed who should put down monks and their cells:

> I am not he shall build the Lord a house
> Or root these locusts from the face of earth;
> But if my dying heart deceive me not,
> From out these loins shall spring a kingly branch
> Whose arms shall reach unto the gates of Rome,
> And with his feet tread down the strumpet's pride
> That sits upon the chair of Babylon. [15.101–7]

This leading idea of the old play is utterly excluded from the new, where the points brought out are those connected with the tenure of the crown; whether it is held by hereditary right of the eldest branch, or the eldest male of the family, or by the accident of possession, fortified by the utility of the state; whether it is forfeited by crimes civil and ecclesiastical, whether such forfeiture is to be adjudged and executed by neighbouring sovereigns, or by the State itself, its peers or its people, or by the Pope. For Shakespeare's play is practically a discussion whether John shall remain King. The grounds of the doubt are not, as in the Chronicles, the general villainy of the King, his cruelty, debauchery, effeminacy, falsehood, extravagance, exactions, and general insufficiency, but two points which do not seem to have weighed a scruple in the minds of John's barons – the defect of his title as against the son of his elder brother, and his supposed murder of that son. The historical quarrel against John as a tyrant is changed into a mythical one against him as a usurper, aggravated by his murder of the right heir.

I will select eight points where Shakespeare deserts the Chronicles, without precisely following the old play, which in some particulars he corrects by the Chronicles; showing that his departures from history were retained with full knowledge and intention.

1. In Shakespeare, John is told by his own mother that he must rely on his 'strong possession' [1.1.40] not on his right, and the suggestion of the old play that Arthur, being 'but young and yet unmeet to reign' [2.339], was therefore to be passed over, is thrown out.

2. Elinor tells Constance that she can 'produce a will that bars the title' of Arthur [2.1.191ff.].

3. History is altered to heighten and refine the characters of Arthur and Constance.

4. John's loss of his French possessions is accentuated by the exaggeration of the dowry given to Blanch.

5. The scenes where John first persuades Hubert to murder Arthur, and then reproaches him for it, are inventions of Shakespeare.

6. The compression of John's four wars into two, though absolutely necessary for dramatic arrangement, is so managed as to have an Elizabethan bearing. Of these two wars the poet makes the first to concern Arthur's title, without any religious or ecclesiastical motive. The second he makes to be in revenge for Arthur's death, with an ecclesiastical motive added in John's excommunication. This is wholly unhistorical. No English lord interfered in behalf of Arthur, whose death raised no commotion in England, and was long passed and forgotten before the controversy with the Pope about Langton began. The confederacy between the barons and Lewis was ten years after Arthur's death, with which it had nothing to do. The Shakespearian representation of the troubles of John is that he had first to defend the legitimacy of his title; then that he had to fight his own barons, who revolted from him because he had murdered the heir they acknowledged, and allied themselves with Lewis the Dauphin, who, now Arthur was dead, could claim, in right of his wife, the Spanish Blanch, the throne which John had forfeited by excommunication. The facts of this excommunication are misrepresented in the play. Really, John's kingdom was first put under

interdict; a year afterwards he was excommunicated; but he prevented the document entering the realm, and his theologians maintained that it was void. After four years, Innocent absolved John's vassals from their oath of fealty, and exhorted all Christian knights to assist in dethroning him, and substituting a more worthy successor. John was not proclaimed a heretic, neither was secret assassination of him publicly recommended.

7. Pandulph insinuates to Lewis that it is his interest to abstain from interference till John's murder of his nephew should make interference profitable to himself.

8. Melun's confession of Lewis's intended treachery to the barons is the occasion of their return to allegiance.

Every one of these points, in which the poet deviates from the Chronicles, is so turned as to contain indirect references and allusions to contemporary politics, or to events which had a decisive influence on them.

Thus, 1. It was not the legitimacy of John's title that was the real object of interest to Shakespeare or his audience. Hecuba was nought to them. Elizabeth's title, and the succession to her crown, were the great questions of the day. Her father and brother were the only sovereigns since Richard II., whose titles had been undisputed.

2. The title of Mary of Scotland had been barred by the will of Henry VIII.

3. The helplessness and wrongs of Constance and Arthur are so managed as to suggest parallels with Mary of Scotland, Catherine Grey, or Arabella Stuart.

4. John Lackland's easy renunciation of all his French possessions (exaggerated by Shakespeare) must have suggested a reference to the widely-blamed proceedings by which Calais was lost by Elizabeth's advisers. Leicester is accused of having sold it to the French in 1559 (*Leicester's Commonwealth*, p. 62).[1] We may read George Sanders' ironical description of the French treatment of the Commissioners who went to demand either the money or the town in 1567: 'our gentlemen were but easily entreated there and are returned without either money or possession' (Historical MSS. Commission). Verstegan, in his tract against the Cecilian commonwealth in 1592, returns to this matter three several times, and Bacon in his reply touches it as lightly as possible.[2]

5. The scenes between John and Hubert are considered by Warburton and Malone to be a covert attempt to flatter Elizabeth by throwing on secretary Davison the blame of the Queen of Scots' death.[3] They did not notice that if Hubert is Davison, John is Elizabeth. She cannot be flattered in the second of these scenes unless she is touched by the murderous suggestions of the first. In truth, both fit her completely [3.3.19–73; 4.2.208–69], and it is only wonderful that allusions so plain should have been tolerated.

6. It was no doubt dramatically necessary to abridge and summarize John's wars. But it was not necessary so to abridge them as to make them typify the troubles of Elizabeth. The Shakespearian John has to maintain two quarrels. One for his title, the second for his crown against the agents of the Pope. So it was with Elizabeth. . . .

Up to the year 1569 the doubts of Elizabeth's title were all connected with the validity of her mother's marriage, and the force of her father's testament. In that year Dr Morton was sent over from Rome to denounce to the northern Earls the impending sentence of excommunication, which was actually published against her in 1570. From this time she was declared to have forfeited the crown as a heretic. Dr [Cardinal William] Allen in publishing the Pope's plenary indulgence to all Englishmen who should favour the Spanish invasion of 1588 exhorted 'any person public or private . . . to arrest, put in hold, and deliver up unto the catholic part the said usurper, or any of her complices.'[4] From a princess's prison to her grave is no long journey; and with the proofs of [Roberto di] Ridolfi's commission, and such evidence as the above document, and the notorious teaching of the schools of divinity on tyrannicide, and the examples of the Netherlands and France, it was not wonderful that all the proved or suspected plots to assassinate the Queen, were held to enjoy the connivance, if not the authority, of Rome: and Shakespeare altered the facts of John's interdict, to make them fit the contemporary history of Elizabeth's excommunication. After the execution of the Queen of Scots, Elizabeth's situation was exactly parallel to that of John after the death of Arthur, as (unhistorically) represented by Shakespeare.

7. The politic advice of Pandulph to Lewis to delay interfering till the murder of Arthur should leave Blanch the next claimant, was acted on by Philip II., who prudently delayed his promised intervention in favour of the Queen of Scots, till her death had opened a prospect for the claims of his daughter, the Infanta. Whether Father Parsons was his Pandulph in this counsel, is not clear; but it is certain that Parsons was bitterly hostile to the school of Catholic politicians who would have come into power with the accession of Mary.

8. The intended treachery of Lewis to his English allies is precisely parallel to that intended by Medina Sidonia to the English who might favour his landing. He declared 'that if he might once land in England, both Catholics and heretics that came in his way should be all one to him: his sword could not discern them: so he might make way for his master, all was one to him.' (Wm Watson, *Important Considerations*, p. 73).[5] This declaration was naturally made into a great motive against 'Spaniolation,' as Shakespeare unhistorically makes Lewis's intended treachery the motive for the return of the rebel peers to their allegiance.

One of these points involves a reconstruction of the facts, another a reconstruction of the motives of history. To what end were these liberties taken with the Chronicles? All the changes seem made with a view to the controversy on the title to the crown. This was the standing trouble of Elizabeth's reign. Her own title was controverted, first because she was illegitimate, next because she was excommunicate. The choice of her successor was equally a difficulty. And all the parties, those who opposed her, whether as illegitimate, or as excommunicate and tainted with the murder of the right heir, – those who maintained her, those who advocated the succession of the Scottish King, or Arabella, or the Infanta, or Derby, or Huntingdon, or Essex, all appealed to foreign arbitration. . . .

Amidst these seething anxieties, and before the youthful heirs of the very families on whom the foreigner counted, Shakespeare produced his King John – a king to whom, with Edward II. and Richard II., Philopater and the malcontents were wont to liken the Queen.[6] And he made the example more apposite, and the allusions more telling, by altering history. He showed the faction of Philip, men who thought he had commission

> From that supernal judge that stirs good thoughts
> In any breast of strong authority
> To look into the blots and stains of right. [2.1.112ff.]

that the motive of his interference was not love of right, but 'commodity,' which would make the prince traitor to the cause he pretended to protect, and lightly sacrifice the claimant he backed, on the first scent of gain. Then he showed the Papal faction, the men who invoked the Pope's arbitration as a divine intervention of indifferent justice, that the Pope is and must be indifferent to every cause but his own. He cares not for the legitimacy of the pretender, nor interferes with the usurper who leaves the Church at liberty. John may imprison and murder Arthur, and the Pope is quiescent. But when John refuses to institute Stephen Langton, the Pope comes on the scene with a rival claimant, not more legitimate than John, but likely to be more obedient, a more faithful vassal of the Church. Arthur is too weak for the purpose, so his legitimate claims are disregarded; Lewis seems a fit instrument, and he is selected, and the English barons are commanded to support him. But Lewis thus acquires no title to the Pope's continued support. He may be faithful as Pylades, and valiant as Hercules, John can at any moment cut away the ground from under him by doing penance. An act of politic hypocrisy restores John, makes Lewis an unjust aggressor, and changes the barons from Crusaders and Paladins into insurgents and traitors, handed over to the tender mercies of a false and vindictive tyrant. Such, the poet seems to say, being the result of foreign intervention, civil or ecclesiastical, it follows that home quarrels are to be settled at home, and British wrongs righted by British hands: [Quotes 5.7.112–18: 'This England never did and never shall. . . .']. The moral of the dramatist amounts to this. He seems to say to the malcontents of his day – 'Whatever you think about the justice of your cause or the crimes of your opponents, whatever outrages you have to endure, whatever the merits of the losers or the demerits of the winners – settle your quarrels amongst yourselves, and above all things beware of inviting foreign intervention!' If this was Shakespeare's meaning, it was certainly a lesson eminently needed by, and exactly fitted for, his contemporaries. (397–406)

36 Edward Dowden, the baseness of John

1875

From *Shakespeare: A Critical Study of His Mind and Art* (London, 1875).

Edward Dowden (1843–1913), critic, editor, and poet, was born at Cork and educated at Trinity College, Dublin, where he was appointed to the newly-created chair of English Literature in 1867, only four years after his graduation. An active and industrious scholar who published widely on French, German, and English literature, Dowden disliked Irish nationalism and opposed home rule. He was honored as the first Taylorian Lecturer in the Taylor Institution at Oxford in 1889, and was Clark Lecturer at Trinity College, Cambridge from 1893–6. In addition to his influential work on Shakespeare (which included a biography, popular editions of the *Sonnets*, *Hamlet*, and *Romeo and Juliet*, and numerous short critical pieces and introductions) he also produced editions of Wordsworth, Shelley, and Southey, as well as a large body of criticism on a wide variety of literary subjects and authors. His *Essays Modern and Elizabethan* (London, 1910), published only three years before his death, gives ample evidence of the eclecticism that characterized his scholarly career.

[From Chapter IV: 'The English Historical Plays']

In *King John* the hour of utmost ebb in the national life of England is investigated by the imagination of the poet. The king reigns neither by warrant of a just title, nor, like Bolingbroke, by warrant of the right of the strongest. He knows that his house is founded upon the sand; he knows that he has no justice of God and no virtue of man on which to rely. Therefore he assumes an air of authority and regal grandeur. But within all is rottenness and shame. Unlike the bold usurper Richard, John endeavours to turn away his eyes from facts of which he is yet aware; he dare not gaze into his own wretched and cowardly soul. When threatened by France with war, and now alone with his mother, John exclaims, making an effort to fortify his heart, – 'Our strong possession and our right for us' [1.1.39]. But Elinor, with a woman's courage and directness, forbids the unavailing self-deceit, – 'Your strong possession much more than your right / Or else it must go wrong with you and me' [1.1.40ff.]. King Richard, when he would make away with the young princes, summons Tyrrel to his presence, and enquires with cynical indifference to human sentiment, 'Dar'st thou resolve to kill a friend of mine?' [*Richard III*, 4.2.69], and when Tyrrel accepts the commission, Richard, in a moment of undisguised exultation, breaks forth with 'Thou sing'st sweet music!' [4.2.78]. John would inspire Hubert with his murderous purpose rather like some vague influence than like a personal will, obscurely as some pale mist works which creeps across the fields, and leaves blight behind it in the sunshine. He trembles lest he should have said too much; he trembles lest he should not have said enough; at last the nearer fear prevails, and the words 'death,' 'a grave,' form themselves upon his lips [3.3.65ff.]. Having touched a spring which will produce assassination he furtively withdraws himself from the mechanism of crime. It suits the king's interest afterwards that Arthur should be living, and John adds to his crime the baseness of a miserable attempt by chicanery and timorous sophisms to transfer the responsibility of murder from himself to his instrument and accomplice. He would fain darken the eyes of his conscience and of his understanding.

The show of kingly strength and dignity in which John is clothed in the earlier scenes of the play, must therefore be recognised (although Shakespeare does not obtrude the fact), as no more than a poor pretence of true regal strength and honour. The fact, only hinted in these earlier scenes, becomes afterwards all the more impressive, when the time comes to show this dastard king, who had been so great in the barter of territory, in the sale of cities, in the sacrifice of love and marriage-truth to policy; now changing from pale to red in the presence of his own nobles, now vainly trying to tread back the path of crime, now incapable of enduring the physical suffering of the hour of death. Sensible that he is a king with no inward strength of justice or of virtue, John endeavours to buttress up his power with external supports; against the advice of his nobles he celebrates a second coronation, only forthwith to remove the crown from his head and place it in the hands of an Italian priest. Pandulph 'of fair Millaine cardinal' [3.1.138], who possesses the astuteness and skill to direct the various conflicting forces of the time to his own advantage, Pandulph is the *de facto* master of England, and as he pleases makes peace or announces war.

The country, as in periods of doubt and danger, was 'possessed with rumours, full of idle dreams' [4.2.145]. Peter of Pomfret had announced that before Ascension day at noon the king should deliver up his crown. John submits to the degradation demanded of him, and has the incredible baseness to be pleased that he has done so of his own free will: [Quotes 5.1.25–9: 'Is this Ascension day? . . .]. After this we are not surprised that when the Bastard endeavours to rouse him to manliness and resolution, 'Away and glister like the god of war / When he intendeth to become the field' [5.1.54ff.], John is not ashamed to announce the 'happy peace' [5.1.63] which he has made with the Papal legate, on whom he relies for protection against the invaders of England. Faulconbridge still urges the duty of an effort at self-defence, for the sake of honour, and of safety, and the King, incapable of accepting his own responsibilities and privileges, hands over the care of England to his illegitimate nephew, 'Have thou the ordering of this present time' [5.1.77].

There is little in the play of *King John* which strengthens or gladdens the heart. In the tug of selfish power, hither and thither, amid the struggle of kingly greeds, and priestly pride, amid the sales of cities, the loveless marriage of princes, the rumours and confusion of the people, a pathetic beauty illumines the boyish figure of Arthur, so gracious, so passive, untouched by the adult rapacities and crimes of the others: [Quotes 2.1.163–5: 'Good, my mother, peace! . . .'].

The voice of maternal passion, a woman's voice impotent and shrill, among the unheeding male forces, goes up also from the play. There is the pity of stern, armed men for the ruin of a child's life. These, and the boisterous but genuine and hearty patriotism of Faulconbridge, are the only presences of human virtue or beauty which are to be perceived in the degenerate world depicted by Shakespeare. And the end, like what preceded it, is miserable. The King lies poisoned, overmastered by mere physical agony, agony which leaves little room for any pangs of conscience, were the palsied moral nature of the criminal capable of such nobler suffering: 'I am a scribbled form, drawn with a pen / Upon a parchment, and against this fire / Do I shrink up' [5.7.32ff.]. (169–73)

37 Algernon Charles Swinburne, Shakespeare's art of characterization

1875-6

From 'The Three Stages of Shakespeare', *The Fortnightly Review*, [Part One] 17, NS, No. 101 (1 May, 1875), 613–632; [Part Two] 19, NS, No. 109 (1 January, 1876), 24–45.

Algernon Charles Swinburne (1837–1909), poet and critic, spent three largely unremarkable years at Balliol College, Oxford, leaving in 1860 without taking a degree. But sometime after a tour of Italy during which he met Walter Savage Landor, one of the numerous men of letters who exerted a strong aesthetic influence upon him, he began writing the poetry that was to secure his literary reputation. As a critic Swinburne is unabashedly florid and impressionistic, investing his critical prose with the same aural sensuousness and rhythmical virtuosity that characterizes his poetry. Exhibiting little interest as a critic in emerging scholarly methods or even the pretense of dispassionate judgment (he condemned with relish 'the horny eye' and 'callous finger' of the pedant) Swinburne embraced the rhapsodic, particularly in his writing on Shakespeare. His two-part essay was later reprinted in his *Study of Shakespeare* (London, 1880), essentially forming the basis of that book.

[In Part One of his essay Swinburne defends his critical approach to Shakespeare, arguing that on the basis of internal evidence alone it is possible to divide the dramatist's career into three distinct phases. He places *King John* in the second of these phases, 'that of perfection in comic and historic style', which he treats in Part Two of his essay.]

[From Part Two]

The ripest fruit of historic or national drama, the consummation and the crown of Shakespeare's labours in that line, must of course be recognised and saluted by all students in the supreme and sovereign trilogy of *Henry IV.* and *Henry V.* On a lower degree only than this final and imperial work we find the two chronicle histories which remain to be classed [*King John* and *Henry VIII*]. In style as in structure they bear witness of a power less perfect, a less impeccable hand. They have less of perceptible instinct, less of vivid and vigorous utterance; the breath of their inspiration is less continuous and less direct, the fashion of their eloquence is more deliberate and more prepense; there is more of study and structure apparent in their speech, and less in their general scheme of action. Of all Shakespeare's plays they are the most rhetorical; there is more talk than song in them, less poetry than oratory; more finish than form, less movement than incident. Scene is laid upon scene, and event succeeds event, as stone might be laid on stone and story might succeed story in a building reared by mere might of human handiwork; not as in a city or temple whose walls had risen of themselves to the lyric breath and stroke of a greater than Amphion; moulded out of music by no rule or line of mortal measure, with no sound of axe or anvil, but only of smitten strings; built by harp and not by hand.

The lordly structure of these poems is the work of a royal workman, full of masterdom and might, sublime in the state and strength of its many mansions, but less perfect in proportion and less aërial in build than the very highest fabrics fashioned after his own great will by the supreme architect of song. Of these plays, and of these alone among the maturer works of Shakespeare, it may be said that the best parts are discernible from the rest, divisible by analysis and separable by memory from the scenes which precede them or follow and the characters which surround them or succeed. Constance and Katherine rise up into remembrance apart from their environment and above it, stand clear in our minds of the crowded company with which the poet has begirt their central figures. In all other of his great tragic works, even in *Hamlet*, if we have grace and sense to read it aright and not awry, it is not of any single person or separate passage that we think when we speak of it; it is to the whole masterpiece that the mind turns at mention of its name. The one entire and perfect chrysolite of *Othello* is neither Othello nor Desdemona nor Iago, but each and all; the play of *Hamlet* is more than Hamlet himself, the poem even here is too great to be resumed in the person. But Constance is the jewel of *King John*, and Katherine the crowning blossom of *King Henry VIII*. . . . Not indeed that without these the ground would in either case be barren; but that in either field our eye rests rather on these and other separate ears of wheat that overtop the ranks, than on the waving width of the whole harvest at once. In the one play our memory turns next to the figures of Arthur and the Bastard, in the other to those of Wolsey and his king: the residue in either case is made up of outlines more lightly and slightly drawn. In two scenes the figure of King John rises indeed to the highest height even of Shakespearian tragedy; for the rest of the play, the lines of his character are cut no deeper, the features of his personality stand out in no sharper relief, than those of Elinor or the French king; but the scene in which he tempts Hubert to the edge of the pit of hell sounds a deeper note and touches a subtler string in the tragic nature of man than had been struck by any poet save Dante alone, since the reign of the Greek tragedians. The cunning and profound simplicity of the few last weighty words which drop like flakes of poison that blister where they fall from the deadly lips of the king is a new quality in our tragic verse; there was no foretaste of such a thing in the passionate imagination which clothed itself in the mighty music of Marlowe's burning song. The elder master might indeed have written the magnificent speech which ushers in with gradual rhetoric and splendid reticence the black suggestion of a deed without a name; his hand might have woven with no less imperial skill the elaborate raiment of words and images which wraps up in fold upon fold, as with swaddling-bands of purple and golden embroidery, the shapeless and miscreated birth of a murderous purpose that labours into light even while it loathes the light and itself; but Shakespeare alone has given us the first sample of that more secret and terrible knowledge which reveals itself in the brief heavy whispers that seal the commission and sign the warrant of the king. Webster alone of all our tragic poets has had strength to emulate in this darkest line of art the handiwork of his master. We find nowhere such an echo or reflection of the spirit of this scene as in the last tremendous dialogue of Bosola with Ferdinand in the house of murder and madness [*The Duchess of Malfi*, 4.2], while their spotted souls yet flutter between conscience and distraction, hovering for an hour as with broken wings on the confines of either province of hell. One pupil at least could put to this awful profit the study of so great a model; but, with the single and sublime exception of that other design from the same great hand, which bares before us the mortal anguish of Bracciano [in Webster's *White Devil*, 5.3], no copy or imitation of the scene in which John dies by poison has ever come near enough to evade the sentence it provokes.... As far beyond the reach of any but his maker's hand is the pattern of a perfect English warrior, set once for all before the eyes of all ages in the figure of the noble Bastard. The national side of Shakespeare's genius, the heroic vein of patriotism that runs like a thread of living fire through the world-wide range of his omnipresent spirit, has never, to my thinking, found vent or expression to such glorious purpose as here. Not even in Hotspur or Prince Hal has he mixed with more godlike sleight of hand all the lighter and graver good qualities of the national character, or compounded of them all so lovable a nature as this. In those others we admire and enjoy the same bright fiery temper of soul, the same buoyant and fearless mastery of fate or fortune, the same gladness and glory of life made lovely with all the labour and laughter of its full fresh days; but no quality of theirs binds our hearts to them as they are bound to Philip – not by his loyal valour, his keen young wit, his kindliness, constancy, readiness of service, as swift and sure in the day of his master's bitterest shame and shamefullest trouble as in the blithest hour of battle and that first good fight which won back his father's spoils from his father's slayer; but more than all these, for that lightning of divine rage and pity, of tenderness that speaks in thunder and indignation that makes fire of its tears, in the horror of great compassion which falls on him, the tempest and storm of a beautiful and godlike anger which shakes his strength of spirit and bows his high heart down at sight of Arthur dead. Being thus, as he is; the English masterwork of Shakespeare's hand, we may well accept him as the best man known to us that England ever made; the hero that Nelson must have been had he never come too near Naples.

I am not minded to say much of Shakespeare's Arthur; there are one or two figures in the world of his work of which there are no words that would be fit or good to say. Another of these is Cordelia. The place they have in our lives and thoughts is not one for talk; the niche set apart for them to inhabit in our secret hearts is not penetrable by the lights and noises of common day. There are chapels in the cathedral of man's highest art as in that of his inmost life, not made to be set open to the eyes and feet of the world. Love and death and memory keep charge for us in silence of some beloved names. It is the crowning glory of genius, the final miracle and transcendent gift of poetry, that it can add to the number of these and engrave on the very heart of our remembrance fresh names and memories of its own creation. . . .

We have come now to that point at the opening of the second stage in his work where the supreme genius of all time begins first to meddle with the mysteries and varieties of human character, to handle its finer and more subtle qualities, to harmonize its more untuned and jarring discords; giving here and thus the first proof of a power never shared in like measure by the mightiest among the sons of men, a sovereign and serene capacity to fathom the else unfathomable depths of spiritual nature, to solve its else insoluble riddles, to reconcile its else irreconcilable discrepancies. In his first stage Shakespeare had dropped his plummet no deeper into the sea of the spirit of man than Marlowe had sounded before him; and in the channel of simple emotion no poet could cast surer line with steadier hand than he. Further down in the dark and fiery depths of human pain and mortal passion no soul could search than his who first rendered into speech the aspirations and the agonies of a ruined and revolted spirit. And until Shakespeare found in himself the strength of eyesight to read and the cunning of handiwork to render those wider diversities of emotion and those further complexities of character which lay outside the range of Marlowe, he certainly cannot be said to have outrun the winged feet, outstripped the fiery flight of his forerunner. In the heaven of our tragic song the first-born star on the forehead of its herald god was not outshone till the full midsummer meridian of that greater godhead before whom he was sent to prepare a pathway for the sun. Through all the forenoon of our triumphant day, till the utter consummation and ultimate ascension of dramatic poetry incarnate and transfigured in the mastersinger of the world, the quality of his tragedy was as that of Marlowe's, broad, single, and intense; large of hand, voluble of tongue, direct of purpose. . . .

[Swinburne continues in this vein for some time before finally returning to the play, specifically the character of the Bastard.]

. . . But the character of the Bastard, clear and simple as broad sunlight though it be, has in it other features than [a] single and beautiful likeness of frank young manhood; his love of country and loathing of the Church that would bring it into subjection are two sides of the same national quality that has made and will always make every Englishman of his type such another as he was in belief and in unbelief, patriot and priest-hater; and no part of the design bears such witness to the full-grown perfection of his creator's power and skill as the touch that combines and fuses into absolute unity of concord the high and various elements of faith in England, loyalty to the wretched lord who has made him knight and acknowledged him kinsman, contempt for his abjection at the foul feet of the Church, abhorrence of his crime and constancy to his cause for something better worth the proof of war than his miserable sake who hardly can be roused, even by such exhortation as might put life and spirit into the dust of dead men's bones, to bid his betters stand and strike in defence of the country dishonoured by his reign.

It is this new element of variety in unity, this study of the complex and diverse shades in a single nature, which requires from any criticism worth attention some inquisition of character as complement to the investigation of style. Analysis of any sort would be inapplicable to the actors who bear their parts in the comic, the tragic or historic plays of the first period. There is nothing in them to analyse; they are, as we have seen, like all the characters represented by Marlowe, the embodiments or the exponents of single qualities and simple forces. The question of style also is therefore so far a simple question; but with the change and advance in thought and all matter of spiritual study and speculation this question also becomes complex, and inseparable, if we would pursue it to any good end, from the analysis of character and subject. In the debate on which we are now to enter, the question of style and the question of character, or as we might say the questions of matter and of spirit, are more than ever indivisible from each other, more inextricably interwoven than elsewhere into the one most difficult question of authorship which has ever been disputed in the dense and noisy school or fought out in the wide and windy field of Shakespearian controversy. (31–37)

38 John Weiss, Constance and the nature of woman

1876

From *Wit, Humor, and Shakespeare. Twelve Essays* (Boston, 1876).

John Weiss (1818–79), author and Unitarian minister, was the descendant of a Jewish immigrant grandfather who came to America from Germany as a political refugee. Weiss graduated from Harvard in 1837, and also for a time attended Harvard Divinity School and the University of Heidelberg. Zealous and high-minded by nature (he openly opposed slavery), Weiss was a witty, eloquent, and often satirical homilist, who, despite his considerable rhetorical skills, had difficulty maintaining a congregation. He turned to writing and lecturing as a means of support, contributing numerous articles to some of the leading periodicals of the day, and publishing several books, the most notable of which was his impressive *Life and Correspondence of Theodore Parker* (2 vols, London, 1863). As a critic Weiss is both eccentric and sententious; his love for digression, rhetorical embroidery, and decorous wit, often enough leads him to a provocative if idiosyncratic point, and seldom fails to entertain.

[From Essay VII, 'Women and Men']

... None of the women in the historical plays stand by the side of the men so emphasized as the mother of Arthur is: she agitates his claims with an impetuous sincerity that ought to have kept him alive to reign.

A high-minded man who claims his rights, and a high-minded woman who does the same, express themselves in different styles. The feminine style is shown in Constance with great discrimination. Both sexes can hate injustice, and may be opposed to compromises. Both can have indignation for a crime. But see how Constance puts into these moral feelings a scorn and a swiftness of dissent, urged by a volubility more native to a woman than to a man. Woman is apt, indeed, to be too voluble: each minute of her phrases breeds new ones; so she does not stop to notice that her indictment is shorter than her breath. Therefore men are apt to notice and to complain that her indictment does not reach up to the tide-mark of her breath. But the invective of Constance is the swift weapon-play of maternity: it flashes through every guard, touches rapidly to and fro, and draws blood at every unexpected touch.

A man's moral disposition has not been nourished and toned by the additional organs which impose wifehood and motherhood upon a woman. In her, more nerve centres are involved, with an exquisite sensibility for pain and pleasure which the average man's life seldom reaches. His bosom is not ample enough to contain such throbs of acquiescence or revolt. Every fount of feeling is twinned in woman, and sweet as the milk is, mingled by love, so sharp and bitter is its flavor made by hate. Her nerves revenge the violence of acts which she supposes dishonorable: she can fight with glances more searching and words more unequivocal than the cooler man will furnish. No doubt that his disdains, too, can summon all his blood to blush and lower magnificently on the cheek. But her blood seems richer in the red corpuscles: it wins, therefore, and is more visited by, the air of heaven. There is no blush so daunting, no look so penetrating to dissolve, no silence of a surprised conscience so unanswerable. And when she grieves, it seems as if the eyes were re-enforced, for all the founts of motherhood are weeping.

This ability to vindicate the right and to repudiate the wrong can easily become absurd to the spectators when it is charged with some excess of temper. Literature does ample justice to the termagant vein, and shows that it is ludicrous because it devotes a high degree of choler to a low measure of affront. In pantomimes, an enormous gun is pointed toward the audience, with extravagant anticipation of its exploit on the faces of the performers. For a moment we are cowed, but laughter fills the vast space between the faint puff and the noise we expected. . . .

Shakespeare shows the exaggeration of the protesting temper in woman by means of the little spat between Queen Elinor and Constance [2.1].

A woman's language becomes exacerbated because she is so inadequate to protest by actions. The weakness rolls itself into a bristling defence of words. Men do not drip so profusely into words because they are reservoirs of force and competency. They know that by fair means or foul they can effect purposes from which women are debarred by seclusion, strangeness of habit, and innate reserve. Among women there is a certain resentment at this civic and social disability which does not stint expression.

When, however, a noble woman with a level countenance repudiates an unjust charge, she transfers herself from the bar to the bench, and unseats her summoners. Their purpose quails before this innocence that is so weak, yet grows so overpowering, as in the beauty of Madame Roland[1] and the prison-blanched majesty of Marie Antoinette. The rebuke pulls down the accuser's eyes from their threat, and they seem to go wandering into corners furtively for refuge. Joan of Arc burns in court before the deluded men who claim her as an imp of witchcraft have time to pile their faggots: the passionless chastity gives out blinding sparks when thus enforced; the cheeks of by-standers are reached by them and set aglow. No man who has been unjustly dealt with, and selected for foul practice, can reach such palsying dignity of behavior that turns the axe's edge or holds the arm suspended in mid-resolve. There is a high manly scorn which is beyond refuting: it can kindle admiration in unwilling minds, and compel baseness to pause and to confer. But woman's beauty, planted in the breastplate of an untainted heart, becomes a petrifying image; and whoso meets the ruthless look will remember it even in the moment of a consummated revenge. Nothing helps bad men at such a sight but the poor subterfuge of flying into a rage, as if to muster in that way momentum enough to huddle her off, to get her where the condemning head shall fall before its eyes or lips can utter another protest. They shear it at the neck, never reflecting that they thus untether it to range in other skies, to unkennel heaven sleuth-hounds at last and drag them down: [Quotes 3.1.68–74: ' I will instruct my sorrows to be proud. . . .']. (240–4)

39 Frederick James Furnivall, *King John*, *Richard III*, and character

1877

From *The Leopold Shakespeare. The Poet's Works, in Chronological Order, from the Text of Professor Delius, with 'The Two Noble Kinsmen' and 'Edward III.,' and an Introduction by F. J. Furnivall. Illustrated* (London, 1877).

Frederick James Furnivall (1825–1910) was one of the most zealous and tireless exponents of both social egalitarianism and the need to preserve early English texts, devoting virtually his whole adult life to both causes. In addition to his prodigious output as an editor and scholar, Furnivall founded a number of societies and institutions, among them the Working Men's College, the Early English Text Society, the Chaucer Society, the Ballad Society, the New Shakespeare Society, and the Shelley Society. His dedication to the reform of English spelling along phonetic lines and his faith in metrical tests as aids in the dating of Shakespeare's plays often drew scorn from so-called 'aesthetic' critics, most notably Swinburne (No. 37 above), who engaged in a prolonged journalistic war with Furnivall over scholarly methods from 1876–81 that also included J. O. Halliwell-Phillips as an adherent of Swinburne. Furnivall was a contentious and often dismissive critic; yet his contribution to literary scholarship is unchallenged. It is largely to his energy and foresight that we owe the existence today of reliable editions of many early English texts, and he was the first to begin work on what eventually became the *New English Dictionary*, a project to which he contributed throughout his life.

[From the 'Introduction']

KING JOHN. – With this play of pathos and patriotism we open Shakespeare's Second Period, – looking on *Richard II.* as the last play in which ryme plays a prominent part, we take the series of *Henry VI.* and *Richard III.* as the transition to the Second Period; – and on opening it we are struck with a greater fulness of characterisation and power than we saw in the First-Period plays. But the whole work of Shakespeare is continuous. *King John* is very closely linkt with *Richard III*. In both plays we have cruel uncles planning their nephews' murder, because the boys stand between them and the Crown. In both we have distracted mothers overwhelmd with grief. In both we have prophecies of ruin and curses on the murderers, and in both the fulfilment of these. In both we have the kingdom divided against itself, and the horrors of civil war. In both we have the same lesson of the danger of division taught to the discontented English parties of Shakespeare's own day. *Richard III.* is an example of the misgovernment of a cruel tyrant; *King John* of the misgovernment of a selfish coward. But in *John* we have the mother's pathetic lament for her child far developed above that of Queen Elizabeth's for her murdered innocents, and far more touching than the laments of Queen Margaret and the Duchess of York, while the pathos of the stifled children's death is heightened in that of Arthur. The temptation scene of John and Hubert, repeats that of Richard and Tyrrel. The Bastard's statement of his motives, 'Gain be my lord,' &c. [2.1.598], is like that of Richard the Third's about his villainy. (The Bastard's speech on commodity may be compared with Lucrece's reproaches to opportunity.) Besides the boy's pleading for his life, besides his piteous death and the mother's cry for him, which comes home to every parent who has lost a child,[1] we have in the play the spirit of Elizabethan England's defiance to the foreigner[2] and the Pope. . . .

[Furnivall briefly treats Shakespeare's departures from *The Troublesome Raigne*, citing Simpson (No. 35 above) and Lloyd (No. 27 above) favorably, then moves on to a discussion of character.]

So long as John is the impersonator of England, of defiance to the foreigner, and opposition to the Pope, so long is he a hero. But he is bold outside only, only politically; inside, morally, he is a coward, sneak, and skunk. See how his nature comes out in the hints for the murder of Arthur, his turning on Hubert when he thinks the murder will bring evil to himself, and his imploring Faulconbridge to deny it. His death ought, of course, dramatically to have followed from some act of his in the play, as revenge for the murder of Arthur, or his plundering the abbots or abbeys, or opposing the Pope. The author of *The Troublesome Raigne*, with a true instinct, made a monk murder John out of revenge for his anti-Papal patriotism.[3] But Shakespeare, unfortunately, set this story aside, though there was some warrant for it in Holinshed, and thus left a serious blot on his drama which it is impossible to remove. The character which to me stands foremost in *John* is Constance, with that most touching expression of grief for the son she had lost. Beside her cry, the tender pleading of Arthur for his life is heard, and both are backed by the rough voice of Faulconbridge, who, Englishman-like, depreciates his own motives at first, but is lifted by patriotism into a gallant soldier, while his deep moral nature shows itself in his heartfelt indignation at Arthur's supposed murder. The rhetoric of the earlier historical plays is kept up in *King John*, and also Shakespeare's power of creating situations, which he had possessed from the first. . . . (xl)

[Furnivall concludes his remarks on *King John* by quoting extensively and approvingly from Jameson's discussion of Constance (No. 14 above), and conjecturing that the play was probably written in 1595.]

40 Denton Jaques Snider, the theme of nationality

1877

From *System of Shakespeare's Dramas* (2 vols, St. Louis, 1877).

Denton Jaques Snider (1841–1925), philosopher and Hellenist, was one of the original members of the St. Louis Philosophical Society, bringing to the St. Louis movement a literary perspective and broadness of outlook often lacking in its older members. As both a compelling public lecturer and educational reformer, Snider introduced the idealism of the St. Louis movement as well as his particular brand of aesthetic literary criticism to many places throughout the American Middle West. He spent nearly the last thirty years of his life living and writing in an immigrant boarding house in St. Louis, often publishing his books (under the imprint of the Sigma Publishing Company) at his own expense. *System of Shakespeare's Dramas* falls in the middle period of Snider's career, between his early work on classical subjects and his many later books on philosophy which outline his grand 'psychologic' system.

[From the Chapter entitled '*King John*']

King John strikes the key-note of the whole series of English Historical plays, namely, nationality. Its very beginning utters a defiance against France, the hereditary foe of England. The glory and supremacy of Fatherland constitute the theme; there is a glow of patriotic exultation, which makes many verses shine like diamonds, while the spirit of the whole work is one grand outburst of the love of country. There is in it the intense consciousness of English greatness, English freedom, English manhood. The style, though varied, is always an exalted reflection of its thought and feeling; the poetic fervor rises at times to a sort of national ecstasy. Other strong passions of the human soul are portrayed in the play, but they are all subordinated to supreme devotion to country. Such is the atmosphere which we here breathe, and which nerves the spirit with a new inspiration. Indeed, there is a special character introduced as the representative of nationality – a character which gives tone to the entire drama. It is Faulconbridge, whose story is the golden thread which both illumines and holds together the other parts of the action. Following his career, we are perpetually reminded of the theme which furnishes life and unity to the work.

In reading *King John* the chief disappointment seems to arise from the fact that nothing is said of the Great Charter. . . .

Personal liberty, in its universal sense, was certainly not the essential point in the conflict between King John and his barons; that conflict arose between the rights of the nobility and the rights of the crown. The people, as such, occupy no prominent place in the Great Charter. But in the time of the Stuarts the struggle lay between the people on the one side, and the crown and nobility on the other. Had the poet lived earlier or later, he might have taken one or the other form of this collision; as the case stands, he takes neither. The age of Elizabeth was not a struggle between the throne and the barons, nor between these united and the people. The elements of the nation were in harmony, hence it was a period of internal peace and national development. But there was a dynastic conflict with a foreign State, and a religious conflict with a foreign Church. The consciousness arising from this condition of affairs is precisely the foundation of the present drama; hence its theme is, primarily, the Right of Succession to the crown.[1] Must the title vest absolutely in the eldest of the line? Is it necessary or just that the heir should always be monarch? Here the answer will be given by Shakespeare. Secondary, but important, is the conflict with the See of Rome. The Poet cannot live out of his own time, in any true sense of the term; he writes his play, though it be historical, from the standpoint of his age.

The action will show the nation upholding the king, both against the legal heir of the throne and against the Church, as long as that king, in so doing, maintains the right and supremacy of the State. It will also show the nation falling off from the sovereign when the latter abandons his national principle and seeks to support his authority by violence and by external power. Thus there will be a transition from the true monarch of the people to the unfit occupant of a throne. The consciousness which underlies the whole fabric is that the right of a nation to a ruler is superior to the right of an heir to the crown. A kingdom is not a mere piece of personal property, subject to the laws of inheritance, or even of possession. Such is the conflict, plainly indicated; it is the universal right of the State against the individual right of the heir or of the possessor.

The drama has two well-marked movements – the one portraying the external struggle of the nation, the other portraying its internal struggle. Each movement has also two threads – the English and the foreign – and upon these threads the action takes its course. The first movement shows the king in conflict with the two extraneous powers – France and the Church – the political and the religious enemy. Both unite against England – the one supporting the right of Arthur as the legal heir to the throne, the other asserting the claim of Papal domination. King John steps forth as the defender of imperilled nationality; the people support him; he wins a complete victory over his combined enemies. This victory is brought about chiefly by Faulconbridge, the type of the English national hero. Such is the first movement; the nation supports the king against the heir and against the Pope. The second movement now begins; it will show the change of character in the monarch, and the consequent disruption of the country internally. As long as John maintained the honor of England abroad, and took nationality as his guiding principle, he retained the unswerving allegiance of the English people. But he has the misfortune to capture the true heir, and at once he plots the young prince's murder to secure his throne. Thus, by his own act, he makes title of supreme importance; and, as he has not the legal title in himself, he logically destroys his own cause. He abandons his national principle for the principle of inheritance, which he had himself previously nullified. His title is now questioned, since it is his own deed which calls attention to its defect. Revolt of the nobles follows; disaffection of the people shows itself in dark forebodings. Then comes foreign invasion added to domestic strife, and, finally, an ignoble submission to the Church – that is, the victory which ended the first movement is completely reversed. John is no longer the true ruler, though he may now be the true heir after the death of Arthur; the nation is assailed from within and from without, and seems on the point of succumbing to the foreign political and to the foreign religious power – to France and to Rome. Nothing now remains to the king – who has sacrificed his most glorious national attribute, namely, the maintenance of the independence of England against all foes, internal and external – but death. Still, the nation cannot perish with him; the national hero, Faulconbridge, again comes to the rescue of the drooping country; the enemy is worsted and retires, the nobles return to loyalty, a new king is crowned, and England is once more free from dissension and war. The very last speech of the play echoes the spirit of the whole; it is the exultant declaration of this same Faulconbridge, the embodiment of English nationality, wherein he utters a parting shout of triumph and defiance: [Quotes 5.7.112–18: 'This England never did. . . .'].

I. 1. We can now proceed to the detailed elaboration of the plan which has just been outlined. Let us follow out the English thread of the first movement. The beginning of the play ushers in at once the national conflict between France and England – a conflict which is continually reappearing throughout this whole series of historical dramas; hence the little scene here given is a kind of introduction to all which is to follow. The pretext on the part of France now is the claim of young Arthur to the throne. The simple legality of this claim is unquestioned. It is admitted by Queen Elinor, by Faulconbridge, and, indirectly, by John himself; indeed, the pith of the play would be destroyed by a denial of it. But the assertion of Arthur's title by France is assailing the autonomy of England, since a foreign potentate thus dictates who shall be her ruler. A legitimate king who owes his throne to external support cannot be the true representative of the State; thus there arises a struggle between the right of inheritance and the right of the nation.

John is now forced, as it were, into becoming the defender of his country, and, hence, the bearer of nationality. This is his only claim – and, indeed, it is the highest claim – to the throne; but he will lose sight of it – he will prove unequal to his lofty position. England is ready to ratify his title if he have the mettle of a ruler. It is at this point that we see the defect of his character; he starts well, but breaks down. The poem, however, must have a man without this flaw – a true and persistent representative of the national spirit – in order to supply what is wanting in the King. Here he comes, just after the defiance given to France; it is Faulconbridge, to whose origin and personal qualities a long scene is devoted – not without purpose.

Let us scan him closely, therefore, and note every essential peculiarity with which the Poet has endowed him, for his character and actions belong not to History. The traits, physical and mental, which he manifests are so pronounced that the Queen-mother at once recognizes the young stranger to be the son of her son, Richard

Cœur-de-Lion, whose exploits in the Holy Land had made him the English national hero. The descent of Faulconbridge is finally established by the confession of his own mother. Thus both his ancestry and his character point him out as the heir and supporter of English nationality. But the circumstance which is dwelt upon with special emphasis is his illegitimacy. The use to which the Poet puts this incident is in every way noteworthy, since it would seem to be a perilous fact to meddle with in a drama.

The object is manifestly to sever the heroic individual from the ethical relation of the Family in order to consecrate him more exclusively to the State. Faulconbridge is first introduced to us disputing the claim of his legitimate brother to the paternal estate. His title to the property is based upon the fact that he is the elder son, which fact would ordinarily make out a clear sense of right; but his sonship is questioned, and, what is more, is wholly disproved. He manifestly does not believe in his own claim; he very soon abandons it and accepts sonship derived from the great King Richard, outside of the pale of the Family. Thus he is declared the heir of that man whom the nation delights to call its hero, and now he will begin life anew as the champion of nationality. The frail-bodied, weak-spirited brother takes the inheritance of the Family, while Faulconbridge himself is adopted into the great national family of the Plantagenets. The English humor which previously added such a healthy flavor to his English good sense now overflows his whole being, yet he is imbued with a hearty earnestness in every fiber. He takes pride in his birth; he would not choose any other if he could. Legitimacy only is derived from the Family; his institution, the State, is something more exalted and more worthy of a great character. His origin, therefore, is national – as near as such a thing is possible – and not domestic; his career must be national, and not domestic.

In other plays the Poet has introduced the Bastard, but has endowed him with a character altogether different. In *Lear* and in *Much Ado About Nothing* he is portrayed as the natural villain, in hostility with the whole Ethical World. Since both Family and State disown him, deride him, oppress him without any fault of his own, he turns against them both and tries to destroy them. Such is the logical result of illegitimacy amid social institutions – their victim becomes their bitterest foe. But in the present play the Bastard is rescued by being elevated into a national existence, which is the more intense and vigorous because of his total separation from the domestic bond. He thus can have an institutional – and, hence, a truly national – life. Such is the meaning of his adoption into the Plantagenets – the royal family is national rather than domestic; but even in it he is still not legitimate.

The third character of this English group will express a new relation between Family and State. It is now a woman – Elinor – usually called the Queen-mother; that is, both queen and mother. Thus there are united in her person two relations – the political and the maternal – which are always incompatible and often in collision. On the French side is her counterpart, Constance, who also is, or aspires to be, Queen-mother. Each is the real power behind the throne, and each without doubt justly blames the other for the troubles which have sprung up; both have equal hate, yet both show a touch of horror at the war. The effect of this political relation of the mother upon the Family is now seen – its members are torn asunder with the passions of civil strife; Elinor opposes the claim of her grandchild, Constance goes to war with her son's kindred. Elinor is now Queen-mother, but, if Arthur possesses the crown, then she will no longer be Queen-mother, but Constance will be. Thus political ambition is the motive which drives her to disrupt her own family – to violate the right of her own grandson, a right which she herself acknowledges to be valid. Domestic life is impossible in such a condition of affairs; the tender maternal relation loses its sweetness and beauty; its vital warmth is deadened by a political relation. Womanhood, too, drops its highest, most glorious, principle – devotion to the Family; its purity is sullied with rancor and intrigue; the female emotional nature turns to gall and becomes the source of the most bitter passion.

It is not to be denied, however, that a rational ground can be given for introducing the domestic into the political relation in the case of royal families; indeed, such a procedure is inwoven into the very fabric of the customs, laws, and institutions of modern Europe. Still, it means the sacrifice of the woman in the subordination of Family to State, for thus her world is destroyed or plunged into an atmosphere poisonous to its organization. Such is the English thread. . . .
[Snider now discusses the 'French thread' of his interpretive scheme, starting with Constance, whom he regards as a woman of great ambition and passion who is nonetheless made the instrument of France. After briefly treating Austria as a foil to the Bastard, he takes up the characters of Philip and Lewis.]

Next comes the French rulers, father and son, whose contrast lies chiefly in their moral natures. The King is a man of conscience; his actions proceed from his convictions of duty; his ground for maintaining the title of Arthur is justice. He is also deeply religious in his feelings, but the essence of religion for him lies in its moral significance, and not in devotion to an ecclesiastical organization. With the latter, indeed, he will collide in the course of the play. He considers himself to be the guardian of right, violated in the person of a helpless boy, and his commission he holds 'From that supernal judge that stirs good thoughts / In any breast of strong authority, / To look into the blots and stains of right' [2.1.112ff.].

The character of the man in other situations can leave no doubt concerning the sincerity of these words; it is the religious conscience which speaks in him and directs his actions. He, therefore, will develop a twofold conflict with the influences of his own party, besides his struggle with John. He is not a mere politician – hence he will collide with the political selfishness which is seeking to control the French expedition; nor is he a mere devotee of the Church – hence he will oppose its violation of good faith and moral rectitude. Conscience thus arrays him against the policy of the Dauphin and the policy of the Legate.

His son, Lewis the Dauphin, is of quite the opposite character; the moral element is simply cut out of his spiritual nature. He is a most obedient son of the Church when the Church falls in with his schemes of aggrandizement, but he sets aside her authority without the least hesitation if she oppose his designs. He is restrained by no delicate scruples of truth or honor from gaining a personal advantage; his plighted faith is merely a means of deception. He, therefore, disregards the conscience of his father on the one hand, and the authority of the Church on the other hand, if either should happen to stand in the way of his personal ambition; he is a self-seeker in politics and a hypocrite in religion. He has no great national end to excuse or sanction his ethical violations; his object is an individual one, to which he is ready to sacrifice both principles and institutions. . . .

[What follows is a rather prolix sequence of plot-summary in which Snider discusses Pandulph as a master of cunning and casuistry, then moves on to summarize the action of the play, with emphasis upon the events before Angiers and the responses of Faulconbridge, Constance, and Pandulph to the marriage of Lewis and Blanch. He then returns to his discussion of Philip and Lewis.]

. . . Let us now watch the father and son – Philip and Lewis – acting in accordance with their different principles. The son is without conscience. He sees in the present turn of affairs an opportunity for personal advantage greater than those which the fulfillment of the marriage contract offered – he uses the Church as a means. At once he becomes very pious, and insists upon obedience to Pandulph's order [the excommunication of John and threat on his life (3.1.172–9)]. To be sure, he violates good faith, and endangers the new-born Family to which he has pledged his sacred fealty; but these are moral considerations, which have not the weight of a feather against his self-interest.

Passing to the father, we observe one of the most profound collisions to be met with in the works of Shakespeare. Philip possesses a powerful – indeed, controlling – principle in conscience. Good faith, amity, oaths, are spiritual elements which he cannot disregard. But here is the Church, which commands him to break them; and the Church, too, is a principle which he acknowledges most devoutly. What is he to do? Philip hesitates to obey the mandate of Pandulph, and maintains the right of moral obligation as revealed in the human heart. It is the great function of the Church to foster and enforce the moral conscience of man; but the Church now has a political end, to which it subordinates its religious end. It is thus in contradiction with itself, and is really destroying the purpose of its existence. The King of France, therefore, asserts the internal spirit of the Church against its formal authority.

But Pandulph is just the man – who has been trained by a rigid scholastic discipline – to meet and put down such cases of rebellious conscience. His argument goes to enforce the submission of private judgment to ecclesiastical control, and to assert the supremacy of the external organization of religion to its internal behests. Most subtly does he point out the contradiction between these two principles: [Quotes 3.1.279–83: 'It is religion that doth make vows kept. . . .'].

The form also is most happy; the bald, logical utterances of scholastic divinity echo from every line, the vein of fine-spun casuistry, confusing the head and misleading the heart, gives a suspicious subtlety to the whole speech. But it is far from being a mere sophistical jingle of words; on the contrary, it is a genuine statement of the right of religious authority against the right of individual opinion. There is, however, a most important suppression in the argument of the Legate. It is that the prime duty of religion is to quicken the conscience of man; and when the organization of religion – the Church – for its own purposes seeks to deaden that conscience, its right of existence has ceased. Philip is manifestly not convinced, but withdraws his opposition, and henceforward drops out of the play.

The mandate of Pandulph causes still another struggle – it threatens the disruption of the Family, here represented by the Lady Blanch. The agreement whereby her marriage took place is broken – broken by order of the Church which makes marriage a sacrament. Which shall she follow? Husband or kindred? It tears her heart asunder to decide. Blanch differs from the other women of the drama in having no political ambition; she is the true woman – devotion to the Family is her whole nature. But the Family is now at war with itself; so must she be. Both Church and State sacrifice her to their purposes. She was born to be an offering; her lovely form is mangled in the conflict of nations; the last note that we hear from her is a wail of agony over her situation.

If we now sum up the collision in which the Church is involved, we find it to have three phases – the collision with State, Family, and Morality. A political supremacy is the ultimate object of the See of Rome. In carrying out this object it comes into conflict with the entire sphere of ethical relations. It compels the individual to fight against his nation; to disregard his domestic ties; to surrender his conscience. Now, since religion must have these ethical principles as its only true content, it has reached a condition of absolute self-contradiction – its organization has turned into the bitterest foe of that which it was created to secure. The opposition between form and spirit is carried to the point at which they entirely fall asunder, and a breach is inevitable. But the Church, for the present, triumphs over all its obstacles – it subordinates State, Family, and Conscience to its designs; the schism within it has not yet sunk into the mind of Europe.

This great conflict is not portrayed by the Poet with partisan bigotry and malice, but it is shown in its simple purity – in its true colliding principles. The old play of *King John* [i.e., *The Troublesome Raigne*] which Shakespeare probably took as the foundation of the present work, is full of Protestant rancor and one-sidedness. But here each element is given in its validity as well as in its inadequacy. The result is curious: Shakespeare has been claimed to be both a Catholic and a Protestant, but he is neither; he is the Poet who sees in every great struggle two conflicting principles, each of which has its truth and its error, its right and its wrong, yet one of which is supreme. His oath to his genius is: I shall show both sides as they are, by the eternal gods.

No doubt here is witnessed the same contest logically which is known in history as the Reformation. That movement was a protest of Conscience, Family, and State against the crushing formalism of the Church. The result of it was that it established, in a part of Europe, at least, the subordination of Church to State; it justified the Family by abolishing celibacy; it generally upheld the right of private judgment in regard to matters of Conscience. But, on the other hand, the Church is not without its strong justification, and Protestantism is not without its serious weakness. The Poet has taken the precaution to throw the struggle into a period long antecedent to the Reformation, and thus exhibit purely the principles at issue, without exciting the blinding passions of theological controversy which the real event would awaken. Nor are the principles confined to Englishmen. King Philip of France is a Protestant, uttering the protest of Conscience in a far higher sense than King John. . . .

[Snider now summarizes the remaining plot of the play at great length, again focusing upon the English and French 'threads' and how these two lines of action raise the issues of nationalism, conscience, and religion discussed earlier. He then, with typical repetitiveness, draws his essay to a close.]

But now we are to have a final exhibition of the Legate and the Dauphin. John submits to Rome; Pandulph orders the French army to withdraw. The Dauphin, from the obedient son of the Church, becomes, in a breath, its most refractory child. What is the matter? His political interest now conflicts with religious authority, and he, in his turn, has now come to refuse subordination to Rome; he is just where John was before. The Dauphin has no conscience; the Church is employed by him simply as an instrument. But Pandulph is truly a comic figure; here his deep policy has swallowed itself. The State which he invoked to subject State to Church very naturally refuses to be subjected itself. This is just the old struggle over again – the Legate is exactly where he began. Such is the outcome of the political authority of the Church; it shows indeed a comic retribution. When the end is supposed to be gained, it is simply lost. Pandulph vanishes, and Lewis declares for battle.

England, therefore, must look for defense to her own stalwart arm; an Italian priest cannot secure natural autonomy. Now is the time for the hero to enter and assert his principle. On the spot he appears, uttering the defiant voice of the nation against France, the Church, and domestic traitors. Faulconbridge was deeply disgusted at the submission of John, but that could not taint his devotion to his country. His moral indignation also was intensely aroused when he beheld the dead form of Prince Arthur lying upon the rocks, but he never entertained the thought, for that reason, of deserting to the hereditary foe of his native land. In all his actions there is seen the same adamantine fidelity to England, and his extravagant laudation of her valor and greatness comes from his innermost soul. As opposed to the ecclesiastical, domestic, and moral person – all of whom are represented in the drama – he is national. This does not mean that he wantonly disregards these other principles, but, in case of a conflict between them and the nation, he goes with the nation.

Under his leadership England triumphs a second time over France, and the kingdom is brought back to internal harmony. Corresponding to this national restoration is the death of the sovereign who was unable to uphold the principle of his country. A new king must begin the new epoch; he is the son of John, and, hence, the conflict between inheritance and possession, which opened the play, is now solved. But, at the same time, it is announced in thunder-tones that the heir must be a ruler; that he must truly represent the deepest national aspiration; that the loss of birthright shall follow like destiny upon his desertion of nationality. It is the same lesson both in the case of Arthur and in the case of John – the right of succession is valid within its limitation; but, when it conflicts with the right of the nation, it must be set aside. Such has always been the fundamental principle of the English people, though to maintain it has cost many an intestine struggle. The final solution came by taking away from the king political power, so that he could not be the supreme representative of the nation, and leaving to him the empty right of inheritance. But this revolution was destined to take place long after the time of Shakespeare. The play ends – the last person to leave the stage is Faulconbridge; there he stands, speaking to future England and inspiring it with his own lofty spirit of nationality, as he utters words which stir the breast like the trumpet-call of battle. (II, 287–316)

41 George Wilkes, *King John* and Roman Catholicism

1877

From *Shakespeare, from an American Point of View; Including an Inquiry as to His Religious Faith, and His Knowledge of Law: with the Baconian Theory Considered* (London, 1877; New York, 1877).

George Wilkes (1817–85), lawyer, editor, and essayist, relished the sort of rogue journalism that earned him thirty days' confinement for libel in the New York City Tombs. Dubbed 'the fighting cock of journalism', he co-founded the *National Police Gazette* in 1845 and served as its editor until 1857, during which time he managed to incur the wrath of the lawless and law-abiding alike. Wilkes published eclectically and sometimes inaccurately; but his work always reflected his characteristic audacity and stylistic verve. His most influential articles appeared in the sporting paper *The Spirit of the Times* (later *Wilkes' Spirit of the Times*), which he purchased in 1856, and soon thereafter invested with a sharp political edge. It was for this paper that Wilkes himself covered many of the chief battles of the American Civil War, treating these bloody encounters as if they were sporting events. His book on Shakespeare, the product of a lifelong interest, is a highly entertaining mixture of serious inquiry and scholarly pugnaciousness. A strong Protestant all his life, Wilkes reportedly converted to Roman Catholicism on his deathbed, but was given a Baptist funeral at the insistence of incredulous friends.

[The object of Wilkes's book is to demonstrate that Francis Bacon could not possibly have been the author of Shakespeare's plays. He argues that since Bacon was 'a Protestant of an extreme type' (10), the key to illustrating Shakespeare's authorship is to prove that he was a Roman Catholic.]

[From 'Chapter VII: Evening Mass']

. . . There is another piece of textual testimony which the Protestant biographers of Shakespeare refer to, in order to resist the theory that he was of the Roman Catholic faith. It is put forward in its most prominent form by Charles Knight, who, combatting the inferences of Chalmers and Drake in favour of Shakespeare's Romanism as evinced in his frequent references to 'purgatory,' 'shrift,' 'confession,' &c., in his dramas, says, 'Surely the poet might exhibit this familiarity with the ancient language of all Christendom without thus speaking "from the overflow of Roman Catholic zeal."

Was it "Roman Catholic zeal" which induced him to write those strong lines in *King John* against the "Italian priest," and against those who "Purchase corrupted pardon of a man" [3.1.153, 166]? Was it "Roman Catholic zeal" which made him introduce these words into the famous prophecy of the glory and happiness of the reign of Elizabeth – "God shall be truly known" [*Henry VIII*, 5.4.36]?[1]

The first of the quotations by Knight looks very formidable; and when I read the above artificial presentation of it I fancied I had run against an insurmountable obstacle to the theory that Shakespeare was a Roman Catholic. But turning to the fountain of the phrase in the body of the text, I found that the quotation had been warped from its true meaning by the critic, and made, by a few accompanying words, to present a proposition which was not the author's. No one could read Knight's presentation of the quotation, along with his unwarranted words, without supposing it was launched not only against the one person addressed, but against *all* '*those* who purchased "corrupted" pardon of a man,' or without coming to the conclusion that Shakespeare meant to deride and reject the sanctity of that vital principle of the Roman Catholic faith, the rite of confession – and the consequent prerogatives of punishment and absolution! And I readily admit that no Roman Catholic writer could ever have permitted himself to do this under any pressure of poetical necessity. But William Shakespeare never did it – never in the plays ascribed to him, at least.

The line above quoted by Knight against Shakespeare's Catholicity is addressed by King John to King Philip Augustus of France, and applies to Pandulph, the Legate of the Pope, who had then recently been despatched from Rome to England, to demand of King John the immediate appointment of Stephen Langton, the Pope's nominee, to the archbishopric of Canterbury on pain of excommunication; and also to interrogate him (King John) why he had thus far been contumacious to the supreme orders of his Holiness in this respect. Pandulph, in pursuance of this insolent commission, finds John in France, at the head of an English army of invasion, confronting a like array of the French legions under the command of Philip. Seizing the opportunity thus afforded him of making his insolence the more conspicuous, Pandulph, in the presence of the two kings, surrounded by their respected nobles, delivers his arrogant message. The English king is naturally roused to anger and resistance by this insult, whereupon Shakespeare, through the mouth of John, treats the prelate in the political attitude he had assumed, and makes John speak with the spirit and dignity which became an English king. The practice of 'fitting' his characters, is invariable with our poet, and is also in full accordance with dramatic rules and common sense. It is in agreement, likewise, with the practice of other Roman Catholic writers, as may be seen in the treatment given by Dumas to the Cardinals Mazarin and Richelieu.[2] When the churchman sinks his profession in the character of an ambassador, he is dealt with as a politician; and when a king (whom, as a king, Shakespeare always worships upon bended knees) abandons himself to crime and despotism, he is always, as in the case of Richard III. and of John also, treated as a tyrant and a murderer. In these crimes the assassin sinks the king; as the primate, by his ambition, veils the priest. It was the only method by which the poet could protect his faith from the necessities of history, and consequently the epithets he uses through the mouths of his incensed characters, as 'false priest' and 'meddling priest' [3.1.163], are only such as are irresistible to anger under any and all circumstances. Shakespeare was too well versed in human nature not to know that an inflamed mind will always assail its enemy where he is most false, and consequently where he is most weak – always preferring an accusation of hypocrisy to any other. But here I prefer to let the text speak to the reader for itself: [Quotes 3.1.135–323: where Pandulph convinces Philip to abandon his treaty with John].

In the light of these quotations it becomes obvious that Knight's presentation of the first italicized line ['Purchase corrupted pardon of a man'], with its inferential words, had the object of making it appear that Shakespeare was deriding and mocking at the sanctity of the rite of confession; and this plain perversion of the author's meaning was, consequently, not only an abuse of the truth, but an insult, by Mr. Knight, to the understanding of his readers. The whole scene represents no independent sentiment of Shakespeare as a writer, any more than does the language of John, when he orders Hubert to commit murder upon Arthur, represent Shakespeare's sentiments; or than the words of Richard III. represent the poet's principles, when Richard directs the assassination of the Princes in the Tower. But we can perceive by the course of the play of *King John*, where the poet *does* step in and take sides; and, when he does make his individual inclinations thus seen, he decides most signally in favour of the Prelate and the Church. He shows that John, on the contrary, with all his resolution and surroundings, cannot withstand its power, but surrenders to it, humbles himself abjectly before the Legate, and is finally consigned to an ignominious death. In the scene immediately following the above, we find King John, while still in the height of his resentment, giving an order to his creature, Faulconbridge, to hasten to England, and ransack and plunder the monasteries: [Quotes 3.3.6–13].

At the opening of Act V. we find that King John, unable to contend any longer, even in his own dominions, against the power of the Pope, makes absolute submission and resigns his crown, in order that he may undergo the utter humiliation of receiving it back from his haughty hands and of holding it subject to his breath: [Quotes 5.1.1–24].

Here the Pope's Legate finishes with John. Now let us see what luck the poet assigns to Pandulph, in his assumptions of Papal supremacy over the King of France. Carrying out his contract with King John, Pandulph next appears before the French forces, which, under the charge of Lewis the Dauphin, have invaded England, and are lying in camp near St. Edmunds-Bury: [Quotes 5.2.64–116: the episode in which Lewis ignores Pandulph's request to make peace].

The Legate then curses the other side, whereupon the fight takes place, and the French, as becomes them, under the effects of Pandulph's new anathema, get the worst of it; but King John is led from the field sick during the middle of the mêlée, and retires to Swinstead Abbey in the neighbourhood. In the following scene his approaching death is thus described, and the lines I have italicized are those which the Protestant biographers stoutly rely upon to show that Shakespeare could not have been a Roman Catholic:

> Hubert.   *The king, I fear, is poisoned by a monk*:
>   I left him almost speechless, and broke out

	To acquaint you with this evil, that you might
	The better arm you to the sudden time,
	Than if you had at leisure known of this.
Bastard.	How did he take it? Who did *taste* to him?
Hubert.	*A monk, I tell you; a resolved villain,*
	Whose bowels suddenly burst out: the king
	Yet speaks, and peradventure may recover. [5.6.23ff.]

The monk who did this deed had evidently prepared himself to carry out Pandulph's curse of excommunication, and also to revenge John's sacrilegious plunder of the monasteries. In those days of the absence of newspapers, this monk doubtless had not been informed of the very recent pardon of John by Pandulph, and therefore, instead of being regarded as 'a resolved villain,' as Hubert, King John's minion, naturally terms him, he would be esteemed by the faithful, for this brave devotion of himself, as being worthy rather of 'canonization' (which, indeed, was promised by Pandulph) [3.1.177] and a high place 'among the glorious company of the apostles' than of harsh terms, or any form of condemnation whatsoever. That the monk had long been 'resolved' in his purpose of poisoning the King and to that extent was 'a resolved villain,' is evident from the fact that it must have cost him much time and considerable court influence to become 'taster' to his Majesty [5.6.28], as a preliminary to the glorious canonization which he expected, for carrying out the orders of the Legate, at the expense of his own life. (50–7)

[From 'Chapter XIX: The Historical Plays – *King John*']

This first of the historical plays of Shakespeare was founded on an anonymous play [*The Troublesome Raigne*]. Shakespeare followed this old tragedy pretty closely, though he was careful to exclude a scene of the original which irreverently alludes to 'the merry nuns and brothers' when Faulconbridge is practising his extortions on the clergy. The exclusion of this scene is attributed by Gervinus, from whom I quote the above expression, to a very different motive from the one which I fancy is most obvious. The German commentator, who is evidently a good Protestant, says, 'But Shakespeare did not go so far as to make a farce of Faulconbridge's extortions from the clergy: the old piece here offered him *a scene in which merry nuns and brothers burst forth from the opened coffers of the "hoarding abbots,"* a scene certainly very amusing to the fresh Protestant feelings of the time; but to our poet's impartial mind the dignity of the clergy, nay, even the contemplativeness of cloister life, was a matter too sacred for him to introduce it in a ridiculous form into the seriousness of history.'[3]

From the light heretofore thrown upon the religious faith of our poet, I read the motive for the exclusion of this Catholic scandal differently from the learned German Professor. Shakespeare's motive here seems to be located in the sensitiveness of a Catholic for the decorums of his sect – a religious sensitiveness which, be it observed, did not operate to protect the 'dignity' of the Protestant clergy, when derision was to be cast upon Sir Hugh, 'the jack priest' of the *Merry Wives* [2.3.31]; upon Sir Nathaniel, the curate, in *Love's Labor's Lost*; upon Sir Oliver Martext, the Puritan preacher, in *As You Like It*; or upon the illusory Sir Topaz, in *Twelfth Night*.

Hunter [No. 20 above], like Gervinus, also exhibits the common concern of the English commentators to protect Shakespeare from the suspicion of Roman Catholic convictions. Nevertheless, the evidences of Catholicism in this play insensibly operate upon even Hunter's mind, and develop their force as follows: [Here Wilkes quotes verbatim Hunter's discussion of the Jesuit 'Chamber of Meditation' and his ensuing gloss on 'convertite'.].

. . . These extracts close our illustrations from *King John* on the subject of religion. We come now to those which exhibit Shakespeare's proclivity to deify and worship kings, and demonstrate his utter want of sympathy with any movement tending to popular liberty. The first and most striking proof this play gives of this latter tendency is, that in the same spirit which directs him to protect the Roman Catholic faith from derision (by leaving out from the old play, which was his model, the scene that scandalized the nuns and monks), he refrains from making the slightest allusion, in *his* version of *King John*, to the signing of Magna Charta; an event, unquestionably, the most momentous as well as the most dramatic of his entire reign. . . . (177–9)

[Wilkes concludes his discussion of *King John* by dismissing John Lord Campbell's citations of the play in his *Shakespeare's Legal Acquirements Considered* (London, 1859), as inadequate to demonstrate Campbell's contention that Shakespeare was a lawyer.]

42 Frederick Gard Fleay, literary and historical background to *King John*

1878

From *'The Life and Death of King John'. By William Shakespeare. Together with the 'Troublesome Raigne of King John', As Acted by the Queen's Players, c. 1589. Edited with Notes, Introductions, Excerpts from Holinshed, Metrical Analysis, and Notices of Contemporary Plays and Players, by F. G. Fleay, M.A., Author of 'The Shakespeare Manual', etc., etc.* (London and Glasgow, 1878).

Frederick Gard Fleay (1831–1909), a trained mathemetician, spent much of his life as a schoolmaster and priest, both of which callings he relinquished for a career in literary studies. A dedicated student of philology, Fleay strongly advocated the reform of English orthography, publishing frequently on the topic and serving as editor of the *Spelling Reformer* (1880–1). As a Shakespearian Fleay shunned interpretive criticism, preferring instead exacting and detailed studies of metre, phraseology, historical background, and topical allusion. These he applied, often with great erudition, to problems of authorship and chronology, which along with such matters as the composition of acting companies, the practical details of performance, and the history of the stage, comprised some of his most avid scholarly interests.

[From the Introduction]

SOURCES OF THE PLOT.

The plot is taken with scarcely any important deviations from the older play [i.e., *The Troublesome Raigne*]. I also give below the main parts of Holinshed which bear on the events introduced by Shakespeare. I do this chiefly because the incomplete and unsatisfactory way in which it has been done by former editors is misleading to the reader. It should be noticed, however, that editors always speak of Shakespeare's having appropriated the plot of the older play as a sort of plagiarism, but they never give any ground for supposing that it is not Shakespeare's own. They admit that Peele, Greene, and Lodge are the most likely claimants to the authorship of the older drama; they put prominently forward their arguments that Shakespeare joined these very men in writing *Henry VI*, yet they give no shadow of reason for supposing that in this case, to which there is no parallel, Shakespeare took anything but what he had originally given – the platform or plot of the play. Having in view the very different manner in which he treated plays, as to which we know that he had no share whatever in their earlier form (such as, for instance, *Promos and Cassandra*, which he used in writing *Measure for Measure*), I shall, until some reason is advanced to the contrary, hold that in his *King John* the original plot was laid down for the early play by Shakespeare himself. What he did take from the old *John*, which was not originally his own, is its version of facts. Shakespeare was no historical investigator. In making his early plot he probably used Holinshed, as he did in his later plays. The writers who worked on his plot certainly used more recondite sources of information, which it forms no part of my plan to examine, but which would be well worth examination by some member of our numerous literary societies. Shakespeare then took the play as they had made it, with the help of a bit here and there from Holinshed, as his sole authority for the facts. (11–12)

* * *

[From] DISTRIBUTION OF THE PARTS.

[Fleay, in his characteristic manner, provides exhaustive charts and graphs for both *The Troublesome Raigne* and *King John* illustrating speaking and non-speaking roles by act and scene, which he uses to analyze the cast size and distribution of parts for each play. These comparisons provide the basis for a discussion of Shakespeare's alterations of the plot of *The Troublesome Raigne*, followed by a scene-by-scene analysis of the changes. A table follows, indicating 'the parallel scenes in the two plays, with a conjectural division of the earlier one into acts and scenes' (26).]
 . . . From these details the reader can easily judge (especially if he consults the older play) how vastly the stage business of this plot was improved in the later version. But I do not say this as if I thought Shakespeare always perfect in this respect. On the contrary, I think it sometimes his weak point. But in this play see how much it conduces to unity and tragic effect, not to dwell on the revenge of the friars for the perquisitions made on them by John, but to keep before the spectator the great crime of the murder of Arthur, as chief cause of his downfall. Yet I have seen this alteration denounced as a mistaken omission.[1] So widely do æsthetic views, in their present anarchical state, differ from each other. Much fuller details than can here be given are announced in a paper by Mr Rose, for the New Shakespeare Society [No. 43 below]. I regret that it has not been issued soon enough for me to make use of it. (27)

ON THE NAMES OF THE DRAMATIS PERSONÆ AS THEY ARE PREFIXED TO THE SPEECHES.

Variations in this matter are sometimes very important, though most editors have neglected them, or at most given them but a passing notice. Some in this play are of little import. Occasional variations of spelling, such as *Dolphin* and *Daulphin*, *Elinor*, *Elenor*, and *Eleanor*, may be due to the printers. The alternation between *K. John* and *John* has probably arisen from the same cause. The substitution of *Hubert* for *Citizen* in II.i[2] indicates that these two parts were taken by the same actor. The solitary instances in which Elinor is called *Old Queen*, and John *England*, do not show any further consequences to be deduced. But there are other variations bearing on questions of some consequence.

1. Philip Faulconbridge is sometimes called *Philip*, sometimes *Bastard*. The alteration was of course made to prevent confusion with *King Philip* of France; but it was made in the old play, and not by Shakespeare, who has retained just whichever happened to be done before him, when he was writing his own play from the elder one, as is manifest on comparing the two; for example, in I.i. There is, however, a further confusion in the text. Philip is knighted as Sir Richard in I.i.162, and is so called in I.i.178; IV.iii.41; and V.iii.12. Yet in III.ii.4, John calls him Philip.

2. In I.ii.1–200 [i.e., 2.1.1–200], and in no other scene, Elinor is called *Queen* and *Queen Mother*, in the stage directions as well as in the names prefixed to the speeches.

3. In the same scene . . . the King of France is called *Lewis* in the text, line 149, and in the prefixed names, lines 1, 18, 150. In this scene only are some of his speeches assigned to *King* simply. Editors have tried emendation unsuccessfully. They either make *Lewis* two syllables, or *Philip* one; neither of which are admissible in the metre of this play.

It seems more reasonable to infer that I.ii.1–200 [i.e., 2.1.1–200], and III.ii.1–10, were inserted hurriedly after the rest of the play had been written. This would also account for the confusion in the division into acts and scenes, already noticed. A reference to the metrical table, which shows only two rhymes in the 200 lines in I.ii [2.1], and no rhyme in III.ii, confirms the conjecture; and when we consider that the celebrated passage alluding to the English fleet of 1596 (lines 71–75) is also contained in I.ii [2.1], I feel little doubt that these subsequent insertions were made after Hamnet's death, and that the blunders of *Philip* for *Richard*, and *Lewis* for *Philip*, are to be attributed to the confusion caused by grief in Shakespeare's mind. None but those who have had to write compulsorily under similar bereavements, can tell how errors do creep in at such times. That the errors remained uncorrected causes no difficulty; for this play was not printed during Shakespeare's life, and its probable revivals in 1611 and 1622 took place after his retirement from the theatre, according to the most probable chronology, which gives 1611 for the production of his last complete play; the two plays produced afterwards being finished by Fletcher. . . . The excision of the character of Essex from this play may also have been made after August 1596, and with the same want of care; which would account for his name being left in the prefix to I.i.44. (27–8)

[From] METRE

. . . The only important metrical point (except for comparison with other plays, a matter with which we are not here concerned) is the great preponderance of rhymes in the early part of the play. In the first five scenes there are 47 rhymes (94 lines) in 1221 lines – one rhyme to every 26 lines: in the rest of the play this proportion falls off to one rhyme in 74 lines. This gives us further reason to suppose that there was a break between the composition of the earlier and later parts of the play, caused possibly by the death of Hamnet Shakespeare, but certainly not a break of long duration. Note also the dying out of the use of alternate rhymes by Shakespeare. In *Love's Labor's Lost* he introduced fifty-nine quatrains: here he has only four.[3] His last use of them is in *As You Like It.* . . . (31)

PROBABLE REVIVALS OF THE PLAY.

The older play was reprinted in 1611 with 'W. Sh.' on the title-page, and in 1622 with 'William Shakespeare' in full. The most probable reason for such reprints (or re-issues with new title-pages) of a not very popular play is that the bookseller endeavoured to get rid of copies under Shakespeare's name at times when his (unprinted[4]) play was being performed. And there is confirmatory grounds for the likelihood of revivals at two dates in the contemporary events.

The special political references in both plays are to fears of Spanish invasions dissipated, and hope restored by English successes as soon as the English people show themselves united; they also display strong hostility to the pope.

Now, after Elizabeth's death to the date of the printing of the Folio, 1623, there were two periods similar in hopes and fears to those already alluded to [i.e., 1588 and 1595] – namely, 1611 and 1622.

In 1610 Prince Henry was made Prince of Wales, and negotiations were set on foot for a marriage between him and the Infanta of Spain. In the same year Henry IV was assassinated by Ravaillac. In 1611 the negotiations for the marriage had been broken off; and the people were excited against Spain; still more against the Jesuits, on account of the assassination; against the pope as the supporter of both; and even in October 1610 they had begun in Parliament their resistance to the encroachments of the Stuarts on the public liberty. What fitter time for a revival of *King John*? In 1622 the match between Prince Charles and another Infanta was, after long negotiation, likely to be effected; but the English hated it and everything Spanish; they were enraged with the king for allowing his subjects (especially Papists) to assist in the wars against the Palatine, for the anti-Puritan tendency of the court, and for the loss of his son-in-law's dominions. Moreover, in the event of the marriage negotiation not being successful, the likelihood of a new armada was already talked of. . . . At these two dates, in fact, and these alone, were revivals of this play likely to take place. (32)

43 Edward Rose, Shakespeare's adaptation of *The Troublesome Raigne*

1878

From 'Shakespeare as an Adapter', *Macmillan's Magazine*, 39, No. 229 (November 1878), 69–77.

Edward Rose (1849–1904) was a dramatist, actor, and theatre critic whose articles on Shakespeare, consisting mainly of papers delivered before the New Shakespeare Society in the late 70s and early 80s, frequently addressed the issue of dramatic construction. Rose early abandoned a career in law, devoting himself to the writing of plays from 1869 until the late 1890s. Some of his best known dramas are adaptations of prose works: *Vice Versa* (1883), from the story by Thomas Anstey Guthrie; *Under the Red Robe* (1897), from the novel by Stanley Weyman; and *Souvenir of The Prisoner of Zenda* (1896) from the novel by Anthony Hope Hopkins. Rose's essay was reprinted by Charles Praetorius in his facsimile edition of the 1591 quarto of *The Troublesome Raigne of John, King of England*, 2 vols (London, 1888), I, v–xvii.

[Rose opens his essay with praise for Shakespeare as a 'practical dramatist'; that is, 'a really good stage-manager' whose art demonstrates mastery of 'the principles and details of the construction of plays for the stage' (69). He then proceeds to examine Shakespeare's abilities in this regard with reference to his adaptation of *The Troublesome Raigne*.]

... If we take for consideration this anonymous play and compare it with Shakespeare's, we shall find how perfectly he understood his art; and we may learn by his example not only what dramatic material to choose, and how to shape it, but – which is by no means so usual with our poet – what to avoid; for *King John*, as it now stands, though it is in many ways a model of construction, and contains at least two of his finest characters and some of his noblest poetry, can hardly be called a successful stage-play. . . .

The chief faults of the old play are these: it has no hero – there is not enough to bind the scenes together, and make an interesting whole of them. It is throughout filled with an anti-Romish spirit, violent and vulgar, and entirely out of place in a work of art, though no doubt adding much to the play's temporary popularity. The characters are mere rough outlines, wanting in fulness and consistency; and there is no one in the play, except here and there Faulconbridge, in whom you can take much interest. The dialogue is rather dull, and lacking in variety and finish; and, finally, the play is much too long – its Second Part especially – and wants neatness and clearness of construction.

It is characteristic of Shakespeare that, in remedying these faults, he does not for a moment depart from the lines the original author has laid down. He does not go to history for fresh facts to strengthen his plot – he absolutely adds no word of allusion to the Great Charter, which might, one would think, have been worked up into a grand scene. Indeed, the only alteration of fact that he makes is a perversion of history; Arthur was not a mere child, but a young man, as, if we may judge by his conversation with Hubert, the original makes him.

The old play is divided into two parts, each of which is about the length of, and may have been split up into, five short acts. Although he has greatly extended almost every important scene, and has doubled the length of two leading characters, Shakespeare has compressed these ten acts into five of reasonable length; arranged, with a curious instinct which seems prophetic, in almost exact accordance with modern scenic requirements, except as regards the last act. Acts i. and ii. have but one scene apiece, acts iii. and iv. each three, of which the middle ones may well be flat or 'carpenter's' scenes; and even in the fifth act the scenery is not very difficult.[1]

It is a very noticeable difference between the two plays, that while in the elder we find no systematic division (except that into two rather unequal halves), in the later Shakespeare – who I believe always paid great attention to the construction of his acts – has made the inter-acts divide the story into five complete and symmetrical parts. Act i. gives us the French king's challenge and its acceptance by John, with the story of the bastard Philip and his brother. Act ii. shows the commencement of hostilities, and the mutual attack upon Angiers; then the arrangement come to between the kings – the peace made on the marriage between Lewis and Blanch. In Act iii. the influence of Rome breaks off this peace; there is a battle in which the French are defeated, and Constance mourns the loss of her son. Act iv. brings us back to England, and gives us the remainder of Arthur's story, and the revolt of the barons at his death. Act v. shows the advance of the French in England, with their allies the rebellious lords; the murder of the king; and the final mishap to the Dauphin's army, which causes him to offer terms of peace.

In reconstructing the play, the great want which struck Shakespeare seems to have been that of a strong central figure. He was attracted by the rough, powerful nature which he could see the Bastard's must have been; almost like a modern dramatist 'writing up' a part for a star actor, he introduced Faulconbridge wherever it was possible, gave him the end of every act (except the third), and created, from a rude and inconsistent sketch, a character as strong, as complete, and as original as even he ever drew. Throughout a series of scenes, not otherwise very closely connected, this wonderfully real type of faulty, combative, not ignoble manhood is developed, a support and addition to the scenes in which he has least to say, a great power where he is prominent.

This is the most striking example of his development of a character, but his treatment of Constance, Arthur, Hubert, Pandulph, and of some portions of the character of John himself, is very noticeable. The entire wonderful scene in which Constance laments the loss of her child is founded upon the seven lines: − [Quotes 5.24–30: 'My tongue is tuned to story forth mishap. . . .'].

The somewhat sinister wisdom of Pandulph is carefully and at length elaborated, and one of several indistinguishable barons (Salisbury) has been made chief spokesman of the revolt caused by the murder of Arthur. Hubert now stands out with a rough manhood which is very sympathetic; and many subtle touches are added to the King's character − of which more hereafter.

And now let us see what were the principal alterations, 'cuts,' and extensions which the adapter of this old play made, and why he made them − going straight through the piece, and studying each scene in which noticeable improvement has been effected by these means. I may here remark that he only omits four entire scenes, and introduces none, except the dialogue between Faulconbridge and Hubert which concludes Act iv.

The plays both begin with the same incident − the King of France claiming the English crown for Arthur; but, while the earlier author opens with twenty lines about the death of Richard and the succession of John, Shakespeare dashes at once into the heart of his subject: − [Quotes 1.1.1–4]. And throughout the play there is the same exchange of tediousness for spirit and brilliancy; very markedly in the succeeding discussion as to the legitimacy of Faulconbridge, during which discussion Shakespeare, writing for an audience he was himself making tender and refined, does not bring the mother upon the stage, as did the elder dramatist. There is, in the midst of the said discussion in the original play, a long 'aside' of the Bastard's, which is most interesting. Shakespeare omits it altogether, partly no doubt because it *is* a long 'aside;' but how it influenced his conception of the character, and how he yet altered that character, are evident. I quote the soliloquy entire. [Quotes 1.241–71: where the Bastard debates with himself whether or not to claim Richard as his father, and concludes that he should deny his royal heritage in order to obtain Faulconbridge's land]. However, when he is directly asked who was his father, he proudly claims Richard.

In the scenes in France, which form the second and third acts, Shakespeare has very closely followed his original in construction, though he has greatly extended some passages and compressed others. Many of the details of his workmanship are very ingenious; for example, when the treaty of marriage between Lewis and Blanch is made he keeps Constance off the stage, because, as he says, 'the match made up, her presence would have interrupted much' [2.1.541ff.] He tells in three lines, too [3.2.5–7], a scene of the original in which Elinor is captured by the French, and afterwards rescued by Faulconbridge; the representation of which would probably only have the effect of making the audience uncertain which side was winning.

Then follows perhaps the most important 'cut' in the play, that of a scene in which Faulconbridge carries out the raid upon the clergy, spoken of here in two lines only [3.4.171–2]. In this place, and throughout the play, Shakespeare has removed the attacks on the Church of Rome to so great an extent that the Catholics claim him for themselves; but it was probably more his hatred of vulgarity and buffoonery than of Protestantism that made him strike out the scene in which the Bastard, ransacking the monasteries, finds a nun in the abbot's chest, a priest in a nun's; and in which a pious friar, horror stricken remarks [Quotes 6.44–51: 'Oh, I am undone. . . .']. And, with regard to John's strong speeches against Popery at the end of the old play, they would probably make him more popular with the audience than Shakespeare could permit such a villain to be.

A great deal of valuable space occupied by the prophet, Peter of Pomfret, is also saved. He was originally brought on in the convent-scene (where his introduction seems to show that dramatists even then felt that it was better not to change the scene too often), and in two subsequent scenes he made long speeches to John, embodying the prophecy that he should give up his crown on Ascension Day, and embodied by Shakespeare, as far as Peter himself is concerned, in one single line [4.2.154], which was probably introduced because the audience had got used to their prophet, and would not have liked to part with him entirely.

The prettiness and pathos of the great scene which follows, between Hubert and Arthur, are quite lost when the prince is made a philosophic young man instead of a winning and tender boy – the sweetest, in Shakespeare's hands, of all pathetic children who have pleaded for their life in plays. Such arguments as the following, however sound and sensible, are not particularly touching: – [Quotes 7.77–84: the discussion between Hubert and Arthur over whether God's will or the king's is predominant]. And so on, for a page of controversial epigrams. It is perhaps worth noticing that even so vague an expression of religious speculation as the terming God 'that Essence' [7.83] is hardly to be found in Shakespeare's writings.

The next scene is substantially the same as the present, Act iv. sc. 2; but the difference in the skill of their workmanship makes it worth while to examine them in detail. In the first place, using the simple stage expedient of announcing a thing as just done instead of doing it, Shakespeare makes the king come on immediately after his second coronation instead of before it – thus saving a good deal of time and losing absolutely nothing: there was no gain of pageantry in the old arrangement, and the discussion between Pembroke and the others is brought in quite as naturally now. Then, in accordance with the modern stage-rule (which, as a French critic tells us, has taken the place of the ancient rule of the three unities), that there must be no more entrances and exits than are absolutely necessary, Faulconbridge's two entrances are reduced to one. The five moons, also, which make their actual appearance in the old play, are, like some of the characters in Ben Jonson's lists of *dramatis personæ*, 'only talked on;' and a few lines take the place of an entire later scene (the second of the Second Part), in which occurred the speech already quoted, describing the manifold evils which are making England miserable. Of the reduction of Peter of Pomfret I have already spoken.

But the most important alteration in this scene is the way in which the false tidings of Arthur's death are treated. . . .

[Here Rose quotes extensively from *The Troublesome Raigne* (8.208–27) and *King John* (4.2.69–102), contending that Shakespeare's treatment of the episode is 'far less jerky' (74) than that of the earlier play.]

. . . Whoever will read this entire scene as it stands in Shakespeare cannot fail to find how very much he has improved it in neatness of construction, in probability, in effectiveness, and even in brevity, though he has doubled the dignity and philosophic fulness of nearly all the chief speeches. And throughout the Second Part (which begins with Arthur's death) his alterations are at least as important and successful. Arthur does not make a speech of fifteen lines after he has leapt from the walls – he is a much less 'unconscionable time a-dying;'[2] and an immense improvement has been made in the subsequent scene [4.3] between Hubert and the barons, by the introduction of Faulconbridge.

In the first scene of Act v. Shakespeare repeats the stage expedient I have already spoken of – he makes John come on just as he has yielded up his crown to Pandulph; and indeed this scene and the next are altogether very neatly constructed. Instead of them we have, in the old piece, first a long scene in which John (after hanging poor Peter of Pomfret) describes his misfortunes, and, under great pressure, consents to become the Pope's vassal; then another in which are set forth most elaborately the appeal to Lewis by the English barons, their oath, and his treachery; and a third, showing John's acceptance of the crown at Pandulph's hands, and the refusal of Lewis to retire at the Pope's bidding.

The fifth and seventh scenes of this Second Part [i.e., 12.90–155 and 14],[3] giving the progress of the struggle between John and the French and rebels, correspond closely to the fourth and fifth of Shakespeare's Act v.; the sixth and eighth [i.e., 13 and 15] show at great length how John took refuge in Swinstead Abbey; how a certain monk, with the connivance of his abbot, poisoned the king's drink, and, tasting it first himself, with the historic cry of 'Wassell!' died, remarking aside, 'If the inwards of a toad be a compound of any proof – why, so: it works!' [15.31; 39ff.]; how Faulconbridge, very naturally, killed the abbot; how the king died, after some long and powerful speeches, rather like those of Sir Giles Overreach,[4] but very strongly anti-Catholic; and how, as he was dying, Henry and the revolted barons came, and John lifted his hand in token of forgiveness, and again as a sign that he died Christ's servant.

Now, these long scenes of meditated murder, and of murder itself and its reward, form a particularly unpleasant conclusion to a play which has already had quite its full share of treachery and crime; and their compression speaks as well for Shakespeare's healthy and manly feeling as for his skill as a dramatist. This skill is again displayed in the neatness with which he throws into a few lines, without change of scene, the establishment of Henry as king, which in the original play occupies a ninth scene [16], coming as an awkward anticlimax after the death of the hero. The 'tag,' given in both plays by Faulconbridge, shows how commonplace verse can be converted into splendid poetry. . . . [Quotes 16.45–54 and 5.7.112–18].

Before I leave these details of construction, I should like to remark three points in which Shakespeare, in compressing the original, has left matters a little less clear than he found them.

In the first place, does it strike one why Faulconbridge makes such a dead set at Austria – or Lymoges, as Shakespeare, repeating his predecessor's blunder, sometimes calls him? Are we not apt to fancy that it was chiefly because the Bastard was a bullying sort of fellow, and saw that Austria was a coward? But in the old play it is at once and fully shown that he wanted to avenge the duke's cruelty to his father, Richard

I.; Austria is indeed wearing the skin of the lion which Richard killed, and which gave him his famous surname.

Then – it is a very minor matter – but one does not quite know why Faulconbridge should be so much annoyed at the bethrothal of Blanch to the Dauphin; nor why Blanch should have backed up Faulconbridge in his apparently unjustifiable attack upon Austria. In the original, we find that Elinor had half promised Blanch's hand to the Bastard, whom the lady gave up for Lewis with some reluctance.

Lastly – and this is a good deal more important – Shakespeare does not at all explain *why* the monk poisoned King John. Has not one been rather startled, on seeing the play acted, by its sudden termination? Just when his fortunes are at their most critical point, the hero without rhyme or reason dies: some one comes in casually and says that the king is dying, murdered by an anonymous monk, who is indeed described as a 'resolved villain' [5.6.29], but who is not shown to have had any motive whatever for his deed. It is as if the Gravedigger should suddenly brain Hamlet with his pickaxe, in the midst of their conversation, and decline to give any reason for his conduct. The author of *The Troublesome Raigne*, besides giving at length the scene of the ransacking the monasteries by the king's command, tells us in so many words that the murderous monk expected to be 'canonized for a holy saint' for poisoning the king that did 'contemn the pope' and 'never loved a friar' [13.84–95], and shows us his conception of and preparation for the crime.

Having thus gone through the principal alterations which Shakespeare made in adapting this rough and diffuse old 'history' for his own theatre, and having tried to show how greatly he improved it, even from the point of view of a modern stage-manager, I must explain why his example in this case seems to me, as I have said, a warning as well as a lesson to dramatists. What is it that has neutralised his efforts to make of *King John* a stage-play as successful and enduringly popular as, for example, *Richard III.*? It must be either the subject itself, or the way in which it has been dealt with in the original piece – which, in its broad outlines, he has not attempted to alter.

The subject is perhaps not altogether a good one. The king's great crime is so dastardly, the leading cause of his misfortunes (his quarrel with Rome about Stephen Langton) is so undramatic, and his nature breaks down so entirely at the end – when even a villain like Richard III. fights nobly and forces some sort of respect from the audience – that it may be that no poet could have made a strong play of the story of his life. As it is, in Acts i. and ii. he is a nonentity. Faulconbridge filling the first act, and nobody being very prominent in the second; in the third act Constance is supreme, and in the fourth Arthur; while even in the fifth the king is not of very great importance, his death-scene being much weakened in effect (however it may gain in refinement) by the removal of his violently remorseful and Protestant speeches. Indeed, it must be confessed that the omission from the play of the constant attacks on Popery, though an improvement from a purely literary point of view, destroys to a certain extent its *raison d'être*, the spirit that helped to animate its old straggling mass, and, as has been pointed out, the motive of its *dénoûment*.

The effort, too, to give the piece a hero in Faulconbridge, is a failure, because, as long experience teaches, you *cannot* force a character out of the position he would naturally occupy in a play. Faulconbridge is properly little more than a chorus, a cynical critic of a wicked age – he might be entirely omitted without in the least degree altering the substance of the plot – and it is therefore impossible to make the story centre in him, as should every story in some one figure, or inseparably-connected group of figures.

Shakespeare has no doubt kept so closely to the lines of the older play because it was a favourite with his audience, and they had grown to accept its history as absolute fact; but one can hardly help thinking that had he boldly thrown aside these trammels and taken John as his hero, his great central figure; had he analysed and built up before us the mass of power, craft, passion, and devilry which made up the worst of the Plantagenets; had he dramatised the grand scene of the signing of the Charter, and shown vividly the gloom and horror which overhung the excommunicated land; had he painted John's last despairing struggles against rebels and invaders, as he had given us the fiery end of Macbeth's life – we might have had another Macbeth, another Richard, who would by his terrible personality have welded the play together, and carried us along breathlessly through his scenes of successive victory and defeat.

That by this means something would be lost is true – Faulconbridge, for example, would certainly be lessened – but the worth of a real work of art is greater than the worth of any part of it; and Constance and Hubert probably need not suffer, while the influence of the death of Arthur might very likely be made to penetrate more thoroughly the entire play. In *Macbeth*, *Henry V.*, *Richard III.*, *Coriolanus*, everything is subordinated to the centre, the mainspring of the plot; in *King John* each act has a different hero. What could be more fatal to the interest of the whole?

To some it may seem presumptuous thus to criticise Shakespeare; but is it not indeed the only way to make sure that one really appreciates him? Of such appreciation I wish my unsparing criticism of his work to be a proof; it is a poor faith that dares not listen to and seek out every accusation against its idol. (70–7)

44 George Henry Calvert, high praise for *King John*

1879

From *Shakespeare: A Biographic Æsthetic Study* (Boston, 1879).

George Henry Calvert (1803–89), poet and critic, was born into a privileged American family, and spent much of his life writing and traveling. His modest involvement in politics as mayor of Newport, R.I. (1853–4) and as chairman of the Newport School Committee seems to have presented no obstacle to his literary endeavors. Calvert produced a large body of lyric and narrative verse modeled after Tennyson's, and 'biographic æsthetic' studies of numerous writers in addition to Shakespeare, including *Wordsworth* (Boston, 1878) and *Coleridge, Shelley, Goethe* (Boston, 1880). Calvert's criticism is unabashedly impressionistic, digressive, and encomiastic, clearly the work of a gentleman-critic whose interests lay in the cultivation of refinement and 'taste'; yet at times, and on its own terms, it manages to join the scholarly debate.

[From Chapter III: '*King John*']

Reading lately *King John*, it seemed to me that I had never before enough admired this tumultuous prophetic prologue to the grand series of Shakespeare's historic dramas. In its rhythm there was a deeper music than ever, in its reflections a wider range, in its sentiment a wiser truth, its grandeur as a whole was more imposing. Like the earth's air, Shakespeare is inexhaustible; like the air, he renews himself from infinite reservoirs. At every contact with him we inbreathe fresh life.

One of his richest plays in passages of power, *King John* is more dramatic than most of the historic dramas; that is, the individuality of its personages brings about its collisions, and shapes their issues, more distinctly than in the others, in which the strongest wills, dominated by historic fatality, are swept on in a resistless *epic* current. Elinor, Pandulph, King John, Hubert, Philip of France, Constance, Lewis, Salisbury, – here is a company of lively dramatic agencies. And then, besides the collisions of individuals, there is the direct terrible collision of kingdoms; while, through his active personality, the colossal Faulconbridge sways the whole movement, literally uplifting the entire action on his Herculean shoulders. Faulconbridge is one of the supreme splendors of Shakespeare, one of those ideal realities in which is most vividly exhibited the creative genius of this mighty mind.

In the first thirty lines of the opening scene are epitomized the drift and substance of the whole play. [Quotes 1.1.1–43, followed by lengthy praise for Shakespeare's 'subtle, gorgeous, myriad-minded genius' (126)]. . . .

Observe how this opening scene is enlivened by the interruption of Elinor: 'A strange beginning! borrowed majesty?' [1.1.5] an interruption which Shakespeare would not have allowed her to make, had she not, in making it, given a strong taste of her quality as a proud, grasping, intermeddling Queen-dowager. While adding life to the scene, the line she utters characterizes herself. Shakespeare thus kills two birds with one stone, and both game birds, a proceeding which he repeats oftener than – I had almost said – all other poets put together. What a double-edged weapon is his pen, the instrument of such penetrating thought, of such a far-ranging keen perception!

The plan and movement of the whole piece being succinctly prefigured in the first scene, the second presents to us the protagonist of the play, the stalwart champion of England, a very prototype of English independence, strength, humor, earnestness, pluck. History makes slight mention of Faulconbridge. A natural son of Richard Cœur-de-Lion there was who fought in John's French wars, and who is one of the dramatic personages in an older play of King John which Shakespeare largely used; and a prose romance about a Lord Faulconbridge was early published. Our Faulconbridge is a child of Shakespeare, and one of his most vigorous offspring. No creation of his is more deeply stamped with the fiery mark of his plastic potency. . . . [Calvert now quotes 1.1.44–57 and 1.1.84–91: the Bastard's argument with Robert Faulconbridge over their inheritance.]

. . . [any further] exhibition of racy humor and peerless art of characterization we are prohibited from reproducing here by the plainness of speech required for such a discussion of paternity, a plainness broadened by the freedom of that age, and, it may be added, by the temptations of wit.

Shakespeare is almost uniquely illustrious for two qualities, delicacy of feeling and depth of feeling. The bane of literature is its superficiality, palpable in much of the verse and prose of all ages, and especially notable latterly in the unceasing flood of pretentious novels, which one might suspect are easily produced, so easily are they forgotten.

This very scene, somewhat gross as it unavoidably is, exemplifies Shakespeare's delicacy, – that refinement of feeling which is an endowment indispensable to high attainment in art. In his admirable commentary on Shakespeare, Gervinus [No. 31 above] refers to several passages in the old play that were modified by Shakespeare in the spirit of this refinement.

On the same page Gervinus writes: 'Shakespeare delineates his Faulconbridge (and himself in him).' In this, it seems to me, the eminent German critic says too much. He could hardly mean to affirm that in Faulconbridge Shakespeare drew his own portrait; and yet, his words will bear that construction. To contract himself into any one of his personages is an impossibility to Shakespeare. The fuller and greater the character, the more of himself will there be in it, as in Faulconbridge, Henry V., Prospero, Hamlet; but in all his work the great objective artist ever presides imperially, condescending never to one-sided, egotistic self-portraiture. . . .

[After a brief digression during which Calvert praises Shakespeare as a supremely objective artist who dwells 'in a beatific sphere inaccessible to worldly footsteps' (130–1), he returns to his subject.]

In the interview between the Bastard and his mother Shakespeare again gives proof of superior refinement and his high quality as artist. In the old play, which supplied so much material to his animating mastery, the son, in order to draw from Lady Faulconbridge the secret of his birth, threatens her life. The occasion of the disclosure Shakespeare has converted into a humorous scene.

Shakespeare is the most genial as well as the most skillful of literary distillers: he extracts the substance out of a vast body of loose material, encloses in a phial the essence of a flood of fluid, imparting to it in the process of extraction that tonic fragrance which naught but poetry exhales.

The scene now shifts to France. The second Act opens before the walls of Angiers. France and Austria are allied to uphold the rights of the boy Arthur against usurping John. They are just about to bend their cannon 'against the brow of this resisting town' [2.1.38] when Chatillion, the ambassador, returned from England, enters and announces that England 'hath put himself in arms' [2.1.57], and is close at hand.

The trumpet and the drum always wake the warrior in Shakespeare. When he writes of battles and precipitated squadrons his verse has the bound and swing of cavalry charging: there is in it the music of a forest swept by a gale. He gives these combatants the help of gunpowder at the end of the twelfth century. In war cannon is a poetical element: its thunderous sound is a token of its might; and so Shakespeare anticipates the terrific play of artillery by more than a century. Had he been reminded of this he would have answered: 'I know it, but I am not writing a chronological history of inventions.'

The speech of Chatillion is cut short by the 'churlish drums' [2.1.76] of England, and thereupon enter King John, Elinor, Bastard, etc. [Quotes 2.1.84–92: the greeting betwen John and Philip].

This mutual greeting of the two adverse sovereigns, how Shakespearean! Privileged kings, to have such a spokesman! In music and distinction these regal salutations are as much above the usual greetings of kings as the habitual utterance of Shakespeare's personages is above the customary speech of men. Shakespeare has been called *the Expresser*, and he deserves the designation; at the same time, his diction owes its brilliancy and effect to the beauty and weight of the substance to be expressed. In his capacious, luminous brain he carried more, and more compact, ideals than were ever carried by man. To his words splendor is imparted by the unique richness of his deeper resources. His words would not uplift us were they not themselves the sun-lit billows of a broad, fathomless sea of upmounting thought. . . .

[Calvert goes on at some length about the transcendent power of poetry, Shakespeare's poetic and visionary insights, his intuition and fineness of feeling, and his love and empathy for his characters.]

Here let me (with due deference) protest against the oft-quoted dictum of Aristotle, that by scenes of pain and agony on the tragic stage, through the pity and fear they excite, the sensibilities of the beholders are purged. On the contrary, the beholding of such scenes would, as such, be demoralizing and hardening. Then, and only then, do they become purifying when they are touched and penetrated by the transfiguring light, the spiritual light, the divine light, of the beautiful. Aristotle's celebrated treatise on poetry places the essence of poetry in imitation; whereas the essence of the poetical is not in imitating, copying, nature, but in reproducing nature in the spirit of the original production, – a reproduction which is only possible to a mind so genially capable of sympathy with the creative process, as to be thereby exalted and inspired to lively re-animation, thus becoming, in its sphere, maker or poet. Far deeper than imitation is this mental action; it uses imitation as its instrument. In Plato's dialogues are to be met with deeper and sounder views on poetry than in the formal treatise of Aristotle. Aristotle's mind, vast as it was, had by no means so much as Plato's of that gift which elevates and enlivens and enlightens all other mental gifts: he was less of a poet than Plato.

This gift which exalts and illumines all other gifts is the decisive gift in high literature and fine art; for art is not fine art except it be poetical. It is the idealizing gift, whereby, through the insight and synthetic power it imparts, the delineator is enabled to see the person or thing before him more distinctly; and this, whether what is before him be a flesh-and-blood reality or a conception of his brain. Thus, the portrait-painter, in order to see his subject more thoroughly as he is, needs the illumination of this idealizing light. Hereby he is empowered to throw a flame into the interior of his subject and thus bring out into clearer individuality the outward features. In short, through his idealizing aptitude, he, like the delineator with pen, realizes reality more truly. He becomes not only a more brilliant but a more faithful limner. On the page of Shakespeare Antony and Henry IV. and Richard II. and King John stand more vividly present than on the page of prosaic history. All his personages, all his scenes, all his dialogues, are steeped in this illuminative idealization, which perfuses them with its beams as the landscape is perfused at daybreak with the auroral splendor which makes the earth to sparkle in its inborn glory.

Shakespeare delights in making kings confront each other to bandy high words. In the times he depicts kings were not merely representative, they were the personal controllers of national destinies. By their almost unrestricted sway they then were real Majesties, not what they have now become in Europe, nominal Majesties. In the scene before us where the rival kings, with their royal and noble attendants, present a picture of irreconcilable ambitions and jealousies, the effect is deepened by the interchange of sharp, very sharp, words between those royal ladies, Elinor and Constance; an interchange which is a lively type of feminine vituperation, an ideal of recriminative give and take. The quality of their logomachy may be inferred from the conclusion: [Quotes 2.1.191–197].

An important figure in the play of *King John* is Cardinal Pandulph, the Pope's legate. At that period papal power was paramount. Of Pandulph Shakespeare avails himself to represent a typical priest, that is, a man who assumes that he is empowered by Heaven to be the exclusive, infallible expounder and interpreter of heavenly things, to guide and rule the spirituality of other men, – an assumption which, concentrating in itself the guilt of usurpation with the iniquity of despotism, is a blasphemy towards God and an offense and an insult to man. One wonders at the ignominious moral subjection of an age that bowed before such tyranny; but a show of indignant scorn at its weakness and superstition is checked by the sudden reflection that ourselves live in the shadow of this tyranny, and that, if incorporated sacerdotalism has, through the working of mental emancipation, the strengthening and purifying of the individual conscience, been shorn of much of its authority, its black shadow shortened and thinned, still itself has not foregone a tittle of its inhuman pretention, and perseveres in grasping at supreme control, political as well as moral, crippling the wills of men even to paralysis, that it may sway their minds, ever ravenous of power, its master-passion an unholy ambition.

Writing in the aroused forceful age of Elizabeth, Shakespeare becomes the spokesman of English independence, of Protestant manliness, and, in a passage quivering with eloquent patriotism, makes the King of England defy the papal legate and his chief. Passages like this, – of which there are others in his works, – set forth the greatest poet and deepest dramatist of the world as not only the foremost national poet of England, but the champion of Protestantism or free religion: [Quotes 3.1.147–71: John's defiance of the Pope].

Whether the movement be tragic grandeur, pathetic tenderness, patriotic fervor, with what ease this mighty penman rises to the elevation demanded by the occasion. Manly, stirring, burning words like these endear Shakespeare, with something of the warmth of personal affection and gratitude, to Englishmen forever, and to those who, in other hemispheres, drawing originally from that rich island-centre principles of religious and political freedom, enjoy as their dearest birthright the privilege of learning from their mothers' lips the language that Shakespeare spoke and wrote.

At the conclusion of King John's manly, sonorous defiance, when Pandulph excommunicates and curses him, Constance exclaims: [Quotes 3.1.179–84: 'Oh lawful let it be. . . .' and Pandulph's reply, 'There's law and warrant, lady for my curse'].

How profoundly must the humane, truly Christian Shakespeare have felt the secret irony of this answer of Pandulph to Constance. Law and warrant for cursing a fellow-man! The bitterness of the fruit proves the poison of the ripening sap, – the monstrous, unhuman assumption of one man to govern the soul of any fellow-man. For the curse of poor Constance there is some warrant, the warrant issued by the wronged, bleeding heart of a mother.

Constance is another of Shakespeare's wonderful ideals that are more real than the historic report of the reality. She is an everlasting mouthpiece of maternal agony, an agony out of which, to the reader or spectator, the sting is taken by the balm of the beautiful. Of this surpassing scene, in which acutest affliction and grief are clothed with radiance, I make room for the conclusion: [Quotes 3.4.76–100: Constance's defense of her extreme grief against the objections of Philip and Pandulph].

Here we have the transmuting virtue there is in poetry that it can make suffering spiritually attractive, draw a beatitude out of intense misery. Carrying dormant in his broad, deep manhood the joys and sorrows his fellow-men are liable to, when Shakespeare depicted a Lear or a Constance a poetic light shone upon his fellow-feeling and wakened it to such rhythmic moans that the deepest pangs of the heart become transfigured into beauty, mankind eagerly welcoming them to its breast, and appropriating them in their exquisiteness as a purifying cordial. In such passages

Shakespeare's doing may be likened to that of some radiant Titan who, grasping the trunk of an oak, through a latent might in his nervous arm should by shaking it make it, instead of acorns, drop glittering diamonds, to the wonder, delight, and enrichment of the beholders.

This great play abounds in scenes of tender or terrible pathos. What a picture of the tartarean interior of an assassin's brain, bemastered by thoughts too damnable for utterance, when King John puts Arthur into the keeping of Hubert! [Quotes 3.3.33–53].

This scene, like all his greatest scenes, is pure Shakespearean invention. Arthur's end is shrouded in mystery, which only the conscience of John can penetrate. History does not know how his death was brought about. It knows that John took him prisoner; and that was the last heard of him.

With such a picture before us as that of Constance, all glistening with poetic tears, we pause and say, 'here the poet must have reached the maximum of excellence,' when, only a few pages further, listening, in exquisite awe, to the talk of John to Hubert, we find ourselves reveling with delight in the inmost hideousness of the blackest of murderers. And still a few pages further, this Proteus – far more mobile and mutable than the Greek sea-god – transforms himself out of the ghastly, royal assassin, not into Prince Arthur, – for no Prince ever spoke such words as does this 'pretty child' [4.1.129] of Shakespeare when pleading with Hubert for his eyes, – but into one of the most heavenly creations of Art, so simple and soulful that it stands for every bright-minded, innocent boy that ever was or ever will be, and yet, so poetical that, while within the bounds of nature, it transcends by its truthful perfection the reality of any reported boyhood.

Nevertheless the chief power of the play is Faulconbridge. Him Shakespeare makes the plenipotentiary of England, to represent and act out English backbone, courage, common sense, patriotism. . . .

[Calvert here quotes liberally from the play to illustrate Faulconbridge's integrity, bravery, and sensitivity, then moves on to his concluding remarks.]

Nowhere does Shakespeare exhibit with more distinctness his intellectual lucidity and his artistic mastership than in foreshortening history. He condenses a decade or a reign into five acts, with such picturesque perception and historic grasp that we get the spirit of a period compactly bound, but faithfully preserved, in a poetic condensation.

Looking from a height over a mountainous region the eye seizes the peaks; the lower hills out of which they rise are scarcely seen. So in a genuine historical drama only the altitudes of history are noted by one looking from the sunny summit of poetry, and these, with the vigorous personages who make the altitudes, give the reader the most vivid view of a marked period and the actors in it. A variously and brilliantly and deeply gifted man, Shakespeare, in the majestic strength of his large manhood, stood above history. History, owing its interest and significance to the unfolded faculties of man, Shakespeare, through his fellow-feeling with all humanity, and thence his sure insight into it, dominated history, and as poet-thinker reproduced its very spirit, as he does in *King John*. . . . (123–50)

45 Henry John Hardy, on Pandulph and history

1887

From 'Shakespeare as a Historian', in *Winchester College Shakespeare Society. Noctes Shakesperianæ. A Series of Papers by Late and Present Members.* Edited by Charles Halford Hawkins (Winchester and London, 1887), pp. 109–118.

Henry John Hardy (b. 1860) was the author of *A Latin Reader for Lower Forms in Schools* (London, 1888) and *Winchester College 1867–1920: A Register Edited on Behalf of the Warden and Fellows of the College* (Winchester, 1923). His sole contribution to Shakespeare studies would appear to be the essay excerpted below, which comprises a chapter in a volume commemorating the twenty-fifth anniversary of the Winchester College Shakespeare Society.

[Hardy begins his essay by raising the issue of whether the historian should 'chronicle facts with a most rigid accuracy' or present a picture of historical events 'with some of the shadows exaggerated and some of the colours brightened, in order that the general effect may be the more vivid and attractive' (109).[1] In addressing this problem he discusses Shakespeare in general, contending that it is 'shallow criticism to convict Shakespeare of small lapses and tiny offences against historical fact' (112); regarding *King John* in particular he contends that here Shakespeare 'distorts the facts as by a prism, in order that the single rays may be manifest and the particular purposes of the poet may be subserved' (115).]

... Thus a series of divergences from history come into prominence in *King John*, in order that the events recorded may be made subservient to the principles they are taken to illustrate. The action of the play ranges over sixteen years (1199–1215); these years are compressed that the events should pass rapidly before the mind; the two occasions of the war with France (springing out of the position of Philip as Arthur's guardian, and out of the deposition of John by Innocent III) are represented as closely consequent when they were, as a matter of fact, separated by many years. ... (115) [Hardy now takes up some key figures in the play, seeing John's historical character as somewhat ameliorated by Shakespeare, and Arthur, Constance, and Austria all altered from history to fit dramatic purposes.]

Lastly, Pandulph, who comes in as 'Cardinal of fair Milan and from Pope Innocent the legate here' [3.1.138ff.], was in 1215 nothing more than Master Pandulph, 'our Lord Pope's subdeacon and familiar'; his ability in changing with Protean subtlety from a sophist to a politician, uniting the arguments learnt in the schools of Occam and Roscellinus[2] with the statecraft of a Machiavelli is very noteworthy; his language seems a caricature of the so-called casuistry of the day with the ulterior object of throwing disgrace on the Roman system.

The character of Pandulph will suggest a point of view from which we may regard all the chief personages of the play. They are all in a sense historical characters; but it is no less true that they are representatives of classes or of institutions then to be found in England – they are, indeed,rather types than individuals.[3] But by clothing his types in flesh and blood Shakespeare avoids the abstract and cold impersonality pervading the characters of Aristotle and Theophrastus, without sacrificing the general lessons which such delineation of character teaches. If Pandulph is not historical, he is typical of a system whose borders were wide enough to include theological logicians who speculated whether the feathers in an angel's wing were the same in the morning and the evening. . . . (117)

46 Henry Morley, on commodity

1887

From *The Life and Death of King John* (London, 1877).

Henry Morley (1822–94) was one of the most productive men of letters of the nineteenth century. Abandoning an unhappy career in medicine, he established a school at Manchester in 1848, and began to devote himself to the two abiding interests of his life, education and literary studies. Morley had an active hand in numerous periodicals, including *Household Words*, *All the Year Round*, and *The Examiner*, serving as editor of the latter for a number of years; he also taught English literature at King's College, London, University College, London, and Queen's College, London. Perhaps his most important scholarly undertaking was the ambitious *English Writers*, an eleven-volume history of English literature on which he labored from 1864–93, and which was completed by W. Hall Griffin in 1895, the year after Morley's death. Hardly less noteworthy was Morley's involvement in two long and ongoing publishing enterprises designed to offer inexpensive editions of English and foreign 'classics' in an accessible scholarly format: 'Morley's Universal Library' (64 vols, London, 1883–8) and 'Cassell's National Library' (214 vols, London, 1886–92); for each of these two hundred and seventy-eight volumes Morley prepared a critical introduction.

[From the Introduction]

... One source of strength in the play is the harmony produced by a clear reference of all its parts to the point of view from which the whole picture is taken. The point of view in every play of Shakespeare's is some strength or weakness of our common humanity that lies at the heart of life, and helps or hinders in the battle we have all to fight. He never founds a play upon a mere philosophical subtlety, or a historical theory, or anything that is not common to the humanity of rich and poor, gentle and simple, that cannot, in short, speak to us all. His are the truths of life that speak to us who live.

In the story of *King John*, the point upon which Shakespeare fixed attention was expediency as a motive of action; there moves throughout the play 'That smooth-faced gentleman, tickling Commodity, / Commodity, the bias of the world' [2.1.573ff.].

The play begins, in its old form as in Shakespeare, with a son who finds it expedient to defame his mother that he may obtain possession of his father's lands; and in the old form, as in Shakespeare, there are two cases of solemn swearing, followed in half an hour by solemn counter-swearing, each at the bidding of expediency and not of right. Shakespeare, observing this, drew from it the keynote of his play. The writer of the older play had not observed this, and had no such keynote. When we have learned the harmonies of Shakespeare's *King John*, no force of a strained ingenuity can help us to read them into the earlier play. Its author only felt that he had good scope for action and passion, in a play that would give occasion for much battering at the Pope and the monks, and much assertion of the strength of England if all Englishmen would hold together. Now it is not one of the fundamental truths of life that the Pope is a 'Pagan full of pride,' or that a monk is treacherous, or that an Englishman is a great creature. Shakespeare silences the whole battery of class hatred; but he loved his country, and often emphatically spoke his love, and he did not remove his hand from the suggestion of strength in union, that arose incidentally from the last part of the story of the play; indeed, he summed it all up in its closing lines which said – [Quotes 5.7.116–118: from the Bastard's final speech on national unity].

England true to itself; – a life true to itself. Does that mean following the whisper of the smooth-faced gentleman, Commodity, Expediency, when he rounds us in the ear, or does it mean God and the Right, Right for its own sake only? In *Julius Cæsar*, Shakespeare takes the noblest example in all history of evil done that good may follow, and shows the tragedy of that mistake in the first principles of human action.

In *King John* there is first the defiance of France in the maintenance of an unjust claim. Shakespeare marks clearly at the first his intention to represent John as the false royalty, as afterwards in Arthur he as clearly represents the true. . . .

Shakespeare then follows the older play in representing the claim of Robert Faulconbridge, who shames his mother for a gain of land; and Philip Faulconbridge, as bastard son of Cœur-de-Lion, takes his place among the followers of John. His place in the old play was a large one; the poet dwelt upon his antagonism to the Arch-Duke of Austria whose captive Cœur-de-Lion had been, and who wears the dead Cœur-de-Lion's lion-hide. This, which was part of the substance of the earlier play, Shakespeare treats with a few touches, confined to a dozen scattered sentences. Shakespeare's Faulconbridge is a blunt soldier, faithful and fearless, with no nice conscience, but a rough natural sense of what is firm and square. Such a man, in whom there are no turnings and windings, Shakespeare uses as a person of the story, who serves as a foil to the men of low and secret policy, – as Fortinbras, the man of action without thought, is foil to Hamlet, the man of thought without action, – and the Bastard, by his comments upon their tortuous ways, becomes now and then a sort of chorus to the play. . . .

[Morley now summarizes the action of 2.1 before the walls of Angiers, seeing 'Commodity' as governing the behavior of Hubert – a fact underscored by the Bastard in his soliloquy at 2.1.561–98. He then moves on to 3.1.]

Discord enters in the person of Cardinal Pandulph. For his plunder of the Church John is threatened with excommunication. He defies the Pope's authority over a king of England in stout words. But Shakespeare, while he puts them in his mouth, has mainly in view a reversal to come, at the bidding of expediency, when John will be shown humbly taking his crown from the Pope at Pandulph's hands. It is not in the strong defiance of the Pope that the thought of the play here lies, but in the fact that all these brave words are to be eaten abjectly, as soon as it appears to John that he can get for himself by submission to the Pope what he is afraid he shall lose by resistance. The more emphatic and earnest his protest, the more his heart goes with his defiance, the more complete the illustration of the power of that smooth-faced gentleman, tickling Commodity. King John is not true to himself.

Pandulph's demand that, on pain of excommunication, Philip of France let go the hand of John, is supported by the Dauphin's plea of expediency: – [Quotes 3.1.204–7]. The vows are broken almost as soon as sworn. War became peace, peace becomes war, at each new turn of the weathercock that points to private gain. The chance of renewed war gives John the advantage. Arthur becomes his prisoner, and the smooth-faced gentleman suggests at once the expediency of murder. Arthur in the old play reasons out his right in set terms. In Shakespeare's play he is the opposite to John. John's is the false royalty that seeks ill gains by following, without regard to right, at every point, the way that seems to lead to earthly gain. Arthur's is the true royalty of life, that lies in simple, childlike innocence and the strong spirit of unselfish love. Almost the first words of Arthur in the play are of flinching from the feuds and hatreds that surround him: – [Quotes 2.1.163–5]. When he is made prisoner in the battle his thought is not for himself, but 'O, this will make my mother die with grief!' [3.3.5]. But, fresh from sight of the mother's grief, Pandulph suggests to France the great commodity there is in the child's murder. John certainly will murder Arthur. That is a good thing for them. England will turn from John, and then will come to France the opportunity of gain. So the Act ends with the murder of Arthur, who represents the cause of right and the true spirit of love and innocence, planned by John, and anticipated by those who had called themselves his champions, with equal relish, there being on each side arguments of Commodity.

In the Fourth Act the touching scene between Hubert and Arthur brings into clearest light the true royalty of life, as it is in every soul that can enter the kingdom of God as one of these little ones. The words of Arthur breathe still a childlike innocence and the pure spirit of love.

When the nobles ask liberty for Arthur, are told of his death, and turn from John to become rebels, inviting aid from France, Commodity has tempted them to bring the common enemy into their country for their own advantage in domestic feud. John repents of a murder that has not brought him the expected gain; but when he learns that Arthur lives, his first thought is not of a conscience relieved. Commodity points instantly to the advantage to be got, and his cry is – [Quotes 4.2.260–2: 'Doth Arthur live? . . .']. Arthur falls in attempting his escape from prison walls, and the true royalty lies bleeding on the stones. He is found dead by the peers, who are deaf, therefore, to John's plea.

In the Fifth Act, Commodity brings John to humble yielding of his crown into the Pope's hand, that he may receive it again from Pandulph, and gain thereby the influence of Pandulph in staying the invasion by the French, in league with the rebellious English lords. The breath that blew the coal wants power to quench the fire. War is a-foot. The Dauphin and the French join with the English nobles and swear league before the altar at Bury St. Edmunds. Their battle is half won, when the English learn that the oath was, for commodity, unsworn by the French within the hour in which it was sworn. Before they left the altar, the French had vowed that the rebellious nobles should not live a day beyond the victory they helped to win, since traitors to one sovereign could not be trusted by another. The nobles changed their side, and changed the issue of the conflict. But Commodity suggested to a monk a great advantage to the Church in putting out of the way a monarch who found it expedient to plunder churches. At last, therefore, in the person of a monk, Commodity destroyed King John.

Thus it is that unity of design is to be found in the main structure and in every detail of Shakespeare's play. Men false to their country make ill compacts with the enemy, looking only to the moment's fair show of expediency. So do men false to their conscience, in which the true self speaks. Right, for its own sake, is the aim of life, whatever the smooth-faced gentleman may say. . . . (7–14)

47 Francis Albert Marshall, a balanced assessment of *King John*

1888

From *The Works of William Shakespeare. Edited by Henry Irving and Frank A. Marshall. With Notes and Introductions to Each Play by F. A. Marshall and Other Shakespearian Scholars, and Numerous Illustrations by Gordon Browne* (8 vols, London, 1888–90; 8 vols, New York, 1888–90). Volume III. *King Richard III*; *King John*; *The Merchant of Venice*; *1 Henry IV*; *2 Henry IV* (1888).

Francis Albert Marshall (1840–89) resigned his position as a clerk in the audit office in Somerset House in 1868 for a career as a playwright. He served for a time as dramatic critic for the *London Figaro*, and either authored or co-authored some eleven plays, the most noteworthy of which were comedies or farces such as *Mad as a Hatter* (1863), *Q.E.D., or, All a Mistake* (1871); and *False Shame* (1872). In addition to his work on 'The Henry Irving Shakespeare', Marshall also edited a stage version of *Hamlet* presented at the Lyceum Theatre and arranged by Irving (London, 1879), and *Henry Irving, Actor and Manager. A Criticism of a Critic's Criticism. By an Irvingite* (London, 1883).

[From the Introduction to *King John*: 'Critical Remarks']

This play, which, if the historical sequence is followed, should go before *Richard II.*, seems to me, on the whole, to be clearly a later work of Shakespeare's than that tragedy. It certainly displays a far greater mastery of dramatic characterization than *Richard II.*: it has fewer rhymed lines; according to Mr. Fleay [No. 42 above] out of 2553 lines it contains 2403 in blank verse. Like *Richard II.* it has no passages written in prose: it has not even any passage like that in *Richard II.* [2.2.108–20], which, though printed as verse, is so unrhythmical as to read like prose. There are very few double endings. Whether this play was written before or after *Richard III.* is doubtful; most editors consider the latter to be the earlier play. Setting aside, however, the exact position which *King John* should occupy among Shakespeare's plays as strictly arranged according to the order of their production, we may fairly consider it as belonging to that period of his literary development in which we have placed it. As a drama, it exhibits a marked superiority to any of the other historical plays except Parts I. and II. of *Henry IV.*, *Richard III.*, and, perhaps, *Henry V.* It contains three characters which will live as long as any of Shakespeare's creations; namely, the Bastard

Faulconbridge, Constance, and Arthur; while it certainly contains one scene, that between Hubert and Arthur [4.1], which is among the most popular and most admired of any in Shakespeare's plays; yet, in spite of its admirable characterization, its many pathetic and vigorous scenes, and in spite of its containing two parts, those of the Bastard and Constance, most effective for an actor and actress respectively, it does not seem to have been a popular play in Shakespeare's own time; and, as will be seen from the stage history of the play, was left for a very long period altogether neglected and practically excluded from the repertory of our theatres. This is the more to be wondered at, because there is a sturdy Protestant spirit in the play, and an heroic strain of patriotism which, one would have thought, could not fail to secure for a very much worse play undying popularity with an English audience. It is true that Shakespeare, following his large-hearted and truly artistic instincts, has modified considerably the bitter anti-papal tone of the old play on which he founded *King John*; but he seems, at the same time, to have given to the political aspect of the play a much closer application to Elizabethan times than is to be found in *The Troublesome Raigne*. In fact, as Mr. Simpson has pointed out [No. 35 above], in his paper on the Politics of Shakespeare's Plays, Shakespeare altered the whole political motive of the old play; and made the quarrel between John and his subjects turn more upon the question of his defective title to the throne than, as it did really, on his own abominable character; but here Shakespeare's inherent honesty of mind stood him in bad stead; for, however much he might change the political motive of the play, he could not bring himself to represent John as anything but a mean and detestable tyrant. All the king's bluster against the pope goes for very little when we find him, a short time afterwards, handing over his crown to the pope's legate, and consenting to receive it again at his hands as if from a suzerain. In fact John is ready to submit to any degradation, in order to obtain a powerful ally against his rebellious barons; and though some of those barons stoop so low as to intrigue with the enemy of their country, and to fight under the standard of France against their sovereign, yet John's crimes have so alienated our sympathies from him that we shut our eyes to the dishonourable treason of Salisbury and his accomplices, and readily forgive them, when they abjure their treason and swear allegiance to the young Prince Henry. There is no doubt that in the unsympathetic character of John lies the weakness of this play. Constance and Arthur both fade out of it some time before the end is reached; and though the Bastard still remains to represent unflinching courage and loyalty, the chief character, the king himself, who ought to be the object of our interest and sympathy, has failed to enlist either one or the other on his behalf; and so the play terminates without that effective climax, which is essential to the success of a drama intended to be acted as well as read.

The character of Constance has always been a very favourite one with the readers of Shakespeare; if it proves less attractive on the stage, it is only because her share in the action ceases at comparatively so early a period of the play. Mrs. Jameson [No. 14 above] in her *Characteristics of Women* has a very interesting essay on the character of Constance, an essay which exhibits considerable power of moral analysis. Mrs. Jameson is quite right in repudiating the theory that the leading motive of Constance's conduct is ambition. On the contrary, she seems, as far as Shakespeare has drawn her, singularly devoid of any personal seeking after power such as Elinor would attribute to her. Her nature is evidently impulsive and passionate; above all she is animated by that keen sense of injustice which is so very commonly found in such natures. She is vehement in the assertion of her son's rights, not so much from any ambition to exercise the power which would naturally belong to her as his mother, but simply because she loves and, indeed, idolizes him; she feels most keenly that she is the only person left to plead for his rights, and to defend him from the mean and overreaching schemes of his detestable uncle. Her passionate sense of the wrong which has been done to her son makes her at once eager in expressing her gratitude to King Philip and the Dauphin, as well as to Austria, when they offer their support to Arthur's just claim, and at the same time vehemently resentful of their cowardly desertion of his cause, when their own selfish interest points in the other direction. In all her pleadings and her remonstrances there is the same want of self-control, the same almost exaggerated indignation because she cannot, for one moment, tolerate the doctrine of expediency which so completely governs the conduct of those with whom she is associated. In fact she is one of those many characters on which Shakespeare seems to have lavished his utmost power of poetic eloquence, because they represent that utter unconventionality, that passionate rebellion against the accepted morality of the world, which must have been one of the strongest traits in his own nature. It is only a very short-sighted criticism that can find in the reticence of Arthur, throughout the only two scenes in which Shakespeare has introduced him in the company of Constance, any proof that the son returns but feebly the passionate affection of his mother. It is only natural that a boy, such as Shakespeare has represented Arthur to be, should feel somewhat timid and awed in the presence of such vehement indignation as Constance displays; but the fact that when he is taken prisoner, the boy's first thought is for his mother and not for himself [3.3.5], is sufficient to prove that Shakespeare did not intend to represent Arthur as at all lacking in filial devotion. We may regret that the poet could not reconcile with his scheme of the dramatic action of this play, the possibility of giving us a scene between mother and son. Such an omission may have been the result of hasty execution; or it may have been the deliberate judgment of a dramatist who, however long his plays may seem to the fastidious intolerance of a modern audience, yet had a very keen sense of the virtue of dramatic concentration. It would certainly seem as if Shakespeare felt himself rather hampered by the amount of material that he had at hand in the construction of this play; otherwise he would not have been content with merely imitating through the mouth of a messenger [4.2.122] the rumour of the death of so important a character as Constance. She was a creation, to the power of which he could not have been himself insensible; yet he allows her to disappear with the end of the third act; and the injury to the play, involved in the absence of all female interest in the two last acts, is one which no doubt has proved fatal to its permanent popularity upon the stage: it is one of which I cannot help thinking the poet's maturer judgment would not have approved.

 The character of the Bastard is more elaborated than that of Constance, and seems to have engaged more of the author's energy; perhaps too of that fondness which every poet is apt to display, with more or less caprice, towards the various beings of his own creation. The boldness of Philip Faulconbridge, his recklessness, his audacious outspokenness, may have been inherited from his father, Richard Cœur-de-Lion; but it is probable that Shakespeare emphasized these characteristics as natural in a man, the circumstances of whose birth placed him in a more or less false position, and impelled him to constant self-assertion. It would be very interesting to compare the character of the Bastard Faulconbridge with that of Edmund in *King Lear.* Both suffer from the stigma of illegitimacy; but what a different effect the consciousness of this stigma exercises on their respective natures! While Edmund is sullen, malicious, and cruel, Faulconbridge is, at the worst, impudent, at the best, fearless.

One point has been much insisted upon in connection with this play, and that is its bearing upon the question of to what were Shakespeare's religious opinions. Some have deduced from the eloquent denunciations of papal interference, which are placed in the mouth of King John, the conclusion that he was a strong Protestant; and the extreme opponents of the Church of Rome have even claimed him as one of their most zealous partisans. On the other hand, some Roman Catholics have maintained that his careful omission of the more offensive portions of the old play shows that he was, at heart, one of themselves.

The probability is that the truth lies between these two extremes; and that Shakespeare, while he thoroughly sympathized with the political aspect of the Reformation, was, in no strict sense of the word, a strong Protestant. I have heard it maintained with some show of probability, and much show of ingenuity, that Shakespeare was, in fact, a lax Roman Catholic, who did not care to face the political and social penalties involved in a strict fidelity to what was then a proscribed religion. It may be doubted whether, in the case of a poet who shows such very wide human sympathies, it is a profitable occupation of one's time to argue this question at all. Suffice it to say, that the whole world has to be thankful that Shakespeare was too large-hearted to identify himself with any form of bigotry; and that, writing as he did for all mankind; he was as scrupulous as possible in avoiding the great error of giving unnecessary offence to any creed which embraced amongst its believers men of large heart as well as of great intellect. As a true poet, loving all that was beautiful and good, he could not help sympathizing with that religion which had so long represented the only form of Christianity in the world. On the other hand his enthusiastic love for his country, which is so often manifested throughout his plays, led him to sympathize more or less with that resentment of all foreign interference in politics which really formed the backbone, in England at least, of that movement which is commonly known as the Reformation. With Puritanism, the great religious factor in that movement, Shakespeare had positively no sympathy whatever; any more than he had with that strict submission to the supreme head of the Church, on the part of Roman Catholics, to which in modern times the name of Ultramontanism has been given. (156–9)

48 Hiram Corson, on Constance and Arthur

1889

From *An Introduction to the Study of Shakespeare* (Boston, 1889).

Hiram Corson (1828–1911) was professor of literature at Cornell University for over thirty years (1870–1903). A political liberal and friend of Walt Whitman, he denounced slavery, organized religion, and concentrated wealth. In his later years he developed a strong belief in spiritualism, the practice of which he set forth in his posthumous book *Spirit Messages* (Rochester, N.Y., 1911), which describes twenty-four seances in which he, his deceased wife, and a number of others took part. Corson was also an early admirer of Browning, and published a critical appreciation of the poet, *An Introduction to the Study of Robert Browning's Poetry* (Boston, 1886); his other noteworthy critical books, in addition to his study of Shakespeare, are the *Primer of English Verse* (Boston, 1892) and the *Aims of Literary Study* (New York, 1895).

[Corson's chapter on *King John* begins by treating its relationship to *The Troublesome Raigne*, arguing that Shakespeare's depiction of John's reign is motivated by patriotism rather than the anti-Catholic bias of the earlier play. Corson then proceeds to a critical evaluation of *King John*.]

... Shakespeare's opening scenes must always receive special attention, in studying the dramatic action of his Plays, as in them the keynote of the whole action is usually and distinctly struck.

In the first 43 lines of *King John*, the entire action of the play is presented in germ. [Quotes 1.1.43].

We have seen that the Play on its political side quite ignores the facts of history. So, on the personal side, there is an ignoring, to a greater or less degree, of the characters, as represented by history, of some of the dramatis personæ; and this is especially so in the case of Constance and Arthur, who must be estimated independently of history, and almost as purely fictitious. We must not inquire of history what manner of woman Constance was – we must consider exclusively what she is in the play. And the same may be said of Arthur. Again, as I read the play, I see a purpose throughout to intensify the injustice, and crime, and baseness of John's usurpation, through the characters given to Constance and Arthur. [Quotes 1.1.31–4: Elinor's characterization of Constance as 'ambitious'; and 2.1.117–23: the beginning of the scolding match between Elinor and Constance].

These words have, I think, misled many commentators; and they have made ambition the ruling motive of Constance.

It is not safe to take the opinions which hostile characters in Shakespeare's Plays, and sometimes characters which are not hostile, are made to express of each other, as opinions which must go for anything in our estimation of the characters; quite as unsafe as it sometimes is in real life to judge of people by what we hear others say of them. In Shakespeare's Plays, what characters say must often be taken as representing themselves rather than others. This is especially true in the case of Elinor. We don't learn what others are from what she says of them; we certainly don't learn what manner of woman Constance really is; but we learn a great deal of what *she* is. . . . [A digression follows in which Corson applies this principle of interpretation to Lady Macbeth's statements about her husband.]

No careful reader of the play of *King John*, will, I am assured, take Elinor's accusations as at all representing the poet's dramatic purpose in Constance. The old Elinor is the political genius and guide of her son John, 'an Ate, stirring him to blood and strife,' as Chatillion describes her in the play [2.1.63], and we must not look for the truth from *her*, in regard to Constance, whom she charges with seeking the throne for her son, only with the ambitious design of ruling herself and kindling all the world. But what Constance says of Elinor [2.1.174–90], we can take as the truth in regard to the old queen mother.

What Ulrici [No. 21 above] says of Constance and Arthur is wide of the mark. I don't find in this German critic much evidence of insight into Shakespeare's dramatic motives, though he has ranked high as a Shakespearian critic. This is what he says, and all that he says:

'As to the fortunes of Constance and Arthur, although they are primarily but an episode in the life and character of John [that is not correct, for they constitute an inseparable part of the main action],[1] yet it is with great significance that they *appear to be thus interwoven* with the history of the state. The instruction they furnish forms a pendant to the general lesson of the piece; for they teach us [Ulrici's interest is always directed to the didactic, in a play, rather than to the dramatic action], that nothing in history more invariably meets its due punishment than *weakness* and *passion – those hereditary failings of the female character*. Women ought not to interfere in history, for history demands action, and for that they are constitutionally disqualified.'

It's a pity Ulrici could not have had a John Ruskin to teach him what he sets forth, somewhat strongly, to be sure, in his *Sesame and Lilies*, in regard to Shakespeare's heroines.[2] Ulrici goes on:

'The haste and impatience with which Constance labors to *establish* her son's rights . . . justly involves him as well as herself in ruin. Arthur, therefore, although preserved by the compassion of Hubert, must nevertheless perish. Had his mother but had the prudence to wait until he could himself have asserted his own rights by his own arm, and *when alone he could have possessed a perfect title*, he could have gained for himself and her what lawfully belonged to them.'

Constance labors, he says, to *establish* her son's rights. But the play throughout *assumes* that those rights *are* established; and the point upon which the whole play turns is, that her son has been unjustly deprived of them. In history, Arthur's rights were not established, and John was not regarded by his disaffected barons in the light of a usurper, but of a tyrant. But the critic of Shakespeare's play has nothing to do with authentic history; he has to do with the play, in itself considered. What are the poet's postulates and assumptions, is the question to be asked. Ulrici repeats the same mistake further on in the passage I've quoted: 'If Arthur's mother had had the good sense to wait until he could himself have asserted his own rights by his own arm, *and when alone he could have possessed a perfect title,*' etc.

Such criticism as that is on a level with Gustav Rümelin's, on *Romeo and Juliet*, in his *Shakespearestudien*,[3] which I may cite here as, along with Ulrici's on *King John*, a good specimen of a species of criticism which interests itself in everything in a play of Shakespeare, except its own independent dramatic vitality....

[Corson briefly and disparagingly summarizes Rümelin's remarks on *Romeo and Juliet*, then cites Gervinus's contention [No. 31 above] that Constance is ambitious, vain, overly passionate, coarse, and violent in nature.]

Is this the Constance as she is understood by the unphilosophical but sympathetic reader, with no critical theories to maintain? I think not.

The play, let me repeat, turns upon the usurpation of John and the consequent murder of Arthur, the rightful heir. The usurpation is *assumed* – the validity of Arthur's title to the crown is *assumed*, and this assumption on the part of the dramatist must not be lost sight of, authentic history to the contrary notwithstanding. It cannot then be said that Constance is ambitious for the crown, either for her son's sake or for her own sake. What she claims and contends for, and agonizes for, is her son's rights, of which he has been basely deprived. Even the queen mother, Elinor, is made, as we have seen, to express to John her sense of the usurpation, in the opening scene, after Chatillion, the ambassador from Philip of France, has gone from the royal presence. What she afterwards says to Constance should go for nothing in the case. She says what she does as a matter of course.

Faulconbridge adheres firmly to John throughout the play; but he is made to reveal, very distinctly, in his speeches, his secret sense of the injustice done to Arthur. He knows that John is a usurper; he knows that he is compounded of baseness, injustice, and treachery; but so long as he has possession of the throne, whether that possession be just or unjust, he is to him the impersonation of the state, to whom loyalty is due.

Shakespeare, it is evident, made Faulconbridge voice the feelings of the English people, *in his own time*, against foreign interference in church and state....

[After linking the Bastard's patriotic speeches to nationalistic pride over the defeat of the Spanish Armada in 1588, Corson goes on to provide a list of all the scenes in the play which include either Constance or Arthur.]

... These scenes evidence with an entire conclusiveness, I think, that Shakespeare's dramatic purpose in Constance was to exhibit *outraged maternal affection*, independently of any ambition on her part. For her to show personal ambition for the crown, would mar the artistic symmetry and the whole moral tone of the play. We shall see that there is not a single speech of hers which indicates directly or by implication, any personal ambition. She is 'oppressed with wrongs' [3.1.13] done to her beloved

Arthur, whom the poet, in the service of his art, represents as possessing all those charms of person and all those qualities of mind and heart which intensify a mother's affection and devotion.

In comparing Shakespeare's Arthur with the Arthur of the old play, we can easily see the dramatic purpose which determined the poet in making him what he does. And Augustine Skottowe [No. 10 above] well remarks: 'The maternal distress of Constance, in the old play, is clamorous and passionate, vindictive and contumelious. The hand of Shakespeare tempered her rage into vehemence, attuned her clamour to eloquence, and modulated her coarse vindictiveness into a deep sense of gross injuries and undeserved misfortunes.'

From the accounts we have of Mrs. Siddons's impersonation of Constance, it appears that she made strong-willed ambition her ruling motive, rather than maternal affection. The impersonation, in the last generation, by Miss Helen Faucit, now Lady Martin, the wife of Sir Theodore Martin, the biographer of the Prince Consort, appears to have been a truer one than that of Mrs. Siddons. From the dramatic criticism of the time (1843 and later) we learn that maternal tenderness and affection alone motivated and informed her impersonation.[4]

The situation in [3.1], which has been led up to by the marriage of the Dauphin and Blanch, is, perhaps, unsurpassed as a dramatic situation, in all Shakespeare. To Constance, when, deserted and betrayed, she stands alone in her despair, amid her false friends and her ruthless enemies, Mrs Jameson [No. 14 above] applies, most appropriately, the image of the mother eagle, wounded and bleeding to death, yet stretched over her young in an attitude of defiance, while all the baser birds of prey are clamoring around her eyrie. The noble Bastard, whose heart seems to be always in the right place, feels deeply the injustice of the act of the two kings: [Quotes 2.1.561–74: from the speech on Commodity].

There's a sort of reflex action induced in his mind, which causes him to slander himself. After representing self-interest as the bias of the world, he continues: [Quotes 2.1.587–98: the conclusion of the same speech].

All this is pure self-slander, as his subsequent disinterested and magnanimous acts and words show. . . .

[Corson now summarizes the action from 2.1 to 3.1, then turns to the character of John.]

. . . He passes, irresistibly, into the power of an avenging fate. The dramatic situation, at this stage of the play, is in Shakespeare's best tragic manner. The moral baseness of John, which seals his doom, may be said to be gathered up, and exhibited in its extreme intensity, in the scene with Hubert, the 3d of the 3d Act, in which he intimates to Hubert his wish to have the little prince put out of the way: and in the 2d Scene of the 4th Act, where he accuses the aptness of the instrument as the cause of the suggestion. I would call special attention to the last 19 verses of John's long speech [3.3.37–55] beginning, 'If the midnight bell.' The thought keeps on the wing through all these 19 verses. There is a moral significance in the suspended construction of the language. The mind of the dastard king hovers over the subject of the ungodly act and dares not alight upon it; and the verse, in its uncadenced movement, admirably registers the speaker's state of mind: [Quotes 3.3.37–55].

The loveliness of Arthur is the most fully exhibited in the scene with Hubert, the 1st in the 4th Act, where he entreats Hubert to spare his eyes. The pathos of the situation is pushed to the verge of the painful. The highest art was demanded here to keep the treatment of the subject within the domain of the beautiful. And it is so kept.

I need not trace the dramatic action further. From the point reached, to the end, there are no new movements. King John is now in a current which he cannot stem, and will be swept helplessly along to the bitter end.

Shakespeare is always true to the fatality of overmastering passion of every kind. To the extent that his characters forfeit the power of self-assertion, do they become subject to fate, and are swept along by circumstances. This, of course, is a universal, an obvious, a self-evident, truth; but it is a truth which the inferior sort of dramatists do not always observe, in their treatment of great passions, and their work is, in consequence, wanting in moral proportion. . . . (163–75)

49 Walter Horatio Pater, kingship, personality, and the human condition

1889

From *Appreciations. With an Essay on Style* (London, 1889).

Walter Horatio Pater (1839–94) was one of the most influential literary critics of the late Victorian period. Educated at Oxford, where he was a student of Matthew Arnold, he became a fellow of Brasenose College in 1864 and taught Classics there for most of his adult life. A chief tenet of Pater's critical creed was the belief that all truth is relative and that our short period of life should be spent relishing its sensations, especially the aesthetic sensations produced by art. This view is particularly evident in his historical novel *Marius the Epicurean* (London, 1885), and, in one way or another, informs all of his critical thinking. Pater was a painstaking stylist, often laboring over his elaborate sentences in order to achieve a precise rhythmic or semantic effect. The rhetorically self-conscious essays in *Appreciations* are superb examples of the highly impressionistic style of late Victorian criticism in which Pater excelled.

[From 'Shakespeare's English Kings']

... The irony of kingship – average human nature, flung with a wonderfully pathetic effect into the vortex of great events; tragedy of everyday quality heightened in degree only by the conspicuous scene which does but make those who play their parts there conspicuously unfortunate; the utterance of common humanity straight from the heart, but refined like other common things for kingly uses by Shakespeare's unfailing eloquence: such, unconsciously for the most part, though palpably enough to the careful reader, is the conception under which Shakespeare has arranged the lights and shadows of the story of the English kings, emphasising merely the light and shadow inherent in it, and keeping very close to the original authorities, not simply in the general outline of these dramatic histories but sometimes in their very expression. Certainly the history itself, as he found it in Hall, Holinshed, and Stowe, those somewhat picturesque old chroniclers who had themselves an eye for the dramatic 'effects' of human life, has much of this sentiment already about it. What he did not find there was the natural prerogative – such justification, in kingly, that is to say, in exceptional, qualities, of the exceptional position, as makes it practicable in the result. It is no *Henriade*, he writes, and no history of the English people, but the sad fortune of some English kings as conspicuous examples of the ordinary human condition. As in a children's story, all princes are in extremes. Delightful in the sunshine above the wall into which chance lifts the flower for a season, they can but plead somewhat more touchingly than others their everyday weakness in the storm. Such is the motive that gives unity to these unequal and intermittent contributions toward a slowly evolved dramatic chronicle, which it would have taken many days to rehearse; a not distant story from real life still well remembered in its general course, to which people might listen now and again, as long as they cared, finding human nature at least wherever their attention struck ground in it.

He begins with John, and allows indeed to the first of these English kings a kind of greatness, making the development of the play centre in the counteraction of his natural gifts – that something of heroic force about him – by a madness which takes the shape of reckless impiety, forced especially on men's attention by the terrible circumstances of his end, in the delineation of which Shakespeare triumphs, setting, with true poetic tact, this incident of the king's death, in all the horror of a violent one, amid a scene delicately suggestive of what is perennially peaceful and genial in the outward world. Like the sensual humours of Falstaff in another play, the presence of the bastard Faulconbridge, with his physical energy and his unmistakable family likeness – 'those limbs which Sir Robert never holp to make' [1.1.239ff.][1] – contributes to an almost coarse assertion of the force of nature, of the somewhat ironic preponderance of nature and circumstance over men's artificial arrangements, to the recognition of a certain potent natural aristocracy, which is far from being always identical with that more formal, heraldic one. And what is a coarse fact in the case of Faulconbridge becomes a motive of pathetic appeal in the wan and babyish Arthur. The magic with which nature models tiny and delicate children to the likeness of their rough fathers is nowhere more more justly expressed than in the words of King Philip. – [Quotes 2.1.99–103: 'Look here upon thy brother Geffrey's face. . . .'].

It was perhaps something of a boyish memory of the shocking end of his father that had distorted the piety of Henry the Third into superstitious terror. A frightened soul, himself touched with the contrary sort of religious madness, doting on all that was alien from his father's huge ferocity, on the genialities, the soft gilding, of life, on the genuine interests of art and poetry, to be credited more than any other person with the deep religious expression of Westminster Abbey, Henry the Third, picturesque though useless, but certainly touching, might have furnished Shakespeare, had he filled up this interval in his series, with precisely the kind of effect he tends toward in his English plays. . . . (193–6)

50 Oliver Elton, the artistic excellence of *King John*

1890

From *The Tragedy of King John* (London, 1890).

Oliver Elton (1861–1945), translator, critic, and editor, enjoyed a scholarly career of noteworthy eclecticism and considerable duration. Among his most significant accomplishments were a translation of *The First Nine Books of the Danish History of Saxo Grammaticus* (London, 1894), *The Augustan Ages* (Edinburgh, 1899), and a six-volume *Survey of English Literature* covering the period 1730–1880, published in three separate installments (London, 1912, 1920, 1928). Elton succeeded Sir Walter Raleigh as King Alfred professor of English Literature at Liverpool, and was an extremely popular lecturer and visiting professor in many colleges and universities throughout England and America. His edition of *King John*, like his earlier edition of *1 Henry IV* (London, 1889), both of which were designed for use in schools, display the liveliness, concision, and argumentative edge typical of virtually all of Elton's critical prose.

[From the Introduction]

The Life and Death of King John is perhaps the most breathless of all Shakespeare's historical plays. It is full of tempestuous haste, of swiftly-changing pageantry. The life of years is condensed into a few hours. The embassy of Chatillion; the field before Angiers, the league against the town; the backsliding of Philip, first from Constance, and then from John; the capture of Arthur, his pleading, his rescue and death; the invasion of England; the vacillations of Fortune; the death-agony of John; and the tranquil note of assured patriotism and hope with which the play ceases – all these scenes fly like thought, like the tumult of a great storm which crushes good and evil impartially, and breaks at the last moment suddenly, displaced by daylight and the orderly march of nature.

This mark of Shakespeare, which he shares with the Greek dramatists and with Goethe, namely, an astonishing naturalness, hopefulness, and serenity at the end of his tragedies, is not for a moment to be confounded with vulgar 'poetic justice.' Poetic justice, which exhibits the good receiving good in this world according to their deserts, and the evil receiving evil, is of course a pleasant but puerile account of the matter; and Shakespeare is the last person to give us this kind of consolation. Arthur's beautiful life is spilt without anyone or anything being the better for it. John dies in misery, but so does Constance, who is guiltless. 'There is one end of one and all.'

A theologian would have his answer to the feelings raised by this heart-breaking spectacle, a modern pessimist would have his; but Shakespeare's is equally remote from both. He simply shows us the world going on again, ready for a new departure; nor does any writer fill us with such a sense of the extravagance and the inexhaustibility of nature.

Shakespeare, however, did not write in order to evoke these moral reflections; he wrote in order to ease his mind of the burning poetry, the patriotism, the gorgeous scenery that crowded it. Nor does he ever supply us with direct choric meditation upon the religious issues of his dramas. It is very seldom that we seem to detect any of the characters speaking the whole mind of the author. Even his most reverend personages have to give and take like others, and we hear of them as fallible or grotesque. In *Measure for Measure*, 'the old duke of dark corners'[4.3.157], the agent of justice and redress, the cowled providence of the play, even he hears of himself on the lips of Lucio; and of Prospero himself we have the views of Caliban. In Shakespeare, as in life, the wise never have it all their own way, and we are rather relieved that they do not.

In *King John* there is a certain approach to a chorus in the person of the Bastard Faulconbridge. He is the keenest-witted and almost the only honest person in the play; an honest buccaneer, he worships 'commodity' for himself; he is the loyal servant of the tyrant; he goes pillaging and blustering like any other buccaneer of his day. Yet no one else, unless it be the injured Constance, sees the wildly shameful and solemnly infernal injustice of Arthur's treatment by the kings. He cries – [Quotes 2.1.561: from the speech on Commodity; and 4.3.143–5: his reaction to Arthur's death].

Yet the speaker goes on to bear his own part in the tragi-comedy; he identifies his 'commodity' with his master's; loyalty and self-advancement work to one end; and at the close of the chaotic warfare, where justice seems nowhere, and righteousness fled to heaven, the Bastard reappears to speak for a moment with the heart of the lion his father, with the accent of courage, fidelity, and hope – [Quotes 5.7.101–2, 117–8: where the Bastard pledges first loyalty to Prince Henry and then love of country].

King John, though written before Shakespeare had gone half-way through his poetic career, and long before he had entered upon the period of *Othello* and *Lear*, is in its way as passionately poetical as *Romeo and Juliet*, which is earlier yet. It is quite possible, indeed, to lay too much stress upon the different periods of Shakespeare's genius. He had the power of saying great things from the first, and from the first he was ready to be interested in high passions and high actions. From the first also, no doubt, he was a patriot; and from the moment that he began to speak about England, he could not help his language rising to his theme. The peculiarity of *King John* is, that it is the first play in which both the personal and the patriotic interests are found at their height. In *Richard III.*, which perhaps was written a year or two before, the interest is centered upon the title character; in *Richard II.*, written about the same time as *King John*, the element of passion is comparatively feeble. But in *King John* we never know which to expect next, the thrill of patriotism or the thrill of pathos. . . .

In teaching a historical play of Shakespeare, it is well to make clear, first, that the poet does not care two straws for historical fact, and secondly, that he has no business to. In composing *King John*, for instance, he not only studies history in a loose and second-hand manner, but he manipulates it just as he chooses. Various instances of this practice will be pointed out in the notes; but once the pupil has grasped the principle of it, they matter very little. What was it to Shakespeare that a thing had, or had not, grossly happened? If he wanted, he could invent something a thousand times more to the purpose than any miserable occurrence. It would not even be true to say that he was a faithful portrayer of character. He did not care for an accurate, historical picture of character; but he did care for colour, passion, gallantry of character, regardless whether he created these or found them ready to his hand. Hence it seems a mistake to treat these historical plays as occasions for lessons in English history; and if it be deemed necessary (since most people's idea of early English history is a thing of Shakespeare's making) to inform the pupil accurately upon the facts of the case, this should be done as a separate discipline, and not as though in a spirit of setting Shakespeare right. . . . (v–xi)

51 James Appleton Morgan, *The Troublesome Raigne* and *King John*

1892

From *The Comedies, Histories, and Tragedies of Mr. William Shakespeare As Presented at the Globe and Blackfriars Theatres*, circa *1591–1623. Being the Text Furnished the Players, in Parallel Pages with the First Revised Folio Text, with Critical Introductions. The Bankside Shakespeare. Edited by Appleton Morgan* (22 vols, New York, 1888–1906). Volume XVIII. *The Life and Death of King John (The Players' Text of The Troublesome Raigne, &c., of 1591, with the Heminges and Condell Text of the King John of 1623). With an Introduction Touching the Adaptations of the Quarto into the Folio. By Appleton Morgan*, etc. (1892).

James Appleton Morgan (1845–1928) graduated from Columbia Law School in 1869 and practiced law in New York City. He founded the Shakespeare Society of New York in 1885 and served as its president until 1910. The Society published *The Bankside Shakespeare* as well as a later edition that Morgan co-edited with Willis Vickery, *The Bankside-Restoration Shakespeare* (5 vols, 1907–8), containing the texts of Shakespearian plays either rewritten or rearranged during the Restoration along with the text of the First Folio. This edition was discontinued after the publication of the first five volumes, none of which includes a text of *King John*. Morgan had an active scholarly life, publishing frequently on legal matters as well as on Shakespeare, particularly the Bacon controversy and other topical and historical issues relating to the poet and his times.

[From the Introduction to *King John*]

...It is very curious to observe that, in adapting this piece [*The Troublesome Raigne*], Shakespeare did not, as is the case of *The Famous Victories*, recast the entire story and supply a new action. On the other hand, he seems to have been perfectly satisfied with the action as it stood, and the parallelization shows an almost perfect following of the order of incidents of the old play in the new one (though, as we shall see, he sometimes put a speech for a scene or a scene for a speech in the rewriting).

But while retaining the action, Shakespeare absolutely rewrote the dialogue from beginning to end. So complete, indeed, is this rewriting of the entire play, that our parallelization detects but three absolute identities, and one, perhaps, only a typographical variation: – [Morgan cites the following parallel passages: *TR*, 1.33–4 and *KJ*, 1.1.11; *TR*, 2.409–10 and *KJ*, 2.1.527–8; *TR*, 12.117 and *KJ*, 5.4.42].

With the formal demand, however, which Cardinal Pandulph, acting as papal Legate, makes upon King John, to show cause why he has overruled the selection of Stephen Langton as Archbishop of Canterbury, Shakespeare is careful – while putting it into the blank verse which the revision required – to tamper very little. Freed from the archaic typography, the two stand thus: – [Quotes *TR*, 3.65–72 and *KJ*, 3.1.138–146].

In this versed form, Shakespeare strictly preserves the words of import – those which, that is, lay the stress precisely upon the claim of jurisdiction for the Pope – for the Legate upon the credentials of Langton, upon the 'disannulling' (that is, the preventing, by force, Langton's possession of the See), and upon the notice to show cause why, etc. And it will be interesting to those who please themselves by culling legalisms from the Plays, to observe the King, in the first line of his Folio [i.e., *King John*] answer, recognizing the legal intendment and solemnity of the notice delivered by the Legate: – 'What earthly name to Interrogatories / Can taste the free breath of a sacred King' [3.1.147ff.] – 'Interrogatories' being the technical name, to this day, for questions which are constructively asked by a court of competent jurisdiction, and which cannot be ignored or left unanswered. And the answer he as king proceeds to give, in both the Quarto [i.e., *The Troublesome Raigne*] and Folio versions, is clearly and emphatically that, as king, he will have no Italian Priest to lay taxes ('have tythe, toll, or poling penie out of England,' as the Quarto says [3.78ff.]; 'Shall tythe or toll in our dominions,' as the Folio [3.1.154]). The spiritual power of the Pope the King distinctly considers, excepting it from his answer, in the Folio, instead of including it in his denial, as in the Quarto.

Had any lingering doubt, therefore, been possible as to the Shakespearian authorship of *The Troublesome Raigne*, this fact would have alone sufficed to dispel it. That a dramatist would rewrite his own play from beginning to end, without retaining a single word or figure of speech, is all but inconceivable. With the above trifling exceptions, it will be perceived that our parallelization is necessarily tentative and approximate only, not to say largely conjectural; relying rather upon similar points in the progress of the action, or the narrative, than upon similarities in the texts. . . . (XVIII, viii–x)

The old play is, of course, what was known as a Chronicle History. It must have been written earlier than would be indicated by the reference in the prologue to Part I., 'To the Gentlemen Readers,' to Marlowe's *Tamburlaine*, which was performed in 1590. Indeed, I think that this prologue or preface was only added on publication of the play. I think it highly impossible that the old play, with its emphatic libels upon and bold speeches denunciatory of the Old Faith and of the Catholic Church could have been performed after Elizabeth's proclamations of April 7 and May 16, 1599,[1] in which all plays were forbidden 'wherein matters of religion or of the government of the Commonwealth are handled or treated,' which may account – and, to me, does entirely and satisfactorily account – for the removal of the scurrilous scenes libelling the Roman Church without the load of discussion as to whether Shakespeare was Catholic or Protestant, with which a commentary upon this play is usually burdened.

The removal need not, however, be referred even to this simplest of explanations. For the scandalous matter of the monk and the nun in each other's private apartments occurs in the course of the long details as to Faulconbridge's raid upon the religious houses, which he had been ordered to make to meet the King's expenses. The one hundred and seventeen lines [*TR*, 6.1–121] which dilate upon these details, Shakespeare rejected, covering the entire episode with just three lines: – [Quotes 3.4.171–3] and then with two more, being a speech of Faulconbridge's announcing the success of his rapine: – [Quotes 4.2.141–2].

With the charge that the monks of Swinstead poisoned the King when he was in their power, Shakespeare, as the charge was never either proven or disproven, deals perhaps more gingerly, but he even more ruthlessly abridges the allotment to them of the old play. Here the one hundred and fifteen Quarto lines [15.1–148] which show us the King at the Abbey, his reception there, the banquet in the garden, the cup of drink concocted from the entrails of a toad, the death of the monk who officiated as the King's taster, the death of the King himself, and the stabbing of the Abbot by Faulconbridge in revenge, are entirely discarded and their place in the action supplied by the single line spoken by Hubert to the Bastard, – 'The King I feare is poyson'd by a Monke' [5.6.23].

In short, whatever reason may be assigned for the excision of all the reflections upon the Roman Catholic Church – or however the excision may afford opportunity for argument as to Shakespeare's personal religious preferences – the Play, as Shakespeare left it, is patriotic, not polemical, in spirit. The protest is against the Pope as a foreign power, and so as a temporal, not as a spiritual usurper in England. So far as one may judge of Shakespeare from his dramatic works, he was a man who kept his religious opinions – if he had any – strictly to himself!

This old play Shakespeare now took for his own stage and proceeded, as we have said, to rewrite it from beginning to end. The old play opens with some fifty or sixty lines of rambling dialogue, from which the reader may draw that the King of France desires some sort of conference or 'dicker' with King John, relative to the old claims of France to the English crown, and of England to the French crown (which were continually being bandied about, back and forth, in the old Plantagenet days, and concerning which the Historical plays have always so much to say). Shakespeare drew his pen through all this dialogue and opened the play with the single sentence, – 'Now say, Chatillion, what would France with us?' [1.1.1] – a splendid and imperious utterance, which at once states the situation, and tells us at once that France desires an interview not only, but that England does not, and is disposed not only to refuse it, but, if reluctantly granted, to maintain a stern opposition to whatever France may intend to offer or to urge. All this is fairly implied and conveyed to the audience in eight short words of that dramatic diction which the consummate artist playwright uses to at once carry his action along, and to state his situation and infer to the spectator the motive which he finds adverse to him and proposes to thwart, as well as his own probable course, whether straightforward or adroit, in thwarting it. Here (and I, for my part, cannot imagine a more capital specimen) is an exemplification of the Art Dramatic: the art of telling a story to ear, eye, and intelligence at once, an art which, the more I study

Shakespeare, seems to me to have been created by him, independently of its evolution from classic or anterior models.

But something else is wanting, besides narrative and action, to a perfect drama. There must be a central character for hero: that is to say, a strong individuality to which the sympathy of the audience may cling – one whose fortunes each individual of the audience will follow, and in whose success, moral or material, each spectator is himself to feel rewarded. There was no such personage in *The Troublesome Raigne*. There was, however, a character, Faulconbridge, who, after a rambling sort of fashion, met and surmounted obstacles, and this personage Shakespeare immediately seized upon, and around him he grouped the entire action of his play, making the success of his motive – this character's personal success, and the triumph of the purpose of the play – his personal triumph: which for stage availability must always be the successful end and aim of every true dramatic production. But there is more yet. The perfect piece of dramatic work, written not for the closet, but for the stage and the spectator, must not only avoid obscurity, and allot certain situations to words, certain other to action, and certain other to stage scenery or stage effect, and unite all these upon every movement, but it must so unify all these that no situation shall be introduced except as the result of a preceding, and the exciting cause of a future, situation. No matter how pathetic, comic, or eloquent a scene, if it do not belong in the dramatic progress, it will weary the spectator and kill the piece. Now, *The Troublesome Raigne* gives several scenes in which Prince Arthur – not a frail child to work upon our sympathies, as Shakespeare saw the opportunity of making him, but a rather colorless young man, with very little to say for himself – figures. In one of them Hubert is sent to put out his eyes in prison. In the old play Arthur objects upon what we would say were rather intellectual grounds for a young man about to be tortured.[2] Upon being apprised of his errand he says to Hubert: –

	Advise thee, Hubert, for the case is hard –
	To lose salvation for a king's reward.
Hubert.	My lord, a subject dwelling in the land
	Is tied to execute the king's command.
Arthur.	Yet God commands, whose power reacheth further,
	That no command should stand in force to murther.
Hubert.	But that same Essence hath ordained a law,
	A death for guilt, to keep the world in awe. (7.77–84).

This may be exemplary, but it is not dramatic. We all know what Shakespeare made of it: a piteous pleading and a relenting, which nowhere in literature or poetry can be touched for pathos. And I may add that Hubert himself, from a mere figure in the old play, is rewritten into a human being; and into a rugged, honest, and rather praiseworthy person.

Again, in the old play Queen Constance holds a sort of short didactic dialogue with herself as to whether, upon classical precedent, she would be justified in shedding a few tears for the loss of her child! [Quotes 5.24–30]. Those seven stilted and impossible lines Shakespeare rewrote into that expression of poignant grief whose eloquence has no match in literature, and which has made Constance's grief for her child a synonym for the acme of maternal bereavement, and will always keep it so! And, in closing the parallelization, what shall we say of the genius, not only for stage art, but for that summit of the sublime which could mould over such commonplaces as [Quotes 16.45–6; 53–4; from the Bastard's closing speech in *The Troublesome Raigne*] into the glorious [Quotes 5.7.112–14; 116–8: from the Bastard's closing speech in *King John*].

In the rewriting, Shakespeare makes the ten acts of the old play over into five – the regulation number in which all his other plays are given. But, although curtailing and cutting very liberally, it is curious to see that Shakespeare is perfectly willing to take the sequence of the play as cut. He only really adds on his own account one new scene: that between Faulconbridge and Hubert to wit: [5.6].

Among the minor points where Shakespeare next saw room for improvement: he forced a tedious old prophet in the earlier play – Peter of Pomfret, who makes, in all, three long speeches – to content himself with just one line before he takes himself and his five moons off the stage forever: cut away the long *aside* soliloquies of Faulconbridge as against all stage form – and there is no canon so inexorable to-day in stage art as that soliloquy is to be admitted very charily. One more example of this prophetic knowledge, as we might call it: a case where Shakespeare does exactly what a stagewright or stage manager of to-day would do, were that old play brought to him for mounting. Turn to the scene where there is a confusion and a hand-to-hand struggle on the battlefield, Queen Elinor is captured by a party of the enemy – then Faulconbridge [i.e., John] recaptures her [3.158–90]. The point, all that is necessary to the course of the story, is that Elinor has been captured and recaptured. This being all that Shakespeare wants, he simply brings in a person [the Bastard] who makes that statement [3.2.7]. Thus a long episode of purposeless action, which would only delay, is cut out quite as peremptorily as Mr. Puff cut out pages of dialogue with his striking clock.[3]

Nor did Shakespeare's refining hand omit to remedy the smaller points, where taste and delicacy might be appealed to. In the old play, for example, there is a scene where two brothers dispute, in their mother's presence, concerning their own legitimacy, one of them going so far as to threaten her with death if she do not reveal the truth to him. Such a scene as this, so repulsive to the least filial or manly instinct, we may be sure went by the board when the great Dramatist, great in every item and phase and department of his Art, adapted and made *The Troublesome Raigne* over into his sombre and splendid KING JOHN. (XVII, xiv–xx)

52 Louis Lewes, on Constance, Elinor, and Blanch

1894

From *The Women of Shakespeare. By Louis Lewes, Ph.D. Translated from the German by Helen Zimmern* (London, 1894).

Louis Lewes (1834–94), noted German critic, published two influential books on women in literature within a year of each other, *Shakespeares Frauengestalten* (Stuttgart, 1893) and *Goethes Frauengestalten* (Stuttgart, 1894). Some measure of the former's perceived importance may be gleaned from its translation by Helen Zimmern into English only a year after its first German appearance. Lewes also published a short biographical sketch of Byron (Hamburg, 1897).

[From 'The Women in *King John*']

Independent, each complete in itself, [*King John* and *Henry VIII*] stand beside the mighty series of eight royal dramas which portray the course of English history from the accession of the House of Lancaster, through the terrible wars of the White and Red Roses, to the accession of the Tudor, Henry VIII., a couple of dramas that bring before our eyes two important movements in the history and development of England. *King John* shows how the realm, which had gained almost infinite power through a line of wise, prudent, and powerful monarchs, had fallen under a weak sovereign, from this majestic height. They tell how this once proud England submitted herself to papal authority; how the politicians of Rome, with that diplomatic skill which distinguished them in all ages, cleverly manipulated the difficulties of the king and the internal confusion of England, to reduce the monarch to submission. On the other hand, the great barons of the realm exacted from this same king, in Magna Charta, the unalterable foundations of a monarchy constitutionally controlled by Parliament. *Henry VIII.* brings before us a powerful, energetic monarch, who, to gratify his passions, is made the unwilling instrument through which is accomplished one of the greatest and most important movements for the future of England, the Reformation, and the loosening of the land from the rule of the Papal See. *King John* has a purely political action, hence the women here are somewhat in the background. In *Henry VIII.* the monarch's passion for Anne Bullen is the leading motive. Consequently the ambition of Anne Bullen, who cleverly exploits Henry's love, and the touching patience and noble dignity with which Queen Catherine meets her fate, play a prominent part. Still the women in *King John* have also an importance that enables us to admire the art of character-painting, and the power with which the exceedingly scant historical materials have been used. When we examine the most prominent female character in *King John*, Constance, the mother of Prince Arthur, whose place has been usurped by his uncle, the king, we are struck with her resemblance to Volumnia, the mother of Coriolanus.[1] In both a powerful pride, a destructive ambition, a glowing maternal love, an unbending strength of will, are distinguishing characteristics. But the great difference between these two characters lies in the circumstance, that while Volumnia, who, with her great and hard characteristics, exhibits only a part of the qualities of her people, and that its patrician portion, has grown by natural development, Constance is a more self-contained being, for she draws her strong passions, her peculiarities as well as her weaknesses, from her personal fate. This history Shakespeare has set forth with all its attendant circumstances in a true and lively manner, in accordance with the materials at his command. These materials, certainly, gave him only scattered and somewhat vague hints and indications, but he manipulated them so skilfully in the portrayal of her personality and character, that there is no doubt the picture given agrees fully with the historic background from which it arises, and also comes very near historic truth when compared with the results of later researches into the history and character of Constance. Shakespeare shows us Constance in a few scenes only, but these suffice to impress us with the conviction that we have here before us the result of a life singularly diversified and full of meaning – an uncontrollable will, a wild passionate temper, that fights unweariedly, undeterred by defeat, against inimical and victorious forces. . . .

[A long digression follows in which Lewes traces in detail the life and times of the historical Constance, ending at the point where the play begins.]

. . . Before we examine Constance, as Shakespeare has shown her to us, let us consider the historical personality here set before us as accurately as is possible with the materials to hand. We find, first of all, that she can never be accused of wilful or unjust conduct, of vice or crime, but rather that during the short time she was permitted to rule her country independently, and in her own way, she proved herself a wise and benevolent princess, who restored prosperity to her dominions, as far as this was possible, in so brief a period, and was, on this account, rewarded by the love and confidence of all her subjects, high and low. The light conduct of which so many of her female ancestors were guilty, did not descend to her; we hear nothing of a stain upon her reputation or her conjugal honour. Nevertheless, her character has shadows as well as lights. She was wanting in self-control, that virtue without which all others, especially in woman, lose much worth. Her speech was often unmeasured and rough to an unfeminine degree; her impulses were thoughtless and precipitate. In spite of her strength of will, she thus became, unconsciously, the tool of her enemies, whose superior cunning she could not cope with, owing to this very want of self-control. We shall see how Shakespeare has used the materials left him by history in drawing the character of Constance. The principal personages in *King John* are the king himself, the bastard son of Richard the Lion-hearted, Faulconbridge, a character evidently a favourite with the poet, and Constance herself. The latter, who appears in history only in faint, vague, hardly recognisable outlines, stands out in Shakespeare's lively portrayal with sharply-defined distinctness, and appeals to us like a being of flesh and blood. But all the sympathy that Constance wins is founded on one single point, her devotion to her son. As in some other of Shakespeare's female characters whose supreme object in life is passionate love for some man, so in Constance this maternal love is the only reason for her life. Nay, it is to her life itself. All that occurs around her has a meaning for her only in so far as it exerts a favourable or unfavourable influence upon her son's fortunes. All the people she meets play a part for her only in so far as they have power and intention to aid her son in obtaining his rights to the crown of England. In her passionate conviction of her boy's undoubted claim, she holds it a sacred duty for all who have the power to fight for this, utterly regardless whether it be to their own advantage or the reverse. Every one, according to her, is pledged to sacrifice all for the sake of the cruel violence of which her amiable boy is a victim.

In all the scenes in which she appears, we hear her speak of nothing but her son's rights; she fears nothing, trembles for nothing but her son's life.

But, in spite of the overpowering, or rather entire prominence of maternal love which shows itself in Constance's demeanour and words, it reveals itself in a fashion through which we recognise clearly the other features of her character. One quality is reflected plainly in all her expressions, and that is an energy transcending that common to her sex. But this energy is unequally developed; it manifests itself in an inordinate imagination, in fixity of will, in an untameable glow of passion. She is lacking in the moral power which leads to self-control. Feeling and imagination are so highly developed in this woman, that her other qualities fall into the background. She is conscious of womanly weakness, and this consciousness is the source of the distrust to which she often yields; of the despair which often consumes her. In all her outbreaks of passion, in all the rages into which she falls, she always remains within the bounds of feminine nature. In her exclusive maternal love, she deems it self-evident that others should be sacrificed to her son. Hence she loses her intellectual impartiality, whenever she meets any obstacle or delay. She has neither patience to await the development of affairs, which do not, as she imagines, revolve exclusively around the fortunes of her son as their natural centre, nor steadfastness enough to endure an unfavourable turn of events. Hence arise the many apparent contradictions in her expressions. She beholds everything solely from the point of view of her son's interest. At one moment she counsels, with great decision, measures which the next moment she as decidedly advises against. For instance, she urges the King of France to keep the peace and await the answer to Chatillion's embassy, for she expects a favourable reply; later on, when she conceives herself to have suffered injustice, and all her passions have been heated to the highest pitch, she calls out in ungovernable rage, 'War! war! no peace; peace is to me a war' [3.1.113]. Some have maintained that Constance is ambitious, not only for her son, but also for herself, that she desires dominion for its own sake; but this view seems to me unjust. She proclaims with the energy of a loving mother and a proud woman the rights of her son, but when she has lost him, her pain at his loss is her sole thought, beside which no other finds place, not even desire of vengeance. Madness, too, which involuntarily brings the innermost thoughts of men to their lips, forces only lamentations from her. She says to the Cardinal: [Quotes 3.4.76–89: 'Father Cardinal, I have heard you say. . . .'].

The unbounded liveliness of her imagination turns her grief to madness, and yet she is not mad. She says: [Quotes 3.4.44–60: 'I am not mad: this hair I tear is mine. . . .'].

Her eloquence rises to the highest flights of metaphor. Listen, for example, to these passages: [Quotes 3.1.68–74: 'I will instruct my sorrows to be proud. . . .' and 3.4.38–42: 'O that my tongue were in the thunder's mouth. . . .'].

Death will be welcome, but she paints him in hideous colours: [Quotes 3.4.25–36: 'Death, death: O amiable lovely death. . . .'].

Resuming this whole description, we find that pride and maternal love are the foundations of Constance's personality, but owing to her unusual intellectual capacity, the strength of her passions, and the powerful flights of her imagination, these qualities, which she has in common with others, are carried to a high, nay, a terrible pitch.

The other female characters of this play, old Queen Elinor and the young Princess Blanch of Castile, are traced only in outline, but they are historically faithful. Elinor is seventy; her passionate character, which led her in youth into many imprudences, is but slightly chastened by age. She has a strong understanding, but little education, and an uncontrolled appetite for power. The old chronicles say that she had a personal hatred for Constance, and that she transmitted this hatred to Arthur. Shakespeare has preserved these characteristics and portrayed them in masterly mode. Blanch of Castile was the daughter of King Alphonse of Castile and Elinor's grandchild. Her marriage with the Dauphin Louis, afterwards Louis VIII., took place as suddenly as described in the play. She was marvellously beautiful; her reputation was unstained. She was proud of her lineage and rank, deeply religious, and filled with boundless desire to rule. Later on she played a great part in European history as Regent of France, and is one of the most celebrated women of her own or of any time. (210–22)

53 Beverley Ellison Warner, historical character and dramatic character

1894

From *English History in Shakespeare's Plays* (New York, 1894).

Beverley Ellison Warner (1855–1910) was ordained a priest in the Episcopal Church in 1880, serving as rector in various parishes in Connecticut before moving to Trinity Church in New Orleans in 1893 where he remained until his death. Throughout his career as a clergyman Warner maintained an active literary life, publishing a novel, *Troubled Waters* (Philadelphia, 1885), as well as *The Young Man in Modern Life* (New York, 1902) and *The Young Woman in Modern Life* (New York, 1903). In addition to his frequent papers and public lectures on Shakespeare he also published on such diverse matters as industrial experiments, religious rationalism, and practical pessimism. *English History in Shakespeare's Plays*, however, was unquestionably Warner's most successful book, going through several reissues up to 1909.

[From Chapter II, '*King John* – The Transition Period']

[Warner's approach to Shakespeare's histories and to *King John* in particular is similar to Courtenay's (No. 17 above). He is concerned to illustrate Shakespeare's departures from actual history in order to provide 'a proper appreciation' of the 'historical accuracy' of *King John* (19). In so doing he spends a great deal of time on the historical background of the play as well as on its relationship to *The Troublesome Raigne*. Warner sees *King John* as dramatizing 'the great turning point of English historical development' (18), that is, the period after the integration of Saxon and Norman into a distinctly 'English' nation, but preceding the dissociation of the English crown from Normandy, an occurrence which finally invested the nation with 'a greater identity of aim' (22). Much of Warner's essay is highly derivative, particularly his treatment of *The Troublesome Raigne*; but despite the unoriginality of many of his remarks, they can at times shed a thin ray of critical light. This is particularly so when he warms to one of his guiding ideas: that Shakespeare, while grossly violating historical facts in many individual instances, somehow captures the 'essential spirit' and 'broad movements of English life' (29–30) in the play as a whole.]

. . . Shakespeare keeps Arthur alive, after the fashion of the old play, for some years after the real date of his death, and uses him as a dramatic puppet in events which had no relation whatever with him or his claims upon the English throne. Indeed this use of Arthur Plantagenet is the great puzzle in any effort to discriminate between what is historical in the play and what is purely dramatic license. The reader of the play must infer that this twelve-year old boy was the central figure of human and political interest in the England of that day. He was nothing of the kind. He was of very small importance in the actual shuffling of the cards. But he offered dramatic material of considerable value, and Shakespeare used him, as the older dramatist did, without reference to the chronicles and with no attempt at preserving the real perspective of history.

Thus the assumed position of Arthur, as an abused and oppressed rightful claimant to the throne, is connected, on no legitimate grounds whatever, with the quarrel between the Pope and King John; and also with the revolts of the Barons. All the critics note the importance attributed by the play to Arthur's movements, but not all of them point out the gross anachronism thus involved.

To illustrate the tortuous politics of those times – which, with many a misdate, overdate, and prolepsis, Shakespeare still preserves in their essential spirit, presenting withal a tolerable estimate of how life in camps and courts was carried on – the speech of Faulconbridge at the end of the second act may be quoted. It is a summing up of what had been accomplished as well as attempted in the royal quarrels over Arthur, and a most just estimate of the reliance to be placed upon the sworn faith of king and noble in the twelfth and thirteenth centuries. [Quotes 2.1.561–98: the speech on Commodity]. In such a passage as this we are able to weigh and estimate the value of Shakespeare's contribution to the philosophy of history. We are often bewildered in his pages by a confusion of dates and events, but history rightly studied is something more than mere annals or chronicles. These are the raw materials which the historian must explain and interpret or he be no true historian. . . . (30–2)

The character of Philip Faulconbridge, the natural son of Richard the Lion Heart, is looked upon as an ideal of the poet's brain, with no other foundation than the fact of the existence of such a person who was not at all conspicuous in history. But Faulconbridge seems to have been more than an ideal. He did really exist, not as a faithful servant of King John, as in the play, but in hundreds and thousands of loyal steadfast men, citizens of England. Not nobles, nor barons, nor degraded serfs, but men. The forgotten men of most historic records. The men who are ploughing and sowing; buying and selling; marrying and bringing up sons and daughters like themselves; paying the taxes of despotism and suffering the inconveniences of oppression, while doing their duty in that state of life to which it had pleased God to call them. Men who faced the daily problems of life, and as God gave them strength sought to deal with them, not complaining over much. Even giving their bodies to be set up as targets at the king's will, because he was the king, and they were loyal to him as sons of the soil.

Philip Faulconbridge is an interesting study. It would appear that Shakespeare intended to have him represent the sturdy heart of English manhood, which, while often misused, humiliated, and beaten back, finally conquered and rose to its proper place in the making of later and nobler England, as the commons; not the legislature of that name narrowly, but the makers of legislatures. So while Philip Faulconbridge was an imaginary character he was not an imaginary force.

Another set of characters in this play are of more than passing interest, the women. Of Blanch we have already spoken; how her youth and innocence were played with as common pawns to advance the interests of worldly-wise bishops and designing kings. But of Constance, the mother of Arthur, and Elinor, the mother of John, and hence grandmother of Arthur, something remains to be said. In the actual history of the times they did not play so important a part as is attributed to them by the dramatist. But that they exerted some influence upon the politics of their day cannot be doubted. Women have, noticeably, always managed to influence for good or evil the affairs of kingdoms and the actions of kings.

The picture Shakespeare draws of Constance is touching in the extreme. Her grief over the death of Arthur is one of the finest outbursts of the poet's genius. But we must read it apart from the other scenes in which the fair lady appears, or our sympathies will receive a shock. There are passages-at-arms between Constance and Elinor which exceed, in not always refined Billingsgate, the choicest scoldings of literature. . . .

Throughout the plays we see, however, that the women were not without influence in the adjustment or maladjustment of the affairs of state. A fact which is true to history then as now, and another evidence that Shakespeare paid more attention to the underlying philosophy than the outward accuracy of his chronicle plays.

The moral of the play, if we may so regard it, is the exaltation of England's place among the nations of the world and the inspiring of England's sons to attain this bright ideal. To illustrate this, and as one more comparison of the paraphrasing of the words of others to his own use − paraphrasing which under his genius became original − compare the last lines of *The Troublesome Raigne* and the parallel passage from Shakespeare's play. [Quotes *The Troublesome Raigne*, 16.43−54 and *King John*, 5.7.112−18]. (50−53)

54 Barrett Wendell, the oddities of *King John*

1894

From *William Shakespeare. A Study in Elizabethan Literature* (New York, 1894).

Barrett Wendell (1855–1921), professor of English at Harvard, was a respected teacher and scholar renowned for his humanity, eclecticism, and sense of innovation. His most important contributions to literary study, in addition to his book on Shakespeare, include the revisionist *Cotton Mather, the Puritan Priest* (New York, 1891), *A Literary History of America* (New York, 1900), which derived from his ground-breaking course on American literature at Harvard, and *The Temper of the Seventeenth Century in English Literature* (London, 1904), consisting of the Clark Lectures he gave at Trinity College, Cambridge, in 1902–3. Other important studies – on education, politics, and society, as well as on literature – followed, none more noteworthy than *The Traditions of European Literature from Homer to Dante* (New York, 1920), the capstone to Wendell's scholarly career.

[From Chapter VII; Part VI: '*King John*']

Less careful, less constantly sustained than *Richard II.*, *King John* often impresses one as queerer, more archaic, more puzzling than any other of Shakespeare's chronicle-histories. This impression, of course, may be chiefly due to the accident that in most editions of the series it is printed first, and so that one is apt to read it with no preparation for its conventions. As we shall see, however, there are reasons enough in the play as it stands to make it seem at first sight more strange than what we have already considered, and yet, on inspection, to prove it a distinct step forward in the development of chronicle-history.

One cause for its oddity of effect lies in its origin. Instead of translating directly from the chronicles, Shakespeare clearly did not trouble himself about them at all; but only adapted a clumsy old play to the improving conditions of the stage. At the time, the subject of this play was accidentally popular. Though tradition generally confirms history in declaring John to have been the worst king England ever had, tradition and history equally agree in preserving a suspicion that he came to his end by poison, administered by an ecclesiastic who had been enraged beyond measure by John's attacks on the vested property of the Church. When England broke away from the Church of Rome, then, John, by an obvious distortion of tradition, became something like a Protestant hero. In the early editions of Foxe's *Book of Martyrs* there is a full page of illustrations, showing how the wicked monk, duly absolved to begin with, took the poison from a toad, put it in the king's wine-cup, tasted the liquor to disarm suspicion, died at the same time with the king, and had masses regularly said for his traitorous, murderous soul. This view of things was presented, among others, in the *Troublesome Raigne*.

The old play, thus for the moment popular, was in two parts. In adapting it, Shakespeare reduced it to the limits of a single performance. However he may have improved it in many ways, he managed in one way to make it decidedly less intelligible than before. In the *Troublesome Raigne* there are a number of ribald scenes where the Bastard sacks religious houses, and incidentally discovers there a state of morals agreeable at once to the principles of Elizabethan Protestants and to the taste of Elizabethan audiences. This proceeding so excites the clergy that they compass the king's death. In Shakespeare's play, this whole matter is compressed into two short passages: – [Quotes 3.3.6–13 and 4.2.141–2]. The poisoning of the king, then, comes without very obvious cause. In this respect the old play is the better.

Nor is this the only instance in which Shakespeare did not improve things. Shakespeare's Constance, in general, however her rhetoric may be admired, certainly rants; like so many passages in the earlier chronicle-histories, her long speeches belong rather to grand opera than to tragedy proper. The Constance of the *Troublesome Raigne*, on the other hand, though less eloquent, is more human. Compare, for example, the last appearance of Constance in the two plays: it is when her heart has been broken by the capture of Arthur. Here is her last speech in the *Troublesome Raigne*: –

> Lewes. Have patience, Madame, this is chaunce of warre:
> He may be ransomde, we revenge his wrong.
> Constance. Be it ner so soone, I shall not live so long. [5.31ff.]

In *King John* this pathetic utterance is expanded into five speeches, which comprise above fifty lines of tremendous declamation, beginning: – [Quotes 3.4.37–41]. Whatever Shakespeare's Constance may be at heart, she is not always so human in expression as the Constance of the *Troublesome Raigne*.

In general, however, Shakespeare's play is by far the better. To find such instances as we have just glanced at, one must seek. Taking the two plays as a spectator or a hasty reader would take them, they differ in effect much as *Romeo and Juliet* differs from *Titus Andronicus*. The old play has so little vitality of imagination that it is hardly ever plausible; *King John*, on the other hand, is full of touches which, when we once accept the old conventions, waken characters and scenes alike into something far nearer real life than we have yet found in chronicle-history. Character after character emerges into consistent individuality. Best of all, of course, is the Bastard, who from a rather lifeless comic personage becomes one of Shakespeare's own living men. Arthur, whose situation and fate recall those of the young princes in *Richard III.*, is at once so human and so pathetic that many modern critics are set to wondering whether the tender sense of boyish charm and parental bereavement hereby revealed may not have been awakened by the illness and death in 1596 of Shakespeare's only son. Elinor is thoroughly alive too;[1] so is the intriguing Cardinal Pandulph;[2] so is

Hubert, whose scenes with the King and with Arthur remain dramatically effective;[3] so is King John himself; and so often, in spite of her rant, is Constance. In no earlier chronicle-history, for example, is there anything like so human a touch as in the scene where Elinor tries to entice Arthur from Constance: – [Quotes 2.1.159–63]. In the *Troublesome Raigne* there is no hint of these speeches. They are all Shakespeare's.

As concrete an example as any of what Shakespeare has done in *King John* may be found in the very opening line. The *Troublesome Raigne* opens with a formal speech by Elinor: – [Quotes 1.1–3: 'Barons of England, and my noble Lords. . . .']. In general manner, this is very much like the opening of *Richard II.*: – 'Old John of Gaunt, time-honour'd Lancaster' [1.1.1], etc. Shakespeare's *King John*, on the other hand, opens with an improved version of the forty-first line of the *Troublesome Raigne*, the line with which the action begins: – 'Now say, Chatillion, what would France with us?' [1.1.1]. By the eighth line, the passionate temperaments of John and Elinor have been revealed by two characteristic outbursts [1.1.5, 6] for which the *Troublesome Raigne* affords no suggestion. The example is sufficient: what has happened in *King John* is what happened in *Romeo and Juliet*. Creative imagination, to all appearances spontaneous, has made real, living people out of what had previously been stage types.

In this very fact lies the reason why *King John* generally impresses one as more archaic, or at least as more queer, than *Richard II*. Such a phrase as Richard's 'Old John of Gaunt, time-honour'd Lancaster,' could never have been uttered by any real man; such a phrase as John's 'Now say, Chatillion, what would France with us?' might be uttered by anybody still. In *Richard II.*, then, the consistent conventionality of everything makes us accept the whole play if we accept any part of it. In *King John* the continual confusion of real, human vitality with the old quasi-operatic conventions combines with the general carelessness of construction to make each kind of thing seem more out of place than it would seem by itself. Like any other transitional incongruity, *King John* is often harder to accept than the consistent conventions from which it departs. Its very excellences emphasize its faults and its oddities.

In *King John*, then, we find Shakespeare's creative energy awake, much as we found it in *Romeo and Juliet*; and somewhat as we found it in the *Midsummer Night's Dream*, in *Richard III.*, and in *Richard II*. From the fact that *King John*, while in some respects as vital as any of these, is less careful, we may infer that this creative energy was growing more spontaneously strong. Clearly, though, it has not here produced a work which for ripeness of development can compare with the comedy or the tragedy already before us. To understand this slowness in the development of chronicle-history, we may conveniently turn to the next play in our study. If our chronology be right, *King John* belongs to the same period as the *Merchant of Venice*. (137–43)

55 Frederick Samuel Boas, on the principal characters

1896

From *Shakespeare and His Predecessors* (London, 1896).

Frederick Samuel Boas (1862–1957) was born in Belfast, Ireland, and taught History and English Literature at Queen's College, Belfast (1901–5), before serving as inspector for the London County Council Education Department (1905–27). A prominent and active man of letters, Boas edited *The Year's Work in English Studies* for thirty-three years (1922–55), during which time he also produced some of his most important book-length 'Introductions' to literary figures and periods, as well as many other respected studies of an historical, biographical, or editorial nature. *Shakespeare and His Predecessors*, was one of Boas's most popular and influential books, enjoying frequent reprintings well into the twentieth century.

[From Chapter XI: 'The Chief Group of Chronicle-History Plays']

. . . In its main subject [*King John*] recalls *Richard III*, while the character of Constance anticipates that of Richard II. It resembles *Richard III* also in the prominence given to rivalries of women, but the grouping is less studiously monumental, and the curious strophic balance of lamentation has disappeared. The blank verse is still overloaded with rhetoric, which has however lost the peculiar lurid tinge of the earlier play. Rhyme is almost entirely confined to the pithy rejoinders and epigrams of the Bastard, in whose person the element of popular humour enters for the first time an entirely Shakespearian historical play. There is as yet, however, no hint of the use of prose as the fittest vehicle for this humour. Thus the internal evidence stamps *King John* as a link between the earlier and later Histories, and it may be assigned to about the year 1595. . . .

[Boas briefly treats Shakespeare's adaptation of *The Troublesome Raigne*, then turns to the dramatist's conception of John, which unlike that of Richard III, 'is designed on no similar scale of lonely grandeur in crime' (239).]

For a time, indeed, John plays the part of a vigorous and able soldier. He crosses to France with a speed that disconcerts his enemies, and the fact that he is followed by a brave 'choice of dauntless spirits' [2.1.72] shows that he can attract supporters to his cause. Shakespeare himself, fully alive to the national dangers involved in the succession of a minor, is inclined to weigh in equal balance the claims of uncle and nephew. If John has an evil angel in his mother, so has Arthur, for the hysterical passion of Constance is as dangerous as Elinor's unscrupulous ambition, and her appeal to foreign aid in support of her son's rights estranges from her all national sympathies. . . .

. . . But the portraiture of John in the earlier scenes of the play, where in spite of duplicity and self-seeking he shows a certain soldierly dignity, scarcely prepares us for the revelation of craven cruelty in his dealings with his captive nephew. This partial inconsistency, however, overlooked, John's attitude in his interview with Hubert is portrayed with wonderful subtlety. In a similar situation Richard III had blurted out his purposes to Tyrrel with almost cheery frankness. John stealthily approaches the theme of Arthur's murder by torturous paths, advancing and retreating by turns; he pauses just long enough at his goal to drop monosyllabic hints of 'death' and 'a grave' [3.3.65–6], and then, as if terrified at the sound of his own voice, slinks hurriedly away. Thus, when the report of Arthur's death by violence is noised abroad, alienating the nobles and stirring the populace to disaffection; when the conscience-stricken king realizes that 'there is no sure foundation set on blood' [4.2.104], he can turn upon his agent with base reproaches for having translated a momentary hint into a fixed warrant for the fatal deed. The discovery that the child's life has been spared lights up his terrified soul with a ray of hope, but the disastrous consequences of his purpose are beyond recall. . . .

But it has attracted universal notice that Shakespeare passes very lightly over those misdeeds of the king which have given him so sinister a prominence in history. His extortions from clergy and laity are merely touched upon incidentally, and not the faintest allusion is made to the constitutional struggle which ended in the grant of the Great Charter. Startling as it sounds to modern ears, it is almost certain that Shakespeare had small knowledge of that document, and a very inadequate sense of its importance. A strong monarchical rule was the ideal of the Tudor period, and the power of the Crown was limited not by strictly defined clauses, but by hearty popular sympathies in the sovereign. It was only under the Stuarts, when this communion of feeling between ruler and ruled ceased to exist, that the champions of national liberty were forced to entrench themselves behind their traditional rights, and drag again into prominence the parchment-scrolls wherein these were embodied. Thus the significance of John's reign for Shakespeare lay far less in constitutional struggles than in foreign relations, and its supreme event was not the signing of the Charter, but the surrender of the English crown, when the recreant king, eating all his brave words of an earlier date, resigned the symbol of royalty into the hands of Pandulph, to receive it back again as a vassal of the Pope. . . .

[After a short passage of plot summary, Boas turns to the death of John.]

. . . Poisoned by a monk, he dies at Swinstead Abbey, in torturing pain which wrings from him agonized cries unworthy of a soldier and a king. But the scene would make a deeper impression were it in more organic connexion with what has gone before. In the old play, where so much prominence had been given to the attack upon the religious houses, the death of John at the hands of a monk was a dramatically fitting Nemesis. But one of the very few mistakes made by Shakespeare in working up older materials was that he here retained the original version of John's murder, while omitting all that had led up to it. We feel that the king's ignoble end should have had more intimate relation to his design upon Arthur, or some other misdeed, emphasized in the play.

Thus the intermixture of historical and political considerations with those of a purely dramatic kind makes Shakespeare's picture of John the least consistent in his gallery of English kings. He was more unfettered in his treatment of lesser personages, at whose head stands Constance, mother of the rival claimant to the throne. Constance is drawn with far more delicate insight than any of the women in *Richard III*, and is the most highly elaborated female figure in the historical plays. She is another of that numerous company in Shakespeare's earlier dramas whose sensibilities are developed to an extravagant degree. Her instinct of maternal affection is not chastened by reason into a moral principle, but is inflamed by an imagination of hectic brilliance into an abnormal passion that swallows up every thought and energy. It is this exaggerated imagination, as Mrs. Jameson has rightly insisted [No. 14 above], that is the controlling force in the nature of Constance. The impetuous ardour of her fancy gives a special quality to her maternal love. The very attribute that is wont to be the source of all that is tenderest in womanhood breeds in her ambition, scorn, and hysterical passion, till at last it consumes her in its fires.

But her imaginative sensibility, though the deepest element in her nature, is not made prominent at first. In the quarrel scene between her and Elinor she figures as a genuine vixen, whose bitter rush of invective amply earns the abusive epithets of her foes, and even irritates her friends. Her imperious temper on this occasion augurs ill for her future bearing in the event of fortune favouring her cause, but the disappointment of her hopes turns her emotion into a more seductive, though no less vehement course. When she hears from Salisbury that Philip has been false to his oath, there sweeps over her the overwhelming sense of her powerlessness, shaking her as a reed before the wind: [Quotes 3.1.12–4: 'For I am sick. . . .']. Yet out of this weakness is born a strange grandeur. The imagination of Constance playing upon her misery wraps her, as it were, in a haze whence she looms large upon our view. The 'unadvised scold' [2.1.191] of the earlier scene rises to wellnigh tragic stature as she flings herself on the ground and cries aloud: [Quotes 3.1.70–4: 'To me, and to the state of my great grief. . . .']. In a similar vein, half-tragic, half-grandiose, is her appeal to the heavens to be the widow's husband, and to arm against the perjured kings. And when the heavens are deaf to her cries, with still more daring luxuriance of imagery she invokes 'amiable lovely Death' to be her mate; whom she may 'buss' as wife [3.4.25, 35].

It is remarkable throughout these speeches how seldom the thoughts of Constance are turned directly towards Arthur; it is her own widowed lot which forms the centre of her exuberant riot of fancy. This is in itself proof that her maternal impulse does not well up, pure and strong, from unfathomable depths in her being. How largely it is fed from merely æsthetic sources is shown by her own declaration that had Arthur been ugly, 'slanderous' to her womb [3.1.44], she would not have loved him, or deemed him worthy of a crown. And when the fortune of war tears him from her arms, her grief at his loss is strangely mingled with the fantastic thought that sorrow will so despoil him of his beauty that she will not know him when they meet in heaven. King Philip's rebuke, 'You are as fond of grief as of your child' [3.4.92], is well deserved, but Constance catches in self-defence at the implicit personification of sorrow and expands it, with pathetic rhetoric, into the picture of grief filling up the room of her absent child, and acting his every part. But the vehemence of her passion, powerless against others, reacts with deadly shock upon her frail nature, and the spectral bridegroom whom she has so passionately invoked, claims her as his own.

In the world of intrigues, ambitions, and passions Arthur shines forth as a being from another sphere. In depicting the boy, Shakespeare was met with the difficulty that in the young princes in *Richard III* he had already drawn types of youthful innocence cruelly done to death. But his exquisite tact in the variation of details prevents all monotonous repetition. The nephews of Richard were marked by an ability and spirit beyond their years, and the elder already bore himself with a true touch of regal dignity. Arthur is of an essentially different nature. He is a saintly, gentle child, without a spark of worldly ambition. The passionate altercation between his mother and grandmother draws tears from his eyes, and forces from his lips the plaintive murmur that he is not worth the coil that is made for him. So when Constance is heaping frenzied reproaches upon those who have broken faith with her, Arthur beseeches her to be content, and, when he is taken captive, his one thought is that his mother will die of grief. Prison itself would have no terror for him, were it not for fear of some feller evils lurking in the background, and if he covets freedom, it is only that he may keep sheep. His gentle heart goes out to his gaoler Hubert, and shows its love in numberless tender offices. It is the memory of these that pleads most powerfully on his behalf against the savage warrant for the branding of his eyes. The boy's recital of his past deeds of loving kindness, his terror at the entry of the attendants bearing the instruments of torture, his entreaty not to be bound, his offer to sacrifice his tongue, if so he may keep his eyes, are all touches of the purest, deepest pathos which have lost no jot of their moving power. But less happy in the eyes of an age more realistic than the Elizabethan, are those appeals of Arthur, in which, showing himself a true son of his mother, he speaks in metaphors and figures unsuited to his years or to the fierceness of the crisis. Thus, when Hubert prepares to heat the iron, he declares that the fire is dead with grief, and that to revive its glow will be but to make it blush with shame of these proceedings. The innocence of boyhood does not need to borrow such weapons from the rhetorician's armoury; it has a more potent advocate in its own inherent charm. Arthur escapes the cruel doom of blinding, but we feel instinctively that he is one of the saintly creatures who are not long for this world. Thus Shakespeare showed his usual fine tact in choosing the tradition which represented him as perishing in an attempt to leap from his prison walls. With a last flash of precocious fancy he finds his 'uncle's spirit' [4.3.9] in the stones upon which he sinks in death.

How cheerless a panorama has been unfolded before us! On the one hand a group of highly-placed personages, John, Philip, Pandulph, Constance, swayed by passion or self-interest; on the other an innocent child crushed beneath the iron forces of the world. Is there no middle path in which the man of sturdy morality and truth may walk with safety? The answer is given in the elaborate portrait of the Bastard, Faulconbridge. From the purely dramatic point of view his figure is scarcely necessary, but morally he is the very salt of the play. At first that salt would seem to be of somewhat coarse savour. The scene in which he discusses the question of his legitimacy in the presence of John and the Queen-mother is undeniably pungent, though Shakespeare, with greater delicacy than the elder dramatist, excludes the lady whose honour is at stake. It is characteristic of Faulconbridge that he decides to reject legitimacy and the material advantages that go with it, in order that he may claim descent from the heroic Richard. He disdains a father who can only transmit 'a half-face' like his brother's instead of his own 'large composition,' even though it be derived 'something about, a little from the right' [1.1.92, 88, 170]. Thus throughout he prefers what is substantial and genuine, even if it will not stand the most delicate scrutiny, to all that smacks of conventionality or artifice. His character is in entire accord with the origin to which he lays claim. His royal blood gives him his daring in battle, and his stern fidelity to duty in the crisis of his country's fortunes; while from his mother's side he draws his hearty, practical common-sense, and his thoroughly popular turn of humour. The latter qualities are shown especially in his soliloquies, as when after being dubbed knight he moralizes on his unfitness for this new honour, because he doth not 'smack of observation' [1.1.208] according to the prescribed standard of fashion; or when he rails against the 'mad kings,' John and Philip, with their 'mad composition' [2.1.561] against Arthur's interests. It is here that he unfolds his practical political philosophy, in which he traces all errors in the well-peised world to the 'vile-drawing bias,' the 'daily break-vow,' commodity [2.1.577, 569]. With bluff sincerity he admits that, with similar temptation, he would similarly fall, though we feel that in this he does himself a wrong. He would never compromise his honour, though his morality is far from thin-skinned. He proposes to the kings a combined assault upon Angiers, because its scroyles flout them, and he makes no scruple of carrying out John's behest to shake the bags of hoarding abbots. But that he has at bottom a tender heart is shown in his words to Hubert, as they stand together over Arthur's body: [Quotes 4.3.116–19: 'Knew you of this fair work? . . .'].

This crowning catastrophe, and the revolt of the nobles for which it gives the signal, perplex the honest soldier. This child of nature loses his way amidst the thorns and dangers of the world. He is confronted by intricacies which demand an intellect more subtle than his. He feels darkly that all is not well with John and the English cause, but he has too much patriotism to imitate the nobles and join his country's foes. Rather, the blacker the dangers that threaten, the higher does his spirit mount, till in the end he fills the rôle, vacated by John's poltroonery, of national leader and hero. It is he who seeks to stir the recreant king to be 'great in act,' in face of the invader, and who bids him 'away and glister like the god of war' [5.1.45, 54]. It is he who, giving voice to the popular instinct, pours contempt upon the 'inglorious league' [5.1.65] which John makes with Pandulph, in order to buy off the assault of a beardless boy. And when the Dauphin refuses to be bound by the compact made over his head, it is the Bastard who, clothing the king in attributes borrowed from his own high-souled temper, describes him as an eagle towering o'er his aiery, 'to souse annoyance that comes near his nest' [5.2.150]. The 'pigmy arms' [5.2.135] of the French he ridicules with much of the old saucy insolence, and for the revolted lords he has epithets of burning indignation. How far his sturdy patriotism transcends their disloyalty, springing though it does from a moral motive, is made palpable when on the field of battle the dying Count Melun reveals the treacherous doom with which the Dauphin purposes to reward their treacherous aid. Under such sharp stimulus they rally again to the cause which the Bastard has so gallantly upheld, and, though John pays the last penalty of his misdeeds, the nation renews its youth. The foreigner retreats; unity is re-established, and the accession of the young Prince Henry marks the dawn of a nobler era thrilled by the spirit of the Bastard's closing words, which strike the very keynote of the whole group of historical plays: [Quotes 5.7.112–18: 'This England never did, nor never shall. . . .']. (238–49)

56 Georg Morris Cohen Brandes, Shakespeare's uneven artistry

1898

From *William Shakespeare. A Critical Study* [Translated from the Danish by William Archer, Mary Morrison, and Diana White] (2 vols, New York, 1898).

Georg Morris Cohen Brandes (1842–1927), Danish critic and philosopher, was one of the foremost literary thinkers of his time. He produced several landmark studies on aesthetics and social issues, demonstrating in much of his work the strong influence of Kierkegaard, Taine, and Mill. Brandes was denied the Chair of Aesthetics at the University of Copenhagen in 1872 on unclear grounds; the fact that he was Jewish and suspected of dangerously radical ideas, including atheism, almost certainly worked against him. This incident, however, only succeeded in making Brandes something of a literary celebrity; and his scholarly writings, particularly *Main Currents in Nineteenth-Century Literature* (first English edition; 6 vols, London, 1901–5) began to attract even greater attention. Many important literary and critical studies ensued, among which *William Shakespeare* (first Danish edition; 3 vols, Copenhagen, 1895–6) has always occupied a secure position. The excerpt below is taken from the New York edition published by Macmillan.

[From Volume I, Chapter XIX]

[Brandes begins his discussion of *King John* by arguing that the death of Shakespeare's son Hamnet in 1596 clearly affected his writing of the play. The dramatist's sorrow over the loss of his son may be seen in Arthur's appeals to Hubert and in the lamentations of Constance. Brandes then turns to the influence of *The Troublesome Raigne* on *King John*.]

... The old play was a mere Protestant tendency-drama directed against Catholic aggression, and full of the cruel hatred and coarse ridicule of monks and nuns characteristic of the Reformation period. Shakespeare, with his usual tact, has suppressed the religious element, and retained only the national and political attack upon Roman Catholicism, so that the play had no slight actuality for the Elizabethan public. But he has also displaced the centre of gravity of the old play. Everything in Shakespeare turns upon John's defective right to the throne: therein lies the motive for the atrocity he plans, which leads (although it is not carried out as he intended) to the barons' desertion of his cause.

Despite its great dramatic advantages over *Richard II.*, the play suffers from the same radical weakness, and in an even greater degree: the figure of the King is too unsympathetic to serve as the centre-point of a drama. His despicable infirmity of purpose, which makes him kneel to receive his crown at the hands of the same Papal legate whom he has shortly before defied in blusterous terms; his infamous scheme to assassinate an innocent child, and his repentance when he sees that its supposed execution has alienated the chief supporters of his throne – all this hideous baseness, unredeemed by any higher characteristics, leads the spectator rather to attach his interest to the subordinate characters, and thus the action is frittered away before his eyes. It lacks unity, because the King is powerless to hold it together.

He himself is depicted for all time in the masterly scene where he seeks, without putting his thought into plain words, to make Hubert understand that he would fain have Arthur murdered: – [Quotes 3.3.48–54].

Hubert protests his fidelity and devotion. Even if he were to die for the deed, he would execute it for the King's sake. Then John's manner becomes hearty, almost affectionate. 'Good Hubert, Hubert!' he says caressingly. He points to Arthur, bidding Hubert 'throw his eye on yon young boy' [3.3.59–60]; and then follows this masterly dialogue: – [Quotes 3.3.60–71].

The character that bears the weight of the piece, as an acting play, is the illegitimate son of Richard Cœur-de-Lion, Philip Faulconbridge. He is John Bull himself in the guise of a mediæval knight, equipped with great strength and a racy English humour, not the wit of a Mercutio, a gay Italianising cavalier, but the irrepressible ebullitions of rude health and blunt gaiety befitting an English Hercules. The scene in the first act, in which he appears along with his brother, who seeks to deprive him of his inheritance as a Faulconbridge on the ground of his alleged illegitimacy, and the subsequent scene with his mother, from whom he tries to wring the secret of his paternity, both appear in the old play; but in it everything that the Bastard says is in grim earnest – the embroidery of wit belongs to Shakespeare alone. It is he who has placed in Faulconbridge's mouth such sayings as this: –

> Madam, I was not old Sir Robert's son:
> Sir Robert might have eat his part in me
> Upon Good Friday, and ne'er broke his fast. [1.1.233ff.]

And it is quite in Shakespeare's spirit when the son, after her confession, thus consoles his mother: –

> Madam, I would not wish a better father.
> Some sins do bear their privilege on earth,
> And so doth yours. [1.1.260ff.]

In later years, at a time when his outlook upon life was darkened, Shakespeare accounted for the villainy of Edmund, in *King Lear*, and for his aloofness from anything like normal humanity, on the ground of his irregular birth; in the Bastard of this play, on the contrary, his aim was to present a picture of all that health, vigour, and full-blooded vitality which popular belief attributes to a 'love-child.'

The antithesis to this national hero is Limoges, Archduke of Austria, in whom Shakespeare, following the old play, has mixed up two entirely distinct personalities. . . .

Faulconbridge is at first full of youthful insolence, the true mediæval nobleman, who despises the burgess class simply as such. When the inhabitants of Angiers refuse to open their gates either to King John or to King Philip of France, who has espoused the cause of Arthur, the Bastard is so indignant at this peace-loving circumspection that he urges the kings to join their forces against the unlucky town, and cry truce to their feud until the ramparts are levelled to the earth. But in the course of the action he ripens more and more, and displays ever greater and more estimable qualities – humanity, right-mindedness, and a fidelity to the King which does not interfere with generous freedom of speech towards him.

His method of expression is always highly imaginative, more so than that of the other male characters in the play. Even the most abstract ideas he personifies. Thus he talks of – 'Old Time, the clock-setter, that bald sexton Time' [3.1.324]. In the old play whole scenes are devoted to his execution of the task here allotted him of visiting the monasteries of England and lightening the abbots' bursting money-bags. Shakespeare has suppressed these ebullitions of an anti-Catholic fervour, which he did not share. On the other hand, he has endowed Faulconbridge with genuine moral superiority. At first he is only a cheery, fresh-natured, robust personality, who tramples upon all social conventions, phrases, and affectations; and indeed he preserves to the last something of that contempt for 'cockered silken wantons' [5.1.70] which Shakespeare afterwards elaborates so magnificently in Henry Percy. But there is real greatness in his attitude when, at the close of the play, he addresses the vacillating John in this manly strain: – [Quotes 5.1.46–53: 'Let not the world see fear, and sad distrust. . . .']. . . .

Next to Faulconbridge, Constance is the character who bears the weight of the play; and its weakness arises in great part from the fact that Shakespeare has killed her at the end of the third act. So lightly is her death treated, that it is merely announced in passing by the mouth of a messenger. She does not appear at all after her son Arthur is put out of the way, possibly because Shakespeare feared to lengthen the list of sorrowing and vengeful mothers already presented in his earlier histories.

He has treated this figure with a marked predilection, such as he usually manifests for those characters which, in one way or another, forcibly oppose every compromise with lax worldliness and euphemistic conventionality. He has not only endowed her with the most passionate and enthusiastic motherly love, but with a wealth of feeling and of imagination which gives her words a certain poetic magnificence. She wishes that 'her tongue were in the thunder's mouth, / Then with a passion would she shake the world' [3.4.39ff.]. She is sublime in her grief for the loss of her son: – [Quotes 3.1.68–74: 'I will instruct my sorrows to be proud. . . .']. Yet Shakespeare is already preparing us, in the overstrained violence of these expressions, for her madness and death.

The third figure which fascinates the reader of *King John* is that of Arthur. All the scenes in which the child appears are contained in the old play of the same name, and, among the rest, the first scene of the second act, which seems to dispose of Fleay's conjecture [No. 42 above] that the first two hundred lines of the act were hastily inserted after Shakespeare had lost his son. Nevertheless almost all that is gracious and touching in the figure is due to the great reviser. The old text is at its best in the scene where Arthur meets his death by jumping from the walls of the castle. Shakespeare has here confined himself for the most part to free curtailment; in the old *King John*, his fatal fall does not prevent Arthur from pouring forth copious lamentations to his absent mother and prayers to 'sweete Iesu' [9.20]. Shakespeare gives him only two lines to speak after his fall.

In this play, as in almost all the works of Shakespeare's younger years, the reader is perpetually amazed to find the finest poetical and rhetorical passages side by side with the most intolerable euphuistic affectations. And we cannot allege the excuse that these are legacies from the older play. On the contrary, there is nothing of the kind to be found in it; they are added by Shakespeare, evidently with the express purpose of displaying delicacy and profundity of thought. In the scenes before the walls of Angiers, he has on the whole kept close to the old drama, and has even followed faithfully the sense of all the more important speeches. For example, it is a citizen on the ramparts, who, in the old play, suggests the marriage between Blanch and the Dauphin; Shakespeare merely re-writes his speech, introducing into it these beautiful lines: – [Quotes 2.1.426–31: 'If lusty love should go in quest of beauty. . . .']. The surprising thing is that the same hand which has just written these verses should forthwith lose itself in a tasteless tangle of affectations like this: –

> Such as she is, in beauty, virtue, birth,
> Is the young Dauphin every way complete:
> If not complete of, say, he is not she;
> And she again wants nothing, to name want,
> If want it be not, that she is not he. [2.1.432ff.]

and this profound thought is further spun out with a profusion of images. Can we wonder that Voltaire and the French critics of the eighteenth century were offended by a style like this, even to the point of letting it blind them to the wealth of genius elsewhere manifested?

Even the touching scene between Arthur and Hubert is disfigured by false cleverness of this sort. The little boy, kneeling to the man who threatens to sear out his eyes, introduces, in the midst of the most moving appeals, such far-fetched and contorted phrases as this: –

> The iron of itself, though heat red-hot,
> Approaching near these eyes, would drink my tears,
> And quench this fiery indignation
> Even in the manner of mine innocence;
> Nay, after that, consume away in rust,
> But for containing fire to harm mine eye. [4.1.61ff.]

And again, when Hubert proposes to reheat the iron: –

> An if you do, you will but make it blush,
> And glow with shame of your proceedings, Hubert. [4.1.112ff.]

The taste of the age must indeed have pressed strongly upon Shakespeare's spirit to prevent him from feeling the impossibility of these quibbles upon the lips of a child imploring in deadly fear that his eyes may be spared to him.

As regards their ethical point of view, there is no essential difference between the old play and Shakespeare's. The King's defeat and painful death is in both a punishment for his wrongdoing. There has only been, as already mentioned, a certain displacement of the centre of gravity. In the old play, the dying John stammers out an explicit confession that from the moment he surrendered to the Roman priest he has had no more happiness on earth; for the Pope's curse is a blessing, and his blessing a curse. In Shakespeare the emphasis is laid, not upon the King's weakness in the religio-political struggle, but upon the wrong to Arthur. Faulconbridge gives utterance to the fundamental idea of the play when he says: –

> From forth this morsel of dead royalty,
> The life, the right, and truth of all this realm
> Is fled to heaven. [4.3.143ff.]

Shakespeare's political standpoint is precisely that of the earlier writer, and indeed, we may add, of his whole age.

The most important contrasts and events of the period he seeks to represent do not exist for him. He naïvely accepts the first kings of the House of Plantagenet, and the Norman princes in general, as English national heroes, and has evidently no suspicion of the deep gulf that separated the Normans from the Anglo-Saxons down to this very reign, when the two hostile races, equally oppressed by the King's tyranny, began to fuse into one people.[1] What would Shakespeare have thought had he known that Richard Cœur-de-Lion's favourite formula of denial was 'Do you take me for an Englishman?' while his pet oath, and that of his Norman followers, was 'May I become an Englishman if – ,' &c.?

[Brandes concludes his essay with a brief and derivative explanation as to why Shakespeare omitted any mention of Magna Carta from the play. First, he was following *The Troublesome Raigne*, which also omits mention of it; second, he did not understand its real importance; and third, 'Elizabeth did not care to be reminded of it' (176).] (169–76)

57 Henry Sebastian Bowden, Shakespeare's Roman Catholicism

1899

From *The Religion of Shakespeare. Chiefly from the Writings of the Late Mr. Richard Simpson, M.A. By Henry Sebastian Bowden of the Oratory* (London, 1899).

Henry Sebastian Bowden (1836–1919), also known as Henry George Bowden or 'Father Sebastian Bowden', was an active Roman Catholic writer and apologist. In addition to the many prefaces and introductions he wrote for books of a spiritual or religious nature, Bowden also edited F. L. Hettinger's German translation of *The Divine Comedy* (London, 1887) as well as an English translation of Hettinger's *Apologie des Christenthums* (London, 1890). *The Religion of Shakespeare* consists mainly of reprinted or newly-edited (but previously unpublished) essays by Richard Simpson (No. 35 above), including those on Shakespeare's histories first published in the *New Shakespeare Society's Transactions* (London, 1874). Some sections of the book, however, such as the excerpt reprinted below, are the work of Bowden, who acknowledges having received 'valuable assistance' from Simpson's MSS (viii).

[From Chapter III: 'Contemporary Dramatists']

. . . It was Shakespeare's well-known custom to alter and adapt existing plays; and by comparing his alterations with the original matter, we discover the strength and direction of his own opinions. One play thus altered and adapted by Shakespeare is that of *King John*, a piece commonly instanced as proving beyond question Shakespeare's Protestantism, especially in the two speeches of King John and Pandulph. The latter, the Legate of Innocent III., was sent to call the king to account for refusing Stephen Langton, Archbishop of Canterbury, admission to his See, and for appropriating its revenues. King John replies thus: – [Quotes 3.1.147–60: 'What earthly name to interrogatories / Can task the free breath of a sacred King? . . .']. . . . These lines have indeed furnished quotation for anti-Catholic declamations of Prime Ministers, Lord Chancellors, and Archbishops in our own time. Their value as representing Shakespeare's opinions, however, assume a different complexion if we apply one of Aristotle's canons of criticism, and inquire not what the speech is in itself, but who spoke it, and with what end it was spoken. The language and action of a hero may be supposed to represent the poet's type of what is good and noble, and therefore of what he would wish his own language and action to be. The sentiments of a scoundrel, on the other hand, are intentionally drawn as false, base, and treacherous, and therefore presumably not those of the poet's ideal self. Now we are quite content that Shakespeare should be judged by this rule throughout his plays, but this rule must be uniformly applied. According to some critics, if Henry V. speaks as a Catholic, this is only from dramatic necessity, or because the poet is following Holinshed's *Chronicles*, and such speeches therefore give us no clue as to his own judgment. Does John, however, rant in true Exeter Hall fashion, or Duke Humphrey malign Cardinal Beaufort, or an added scene in *Henry VIII.* extol Elizabeth, there we have the poet himself. With such a method of argument Shakespeare can be proved as rabid a bigot as these writers desire. But if the canon be impartially applied, an opposite result is, we believe, attained.

In this particular instance is John a hero or a villain? 'He begins,' says Kreyssig, 'as an ordinary and respectable man of the world, and he ends as an ordinary criminal; he is not only a villain, but a mean villain. The satanic grandeur of an Edmund or Macbeth is wholly beyond him. His criminal designs are pursued with the instinct common to selfish natures, but without any clear, far-reaching intelligence.'[1] His bold defiance proves mere bombast; he ends by eating his words. He humbles himself to the dust before the Legate, and as a penitent receives the crown again at his hands, and his kingdom in fief from the Pope. John's anti-Catholic speeches, then, no more prove Shakespeare a Protestant than the fool's saying in his heart 'There is no God,' makes David a sceptic [Psalms 14.1].

We now come to the composition of the original play and its alterations by Shakespeare. We must premise that *The Troublesome Raigne of King John* which Shakespeare adapted must not be confounded with the earlier *King John* of 'Bilious' Bale (1495–1563), a quondam friar who took a wife, became Protestant Bishop of Ossory, and wrote, besides various acrid controversial works, several plays[2] alike doggerel and indecent.

The Troublesome Raigne of King John, the original of Shakespeare's play, was composed, like that of Bale, to glorify Protestantism and vilify the ancient faith. Shakespeare, in adapting it, had only to leave untouched its virulent bigotry and its ribald stories of friars and nuns to secure its popularity, yet as a fact he carefully excludes the anti-Catholic passages and allusions, and acts throughout as a rigid censor on behalf of the Church. . . .

[Bowden now mentions that Shakespeare omits from *King John* the earlier play's emphasis on John's claims of spiritual and temporal supremacy, his contemptuous reply to his excommunication, and his declared purpose of despoiling the monasteries and sending the monks as prisoners to the Pope.]

. . . In Shakespeare's play King John makes no reply to the prelate after the excommunication is pronounced, and is singularly silent till he threatens Philip at the close of the scene. The excommunication itself, however, is taken by Hunter [No 20 above] and others as conclusive proof of Shakespeare's Protestantism. It runs thus: – [Quotes 3.1.174–9: where Pandulph advocates treason and even tyrannicide against John]. These words, we admit, at first sight seem difficult to reconcile with the theory of Shakespeare's religious opinions which we are defending. For here it is Pandulph, the Legate himself, who is giving utterance to the very doctrines attributed to the Church by its enemies. Nor is it any answer to say that the speech was in substance in the old play, for our point has been that Shakespeare, in so far as he follows the original piece, uniformly expurgates it of any anti-Catholic virus. Why then, while rejecting so much which, as Gervinus says [No. 31 above], was particularly agreeable to the Protestant audiences of the time, did he allow this one passage to remain?

First, then, it might, we think, be urged that a regard to his personal safety prompted the inclusion of the speech in question. His play of *Richard II.* had already, as we have seen, been condemned as treasonable, and though Hayward was in that instance the victim,[3] might not Shakespeare himself be the next victim, if he left no Protestant sentiment to satisfy the royal sensitiveness? Such a motive is indeed unworthy of a bold and fearless champion of the Faith; but we have neither regarded nor represented Shakespeare in such a light, but rather as one who, whatever his convictions, was desirous, as far as possible, of avoiding any suspicion of recusancy. . . .

But yet another motive for the insertion of Pandulph's speech suggests itself. Might not his words represent Shakespeare's own feeling with regard to Elizabeth? The lawfulness of tyrannicide was advocated in the sixteenth century by individuals of every creed, and, though on entirely different grounds, by Protestants of every shade, as well as by some Catholics. . . . What then was Elizabeth in Shakespeare's judgment? In the eyes of his kinsfolk, friends, and associates she was illegitimate, excommunicate, an usurping, cruel tyrant. Nor would his reiterated condemnation of rebellion in theory, as fatal to its perpetrators and disastrous in its results, hinder his having the warmest sympathy with those who pursued such a line of action. Before the poet's mind, at the thought of Elizabeth, would have arisen a vision of victims more numerous than the spectres which haunted the last moments of Richard III. . . .

[After mentioning a number of the victims of Elizabeth's cruelty, Bowden goes on to suggest that Richmond's indictment of Richard III as 'a bloody tyrant and a homicide' (*Richard III*, 5.3.246) may represent Shakespeare's feelings about the queen.]

If these were the poet's own feelings with respect to Elizabeth, they would gain weight by being spoken by a prelate whom Shakespeare portrays as a man of dignity and worth. In any case, the two interpretations suggested do not exclude each other, and Pandulph's speech may have had the double purpose of securing the poet's personal safety, and of expressing to those who knew him his own personal condemnation of the Tudor queen.

In the same scene Pandulph calls on King Philip to break with John, and declares the alliance sworn with him void, but not, as in the old play, because 'the oath was made with a heretic' [3.108ff.]. This popular calumny against Catholic doctrine Shakespeare utterly repudiates, and instead he substitutes a careful, accurate, and detailed disquisition on the obligations of an oath, drawn out according to the Church's teaching. An oath is invalid, Pandulph says, when it is contrary to a former oath, or to a prior moral obligation. On both heads Philip's oath to John was invalid. It forswore his previous oath of allegiance to the Church – [Quotes 3.1.288–9]. And again the calling God to witness that he would attack the Church was by its nature null and void as an oath. . . . [Morally sound] is the Cardinal's teaching that an oath, though unlawful when sworn to, may by a notable change of circumstance become lawful, and be rightly carried out, not *vi juramenti*,[4] but because of the altered nature of the act; while when the matter of the oath remains unlawful, it is best kept by non performance.[5] [Quotes 3.1.270–3: 'For that, which thou hast sworn to do amiss. . . .'].

After his victory over the French, John in the old play pours a flood of jeers and invectives over the 'mischievous Priest in Italy who calls himself Christ's Vicar' [8.7ff., loosely quoted], and is now hard at work with Dirges, Masses, Octaves, and Requiems, to assuage the flames of Purgatory for those who have fallen in battle. To this succeeds a round of abuse of those princes who 'formerly bore the yoke of the servile priest' [8.19ff., loosely quoted], and in foolish piety submitted to the See of Rome. Shakespeare simply cuts out all this. . . . The old play makes Pandulph a hypocrite and a Machiavellian simply because he is a Catholic prelate. In Shakespeare he appears as an experienced, far-sighted statesman, but also as a ghostly Father, full of sympathy for the afflicted. He grieves for Arthur's capture and pities Constance, whose maternal beautiful and pathetic appeal proves that she saw in him a spiritual consoler, and not a mere cold-hearted, calculating politician – [Quotes 3.4.76–89: 'And, Father Cardinal. . . .']. Again Lewis, though he changes his tone afterwards, fully recognizes the Legate's spiritual character – [Quotes 5.2.64–8: 'And even there, methinks, an angel spake. . . .']. In his speech to the Dauphin the Cardinal shows his political foresight, and his knowledge of the ways of Providence in the conduct of human affairs. The lost battle and Arthur's imprisonment do not deceive him.[6] He knows 'that whiles warm life plays in that infant's veins' John cannot enjoy a peaceful moment – 'That John may stand, then, Arthur needs must fall; / So be it, for it cannot but be so' [3.4.132ff.]. He forsees that the King's treatment of Arthur will estrange all hearts from him, and beget a rebellion against the usurper; and the event fully justifies his prophecy. Arthur is scarcely in the King's power before the latter has engaged his executioner, and from that moment John himself becomes the victim of a vengeful nemesis. According to Kreyssig and other critics, John's fall was in no way due 'to the excommunication, or the word of the priest, but merely to the natural revulsion of popular feeling consequent on the murder of Arthur. The Pope's failure is in fact a point in the play.' Yet the Church's curse was believed in the Middle Ages to be no idle threat. The Divine vengeance might be delayed, and when it came it might be accomplished, not by any direct supernatural intervention, but by what seemed merely natural means. . . .

No sooner has the seat of war been shifted to England than Fortune changes. The king is forsaken by the nobles, on account both of the excommunication and of Arthur's murder, and finds himself vanquished. . . .

It is no less instructive to remark the poet's representation of Faulconbridge. In the older play he rails at the Pope and the Legate, he discovers the scandals and ludicrous scenes in the monasteries, and is never wearied of declaiming against the arrogance and greed of Rome. In Shakespeare he is represented indeed as ready to levy contributions on the monasteries – [Quotes 3.3.12–13]. He is a reckless, careless soldier, but he is not a Protestant bigot. On the contrary, instead of expressing indignant contempt – as he does in the old play – at John's submission to the Legate, by which 'friars are made kings, and kings friars' [12.8ff., loosely quoted], Faulconbridge looks upon Pandulph as the friend of England and an honourable peace-maker. The anger of the Bastard is reserved exclusively for France and the Dauphin – [Quotes 5.1.65–70: 'O inglorious league! . . .'].

And the action of the Cardinal with the Dauphin justifies the Bastard's view of him. Instead of mutually cursing each other to their 'bellyful' as in the old plays, in Shakespeare the Cardinal tells the Dauphin that he looks at but 'the outside of the work' [5.2.109], and persuades him though victorious to offer England terms of honourable peace. The death of John marks the final contrast between the two plays. In the older piece the Monk obtains the Abbot's blessing and the promise of heaven as the reward for murdering the King. John dies ascribing all his miseries to his submission to the Pope, and the Bastard stabs the Abbot. In Shakespeare's play the murderer, 'the resolved villain' [5.6.29] is alluded to in one line; and the Bastard, instead of expressing indignation at the crime, seems rather to see in it the punishment of a just God, and prays – 'Withold thine indignation, mighty Heaven, / And tempt us not to bear above our power!' [5.6.37ff.]. Finally, John dies, not a defiant prophet cursing Rome, but desolate and despairing, his torments intensified by the impotent sympathy of his friends – [Quotes 5.7.30–48: John's painful exclamations at his death]. . . .

Having now compared the two plays, we can judge of their respective application. The moral of the old play was, that as David was the forerunner of Solomon, so John began the noble work which was to be fully accomplished by the more worthy hands of his descendant Henry VIII., 'Whose arms shall reach unto the Gates of Rome / And with his feet tread down the strumpet's pride, / That sits upon the Chair of Babylon' [15.105ff.]. And the play was intended to keep alive the burning hatred of Popery, as was the account of the same transactions in the *Homilies*.[7] With Shakespeare all this disappears; in his hands the play becomes a moral and political essay on the events and questions of his time. The slaying of Arthur is closely parallel to that of Mary, Queen of Scots; John, like Elizabeth, first suggests, then commands the deed, afterwards feigns horror at its accomplishment and repudiates the perpetrators. John disowned Hubert, as Elizabeth did Davison,[8] though in both cases the order for the murder was given under the royal hand and seal. In fact, Sir Amyas Paulett, the governor of Fotheringay, knowing his mistress's way, refused to carry out Mary's execution till he had Elizabeth's warrant for the same, which angered her much and she complained of him as a 'dainty precise fellow' for his insistence. Again, Philip's disinclination after the loss of Angiers, to prosecute the war till the prospect of Arthur's death opens his son's claim to the English crown, resembles the delay of Philip II. of Spain to make any serious attack on England till Mary Stuart's death made the Infanta or Duke of Parma possible claimants for the English throne. Lewis' intended slaughter of his allies, the English rebel nobles, finds a parallel in the reported intention of the Duke of Medina Sidonia, Commander of the Armada, who declared that, once landed in England, all Catholics and heretics should be one to him, his sword would not discern them! so that he might make way for his master.[9]

But Shakespeare's *King John* extends beyond historical parallels and discusses principles. In the case of an usurping ruler, who is to decide between him and the nation what power has commission – [Quotes 2.1.112–14:].

And the answer is found not in the alliance of princes which dissolve when 'That smooth-faced gentleman, tickling Commodity, / Commodity, the bias of the world'

[2.1.573ff.] insinuates the prospect of gain to any of the contracting parties — but as we think with Raich,[10] in the action of the Legate. Here we disagree with Mr. Simpson [No. 35 above], who thinks the play teaches, among other lessons, the futility of Papal interference in national disputes. We know that Pandulph is regarded generally as being also a slave to commodity, and of changing sides merely as suited the interests of the Church. No doubt those interests were first with him, but with them were bound up the claims of justice and right and the liberties of the people. He is allied with France to enforce John to submit, but on John's submission he orders, as he was bound, the Dauphin to withdraw his invading force. His mission is completely successful. England is reconciled to the Church, France and England are friends again, the rebel nobles are pardoned, the rightful heir ascends the English throne, and all this is effected by the offices of the Legate and the action of Faulconbridge, the typical Englishman, of whom the poet is so fond. Shakespeare, then, on our view, appears to have thought that the appeal to an international tribunal in the person of the Pope was not without its advantages; that the disputes between people and rulers, or between rival sovereigns, found safer, speedier, and more equitable adjustment when settled by a recognised arbitrator, himself the common-head of Christendom, than when decided between the contending parties themselves by rebellion or war. (117–35)

58 Charles Harold Herford, Shakespeare's maturing artistry

1899

From *The Works of Shakespeare. Edited with Introductions and Notes by C. H. Herford, Litt.D.*, etc. (10 vols, London, 1899).

Charles Harold Herford (1853–1931) was professor of English Language and Literature at University College, Aberystwyth, from 1887 to 1901, after which he spent twenty years at Manchester University before retiring in 1921. Even during his retirement he served as the literary critic for *The Manchester Guardian*, and maintained an active scholarly life until his death. Herford was a highly respected and industrious critic and editor, whose interests ranged widely, both within and without the English tradition. The so-called 'Eversley' edition of 1899 was perhaps his most important Shakespearian scholarly project, particularly when one takes into account the judicious and polished introductions to the plays that, taken as a whole, could easily stand as a fine book-length study of Shakespeare's dramatic development.

[From the Introduction to *King John*]

. . . Far more clearly than *Richard II.*, *King John* belongs to the interim between the first and second group of Histories. It has palpable links with both. The absence of prose, the rarity of rhyme, the approximation to tragedy, connect it with the earlier, Marlowesque, group; the wealth of humour, the plastic characterisation, with the later. John is modelled with a maturer touch than Richard II.; but the tragedy of which he is the contriver has striking affinities of situation to that of Richard, and continually recalls it in spite of equally striking diversities of treatment. Constance is not Margaret, nor Arthur Edward, but they are new and poignant melodies upon the same motifs; the frenzied mother, the assassin uncle, are still dominant and unexhausted themes. On the other hand, the character of Faulconbridge links the play yet more closely to the great trilogy of [the *Henry IV* plays and] *Henry V*. The madcap prince who shows himself a master of war and of peace the moment the need arrives, is of the same mould as the blunt soldier 'one way Plantagenet' [5.6.11] whose motley covered the lion's heart of Cordelion; the mythical Bastard foreshadows the historical conqueror of Agincourt. He opens the cycle of Histories founded upon humour and heroism, as John closes the cycle founded upon anguish and crime. These considerations tend to fix *King John* near the middle of the probable interval between the last of the earlier group and the first of the later, *i.e.* about 1595.

King John is probably, of all Shakespeare's Histories, the most distantly related to History. Theological fanaticism, that potent myth-maker, had, since the middle of the century, laid a powerful grasp upon the tradition, already not without its mythic elements, recorded in the Chronicles; and the wonderful transformation which this legend underwent in Shakespeare's hands was certainly not undertaken in the interest of historical truth. Indeed his most striking alterations only serve to detach it more completely from the Chronicles, and to draw it more explicitly into the sphere of irresponsible poetry. What manner of legend it was that underwent this apotheosis may be gathered from two dramas, one of them certainly unknown to Shakespeare, the other the immediate basis of his work. . . .

[Herford now discusses Bale's *King Johan* and *The Troublesome Raigne*, noting the 'incoherent' and 'frenzied' (7) anti-Catholic virulence of the former, and the influence of the Armada, nationalistic Protestantism, and Marlowe on the latter. After a pithy and carefully detailed assessment of *The Troublesome Raigne*, Herford takes up its influence on Shakespeare.]

The Troublesome Raigne thus provided the entire material of *King John*. Shakespeare has followed his original almost scene for scene, retaining the outer mechanism of the plot unchanged, or at most dismissing into the background events which the earlier dramatist exhibited with genial prolixity on the stage.[1] But he has essentially altered the significance of the action, and immensely strengthened and vitalised what he retained. We may say, generally, that, while the *Troublesome Raigne* is patriotic, Protestant, and Marlowesque, *King John* is the work of a man whose patriotism was more fervent, whose Protestantism was less fanatical, and who had definitely broken through the charmed circle of Marlowe. Shakespeare entirely adopts the bold device of his predecessor for saving the unpatriotic surrender of John. The Bastard plays an even more imposing part, and his energy pervades and animates the whole drama. As a character he belongs altogether to Shakespeare. The earlier Faulconbridge's alternate accesses of mysticism and horseplay disappear in the brimming vitality of this frank and burly Plantagenet. Shakespeare's Bastard discovers his father not from rustling leaves, but by the contrast between his own giant frame and that of his mannikin brother, slays Austria without invoking his father's shade, and does battle without the ægis of his father's fortune. The grounds of his animosity to Austria are indeed rather hinted than explained. And with these mystic touches disappears the horseplay of the scene in the monastery. But the character of Faulconbridge is put to uses of which the earlier writer did not dream. His prototype is indeed already in some sense the mouthpiece of England, and rudely anticipates the magnificent closing assurance that [Quotes 5.7.112–14: 'This England never did, nor never shall. . . .']. Shakespeare's Faulconbridge, however, stands not merely for the cause of England but for English character; for bluff, straightforward manliness against subtle shifts and unmeaning phrase: he has his jest at the rhetoric of the Angiers citizen who 'Talks as familiarly of roaring lions / As maids of thirteen do of puppy-dogs' [2.1.459ff.]; and the subtle diplomatic chicaneries of Pandulph are thrown into relief with caustic effect by the trenchant humour of the Bastard's famous exposure of 'commodity.' Notwithstanding the jocose profession which closes that speech, private ends have little to do with his action; and with great judgment Shakespeare excised the earlier playwright's explanation of his indignation at the match between Blanch and Lewis as arising from a previous bethrothal of Blanch to himself.

But while *King John* is informed with a yet keener patriotism, it is less aggressively Protestant than the *Troublesome Raigne*. The gross burlesque of Faulconbridge's raid upon the 'fat Franciscans' [6.1] is altogether excised. John's relations with Rome remain unchanged, but it is no longer here that the principal ethical purport of the play is to be found. In the eyes of the earlier writer, John's surrender of his birthright to Philip, his surrender of his crown to Pandulph, and his betrayal of Arthur, seem coordinate causes of his fall.[2] Shakespeare exposes his errors with at least equal trenchancy, but makes clear that the more deadly step is not the surrender but the crime. It is this which alienates his subjects, and gives the French invasion its sole chance of success. The thunders of Pandulph on either side do not affect the issue. The earlier dramatist treats the crafty legate with malignant hatred, as a 'curse' happily evaded;[3] the later manages him with fine irony, as the wielder of an imposing but not really formidable authority, easily rendered innocuous, incapable of injuring a people true to themselves. And though John still meets his death at the hands of a monk, the act is dismissed with a studiously casual allusion, so that the 'resolved villain' [5.6.29] seems merely the executant of Nemesis. Whereas in the *Troublesome Raigne* he dies to satisfy the vengeance of an incensed ecclesiastic, who has vowed never to let escape 'the king that never loved a friar, the man that did contemn the pope' [13.84ff.]. Naturally, Shakespeare ignores the 'moral' which this suggests to the Bastard: —

> This is the fruit of Poperie, when true kings
> Are slain and shouldered out by Monks and friars. [15.113ff.]

Nor does his John indulge any vision of a more fortunate Protestant successor.

The Shakespearian Pandulph, finally, would suffice to show that Shakespeare was no longer under the spell of the fiery but nowise subtle intellect of Marlowe. If Marlowe was the first English dramatist who commanded the language of impetuous passion, Shakespeare was the first master of the language of polished and astute debate, of high-bred conversation, of courtly ceremony. The earlier John retains not a little of the lofty insolence of Tamburlaine: how kingly on the other hand is the later John's dismissal of Chatillion; — dignified defiance, injunction, valiant forecast, courteous attention and farewell, all concentrated in eight lines [1.1.23–30]. The two great creations Constance and Arthur, also, are touched with an intensity of pathos still strange to the Shakespeare of *Henry VI.* and of *Richard III*. The situation of Margaret after Tewksbury, of Elizabeth after the murders in the Tower, resemble that of Constance; but Margaret utters her passion for vengeance more poignantly than the agony of her loss, and Elizabeth's outraged motherhood finds expression merely in sullen resentment. Constance is the Juliet of maternal love. Love for Arthur dominates her whole being, and the agony of bereavement finds utterance through phrases that burn in the fire of an imagination familiar with wild grief. Arthur's situation similarly recalls that of the young princes. The Arthur of the *Troublesome*

Raigne does, in fact, bear himself like the young Duke of York in *Richard III.*, boldly bearding his dangerous uncle, and incurring reproof from Elinor for his vehemence ('Peace, Arthur, peace,' etc. *Troublesome Raigne* [2.108]). Shakespeare has endowed his Arthur not with the charm of precocious talent, but with the pathos and shrinking tenderness of childhood: 'I am not worth this coil that's made for me' [2.1.165]; and, instead of incurring reproof, it is he who, almost in Elinor's words, appeals to his own fiery advocate to cease pleading: 'Good my mother, peace!' [2.1.163]. Of the death of the princes we have in the earlier play no more than a brief though exquisite picture; but Arthur's perilous captivity is displayed in the most tender and sympathetic dramatic detail; and the pathos of the scene is derived, not from an accumulation of harrowing details, as to some extent it is in the grim finale of *Edward II.*, but from the ideal loveliness of childlike character which unfolds itself under the stress of Hubert's threat. (VI, 5–14)

59 Hamilton Wright Mabie, *King John* as a transitional play

1900

From *William Shakespeare: Poet, Dramatist, and Man* (New York, 1900).

Hamilton Wright Mabie (1845–1916) abandoned a career as a lawyer in 1879 to join the staff of *The Christian Union* (renamed *The Outlook* in 1893), serving in a variety of capacities until he eventually became associate editor, a post he occupied until his death. Mabie was a popular writer of children's literature but also published a number of books on literary and cultural matters, among them *Essays in Literary Interpretation* (New York, 1892), *Nature and Culture* (New York, 1896), *Books and Culture* (New York, 1896), and *Introductions to Notable Poems* (New York, 1909). *William Shakespeare*, like much of Mabie's critical work, is accessible and unpretentious, a fit vehicle for one of his chief scholarly objectives, the fostering of a sense of literary culture in the United States.

[From Chapter X: 'The Historical Plays']

[Mabie, following Herford (No. 58 above), sees Shakespeare as a dramatist 'working out his artistic emancipation' (233) from Marlowe at about the time he was writing *Richard II*, and assigns *King John* to roughly the same period.]

... To this period belongs *King John*, which was probably completed about 1595, and which was a recast of the older play of *The Troublesome Raigne of John, King of England*, published in 1591. The conventional construction was not greatly modified by Shakespeare, but the play marks the transition from the chronicle play to the true drama; in which incidents and characters are selected for their dramatic significance, a dramatic motive introduced, dramatic movement traced, and a climax reached. The older playwrights, dealing with the events of a whole reign, would have given the play an epical or narrative quality; Shakespeare selected, compressed, foreshortened, and grouped events and figures in such a way as to secure connected action, the development of character, and a final catastrophe which is impressive, if not intrinsically dramatic. He instinctively omitted certain coarse scenes which were in the older play; he brought into clear light and consistency certain characters which were roughly sketched in the earlier work; in the scene between Hubert and Arthur he struck a new note of tenderness and pathos; while in giving marked prominence to the humour of Faulconbridge he opened the way for that blending of comedy with tragedy and history which is one of the marks, not only of his maturity, but of his greatness. The play has no hero, and is not free from the faults of the long line of dramas from which it descended and to which it belongs, but Shakespeare's creative energy is distinctly at work in it. (233–4)

60 George Charles Moore Smith, weaknesses and strengths of *King John*

1900

From *King John. Edited by G. C. Moore Smith, M.A. Professor of English Language and Literature in University College Sheffield* (Boston, 1900).

George Charles Moore Smith (1858–1940) produced two highly competent editions of individual Shakespearian plays (*Henry V* [1896] and *King John* [1900]), published in London by Blackie as 'The Warwick Shakespeare' and in Boston by D.C. Heath as 'Heath's English Classics' (both also referred to as 'The Arden Shakespeare', but not to be confused with the later twentieth-century edition of the same name). Smith is a careful and astute critic, yet one who graciously credits others when he regards their work to be of superior quality, as he does in the case of Edward Rose (No. 43 above) and Heinrich Bulthaupt, the German scholar whose critical remarks on *King John* receive their only English translation in Smith's edition.

[From the Introduction]

[Smith begins by dating *King John* between 1594–6 on the basis of internal evidence, then proceeds to a detailed and instructive analysis of *The Troublesome Raigne*, beginning with its source in Holinshed and concluding with Shakespeare's adaptation of it. The discussion contains extensive quotation from Rose's essay, the judiciousness of which Smith fully endorses.]

... As supplementing Mr. Rose's paper, I may here call attention to the part played by the Bastard during the dispute as to his legitimacy in the old play and in Shakespeare. In the old play Philip at first wishes the charge of bastardy to be dismissed: [Quotes 1.146–8]. His brother Robert's reasons are dismissed by King John as inconclusive, his mother asserts his legitimacy, and all that is required is a plain statement from Philip that he considers Faulconbridge his father. At this point he falls into a state of absent-mindedness, during which, in an *aside*, he sets forth the contention between his instinctive feeling that he was a king's son, and his common sense, which makes him unwilling to throw away his inheritance. The *aside* is highly poetical:

> Birds, bubbles, leaues and mountaines, Eccho, all
> Ring in mine eares, that I am Richards Sonne.

> Fond man, ah whither art thou carried? . . .
> These thoughts are farre vnfitting Fauconbridge.
> No, keepe thy land, though Richard were thy Sire,
> What ere thou thinkst, say thou art Fauconbridge. [1.257ff.]

But when John interrupts him, 'Speake man, be sodaine, who thy father was' [1.272], Philip cannot bring out the name: [Quotes 1.274–8]. Shakespeare probably cut out the passage partly, as Mr. Rose says, just because it was a long 'aside', partly because it was too lyrical for Philip's character. But his whole treatment is different. Instead of showing us the contest of feelings in Philip's breast, and his final following of an inner call even against all his worldly interests, he seems to represent him as having no serious intention from the beginning of denying his illegitimacy, but determined not to give up his land without at least pleading before the king. The ironical humour which Shakespeare has imparted to his character has given quite a new turn to the old scene. . . . (xxi–xxii)

[After further extensive quotation from Rose's essay, Smith concludes his discussion of Shakespeare's sources by arguing that the dramatist's likely reliance upon Holinshed was negligible at best. He then begins a 'critical appreciation' of *King John*, again citing Rose's contention that despite its considerable merits the play is in many respects flawed.]

But if *King John*, considered as an artistic whole, has such serious faults, on what does it depend for the profound impression which again and again it makes on us? The answer is: in the imaginative power with which Shakespeare seized on some of the characters of the old play – John himself, Constance, Arthur, Pandulph, and above all the Bastard – and made out of comparatively slight sketches immortal types of guilt, anguish, pleading innocence, diplomatic foresight, and devil-may-care honesty and patriotism. By compressing what was unimportant, he left himself room to draw great pictures of the working of human passions, such as are found in the two scenes between John and Hubert [3.3; 4.2], in the scene between Hubert and Arthur [4.1], in the scenes of Constance's agonized lamentations [3.1; 3.4], in that in which the lords find the body of Arthur [4.3]. In vain did the poet heighten the virtues and soften some of the vices of John, in vain suppress some of his violent expressions of the spirit of sixteenth-century Protestantism: he left the character at the end perhaps more unheroic than he found it. And so the play remains without a centre, but great, even supremely great, in its parts.[1]

I conclude with a very judicious estimate of the weakness and strength of the play, which Dr. Heinrich Bulthaupt, of Bremen, has kindly allowed me to transfer to these pages from his *Dramaturgie des Schauspiels*. . . .[2]

'Shakespeare did not succeed in so narrowing down the material offered him as to make it present a single action, developing itself surely and consequently to a single end, and so it is a difficult matter to extract the kernel from the entanglement of the episodes, as in *Richard II* – a much better constructed play – one can find a central idea in the struggle between usurpation and hereditary rights.

'The powerful rapid opening would lead one to assume that the central interest of the piece was to be the contest about the hereditary claims of Arthur. It is on his account that the campaign is undertaken, it is his imprisonment and supposed murder which provoke the revolt of the nobility from John. Very soon, however, nay in the very first act, side by side with this action but in no way connected with it, we have the humorous episode of the legitimacy contest, and when we reach the third act the centre of equilibrium of the action seems to be completely displaced by the appearance of Pandulph. Our chief interest now is John's resistance to the Papacy, and Arthur is forgotten. It is true that in the fourth act Arthur's personality comes again to the foreground, but the poet (following his text *The Troublesome Raigne*) has here deviated from the almost symbolic poeticization of the action which history offers, viz. the murdering of Arthur by John himself, and offers in place of it the Blinding-scene, a magnificent scene considered in itself, but one which stands in no relation to the almost sketchy treatment of Arthur in the preceding acts. Then suddenly the attitude of the Barons, their revolt from John, their desertion to the Dauphin, becomes the main action; but this also runs dry, and in the last act there is no further trace of any connexion with the opening of the play. John's death, through the agency of a shameless monk, has nothing to do with Arthur's legal claims: the bond between cause and effect is wanting.

'The impression made by the motiveless zigzagging of the action is intensified when we examine the play more closely. In almost every act a new side-issue is treated with such breadth as to become the main issue: in the first act Sir Robert's dispute with the Bastard Faulconbridge (which is treated in itself with freshness and most charming good-humour); in the second, the immoderate delay caused by the mere word-sparring before Angiers, which does not carry the action an inch further, and is doubly uneconomical inasmuch as, after the ensuing battle has been left doubtful, we are brought back to the same position as before; in the third, Constance's outbursts of rage and complaints; in the fourth, the Blinding-scene. Indeed, even this scene appears to be merely an episode, although it is concerned with the fate of Arthur, the innocent cause of the war. For, in the first place, it is a scene of needless and soul-torturing barbarity, which, even if it had been carried out, would still not have advanced the action – nothing short of Arthur's *death* would have made John safe from his claims; and in the second place it is *not* carried out, and accordingly (brilliantly as the charms of Shakespearian poetry are disclosed in the touching tones of childish supplication) it appears from a dramatic point of view to be once more in this respect a mere postponement of the action of the play.

'Finally comes the unevenness of the dramatic style. Here we have the most delicately wrought-out detail, here a coarse sketch, here the most realistic draughtsmanship, here impressionist painting which does little more than symbolize what it professes to represent. Read the glorious third scene of the third act with its deep penetration into the most secret recesses of the heart, its slow steady march, its moving laconic conclusion: [Quotes 3.3.63–6: where John asks Hubert to murder Arthur]. Only consider this scene and the wonderful Blinding-scene, or the concluding scene of the fourth act (the finding of Arthur's corpse), side by side with the marionette style in which the ambassadors introduce themselves, *e.g.* Chatillion before Angiers, who (as though this was the most natural thing in the world) delivers his message without a word of introduction on the instant of his arrival from England;

with the naive swiftness with which John, as though shot from a pistol, appears in France, and at once, like a wound-up clock, rattles off his sermon; with what, in spite of all excitement on the part of the women, one must call, considering the situation, the amiable manner in which the hostile parties and the citizens of Angiers carry on their negotiations; with the mysterious haste with which Lewis' bethrothal to Blanch is brought about. The inequality of the treatment is surely glaring. And when one reflects that the personality of the king himself is utterly without truly dramatic qualities such as might carry our interest along through all the zigzag paths of the action, one feels that one would be badly off indeed if there were not one figure who, with strong arms, held the structure together, a figure – not of principal importance to the action, but yet the soul of the play – the Bastard: a complete man bubbling over with life, one of those who have received in "the lusty stealth of nature", as Edmund says in *Lear* [1.2.11], a spirit of the most fiery quality. Full of a cheery daring, he gives away lightheartedly the inheritance of Sir Robert Faulconbridge, but he never becomes a mere characterless adventurer. For such a rôle his moral feeling is too genuine. Excellently does he mock at the 'mad world' of the 'mad kings' after the criminally hasty alliance of Angiers [2.1.561]; but, like all men of action and grit, who follow rather their own impulse than any ethical system, he takes no satisfaction in making himself out as a virtuous foil to this company of promise-breakers; he considers himself no less weak than the rest, and thinks that up till now he has merely lacked the opportunity of getting his own advantage from the broker. One does not believe him. It is only the inner modesty of his nature which here overshoots the mark. There are men who make themselves out worse than they are; without any affectation they are the antipodes of the self-righteous and the wise in their own conceit; they are honest judges of human frailty, who take account of the tendencies which determine human life, often too indulgent towards others, but never towards themselves. If anyone has any doubts, let him mark the deep thrilling excitement which takes possession of this strong nature after the death of Arthur, let him hear the passionate curse with which he overwhelms Hubert, the moving confession, [Quotes 4.3.140–1: 'I am amazed. . . .']. The same man who will deliver 'sweet, sweet, sweet poison' for the age's tooth [1.1.213], how differently does he behave in reality, with what rectitude, what disregard of self! He gives his opinion, often indeed rather too loudly, to all, to the cannoneers of Angiers, the Barons, the Legate, the Dauphin, and above all to the luckless Austria. It is quite surprising how his genuine unadorned nature rises in revolt against the strutting heroics of this woman in the lion-skin of Hercules, and how this instinctive antipathy unites itself with his rancour against the murderer of his father. Every desire to spare another's feelings here deserts him; with a real joy he seizes every opportunity to show his hated antagonist how much he despises him. How that famous 'Hang a calf's-skin on his recreant limbs' [3.1.199] sounds like an angry battle-cry of Nature against the paint and the disguises of fashion! So he stands, a sort of Chorus in the restless ebb and flow of parties, a firm support for the complicated texture of the actions of the play.

'And just as the Bastard owes the imposing part which he plays in the piece not to his share in the action, but purely to the power with which his character is drawn, so everything else in the work which lays hold of one and touches one and stirs one's wonder is to be ascribed to the same source – Shakespeare's astounding art in drawing human beings. The awkward, reserved, lumbering Hubert, the tender, soft-hearted boy, the French king, John's warlike mother – how clearly one seizes them all in one's mind! It is not so, however, with all the others. Pembroke, Bigot, Melun, Prince Henry, Blanch, speak Shakespearian lines, but as figures they are not sufficiently sharply defined. Austria, however, is drawn excellently – and on the whole the Dauphin also, who shows himself alike cold and crafty, bold and enterprising.

'The few words which he addresses to his betrothed [2.1.496–503] ring less of the lover than of the man of fashion. They play with an image which is not original. This, however, is English, in the spirit of Elizabeth's time and of Shakespeare's inclination – even when he is not specially thinking of it – to make fun of his characters. In this same *King John* even the dying Melun makes puns. When the Bastard ridicules the Dauphin [2.1.504–9], he is really ridiculing only a fault of his poet's, which the latter, even in his best works after he had attained to the full possession of his poetical powers, never succeeded in completely renouncing. Even the characteristic outlines of the drawing of Constance grow faint in the rich copiousness of her expression. Her eloquent, pathetic words correspond to the mother's disappointed hope and overmastering pain – but they are not distinctly individual. In the loathsome picture in the first scene of the third act ('If thou, that bidst me be content, wert grim' [3.1.43]), in the invocation of Death, 'Thou odoriferous stench! sound rottenness!' [3.4.26], it is rather the poet who speaks than the *dramatis persona*.

'The most glorious part of the play, and at the same time that which is most open to criticism in the matter of poetical expression, is furnished by the Blinding-scene. Whoever has heard the eloquence of breathless anxiety, which feels the ground slipping beneath its feet and seeks wildly for some support for the fainting hands, when everything is poured forth confusedly in a continuous stream of words, such an one knows how true to the very depths is Arthur's touching supplication. Only even here Shakespeare exercises the poet's craft of unfolding thought in poetical language.

'Everything that the boy could press into service in his cry of lamentation takes a concrete form: I did you kindness, I, a Prince, and you wish to blind me! how the eyes smart at the smallest pain! why the eyes? – rather take my tongue! Everywhere the feeling is most genuine. Just as close to nature is it when the boy points out that the fire will not assist the deed, for it has gone out. But it is a trick of the *Poet's* to draw mannered, far-fetched similitudes from the fact of the glowing and cooling of the coal and iron – the breath of heaven has strewn ashes of repentance on the head of the coal; the iron is blushing for shame, and will sparkle in Hubert's eyes like a dog who snatches at his master, – comparisons which, instead of heightening, weaken the effect of the dramatic action. These are vices of style which can only be outweighed by the pithy unadorned intensity of the language in other parts of the play, and by those magnificent soul-revelations – the secret of which is granted only to a born poet – in which the play is so rich.' (xxx–xxxvi)

61 J. Lytelton Etty, the character of John

1901

From 'Studies in Shakespeare's History. V. – KING JOHN', *Macmillan's Magazine*, 84, No. 504 (October 1901), 462–70.

J. Lytelton Etty, of Swindon, Wiltshire, contributed a series of articles to *Macmillan's Magazine* from 1900 to 1904 on the relationship between selected Shakespearian plays on English and Roman history and their actual historical backgrounds. The essay on *King John* is the fifth in a sequence of essays too often neglected by critics. Unlike Courtenay (No. 17 above), who rather pedantically documents Shakespeare's departures from historical fact, Etty regards history as the foundation of aesthetic concerns, particularly Shakespeare's art of characterization.

[Etty sees the period of the early Plantagenet kings as 'an age of great personalities', among them King John, whom he describes as 'morally contemptible' yet endowed with 'tireless energy', 'intellectual alertness', and 'adroit self-helpfulness' (462).]

. . . Wise man or fool, such a character is necessarily of considerable psychological interest and, at first sight, admirably fitted to be the hero in a play written by one who was a great thinker as well as a great dramatist. But a closer study of the man shows pretty clearly that, interesting as his character is from what may almost be called a scientific point of view, he was very little suited to become the hero of a play, nor was his life particularly adapted for dramatic presentment. For though John is a striking figure in history, it is only occasionally that he is an interesting one; his wickedness does not arouse our hatred, nor his fate our pity, while his ingenuity calls forth a cold admiration quite untouched by emotion. There is but little human interest in his life; he knows neither real love nor true friendship; his ambition is merely negative, a dogged determination not to be beaten. And thus he is something alien, something rather remote, less human than Milton's Satan because without his eloquence; and it is chiefly for this reason, I suppose, that Shakespeare's *King John* is among the least admirable of his plays, being both unconvincing and undramatic. One feels in reading the play, and even when seeing it acted, as if the dramatist had striven vainly to make dry bones live, to make the historical King John a real and living figure, and to energise the old drama upon which his play is founded. But the material he had to deal with baffled even his genius, and King John remains a lay-figure in all but a few passages; he is indeed the protagonist only in name,

Faulconbridge being the chief speaker and the characteristic channel of Shakespeare's philosophy.

The play is based on two motives; the most prominent, of which Faulconbridge is the principal exponent, being the virtue of patriotism. The Bastard is typical of that somewhat aggressive loyalty so inherent in the Elizabethans during and after the long struggle with Spain: [Quotes 5.7.112–14: 'This England never did, nor never shall. . . .']. And his patriotism is even more violent earlier in the play when, in braving the Dauphin, he allows his imagination to get the better of him and describes his master, the loser of Normandy, John Sansterre, as [Quotes 5.2.137–45: 'That hand which had the strength, even at your door. . . .]. . . .

But the utterance of that strong national sentiment common in most of Shakespeare's historical plays is not confined to the Bastard alone. King John himself, before he has been forced to his knees, expresses the anti-papal feeling of Shakespeare's time when he refuses to accept Stephen Langton as Archbishop of Canterbury. His language calls to mind both the statutes of Henry the Eighth and the theories of the Stewarts: [Quotes 3.1.147–60: 'What earthy name to interrogatories. . . .'].

But the secondary motive, the study of the character of the king himself, is far more interesting, even if, from a dramatic point of view, it is unsatisfactorily developed. Of course, in order to bring the action of his play within a moderate limit of time, Shakespeare began his story of King John when he was grown up and his character fixed, and, even so, has crowded the events of years into a few months. Had the dramatic presentment been possible, how interesting would it have been to know Shakespeare's conception of John in his youth! What started him on the course which led him to a cynical treachery to his father, his brother, and his subjects? These and other questions might Shakespeare have solved for us, had he chosen to go back beyond the old play upon which he based his work. The youth of John might have been as interesting as that of Henry the Fifth. But, even within the limits which he took for his play, Shakespeare seems to have found the material so difficult to deal with that we can well believe he regarded a trilogy like the two parts of *Henry the Fourth* and *Henry the Fifth* as impossible. . . .

[Etty now briefly explains that John's title was not a very doubtful one, but that the murder of Arthur gave his enemies a pretense for further challenging his claim. The historical John is depicted by Etty as venal, passionate, fatally lacking in patience, and destructively impulsive.]

The tragedy of the rapid disappearance of the Angevin empire seems hardly to have been appreciated by Shakespeare; its loss he regards merely as a testimony to John's incapacity. His indifference is probably due to the fact that it was a purely dynastic, not a national possession and of little interest to the English people. But, further, it is perhaps not too fanciful to suppose that, like most of our historians, he regarded its loss as a national advantage. The severing of the direct connection of England with the continent is in any case mainly responsible for what is called the insularity of the English character; and we may note that in the reign succeeding this the dislike for foreigners was particularly pronounced, exactly as it was in the reign of Elizabeth, when Mary's death without children had just saved England from becoming a province of the Spanish empire. . . .

But, to return to John, the murder of Arthur is the chief point on which Shakespeare's slight sketch of his character rests. We see little of the real man in the war and reconciliation with Philip; that is but an instance of the universal sway of 'That smooth-faced gentleman, tickling Commodity' [2.1.573]. But it is when, in his desire for murder and yet fear to order it (for he already shirks the responsibility), he conveys his wish to Hubert de Burgh in a web of hints and flatteries, talking to drown his own conscience, silencing his horrid fear with words, that we begin to understand Shakespeare's conception of him, the meanness, the cowardice, and the self-consciousness which would make of his own thoughts an audience to be conciliated: 'I had a thing to say, / But I will fit it with some better time' [3.3.25ff.]. And then notice the curious nervousness which makes him break off and feign, with the most feebly transparent pretence of emotion, to be almost overcome by his friendship for Hubert: [Quotes 3.3.27–55: John's speech to Hubert in which he obliquely suggests the murder of Arthur]. Thus he reveals his desire in riddles, and yet in the end is forced to be explicit and utter those words his tongue will scarcely form, 'Death, a grave' [3.3.65ff.].

Shakespeare has taken no greater liberty with history in this play, notorious for its inaccuracies, than in the part which he assigns to Hubert De Burgh, a great baron and a man of noble character, who it is absurd to think could ever have been appointed gaoler and murderer. The scene in which he attempts to blind Arthur is without any historical foundation; some of us may also perhaps consider it a piece of unattractive melodrama unworthy of Shakespeare. But, keeping to Shakespeare's story, although Hubert does not murder Arthur, he is forced to pretend to have done so for fear of the King's wrath, and the poet makes most excellent use of John's reception of the news for the further portrayal of his character. The Earls of Salisbury and Pembroke, suspecting foul play, are begging for Arthur's liberation when Hubert enters to announce his death. . . .

[Here Etty recounts the episode at 4.2.82–241 where John tries unsuccessfully to convince the lords that he is innocent of Arthur's murder and then attempts to shift the blame for the murder to Hubert.]

The tragic episode is complete here, the real inner tragedy of John's life. It matters little now if Arthur be alive or dead, though the news that he yet lives at once restores Hubert to favour. It matters little if John succeed or fail. For morally his failure is now achieved. Hitherto he has been a villain certainly, but he has not lacked a certain grand consistency in his wickedness together with traces of intellectual power. But now in the revelation of his feebleness, of his absolute inability to abide by the result of his actions, John ceases to be in any sense respectable. The attitude in which Shakespeare draws him here tallies with his abject submission to the Pope after defying him for years; neither his submission in the one instance nor his repentance in the other would make him contemptible, were it not for the violence which came first. Audacity can scarcely be reckoned a virtue, but persistent courage even in crime ennobles what it cannot excuse. . . .

[After recounting some of the critical blunders and mishaps of John's reign, Etty describes the king's fatal illness.]

His death was terrible. He had failed in his own objects, and he had injured his country continuously for seventeen years. The tradition of the horror of his death is said to have lasted for many generations, growing more awful doubtless with the years, like the deaths of those who had offended the Church so deeply that the avenging devils were permitted to invade the last moments of their lives. But Shakespeare has softened the grimness of the end by transferring it from Newark to the orchard of Swinstead Abbey, which, as a matter of fact, John left a day or two before his death, and in his story the King is forced to seek a place to die in from the hospitality of the class which he had most oppressed.

It is a very fine scene in which John takes his departure from a world most justly weary of him, standing, together with the scene of the subornation of Hubert for Arthur's murder and that in which the King reviles him for carrying out his desire, far above the level of the rest of the play. In his last moments John acquires that eloquence which Walter Pater noted as 'a gracious prerogative' common to Shakespeare's English kings,[1] but a bitter, ineffective eloquence, characteristic of one who had striven alone for no noble end and had failed. There is a certain tremendous force about him, a huge vitality which prolongs the last struggle, forbidding him to die at peace within the walls of any house. . . .

While far from standing in the front rank of the historical plays, *King John* is interesting from its suggestiveness. Shakespeare's sketch of John's life is in reality of the slightest, but it tempts to endless speculations as to his real character and motives, and the reasons for the completeness of his failure. Such speculations I have already indulged in at sufficient length and recapitulation is unnecessary. I would, however, suggest that the explanation of his curiously disappointing failures and his ultimate ruin lies in the fact that he was after all an incomplete hypocrite. He could plot, deceive, and beguile with the utmost subtlety; he could manufacture complicated schemes for out-witting his enemies with complete patience, – in fact in action his ingenuity was consummate. But of a merely passive hypocrisy he was incapable; his natural impatience had to find a vent in plots and deep designs; when his mind was not so occupied, he was unable to conceal his real nature.

I said in a former paper that the Elizabethan dramatists were frequently fascinated by the study of evil characters, and that in their plays such characters are apt to assume an excessive importance, excessive because absolute wickedness is neither very interesting nor, perhaps, possible. As examples of this tendency I instanced *Titus Andronicus* and *Richard the Third*, and to them KING JOHN may, I think, be added. Both John and Richard were, to quote Pater again, 'spoiled by something of criminal madness.'[2] Richard destroyed himself by piling crime on crime with the fury of a madman; while John, when he might have escaped the reward of his deeds, would not earn impunity by a timely hypocrisy and a patient pretence of virtue. (462–70)

62 Felix Emanuel Schelling, Shakespeare and Davenport

1902

From *The English Chronicle Play. A Study in the Popular Historical Literature Environing Shakespeare* (New York, 1902).

Felix Emanuel Schelling (1858–1945) abandoned the practice of law in 1886 to teach English at the University of Pennsylvania, a position he occupied until his retirement in 1934 as John Welsh Centennial Professor of History and English Literature. A resourceful and powerful academic leader, he changed the face of the Pennsylvania English department by instituting its first doctoral program as well as innovative courses in the modern novel and even American literature. Schelling was a prolific scholar who produced a number of authoritative books on Shakespeare and the Elizabethan dramatists, none more important than his *Elizabethan Drama, 1558–1642* (2 vols, Boston, 1908), one of the landmark studies of its time.

[From Chapter IX: 'Plays on Henry VIII and Later Historical Dramas']

... [John Davenport's] *King John and Matilda* [1624?; published 1655] is a tragedy of genuine merit and exemplifies in its treatment the long step which had been taken by Shakespeare, Fletcher and others from the use of drama to illustrate a succession of historical events to the employment of historical material for the dramatic delineation of human passion. Despite the subtle portraiture of the most ignoble of English kings, the touching story of Prince Arthur and the lyricism of the grief of Constance, Shakespeare's *King John* is a typical chronicle play. The subject-matter concerns the public life of that king, his relation to France, to Rome and to his rebellious barons at home; the sequence of events is chronological. What little unity there is centers in the royal malefactor and in his loyal attendant, 'Cordelions Base sonne,'[1] whose humorous, honest, and clear-sighted view of the wrongs and intricacies about him serves the twofold function of comedy and chorus, and affords at once a contrast to the somber tone of the rest of the play and a normal standard by which to judge among the contending parties. The epic quality of the Chronicle Drama, already so often adverted to, is characteristic of this play of Shakespeare to a remarkable degree. There is substantially no action in the second act, in which the French and English armies meet before the walls of Angiers and bandy taunts, negotiate and parley, while, during the long conversations of other parts of the play, the action halts or is narrated rather than presented on the stage. In *King John and Matilda* all this is changed. It is the character of John as a man, not as a king, which is the central theme; his unlawful pursuit of the steadfast and resourceful Matilda. Davenport does not lose sight of the fact that his protagonist is a king and he presents us with vividness, though only in the background, that portion of the reign of John in which was concentrated England's deepest degradation: the removal of the papal interdict and John's acceptance of his crown at the hands of Cardinal Pandulph as vassal of Rome. In a word, though dealing with historical material, this play is primarily concerned with the portrayal of passion. Without raising any question of comparative literary or poetical excellence – a matter which does not concern us here – Davenport's tragedy is far less epical than Shakespeare's and must be pronounced unhesitatingly more dramatic. (258–60)

63 Richard Green Moulton, the pendulum of history in *King John*

1903

From *The Moral System of Shakespeare. A Popular Illustration of Fiction as the Experimental Side of Philosophy* (New York, 1903).

Richard Green Moulton (1849–1924) was born in Preston, England, graduating from London University in 1869 and Christ College, Cambridge, in 1874. Moulton was always a popular lecturer, an accomplishment that greatly enhanced his reputation upon his arrival in America in 1890 and throughout his academic career at the University of Chicago (1892–1919). At Chicago he became head of the Department of General Literature and Professor of Literary Theory and Interpretation, establishing himself as one of the foremost biblical scholars of his day as well as a respected critic of Shakespeare and the classical drama. Moulton's chief aim as a scholar was to popularize the study of literature as a means toward moral, spiritual, and cultural growth. This he did most effectively in *The Modern Reader's Bible* (21 vols, New York, c.,1895–8), which, like *The Moral System of Shakespeare*, was often reprinted, the latter under the new title *Shakespeare as a Dramatic Thinker*.

[From Chapter XIII: 'The Pendulum of History']

. . . A certain principle of history, simple yet highly impressive, appears dramatically enunciated in the prologue play [*King John*], worked over on the largest scale in the succession of eight historic dramas, and recast with a striking variation in the play which serves as epilogue [*Henry VIII*]. The principle is best expressed in metaphorical language: it is the pendulum swing of events between one and the other of two rival interests; a deep-seated alternation in the natural course of things. Such a principle needs, however, a corollary. If the general movement is to be a pendulum-like alternation, this will be the more impressive dramatically if it is broken at intervals by what appears like a position of rest: not rest in the negative sense, – as if the alternation at that point was merely not perceptible, – but a peculiar, striking, exceptional evenness between things which before and after are seen rising and falling. Or it may be that there is a pause to gather in fresh material, which is itself presently to become the subject of rapid mutation. This then is the nature of the movement I am seeking in this chapter to trace through the succession of historic plays; a persistent swing in the course of history to and fro, broken by parentheses of emphasised rest, or other preparation for fresh alternation.

It is the play of *King John* which serves as prologue for the historic succession. Here we have very clearly marked the two interests between which the movement of the plot is to alternate. England and France are throughout Shakespeare treated as rival countries; the rivalry in the present case is enhanced by a double claim to the English crown; France has backed the cause of young Arthur, while John has his claim supported by the strong argument of possession. Yet other forces are added to both sides, to make the scale more even. Feminine influence is strong for either cause; the passionate young motherhood of Constance is a bulwark for Arthur; the queen mother Elinor brings to John the strength of maturity and political capacity. Again, France has an ally, the Duke of Austria, who appears always in his robe of lion's skin, in token of the proud feat by which he held prisoner the magnificent Cœur-de-lion; naturally he is the enemy of the King who is his prisoner's brother. On the other hand the English army contains Faulconbridge, bastard son of this Cœur-de-lion, whose rude humour loses no opportunity of mocking the lion-like pretensions of Austria, while his rough valour eventually brings the boaster to his doom. Between these evenly balanced interests – England with its allies, France with its allies – the pendulum of fortune is to be seen swinging.[1]

But, as we have seen, the alternation will be the more dramatically impressive if the movement can start in some evenness of poise between the interests that are afterwards to rise and fall. This is secured by the curious incident of Angiers, which occupies the second act of the play. This Angiers is a fortified city in that part of the land of France which at the period of the play was an appanage of the English crown. The French King has begun the war against John by besieging this place; his ally and the French court are with him in the field. And it is here that King John, with his court and his army of invasion, encounters his rival. First, there is a discussion of rights and claims between the two courts, feminine bitterness and rough humour bearing their part in the dialogue. Words proving vain, both armies turn to force, and the city is summoned with blast of trumpet: [Quotes 2.1.201–6; 267–72 and 329–33 and describes the negotiations with the citizens of Angiers]. Nothing could emphasise more dramatically the even poise of the scales in which England and France are being weighed than the possibility of a single city thus defying three potentates and their armies. Faulconbridge catches the situation, and asks why the rival kings let 'these scroyles of Angiers' [2.1.373] flout them, and why they do not unite their forces to level the insolent fort to the ground, and afterwards fight out their own quarrel. The counsel suits the spirit of the times; there is a movement for carrying it into effect, when the citizens feel the peril of their position, and meet the crisis with a proposal of their own. In parley with the kings they point to two youthful figures in the rival courts, the French Dauphin, and Blanch, niece of the English King: [Quotes 2.1.437–40]. In pompous oratory it is suggested that a union of these two persons would heal the breach between two kingdoms and be more powerful than cannon to open the fortress gates. The policy of such a match attracts the elders; youth and beauty work upon the parties concerned; the project gains ground, and articles of treaty are discussed. The evenly balanced conflict has ended in compromise,

Faulconbridge alone catching the humour of the situation: that King John to bar a title to the whole has voluntarily surrendered a part, while the champion of conscience has exchanged a holy war for a vile peace, all through that great bias of the world – Commodity!

Now it is precisely with this proposal from the men of Angiers that the peculiar movement of the play has started from its position of rest. Up to this point, all has gone to emphasise the even balance of the two parties; when this compromise has been accepted, we have the whole power of England, of France, of Austria, concentrated on one side, while on the other side young Arthur is left helpless and alone. It is in vain that they talk to Constance of the blessedness of peace, and declare that the day which has brought it shall be a perpetual holiday: [Quotes 3.1.83–95: Constance's 'A wicked day, and not a holy day. . . .']. The passion of Constance is the precise measure of the degree to which the pendulum of fortune has swung to the side opposed to Arthur. Yet it is in the midst of this scene of bitterness between Arthur's mother and her former allies that a diversion takes place, and, in reality, the sway of movement has begun to turn in an opposite direction.

The diversion has been made by the entrance of the papal legate: on his way to England he has met its king in company with the King of France. In presence of the two monarchs and their courts the legate blurts out certain demands respecting quarrels between the English crown and primate. John is represented in this drama as the mouthpiece of England's antagonism to papal pretensions: [Quotes 3.1.147–8: 'What earthly name. . . .']. When Philip is shocked at resistance to Holy Church, John speaks with more and more of defiance, until the legate thunders excommunication, and King Philip is commanded to loose the hand of an arch-heretic. It had happened that the papal legate entered at the very moment in which the two kings by a ceremonious hand-clasp were signifying their new peace and alliance: round that hand-clasp a great contest now wages – Pandulph against John, Constance against Elinor, Austria against Faulconbridge; the newly pledged lover and his prospective bride take opposite sides. . . . The loosing of this hand-clasp has symbolised a swing of the pendulum from one extreme to the very opposite: a moment before Arthur was alone, and all power massed on the side of John; by this change we see the whole strength of France and Austria transferred to the support of Arthur, with the addition of the spiritual power of Rome and Holy Church, while John must face this vast combination without a single ally.

There is another turning-point, and the pendulum swings back. This time it is by 'the fortune of war': providence is not always on the side of the big battalions, and, though France, Austria, and Rome are all against England, in the actual fight it is England that wins. A roaring tempest shatters the French fleet; their armies are disgracefully defeated in the field; the Duke of Austria is slain in battle by Faulconbridge. This Faulconbridge, as a man not likely to be frightened by bell, book, and candle, is sent to England to seize the wealth of the Church. . . .

[Moulton now briefly traces ensuing events: Arthur's imprisonment, Constance's suffering, and the Dauphin's expression of despair at 3.4.108–9: 'Life is as tedious as a twice-told tale. . . .']

Now, it is just at the close of this speech of the Dauphin that one more turning-point of the plot must be placed; the pendulum of events prepares to swing again from one extreme to the opposite. This time the change comes through that hidden force in things we call 'reaction': the sagacious legate sees how the very completeness of John's good fortune will make him reckless and unscrupulous; something will happen to Arthur, there will be a revulsion of feeling in England against the evil King, and the French prince may claim the crown by virtue of his marriage with Lady Blanch. And events turn out precisely as Pandulph prophesies. The fourth act is filled with dramatic interest of detail, especially with reference to the character of Hubert as a man of mystery, who plays a deeper part than appears on the surface. But the drift of this act in the general plot is to present Arthur dead, the blame of it fixed by the national voice on the King, the French invading in force, and the English nobles – who constitute the military force of the country – deserting in mass to the enemy. John is left helpless, with a hostile people behind him, and in front an enemy already landed on his shores.

An adroit device of a desperate man makes another turning-point, and introduces one more reversal of the scale of fortune. In flat contradiction to his late position as representative of national independence, King John in this extremity surrenders his crown to Rome, and, at the opening of the fifth act, is seen receiving it back as Rome's vassal. Thus one powerful element of the combination against him is not only removed, but transferred to King John's side: [Quotes 5.1.17–21: Pandulph's determination to make the French lay down their arms]. Of course, the invading prince of France resents thus being made a puppet of Roman diplomacy. But meanwhile Faulconbridge, embodying the patriotic spirit which repels invasion under any pretext, has raised a powerful force to confront Lewis. Providence takes the English side, and the French reinforcements are wrecked on the Goodwin sands. More strange still: a dying nobleman of the French army reveals to the English a treacherous plot against the nobles who had deserted to France: [Quotes 5.4.10–20 and 40–3: from Melun's remarks to the English lords]. Thus at this point it is the representative of France who is defeated, deserted, and helpless, and all power has gravitated to the English side.

Yet the course of events dramatised in this play is to see just one more swing of the pendulum. King John, victorious against the French and in the restored allegiance of his nobles, is suddenly conscious that he is doomed never to reap the fruits of victory: [Quotes 5.7.35–41 and 52–6: John's dying scene where the Bastard enters in haste with news of battle]. The news Faulconbridge brings is that the forces he was leading to meet [the] fresh advance of the Dauphin have been overpowered by a flood as the Wash was being crossed. At the shock of this loss the King dies, and the pendulum swing of the plot ceases. It only remains for the papal legate to make peace between the countries, and Henry reigns in his father's stead.

To the modern reader Shakespeare's dramatisation of the reign of King John comes as a surprise. There is not a hint of what we are accustomed to consider as the characteristic of that reign, making it the most critical period of English history; on the other hand, what would seem matter of inferior moment is treated with fine workmanship and dramatic vigour. The explanation is easy, if this play is to stand as prologue to the succession of histories, and if the spirit of history, as conceived by Elizabethan dramatists, consisted in the pendulum-like alternation of fortune. Nowhere else do we find the rival interests so evenly balanced, nor the balance so constantly emphasised; nowhere else do we see such sharp turns in events, and such great mutations realised in such brief intervals. Moreover the whole of this manifold alternation is within the limits of a single play, and centres around the single personality of King John. (270–9)

64 Edmund Kerchever Chambers, the formlessness of *King John*

1906

From *The Life and Death of King John* (London, 1906).

Edmund Kerchever Chambers (1866–1954) combined a career as a civil servant in the Department of Education with a remarkably productive life as a scholar and editor. Chambers published a series of seminal books on the the factual, documentary, social, and literary backgrounds of Shakespeare and early English drama that remain indispensable to this day: *The Medieval Stage* (2 vols, London, 1903); *The Elizabethan Stage* (4 vols, Oxford, 1923); and *William Shakespeare* (2 vols, Oxford, 1930). He was the first president of the Malone Society (1906–39), as well as a frequent contributor to the series of dramatic documents and playtexts published in its *Collections*. Chambers's introduction to *King John*, along with the other introductions to the plays from his 'Red Letter Shakespeare', was reprinted in *Shakespeare: A Survey* (London, 1925).

[From the Introduction]

For the sake of the wild and whirling words of Constance and the boyish pathos of Arthur's struggle against death, it is possible that *King John* may always continue to have its share of devotion from readers of Shakespeare. The sentimentalism of commentators is apt to find in the play a reflection of the natural sorrow of the poet at the death of his own son Hamnet. But the sentimentalist is a dangerous leader in the slippery ways of literary biography. Hamnet Shakespeare died, at between eleven and twelve years of age, in August, 1596, and it is difficult, with due regard to the evidence of style, to suppose that *King John* was not already written some year or two before this date. Moreover, the psychological theory implied is a fantastic one. The grief of Constance rings true enough; but, after all, her hint of woe is common, and it must certainly not be assumed that a dramatist can only convince by reproducing just those emotions which he has seen at play in his own household. It is safest to regard the tragic figure of the weeping mother as based rather upon broad human sympathies than upon personal experience; but whatever its origin, the part of Constance, like that, almost contemporary, of the unkinged Richard the Second, affords an ideal mouthpiece for the flood of splendid emotional declamation, which is one of the finest and most enduring qualities of the Elizabethan stage: [Quotes

3.4.76–89: 'And, father cardinal, I have heard you say. . . .']. This has the authentic thrill in it; but there is much in *King John* which is far away indeed from such fine rhetoric. Rarely, for example, did Shakespeare write anything more frigid than the casuistries of Pandulph, with their baffling and bewildering reliance upon verbal ingenuities: [Quotes 3.1.279–87: 'It is religion that doth make vows kept. . . .'].

But, whatever the merits or demerits of *King John* as regards phrasing and the handling of individual episodes, there can be no doubt that there is hardly any mature play of Shakespeare the total dramatic effect of which is so disappointing. Something of the epic chronicle, it must be admitted, hangs about all the Histories; but for the most part, whatever room may be left for alarums and excursions and other irrelevancies, there is nevertheless some intellectual core, some recognizable attempt to body forth a central idea in dramatic form. But what is the intellectual bearing of *King John*? Plainly it is conceived as a tragedy, but wherein does the tragedy consist? Is John himself the villain or the hero? Are we, as in *Richard the Third*, face to face with the nemesis that waits upon wickedness in high places? And if so, why do many of the scenes, and in particular the closing lines, with their emphasis upon England's dissensions as the cause of England's woes, seem to strike another note, and to point out not John, but those who plot against John, as the workers of the tragic evil? One fears the answer is, that no answer can be given, and that the infirmity of double purpose here suggested is indeed inherent in the backboneless structure of the piece. The explanation of this want of grip and dramatic unity in *King John* is probably to be found in the fact that Shakespeare has put, and perhaps from the conditions under which he worked was only in a position to put, but little of himself into the play. Standing aloof as it does from both of the two great tetralogies into which the bulk of the poet's dramatic comment upon English history was cast, that of York and that of Lancaster, it is hardly more than a bit of hack work. Herein, indeed, it stands upon much the same footing as *Henry the Sixth* itself, in the two latter parts of which, at least, Shakespeare seems to have been but learning his trade by rewriting, scene for scene, the two parts of the older chronicle play known as *The Contention of York and Lancaster*. Quite similarly it is probable that *King John*, from the points of view alike of the actors, of the booksellers, and of the dramatist himself, was not an independent creation, but only a revision of another old chronicle play, still extant under the title of *The Troublesome Raigne of King John*. A comparative reading leaves the relation between the model and the copy clear enough. Obviously Shakespeare has advanced enormously in authority and in manipulative dexterity since he was set to tinker at *The Contention*. So far as the rewriting of the dialogue is concerned he takes a very free hand, and only here and there retains a turn of speech of his predecessor. Moreover he omits many scenes and liberally clips others, with a view to compressing the matter of two performances within the limits of one, and of course the gain in dramatic concentration and vigour is considerable. But when all is said and done, the old play remains the model; and indeed, so far as structure goes, the parallelism is quite complete. Somewhat different value is given to the motives and situations in *King John*, but there is hardly one which *The Troublesome Raigne* did not originally dictate.

The Troublesome Raigne, although not without its merits, belongs wholly to the chronicle history *genre*, and it is not surprising to find that it already displays that invertebracy of purpose of which one is inclined to complain in *King John*. . . . [Chambers now briefly discusses the overt Protestantism and nationalism of the play, attributing these to feelings aroused by the Spanish Armada of 1588. Noting the same qualities in Bale's earlier *Kynge Johan*, he contends that the later playwright lacked Bale's ability to select only those details of plot that specifically served his purpose.]

Shakespeare, as has been said, adopts the full structural outlines of his predecessor, and with them this historic incongruity in the presentment of the principal character which is so destructive of all true dramatic unity. But he alters the distribution of the emphasis, pruning the obsolete Protestantism, and bringing the Arthur theme with its capacities for emotional treatment into the foreground of his design, where it repeats the somewhat melodramatic pattern already made use of in *Richard the Third*. The limitations of the adapter do not, of course, allow this process to be complete. During large tracts of the play John, or the English spirit which John is made to typify, is still conceived in the heroic vein. The theological rancour has in the main disappeared, in spite of the king's defiance of the 'usurped authority' [3.1.160] of the Pope, and his expressed determination – 'that no Italian priest / Shall tithe or toll in our dominions' [3.1.153ff.]. But the note of nationalism is there still, and if the play looks back to *Richard the Third*, it looks forward just as much to *Henry the Fifth*. It contains the first of those glorifications of the island realm which Shakespeare, as often as not, prefers to put in the mouth of a foreigner. It is Austria who vows – [Quotes 2.1.21–30: Austria's expression of allegiance to Arthur that includes praise for England as a secure and confident island nation].

Even so does John of Gaunt himself extol, in *Richard the Second* – [Quotes 2.1.40–9: 'This royal throne of kings. . . .'].

There is an Anglo-Saxon ring, too, in the description of the triumphant evening of battle upon which, as from a day's sport in the chase – 'like a jolly troop of huntsmen, come / Our lusty English, all with purpled hands, / Dyed in the dying slaughter of their foes' [2.1.321ff.]; and in that of the light-hearted gentlemen who cast their fortunes with John's expedition in the eternal spirit of knight-errantry – 'Rash, inconsiderate, fiery voluntaries, / With ladies' faces and fierce dragons' spleens' [2.1.67ff.].

It is perhaps from a consciousness of the ambiguous place which John must necessarily fill in the play, that Shakespeare throws a large share of the burden of his nationalism upon the Bastard. This tall man of his hands, with his blusterous humours and his shrewd mother-wit, is clearly intended to be typical of the stout Anglo-Saxon race. He has the blood of her kings, even though it came to him a little o'er the hatch, and the very spirit of Plantagenet, and in his large composition there are tokens of the greatest of her heroes, Richard Cœur-de-lion himself. So he stands for England throughout. The sins of his king do not, as in the case of some greater nobles, turn him from loyalty to his country. It is he who throws down the glove of undying defiance to the foreign invader, and as the curtain falls voices the watch-word of England's peace – [5.7.112–18: 'This England never did, nor never shall. . . .'].

But in a drama faults of structure are irreparable, even by a Shakespeare; and neither Constance nor the Bastard can really redeem the incoherent patchwork from ineffectiveness. (5–14)

65 George Pierce Baker, Shakespeare's dramatic development

1907

From *The Development of Shakespeare as a Dramatist* (New York, 1907).

George Pierce Baker (1866–1935) graduated from Harvard in 1887 and became an instructor in English there the following year. Although he both wrote and edited several books on drama, Baker was perhaps best known for 'English 47', his pioneering course at Harvard on playwriting, the first of its type in an American university. Among his students were Eugene O'Neill, Sidney Howard, and George Abbott, as well as scores of other playwrights and pedagogues who profited from his instruction either at Harvard, or later at Yale, where Baker went in 1925 to establish a department of drama. He retired from Yale in 1933, widely regarded as one of the most respected and influential figures of the contemporary American theatre.

[From Chapter IV: 'The Chronicle Plays']

. . . In *King John*, though Shakespeare gains decidedly in dramatic skill, some of the old weaknesses persist. Again we face in John a weakling who can only slightly command our sympathy and whose death is far less touching than it would be had he in the earlier scenes been of larger mould. There can be no question that Faulconbridge is the strength of the play as a play. As any reader knows who has compared Shakespeare's *John* with the earlier play in two parts, from which he skillfully condensed it, *The Troublesome Raigne of King John*, and with the historical material in Holinshed,[1] Faulconbridge is Shakespeare's creation from vague and inadequate suggestions. But it is not merely the courage, resourcefulness, and wit of Faulconbridge, – in a word his characterization – which make him memorable: it is he who passes straight through the play, carrying our sympathies and affection with him and giving to it a kind of unity. But he cannot give it that essential unity which would come from a compelling central figure indispensable to all the important scenes, without whom the play could have no being.

Particularly noticeable is the development of the comic in this play. Part I of *Henry VI* showed only touches, and those coarse; Part III lacked it; and in Part II Cade's followers provided comic relief. *Richard II* lacks it, and in *Richard III* its place is taken by the sardonic irony of the king himself. In *Henry V*, as it stands, the comic alternates with the graver scenes. Thus far, then, the really comic has come almost entirely, if present at all, from people not closely involved with the main plot. In *King John* it is Faulconbridge himself, an important person in nearly all the main scenes, who brings the comic relief. This recognition that the comic is desirable for contrast and that it may relax tense emotion till a hearer may again be wrought upon with effect, Shakespeare, in part, owes the author of *The Troublesome Raigne*; but a few years later in *The Merchant of Venice* he will show us in the trial scene that the comic and the tragic depend not upon the person who is looked at, but [upon] the sympathies of the person who looks at him.

Growing maturity is seen also in *King John* in the scene of Arthur and Hubert, by the subordination of mere physical horror to working upon us through sympathies with the lad himself. There are, too, repeated instances which show increasing sureness of theatrical knowledge. In the original of the Hubert-Arthur scene, the murderers enter shortly after Hubert begins to speak with the lad and seize upon the boy. Shakespeare holds them back till just as Hubert is beginning to yield. Their coming fills an audience with dread lest it strengthen Hubert's weakening purpose. Our eager watching of Hubert relaxes only when he orders out the murderers, for then we know that he will yield. In the first chapter I pointed out that the earlier dramatists seem not to have understood how to make an entrance or an exit dramatically effective. Here Shakespeare proves that he knows how to make both significant for their scene. In this play, too, Shakespeare shows marked alertness to motivate the details of his story; for example, when Philip breaks his bond with John. In the original Philip breaks it promptly and with no conscience; in Shakespeare he yields only after appeals to him from all his friends and followers. This care for motivation in characters other than the title part is noteworthy because unusual in the preceding work both of Shakespeare and his contemporaries. In brief, *King John*, except in not providing for the title part a person who holds us to the end thoroughly sympathetic or fascinated by his evil doing, and in the momentary abeyance of rich poetic expression, shows dramatic gain by Shakespeare. (154–6)

66 Henry Charles Beeching, on the religion of Shakespeare

1907

From 'The Religion of Shakespeare', in *The Works of William Shakespeare in Ten Volumes*, edited by A. H. Bullen, (10 vols, Stratford-on-Avon, 1904–7), X, 335–49.

Henry Charles Beeching (1859–1919), Dean of Norwich, poet, essayist, and literary scholar, was respected both as a churchman and as a man of letters. He published several books of poetry, the best known being *In a Garden and Other Poems* (London, 1895). Beeching was also an active editor of literary texts, producing *The Poetical Works of John Milton* (Oxford, 1900), *George Herbert's Country Parson* (Oxford, 1898), and *A Selection from the Poetry of Samuel Daniel and Michael Drayton* (London, 1899) among others. He had a considerable reputation as a witty, precise, and learned orator and literary critic, often contributing essays and introductions to a number of books and periodicals, as he did in the present instance for the so-called 'Stratford Town Edition' of Shakespeare's works.

[Beeching's essay consists of a brief but systematic refutation of the views of Thomas Carter[1] and of Henry Sebastian Bowden (No. 57 above). Carter undertook to demonstrate that Shakespeare was a sincere Puritan, while Bowden maintained that he was a conscientious Roman Catholic. Near the end of his essay Beeching addresses questions raised by Bowden that are pertinent to *King John*.]

. . . A somewhat more substantial case is made out by Mr. Bowden for Shakespeare's alleged sympathy with Rome, from the changes he introduced in re-casting the old play of *King John*. Shakespeare omits all the ribald abuse of monks and nuns, which is a prominent feature of the earlier play; he omits also such fine Tudor sentiments as this: 'As I am king so will I reign next unto God, Supreme Head both over spiritual and temporal; and he that contradicts me in them, I will make him hop headless' [3.79–82]. But while Shakespeare undoubtedly refuses to make of his play a mere Protestant tract, can it be said that he reveals in it any sympathy with the papal cause? If the character of the legate Pandulph is made less of a caricature, is it made any more attractive? Prof. Herford [No. 58 above] seems to hit the mark exactly when he says of the two plays: 'The earlier dramatist treats the crafty legate with malignant hatred, as a curse happily evaded; the latter manages him with fine irony as the wielder of an imposing but not really formidable authority, easily rendered innocuous, incapable of injuring a people true to themselves.' Shakespeare had enough respect for historical verisimilitude not to antedate by some three centuries the English breach with Rome, and not to represent any of the English nobles, even Faulconbridge, as disrespectful to a Cardinal legate. But is it credible that any Roman Catholic dramatist would have allowed Pandulph to play so ignominious a part as Shakespeare has assigned him? After John has made his submission, Pandulph says: – [Quotes 5.1.17–24: 'It was my breath that blew this tempest up. . . .']. But the next scene shows him quite powerless to fulfil his boast. Earlier in the play we have John's defiance of the Pope, which contains the lines – 'And from the mouth of England / Add this much more, – that no Italian priest / Shall tithe or toll in our dominions' [3.1.152ff.]; and following on this the solemn excommunication: – [Quotes 3.1.172–9]. As to the second of these passages Mr. Bowden urges that it represents the poet's own feelings toward Elizabeth; in which case it must be reckoned a very undramatic expression of them, for the speech would have aroused no sympathy in the audience, who still had occasion to remember Pius V.'s bull of deposition. But there is no evidence at all that Shakespeare detested the Queen, while Sonnet 124 ['If my dear love were but the child of state'] is evidence that he detested the ultramontane policy. The first passage Mr. Bowden considers a concession to Protestant sentiment, prompted by the dramatist's concern for his own safety. But in that case, one asks why he should have meddled with the subject of King John at all, which obliged him to please his audience by affronting his own conscience. Alternatively, Mr. Bowden argues that as King John was a villain, he must not be held to express the sentiments of the dramatist. But Shakespeare is always careful to make it plain to the audience when he does not agree with his villains. Has the audience any doubt as to the dramatist's opinion about John's treatment of Arthur? Hubert's conduct and the barons' revolt are commentary enough. But when John defies Pandulph, he does so 'from the mouth of England' [3.1.152], and no English voice is roused in protest at the time or afterwards. These are very elementary considerations; but Mr. Bowden's special pleading recognises no principles of criticism, even the most elementary. (346–7)

67 Richard Garnett, introduction to *King John*

1907

From *The Complete Works of William Shakespeare with Annotations and a General Introduction by Sidney Lee* (40 vols, London, 1906–9). Volume XXII. *The Life and Death of King John with a Special Introduction by Richard Garnett and an Original Frontpiece by W. H. Margetson* (1907).

Richard Garnett (1835–1906), keeper of printed books at the British Museum, was also an accomplished linguist and literary scholar. Although Garnett was a poet of some note, it was as an editor, critic, and later as a writer of fiction that he made his literary reputation. He wrote essays for numerous periodicals on various aspects of continental and English literature, biographies of historical and literary figures, and many introductions for popular reprints of standard authors. His best known works are the *Relics of Shelley* (London, 1862), a collection of Shelley's previously unpublished verse, and *The Twilight of the Gods* (London, 1888), a series of moral fables that established Garnett as a recognized writer of fiction. Lee's edition of Shakespeare, with introductions to the plays and poems by various hands, was often reprinted in England and America as either 'The Renaissance Edition', 'The Harper Edition', or 'The University Press Shakespeare'.

[From the Introduction]

[Garnett endorses Schlegel's view [No. 6 above] of the histories as comprising a national epic in dramatic form, with *King John* as a sort of prologue to the group, even though this structure may not have originally been envisioned by Shakespeare when he began the plays.]

 . . . *King John* may nevertheless be regarded as in some measure a prologue, not merely or chiefly because the action precedes that of the other plays in order of time, but because it embodies in the most concentrated form the patriotic idea by which the entire series is animated.

Not more than seven or eight of Shakespeare's plays betray a direct purpose, and whenever this purpose exists it has reference to public affairs. We have seen the drift of *King Henry V* and *King Henry VIII*. The purpose of *King John* is much more profound. The play is a veiled exhibition of Queen Elizabeth's conflict with the Pope and the Spaniard, and its moral is the impotence of the foreign foe but for domestic treason. . . .

[Garnett now discusses the relationship of *King John* to *The Troublesome Raigne*, the latter of which contains 'the rudiments of excellence' (xii).]

. . . If Shakespeare had followed the example of his predecessor in placing some effective speeches and soliloquies in the mouth of the stricken king, he would have dignified the latter part of his piece, which is animated indeed, but not so overwhelmingly tragical as he might easily have made it. Perhaps he wrote in haste: perhaps he shrank from carrying the humiliation of the Crown too far in a drama where the Crown represented the nation. He has taken another way of reconciling us as far as may be to his ignoble hero by depicting him as the object of the unswerving loyalty of the personage who morally, as John officially, represents the Englishman. The character of Faulconbridge, which seems to be founded upon a tradition of that unscrupulous soldier of fortune, Faukes de Breauté, a man of might in the days of John, and of extraction sufficiently obscure to pass for illegitimate, belongs substantially to the old dramatist; but while he has only thought of enlivening his action by the introduction of a semi-comic personage, Shakespeare has framed an Englishman so representative of his country in strength and weakness that we must accept his verdict on John as the verdict of the nation. With signal tact, having once established Faulconbridge's lineage, he forbears to remind us that Faulconbridge is John's half-brother, and consequently bound to him by even stronger ties than personal loyalty and zeal for the public welfare. To give more weight to Faulconbridge's action, he has considerably toned down the humorous element in the character as he received it from his predecessor, and in one or two soliloquies has introduced a vein of sardonic criticism on the world's ways, sufficient to show that the speaker is a man of sense and reflection, and not a mere soldier. When upon the death of John such a man exclaims: – [Quotes 5.7.70–3: 'Art thou gone so? . . .'] we feel that a verdict has been rendered which may surprise but which cannot be ignored. England is speaking by the mouth of this most representative Englishman, and absolves her guilty and ill-starred king.

The redemption of John consists in the fact that he, too, is a representative of England. He is even more: he is the prototype of Elizabeth as regards the political situation with which he is grappling, though by no means as regards personal character, and is performing the part ingloriously which she would have performed gloriously. Shakespeare takes the first opportunity of showing that John is his hero, not in virtue of any pretension of his own to the heroic character, but in his official capacity as guardian of the independence of the realm. Scarcely has he appealed to 'our strong possession and our right' [1.1.39] when his shrewd old mother whispers: – 'Your strong possession much more than your right, / Or else it must go wrong with you and me' [1.1.40ff.].

How superior seems his competitor, Arthur, who has not only right but youthful innocence and every amiable quality! But Arthur has a fatal disqualification: he is the tool of the foreigner, and can only hope to succeed by foreign arms. . . .

. . . John, however sorry a personage, represents national independence, and, granted that there may be defects in his title, has a moral claim to the allegiance of the country. Shakespeare has also taken the most favourable view of John's character of which circumstances admitted, overlooking the historians' charges of ferocity, rapacity, and lust. These he could well afford to disregard as not essential to his main action, while his view of such of John's private failings as affected his public character is probably correct. John's chief fault, unkingly as it is, is not so much a vice as an infirmity. It is an excessive timorousness. Under the pressure of fear he commits or rather designs villainous actions without being absolutely a villain. Nor is his the fear that trembles at its own shadow. He is not daunted by the mere threats of his adversaries, nor does his defiance of them evaporate in mere words. Until actually defeated he bears himself proudly and well; but when he is once driven into a perilous strait his quick intelligence shows him the situation, and he is incapable of meeting it in a manly spirit. His sole idea is to disarm the imminent peril, and for this end no manoeuvre is too base. He is not devoid of compassion for Arthur or of shame at the temporary resignation of his crown, but concern for his own safety overbalances both. Shakespeare has done the best possible for him by putting some of the finest poetry of the play into his mouth, especially when circumstances make him the mouthpiece of England: – [Quotes 3.1.153–60: 'No Italian priest / Shall tithe or toll in our dominions. . . .'].

Every auditor knew that this was the position Elizabeth had taken up and was still maintaining, and must have felt that the play's centre of gravity lay there, and that in comparison with it the fate of Arthur, however tragic and pathetic, was but a subordinate detail. Shakespeare has further mitigated John's humiliation by passing over everything relating to Magna Charta, and ascribing the barons' revolt to horror at a crime imputed to him, of which, though in intention guilty, he was in act innocent. Our sympathies run counter to those who support a foreign invader on an imaginary ground, and whatever is lost by the barons is gained by John. It is true that the exhibition of Magna Charta on the stage would not have been suffered by the government in Shakespeare's time; but even if this obstacle had not existed Shakespeare would probably have omitted it on dramatic grounds.

Faulconbridge is not merely the faithful follower who throws the shield of his loyalty over John, but also his complement, who fills up the measure of what is lacking in him. Could John's official and Faulconbridge's personal character be united in the same individual, England would have a perfect representative. As a type of his country, he is made to participate in the most characteristic national faults; he is boisterous, aggressive, and contemptuous of the feelings of others. His animosity to Austria is explained by the Austrian duke's behaviour to his father, strangely exaggerated by the assertion (a legacy from the old play) put into the king of France's mouth that Austria has been accessory to Cœur-de-lion's death. The mixture of truculence and joviality gives a slightly comic tint to the character, and tends to relieve the general gloom of a tragedy full of 'treasons, stratagems, and spoils' [*The Merchant of Venice*, 5.1.85]. The importance of Faulconbridge's part justifies in some measure what appears an artistic fault, the inordinate proportion of the first act devoted to his affairs, which have no connection with the main business of the play. The fault, for such it must be deemed, is partly due to Shakespeare's refined delicacy. The author of the old play saves space by bringing Lady Faulconbridge on the stage while the dispute as to her son's legitimacy is being agitated. Shakespeare, comprehending the awkwardness of the situation, introduces her in a subsequent scene, which mitigates her embarrassment, but prolongs the action.

Faulconbridge thus performs for his master a service somewhat akin to that which Siegfried renders to King Gunther in the *Nibelungen Lied*. John takes lustre from his follower, and appears a less unworthy forerunner of the great conflict of Elizabeth's times. He is further helped by a daring sacrifice of historical to poetical truth. Arthur is represented as laying claim to the Crown of England. This he never did. His pretensions were limited to the French duchies, but so restricted a stage would not have fitted the great contest of Elizabeth with Rome and Spain, which was never to be out of the mind of dramatist or spectator. Shakespeare has again deviated from historical truth for a most obvious reason, in making Arthur little more than a child instead of the adolescent that he really was. But for this the heart-breaking scene with Hubert would lose most of its pathos, which depends less upon the atrocity of the crime than the helplessness of the victim. It is remarkable that the idea of blinding the young prince must have been an after-thought, and that Shakespeare has not been at the trouble to make it consistent with what precedes and follows. John's hints to Hubert, that his nephew must disappear, foreshadow his death; there is no suggestion of his being blinded. When, however, Hubert visits Arthur in prison he presents a warrant for blinding, not killing him; but in the subsequent scene the warrant is for Arthur's death, and John has evidently no idea that his nephew's eyes have been in jeopardy, or that his life has not been taken.

The blinding is borrowed from the old play, and the absence of all endeavour to reconcile the two versions argues that Shakespeare's drama must have been composed in great haste. This is not wholly disadvantageous; if on the one hand some situations are worked out less thoroughly than might have been expected, on the other the language is brilliantly energetic and rapid. . . .

The principal fault of *King John*, viewed as poetry, is an occasional employment of conceits below the dignity of tragedy, which unfortunately insinuate themselves into the finest scenes where simplicity and severity are most called for. In the unutterably pathetic scene just adverted to, the beautiful thought that the iron with which Hubert would brand Arthur's eyes had grown cold, as though the senseless metal refused to be his accomplice, is followed by a number of pretty quaint ingenuities entirely out of keeping with tragic emotion. The distraught Constance calls death *an odoriferous stench* [3.4.26], and follows this up with a tirade that can only be described as a choice specimen of the genus of the forcible feeble. It must be acknowledged that she soon recovers herself, and Shakespeare has seldom reached a greater height of impassioned eloquence than in the thrilling scorn of some of her outbursts and the heart-rending pathos of others. The tragedy queen is a very human personage, and at bottom such as may be encountered in any order of society. With all her grandeur, Constance, in the light in which she is here displayed, is just such a mother as nine-tenths of the mothers of the world. She is not ambitious for herself, all her ambition is concentrated upon her idolised boy; she would not have shown half the emotion for a daughter. The idea that her Arthur should lose an atom of his right is insufferable to her; rather than endure it she will drench kingdoms in blood; and when the wrong is sanctioned by her own friends, her indignation becomes absolute frenzy. It is inconceivable to her that there can be two opinions on the question, or that anything should for a moment be put into competition with the redress of her son's wrongs: – [Quotes 3.1.101–11: 'You are forsworn, forsworn. . . .'].

The shrewishness of Constance in the early scenes is equally in keeping, she is living throughout at a white heat of passionate excitement. She could not bear any strain of conflict indefinitely, but she cannot bear failure, and when her cause is lost she vanishes in death like a lamp deprived of air. The effect of her vehemence is heightened by the contrast with Arthur, the model of gentle innocence. The pathos of the scene where the poor boy, rent and torn among the fierce people about him, exclaims [Quotes 2.1.163–5: 'Good my mother peace. . . .'] is fully as great as that of Constance's famous reply to the not unreasonable admonition of the cold-hearted and worldly King Philip, 'You are as fond of grief as of your child' [3.4.92]: – [Quotes 3.4.93–100: 'Grief fills the room up of my absent child. . . .'].

Constance clearly does herself great injustice when she declares that she could not have loved her son if he had been 'Lame, foolish, crooked, swart, prodigious' [3.1.46]. The maternal instinct would have overcome all such trifling drawbacks, and she would have thought no more of them than the sage and temperate Queen Elinor thinks of the moral deformities of *her* son.

Constance, though a real historical character, is dramatically Shakespeare's creation. Pandulph, the Papal Nuncio, is an historical character in every point of view; or rather, in the absence of direct information respecting him, Shakespeare has been careful to paint him in colours beseeming his function. He appears as the incarnation of Roman arrogance in his assertion of Papal authority, and of Roman unscrupulousness in his readiness to annul every moral obligation inconvenient to the Holy See. With such a sanction, perjury and slaughter become virtues, and there is no moral fibre in Pandulph's character to render such teaching in any way difficult to him. Intellectually he is far superior to any of the people with whom he comes into contact. 'How green you are, and fresh in this old world!' [3.4.145] he says pityingly to the young Dauphin, when the latter laments the captivity of Arthur, which at first sight naturally appears a disaster. But Pandulph has fathomed John's nature, and foresees that his victory will prove his ruin: ''Tis strange to think how much King John hath lost / In this which he accounts so clearly won' [3.4.121ff.]. Pandulph's Italian craft is nevertheless unable to control fiercer and more impulsive natures, and he is left pleading for liberty to speak, which he does not obtain. Although the denunciation of Papal interference in English affairs is the salt and soul of the drama, it has necessarily had the bad effect of excluding one great and noble contemporary figure from Shakespeare's canvas. The introduction of Magna Charta was, as we have seen, impossible in Shakespeare's day, but Stephen Langton, the patriotic Archbishop, and no friend of the Nuncio's, might well have been represented as bringing about the barons' submission to the King, and we should thus have got rid of the offensive and incredible incident of the revelation of the Dauphin's plot to destroy his own English partisans. Shakespeare took this from the old play, where it occupies two scenes: he has shown his usual judgment by reducing these to one, but it is to be wished that he could have banished the awkward contrivance altogether. To have represented a Romish ecclesiastic in a favourable light, nevertheless, would have been to undo with one hand what he had throughout been doing with the other. The poetry and passion of King John will not be surpassed, but there is room for a rehandling of the subject in the calmer atmosphere and with the more ample knowledge of the twentieth century. Pandulph's character, nevertheless, would have to remain as Shakespeare left it, as striking a contrast to Faulconbridge's as the outward man must have been in costume, bearing, and complexion. . . .

This mailed tragedy stands to Shakespeare's other plays of English history in the relation of a prologue, not merely as first in order of period, but as depicting a rudimentary condition of English society. It is Shakespeare's one purely mediæval play, for by Henry IV's time a modern element has come in, and Richard II[1] is rather a study of character than a delineation of contemporary manners. *King John*, on the other hand, gives 'the very form and pressure of the time' [*Hamlet*, 3.2.24]. It is therefore distinguished by the overwhelming force of the passions represented, and also by their simplicity. Every leading character has a single object, which he pursues with no more deviation than the stress of circumstances demands. John would save his crown and Faulconbridge his country; Constance would vindicate her son's rights and Pandulph would subjugate England to the Pope. There is no complication of motives, no hesitation or qualification; passion is primitive, simple, and Titanic. The language is consequently high pitched throughout, but without exaggeration. Everything is on the grand scale, as it ought to be when the interlocutors are kings, queens, princesses, nobles, and cardinals, and there is hardly a person of humble birth or low calling in the piece. The existence of the commonality is not, indeed, unrecognised. The sturdy citizens of Angiers stand up stoutly for themselves against two kings: Pandulph threatens John with the loss of his subjects' hearts, and Hubert reports their discontent in a passage of unsurpassed graphic force: – [Quotes 4.2.187–200: 'Young Arthur's death is common in their mouths. . . .'].

But even this speech shows the speaker's disdain for the common people, except in so far as they may be dangerous, and they hardly appear except as a force in the background. The land is as yet the property of kings and nobles, and the atmosphere of the play is entirely oligarchic. Yet, different as are the conditions from those of his own day, Shakespeare thoroughly carries out his great purpose of admonishing his contemporaries what may become of them if they give place to civil discord. Absorbed in this chief design, he slights every minor attraction. There is no comedy in *King John*, no music, no love-making, no by-play or under-plot to divert attention from the serious action; save for the sallies of the Bastard, there is even no humour. It relies upon its political significance, more apparent to contemporaries than to posterity, upon mediæval picturesqueness and a martial spirit that stirs the blood throughout, upon splendid language and scenes of intense pathos. The brilliant picture of the mediæval world is not morally attractive, and the hard facts of history jar with poetical justice, which is nevertheless vindicated in the end. The plotters and schemers are eventually baffled; the blunt honesty of Faulconbridge gains its desire in the restoration of national concord and independence; and though Arthur is in his grave, another innocent boy [Prince Henry] arises in his place. . . . (x–xxviii)

68 Ivor Bertram John, *King John* and *Richard II*

1907

From *The Life and Death of King John* (London, 1907).

Ivor Bertram John (1875–) produced two editions of Shakespearian plays for the old 'Arden Shakespeare': *King John* and *Richard II* (London, 1912). In addition, he edited *The Mabinogion* (London, 1901), *Macaulay's Lives of Goldsmith and Johnson* (London, 1904), *Macaulay's Lives of Bunyan and Goldsmith* (London, 1914), and a pamphlet on *University Training for Elementary Teachers* (London, 1907).

[From the Introduction]

[John begins his Introduction with an extensive comparison of *King John* and *The Troublesome Raigne*, relating both plays to the historical accounts that lie behind them and the actual amount of historical time they represent (about four months). He then moves on to his critical remarks.]

. . . First of all, it is quite clear that we are dealing with 'early Shakespeare.' Apart from a certain want of definite continuity throughout the play — which in itself might very well be put down to the close following of the older version — we find the 'clenches,' the lengthy speeches, the antithetical answers, the absence of prose, and the more inelastic verse characteristic of Shakespeare's earlier manner. The minute analysis of this last point — verse — the formidable array of perhaps rather too mechanical 'double-ending,' 'light-ending,' and 'broken-line' tests, together with the 'rhyme-test,' lead us to the same conclusion. Professor Herford in his Introduction to the Warwick edition of *Richard II*. [London, 1893] thus tabulates the results of these tests: — [Here John reprints Herford's table giving the percentages of each of the above quoted categories in selected Shakespearian plays, among them *Richard II* and *King John*].

These percentages in the first two cases do not enlighten us much, but we notice that in the last two [i.e., 'light-endings' and 'broken lines'], which are generally supposed to be the more trustworthy, *King John* shares with *Richard II*. the middle place in the series, and on general grounds (following what we might call the 'feeling' test) *Richard II*. and *King John* seem to be grouped together. Authorities unanimous in dating *Richard II*. about 1593–4 are now equally unanimous in dating *John* either immediately before or immediately after *Richard*; we have therefore to choose between a date nearer to 1593 and a date nearer to 1595. Nothing can guide us in our choice except a comparison of the plays in the hope of discovering signs of greater maturity in the treatment of one or the other. But even here we are handicapped; firstly, by the fact that Shakespeare deliberately chose to keep close to his 'source' in so many respects, and therefore did not allow his own genius full play, and secondly, by the fact that, in any case, the plays were written within a very short time of one another. Comparison of the methods and characteristics of the two plays yields the following results: there is a greater consistency and unity in the treatment of Richard's character. He is, all through, the weak, sentimental *poseur*, whose weakness we pity, and whose poses we despise; but we sympsthise with him in his misfortunes because they are brought about not by crime but by incompetence, not by deliberate malice but as a result of sentimental impotence. On the other hand, John is at one and the same time the swift and resolute warrior leaping fearlessly upon his enemy, the champion of his country against Papal aggression, and the vacillating coward far worse than the murderer of Arthur, toadying to Pandulph and detracting from our sympathy with his awful death by the childishness of his unkingly lamentations. John is neither the hero nor the villain of the piece but an unpleasant mixture of both.

Again, the characters in *Richard* appear to be drawn by a hand at once firmer and more subtle.

We get to know Bolingbroke gradually and surely as the play progresses, every action and almost every word add little by little to our conception of his character, and that conception is only completed with the last scene of the last Act. There is no parallel to this in *King John*. We know Faulconbridge as well at the end of the first scene as we do when we close the book. It may be said that every scene is a new revelation of John's character. Granting that, we still find that the revelation is not consistent, natural and inevitable as it is in the case of Bolingbroke. These arguments and others of a similar kind that might be adduced make for the later date of *Richard*.

As opposed to that view it may be held that the mixture of tragedy and comedy in the play brought about by Shakespeare's treatment of the character of the Bastard is a sign of more mature work; besides, the continual and fatiguing drop into rhyme in the earlier part of *Richard* and the uncalled-for puns and conceits in unwelcome places also seem to indicate that *Richard* was earlier than *John*. . . .

A comparison between two similar passages, *King John*, II.i.23 *et seq*. and *Richard II.*, II.i.40 *et seq*. [Austria's short digression in praise of England and Gaunt's longer speech on the same subject], may give a slight hint as to their order. Shakespeare never goes back, and in such cases the more elaborate and fuller passage is always the later. In this case the *Richard* passage is far more fully developed than that in *John*; this seems therefore to make for the later date of *Richard*.

The definite truth, however, 'by our best eyes cannot be censured' [2.1.328], and we must therefore candidly date *John* with a hyphen, 1593–5.

. . . It is true that the play has its defects. We have already partly mentioned the greatest of these, – it has no real 'hero.' John ought to be the hero. He is 'cast' for it, but cannot play the part. Faulconbridge, although prominent, is not quite prominent enough, and, as the provider of continual 'comic relief,' is not dignified enough. Arthur, in order that the pathos of his situation may be more fully developed

– in the scene with Hubert it is absolutely essential that Arthur should be an innocent child – is kept too young, and dies too soon. This want of a commanding central figure gives a certain regrettable looseness of structure to the play. The minor faults of construction we have already noticed, and with them we are at the end of our fault-finding.

When we come to ask what are the strong points of the play, we do not know whether to admire most that breathing of life into the clay figures of the *Raigne*, which stirred into being men and women worthy to take their places in the front ranks of Shakespeare's wondrous array of human creations; or that exhibition of supreme mastery of all the detail of stage-craft to be found in every rejection, acceptation or alteration of the arrangement of the original. Probably the best way to appreciate these things would be to read both plays together, scene for scene and speech for speech; we can hardly illustrate them within the limits of an Introduction. But, apart from comparison, it is quite easy to recognise the touch of genius in the presentation of the character of that 'hardy wild head, tough and venturous' [2.70] as the *Raigne* calls him, – the Bastard; in the revelation of the depths of Constance's love and grief; in the pathetic and innocent pleadings of Arthur for his eyes; and, indeed, in the glib sophistry of Pandulph. (xxix–xxxiv)

69 Charlotte Endymion Porter, the belittling of John

1910

From *The Life and Death of King John* (New York, 1910).

Charlotte Endymion Porter (1857–1942), along with her friend and lifelong companion Helen Archibald Clarke, engaged in a number of literary pursuits, among them the so-called 'First Folio Edition' of Shakespeare (40 vols, New York, 1903–12). Porter was the sole editor of the *King John* volume for this edition, but Clarke collaborated with her on several other volumes in the series. Porter and Clarke were the co-founders of the Browning Society of Philadelphia, and later founded *Poet Lore* magazine in 1889 as a scholarly outlet for their mutual interest in Shakespeare, Browning, and comparative literature. Both became prominent in the growing Browning industry that flourished around the turn of the century, publishing numerous editions of both Elizabeth Barrett and Robert Browning in addition to their ongoing work on Shakespeare and their constant efforts, reflected in the pages of *Poet Lore*, to familiarize American readers with European literature.

[From the Introduction]

Richard Coeur de Lion's unacknowledged and throneless son, Richard Faulconbridge, stands out above the stature of King John in Shakespeare's Play.
    These two Richards are in fact the true kings of the story, in the poetic sense of that word – 'kings.' One of them is alive solely in his fame; yet he lays his mark on the Play by his deep personal effect on his survivors. The other is the only living perpetuator of his heroic mould and hearty directness. Together they count as an obvious source of stout muscle and honest brain to make the nominal king look unexecutive and double-minded. And that cross-reflection upon John's personality Shakespeare must have known and meant.
    The shuffling characteristics of John's career, alternately wilful and paltering, appear so strikingly as they do in this *Life and Death of King John*, partly on account of that cleverly devised background of character-contrast with the famous hero and his obscure illegitimate son. Their straightforward traits contribute very artfully to make John's portrait the clearer.
    Faulconbridge, the unfamed commoner, is really John's right arm and sole true strength. John's left arm proves to be Hubert; his lurking humaneness and disobedience of his Master was a sort of abortive good Providence. Both men, mark you! are

virtually creations of Shakespeare. Faulconbridge is made more independently strong in his devotion to John, than in *The Troublesome Raigne*, and Hubert more exclusively a creature of John's favor. Yet he dares to be humane. Both are emphasized and set in high relief. They are fitted thus to modify and divide the prominence of John. John, himself, moreover, is depressed below his level in *The Troublesome Raigne*. This must be because John is not intended to be the hero of Shakespeare's History, but its dupe. Otherwise, opposite relative arrangement would have been made.

By means of this doughty English challenger, and this merciful French supporter of John's prerogatives, on the one side; and by means, on the other, of the unusually individualized group of masterful peers, who censure John and revolt from him while he clumsily seeks to propitiate them, the peculiarly scattering quality of the interest of this Play is wrought out. This quality is the characterizing color through which the history employed in this Drama is presented to the eye. In this dramatic ground-color the whole action is deeply dyed. If we do not discern this color and its fitness to the design, we miss the clew to Shakespeare's summary of John and his time. . . .

If interest neither centres in John nor holds in any sense along with him against the ups and down[s] of his fortunes, the result is, still, to characterize John. By that very negation of the interest at first aroused in him at the opening of the Play, the confusion of John's fate in the sequel is made manifest. Even at first, the supreme royalty of nature in Constance belittles John, and every figure in the canvas beside. No one else but Faulconbridge is master enough of his soul to count truckling to 'Commoditie' beneath him. Constance's scorn of it degrades John especially because they are the two opposites of the tragic action. She serves to set John down at once at the low appraisal he must bear later with Pandulph in the bargaining for his crown at any cost of honor.

Despite the glamor of John's first bold successes, his mongrel coarseness, neither straightforward nor astute, traps him into crookedness. His murderous suppression of Arthur is worse than an evil deed for John, as Shakespeare clearly shows. It is bad policy. As such only John comes to lament it.

Woe for Arthur next belittles John in England. Yet he never guesses, when it embroils him with the English nobles, that Pandulph has been watching the snare wherein he fell, and that he is the victim of a cleverer Roman Franco-English underhandedness than he would ever have the wit to indulge.

But whether belittled by the nobility of Constance, or the passion of pity for Arthur, the public identification of John with mediocrity is the fruit of the clash of the noble Constance, grief-possessed and justice-inspired with the ignoble John. Shakespeare puts the human dilemma into human embodiments.

John is characterized, and his career and its historic incidents are thus presented by means of the very scattering away of the supreme attention from himself to Constance and Arthur, to his 'discontented Peeres' [4.2.127], the invading Frenchmen, and the resentful clergy. It is all skillfully adjusted to suit and show the muddy unsettled interval between French and native English domination over England, whence, as out of sediment, and the grace of John, better things arose for the English People.

John's lack of distinction in the plot is typical of the curious inefficiency of his rule, the nugatory results of his first warlike deeds in France, and his first vigorous policy against Rome.

In his ecclesiastical program, the John of *The Troublesome Raigne*, unlike Shakespeare's John, enjoys, at least in the better figure he makes as a personality, the effect of his vigor. He is forcible, vivid, and stirring. Shakespeare cancelled all that. He struck out, along with the grossness of the raids upon the Abbeys, most of the tokens of personal power in John, when he recast the earlier Play.

It is commonly supposed that regard for the Church, or for Church-people, influenced the change. It is quite possible; it is obvious, besides, that the omission offered him an easy short cut in his task of reducing a double play to a single play's length. It is worth noticing, however, that there is further room for a deeper reason. The omission harmonizes with the rest of his developments and changes of character. It contributes toward keeping the figure of John in low relief.

Enough modelling for accent, for the proper introduction of the promise of his Kingship is provided liberally for John. In the first blush of his accession to the throne, with the able and positive Queen-Mother, Elinor, backing her favorite, John spiritedly challenges France. With Elinor to advise and inspire him, he carries the war swiftly into the enemy's country. Before Angiers he speaks with impressive readiness. There, in his first heat, he draws strongly to himself the personal friendship of King Philip, and the loyal attachment for life of Hubert.

John, then, is neither stupid nor unmagnetic. Yet, by himself, he is found lacking in nerve, insight, initiative energy, and steering power. These his mother Elinor supplies him in the morning of his career. Later, bold-eyed, showy, and personable animal as he is, his soul cannot hold out and make good. The coarse and shallow nature is unveiled in these fundamental incapacities.

Shakespeare has put in several passing touches to denote how dependent he was on his mother's fostering care. Her death seemed to him an omen of his failure (IV.ii.120–1, 131–2, 189). This touch of nature redeems John. Again at the close of his life his sufferings capture human pity, and the affection Hubert and Faulconbridge yield him influences human sympathy. We remember, at his topmost moment of success, how timid and loath he was to feel his way through blind and groping words to the curt grim ones that put into Hubert's bosom his evil hankerings for Arthur's death. We see, even at the last, how dull his consciousness is to any but the bodily pains of fever and poison. We then gladly give his poor soul 'elbow roome' [5.7.28].

John is so much of a minor character stranded amid the persons and events of his wrecked life that Shakespeare has prompted everybody to talk less of him than several others. Yet it has scarcely been realized that this qualifying of us all to ignore John in his own History is of itself a descriptive master-stroke in this portrait of 'confounded royalty' [5.7.58] . . . . (vii–xv)

70 Frank Harris, Constance and Shakespeare's shrewish wife

1911

From *The Women of Shakespeare* (London, 1911).

James Thomas 'Frank' Harris (c.1856–1931) was the influential editor of *The Evening News* (1882–6), *The Fortnightly Review* (1886–94), and *The Saturday Review* (1894–8). Vain, outspoken, and iconoclastic, Harris openly flouted Victorian conventions (particularly sexual ones) and supported Germany during World War I. He wrote several volumes of short stories, a novel (*The Bomb* [London, 1908]), plays, and biographies of Wilde (2 vols, New York, 1916) and Shaw (London, 1931). The self-proclaimed greatest Shakespearian of his day, Harris wrote a controversial, highly conjectural, but popular biography *The Man Shakespeare* (London, 1909). The excerpt below from *The Women of Shakespeare* is taken from the American edition (New York, 1912).

[From Chapter II]

... *King John* is with some certainty dated about 1596. It was in 1596 that Shakespeare visited Stratford for the first time after an absence of eight or nine years: he was recalled probably by the news that his son Hamnet was very ill. His son's death made a great impression on Shakespeare; it is responsible, I think, for the exquisite tenderness, beauty and pathos with which he has invested the figure of young Arthur, and also for the tragic intensity of the Queen-mother's grief.

Shakespeare took his *King John* from an old play which we still possess, *The Troublesome Raigne of King John*. In it Constance is pictured as high-tempered and Arthur as a bold youth of eighteen or nineteen, but Shakespeare turned Arthur into a young boy, a girl-boy, all affection and tenderness, and at the same time hardened Constance into a 'bedlam' [2.1.183]. Constance is presented to us as so bad-tempered, such a raging wordy termagant that I am forced to believe Shakespeare is again thinking of his own wife. For there is no object in making Constance a shrew; Shakespeare paints her afterwards as a mother mourning for her only son, and evidently tries to bring out all the pathos of her misery; he would have done better, therefore, not to have alienated one's sympathy from her at the beginning by making her an intolerable scold. But he had just been in Stratford, his wife had been before his eyes, and he cannot help depicting her raging violent passion. Constance is as bad-tempered as Adriana [in *The Comedy of Errors*] herself, and that's saying a good deal. From the point of view of art the bad temper of Constance is much more significant. After all Adriana had some reason for her ill-humour. She was passionately in love, madly jealous, and her husband neglected her; but this Constance is a raging termagant without any such cause. We cannot, therefore, understand her ill-humour; we simply dislike her and accordingly have less sympathy with her in her affliction.

Constance comes on the stage at the beginning of the second act. At first she is becomingly grateful for the help offered to her by King Philip and Austria and counsels patience and peace. A moment later she begins to rant and rage; even her gentle son Arthur has to reprove her: [Quotes 2.1.163–5: 'Good my mother, peace. . . .'].

But nothing can stop Constance's tongue. She raves even worse than Margaret [in the *Henry VI* plays] raved, till at last King John pulls her up with 'Bedlam, have done'. She answers him: 'I have but this to say. . . .' [2.1.183] and rages on; she is indeed as Elinor calls her, an 'unadvised scold' [2.1.191]. . . .

She appears again at the opening of the third act. She has learned from Salisbury that peace has been made between France and England, and her temper comes again to show: [Quotes 3.1.1–4: 'Gone to be married! . . .].

After holding forth for a page or so in this strain she attacks Salisbury the messenger, for bringing the tidings: [Quotes 3.1.36–42: her anger at Salisbury and his and Arthur's conciliatory reaction]. But nothing will content her. She raves on [for] page after page, now against Philip, now against Austria, till one wonders how the princes could have stood it, and when Pandulph enters she asks characteristically for leave to curse: 'O, lawful let it be / That I have room with Rome to curse awhile!' [3.1.179ff.]. A raging cursing scold she is, and nothing more.

Suddenly the overloud note is muted: as soon as Arthur is taken prisoner she jumps to the conclusion that he is dead; long before even the famous scene between Hubert and Arthur takes place, she grieves for her child as lost. The agony of her grief is so realized that it carries us all away with it, and turns the furious scold into one of the great tragic figures of our literature.

At first she does not strike the true note. When Philip counsels patience and comfort she raves: [Quotes 3.4.23–8: 'No, I defy all counsel, all redress. . . .'] and so on, plainly the poet talking and not yet in the spirit of the part. But as soon as Constance thinks of her son, her voice falls to mournful sadness, and takes on the very accent of regret: [Quotes 3.4.46–60: 'I was Geffrey's wife. . . .']. King Philip prays her to bind up her hair, and she goes off again: [Quotes 3.4.69–75: 'Yes, that I will. . . .'].

There is distinct individuality now in the scolding verbosity, which characterizes even her grief. But it is when she again talks of the child that she touches the heart: [Quotes 3.4.81–9: 'There was not such a gracious creature born. . . .']. This seems to me Shakespeare's own emotion. The wonderful first line: 'There was not such a *gracious* creature born' is unmistakable, and he will give us that 'gracious' again.

When the mother-grief of Constance swings higher still and reaches the soul of sorrow, to me it is again Shakespeare speaking, Shakespeare lamenting his own loss, at least for the first six lines: [Quotes 3.4.93–105: 'Grief fills the room up of my absent child. . . .'].

The last seven lines are poor stuff, and the last four words out of place, intolerable: but the first lines are all perfect till the poet tries to think himself into the character of Constance. For this Constance lives in a frenzy as the poet takes care to tell us that she dies in a frenzy too. For years his furious scolding wife simply obsessed Shakespeare; but the intense emotion which throbs through these pages is Shakespeare's own emotion – his grief, his agony of bereavement – speaking through the scolding mask. How lovable his young boy must have been to have wrung such a phrase from him: 'There was not such a gracious creature born'.

The sorrow of young Hamnet's loss lived with gentle Shakespeare for the rest of his life. Fourteen or fifteen years later we find it again in *The Winter's Tale* when he describes young Mamillius, who charms every one by telling fairy stories with childish grace and dies through 'thoughts too high for one so tender' [*Winter's Tale*, 3.2.196].

I cannot regard any of the other women characters in *King John* as more than historical lay figures: Elinor is as wooden as she can be, and Blanch is no better.

My readers will notice that all through the piece I take part with Shakespeare against his wife. For a dozen reasons I accept his view that she was a shrew of the worst; one may here suffice. From Jonson and Chettle we know that Shakespeare was very gentle and sweet-tempered, justified indeed in portraying himself as he allows the servant in *The Comedy of Errors* to portray him as the reverse of 'choleric' [2.2.62–7]. This mildness of Shakespeare is attested by other facts. He was criticized again and again by surly Jonson, for instance, now with reason, and now without; yet remained a friend of Jonson's to the end. He preached forgiveness, too, as a duty all through his life, and yet he nursed his dislike of his wife to the grave and beyond it, as I have shown in *The Man Shakespeare* [London, 1909]. She was the one person whom he could never forgive. I am convinced that the Xanthippe of Socrates was not a more violent termagant than Anne Hathaway. (42–50)

71 John Edward Masefield, on treachery and 'Englishness'

1911

From *William Shakespeare* (London, 1911).

John Edward Masefield (1878–1967), poet laureate of England, author of some fifty volumes of verse, over twenty novels, eight plays, and various miscellaneous writings, spent his adolescence as a seaman only to desert ship at seventeen. After a brief stay in America he returned to England where he began the literary career that was to lead to his being named poet laureate in 1930 and a member of the Order of Merit in 1935. Masefield's *William Shakespeare*, which includes a brief life of the poet, a chapter on Elizabethan theatres, and a short essay on each of Shakespeare's works, was considerably revised some forty-three years after its first appearance (London, 1954). The essay on *King John* in this edition is so considerably altered as to constitute a very different critical perspective on the play (see Introduction, note 49).

... Like the best Shakespearian tragedies, *King John* is an intellectual form in which a number of people with obsessions illustrate the idea of treachery. The illustrations are very various. Perhaps the most interesting of them are those subtle ones that illustrate treachery to type, or want of conformity to a standard imagined or established.

In the historical plays, Shakespeare's mind broods on the idea that our tragical kings failed because they did not conform to a type lower than themselves. Henry V conforms to type. He has the qualities that impress the bourgeoisie. He is a success. Henry VI does not conform to type. He has the qualities of the Christian mystic. He is stabbed in the Tower. Edward IV conforms to type. He has the qualities that impress the rabble. He is a success. Richard II does not conform to type. He is a man of ideas. He is done to death at Pomfret. King John does not conform to type. His intellect is bigger than his capacity for affairs. He is poisoned by a monk at Swinstead.

King John presents that most subtle of all the images of treachery, a man who cannot conform to the standard of his own ideas. He fails as a king because his intellect prompts him to attempt what is really beyond the powers of his nature to perform. By his side, with an irony that is seldom praised, Shakespeare places the figure of the Bastard, the man who ought to have been king, the man fitted by nature to rule the English, the man without intellect but with a rough capacity, the man whom we meet again, as a successful king, in the play of *Henry V*.

King John is placed throughout the play in treacherous relations with life. He is a traitor to his brother's son, to his own ideas, to the English idea, and to his oath of kingship. He has a bigger intellect than any one about him. His brain is full of gusts and flaws that blow him beyond his age, and then let him sink below it. Persistence in any one course of treachery would give him the greatness of all well-defined things. He remains a chaos shooting out occasional fire.

The play opens with a scene that displays some of the human results of treachery. John's mother, Elinor, has been treacherous to one of her sons. John has usurped his brother's right, and, in following his own counsel, has been treacherous to his mother. These acts of treachery have betrayed England into a bloody and unjust war. The picture is turned suddenly. Another of the results of human treachery appears in the person of the Bastard, whose mother confesses that she was seduced by the 'long and vehement suit' [1.1.254] of Cœur de Lion. The Bastard's half-brother, another domestic traitor, does not scruple to accuse his mother of adultery in the hope that, by doing so, he may obtain the Bastard's heritage.

The same breaking of faith for advantage gives points to the second act, where the French and English Kings turn from their pledged intention to effect a base alliance. They arrange to marry the Dauphin to Elinor's niece, Blanch of Castile. In the third act, before the fury of the constant has died down upon this treachery, the French King adds another falseness. He breaks away from the newly-made alliance at the bidding of the Pope's legate. The newly-married Dauphin treacherously breaks with his wife's party. In the welter of war that follows, the constant, human and beautiful figures come to heartbreak and death. The common people of England begin to betray their genius for obedience by preparing to rise against the man in power.

The fourth act begins with the famous scene in which Hubert fails to blind Prince Arthur. Even in the act of mercy he is treacherous. He breaks faith with King John, to whom he has vowed to kill the Prince. Later in the act, King John, thinking that the murder has been done, breaks faith with Hubert, by driving him from his presence. In the last act, the English nobles, who have been treacherous to John, betray their new master, the French King. King John is a broken man, unable to make head against misfortune. He betrays his great kingly idea, that the Pope shall not rule here, by begging the Legate to make peace. At this point death sets a term to treachery. A monk treacherously poisons John at a moment when his affairs look brighter. The play ends with the Bastard's well-known brag about England – 'Naught shall make us rue / If England to itself do rest but true' [5.7.117ff.].

This thought is one among many thoughts taken by Shakespeare from the play of *The Troublesome Raigne*, and taken by the author of that play direct from Holinshed's *Chronicles*.

Comedy deals with character and accident; tragedy with passionate moods of the soul in conflict with fate. In this play, as in nearly all poetical plays, the characters that are most minutely articulated are those commoner, more earthy characters, perceived by the daily mind, not uplifted, by brooding, into the rare state of passionate intellectual vision. These characters are triumphant creations; but they come from the commoner qualities in Shakespeare's mind. He did them easily, with his daily nature. What he did on his knees, with contest and bloody sweat, are his great things. The great scheme of the play is the great achievement, not the buxom boor who flouts the Duke of Austria, and takes the national view of his mother's dishonour.

Shakespeare, like other sensitive, intelligent men, saw that our distinctive products, the characters that we set most store by, are very strange. That beautiful kindness, high courage, and devoted service should go so often with real animal boorishness and the incapacity to see more than one thing at a time (mistaken for stupidity by stupid people) puzzled him, as it puzzles the un-English mind to-day. A reader feels that in the figure of the Bastard he set down what he found most significant in the common English character. With the exceptions of Sir Toby Belch and Justice Shallow, the Bastard is the most English figure in the plays. He is the Englishman neither at his best nor at his worst, but at his commonest. The Englishman was never so seen before, nor since. An entirely honest, robust, hearty person, contemptuous of the weak, glad to be a king's bastard, making friends with women (his own mother one of them) with a trusty, good-humoured frankness, fond of fighting, extremely able when told what to do, fond of plain measures – the plainer the better, an honest servant, easily impressed by intellect when found in high place on his own side, but utterly incapable of perceiving intellect in a foreigner, fond of those sorts of humour which generally lead to blows, extremely just, very kind when not fighting, fond of the words 'fair play' [5.2.118], and nobly and exquisitely moved to deep, true poetical feeling by a cruel act done to something helpless and little. The completeness of the portrait is best seen in the suggestion of the man's wisdom in affairs. The Bastard is trying to find out whether Hubert killed Arthur, whose little body lies close beside them. He says that he suspects Hubert 'very grievously' [4.3.134]. Hubert protests. The Bastard tests the protest with one sentence: 'Go bear him in thine arms' [4.3.139]. He utters the commonplace lines – 'I am amaz'd, methinks, and lose my way / Among the thorns and dangers of the world' [4.3.140ff.] – while he watches Hubert's face. Hubert stands the test (the emotional test that none but an Englishman would apply), he picks up the body. Instantly the Bastard is touched to a tenderness that lifts Hubert to a spiritual comradeship with him – 'How easy dost thou take all England up' [4.3.142].

This tragedy of the death of a child causes nearly all that is nobly poetical in the play.

All the passionately-felt scenes are about Arthur or his mother. Some have thought that Shakespeare wrote the play in 1596, shortly after the death of his little son Hamnet, aged eleven. The supposition accuses Shakespeare of a want of heart, of a want of imagination, or of both wants together. He wrote like every other writer, from his sense of what was fitting in an imagined situation. It was no more necessary for him to delay the writing of Prince Arthur till his son had died than it was for Dickens to wait till he had killed a real Little Dorrit by slow poison.

There is a great change in the manner of the poetical passages. The poetry of the *Henry VI* plays is mostly in bright, sweetly running groups of rhetorical lines. In *King John* it is either built up elaborately into an effect of harmony several lines long, or it is put into a single line or couplet. . . .

The characters in this truly noble play daunt the reader with a sense of their creator's power. It is difficult to know intimately any human soul, even with love as a lamp. Shakespeare's mind goes nobly into these souls, bearing his great light. It is very wonderful that the mind who saw man clearest should see him with such exaltation. (76–86)

72 Stopford Augustus Brooke, on John, Faulconbridge, and Constance

1913

From *Ten More Plays of Shakespeare* (London, 1913).

Stopford Augustus Brooke (1832–1916), ordained in 1857, had a successful if sometimes turbulent career as a preacher and writer, finally leaving the Church of England in 1880 over matters of church authority and theological freedom. Although never attaching himself to any new denomination, he had a decided affinity for Unitarianism, and occasionally preached in Unitarian churches. Brooke was an influential and respected writer on a variety of literary subjects, but perhaps his most significant work was the *Life and Letters of Frederick W. Robertson* (2 vols, London, 1865), an important broad church document. *Ten More Plays of Shakespeare* is a companion piece to Brooke's earlier *On Ten Plays of Shakespeare* (London, 1905); the two studies taken together comprise an exhaustive critical assessment of the major plays.

[From Chapter VIII: '*King John*']

... The character of King John is perhaps nearer to historical truth than anything else in the play. Only he is not quite so bad a man in it as he actually was. 'Foul as hell is, hell is made more foul by the presence of John,' was the judgment of his contemporaries. This tradition has so influenced the critics of this play, that they have made the John of Shakespeare much more wicked and vile than the dramatist represented him. They have searched into every line for badness and have found it. But the King in Shakespeare's hands is no such unredeemed a villain. He is, as he really was, an able politician, a wise war-leader, a bold and ready pursuer of his aim. He stands up for England, and when he does submit to the Legate (changing apparently his steadfast mind) it is not so much to bow to Rome, as to overthrow – as he does – the whole of the conspiracy of his foes against the English Crown. He gains his end; his revolting nobles are brought back to his dying bed, and the invaders are forced, raging, to leave the shores of England. Nor is he represented as a coward, as some have said. He is quite as physically though not so morally brave as Faulconbridge.

On the moral side Shakespeare joins with his accusers. On that side he is represented as he is, the ruthless politician, the murderer of Arthur. But even that villainy does not turn Faulconbridge against him; Faulconbridge who stands for England against the whole world! John is a wicked king, but, wicked or no, he represents to Faulconbridge England and her fates. As such he clings to him, supports him when the rest leave him, cheers him in his dismay, reports him to the French as the gallant and victorious king, denounces the revolting lords, – and idealising him thus as the embodiment of England – comes even to love him, when he is ill fortuned, and finally to mourn his death: [Quotes 5.7.70–3: 'Art thou gone so? . . .]. And this double aspect of John – bad and good – under which the Bastard views his master is also Shakespeare's representation of him. It was not his cue, at a time when England stood alone against the envious Continent, to lower the monarchy of England. The case of Richard III. was different. To lower him was to exalt the Tudors, the true heirs of England in the eyes of an Elizabethan. Here King John was against France. He must not then be represented as infamous, even though he slew the rightful heir. The King stands for England.

Therefore John, except as the murderer of Arthur, is not completely blackened in this play. No one, not even Henry V., can speak more kingly, more concisely, than King John to the ambassador of France; nor did Henry V. act as rapidly, more like a great commander-in-chief, than John against France. He is on Philip's back before Philip thinks he has left England. In war, John is pictured as prompt to act, subtle to plan, making victory a certainty; and when, out of a difficult position in which France and the Church are both against him, he has wrung victory, the French confess his genius in war and policy – [Quotes 3.4.10–14: Lewis's praise for John's alacrity in military matters]. It is the description of a great general.

Before the first fifty lines are over, we meet the two matters on which the whole of the play is to turn. First, we understand from Elinor's speech that Arthur's claim to the throne is just, that John holds it against him by force: 'Your strong possession much more than your right' [1.1.40] is your title to the crown. The working out of that is half the play. The second point is that John and the Church are in ruthless opposition. And this is marked by John's cynical phrase – 'Our abbeys and our priories shall pay / This expedition's charge' [1.1.48ff.]. This quarrel rules the other half of the drama. These two points made in the first fifty lines are another illustration of Shakespeare's careful preparation for all that is to follow.

Close upon this, following up John's denial of Arthur's claim to England, is the arrival on the stage of Faulconbridge, John's great supporter, who towers above all the rest, the natural not the legitimate cousin of the King. The scene is a curious one, and John appears in it, not as the rude, truculent villain he was, but as the grave dispenser of law, one who knows a man when he sees him, and welcomes him with frank and ready friendship.

Nor is Shakespeare's King John less dignified, less regal in speech and act when he meets King Philip before Angiers. His defiance of France is grave and courteous, and when war is inevitable, what he says is thoughtful in its sorrow for war, even Christian in its feeling: [Quotes 2.1.283–6: 'Then God forgive the sin of all those souls. . . .']. This is not the speech of the foul king that history has drawn in the colours of hell.

But now, and with a touch, he changes from this high mood into that evil temper which blackens all the good in him. His dominant passion is to keep the crown he has unjustly taken. Any wrong done for that seems right, and the doing away of Arthur is now the first necessity. Murder sits in his heart, ruthless, politic murder. France supports Arthur, and to divide France from Arthur, John agrees to marry Blanch, his niece, to the Dauphin – [Quotes 2.1.562–3]. This peace leaves Arthur unsupported; he is no longer a danger to John; but it earns and develops that maternal rage of Constance, which Shakespeare uses so magnificently.

When the Pope's Legate appears, the second element of the drama takes form. The Church is against John, for he has offended its supremacy. John answers him as Elizabeth's England would have answered. Shakespeare in this lifts high the figure of John. The Legate breaks up the peace. Philip is forced again to support Arthur against John, because John is against the Church. Arthur becomes again a danger; he is taken prisoner in the battle. And then – murder, long debated in alternating thoughts, determines itself for act. The good in John is drowned by the evil. Spite of conscience, of pity, of justice, and of honour, he will make his crown safe. But he is ashamed of the deed, or rather of entrusting it to another. Richard III. has no shame for his murders; Macbeth performs his own, and it is a soldier's honour, and a host's, rather than conscience, which disturbs him. John shrinks from the murder, recoils from innocent blood; conscience touches him, but no pity; policy overtops conscience; 'he has a mighty cause to wish the death of Arthur' [4.2.205ff.]. But he fears his own design, fears to place it in words – wishes for the night to hide his soul from itself; wavers round the telling his desire to Hubert – dreads to hear it in words, for then it is irrevocably shaped. It is a wonderful passage, and it is worth while to compare it – with all its subtle differentiations – with the soliloquy of Macbeth before the slaying of Duncan: [Quotes 3.3.33–66: John's speech and his proposition to Hubert]. What can be more dramatic than those five whispered sentences [3.3.65–6]? They are like the heavy strokes of a death-bell.

Then, free from this fear, John has no remorse till his lords, hearing of the murder, leave him in burning indignation, and join the French invaders. Then he repents, not of the murder, but of the mistake he made. And he turns all his ill temper upon Hubert. His talk is a mingled skein. Now he thinks of his own danger; now his conscience seems to trouble him. . . .

[Brooke now briefly discusses the 'to and fro of policy and conscience in the soul of John', quoting various incidents in the play, and concluding that John is not 'a villain lost to all sense of shame' (239) nor a coward.]

This is Shakespeare's presentation of John – not altogether wicked, good and ill mingled in him; swept into crime by policy, but sometimes repentant; wise in action and thought; brave in battle; not overwhelmed by misfortune; a murderer against his conscience; a king who, because he stood against France and the Papacy for England, is half forgiven by Shakespeare who thinks of him as the Bastard thinks, and for the same reasons. . . .

Faulconbridge is intended by Shakespeare to be, amidst a crowd of selfish kings, princes, and nobles, all pressing to their own advantage, an incarnation of the honest Englishman who loves his country, abjures the foreigner, clings to his king at all hazards because the king represents England; is not indifferent to his own interests; is bluff, outspoken, and brave as a lion, yet has a clear eye to see beyond the follies of the world into the serious heart of affairs. He can philosophise on the mad world, because he really stands apart from all the rest. Amid all the changes of politics, the quarrels which are knit and unknit around him, he is steadily consistent. The principles he lives by remain at the end what they were at the beginning; they change only by development. Nor is he without natural and simple affection, the faithfulness of which is always to be relied on. He loves the King; I have already quoted his passionate farewell to his dead master. He heartens and consoles the King when misfortune lies heavy on him. He is faithful to the last, even when he disapproves [of] the King. Yet when he sees the dead body of Arthur, and thinks that the King is guilty of the murder, his natural pity and indignation break out of his heart. . . . This is the man who, when we first meet him, has come to the court from the country to defend his claim to his father's property – denied to him because he is not his father's son, but a bastard got on his mother by Richard Cœur de Lion. But he loved fame more than property, and when he is recognised by the King as the son of Richard, when Elinor asks him to follow her fortunes and receive knighthood, he flings away his claim, and will live to make his own fortune and his own fame. He rejoices in his sonship to the great warrior; he tells his mother, whom his affection consoles, that she was justified in yielding to the conqueror of the lion, that he is for ever grateful to her; and he leaves her happy and at ease. Brave, ambitious, rough and frank, he has yet a kind heart, and a wise mind in affairs because his heart is kind.

Shakespeare lifts him in this scene out of the country-man into the courtier without lowering his character. No sooner is he in his natural element as a king's son, no sooner does he realise that here, in war and policy, he can fulfil all the dreams he must have had when lost in the solitude of the country, than he flings his old life away for ever with a laugh. He sees the varied movement of the great world open before him like a fan, and his spirit burns to join the mellay. John and Elinor watch his soul rise to his eyes; they see the man emerge from the chrysalis; and they knit him to their side. . . . He laughs at the conventions of society which is chiefly made up of fools, but for that very reason suits a 'mounting spirit' [1.1.206] like himself – one who observes, and will make of his observation means to grow – one who will soothe the world with deceit's sweet poison when it is necessary, yet will, on the whole, be true. The first of his soliloquies paints him as less noble than he becomes.

Shakespeare slowly develops Faulconbridge into a great nobility of character. Great affairs, in which he plays a serious part, lift him into greatness. There is that in him – his honest truthfulness, his unbroken faith – which makes him equal to arduous events, and above them. His large conception of England and of his duty to her and to the King as the image of England, enlarges his mind, strengthens him in difficulty, opens his soul and sets him apart, in dignified separation, from all these kings and nobles who are struggling, without any high idea of country and duty, for their own ends alone. He grows steadily from the brave and self-seeking man of the first Act, from the vainglorious soldier of the third, to the serious patriot and the honourable statesman of the last.

Only one personal matter is at his heart. It is the avenging of his father on Austria, his enemy. . . . When that is done, he has no more personal aims. He is for England only. . . .

... He speaks his mind about Arthur's death to the King with faithfulness, but he does not, like the rest, abandon the King. Even in the murder of Arthur, he feels how fierce was John's temptation. Moreover the King to him is England, and England now is the only mistress of the Bastard's soul. He becomes from henceforth the protagonist of the drama – the real king of events, the centre round which all the action revolves. And his character, purged of its half-cynic selfishness, rises to the level of his position. He speeds to the support of the King. He takes a lofty tone of reproof to the disloyal nobles who are false to their country. When the French land in England, he alone stands against them for England, gathers and arrays the forces of the kingdom. He lifts the despondent King with noble words into courage, bids him contend to the death, make no compromise, let no Cardinal make peace but make it with our own arms. ... He does not despair even when half his power is lost in the Lincoln Washes; and, when the King is dead, his wisdom takes precedence and governs the action of the lords of the kingdom. He incarnates the constancy of England in the play.

And now for Constance. Amid all this hurly-burly of wars, contending kings, selfish interests, walks like a spirit the awful figure of Constance – worn and wasted motherhood maddened by loss and grief; primeval motherhood isolated from everything else in its own passion: [Quotes 3.4.17–19]. When she is present, all the others recede into the background – are only scenery for her wild figure, with disordered garments and hair unbound, and the sound of death in her voice. The actress who should undertake her part is scarcely born in a century. It needs a majestic woman whose soul has lived in the depths; it needs a man's strength to keep up so continuous a frenzy of passion. It needs a self-control, most rarely found in any artist, to prevent the fury of the part, its total abandonment, from carrying away the actress beyond the self-mastery she must hold over her emotion, lest her execution of the part should break down into feebleness, into mere rant and shouting. Moreover, she must have a noble intellect as well as a pitiful heart to act the part adequately; and added to that – a spirit of imagination to feel the poetic passion in the speech of Constance. All she says, in her grief, is steeped in the waters of poetry; the penetrating pity of imagination pierces through her words into the secret recesses of sorrow.

As to the intellect required, the part needs to be conceived on large and simple lines, so as not to lose its grandeur; and yet, within that simplicity, the part is so variously and finely conceived and wrought, that she who acts it must have a hair-dividing, subtle intellect to wind in and out among its changes. Constance is not mad; she is only frenzied with grief, and the frenzy seems sometimes to rise into insanity. But she never loses the clear sequences of thought, and never (as a madwoman would do, as Ophelia does) gambols from the sense. Even her wildest cry, when she apostrophises Death, when she gets nearest to madness, is in intellectual order! Instead of becoming (as a madwoman in excitement would certainly become) more incoherent, she becomes quieter and quieter to the end of the scene, more clear and simple. The changes are as subtle, as delicate as the changes of a cloud; and their infinite interchange of feeling and thought needs a great intellect to conceive them, a passionate heart to follow their intricacy of emotion, and a great, grave, and self-mastering artist to represent them.

When we meet her first, she has no grief, but eager wrath that her son is kept out of his heritage; and keen desire, because she loves him, that he should have it. She does not care, because of any politic reason or desire of power, to make him king, but does care because he is her son, and she his mother. It is her love that is the motive. The motive of Elinor, her opponent, is love of power. Even in their first quarrel these motives are plainly disclosed: Elinor's violence is cool; her policy and not her heart speaks. Every word of Constance is charged with the physical passion of motherhood. Motherhood, universal motherhood, the deep agony of the female in animals and in humanity; – her defence of her young, her desire, her hope for them; her fury at their loss, her rapture at their recovery; motherhood unmodified by civilisation – it was that which rose into Shakespeare's soul and before his imagination, when he pictured Constance. Only, here he did not picture the happy motherhood of Hermione, or the proud joy of Volumnia in her son, but the misery of a mother's loss; the tigress robbed of her whelps.

For, indeed, Constance is a tigress. We do not understand the terrible frenzy into which her sorrow passes till we understand that she has a naturally violent temper. Her attack on Elinor is savage, and Elinor answers her in kind. These fine ladies have foul tongues, but Constance is the most furious. So loud is the battle between these two, and so much more fierce is Constance, that Arthur, the innocent cause, the little peaceful island in these stormy seas, is weary of the noise; – weary, the delicate child, almost of life. . . .

In [3.1] the unregulated violence of her speech is flashing with imagination. The poetry never fails, never weakens. There is not a word out of place; scarcely a word too much. There is no fading into feebleness of the similes. They are crisp and short, and illuminate the passion of the woman. Thought runs to overtake the previous thought before the first has fully shaped itself – a mark of emotion at its height. When we think that she can say no more, she says something more rich and beautiful than she has yet said: [Quotes 3.1.65–74: Constance's refusal to go with Salisbury to see John and Philip]. The Kings enter. She rises from her throne on the ground like a queen of immortal wrath (like Margaret before the Tower), to curse the day when France has beguiled her, 'this day of shame, oppression, perjury' [3.1.88], and cries to the heavens in a splendid invocation: [Quotes 3.1.107–12: 'Arm, arm, you heavens. . . .']. Her wish is fulfilled. The Legate separates the peace, and there is war between France and England. But in the fight Arthur is taken, and the boy knows well what will happen. He loves his mother and he cries – 'O, this will make my mother die of grief' [3.3.5]. And then, we see the grief of Constance. She sees him dead already in his captivity to John. She is dead in his death. Sorrow, only sorrow, passes by, as Constance crosses the stage; and she calls on death, 'Misery's love, / O, come to me' [3.4.35ff.]. Was ever a sadder thing said in this sad world! The full apostrophe to death may be said to be too fantastical – 'O amiable lovely death! / Thou odoriferous stench! sound rottenness' [3.4.25ff.]. It has the sound of madness, but it is only frenzy at its height playing with images. Were it madness, it would not at once be followed by those magnificent lines, charged with imaginative thought, invoking death – 'Arise forth from the couch of lasting night, / Thou hate and terror to prosperity' [3.4.27ff.], nor by her close argument that she is not mad in answer to the Legate's accusation, nor by her clear consciousness that her wit is somewhat disordered, nor by the soft and piteous picture of her sorrow to the Cardinal and the King. On the verge of frenzy, she has as yet a clear mind. There is no madness in this speech, where sorrow and beauty live together – [Quotes 3.4.76–105: 'And father Cardinal. . . .']. With that in her heart, she could not live. She broke her heart and in a frenzy died. But before she dies, Shakespeare, by words of King Philip, has adorned her image with beauty, and veiled it with pity: [Quotes 3.4.61–2: 'Bind up those tresses. . . .'].

Then, finally, judgment falls on John. The misfortune of his realm is doubled to him by the burning poison of which he dies. The last words he hears are of the ruin of his kingdom. He does not live to hear of its salvation. No words of death, of violent death, are more terrible, more poetic, more wild with imagination, than those of John in dying: [Quotes 5.7.34–43: John's description of the hot pain of poison]. (233–51)

73 John James Munro, Shakespeare's use of *The Troublesome Raigne*

1913

From *'The Troublesome Raigne of King John': Being the Original of Shakespeare's 'Life and Death of King John': Edited by F. J. Furnivall and John Munro* (London, 1913).

John James Munro (d. 1956) collaborated with F. J. Furnivall on a number of scholarly projects besides their edition of *The Troublesome Raigne*, most notably the 'Century' Shakespeare (40 vols, London, 1908) for which they contributed introductions and notes as well as a volume on the life and work of the poet. Munro also undertook a complete re-editing of *The Shakespeare Allusion Book* (2 vols, London, 1909), to which he also appended an introduction. His other significant scholarly work includes editions of Arthur Brooke's *Romeus and Juliet* (London, 1908) and William Caxton's translation of Raoul Le Fevre's *History of Jason* (London, 1913). *Frederick James Furnivall: A Volume of Personal Record* (London, 1911) was his biographical tribute to a good friend.

[From the Introduction]

... The view put forward by Mr. R. Simpson in 1874 [No. 35 above] that Shakespeare's purpose in *King John* was to reflect political problems connected with Elizabeth's tenure of the crown, is still sometimes accepted. The comparison of the two plays seriously modifies, if it does not utterly destroy, Mr. Simpson's contentions. The eight points on which his case is based in the main, and which show 'where Shakespeare deserts the Chronicles, without precisely following the old play,' turn out to be minor and unimportant, or points where he does in fact follow *The Troublesome Raigne*.

A study of sources reveals, to a great extent, sameness of treatment by Shakespeare. The same unmistakable methods are adopted in handling Lodge's *Rosalynde*, Greene's *Pandosto*, Brooke's *Romeus, Leir,* and *The Troublesome Raigne*.[1] Convenient headings for the discussion of the matter are, 1, compression; 2, development of characters and introduction of new characters; 3, re-modelling of the story; 4, development of scenes of strong human interest; 5, excision of the undramatic – obscenity, theology, etc.; 6, general improvement in stage-business and handling of parts; 7, introduction of a wider philosophical outlook; 8, intensification of the dialogue, and the introduction of a higher level of poetry; 9, arrangement of the play with a view to effective climax.

1. *Compression*. Without a slavish submission to the unities, Shakespeare usually reduces the dramatic time. Time-compression is generally a necessary part of dramatic intensification. *Romeo* is a conspicuous example. In the case of *King John*, Shakespeare's play occupies seven days with intervals,[2] and the old piece ten days with intervals,[3] the period covered by the two being about the same. In each case the historical time is 1199–1216.

Another means is compression of subject matter. The common fault with poor plays is that they neglect, greatly from lack of insight and power, the moving situations, and waste time on weak display, sententiousness or minor details. It was Shakespeare's business to cut all this away. The prosy speeches of *Rosalynde* and *Romeus*, the preliminaries of *Leir*, and the preliminary talk of *The Troublesome Raigne* are dispensed with, and the dramatist plunges at once into the main course of the action.

Compression is also effected by the excision of whole scenes, which duplicate action, or which can be made up by mention and description elsewhere. Shakespeare is careful to avoid the repetition of the older dramatist in such matters as Lewis's swearing and Melun's confession. His rejection of scenes and passages introduced for other than dramatic purposes also helps in his powerful contraction. . . .

Certain of the characters may also be dispensed with. There is no question but Mr. Fleay's theory that Shakespeare intended to dispense with Essex, is correct [No. 42 above]. The part is restricted to three lines in Act I. sc. i. corresponding to a prose bit of Salisbury's in *The Troublesome Raigne*. Shakespeare has, of course, no need for the characters in the burlesque friary scenes.

But in his scrupulous cutting-down for purposes of intensification and economy, it has been claimed that Shakespeare actually weakened the play in several details. Three points have been discussed by Mr. Edward Rose in his paper, 'Shakespeare as an Adapter',[4] the third also by Dr. F. S. Boas.[5] The first is, that the real cause of the Austria-Bastard dispute, as outlined in the old play – the Duke's cruelty to the Bastard's father, Richard – is omitted in Shakespeare's version. But the facts that Austria actually wears the lion's skin and that definite reference is twice made to Richard in this connexion in sc. ii. of Act I [i.e., 2.1], prove that the dramatist was not forgetful in this connexion. The second point, that the Bastard's antagonism to the betrothal of Blanch was, as expressly shown in *The Troublesome Raigne*, greatly actuated by a previous promise of Elinor's to bestow her on him, and that Shakespeare omits this, – is also a plea of small importance. Shakespeare was certainly right in omitting the talk on the promise; and the Bastard's soliloquy at the end of Act II. sc. i. on the 'Mad world' and Commodity, all in keeping with his own blunt honesty, is enough to show why he objected. The third point, far more serious than the preceding two, is that Shakespeare does not show *why* the monk poisoned John. The earlier dramatist presented the poisoning as a direct nemesis falling upon John at the friary which had been ransacked by his orders. Shakespeare leaves the previous indefinite references to spoilation and the quarrel with papacy and church to supply the motive; and he omits the steps which lead up to the deed. 'We feel,' says Dr. Boas, 'that the King's ignoble end should have had more intimate relation to his design upon Arthur.'

This brings us to a further and more important change by Shakespeare, hitherto, so far [as] I know, overlooked by critics. It concerns the news of Arthur's actual death, which, together with the election of Lewis, forces John in *The Troublesome Raigne* to submit to Pandulph: in Shakespeare's play we pass with extraordinary swiftness from John having learnt that Arthur actually lives (Act IV. sc. ii.) to John having just resigned his crown to Rome (Act V. sc. i.). Between these two scenes Arthur has died (Act IV. sc. iii.); but John does not know of it. The Bastard returns subsequently from his mission to win back the rebels, and John says (Act V. sc. i. ll. 37–8) –

	Would not my lords return to me again,
	After they heard young Arthur was alive?
Bastard.	They found him dead and cast into the streets. . . .
John.	That villain Hubert told me he did live.
Bastard.	So, on my soul, he did, for aught he knew. [5.1.37ff]

John thus submits to Rome still thinking Arthur lives. This is so important and obvious a change that it cannot have been without design. The intention of the dramatist is fairly apparent. The news of Arthur's death smites John down (Act V. sc. i. l. 43, etc.); it paralyses his action: it is now that the energetic and intrepid Bastard comes forward with all the fire of Richard, and steps into John's place as leader; it is now that John begins his decline. The submission of the crown to Rome was but a step on the way, and it is not that step in the main which Shakespeare has in view. What to him is dramatically so important is the final catastrophe. The attempt on Arthur and the consequent secession of nobles drove John to surrender to Rome. Surrender to Rome proved unavailing. But the old John sending back Chatillion 'as lightning in the eyes of France' [1.1.24], and hurling defiance at France and Rome, could yet have arisen as the Bastard objurgated him, to 'outface the brow of bragging horror' [5.1.49ff.]. To all the Bastard's exclamations of shame at compromise with the 'cock'red silken wanton' [5.1.70] of France, John says but this – 'Have thou the ordering of this present time' [5.1.77].

The news of the actual death of Arthur is carried over from the dramatically incidental resignation of the crown to the dramatically important death. The change is part of Shakespeare's attempt to reconcile the brave and aggressive John of the play's beginning with the weakling at its end. It links the death of Arthur with the death of John.

2. *Development of Characters, etc.* Shakespeare still leaves a number of characters mere outlines, but pays especial attention to the main ones. Whatever important traits are insisted upon in the earlier play are developed and knit into the action. The dishonest and permutative adroitness (now called diplomacy) of Pandulph is more subtle and profound. Constance, who in the old piece shares with Ragan [in *King Leir*] the feline desire to scratch out her enemy's eyes,[6] becomes a figure terrific in its comfortless passion. The boyishness of Arthur is specially emphasized, and he is relieved of the theologico-legal alertness he had earlier possessed.[7] John ceases to be the prophetic forerunner of the first English *Defensor*, and becomes the very human central figure of a drama which is of intense emotional interest and devoid of ulterior homiletic purpose, theological or political; an attempt is also made to reconcile the early confident John

with the irresolute latter-day monarch. The most important character so far as development goes, is Philip the Bastard. He is of the same stock as Mumford in *Leir* and Mercutio in *Romeo*. Like the latter, he is intended to provide a contrast and a commentary. It is evidently Shakespeare's intention to make him a sort of backbone to the story; but as his chance only arises after the decline of John, and as this prominence is obviously artificial, the device is not altogether a success. One new character, Gurney, is used to lend realism to the introduction of Lady Faulconbridge.

3. *Remodelling of the Story.* There is little remodelling in *John*. Shakespeare follows his original almost scene by scene; but it is important to notice how completely he re-writes the whole play, and from an entirely different standpoint. Hardly two lines are identical and but few phrases. It looks as though he might have noted down the progress of the action, and written his play from memory of the text and an independent view of the story. *The Taming of the Shrew* represents a different method, and has far more verbal borrowings from its original, which the later dramatist probably had before him as he wrote. *Lear* and *Romeo* are noteworthy as having been freely remodelled in their plots.

4. *Development of Scenes.* Having removed Constance from the negotiations for the betrothal, Shakespeare introduces her apart, where she pours forth her grief and anger. He creates John's subtle innuendoes to Hubert from a mere suggestion. The crafty handling of Lewis by Pandulph is developed in as remarkable a manner. The scene between Arthur and Hubert [4.1] is lifted to a sphere beyond the vision of the first poet, and it is Arthur's tender moving appeal which touches Hubert's heart rather than his appeal for Hubert's immortal soul. Shakespeare's Arthur, after leaping from the walls, utters but eighteen words and dies: the original Arthur (like Peele's Absalom hanging by the hair) indulges in a set speech on his 'tragic overthrow,' not, however, devoid of some true pathos.[8] There is throughout the play the same sensible enlargement of the tragic and determining situations, with condensation or rejection of the accidental. The same criticism applies in greater degree to *Lear*.

5. *Excision of the Undramatic.* With the main end in view Shakespeare could afford to dispense with unessentials. The doggerel and ribaldry of the monastic scenes; the marvels of Peter the Prophet, and the five moons on the stage; Constance's supposed tragic appeal to Dido; the ceremony of coronation, and submission of the crown; the anti-papal invective and the whole of the adscititious theological matter; and John's bombast, could well be relinquished. The removal of these things is a tribute to the dramatist's good taste. It is noteworthy, however, that he retains enough of the theological matter and John's talk of supremacy to maintain the proper atmosphere and historical consistency, and to provide a motive for the monkish assassin.

6. *Improvement in Stage-business.* Shakespeare avoids lengthy 'asides' in the middle scenes (like the Bastard's in Sc. I. of *T.R.*); and the awkward habit of delivering up the dialogue for long to two of the characters. Lady Faulconbridge is absent during the discussion on [of?] Philip's father, and Constance and Arthur are 'off' during the proposals for marriage. Hubert no longer blandly informs the king before the discontented nobles of his fulfillment of the order to blind Arthur. The whole scene [4.2] is much better managed. Other points concerning Peter, Melun, etc., have been touched on above.

7. *New Philosophical Outlook.* In *John* this is effected principally by means of the Bastard. In the older play the Bastard, more than John, had been the mouthpiece of patriotism; in the latter he is none the less its voice, but his patriotism is of a richer, deeper kind. Even Austria [2.1.23–30] has words which are redolent of an affectionate regard for 'that pale, that white-faced shore, Whose foot spurns back the ocean's roaring tides' [2.1.23–4]. But the philosophical note lies in the comments of the Bastard. His utterances on 'tickling commodity . . . the bias of the world' [2.1.573–4] proceed from the application to the affairs of men of that reflective genius which reaches its highest achievement in *Hamlet*.

8. *Intensification of Dialogue, etc.* The forceful brevity with grip and life in it characteristic of Shakespeare at the opening of his scenes, designed to command attention and arouse interest, is conspicuous in *John*. It is most noticeable in the Hubert Arthur scene, where the old play prosily begins: 'My masters! I have showed you what warrant I have for this attempt. I perceive, by your heavy countenances,' etc. [6.1–2]: while Shakespeare's Hubert opens – 'Heat me these irons hot. . . .' [4.1.1]. The beginning of the play itself, and the outcry of Constance – 'Gone to be married? gone to swear a peace? / False blood to false blood joined? . . .' [3.1.1–2] are other examples. This intensification, however, the utterance of people with hearts that burn, is maintained in due degree throughout.

Not less noticeable is the higher level of poetry: the metre is no longer pedestrian; the sentiment no longer artificial; the purple patches, with a few exceptions, are not so obviously superfluous. The patriotism is less bombast and brag: it rings sincere and true.

9. *Arrangement of Plot for Effective Climax.* There is little alteration of the plot other than the Arthur shift mentioned above, and the dramatist's diversion of attention from the crown by the rejection of the second coronation and the submission. The audience's familiarity with the story precluded extensive re-handling: but all of Shakespeare's changes tend to indicate that his interest in *John* was interest in a living human story rather than a legal or theological plea, and that the climax for him lay in the fall and death of John. Patriotic rhetoric is enough to show that he was deeply interested in the national question, – he was above all an Englishman; but none the less a dramatist for that. (xxix–xl)

74 James Brander Matthews, the artistic flaws of *King John*

1913

From *Shakespeare as a Playwright* (New York, 1913).

James Brander Matthews (1852–1929), theatre historian, critic, and playwright, was the first professor of Dramatic Literature at Columbia University (1900–24). Matthews inaugurated the practice of giving lectures and seminars designed specifically for playwrights, and also founded a number of societies for actors, dramatists, and others concerned with the practical life of the theatre. Both as a pedagogue and in his capacity as drama critic for *The New York Times*, he had a major influence on the American stage. Among his most important works are *Actors and Actresses of Great Britain and the United States* (5 vols, New York, 1886), written jointly with Laurence Hutton, *The Development of Drama* (New York, 1903), *Molière* (New York, 1910), *The Principles of Playmaking* (New York, 1919), and an autobiography, *These Many Years* (New York, 1917).

[From Chapter V: 'His Earliest Chronicle-Plays', Part IV]

In *King John* Shakespeare appropriates an old play in two parts and condenses it, without taking pains to make the story coherent or compact. In speech and in character he betters what he borrows; as M. Jusserand has suggested, 'it is a case of the eagle donning the jackdaw's feathers.'[1] With these feathers he is content to skim close to the ground and not to soar aloft on his own strong pinions. The piece is a mere medley of scarcely related scenes, following each other almost in confusion, sometimes powerful in themselves, but even then less potent than they might be if they were properly coördinated and firmly knit together. There is nothing to rivet the attention of the spectators except contrasted characters and abundant eloquence; and in a play these are inadequate substitutes for a controlling motive or for a dominating figure. As Aristotle had asserted many centuries earlier, 'if you string together a set of speeches expressive of character, and well finished in point of diction and thought, you will not produce the essential tragic effect nearly as well as with a play, which, however deficient in these respects, yet has a plot and artistically constructed incidents.'[2]

Plot and artistically constructed incidents had been lacking in most of the chronicle-plays which Shakespeare was following; and yet these earlier pieces had often a forward movement absent from *King John*, because Shakespeare fails to provide any single character to focus our interest. A chronicle-play it is, with all the looseness of that easy form; but a chronicle-play is only a kaleidoscope of battle, murder and sudden death unless it has a central figure, like Richard III or Henry V, to compel our interest. In *King John* the action is wandering and uncertain; it is even more fragmentary than that of *Richard II*; and it is wholly without the huddled swiftness of *Richard III*. Furthermore, King John himself, although not so absolutely unfit to be the leading personage of a play as Richard II, is not so presented as to grip our sympathy; and Faulconbridge, the valiant braggart, who is set before us with assured mastery, is external to the story, such as it is.

The opening scenes cheat us with the belief that Faulconbridge is to take a prominent place in the plot, and we are disappointed when we find that this is impossible, since he is only an outsider, involved in no important situation and useful at best only to give color to certain scenes and to comment upon the events like a chorus. Faulconbridge is a largely conceived character with Shakespeare's unfailing appreciation of a free and unconventional nature; and Shakespeare lends him wit, shrewdness and even eloquence; yet his best bravura passages have but little dramatic value, since he is not firmly tied into the action. He exists for his own sake – for the sake of the vivacity and the variety his presence imparts to the scenes in which he appears. He is a pleasant fellow of an easy and contagious mirth; he has a captivating humor of his own, forecasting that of Mercutio; but his part is so loosely related to the action that he cannot be forced into prominence.

King John is curiously incongruous in the carelessness of its composition. It is in the main a drum-and-trumpet history, with the flourishes of heralds, the challenges to instant battle and the sudden settling of a war by the unexpected betrothal of a prince and a princess who have never before met – a betrothal impertinently proposed by a private citizen and incontinently accepted by the warring kings. Then the fight breaks out again, when the Cardinal most unexpectedly intervenes; the French invade England with the aid of the English nobles, who suddenly turn against them when they are told that the Dauphin has inexplicably planned their needless assassination. The death of King John by poison is casual; it has not been prepared for by the dramatist, and it is therefore feeble in dramatic effect.

The railings and the ravings of Queen Elinor and Queen Constance are unseemly; they are unqueenly, if not unwomanly. At times, these two widows of dead kings are little better than a couple of common scolds, with an unbridled license of speech that even Queen Elizabeth might have thought excessive. Of the two, Constance is the more violent, as she has good reason to be; her later outbreaks are hysteric, even if they are the result of maternal devotion. She is superb in mother-love and eloquent in high-sounding words; but her temper is painfully shrewish and she revels in her opportunities for vehement protest. Her violence therefore detracts not a little from the pathos of her plight, and even from the appeal of her heartfelt plaints. Overdone as they seem to us now, her swelling invectives, excited by a natural emotion, must have been grateful to the boy-actor intrusted with the part (possibly the same youthful performer who was soon to be intrusted with Katherine in the *Taming of the Shrew*).[3]

The characters, however overdrawn they may be and however external to the action, in so far as there is any action, are admirably depicted. They are living men and women; they are no longer merely parts, sketched in outline, to be colored by the personality of the performer; they are truly characters, standing on their own feet and speaking out of their own mouths. The gift of endowing his creations with life itself, of which Shakespeare gave little sign in his earliest plays, is now at last displayed. Equally undeniable is his gift of handling a pathetic situation with a full understanding of its possibilities. Nothing that he had done in any earlier piece foretold the psychologic subtlety of the scene in which King John suggests to Hubert the murder of Arthur or the compassionate handling of the scene in which Hubert undertakes to put out Arthur's eyes and is overcome by the little prince's irresistibly moving plea for mercy. And yet note must be made of the fact that in Shakespeare's play the project of putting out Arthur's eyes is wholly gratuitous; what King John wanted and what Hubert had undertaken to do was to make away with Arthur; and there was no possible excuse for blinding him before killing him. Shakespeare is amplifying a hint he found in the old play, but he carelessly omits the passage in the old play which justified the scene. Probably the episode took shape as it did partly because of the well-known delight the Elizabethan playgoers had in beholding ghastly spectacles of mutilation and torture – a violent delight which Shakespeare again procured them by the plucking out of Gloucester's eyes in the later *King Lear*. (96–9)

75 Horace Howard Furness, Jr., on the Bastard, John, and the play

1919

From *The Life and Death of King John* (Philadelphia, 1919).

Horace Howard Furness, Jr. (1865–1930) joined his father as co-editor of the New Variorum Shakespeare in 1901, becoming sole editor of the project after his father's death in 1912. In an astonishing sixteen-year period he produced variorum editions of *Macbeth* (Philadelphia, 1903), *Richard III* (Philadelphia, 1908), *Julius Caesar* (Philadelphia, 1913), and *King John*. Between these and his edition of *Coriolanus* (Philadelphia, 1928), Furness published a one-act play, *The Gloss of Youth* (Philadelphia, 1920), treating an imagined episode in the lives of Shakespeare and John Fletcher. Although Furness's editorial work never received the acclaim of that of his more notable father, his edition of *King John* nonetheless marks a sort of scholarly watershed in the critical history of the play.

[From the Preface]

. . . Faulconbridge carries all before him from his first scene, where he at once captivates the King and Queen Elinor, to the final words of the play put in his mouth as the one best typifying the rugged warrior Englishman of the time. Critics have not been slow to note the gradual change in his character. The braggart of the early scenes is drawn on the same plan as that of the Faulconbridge of *The Troublesome Raigne*, and in the older play he maintains practically the same character throughout. It was the intuitive perception of Shakespeare that grasped the dramatic possibilities of such a character and showed how a man of Faulconbridge's temperament attains to full strength and fineness by responsibility placed upon him, and by the confidence of one who trusts him implicitly. 'Have thou the ordering of the present time' [5.1.77] are almost the last conscious words addressed to Faulconbridge by the King, as he hands over to him the conduct of the campaign against the Dauphin's invasion, and this after Faulconbridge's scathing comment on the King's announcement that Pandulph has offered to make a compromise with the invaders. Once only can we detect a slight wavering in his allegiance. The dead body of Arthur, found under such suspicious circumstances, almost shakes his faith, and wrings from him the admission that he begins to lose his way amid the thorns and dangers of this world; and that Heaven itself frowns upon the land where such deeds can be committed. His righteous indignation is forgotten as he stands beside the dead body of the King; his last words breathed in the dead ears are, that he but stays to avenge the murder, and then his soul shall wait on his benefactor to heaven as it has been but his servant upon earth. In adapting the older play it must have been at once apparent to the playwright that King John's was not a character which lent itself to dramatic treatment. He was utterly perfidious, a poltroon, and a moral coward without one redeeming feature. Richard, Duke of Gloucester, ruthless and cruel though he was, had at least the saving grace of a grim humor; and his resourcefulness on all occasions excites a dreadful interest in his fate. But John was without even these signs of strength; his defiance of the Pope is mere bluster, he cringes abjectly when he is made actually to realize the power of the Church, and accedes to all the conditions, forcing him to believe that all this was done not on compulsion, but as a voluntary act on his part....

In conclusion let it be admitted that *King John* as an acting play is not to be ranked with the greater productions of Shakespeare, but this is not, by any means, to say that it is lacking in dramatic interest. What other playwright has ever produced the thrilling horror of King John's veiled hints at murder and death in his instigation of Hubert? Where will be found words of grief and despair equalling those of Constance on the loss of Arthur? What moralist could picture a scene of retribution more complete than John's miserable death by poison in the orchard of Swinstead Abbey? These scenes, be it remembered, written by a dramatist not yet thirty-five years old. How incredulous would have been that young playwright had there stood beside his elbow a seer, who in strange words should inform him, as he finished the last ringing lines of his play, that four hundred years from that time those words should still find a responsive echo in the ears of his countrymen. And that he, the humble playwright, and not all the historians, had placed upon King John's unworthy brows the wreath of immortality. (x–xiii)

Notes

1 EDMOND MALONE

1   The first edition of this Essay was published in January 1778 [as part of the Johnson-Steevens edition of Shakespeare, and reprinted with Malone's prefatory apparatus to the 1790 *Plays and Poems*, with a slight change of title].
[2] *Johnson on Shakespeare*, edited by Arthur Sherbo, 2 vols (New Haven, 1968), I, 417. Johnson's note occurs at 3.1.147ff. in reference to the episode in which John flouts the authority of the Pope before Pandulph.
3   'I had as fair a *gold jerkin* on that day as any was worn in the Island Voyage, or Cadiz, none dispraised.' *Silent Woman*, 1609. [See *The Silent Woman* (1.3.61ff.) in *Ben Jonson*, edited by C. H. Herford, Percy Simpson, and Evelyn Simpson, 11 vols, 1925–52 (Oxford, 1947), V, 176.]
[4] Probably Juan Eusebio Nieremberg's *Varones Ilustres de la Compañia de Jesus* 9 vols (Madrid, 1643–1736). See *Johnson on Shakespeare*, edited by Arthur Sherbo, 2 vols (New Haven, 1968), I, 417–18.
[5] *The Insatiate Countess*, edited by Giorgio Melchiori (Manchester, 1984).
[6] See *The Works of Mr William Shakespeare*, 6 vols (London, 1723–5), III, 115.
[7] In those cases when a commentary note from Malone's edition is anticipated in some form, either substantially or partially, in his *Supplement to the Edition of Shakespeare's Plays published in 1778 by Samuel Johnson and George Steevens*, 2 vols (London, 1780), I have indicated the fact as follows: *Supp*. vol., page.
[8] *The Plays of William Shakespeare*, edited by Samuel Johnson and George Steevens, 10 vols (London, 1773), V, 7.
[9] John Monck Mason, *Comments on the Last Edition of Shakespeare's Plays* (Dublin, 1785), p. 153.
[10] *The Works of Shakespeare*, edited by Lewis Theobald, 7 vols (London, 1733), III, 172.
[11] See *William Camden: Remains Concerning Britain*, edited by R. D. Dunn (Toronto, 1984), p. 90.
[12] Theobald, III, 182.
[13] Pope, III, 135.
[14] See *The Plays of William Shakespeare*, edited by Samuel Johnson and George Steevens, 10 vols (London, 1778), V, 39. The emendation first occurs in Tyrwhitt's *Observations and Conjectures upon Some Passages of Shakespeare* (Oxford, 1766), pp. 49–50.
[15] Johnson and Steevens (1778), V, 44.
[16] See Sherbo, I, 415.
[17] *The Works of Mr William Shakespeare*, edited by Thomas Hanmer, 6 vols (Oxford, 1743–4), III, 137.
[18] Theobald, III, 210.
[19] Ritson, *Remarks, Critical and Illustrative, on the Text and Notes of the Last Edition of Shakespeare* (London, 1783), p. 238 note.

[20] Johnson and Steevens (1778), V, 72.
[21] Pope, III, 158.
[22] Pope, III, 159.
[23] Pope, III, 162.
[24] Mason, pp. 159–60.
[25] *The Works of Mr. William Shakespeare*, edited by Nicholas Rowe, 6 vols (London, 1709), III, 1044.

2 JOSEPH RITSON

1 Malone, in this, as in other places, prefers the *nonsense* of the first edition to the *sense* of the second.

3 GEORGE STEEVENS

[1] *The Works of Mr William Shakespeare*, edited by Alexander Pope, 6 vols (London, 1723–5), III, 135.
[2] Pope, III, 162.
[3] the very vestibule and first entrance; perhaps an allusion to the following lines of Virgil's *Aeneid*, 6.273ff.: 'vestibulum ante ipsum primisque in faucibus Orci / Luctus et ultrices posuere cubilia Curae'. . . . ['Just before the entrance, even within the very jaws of Hell, Grief and avenging Cares have made their bed'].
[4] *The Works of Mr William Shakespeare*, edited by Thomas Hanmer, 6 vols (Oxford, 1743–4), III, 186.
[5] substitute or deputy; more precisely used to designate a doctor or clergyman who temporarily fills the office of another.
[6] *The Dramatic Works of Richard Brinsley Sheridan*, edited by Cecil Price, 2 vols (Oxford, 1973), II, 532.
[7] See Malone's note on Gray's supposed error in depicting Death as a female (No.1; item 22 above).
[8] Joseph Spence, *Polymetis* (London, 1747), p. 261.
[9] ll. 24–5: 'Around him stand the Furies and various Deaths in order due, and savage Vengeance thrusts forth her coils of jangling chains'.
[10] William Dobson, *Paradisus Amissus*, 2 vols (Oxford, 1750, 53).
[11] Ovid, *Metamorphoses*, 3.97–8: 'Why, O son of Agenor, dost thou gaze on the serpent thou hast slain? Thou too shalt be a serpent for men to gaze on'.

4 GEORGE CHALMERS

1 Steev. 1793, vol. viii. p. 1 [i.e., 2–3]; [see No. 3 above].
2 Mal. Shak. vol. i. p^t. 1. p. 314 [see No. 1 above].
[3] *The Insatiate Countess*, edited by Giorgio Melchiori (Manchester, 1984).
4 Mal. Shak. vol. i. p^t. 1. p. 312 [see No. 1 above]: Steev. 1793, vol. viii. p. 81 [see No. 3 above; for the note in Johnson's edition see *Johnson on Shakespeare*, edited by Arthur Sherbo, 2 vols (New Haven, 1968), I, 417].
5 Camden in Kennet, vol. ii. p. 601. [Chalmers's references to Camden are taken from *A Complete History of England*, 3 vols (London, 1706); volumes 1 and 2, by various authors, are collected and edited by J. Hughes; volume 3 is the work of White Kennet, Bishop of Peterborough.]

6   Steev. vol. viii. p. 81 [see No. 3 above; see also *Johnson on Shakespeare*, edited by Arthur Sherbo, 2 vols (New Haven, 1968), I, 417].
7   Camden in Kennet, vol. ii. p. 595.
8   Camden in Kennet, vol. ii. p. 594, 597.

6 AUGUST WILHELM VON SCHLEGEL

1   I mean the piece with this title in the collection of his works. There is an older *King John*, in two parts, of which the former is a re-cast: – perhaps a juvenile work of Shakespeare, though not hitherto acknowledged as such by the English critics. See the disquisition appended to this Lecture [in which Schlegel briefly argues that *The Troublesome Raigne* is likely by Shakespeare since it cannot be attributed with confidence to anyone else; Morrison, 446; Black, II, 258–9].

7 NATHAN DRAKE

[1]   Drake considers *King John* to be Shakespeare's sixteenth play in order of composition, falling between *Hamlet*, which he dates at 1597, and *All's Well That Ends Well*, 1598.
2   Chalmers's *Supplemental Apology*, p. 357 [see No. 4 above].
3   Vide Reed's Shakespeare [i.e., Isaac Reed's, *The Plays of William Shakespeare*, 21 vols (London, 1803)], vol. x. p. 362. 'For he is but a bastard to the time, / That doth not smack of observation,' &c. [1.1.207ff.].
4   Reed's Shakespeare, vol. x. p. 413. Act iii. sc. 1.
5   Reed's Shakespeare, vol. x. p. 447. note 9.

8 WILLIAM HAZLITT

[1]   *Timber: or, Discoveries*; see *Ben Jonson*, edited by C. H. Herford, Percy Simpson, and Evelyn Simpson, 11 vols, 1925–52 (Oxford, 1947), VIII, 584. The original is from the elder Seneca, *Controversiae* 4; Preface 7, where the Emperor Augustus, remarking on the headlong and unrestrained oratory of Quintus Haterius, declares 'Haterius noster sufflaminandus est'; i.e., 'Haterius needs a brake'.

9 WILLIAM OXBERRY

[1]   The phrase is Hazlitt's (see No. 8 above).

10 AUGUSTINE SKOTTOWE

[1]   Raphael Holinshed, *Chronicles*, 3 vols (London, 1587), III, 157, 160.

11 SAMUEL WELLER SINGER

[1]   *The Works of Mr William Shakespeare*, edited by Alexander Pope, 6 vols (London, 1723–5), III, 115.
[2]   Richard Farmer, *An Essay on the Learning of Shakespeare*, second enlarged edition (London, 1767), p. 76.
[3]   *Johnson on Shakespeare*, edited by Arthur Sherbo, 2 vols (New Haven, 1968), I, 428.
[4]   Misquoted from Nathan Drake (No. 7 above).

14 ANNA BROWNELL JAMESON

1 Malone [No. 1 above, IV, 449] says, that 'in expanding the character of the bastard, Shakespeare seems to have proceeded on the following slight hint in an old play on the story of King John:

> Next them a bastard of the king's deceased –
> A hardy wild-head, rough and venturous. [2.69ff.]

It is easy to *say* this; yet who but Shakespeare could have expanded the last line into a Faulconbridge?'

2 The Greek *Merope*, which was esteemed one of the finest of the tragedies of Euripides, is unhappily lost; those of Maffei, Alfieri, and Voltaire, are well known. There is another *Merope* in Italian [by Apostolo Zeno (Venice, 1711)], which I have not seen: the English *Merope* [by Aaron Hill (London, 1749)] is merely a bad translation from Voltaire. [Jameson either overlooks or ignores the much maligned *Merope* of George Jeffreys (London, 1731), regarded by many as a source for Voltaire's play.]

3 'Queen Elinor saw that if he were king, how his mother Constance would look to bear the most rule in the realm of England, till her son should come to a lawful age to govern of himself.' – Holinshed, [*Chronicles*, 3 vols (London, 1587), III, 158].

15 THOMAS CAMPBELL

1 Cast of the other parts: King John, Kemble; Faulconbridge, Smith; Hubert, Bensley; King of France, J. Aickin; Dauphin, Barrymore; Pandulph, Palmer; Chatillion, Farren; Queen Elinor, Mrs. Hopkins.

2 The dramatic criticism of our newspapers at that time was as inferior to what it has since been, as the engravings of the same period are inferior to those plates which so exquisitely adorn several modern publications.

[3] For this metaphor Campbell appears indebted to Jameson (No. 14 above).

16 THOMAS CAMPBELL

1 In my estimation of Hume as an historian, I often compare him to Thucydides; but in this part of the reign of John he reminds me of Livy.

17 THOMAS PEREGRINE COURTENAY

1 [James] Boswell's edition, [*The Plays and Poems of William Shakespeare*, 21 vols (London: 1821)], XV, 194.
2 In *Six Old Plays*, [edited by John Nichols, 2 vols (London, 1779)], I, 217.
3 See Pictorial Shakespeare [No. 18 below], [III], 6.
4 J. P. Collier's preface to *King John* [i.e., *Kynge Johan* (London, 1838)], p.vii.
5 See also [William] Blackstone, [*Commentaries on the Laws of England*, nineteenth edition, 4 vols (London, 1836)], I, 200; and [Nicholas Harris Nicolas], *Nicolas' Chronology of History*, [second edition (London, 1838)], p. 306.
6 *Middle Ages*, ii. 473. [i.e., Henry Hallam, *View of the State of Europe During the Middle Ages*, fifth edition, 3 vols (London, 1829), II, 473.]
7 See Bosw[ell], [XV], 221, 270. It appears from the *Patent Rolls* [Thomas Duffus Hardy, *A Description of the Patent Rolls in the Tower of London* (London, 1835)], p. 43 that Limoges

[8] See *The Plays and Poems of William Shakespeare*, edited by Edmond Malone, 11 vols (London, 1790), IV, 467 (No. 1 above).

9 [Roger de] Hoveden, [*Rerum Anglicarum Scriptores post Bedam*, edited by Henry Savile (London, 1596)], p. 791.

10 [Jacques Nicolas Augustin] Thierry, [*Histoire de la Conquête de l'Angleterre, par les Normands*, 4 vols (Paris 1836)], IV, 147.

[11] All citations of Holinshed are to the first edition of the *Chronicles*, 3 vols (London, 1587).

12 Hol[inshed], [III, 161]; Hoveden, p. 814; [Pierre] Daru, [*Histoire de Bretagne*, 3 vols (Paris, 1826)], I, 406, notices the treaty as an abandonment of Arthur and Constance, but he does not represent its terms differently.

13 He had been an ally of John, who now agreed that he should hold of the King of France.

14 See [John] Lingard, [*A History of England*, fourth edition, 13 vols (London, 1837–9)], III, 10. [The sections of Matthew Paris's history treating the events of King John's reign are now generally attributed to Roger of Wendover. See *Roger of Wendover's 'Flowers of History'*, edited by J. A. Giles, 2 vols (London, 1849), I, vii.]

15 Matt[hew] Par[is], [*Historia* (London, 1640)], p. 224; anno 1207.

16 Matt. Paris, p. 208.

17 Bosw[ell], [XV], 327.

18 Hol[inshed], [III, 165]. See Lingard, III, 8.

19 I know not what to infer from the following, which I take from Mr. T. Hardy's *Patent Rolls*, p. 36: – 'The King to Alan Fitz Court and others, and to all those whom they wish to bring with them. Know ye that Furmie, servant of Arthur our nephew, came to us and told us on your part, that you were desirous of speaking with us, provided ye could easily obtain secure and safe conduct to come to us. We therefore inform you that we have granted unto you, and unto all those who may accompany you, safe and secure conduct, in coming to us and in returning, for eight days from Sunday next after the feast of St. Bartholomew; and in testimony hereof, &c. Inform us, however, of the day and place when and where you wish to come, and we will send letters of safe conduct to you thither. *We command you, however, that you do naught whereby evil may befal our nephew Arthur.* Witness ourself at Chinon, this 24th day of August [1202].' – [James] Mackintosh apparently believed John to be the murderer. – See his *Hist.* [i.e., *History of England*, 3 vols (London, 1830)], I, 200.

20 Hov[eden], p. 818.

21 The old play introduces Philip Faulconbridge compelling the friars to produce their hidden stores; and it is otherwise more full in enumerating the offences of the king.

22 Hol[inshed], [III, 177].

23 Of her Breton succession she was deprived by her stepfather, who preferred his own daughter by Constance.

24 The principal occurrence was the battle of Bouvines, in 1214, wherein John and his allies were defeated. – See Lingard, III, 40.

[25] The books referred to are Fortescue's *De Laudibus Legum Angliae* (London, 1567) and Smith's *De Republica Anglorum* (London, 1583).

[26] The principle, paraphrased controversially by Courtenay in his Preface [see the remarks of Knight, No. 18 below], is 'that only striking and poetical events can be pleasantly dramatised'; hence Courtenay concludes, based upon his understanding of Coleridge, that 'it would be necessary to choose for each play at least one great event, important as well as dramatic; and, where a *reign* is represented, that event of the reign with which it is most desirable to impress the young mind' (I, ix).

27 As to John's conduct after signing the charter, I would refer the historian to Hardy's *Patent Rolls*, pp. 71 and 106.
[28] See *Johnson on Shakespeare*, edited by Arthur Sherbo, 2 vols (New Haven, 1968), I, 425.
29 *Characteristics of Women*, II, 238 [No. 14 above].

18 CHARLES KNIGHT

1 See Introductory Notice to *Two Gentlemen of Verona*, [I], 5.
[2] *Twenty of the Plays of Shakespeare*, 4 vols (London, 1766), II, Sig.N7^v.
[3] Although this attempt to date *The Troublesome Raigne*, as Knight says, was made in 1802, it was not published until the appearance of Coleridge's *Literary Remains*, 4 vols (London, 1836), II, 86–7.
4 *Naval History*, vol. iv. p. 39. [i.e., *The British Admirals. With an Introductory View of the Naval History of England*, by Robert Southey continued by R. Bell, 5 vols (London, 1833–40), IV, 39–40; subsequent references are noted within brackets in the text.]
[5] See Richard Hakluyt's *The Principal Navigations, Voyages, Traffiques & Discoveries of Foreign Voyagers*, 10 vols (London, 1927–8), IX, 266.
[6] See *Johnson on Shakespeare*, edited by Arthur Sherbo, 2 vols (New Haven, 1968), I, 417–18.
7 *Supplemental Apology* [No. 4 above], pp. 356–9.
8 'On worthy Master Shakespeare and his Poems', by J. M., S. From the folio of 1632.
9 Observations prefixed to the second edition of Lyrical Ballads.
[10] *Lectures on the History of Literature*, translated by J. G. Lockhart, 2 vols (Edinburgh, 1818), II, 147.
11 *Literary Remains*, vol. ii. p. 161.
[12] *The Works of Shakespeare*, edited by William Warburton, 8 vols (London, 1747), III, 452.
[13] *The Plays and Poems of William Shakespeare*, edited by Edmond Malone, 11 vols (London, 1790), IV, 536 (No. 1 above).
14 [Francis Douce], *Illustrations* [*of Shakespeare, and of Ancient Manners*, 2 vols (London, 1807)], I, 406.
15 Coleridge's *Literary Remains*, vol. ii. p. 77.
16 'Shakespeare's Historical Plays considered historically.' By the Right Hon. T. P. Courtenay. In the *New Monthly Magazine*, 1838. [No. 17 above: I, vi–xii; 251–2. Knight's citations of Schlegel (No. 6 above) are all taken directly from Courtenay.]
[17] J. M. W. Turner (1775–1851), English painter.
18 In the *Troades* of Euripides.
[19] The allusions are to Johnson's 'Preface to Shakespeare'. See *Johnson on Shakespeare*, edited by Arthur Sherbo, 2 vols (New Haven, 1968); the first two occur at I, 75 and I, 68 respectively. Johnson's discussion of Shakespeare's treatment of the three unities of time, place, and action occurs at I, 74–80.

19 GEORGE FLETCHER

[1] First published in *The Athenæum*, 11 February 1843, pp. 137–9.
2 The omission of this passage in acting, mutilates the development of the intellectual part of this interesting character.
3 The omission of these eight lines [51–8] in performance, is another mutilation, of the same nature as the one last-mentioned, and even more injurious.

[4] First published in *The Athenæum*, 18 February 1843, pp. 161–3.

20 JOSEPH HUNTER

[1] John Payne Collier, *The Works of William Shakespeare*, 8 vols (London, 1842–4), IV, 53.
2   [*King John* appears in Volume 4 of Collier's edition, dated 1842.] It is not my intention in the progress of these remarks to enter into further examination of the text of Mr. Collier's edition, or of the illustrations which he has given of this author. I have been called to defend my theories respecting some of these plays against Mr. Collier's objections; and, if I am not greatly mistaken, where we could get at the ground of an opinion adverse to mine I have shewn that it was insufficient. As to the opinion which is mere opinion, its force is greatly weakened by the proofs which this edition exhibits that Mr. Collier cannot have been a long and critical student in these writings, with an affluence of materials prepared beforehand for the purpose, when he ventured on the arduous task of preparing an edition which was to claim to be ranked among the standard editions of this great author. It is to he hoped that this edition will not be taken, either as to text or illustration, as an exhibition of the state of Shakespearian knowledge in the reign of Her Majesty Queen Victoria, although the circumstance of Mr. Collier being the Director of the Shakespeare Society, in which so many respectable names are found, may seem to give it that degree of consequence. And with this protest I leave it, recurring to it hereafter as little as may be, either to confirm my own judgments or for the purpose of correcting its misapprehensions.
3   *Anatomy of Melancholy*, 4to. 1621, p. 738.

21 HERMANN ULRICI

[1] See *Roger of Wendover's 'Flowers of History'* (formerly attributed to Matthew Paris), edited by J. A. Giles, 2 vols (London, 1849), II, 205.
[2] Friedrich Kreyssig, *Vorlesungen über Shakespeare*, 3 vols (Berlin, 1858–60), I, 450–1.
[3] Although Ulrici seems to cite Bale's play here, the apparent reference is to *The Troublesome Raigne*.
[4] Ludwig Tieck, *Alt-Englisches Theater*, 2 vols (Berlin, 1811), I, xvi–xvii.

22 GULIAN CROMMELIN VERPLANCK

[1] Verplanck's note (I, 50) reads as follows: 'In the old *King John*, after his fall, Arthur speaks thus: –

> Ho! who is nigh? Somebody take me up:
> Where is my mother? Let me speak with her:
> Who hurts me thus? – speak, ho! where are you gone?
> Ah me, poor Arthur, I am here alone.
> Why called I mother? how did I forget?
> My fall, my fall hath killed my mother's son.
> How will she weep at tidings of my death!
> Sweet Jesu! save my soul; forgive my rash attempt:
> Comfort my mother; shield her from despair,
> When she shall hear my tragic overthrow. [9.12ff.]

This fond recurrence of the dying youth to his mother is natural and affecting; and I can only account for Shakespeare's throwing it aside, upon the same reason that in *Lear* he has purposely avoided one or two touching incidents of the old play, as thoughts pre-occupied by his predecessors, whose works he had taken for the groundwork of his plot, while it was his aim to give a new and original poetical character to the familiar plot.'

[2] Richard Farmer, *An Essay on the Learning of Shakespeare*, second enlarged edition (London, 1767), p. 76; *The Plays of William Shakespeare*, edited by Samuel Johnson and George Steevens, 15 vols (London, 1793), VIII, B1^v. Here Steevens recants his earlier opinion regarding Shakespeare's authorship expressed in his *Twenty of the Plays of Shakespeare*, 4 vols (London, 1766), II, Sig.N7^v; Knight, *The Pictorial Edition of the Works of Shakespeare*, 8 vols (London, 1838–43), III, 5–6 (No. 18 above); and Collier, *The Works of William Shakespeare*, edited by J. Payne Collier, 8 vols (London, 1842–4), IV, 3–4.

[3] See *The Poetical Works of Charles Churchill*, edited by Douglas Grant (Oxford, 1956), p. 32.

[4] Jacob Van Ruysdael (1628–82), Dutch landscape painter; Thomas Cole (1801–48), American landscape painter.

24 FRANÇOIS PIERRE GUILLAUME GUIZOT

[1] David Hume, *The History of England*, 6 vols (London, 1754–62), I, 367.
[2] Hume, I, 364.
[3] Actually Roger of Wendover. See No. 17, note 14; and No. 27, note [2].

25 HENRY NORMAN HUDSON

[1] Wordsworth, 'It is not to be thought of that the Flood' (11ff.).
[2] Compare Knight's phraseology (No. 18 above), to whom Hudson is strongly indebted here.
[3] The most influential proponent of this view is Ludwig Tieck. See, for example, his remarks in *Shakespeares Dramatische Werke. Übersetzt von August Wilhelm von Schlegel, ergänzt und erläutert von Ludwig Tieck*, 9 vols (Berlin, 1825–33), III, 339.
[4] An echo from *King Lear* (1.1.17–18).
[5] Compare Ulrici (No. 21 above), for an earlier expression of this idea.
[6] The quotation is taken from Knight (No. 18 above).

26 HENRY REED

1 Wordsworth's 'Rob Roy's Grave' [37ff., loosely quoted].
2 Hare's *Guesses at Truth*, First Series, p. 355 [i.e., Julius Charles Hare and Augustus William Hare, *Guesses at Truth, by Two Brothers* (London, 1838; reprinted 1847; 1871). The quotation appears on p. 277 of the 1871 edition.].
3 Franz Horn, [*Shakespeare's Schauspiele*, 5 vols (Leipzig, 1823–31)], II, 196.
4 Wordsworth's Sonnet written in London in 1802 [i.e., 'Milton! thou shouldst be living at this hour' (9)].
5 *Reflections on the French Revolution*, vol iii. p. 98 [i.e., *The Works of the Right Honourable Edmund Burke*, 8 vols, 1792–1827 (London, 1792), III, 98].
6 *Table Talk*, p. 35. Ed. 1852. [i.e., *Specimens of the Table Talk of Samuel Taylor Coleridge* (London, 1851, reprinted in 1852 and often thereafter); *Table Talk* was first edited by

Henry Nelson Coleridge, 2 vols (London, 1835); for a modern citation of this remark see *The Collected Works of Samuel Taylor Coleridge: Table Talk*, edited by Carl Woodring (London and Princeton, N.J., 1990), XIV, part 1, 67.]

[7] Thomas Wolsey (c. 1475–1530); Armand Jean du Plessis de Richelieu (1585–1642); Jules Mazarin (1602–61); Luis Manuel Fernandez de Portocarrero (1635–1709).

8 'In the chroniclers, we have manifold changes of fortune in the life of John, after Arthur of Brittany has fallen. In Shakespeare, Arthur is at once avenged. The heart-broken mother and her boy are not the only sufferers from double courses. The spirit of Constance is appeased by the fall of John. the Niobe of a Gothic age, who vainly thought to shield her child from so stern a destiny as that with which Apollo and Artemis pursued the daughter of Tantalus, may rest in peace.' 'Historical Illustrations' [i.e., 'Supplementary Notice'] to C. Knight's Shakespeare [No. 18 above], vol. iii p. 78. W.B.R.

27 WILLIAM WATKISS LLOYD

[1] All citations of Holinshed are to the first edition of the *Chronicles*, 3 vols (London, 1587).
[2] The relevant passage from Matthew Paris's note in Roger of Wendover's *Flowers of History* reads as follows: 'This wicked freebooter was a Norman by birth, and illegitimate. He even acted much more cruelly against the barons than he had been ordered to, as will be related hereafter. . . .' See *Roger of Wendover's 'Flowers of History'*, edited by J. A. Giles, 2 vols (London, 1849), II, 260.

28 JOHN CHARLES BUCKNILL

[1] (Lat.), you also.
[2] probably Otto Nicolai (1810–49), German composer and conductor, noted for his exacting committment to high standards of performance as well as for his mercurial personality, which fluctuated regularly from assertive self-confidence to deep despondency and self doubt. Bucknill does not elaborate on the odd juxtaposition of Jonson and Nicolai here, although Nicolai's emotional contradictions are recognizable enough in Jonson. But since Bucknill is discussing the phenomenon of hallucination in people of otherwise sound mental health, he may also be recalling a vision Jonson experienced, as reported by Drummond of Hawthornden, in which Jonson's eldest son appeared to him with a bloody cross on his forehead as a grim premonition of the boy's imminent death of plague. See *Ben Jonson's Conversations with William Drummond of Hawthornden* in *Ben Jonson*, edited by C. H. Herford, Percy Simpson, and Evelyn Simpson, 11 vols, 1925–52 (Oxford, 1925), I, 139–40. Drummond also reports on other imaginative extravagances by Jonson, such as his consuming a whole night 'looking to his great toe, about which he hath seen tartars & turks Romans and Carthaginions feight in his imagination' (*Ben Jonson*, I, 141); he later describes him as 'oppressed with fantasie, which hath ever mastered his reason, a generall disease jn many poets' (*Ben Jonson*, I, 151).

29 RICHARD GRANT WHITE

[1] See Charles Gildon's *The Laws of Poetry* (London, 1721), p. 158.
2 Printed by the Camden Society from the original MS. edited by Mr. Collier [London, 1838].
3 *The First and Second Part of the Troublesome Raigne of John, King of England. With the discovery of King Richard Cordelion's base sonne (vulgarly named the Bastard Fawconbridge:)*

Also the Death of King John at Swinestead Abbey. As they were (sundry times) lately acted by the Queenes Majestyes Players. Written by W. Sh. Imprinted at London by Valentine Simmes for John Helme, and are to be sold at his shop in St. Dunstan's Churchyard, in Fleet Street. 1611. . . .

4 The following extracts from the old play will give the reader a notion of its general style, as well as of the Bastard as he there appears, both in his jocose and in his sober moods. [Here White quotes the following passages from *The Troublesome Raigne*: 1.230–58: the episode in which the Bastard identifies himself as Richard's son; and 6.1–16: the episode in the abbey where the Bastard demands to see the abbot's treasure.]

[5] White cites the following passages from *King John* in his Notes: 2.1.5; 2.1.65; 2.1.140–1; 2.1.193–4; 2.1.398; 2.1.527–30; 2.1.538; 3.1.14; 3.1.114; 4.1.121–4; 4.2.215–29; 5.2.104; 5.3.16; 5.4.42; 5.7.112–14.

[6] See *The Works of Shakespeare*, edited by Lewis Theobald, 7 vols (London, 1733), III, 196; the ensuing quotations from Theobald appear on III, 198.

[7] See *Johnson on Shakespeare*, edited by Arthur Sherbo, 2 vols (New Haven, 1968), I, 416; *The Plays and Poems of William Shakespeare*, edited by Edmond Malone, 11 vols (London, 1790), IV, 490 (No. 1 above); and *The Works of William Shakespeare*, edited by J. Payne Collier, 8 vols (London, 1842–4), IV, 39.

30 CHARLES COWDEN CLARKE

[1] *An Essay on Man*: 1.2.
[2] See Hermann Ulrici (No. 20 above).
[3] Henry Norman Hudson (No. 25 above).
4   Mr Macready had previously revived the play of *Henry V*, at Covent Garden Theatre [10 June 1839], with prodigal magnificence and splendour.

31 GEORG GOTTFRIED GERVINUS

[1] See *Voltaire on Shakespeare*, edited by Theodore Besterman, Studies on Voltaire and the Eighteenth Century, Volume LIV (Geneva, 1967), p. 56. The passage comes from the *Discours prononcé à l'Académie française* (1746).

34 HENRY THOMAS HALL

[1] An unacknowledged quotation from Heraud (No. 32 above) to whom Hall is indebted throughout his discussion of John.
[2] See *Annales Monastici*, edited by Henry Luard Richards, 5 vols (London, 1864–69); volume 1 (1864) includes *Annales de Burton, A.D. 1004–1263*.
[3] Hall's discussion of Salisbury is also heavily indebted to Heraud.

35 RICHARD SIMPSON

[1] *Leycesters Commonwealth*, sometimes ascribed to the Jesuit Robert Parsons (1546–1610), was first published in Antwerp (1584); subsequent editions appeared as follows: (London, 1585); (Naples, 1585); (London, 1641). Simpson quotes from the 1641 edition. See also *Leicester's Commonwealth*, edited by D. C. Peck (Athens, Ohio, 1985), p. 110.
[2] Richard Verstegan's *Declaration* (n.p., 1592) was perhaps written by Robert Parsons.
[3] *The Works of Shakespeare*, edited by William Warburton, 8 vols (London, 1747), III,

452; *The Plays and Poems of William Shakespeare*, edited by Edmond Malone, 11 vols (London, 1790), IV, 536 (No. 1 above).
[4] *An Admonition to the Nobility and People of England and Ireland* (Antwerp?, 1588).
[5] First published (London, 1601), 43pp., and frequently reprinted. It is not clear to which later edition Simpson alludes.
[6] Andreas Philopater was a pseudonym of Robert Parsons.

38 JOHN WEISS

[1] Manon Jeanne Philipon Roland de la Platière (1754–93), who, along with her husband Jean Marie (1732–93), were for a time two of the most powerful adherents of republican government in France.

39 FREDERICK JAMES FURNIVALL

[1] Furnivall's daughter Ena died in infancy in 1866.
2 'The great lesson taught in the last lines of the play should be more brought out. King, nobles, claimant, all lean on foreign help, and all find it a broken reed which pierces their hands.' – C. Hargrove. [Furnivall occasionally quotes the critical remarks of his 'friend' Hargrove throughout the introduction, but never provides bibliographic citation for them, as he does for the remarks of his other scholarly acquaintances.] Besides the passage usually cited from Andrew Boorde for these last lines, he has another nearer to Shakespeare's words: 'I think if all the world were set against England, it might neuer be conquered, they beyng treue within them selfe.' – 1542 (pr. 1547) *Introduction*, p. 164 of my edn., 1870. [i.e., *The Fyrst Boke of the Introduction of Knowledge*, edited by Furnivall for the Early English Text Society (London, 1870)].
3 'No, but for his enmity to, and robbery of the monks. See Hazlitt's *Shakespeare Library* [second edition, 6 vols (London, 1875)], Pt. II., vol i., pp. 309–311' – C. Hargrove. I meant to include these as anti-Papal acts.

40 DENTON JAQUES SNIDER

[1] Snider here and to the end of the paragraph is indebted to Simpson (No. 35 above).

41 GEORGE WILKES

[1] Knight's statement appears in his biography of Shakespeare, comprising the last volume of the Pictorial Edition (No. 18 above), VIII, 38. See also George Chalmers, *An Apology for the Believers in the Shakespeare-Papers* (London, 1797), p. 200; and Nathan Drake, *Shakespeare and His Times*, 2 vols (London, 1817), I, 15–16 (No. 7 above).
[2] See No. 26, note [7].
[3] See *Shakespeare Commentaries*, translated by F. E. Bunnett, 2 vols (London, 1863), II, 494 (No. 31 above).

42 FREDERICK GARD FLEAY

[1] It is not clear here to whom Fleay alludes. H. N. Hudson in his 1852 introduction to *King John* (No. 25 above; reprinted with revisions in Hudson's *Shakespeare: His Life, Art, and Characters* [2 vols, Boston, 1872]), briefly disparages Shakespeare's play for distorting

history by placing such a heavy emphasis on the fate of Arthur, but makes no mention of the revenge of the friars (Hudson's introduction, p. 355). Thomas Campbell in his 1838 edition of Shakespeare (No. 16 above) expresses regret that Shakespeare failed to demonstrate in *King John* the 'desolation of the English mind' that followed the papal excommunication against John and England. See also François Guizot (no. 24 above) who claims that the latter portions of *King John* 'are not well arranged'; Guizot sees the poisoning of John by the monk as 'not prepared with that care which Shakespeare usually bestows upon the foundation and justification of the slightest circumstances in his dramas; and there is nothing to indicate the motive which could have led the monk to commit so desperate an action. . . . We cannot tell what could have induced Shakespeare to adopt this story, which has turned to so little account' (pp. 356–7).

[2] Fleay's act, scene, and line designations are generally identical to those in *The Riverside Shakespeare*; where they are not, I have provided the *Riverside* designation after Fleay's in brackets.

3 One of them depends on a conjecture of my own. Hence it was not counted in my table in my *Shakespeare Manual* [London, 1876]. See note on I.i.146. [In his note Fleay explains that his emendation of F's 'face' to 'hand' is necessary in part so that the line can rhyme with 'land' at 144.]

4 Nor ever entered anywhere in the Stationers' Register, which is not the case with any other undisputed play of Shakespeare.

43 EDWARD ROSE

1 Modern editors somewhat unnecessarily divide the third act into four scenes.

[2] An allusion to Thomas Babington Macaulay's description of Charles II's own words on his deathbed; see *The History of England from the Accession of James II*, 5 vols (London, 1849–61), I, 437.

[3] Rose uses the act and scene divisions of Fleay's edition of *The Troublesome Raigne* (No. 42 above).

[4] The unscrupulous villain of Massinger's *A New Way to Pay Old Debts*.

45 HENRY JOHN HARDY

[1] An obvious reference to concerns raised by Courtenay (No. 17 above).

[2] William of Occam (d. *c.*, 1349), English scholastic philosopher, credited with the revival of nominalism; Roscellinus (*c.*, 1050–*c.*, 1122), the most influential early proponent of nominalism.

[3] On the characters in *King John* as representative types see Ulrici (No. 21 above).

48 HIRAM CORSON

[1] The brackets in this paragraph, and all subsequent italics in quotations from Ulrici, are supplied by Corson, who cites the translation of *Shakespeare's Dramatic Art* by A. J. W. Morrison (London, 1846), p. 363.

[2] In 'Of Queens' Gardens', Lecture II of *Sesame and Lilies*, Ruskin asserts that Shakespeare 'has no heroes; – he has only heroines'. He goes on, after giving a brief overview of women and men in the plays, to claim that Shakespeare represents women as 'infallibly faithful and wise counsellors, – incorruptibly just and pure examples – strong always to sanctify, even when they cannot save'. Constance is not mentioned by name, although

several other Shakespearian women are. See *The Works of John Ruskin*, edited by E. T. Cook and Alexander Wedderburn, 39 vols (London, 1903–12), XVIII, 112–14.
[3] *Shakespeare Studien* (Stuttgart, 1866), 65–6.
[4] See, for example, George Fletcher (No. 19 above).

49 WALTER HORATIO PATER

1 *Elinor.* Do you not read some tokens of my son (Cœur-de-Lion)
In the large composition of this man? [1.1.87ff.]

51 JAMES APPLETON MORGAN

1 Vol. i. p. 5. [Here (I, 5ff.) Morgan briefly discusses these proclamations and prints that of 16 May 1599 in full.]
[2] Morgan here appears indebted to Rose (No. 43 above).
3 'I open with a clock striking, to beget an awful attention in the audience – it also marks the time, which is four o'clock in the morning, and saves a description of the rising sun, and a great deal about gilding the eastern hemisphere.' – *The Critic*. [See *The Dramatic Works of Richard Brinsley Sheridan*, edited by Cecil Price, 2 vols (Oxford, 1973), II, 521.]

52 LOUIS LEWES

[1] Compare the beginning of Jameson's discussion (No. 14 above). Lewes is strongly indebted to Jameson throughout his critical remarks.

54 BARRETT WENDELL

1 See I.i.
2 See III.iv.112 seq.
3 III.iii.19 seq.; IV.i.

56 GEORG MORRIS COHEN BRANDES

[1] Compare the remarks of Warner (No. 53 above) on the integration of Saxon and Norman into a distinctly 'English' nation.

57 HENRY SEBASTIAN BOWDEN

1 *Vorlesungen* [i.e., *Vorlesungen über Shakespeare*, 3 vols (Berlin, 1858–60)], I, 462, 559.
2 One of these is entitled *New Comedy, or Interlude concerning the Three Laws of Nature. Moses and Christ corrupted by the Sodomites, Pharysees, and Papists* (1538). London, 1562; and offers further evidence of the bigotry exhibited by dramatists in Shakespeare's time. [See Alfred Harbage, *Annals of English Drama 975–1700*, revised by Samuel Schoenbaum (London, 1964), p. 26; Harbage and Schoenbaum note that Bale's *New Comedy* first appeared in 1538, was revised around 1547, and then again in 1562.]
[3] Sir John Hayward (1560–1627), who in 1599 wrote a short history of King Henry IV that displeased Elizabeth because of volatile political material in it purportedly related to Richard II, Elizabeth, and Essex. See Peter Ure, *King Richard II*, fourth revised edition (Cambridge, Ma., 1956), pp. lviii–lix.

[4] (Lat.), by way of the oath.
5 On the contrary doctrine that an oath always binds, whatever its nature may be, Herod would have been bound, in deference to his oath, to slay St. John Baptist.
6 We have borrowed largely from [J. M.] Raich, '*König Johann*', *Shakespeares Stellung zur Katholischen Religion* [Mainz], 1884, in our interpretation of *King John*.
7 Sixth part of the Sermon against Wilful Rebellion.
8 And as Bolingbroke disowned Exton, the murderer of Richard II.
9 [Wm] Watson's *Important Considerations*, [p.] 73. [first published (London, 1601), 43pp., and frequently reprinted. Bowden takes the reference here from Simpson (No. 35 above), to whom he is strongly indebted throughout this concluding section of his argument. As was the case with Simpson's citation of Watson, it is not clear here to which later edition of *Important Considerations* Bowden alludes.]
10 *Shakespeares Stellung zur Katholischen Religion*, [p.] 167.

58 CHARLES HAROLD HERFORD

1 Four scenes are omitted, or replaced by a mere allusion, *e.g.* the Bastard's visitation of the monasteries. Similarly, the 'five moons,' reported in IV.2.[182], are *presented* in the earlier play. On the other hand, one of the greatest scenes [3.3], John's 'suggestion' [4.2.166] of Arthur's death, is barely hinted in *The Troublesome Raigne*.
2 Cf. John's dying speech: –

> Since John did yield unto the Priest of Rome,
> Nor he nor his have prospered on the earth;
> Curst are his blessings, and his curse is bliss. [15.95ff.]

[3] The word "curse' is used frequently in *The Troublesome Raigne*.

60 GEORGE CHARLES MOORE SMITH

[1] On the play's lack of a dramatic or thematic center compare Rose (No. 43 above) and Brandes (No. 56 above).
[2] 4 vols (Oldenburg and Leipzig, 1897–1902), II, 78ff. Bulthaupt's remarks on *King John* were first published in his *Dramaturgie der Classiker*, 2 vols (Oldenburg, 1883–4), II, 5–32.

61 J. LYTELTON ETTY

[1] *Appreciations. With an Essay on Style* (London, 1889), p. 201 (No. 49 above); the statement appears in Pater's discussion of *Richard II*.
[2] Pater, p. 198.

62 FELIX EMANUEL SCHELLING

[1] The quotation comes from the title page of *The Troublesome Raigne*.

63 RICHARD GREEN MOULTON

[1] In an appendix (p. 365) Moulton provides the 'dividing points and exact references' of the 'scheme' of the pendulum swings in *King John*.

65 GEORGE PIERCE BAKER

1   For a probable source of the dispute of the Bastard and his brother in *The Troublesome Raigne of King John*, see Halle's account of the reign of Henry VI, *Shakespeare's Holinshed*, W. Boswell-Stone, [London, 1896], pp. 48–50.

66 HENRY CHARLES BEECHING

[1] *Shakespeare: Puritan and Recusant* (Edinburgh, 1897).

67 RICHARD GARNETT

[1] Garnett seems to be referring here to the character rather than the play; he places neither 'Henry IV' nor 'Richard II' in quotation marks, which is his customary method for indicating a Shakespearian title.

73 JOHN JAMES MUNRO

[1] The texts of all these works can be found in Geoffrey Bullough's *Narrative and Dramatic Sources of Shakespeare*, 8 vols, (London, 1957–75); Thomas Lodge's *Rosalynde* (1590 edition) in II, 158–256; Robert Greene's *Pandosto* (1588) in VIII, 156–99; Arthur Brooke's *Tragicall Historye of Romeus and Juliet* (1562) in I, 284–363; and the anonymous *True Chronicle Historie of King Leir* (1605) in VII, 337–402.

2   Mr. P. A. Daniel, *Trans. N[ew] Sh[akespeare]. Soc[iety].*, 1877–9, pp. 257–64. [Here Daniel provides an exhaustive and detailed 'time-analysis' of *King John*.]

3   Mr. P. A. Daniel, Appendix II, below [pp. 162–70; here Daniel provides a 'time analysis' for *The Troublesome Raigne* analogous to the one he provides above for *King John*].

4   *Macmillan's Magazine*, Nov. 1878, pp. 69–77; facsimile, by Praetorius, ed. Furnivall, 1888, pp. xv–xvi [see No. 43 above].

5   *Shakespeare and His Predecessors*, pp. 243–4 [see No. 55 above].

[6] See Bullough, VII, 383 (*King Leir*, ll. 1906); cf., *The Troublesome Raigne* (2.394–5).

7   The statement sometimes made that the Arthur of the *T.R.* was a youth is wrong: it was doubtless an error of judgment to bestow adult reason and interests on him; but the earlier dramatist still describes him as a 'boy' [1.50], etc.

[8] See *David and Bethsabe* (ll. 1470ff.), edited by Elmer Blistein, in *The Life and Works of George Peele*, general editor Charles Tyler Prouty, 3 vols, 1952–70 (New Haven, 1970), III, 240–4.

74 JAMES BRANDER MATTHEWS

[1] J. J. Jusserand, *A Literary History of the English People*, second English edition, 3 vols (London, 1906–9), III, 190.

[2] Aristotle, *Poetics*, 6.16.

[3] Matthews gives no precise date for either *King John* or *The Taming of the Shrew*, but he assigns the latter play to roughly the same period as the *Henry IV* plays and *Henry V*, and just before *As You Like It*.

A Select Bibliography

(Page numbers are included for those works which treat *King John* specifically)

(A) HISTORIES OF LITERARY CRITICISM AND BACKGROUND STUDIES

Babcock, Robert Witbeck, *The Genesis of Shakespeare Idolatry*, Chapel Hill, N.C., 1931.
Bate, Jonathan, (ed.), *Shakespeare and the English Romantic Imagination*, Oxford, 1986; revised 1989.
—— *Shakespearean Constitutions*, Oxford, 1989.
—— *The Romantics on Shakespeare*, London, 1992.
Birch, W. J., *An Inquiry Into the Philosophy and Religion of Shakespeare*, London, 1848, pp. 33–4; 253–61.
Bryant, James C., *Tudor Drama and Religious Controversy*, Macon, Ga., 1984, pp. 129–49.
Bucknill, John Charles, *The Medical Knowledge of Shakespeare*, London, 1860, pp. 132–9.
Campbell, John Lord, *Shakespeare's Legal Acquirements Considered*, New York, 1859, pp. 74–8.
Cartwright, Robert, *The Footsteps of Shakespeare*, London, 1862, pp. 183–4; a response to Campbell.
Chambers, E. K., *William Shakespeare*, 2 vols, Oxford, 1930, I, 364–7.
Chesney, J. Portman, *Shakespeare as a Physician*, Chicago, 1884.
Curren-Aquino, Deborah T., (ed.), *'King John': An Annotated Bibliography*, New York, 1994.
Davis, C. K., *The Law in Shakespeare*, Washington, 1883.
de Grazia, Margreta, *Shakespeare Verbatim*, Oxford, 1991.
de Groot, John Harry, *The Shakespeares and 'The Old Faith'*, New York, 1946, pp. 182–223.
Dobson, Michael, *The Making of the National Poet*, Oxford, 1992.
Forsyth, Ebenezer, *Shakespeare: Some Notes on His Character and Writings*, Edinburgh, 1867, p.14.
Franklin, Colin, *Shakespeare Domesticated*, Aldershot, 1991.
Frye, Roland Mushat, *Shakespeare and Christian Doctrine*, Princeton, 1963, pp. 282–8.
Fullom, S.W., *History of William Shakespeare, Player and Poet*, London, 1864, pp. 61ff.
Holinshed, Raphael, *Chronicles*, 3 vols, London, 1587.
Hume, David, *The History of England*, 6 vols, London, 1754–62.
Kemble, Frances Anne, *Records of a Girlhood*, New York, 1883, pp. 517–18 and *passim*; first edition, 3 vols London, 1878.
Mutschman, H. and K. Wentersdorf, *Shakespeare and Catholicism*, New York, 1952, pp. 309–19.
Paris, Matthew, *Historia*, London, 1640.
Ralli, Augustus, (ed.), *A History of Shakespearian Criticism*, 2 vols, London, 1932.
Sherbo, Arthur, (ed.), *Johnson On Shakespeare*, 2 vols, New Haven, 1968, I, 405–28.
—— *The Birth of Shakespeare Studies*, East Lansing, Mi., 1986.
—— *Shakespeare's Midwives*, Newark, De., 1992.
Smith, D. Nichol, (ed.), *Eighteenth Century Essays on Shakespeare*, Glasgow, 1903; reprinted Oxford, 1963: with corrections and additional notes by F. P. Wilson.

Stavisky, Aron Y., *Shakespeare and the Victorians*, Norman, Ok., 1969.
Vickers, Brian, (ed.), *Shakespeare: The Critical Heritage, 1623–1801*, 6 vols, London and Boston, 1974–81.
Wendover, Roger of, *See* Giles (under EDITIONS AND PLAYTEXTS)
White, Edward J., *Commentaries on the Law in Shakespeare*, St. Louis, 1911, pp. 208–25.

(B) EDITIONS AND PLAYTEXTS

Beaurline, L. A., (ed.), *King John*, Cambridge, 1990.
Boswell, James, (ed.), *The Plays and Poems of William Shakespeare*, 21 vols, London, 1821.
Braunmuller, A. R., (ed.), *The Life and Death of King John*, Oxford, 1989.
Cibber, Colley, *Papal Tyranny in the Reign of King John*, London, 1745; an adaptation of Shakespeare's play.
Collier, John Payne, (ed.), *The Works of William Shakespeare*, 8 vols, London, 1842–4.
Evans, G. Blakemore, (ed.), *The Riverside Shakespeare*, Boston, 1974.
Foakes, R. A., (ed.), *The Collected Works of Samuel Taylor Coleridge: Lectures 1808–1819: On Literature*, 2 vols, London and Princeton, 1987, II, 285.
Furness, Horace Howard, Jr., (ed.), *The Life and Death of King John*, Philadelphia, 1919; the most recent variorum edition, invaluable for textual, critical, and performance history.
Giles, J. A., (ed.), *Roger of Wendover's 'Flowers of History'*, 2 vols, London, 1849.
Hanmer, Thomas, (ed.), *The Works of Mr William Shakespeare*, 6 vols, Oxford, 1743–4.
Honigmann, E. A. J., (ed.), *King John*, London, 1954.
Johnson, Samuel, (ed.), *The Plays of William Shakespeare*, 8 vols, London, 1765.
—— and Steevens, George, (eds.), *The Plays of William Shakespeare*, 10 vols, London, 1773.
—— and Steevens, George, (eds.), *The Plays of William Shakespeare*, 10 vols, London, 1778.
Keate, George, *The Poetical Works of George Keate, Esq.*, 2 vols, London, 1781, II, 147–9.
Matchett, William H., (ed.), *The Life and Death of King John*, New York, 1966.
Pope, Alexander, (ed.), *The Works of Mr William Shakespeare*, 6 vols, (1723–5).
Rowe, Nicholas, (ed.), *The Works of Mr. William Shakespeare*, 6 vols, London, 1709; the spurious 'seventh' volume of this edition (1710) contains Charles Gildon's 'Remarks on the Plays of Shakespeare', which include his observations on *King John* (337–41).
Shattuck, Charles H., (ed.), *William Charles Macready's 'King John'*, Urbana, Ill., 1962.
Sider, J. W., (ed.), *The Troublesome Raigne of John, King of England*, New York, 1979.
Smallwood, R. L., (ed.), *King John*, Harmondsworth, 1974.
Steevens, George, (ed.), *Twenty of the Plays of Shakespeare*, 4 vols, London, 1766.
Theobald, Lewis, (ed.), *The Works of Shakespeare*, 7 vols, London, 1733.
Valpy, Richard, *King John*, Reading, 1800; second edition, 1803; an adaptation of Shakespeare's play.
Warburton, William, (ed.), *The Works of Shakespeare*, 8 vols, London, 1747.
Wilson, John Dover, (ed.), *King John*, Cambridge, 1936.
Woodring, Carl, (ed.), *The Collected Works of Samuel Taylor Coleridge: Table Talk*, 2 vols, London and Princeton, 1990, I, 67; II, 57.

(C) CRITICISM AND OTHER SECONDARY WORKS

Alexander, Peter, *Shakespeare's Life and Art*, London, 1939, pp. 85–6.
Anon, *A Letter to Colley Cibber, Esq; on his Transformation of 'King John'*, London, 1745.
Battenhouse, Roy, 'King John: Shakespeare's Perspective and Others'. *Notre Dame English Journal*, 14 (1982), 191–215.

—— 'Religion in *King John*: Shakespeare's View'. *Connotations*, 1 (1991), 140–9.
Billington, Sandra, *Mock Kings in Medieval Society and Renaissance Drama*, Oxford, 1991, pp. 123–34 and *passim*.
Bonjour, Adrien, 'The Road to Swinstead Abbey: A Study of the Sense and Structure of *King John*'. *ELH*, 18 (1951), 253–74.
Bowle, John, *Miscellaneous Pieces of Antient English Poesie*, London, 1764, Sig.A2–A3.
Brown, A. D. J., 'The Little Fellow Has Done Wonders: Pope as Shakespeare Editor'. *Cambridge Quarterly*, 21 (1992), 120–49.
Burckhardt, Sigurd, 'The Ordering of This Present Time'. *ELH*, 33 (1966), 133–53; reprinted in Burckhardt's *Shakespearean Meanings*, Princeton, 1968, pp. 116–43.
Cairncross, Andrew, *The Problem of 'Hamlet': A Solution*, London, 1936, pp. 136–43
Calderwood, James, 'Commodity and Honour in *King John*'. *University of Toronto Quarterly*, 29 (1960), 341–56.
Candido, Joseph, ' "Women and fooles break off your conference": Pope's Degradations and the Form of *King John*'. In *Shakespeare's Histories: A Quest for Form and Genre*, edited by John Velz, Binghamton, N.Y., 1996, pp. 91–109.
Capell, Edward, *Notes and Various Readings to Shakespeare*, 3 vols, London, 1779–83, I, part 2, 115–39.
Champion, Larry S., ' "Confound Their Skill in Covetousness": The Ambivalent Perspective of Shakespeare's *King John*'. *Tennessee Studies in Literature*, 24 (1979), 36–55; this essay forms the basis for the remarks in Champion's *Perspective in Shakespeare's English Histories*, Athens, Ga., 1980, pp. 92–100.
Charlton, H. B., *Shakespearian Tragedy*, Cambridge, 1948, pp. 63–9.
Curren-Aquino, Deborah T., (ed.), *'King John': New Perspectives*, Newark, De., 1989; contains twelve essays on the play.
Davies, Thomas, *Dramatic Miscellanies*, 3 vols, London, 1783–4, I, 1–114.
Dusinberre, Juliet, '*King John* and Embarrassing Women'. *Shakespeare Survey*, 42 (1990), 37–52.
Elliott, John R., 'Shakespeare and the Double Image of King John'. *Shakespeare Studies*, 1 (1965), 64–84.
Farmer, Richard, *An Essay on the Learning of Shakespeare*, second edition, Cambridge, 1767, p. 76.
Gentleman, Francis, *The Dramatic Censor; or Critical Companion*, 2 vols, London, 1770, II, 155–73.
Gildon, Charles, *See* Rowe (under EDITIONS).
Grennan, Eamon, 'Shakespeare's Satirical History: A Reading of *King John*'. *Shakespeare Studies*, 11 (1978), 21–37.
Grey, Zachary, *Critical, Historical, and Explanatory Notes on Shakespeare*, 2 vols, London, 1754, I, 281–93
Griffith, Elizabeth, *The Morality of Shakespeare's Drama Illustrated*, London, 1775, pp. 175–88.
Halio, Jay L. 'Alternative Action: The Tragedy of Missed Opportunities in *King John*'. *Hebrew University Studies in Literature and the Arts*, 11, No. 2 (Spring, 1983), 254–69.
Hamilton, Donna B., *Shakespeare and the Politics of Protestant England*, Lexington, Ky., 1992, pp. 30–58.
Heath, Benjamin, *A Revisal of Shakespeare's Text*, London, 1765, pp. 222–32.
Hodgdon, Barbara, *The End Crowns All: Closure and Contradiction in Shakespeare's History*, Princeton, 1991, pp. 22–43.
Honigmann, E. A. J., *Shakespeare: The 'Lost Years'*, Manchester, 1985, pp. 119–22.
Jones, Emrys, *The Origins of Shakespeare*, Oxford, 1977, pp. 233–62.
Kastan, David Scott, ' "To Set a Form Upon that Indigest": Shakespeare's Fictions of History'. *Comparative Drama*, 17 (1983), 1–16.

Kenrick, William, *A Review of Doctor Johnson's New Edition of Shakespeare*, London, 1765, pp. 129–33.
Langbaine, Gerard, *An Account of the English Dramatic Poets*, Oxford, 1691, p. 467.
Leggatt, Alexander, 'Dramatic Perspective in *King John*'. *English Studies in Canada* (Toronto), 3 (1977), 1–17.
Loftis, John, *Renaissance Drama in England and Spain*, Princeton, 1987, pp. 72–82.
Matchett, William H., 'Richard's Divided Heritage in *King John*'. *Essays in Criticism*, 12 (1962), 231–53.
Palmer, John, *Political Characters of Shakespeare*, London, 1945, pp. 319–35.
Price, Jonathan Reeve, '*King John* and Problematic Art'. *Shakespeare Quarterly*, 21 (1970), 25–8.
Rackin, Phyllis, 'Patriarchal History and Female Subversion in *King John*'. In *'King John': New Perspectives*, edited by Deborah T. Curren-Aquino, Newark, De., 1989, pp. 76–90.
Ranald, Margaret Loftus, 'Women and Political Power in Shakespeare's English Histories'. *Topic*, 36, (1982), 54–65.
Ridley, M. R., *Shakespeare's Plays: A Commentary*, London, 1937, pp. 85–9.
Ritson, Joseph, *Remarks, Critical and Illustrative, on the Text and Notes of the Last Edition of Shakespeare*, London, 1783; challenges Malone on the status of Shakespeare's text.
Roderick, Richard, 'Remarks'. In *Canons of Criticism* by Thomas Edwards, seventh edition, London, 1765, pp. 251–5.
Salter, F. M., 'The Problem of *King John*'. *Proceedings and Transactions of the Royal Society of Canada*, third series, 43, section 2 (June 1949), 115–36.
Smith, Logan Pearsall, *On Reading Shakespeare*, London, 1933, pp. 143–5.
Stauffer, Donald A., *Shakespeare's World of Images*, New York, 1949, pp. 84–8.
Stubblefield, Charles, 'Some Thoughts About *King John*'. *CEA Critic*, 35, No. 3 (1973), 25–8.
Tillyard, E. M. W., *Shakespeare's History Plays*, London, 1944, pp. 215–33.
Upton, John, *Critical Observations on Shakespeare*, London, 1748, pp. 53–7; second corrected edition, 1748.
Van De Water, 'The Bastard in *King John*'. *Shakespeare Quarterly*, 11 (1960), 137–46.
Van Doren, Mark, *Shakespeare*, New York, 1939, pp. 106–15.
Vaughan, Virginia Mason, 'Between Tetralogies: *King John* as Transition'. *Shakespeare Quarterly*, 35 (1984), 407–20.
Welstead, Leonard, *The Works of Dionysius Longinus*, London, 1712, pp. 166–8.
Wixson, Douglas C., '"Calm Words Folded Up in Smoke": Propaganda and Spectator Response in Shakespeare's *King John*'. *Shakespeare Studies*, 14 (1981), 111–27.

Index

The Index is arranged in three parts: I. References to *King John* (including references to its characters as historical figures); II. References to Shakespeare's other works (including references to their characters as historical figures); III. General Index.

In Part II references to individual characters that contain no specific mention of a play or plays are not repeated under the relevant works.

I *KING JOHN*

Arthur, 4, 5, 6, 7, 9, 14, 19, 25nn., 26n., 27n., 32, 34, 37, 46, 51, 53, 55, 57, 59-60, 62, 63, 65-7, 69, 70-2, 73, 77, 78, 79, 81, 83, 84, 85, 86, 87, 89, 90-4, 96, 98, 102, 103, 105-10, 112-13, 119-20, 121, 122-3, 124, 132, 133-4, 138, 141, 143, 144, 145, 147, 150, 151, 152-3, 155-6, 157, 160-1, 164, 165-6, 169-71, 173, 178, 179, 180, 182, 183, 184, 185, 187, 190, 191, 192, 194, 195, 199, 205, 208, 209, 210, 211, 213-14, 216, 217, 220, 224, 226-7, 229, 232, 235, 239, 243, 244, 245, 246, 247, 248, 251, 254, 255, 258, 259, 262, 263, 265-9, 271, 272, 273, 278, 281, 282, 284-5, 286, 288, 289, 290-1, 292, 293, 294, 296, 297, 298-300, 304, 305, 307, 309-10, 311, 314-15, 316, 317, 320, 322, 325, 326-7, 329, 331, 333, 335, 337, 338, 339-40, 341, 343, 344, 346, 347, 348, 349, 352, 353, 355, 356, 357, 358, 359, 360, 363-4, 365, 366, 369, 370, 371, 380n., 383n., 385n.
Arthur (historical figure), 65, 76, 89, 90-1, 94, 110, 129, 138, 143, 150, 155-6, 166, 191, 198, 208, 255, 267, 283, 285, 286, 319, 320, 339, 375n., 376nn., 380n.
Austria, Duke of, *see* Lymoges

Bastard, *see* Faulconbridge
Bigot, 317
Blanch, 20, 61, 66, 81, 84, 90, 112, 118, 123, 133, 169, 170, 172, 178, 179-80, 182, 208, 210, 230-1, 243, 244, 247, 268, 280, 283, 286, 309, 316, 317, 325, 327, 350, 352, 357, 363
Blanch (historical figure), 81, 90, 283, 286

Chatillion, 32, 89, 99, 105, 114, 178, 251, 266, 267, 272, 277, 282, 289, 309, 315, 356, 364, 375n.
Citizen of Angiers, *see* Hubert

Commodity, 6, 14, 17, 19, 21, 29n., 61, 105, 112, 179, 184, 193, 200, 211, 257-60, 268, 273, 285, 294, 305-6, 308, 320, 326, 346, 363, 366
Constance, 1, 2, 3, 4, 5, 6-8, 9-10, 11-12, 13, 14, 17, 18, 23, 24n., 25n., 26n., 27nn., 32, 37, 38, 46, 51, 53, 55, 57, 59-60, 63, 66-7, 69, 70-2, 73-4, 75-81, 82-5, 86, 87, 89, 90, 93, 95-6, 98, 102, 103, 105-7, 108, 110, 111-22, 133-4, 138, 140-1, 143, 144, 147, 149-50, 155, 156-7, 161, 164, 168-74, 178-80, 182-3, 186-7, 190, 191, 192-3, 195, 202-3, 205, 208, 209, 216, 220-2, 224, 228-9, 230, 243, 244, 247, 248, 249, 252, 253-4, 255, 262-3, 265-9, 272, 273, 278-9, 280-3, 286, 288, 289, 290, 291, 292-3, 296, 298, 304, 307, 309, 314, 315, 322, 325, 326, 329-30, 331, 339-40, 341, 344, 346, 348-50, 355, 359-61, 364, 365, 366, 368, 371, 380n., 383n.
Constance (historical figure), 66, 75-7, 89, 90, 93, 94, 96, 191, 255, 281, 286, 375n., 376nn.

Date, 8, 10, 19, 28nn., 31-5, 50-1, 56, 64, 97-101, 134-5, 136-7, 148, 215, 224, 261, 290, 308, 311, 313, 329, 342-3, 348, 353
Dauphin, *see* Lewis, the Dauphin
Dolphin, *see* Lewis, the Dauphin

Elinor, 1, 2, 5, 6, 13, 23, 24n., 25n., 71, 78, 79, 81, 89-90, 91, 105, 112, 113, 114, 116, 118, 120-3, 140-1, 160-1, 168-9, 178, 182, 183, 191, 192, 208, 212, 216, 221, 227, 228-9, 240, 244, 249, 250, 251, 252, 263, 265-6, 267, 280, 283, 286, 288, 289, 290-1, 292, 294, 310, 317, 325, 326, 337, 340, 347, 349, 350, 352, 356, 358, 360, 363, 368, 370, 375n.
Elinor (historical figure), 76, 81, 89, 122, 191, 283, 286, 375n.
Essex, 161, 166, 363

Faulconbridge, 1, 2, 3, 4, 5, 7, 9, 12, 13-14, 18, 21, 22, 24, 24n., 26n., 29n., 34, 35, 44, 46, 51, 52, 53, 55, 57, 60-1, 63, 67, 69, 71-2, 74, 77, 81, 86, 94, 100, 102, 105, 109, 112, 122, 123, 129, 132, 133, 134, 138-9, 131, 141, 143, 144-5, 147, 149, 150-1, 154-5, 157, 160-3, 164, 165, 166-7, 177, 178, 179, 184-6, 190, 191, 193, 195-7, 199, 200-1, 205, 213, 214, 216, 217, 218, 224, 225, 226, 227-8, 230, 232, 235-6, 240, 243, 244, 245, 246-8, 249, 250, 251, 254, 258, 261-2, 263-4, 267, 268, 271, 273, 277, 278, 279, 281, 285-6, 288, 293-5, 297-8, 300, 304-5, 306, 307, 308-9, 312, 313-14, 316, 319, 322, 325, 326, 327, 331, 332-3, 335, 337, 338-9, 341, 343, 344, 345-6, 347, 351-2, 353, 355-6, 357-9, 363-4, 365, 366, 368, 370-1, 375nn.
Faulconbridge (historical figure), *see* Brent, Faukes de (III General Index)
Form, *see* Structure

Gurney, *see* James Gurney

Henry, *see* Prince Henry
History, (accuracy of), 7, 9, 10, 15, 74, 76, 77, 81, 82, 88-96, 102-5, 111-12, 128-30, 140, 142-4, 146-7, 153-4, 156-7, 160, 165-6, 170, 176, 189-91, 198-9, 205, 207-11, 243, 251, 255-6, 265, 267, 273-4, 281, 283, 284-6, 291, 300, 308, 318-21, 339, 355; (views of), 13, 22-4, 54-5, 59, 102-5, 128-34, 140, 152-6, 158-67, 198-201, 206, 255-6, 270-1, 280, 285, 291, 305-6, 318-21, 322, 324-8
Hubert, 4, 5, 6, 7, 9, 19, 25n., 27n., 36, 37, 52-3, 55, 57, 60, 63, 65-7, 68-9, 70, 72, 87, 92-3, 95-6, 101, 102, 106, 107, 108, 109, 112, 122-3, 124-7, 134, 138, 143-4, 149-50, 164, 178, 180, 182, 183, 185, 186, 188, 191, 192, 194-5, 205, 208, 209, 212, 216, 224, 235-6, 240, 243, 244, 245, 246, 248, 249, 254, 258, 259, 262, 266, 268-9, 277, 278,

279, 289, 291, 293, 294, 296, 297, 299-300, 305, 308, 310, 311, 314, 316, 317, 320, 321, 327, 333, 335, 339, 341, 344, 345-6, 347, 349, 352, 353, 357, 365, 366, 369, 371, 375n.
Hubert (historical figure), 92, 95, 143, 166, 320

James Gurney, 8, 12, 154-5, 365
John, *see* King John

King John, 2, 5, 6, 7, 9, 12, 13-15, 16-18, 21, 25n., 28n., 29n., 40, 52, 55, 57, 59-60, 61, 62-3, 65-7, 68-9, 70-2, 74, 77, 81, 84, 86, 87, 89, 90-6, 99, 101-2, 105, 107-10, 112, 114, 115, 116, 120-3, 124-7, 131-4, 138, 141, 143, 145, 149-50, 151, 152-4, 155-7, 160-3, 164, 165, 170, 178, 180, 183, 184, 185, 186, 187-8, 190-2, 193, 195, 196, 199-200, 201, 204, 205, 208, 209, 210, 211, 212-14, 216, 217, 224, 226-7, 229, 231, 232, 234-6, 240, 243, 244, 245, 246, 247, 248, 249, 251, 252, 253, 254, 258-60, 262, 265, 267, 268-9, 271, 272, 276, 277, 285, 287, 288, 289, 290-2, 293, 294, 295, 296-7, 298, 300, 301, 302, 303, 304, 305, 306, 308, 309, 314, 315, 316, 318-21, 325, 326-8, 330, 331, 332, 333, 335, 337-9, 340, 341, 343-4, 345-7, 351-2, 355-8, 359, 360-1, 363-5, 368, 369, 370-1, 372n., 375n., 380n., 381n., 382n., 383n., 385nn.
King John (historical figure), 35, 54, 65, 70, 77, 89, 90-6, 110, 129, 141, 142-3, 145, 149, 152-3, 166, 191, 198-9, 208-10, 255, 305, 318-21, 337-8, 355, 376nn., 377n., 380n., 383n.
King Philip, *see* Philip, King of France

Lady Faulconbridge, 5, 6, 71, 118, 123, 154-5, 178, 196, 228, 244, 251, 297, 338, 352, 353, 358, 365
Language, 6-7, 8, 16, 35-41, 42-4, 45-9, 55, 59, 63, 68-9, 72, 79-80, 95-6, 115-16, 125-7, 134-5, 136-7, 141, 145, 148-9, 150, 169-71, 187, 192-3, 215-16, 220-2, 223, 230, 239-41, 245, 251, 261, 268, 276, 277, 290, 293, 298, 299-300, 309, 317, 329-30, 339, 341, 342-3, 349, 360-1, 383n.
Lewis, the Dauphin, 6, 27n., 36, 46, 66-7, 81, 83, 84, 90, 94, 95, 105, 107, 112, 117-18, 133, 156, 163, 164, 165, 170, 171-2, 178, 179, 182, 183, 195, 200, 208, 209, 210, 211, 229-30, 232, 235, 240, 243, 244, 247, 249, 259, 263, 268, 294, 295, 299, 304, 305, 306, 309, 315, 316, 317, 319, 325, 327, 340, 352, 356, 357, 363, 365, 368, 370, 375n.
Lewis, the Dauphin (historical figure), 46, 94, 166-7, 208, 283
Lymoges (Limoges), 2, 5, 7, 36, 51, 60-1, 65, 66-7, 71, 79, 83, 85, 89, 100, 105, 113, 133-4, 144, 166, 169, 171, 177, 178, 183, 184, 192, 193, 194, 206, 229, 246-7, 251, 255, 258, 263, 298, 308, 316, 317, 325, 326, 331, 338, 343, 349, 353, 358, 363, 366; *see* Widomar, Viscount of Limoges *and* Leopold, Duke of Austria (III General Index) for the historical figures on which this character is based

Melune (Melun), 40, 95, 178, 186, 195, 200, 206, 209, 295, 317, 327, 363, 365
Melune (Melun) (historical figure), 95
Morality, 5-6, 13-14, 17-18, 22-3, 26n., 60-1, 65, 69, 128-34, 156, 181-8, 190-7, 199, 212-14, 229-32, 257-60, 268, 272-3, 298, 305, 309, 320, 355

Nationalism, 9, 12-13, 18, 54-5, 88, 101, 143, 147, 151, 153-4, 157, 158-67, 171, 177, 189, 197, 199-200, 204-6, 211, 217, 223, 224, 225-32, 253, 258, 262, 265, 267, 273, 277, 286, 294-5, 308-9, 319, 331, 336, 337, 356, 358-9, 366

Pandulph, 2, 4, 14, 19, 28n., 40, 51, 57, 60, 72, 78, 81, 85, 91, 94, 99, 106, 107, 115, 118, 127, 132, 134, 156-7, 164, 165, 171, 172, 178, 180, 182, 183, 194, 200, 205, 209, 210, 213, 230, 232, 234-6, 243, 244, 246, 249, 252-3, 255-6, 258-9, 262, 276, 282, 288, 291, 293, 294, 301, 302-6, 308, 309, 314, 315, 316, 326-7, 330, 334-5, 340-1, 343, 344, 346, 349, 352, 355, 357, 360-1, 364, 365, 368, 370, 372n., 375n.
Pandulph (historical figure), 255-6, 301
Patriotism, *see* Nationalism
Pembroke, 108, 109, 134, 161, 185, 187, 199, 245, 317, 320
Pembroke (historical figure), 167
Peter of Pomfret, 134, 138, 163, 178, 213, 245, 246, 279, 365
Philip, King of France, 27n., 32, 36, 37, 46, 60, 66, 71, 81, 83, 84, 85, 89, 90, 94, 99, 105-6, 113, 118, 121, 132, 133, 152, 155, 157, 160, 164, 169-70, 171-2, 173, 179-80, 182, 183, 184, 186, 191, 193, 206, 210, 212, 216, 227, 229, 231, 234-5, 240, 243, 244, 249, 251, 253, 259, 263, 267, 271, 277, 282, 292, 293, 294, 298, 302, 303, 305, 317, 320, 325, 333, 340, 349, 352, 356, 360, 361, 375n.
Philip, King of France (historical figure), 76, 89, 90, 91, 143, 166, 255, 376n.
Philip the Bastard (also called Richard), *see* Faulconbridge
Politics, *see* Nationalism *and* History
Prince Henry, 40, 47, 232, 246, 262, 273, 295, 317, 327, 341
Prince Henry (historical figure), 271; *see also* Henry III (III General Index)
Productions, (at Hackney 1769), 6; (by Macready), 27n., 118, 187-8, 381n.; (by John Philip Kemble), 52-3

Relationship to the other histories, 54-5, 104, 128-9, 130, 131, 158, 161, 163, 175-6, 187-8, 190, 215-16, 223-4, 227, 249, 261, 270-1, 273, 280, 287, 289, 290, 292, 307-8, 321, 324-5, 330, 332-3, 336, 341
Religion, *see* Roman Catholicism *and* Protestantism (III General Index)
Robert Faulconbridge, 51, 178, 182, 228, 243, 250, 258, 294, 297, 308, 315, 352

Salisbury, 6, 61, 94, 106, 108, 109, 134, 161, 164, 165, 170, 171, 179-80, 183, 185, 186-7, 194-5, 197, 199-200, 204, 205-6, 244, 249, 262, 292, 320, 349, 360, 363, 381n.
Sources, 3-4, 7, 16, 17, 19, 21, 31-2, 35, 50, 64-7, 68-9, 70, 75, 86, 88-96, 97-8, 103, 129, 137-9, 144, 147-8, 163, 165-7, 176-8, 181, 198-9, 201, 207-10, 224, 231, 236, 238-9, 242-8, 250, 262, 265, 268, 270, 275-9, 281, 284-6, 287-8, 296, 298-9, 302-5, 308-10, 311, 313-14, 330-1, 332, 337, 340, 342, 344, 346, 347, 348, 352, 362-6, 367, 370, 383n.
Structure, 1-6, 7, 10, 13, 15-17, 18, 20-3, 29n., 62-3, 64-5, 70, 72, 102, 105-7, 141, 145, 201, 216, 226-32, 239, 242-8, 249, 257-60, 262, 265, 278, 279, 291-2, 297, 314-6, 324-8, 330-1, 346-7, 363-6, 367-8, 383n.
Style, 16-17, 25n., 55, 61, 135, 136-7, 139, 141, 145, 148-9, 190, 215-16, 219, 220-2, 223, 245, 250-4, 272, 277-9, 290, 307, 311-12, 315, 317, 333, 341, 342-3, 353, 366; *see also* Language

Topicality, 8, 10, 14, 15, 20, 22, 33-4, 51, 93, 98-102, 148, 207-11, 241, 262, 267, 303, 305, 336, 362

War, (attitudes toward), 183-4

II SHAKESPEARE'S WORKS (EXCLUDING *KING JOHN*)

Adriana (*The Comedy of Errors*), 349
All's Well That Ends Well, 38, 48, 374n.
Anne Bullen (*Henry VIII*), 280
Antony (*Antony and Cleopatra*), 252
Antony and Cleopatra, 83
As You Like It, 40, 111, 236, 241, 386n.

Bolingbroke (*Richard II*), 343, 385n.
Brutus (*Julius Caesar*), 86

Caliban (*The Tempest*), 273
Cardinal Beauford (also 'Beaufort') (*1* and *2 Henry VI*), 302
Cassandra (*Troilus and Cressida*), 171
Chorus (*Henry V*), 127
Comedy of Errors, The, 38, 146, 349, 350
Cordelia (*King Lear*), 217
Coriolanus, 38, 40, 79, 130, 131, 137, 248, 370
Coriolanus (character), 75, 113, 281
Cymbeline, 38, 111, 148

Desdemona (*Othello*), 216
Dromio of Syracuse (*The Comedy of Errors*), 350
Duchess of York (*Richard III*), 224
Duke Frederick (*As You Like It*), 40
Duke Vincentio (*Measure for Measure*), 273
Duncan (*Macbeth*), 357

Edmund (*King Lear*), 200, 264, 297, 302, 316
Edward IV (*3 Henry VI* and *Richard III*), 351
Edward, Prince of Wales (*Richard III*), 194, 235, 288, 293, 307, 309
Elizabeth, Queen (*Richard III*), 224, 309
Erpingham (*Henry V*), 187-8
Exton (*Richard II*), 385n.

Falstaff (*1* and *2 Henry IV*), 21, 71, 151, 271
First Tetralogy, 23, 135, 223, 307-8
Fortinbras (*Hamlet*), 258

Gloucester (*King Lear*), 172, 369
Goneril (*King Lear*), 98
Gravedigger (*Hamlet*), 247

Hamlet, 8, 28n., 46, 47, 48, 100, 137, 138, 147, 212, 216, 261, 341, 366, 374n., 389
Hamlet (character), 216, 247, 250, 258
Henry IV plays, 5, 35, 128, 148, 168, 215, 223, 238, 261, 307, 319, 386n.
Henry IV, part one, 35, 97, 127, 175, 261, 272

Henry IV, part two, 35, 47, 97, 175, 261
Henry IV (character), 2, 252, 341, 351, 386n.
Henry IV (historical figure), 384n.
Henry V, 5, 23, 46, 47, 97, 127, 187-8, 215, 248, 261, 307, 313, 319, 331, 332-3, 336, 351, 381n., 386n.
Henry V (character), 2, 187-8, 250, 302, 307, 319, 351, 356, 368
Henry VI plays, 4, 31, 61, 309, 330, 349, 353; *The Whole Contention betweene the Two Famous Houses, Lancaster and Yorke* (1619), 330
Henry VI, part one, 332
Henry VI, part three, 37, 332
Henry VI (character), 2
Henry VI (historical figure), 386n.
Henry VIII, ix, 3, 4, 8, 37, 54-5, 60, 141, 176, 215, 216, 234, 280, 302, 324, 336
Henry VIII (character), 2, 216
Henry VIII (historical figure), 54, 91, 207, 209, 280, 305, 319
Hermione (*The Winter's Tale*), 80, 150, 360
Horatio (*Hamlet*), 196
Hotspur (*1 Henry IV*), 138, 161, 217, 298
Humphrey, Duke of Gloucester (*1* and *2 Henry VI*), 302

Iago (*Othello*), 138, 216
Imogen (*Cymbeline*), 38

Joan of Arc (historical figure), *see* Joan of Arc (III General Index)
John of Gaunt (*Richard II*), 289, 331, 343
Juliet (*Romeo and Juliet*), 79, 80, 116, 172, 309
Julius Caesar, 86, 258, 370
Justice Shallow (*2 Henry IV*), 353

Katherine (*The Taming of the Shrew*), 368
Katherine (also 'Catherine') (*Henry VIII*), 60, 141, 216, 280
Kent (*King Lear*), 196
King Lear, 35, 98, 106, 137, 172, 200, 228, 264, 273, 297, 316, 365, 369, 379nn.
King Lear (character), 80, 98, 106, 116, 172, 174, 253

Lady Macbeth (*Macbeth*), 266
Lady Macduff (*Macbeth*), 150
Love's Labor's Lost, 38, 137, 236, 241
Lucio (*Measure for Measure*), 273
Lucrece (*The Rape of Lucrece*), 224

Macbeth, 61, 102, 111, 118, 137, 138, 146, 150, 185, 248, 370
Macbeth (character), 248, 266, 302, 357
Mamillius (*The Winter's Tale*), 150, 194, 350
Margaret, Queen (*Henry VI* plays), 168, 309, 349
Margaret, Queen (*Richard III*), 224, 307, 360
Measure for Measure, 41, 239, 273
Merchant of Venice, The, 58, 137, 148, 261, 289, 333, 338
Mercutio (*Romeo and Juliet*), 138, 297, 365, 368

Merry Wives of Windsor, The, 236
Midsummer Night's Dream, A, 36, 46, 127, 289; *Pyramus and Thisbe*, 46
Much Ado About Nothing, 111, 228

Northumberland (*1* and *2 Henry IV*), 161

Ophelia (*Hamlet*), 359
Othello, 85, 119, 137, 138, 216, 273
Othello (character), 47, 80, 116, 216

Pericles, 136
Pistol (*2 Henry IV* and *Henry V*), 177
Polonius (*Hamlet*), 48
Prince Hal (*1* and *2 Henry IV*), 217, 307
Prospero (*The Tempest*), 250, 273

Regan (*King Lear*), 98
Richard II, 5, 8, 23, 61, 97, 141, 175, 190, 223, 261, 273, 287, 289, 297, 303, 307, 311, 314, 331, 342-3, 368, 384n., 385n.
Richard II (character), 2, 12, 190, 192-3, 252, 290, 307, 329, 341, 351, 368, 385n., 386n.
Richard II (historical figure), 54, 209, 210, 384n.
Richard III, 4, 16, 37, 128, 138, 178, 194, 212, 223-4, 247, 248, 261, 273, 288, 289, 290, 292, 293, 309, 321, 330, 331, 332, 368, 370
Richard III (character), 2, 62, 70, 108, 138, 161, 182, 194, 212-13, 224, 234, 235, 247, 248, 290, 291, 293, 303, 356, 357, 368, 371
Richard III (historical figure), 54
Richard, Duke of York (*Richard III*), 194, 235, 288, 293, 309-10
Richmond (*Richard III*), 303
Romeo and Juliet, 38, 80, 111, 137, 212, 267, 273, 288, 289, 363, 365

Second Tetralogy, 23, 307-8
Sir Hugh Evans (*The Merry Wives of Windsor*), 236
Sir Nathaniel (*Love's Labor's Lost*), 236
Sir Oliver Martext (*As You Like It*), 236
Sir Toby Belch (*Twelfth Night*), 353
'Sir Topas' (*Twelfth Night*), 236
Son to Macduff (*Macbeth*), 194
Sonnets, 20, 56, 98, 127, 212

Taming of the Shrew, The, 365, 368, 386n.
Tempest, The, 36, 124, 148
Timon of Athens, 47
Titus Andronicus, 136, 288, 321
Troilus and Cressida, 171
Two Gentlemen of Verona, The, 137, 148, 377n.
Two Noble Kinsman, The, 223
Tybalt (*Romeo and Juliet*), 80
Tyrrel (*Richard III*), 212-13, 224, 291

Volumnia (*Coriolanus*), 75, 79, 113, 281, 360

Warwick (*Henry VI* plays), 161
Westmoreland (*Henry V*), 187
Winter's Tale, The, 146, 148, 150, 194, 350
Wolsey (*Henry VIII*), 141, 216
Wolsey (historical figure), 157, 380n.

III GENERAL INDEX

Abbott, E. A., ix
Abbott, George, 332
Aeneid, The, see Virgil
Agenor, 373n.
Aickin, James, 375n.
Albert, Cardinal Archduke of Austria, 51, 100
Alcides (i.e., Hercules), 35-6, 44; *see also* Hercules
Alexander, Peter, 19, 28n., 388
Alfieri, Vittorio, 375n.; *Merope*, 375n.
Alighieri, Dante, 216, 287; *The Divine Comedy*, 301
All the Year Round (periodical), 257
Allen, William, Cardinal, 210
Alphonso III (King of Castile), 283
Amphion, 216
Anatomy of Melancholy, see Burton, Robert
Andromache, 7, 169
Anglican Church, *see* Church of England
Anjou, Geoffrey, 1st Earl of, 35
Annales de Burton, see Annales Monastici
Annales Monastici, 205, 381n.
Apollo, 110, 380n.
Archer, William, 296
Aristotle, 1, 18, 251-2, 256, 301, 367, 386n.; *Poetics*, 386n.
Artemis, 110, 380n.
Athenæum, The, 111, 198, 377n., 378n.
Atlantic Monthly, 175
Augustus, 1st Roman Emperor, 374n.

Babcock, Robert Witbeck, 387
Bacon, Sir Francis, 68, 98, 201, 209, 233, 275; authorship controversy, 233, 275
Baker, George Pierce, 16, 332-3, 386
Bale, John, 89, 103, 141, 147, 176-7, 302, 308, 331, 378n.; *Kynge Johan* (also *King Johan*), 89, 103, 147, 176-7, 302, 308, 331, 375n.; *New Comedy*, 384n.
Barrymore, William, 375n.
Baskerville, Sir Thomas, 51
Bate, Jonathan, 8, 26n., 387
Battenhouse, Roy, 19, 28n., 388-9

'Battle of the Baltic, The', *see* Campbell, Thomas
Baudissin, Graf W. H., 54
Beaurline, L. A., 19, 28n., 388
Beeching, Henry Charles, 27n., 334-5, 386
Bell, R., 377n.
Bensley, Robert, 375n.
Bertha (grandmother of Constance of Brittany), 76
Besterman, Theodore, 381n.
Billington, Sandra, 29n., 389
Birch, W. J., 27n., 387
Black, John, 54-5, 374n.
Blackstone, William, 375n.
Blake, Henry, 26n.
Blistein, Elmer, 386n.
Blount, Edward, 148
Boaden, James, 9, 73-4
Boas, Frederick Samuel, ix, 15, 28n., 290-5, 363
Bomb, The, *see* Harris, Frank
Bonaparte, Napoleon, *see* Napoleon I
Bonjour, Adrien, 21, 29n., 389
Book of Martyrs, *see* Foxe, John
Boorde, Andrew, 382n.; *The Fyrst Boke of the Introduction of Knowledge*, 382n.
Borgia, Cesare, 77
Boswell, James, 31; *The Life of Johnson*, 31
Boswell, James, Jr., viii, 25n., 31, 125, 375nn., 376n., 388
Boswell-Stone, W., 386n.
Bowden, Henry Sebastian, 14, 19, 27n., 301-6, 334-5, 384, 385n.
Bowle, John, 3-4, 389
Bradley, A. C., ix, 12, 14, 15
Brandes, Georg Morris Cohen, 12, 16, 296-300, 384, 385n.
Braunmuller, A. R., 28n., 388
Brent, Faukes de (also 'Falcasius de Breaute', 'Fawkes de Bréauté', 'Faukes de Breauté', 'Foukes de Brent', 'Falco de Brenta'), 144, 166-7, 337
British Theatre, The, 52
Brooke, Arthur, 362, 386n.; *The Tragicall Historye of Romeus and Juliet*, 362, 363, 386n.
Brooke, Stopford Augustus, 12, 355-61
Brown, A. D. J., 24n., 389
Browne, Gordon, 261
Browning, Elizabeth Barrett, 345
Browning, Robert, 265, 345
Bryant, James C., 28n., 387
Bucknill, John Charles, 12, 27n., 168-74, 380, 380n., 387
Bullen, A. H., viii, 334
Bullough, Geoffrey, 386nn.
Bulthaupt, Heinrich, 16, 313, 314-17, 385n.
Bunnett, F. E., 189, 382n.
Bunyan, John, 342
Burckhardt, Sigurd, 22, 24, 389
Burke, Edmund, 154, 379n.

Burleigh, William Cecil, 99, 209
Burns, Robert, 202
Burton, Robert, *Anatomy of Melancholy*, 378n.
Byron, George Gordon, 98, 280

Cairncross, Andrew, 19, 28n., 389
Calderón de la Barca, Pedro, 128
Calderwood, James, 21, 29n., 389
Calvert, George Henry, 15, 27n., 249-54
Camden, William, 35, 372n., 373n., 374nn.; *Remains Concerning Britain*, 35, 372n.
Campbell, John Lord, 27n., 237, 387
Campbell, Thomas, 9-10, 82-5, 86-7, 116, 117, 375, 375nn., 383n.; *The Pleasures of Hope*, 82; 'Ye Mariners of England',82; 'Hohenlinden', 82; 'The Battle of the Baltic', 82
Candido, Joseph, ix, 24n., 30n., 389
Capell, Edward, 3-4, 25n., 26n., 389
Carlisle, Carol J., 27n.
Carlyle, Thomas, 198
Carter, Thomas, 334
Cartwright, Robert, 27n., 387
Case, R. H., ix
Catholicism, *see* Roman Catholicism
Caxton, William, 362
Cervantes Saavedra, Miguel de, 202
Chalmers, George, 8, 26n., 50-1, 56, 97, 100, 233, 373, 373n., 374n., 382n.
Chambers, Edmund Kerchever, 16, 25n., 329-31, 387
Champion, Larry S., 29n., 30n., 389
Charles II, 383n.
Charles, Duke of York, Prince of Wales (son to James I), 241
Charlton, H. B., 29n., 389
Chaucer, Geoffrey, 38, 44
Chesney, J. Portman, 27n., 387
Chester, Ranulf, Earl of (also 'Randall de Blondeville'; second husband of Constance of Brittany), 66, 76
Chesterfield, Philip, Earl of, 2
Chettle, Henry, 350
Christian Union, The, 311
Chronicles, see Holinshed, Raphael
Church of England, 20, 28n.
Churchill, Charles, 138, 379n.; *The Rosciad*, 138
Churchman, The, 146
Cibber, Colley, 2-3, 4, 7, 8, 10, 16, 20, 25n., 26n, 27n., 102, 388; *Papal Tyranny in the Reign of King John*, 2-3, 7, 10, 20, 25nn., 26n., 27n., 102, 388
Cibber, Susannah, 53, 193
Clark, William George., viii, 175
Clarke, Charles Cowden, 13-14, 181-8, 381n.
Clarke, Helen Archibald, ix, 345
Clarke, John, 181
Clarke, Mary Cowden, ix, 181
Clarke, Sampson, 32

Cleopatra, 7
Clinton, De Witt, 136
Clytemnestra, 7
Coke, Sir Edward, 102
Cole, Thomas, 139, 379n.
Coleridge, Derwent, 140
Coleridge, Hartley, 11, 16, 140-1
Coleridge, Henry Nelson, 380n.
Coleridge, Samuel Taylor, vii, 8, 12, 14, 26nn., 95, 98, 101, 102, 140, 154-5, 198, 249, 376n., 377nn., 379n., 380n., 388; *Lyrical Ballads*, 377n.
Collier, Jeremy, 1
Collier, John Payne, vii, viii, 68, 103, 124, 136, 137, 175, 178, 375n., 378n., 379n., 380n., 381n., 388
Conan, Duke of Brittany (father of Constance of Brittany), 76
Condell, Henry, 275
Congreve, William, 63
Constance (godmother of Constance of Brittany), 76
Controversiae, see Seneca, Lucius Annaeus (the elder)
Cook, E. T., 384n.
Cooke, George Frederick, 52-3
Corson, Hiram, 12, 265-9, 383, 383n.
Country Parson, The, see Herbert, George
Courtenay, Thomas Peregrine, 10, 27n., 88-96, 102, 104-5, 128, 129, 130, 189, 284, 318, 375, 376n., 377n., 383n.
Craig, W. J., ix
Creizenach, Wilhelm, ix
Crëusa, 7
Critic, The, see Sheridan, Richard Brinsley
Cromwell, Oliver, 164
Cumberland's British Theatre, 70
Curll, Edmund, 24n.
Curren-Aquino, Deborah T., xv, 18, 23, 27n., 28n., 29n., 30n., 387, 389

Daily Journal, The, 25n.
Daniel, George, 9, 70-2
Daniel, P. A., 386nn.
Daniel, Samuel, 334
Dante Alighieri, *see* Alighieri, Dante
Dark Lady of the Sonnets, 20
Daru, Pierre, 376n.
D'Avenant, William, 1
Davenport, John, 322; *King John and Matilda*, 322
David, King, 207, 302, 305
David and Bethsabe, see Peele, George
Davies, Thomas, 7-8, 10, 389
Davis, C. K., 27n., 387
Davison, William, 93, 101, 209, 305
de Dol, Count, *see* Dol, Count de
de Gourdon, Bertrand, *see* Gourdon, Bertrand de

de Grazia, Margreta, 26n., 387
de Groot, John Henry, 19, 28n., 387
de Thouars, Guy, *see* Thouars, Guy de
de Tours, Guy, *see* Thouars, Guy de
degli Ubaldini, Ruggiero, Archbishop, *see* Ubaldini, Ruggiero degli, Archbishop
Delius, Nicolaus, viii, 223
Dennis, John, 1
De Quincey, Thomas, 202
Derby, William Stanley, 6th Earl of, 210
'Descent Into Hell, The', *see* Heraud, John Abraham
Deutsche Zeitung, 189
Dewe, Thomas, 32
Dickens, Charles, 353
Dicks, John, viii
Dido, 74, 365
Divine Comedy, The, *see* Alighieri, Dante
Dobson, Michael, 26n., 387
Dobson, William, 49, 373n.; *Paradisus Amissus*, 49, 373n.
Dol, Count de, 76
Douce, Francis, 102, 377n.
Dowden, Edward, viii, ix, 13, 14, 212-14
Drake, Nathan, 9, 56-8, 233, 374, 374nn., 382n.
Drayton, Michael, 334
Drummond of Hawthornden, William, 380n.
Dryden, John, 1, 31
Duchess of Malfi, The, *see* Webster, John
Duke of Milan, The, *see* Massinger, Philip
Dumas, Alexandre, 234
Dunn, R. D., 372n.
Dusinberre, Juliet, 1, 7, 13, 23, 389
Dyce, Alexander, viii, 124

Eastlake, Lady Elizabeth, 75
Edward II, 210
Edward II, *see* Marlowe, Christopher
Edward III (partly Shakespearian?), 223
Edward VI, 103, 177, 209
Edwards, Thomas, 25n.
Elinor (sister to Arthur of Brittany), 94-5
Elizabeth I, 7, 14, 32, 33, 35, 51, 55, 86, 91, 93, 95, 100, 101-2, 129, 140-1, 142, 157, 161, 209-10, 226, 234, 241, 253, 276, 300, 302, 303, 305, 317, 319, 335, 336, 337, 338, 339, 357, 362, 368, 384n.
Elliott, John R., 21, 389
Ellis, Miss (English actress), 118, 122
Elton, Oliver, 272-4
Elze, Karl, ix
Essay on Man, An, *see* Pope, Alexander
Essex, Robert Devereaux, 2nd Earl of, 33, 51, 98, 100, 102, 210, 384n.
Etty, J. Lytelton, ix, 14-15, 16, 17, 318-21, 385

Euripides, 375n., 377n.; *Merope*, 375n.; *Troades*, 377n.
Evans, G. Blakemore, 388
Evening News, The, 348
Examiner, The, 257

Faerie Queene, The, *see* Spenser, Edmund
Fairbrother, Louisa, 118, 123
False Shame, *see* Marshall, Francis Albert
Famous History of Captain Thomas Stukely, The (Anon.), 34
Famous Victories of Henry V, The (Anon.), 275
Farmer, Richard, 3, 4, 25n., 42, 68, 137, 374n., 379n., 389
Farren, William, 375n.
Faucit, Helen, 11, 118-20, 268
Fawkes, Guy, 33
First Folio (1623), 1, 36, 39, 42-4, 46-7, 148, 178, 180, 241, 275, 276, 383n.
Fitz Court, Alan, 376n.
Flanders, Philip, Earl of, 90
Fleay, Frederick Gard, 15, 238-41, 261, 299, 363, 382, 382n., 383nn.
Fletcher, George, 11, 111-23, 377, 384n.
Fletcher, John, ix, 240, 322, 370
Flowers of History, *see* Wendover, Roger of
Foakes, R. A., 26nn., 388
Ford, John, 140
Forsyth, Ebenezer, 27n., 387
Fortescue, Sir John, 95, 376n.
Fortnightly Review, The, 215, 348
Foxe, John; *Book of Martyrs*, 287
Franklin, Colin, 25n., 387
Franz, Wilhelm, ix
Frye, Roland Mushat, 28n., 387
Fullom, S. W., 27n., 387
Furmie (servant to the historical Prince Arthur), 376n.
Furness, Horace Howard, viii, 370
Furness, Horace Howard, Jr., viii, 8, 17, 18, 25n., 27n., 370-1; *The Gloss of Youth*, 370, 388
Furnivall, Frederick James, vii, viii, 15, 16, 28n., 223-4, 362, 382, 382nn., 386n.
Fyrst Boke of the Introduction of Knowledge, The, *see* Boorde, Andrew

Galaxy, The, 175
Garnet, Henry, 33
Garnett, Richard, 12, 336-41, 386, 386n.
Garrick, David, 52-3, 193
Gentleman, Francis, 5, 16, 17, 18, 26nn., 389
Gentleman's Magazine, The, 73
Geoffrey, 1st Earl of Anjou, 35
Geoffrey Plantagenet (first husband of Constance of Brittany), 66, 76, 121, 152, 172, 183
George III, 82
Gervinus, Georg Gottfried, ix, 10, 12, 13-14, 17, 27n., 29n., 128, 135, 189-97, 236-7, 250, 267, 303, 381
Gherardesca, Ugolino della, 76

Gildon, Charles, 1, 2, 3, 4, 5, 7, 9, 15, 24n., 175, 380n., 388, 389
Giles, Henry, 11, 202-3
Giles, J. A., 376n., 378n., 380n., 388
Gloss of Youth, The, see Furness, Horace Howard, Jr.
Glover, John, viii, 175
Godwin, William, 74
Goethe, Johann Wolfgang von, 128, 249, 272, 280
Goldsmith, Oliver, 342
Gould, Robert, 1
Gourdon, Bertrand de, 65
Grant, Douglas, 379n.
Gray, Thomas, 40, 48-9, 373n.; 'Ode on a Distant Prospect of Eton College', 40, 48
Greenblatt, Stephen, 20
Greene, Robert, 34, 165, 238, 362, 386n.; *Pandosto*, 362, 386n.
Grennan, Eamon, 22, 389
Grey, Lady Catherine, 209
Grey, Zachary, 25n., 389
Griffin, W. Hall, 257
Griffith, Elizabeth, 5-6, 7, 26n., 389
Guizot, François Pierre Guillaume, 16, 142-5, 379, 383n.
Guthrie, Thomas Anstey, 242

Hakluyt, Richard, 99, 377n.; *Hakluyt's Voyages*, 99, 377n.
Hakluyt's Voyages, see, Hakluyt, Richard
Halio, Jay L., 29n., 389
Hall (also 'Halle'), Edward, 88, 270, 386n.
Hall, Henry Thomas, 11, 12, 204-6, 381, 381nn.
Hallam, Henry, 89, 375n.
Halliwell-Phillipps, J. O., viii, 223
Hamilton, Donna B., 20, 29n., 389
Handel, George Frederick, 189
Hanmer, Sir Thomas, 38, 42, 47, 372n., 373n., 388
Harbage, Alfred, 384n.
Hardy, Henry John, 10, 255-6, 383
Hardy, Thomas Duffus, 375n., 376n., 377n.
Hare, Augustus William, 379n.
Hare, Julius Charles, 379n.
Hargrove, C., 382nn.
Harris, Frank, 11, 17, 348-50; *The Bomb*, 348
Harvey, William, 136
Haterius, Quintus, 374n.
Hathaway, Anne, 17, 348, 350
Hawkins, Charles Halford, 255
Hawthorne, Nathaniel, 202
Hayward, Sir John, 303, 384n.
Hazlitt, William, vii, 8-9, 13, 28n., 59-61, 108, 149, 150, 374, 374n., 382n.
Heath, Benjamin, 25n., 389
Hecuba, 7, 107
Hegel, Georg Wilhelm Friedrich, 128

Heminges, John, 275
Henneman, John B., 175
Henry II, 35, 89, 122
Henry III, 166, 271
Henry IV (King of France), 51, 241
Henry VII, 54
Henry VIII, *see* Henry VIII (historical figure) (II Shakespeare's Works)
Henry Fitz-Empress, *see* Henry II
Henry, Prince of Wales (son to James I), 241
Heraud, John Abraham, 12-14, 17, 198-201, 204, 381nn.; *The Roman Brother*, 198; *Videna*, 198; 'The Descent Into Hell', 198; 'The Judgment of the Flood', 198
Herbert, George, 334; *The Country Parson*, 334
Herbert, William, Earl of Pembroke, 73
Hercules, 211, 297, 316; *see also* Alcides
Herford, Charles Harold, viii, 12, 307-10, 311, 334-5, 342, 372n., 374n., 380n., 385
Herrick, Robert, 68
Hettinger, F. L., 301
Hewet, H. W., 136
Hickson, Samuel, ix
Hill, Aaron, 375n.; *Merope*, 375n.
Historia, *see* Paris, Matthew
History of Jason, *see* Le Fevre, Raoul
Hodgdon, Barbara, 29n., 389
'Hohenlinden', *see* Campbell, Thomas
Holinshed, Raphael, 35, 64, 65, 88-95, 129, 138, 144, 165-6, 198, 224, 238-9, 270, 302, 313, 314, 332, 352, 374n., 375n., 376nn., 380n., 386n., 387; *Chronicles*, 35, 64-5, 88-95, 129, 138, 144, 165-6, 198, 238-9, 302, 352, 374n., 375n., 376nn., 380n., 387
Home and Foreign Review, 207
Homer, 287
Honigmann, E. A. J., 19, 20, 28n., 29n., 388, 389
Hope, Jonathan, ix
Hopkins, Anthony Hope, 242
Hopkins, Elizabeth, 375n.
Horace, 48, 68
Horn, Franz, 379n.
Household Words, 257
Hoveden, Roger de, 376nn.
Howard, Sidney, 332
Howard, Thomas, Lord, 98
Hudson, Henry Norman, viii, 11, 27n., 28n., 146-51, 379, 379n., 381n., 382n.
Hughes, J., 373n.
Hume, David, 87, 142, 375n., 379nn., 387
Hunt, Leigh, 181
Hunter, Joseph, 27nn., 124-7, 237, 302, 378n.
Huntington, Henry Hastings, 3rd Earl of, 210
Hutton, Laurence, 367
Hyde, Henry, Earl of Clarendon, 68
Hyde, Lawrence, Earl of Rochester, 68

Important Considerations, see Watson, William
Inchbald, Elizabeth, 9, 52-3, 73; *A Simple Story*, 52
Inchbald, Joseph, 52
Infanta of Spain, *see* Isabel Clara Eugenia, Infanta of Spain; *see also* Maria, Infanta of Spain
Innocent III, Pope, 157, 209, 255, 301
Insatiate Countess, The, see Marston, John
Ireland, William Henry, 26n., 31, 50, 73
Irving, Henry, viii, 261
Isabel Clara Eugenia, Infanta of Spain, 210, 241, 305
'It is not to be thought of that the Flood', *see* Wordsworth, William

Jaggard, Isaac, 148
James I, 86, 95, 210
James II, 383n.
Jameson, Anna Brownell, 9-10, 11-12, 13, 18, 23, 27nn., 28n., 75-81, 96, 106, 111, 113-17, 205, 224, 262, 268, 292, 375, 375nn., 384n.
Jameson, Robert, 75
Jeffreys, George, 375n.; *Merope*, 375n.
Joan of Arc, 7, 221
John, Ivor Bertram, 16, 342-4
Johnson, Samuel, viii, 2, 4, 5, 6, 8, 26nn., 31, 33, 37, 42, 45, 51, 59, 68, 96, 99, 100, 178, 342, 372nn., 373nn., 374nn., 377nn., 379n., 381n., 387, 388
Jones, Emrys, 23, 29n., 389
Jonson, Ben, 1, 31, 33, 34, 60, 173, 175, 245, 350, 372n., 374nn., 380.; *The Silent Woman*, 33, 372n.; *Timber: or, Discoveries*, 374n.
Jordan, Dorothy, 73
'Judgment of the Flood, The', *see* Heraud, John Abraham
Jusserand, J. J., 367, 386n.

Kafka, Franz, 29n.
Kastan, David Scott, 29n., 389
Keate, George, 6-7, 26n., 388
Keats, John, vii, 181
Kemble, Charles, 53
Kemble, Frances Anne (Fanny), 9, 27nn., 387
Kemble, John Philip, 52, 73, 82, 375n.
Kennet, White, Bishop of Peterborough, 373n., 374nn.
Kenrick, William, 26n., 390
Kierkegaard, Søren, 296
King John and Matilda, see Davenport, John
Knight, Charles, viii, 10, 14, 27n., 28n., 97-110, 124, 137, 148, 233-5, 376n., 377, 377nn., 379nn., 380n., 382n.
Kreyssig, Friedrich, 129, 302, 304, 378n.
Kyd, Thomas, *The Spanish Tragedy*, 34
Kynge Johan (also *King Johan*), *see* Bale, John

Lamb, Charles, 137, 181
Lamb, Mary Ann, 181
Landor, Walter Savage, 215

Langbaine, Gerard, 1, 4, 19, 25n., 34, 390
Langton, Stephen, Archbishop of Canterbury, 91, 94, 157, 208, 211, 234, 247, 276, 301, 319, 340
Lee, Sidney, viii, 336
Le Fevre, Raoul, 362; *History of Jason*, 362
Leggatt, Alexander, 29n., 390
Leicester, Robert Dudley, Earl of, 209
Leicester's Commonwealth, The, see Parsons, the Reverend Robert
Leopold, Duke of Austria, 7, 65, 89, 129, 144, 166
Lewes, Louis, 12, 280-3, 384, 384n.
Life of Johnson, The, see Boswell, James
Lingard, John, 376nn.
Livy, 87, 375n.
Lloyd, William Watkiss, 12-14, 17-18, 68, 158-67, 224, 380
Lockhart, John Gibson, 198, 377n.
Lodge, Thomas, 165, 238, 362, 386n.; *Rosalynde*, 362, 363, 386n.
Loftis, John, 20, 29n., 390
London Figaro, 261
Lord High Admiral, *see* Nottingham, Charles Howard, Baron of Effingham
Louis VII (first husband of Elinor of Aquitaine), 89, 122
Love's Labour's Wonne (play attributed to Shakespeare), 56
Lucretius, 48
Luther, Martin, 68
Lyly, John, 34
Lyrical Ballads, see Coleridge, Samuel Taylor; and Wordsworth, William

Mabie, Hamilton Wright, 311-12
Mabinogion, The, 342
Macaulay, Thomas Babington, 342, 383n.
Machiavelli, Niccolò, 165, 194, 256
Mackintosh, James, 376n.
Macmillan's Magazine, 242, 318, 386n.
Macready, William Charles, 27n., 70, 118, 187-8, 381n., 388
Mad as a Hatter, see Marshall, Francis Albert
Maffei, Francesco Scipione, 375n.; *Merope*, 375n.
Magna Carta, 7, 64, 86, 95, 102, 129, 132, 137, 142, 164, 225-6, 237, 243, 248, 280, 291, 300, 338, 340
Malone, Edmond, viii, 8, 9, 10, 17, 19, 25n., 26nn., 31-41, 42-4, 45-9, 50-1, 56, 64, 88, 93, 97, 98, 99, 100, 101, 102, 125, 178, 209, 372, 372nn., 373nn., 375n., 376n., 377n., 381n., 382n., 390
Manchester Guardian, The, 307
Manheim, Michael, 30n.
Marbeck, Dr. Roger, 99
Margetson, W. H., 336
Maria, Infanta of Spain, 241
Marie Antoinette, 221
Marius the Epicurean, see Pater, Walter Horatio
Marlowe, Christopher, 40, 165, 276, 307, 308, 309, 311; *Tamburlaine*, 32, 216-17, 218, 219, 276, 309; *Edward II*, 310

Marshall, Francis Albert., viii, 11, 16, 27n., 261-4; *Mad as a Hatter*, 261; *Q.E.D., or, All a Mistake*, 261; *False Shame*, 261
Marston, John, 34, 50; *The Insatiate Countess*, 34, 50, 372n., 373n.
Martin, Sir Theodore, 268
Mary I, 177, 319
Mary, Queen of Scots, 93, 101, 209, 210, 305
Masefield, John, 17, 28n., 351-4
Mason, John Monck, 35, 40, 372n., 373n.
Massinger, Philip, 140, 141, 383n.; *The Duke of Milan*, 141; *A New Way to Pay Old Debts*, 383n.
Matchett, William H., 19, 21, 28nn., 29n., 388, 390
Mather, Cotton, 287
Mathias, T. J., 50
Matilda, Empress (wife to Geoffrey, 1st Earl of Anjou), 35
Matilda of Scotland (wife to Henry I; great-grandmother to Constance of Brittany), 76
Matthews, James Brander, 11, 18, 367-9, 386, 386n.
Maude, Empress, *see* Matilda, Empress
Mazarin, Jules, Cardinal, 157, 234, 380n.
Meadows, Kenny, 136
Medina Sidonia, Alonso Pérez de Guzmán, Duke of, 210, 305
Melchiori, Giorgio, 372n., 373n.
Meres, Francis, 32, 50, 56, 97, 98, 99, 134, 136, 148; *Palladis Tamia: Wit's Treasury*, 50, 148
Merope, *see* Euripides; Maffei, Francesco Scipione; Alfieri, Vittorio; Voltaire, François Marie Alouet de; Zeno, Apostolo; Hill, Aaron; *and* Jeffreys, George
Merope (character), 7, 77, 107
Metamorphoses, *see* Ovid
Metropolitan Magazine, 82
Mill, John Stuart, 296
Miller, Mary Ruth, 86
Mills, Charles, 64
Milton, John, 109, 318, 334, 379n.; *Paradise Lost*, 109, 318
'Milton! thou shouldst be living at this hour', *see* Wordsworth, William
Mitford, Mary Russell, 202
Modern Language Association of America, viii
Molière (i.e., Jean Baptiste Poquelin), 367
Morgan, James Appleton, viii, 27n., 28n., 275-9, 384, 384nn.
Morley, Henry, 14, 17, 28n., 257-60
Morrison, the Reverend A. J. W., 54-5, 128, 130-4, 374n., 383n.
Morrison, Mary, 296
Morton, the Reverend Nicholas, 209-10
Moulton, Richard Green, ix, 324-8, 385, 385n.
Munro, John James, ix, 362-6, 386
Mutschmann, H., 19, 28n., 387

Napoleon I, 9, 27n.
National Police Gazette, 233
Nelson, Horatio Nelson, 217
New Comedy, *see* Bale, John
New English Dictionary, 223

New English Drama, The, 62
New Monthly Magazine, The, 82, 88, 377n.
New Shakespeare Society (i.e., 'New Shakspere Society'), vii, 15, 16, 28n., 239, 242
New Shakespeareana (Shakespeare Society of New York), viii
New Variorum Shakespeare, viii, 370
New Way to Pay Old Debts, A, *see* Massinger, Philip
New York American, The, 136
New York Times, The, 367
Nibelungenlied, 339
Nichola, Lady, 167
Nichols, John, 375n.
Nicolai, Otto, 173, 380n.
Nicolas, Sir Nicholas Harris, 375n.
Nieremberg, Juan Eusebio, 372n.
Niobe, 77, 110, 380n.
Noctes Shakespearianæ (i.e., '*Noctes Shakspearianæ*', Winchester College), vii, 255
North British Review, 207
Nottingham, Charles Howard, Baron of Effingham (Lord High Admiral), 33, 99
Novello, Mary Victoria, *see* Clarke, Mary Cowden

Occam, William of, 255, 383n.
'Ode on a Distant Prospect of Eton College', *see* Gray, Thomas
O'Neill, Eliza, 72
O'Neill, Eugene, 332
Oracle, The, 73
Otway, Thomas, 1
Outlook, The, 311
Ovid, 48, 49, 373n.; *Metamorphoses*, 49, 373n.
Oxberry, William, 9, 27n., 62-3, 374

Palmer, John, 29n., 390
Palmer, (John?), (English actor), 375n.
Palladis Tamia: Wit's Treasury, *see* Meres, Francis
Pandosto, *see* Greene, Robert
Papal Tyranny in the Reign of King John, *see* Cibber, Colley
Paradise Lost, *see* Milton, John
Paradisus Amissus, *see* Dobson, William
Paris, Matthew, 21, 91, 94, 95, 129, 144, 166, 376nn., 378n., 380n., 387; *Historia*, 376n., 387
Parker, Theodore, 220
Parma, Alessandro Farnese, Duke of, 305
Parsons, the Reverend Robert (pseud. 'Andreas Philopater'), 210, 381n., 382n.; *Leicester's Commonwealth* (probable author), 209, 381n.; *see also* Verstegan, Richard
Pater, Walter Horatio, ix, 15, 270-1, 321, 384, 385nn.; *Marius the Epicurean*, 270
Paulett (also 'Paulet'), Sir Amyas, 305
Peck, D. C., 381n.
Peele, George, 34, 165, 238, 365, 386n.; *David and Bethsabe*, 386n.
Pepys, Samuel, 1
Perkins Folio, 68
Petronius, 48

Phaedrus, 48
Philip II (King of Spain), 210, 305
Philopater, Andreas, *see* Parsons, the Reverend Robert
Pichot, Amédée, 142
Pius V, Pope, 335
Plato, 252
Pleasures of Hope, The, *see* Campbell, Thomas
Poet Lore, vii, 345
Poetics, *see* Aristotle
Polymetis, *see* Spence, Joseph
Pope, Alexander, 1, 2, 3-4, 8, 19, 24n., 25nn., 26n., 34, 36, 39, 40, 42, 46, 47, 68, 372n., 373nn., 374n., 388, 389; *An Essay on Man*, 381n.; *Virgilius Restauratus*, 39
Porter, Charlotte Endymion, ix, 16-17, 21, 345-7
Portocarrero, Luis Manuel Fernandez de, Cardinal, 157, 380n.
Praetorius, Charles, 242, 386n.
Price, Cecil, 373n., 384n.
Price, Jonathan Reeve, 22, 390
Promos and Cassandra (George Whetstone), 239
Protestantism, 3, 19-20, 27n., 28n., 147, 171, 176-7, 190, 231, 233, 235, 236, 244, 247, 253, 262, 264, 276, 287-8, 296, 301-4, 308, 309, 314, 331, 334-5
Prouty, Charles Tyler, 386n.
Putnam's Magazine, 175
Pylades, 211

Q.E.D., or, All a Mistake, *see* Marshall, Francis Albert
Queen Elizabeth, *see* Elizabeth I

Rachel, 203
Rackin, Phyllis, 23-4, 390
Raich, J. M., 306, 385n.
Ralegh, Sir Walter, 51
Raleigh, Sir Walter, *see* Ralegh, Sir Walter
Raleigh, Sir Walter (twentieth-century literary scholar), 272
Ralli, Augustus, 26n., 387
Ranald, Margaret Loftus, 30n., 390
Ravaillac, François, 241
Ravenscroft, Edward, 1
Reed, Henry, 12-14, 17, 152-7, 379
Reed, Isaac, 42, 45, 57, 374nn.
Remains, *see* Camden, William
Richard I (Cœur de Lion), 13, 24n., 35, 55, 65, 69, 71, 76, 89, 90, 109, 122, 123, 129, 132, 134, 138-9, 143, 144, 153, 154, 161, 166, 184, 196, 227-8, 244, 246-7, 250, 258, 264, 273, 281, 285, 294, 297, 300, 307, 316, 322, 325, 331, 338, 345, 352, 358, 363, 364, 381n., 384n.
Richards, Henry Luard, 381n.
Richelieu, Armand Jean du Plessis de, Cardinal, 157, 234, 380n.
Riches, William de, 166
Ridley, M. R., 29n., 390
Ridolfi, Roberto di, 210

Ripariis, Margareta de (also 'Margaret de Rivers'), 166
Ritson, Joseph, 8, 26n., 39, 42-4, 125, 372n., 373, 390
'Rob Roy's Grave', *see* Wordsworth, William
Robertson, Frederick W., 355
Roches, William des, 90
Roderick, Richard, 25n., 390
Roland de la Platière, Jean Marie, 382n.
Roland de la Platière, Manon Jeanne Philipon, 221, 382n.
Rolfe, W. J., ix
Roman Brother, The, see Heraud, John Abraham
Roman Catholicism, 2-3, 7, 11, 14, 19-20, 25n., 27nn., 28nn., 40, 65, 71, 89, 91, 102, 127, 130-3, 141, 147, 157, 163-4, 176-7, 182, 190, 198, 207, 209-11, 224, 226, 229-32, 233-7, 242, 244-5, 246, 247, 256, 264, 265, 276-7, 287-8, 296, 298, 301-6, 308, 326, 331, 334-5, 340
Romanticism, vii, 8-9, 54, 59, 82
Rosalynde, see Lodge, Thomas
Roscellinus, 256, 383n.
Rosciad, The, see Churchill, Charles
Rose, Edward, 16, 21, 28n., 239, 242-8, 313-14, 363, 383, 383n., 384n., 385n.; *Vice Versa*, 242; *Under the Red Robe*, 242; *Souvenir of The Prisoner of Zenda*, 242
Rowe, Nicholas, 24n., 25n., 40, 42, 373n., 388
Rowley, William, 3-4, 25nn., 34, 68, 137, 144
Roxana, 7
Ruggiero degli Ubaldini, Archbishop, *see* Ubaldini, Ruggiero degli, Archbishop
Rümelin, Gustav, 267
Ruskin, John, 266, 383n.,; *Sesame and Lilies*, 383n.
Ruysdael, Jacob Van, 139, 379n.
Rymer, Thomas, 1, 24n.

Salter, F. M., 29n., 390
Sanders, George, 209
Sankey, the Reverend William, 28n.
Sarrazin, Gregor, ix
Saturday Review, The, 348
Savile, Henry, 376n.
Schelling, Felix Emanuel, 16, 322-3, 385
Schlegel, August Wilhelm von, ix, 8-9, 12, 28n., 54-5, 59, 64, 91, 101, 104, 128, 148, 158, 336, 374, 374n., 377n., 379n.
Schmidt, Alexander, ix
Schmitz, L. Dora, 13, 128-35
Schoenbaum, Samuel, 384n.
Second Folio (1632), 28n., 36, 39, 42-4, 46-9, 377n.
Sedge, Douglas, vii
Selby, (Mrs. Charles?), (English actress), 118, 123
Seneca, Lucius Annaeus (the elder), 48, 374n.; *Controversiae*, 374n.
Sesame and Lilies, see Ruskin, John
Shadwell, Thomas, 1
Shakespeare, Hamnet, 8, 17, 19, 32, 51, 98, 240, 241, 288, 296, 329, 348, 350, 353
Shakespeare Jahrbuch (Deutsche Shakespeare Gesellschaft), viii

Shakespeare Society, vii, 378n.
Shakespeare Society of New York, viii, 275
Shakespeariana, vii,
Shattuck, Charles, 27n., 388
Shaw, George Bernard, 348
Shelley, Percy Bysshe, 212, 249, 336
Sherbo, Arthur, 25nn., 26nn., 45, 372nn., 373n., 374nn., 377nn., 381n., 387
Sheridan, Richard Brinsley, 373n., 384n.; *The Critic*, 48, 384n.
Siddons, Sarah, 9-10, 11-12, 27nn., 53, 72, 73-4, 82-5, 87, 116-18, 119-20, 149, 193, 268
Sider, J. W., xvi, 24n., 388
Sidney, Sir Philip, 10
Silent Woman, The, *see* Jonson, Ben
Simple Story, A, *see* Inchbald, Elizabeth
Simpson, Evelyn, 372n., 374n., 380n.
Simpson, Percy, 372n., 374n., 380n.
Simpson, Richard, ix, 14, 15, 19, 20, 27n., 207-11, 224, 262, 301, 306, 362, 381, 381n., 382nn., 385n.
Singer, Samuel Weller, 9, 68-9, 158, 374
Skottowe, Augustine, 9, 64-7, 268, 374
Smallwood, R. L., 28n., 388
Smith, D. Nichol, 387
Smith, George Charles Moore, 16, 313-17, 385
Smith, Logan Pearsall, 29n., 390
Smith, Sir Thomas, 95, 376n.
Smith, William, 375n.
Snider, Denton Jaques, 12-13, 27n., 225-32, 382, 382n.
Socrates, 350
Solomon, King, 207, 305
Solyman and Perseda (Anon.), (Thomas Kyd?), 34
Southey, Robert, 98, 99, 198, 212, 377n.
Souvenir of The Prisoner of Zenda, *see* Rose, Edward
Spanish Tragedy, The, *see* Kyd, Thomas
Spectator (London), 175
Spedding, James, ix
Spelling Reformer, 238
Spence, Joseph, 48, 373n.; *Polymetis*, 48, 373n.
Spenser, Edmund, 25n.; *The Faerie Queene*, 25n.
Spevack, Marvin, ix
Spirit of the Times, The, 233
Statius, 48-9
Stauffer, Donald A., 29n., 390
Staunton, Howard, viii
Stavisky, Aron Y., 14, 28n., 388
Steevens, George, viii, 8, 26nn., 31, 35, 37-8, 39, 42, 45-9, 50, 57, 73, 88, 98, 137, 372nn., 373, 373nn., 374n., 379n., 388
Stow, John, 88, 270
Strachey, Lytton, ix
Stuart, Lady Arabella, 209, 210
Stuart, Charles Edward, 2

Stubblefield, Charles, 29n., 390
Stukeley (also 'Stukely'), Captain Thomas, 34, 207
Swinburne, Algernon Charles, 15, 16, 215-19, 223
Symmons, Charles, 68

Taine, Hippolyte Adolphe, 296
Tamburlaine, see Marlowe, Christopher
Tantalus, 110, 380n.
Tate, Nahum, 1
Temple, Sir William, 88
Tennyson, Alfred, 249
Theobald, Lewis, 2, 35-6, 38, 39, 42, 125, 178-80, 372nn., 381n., 388
Theophrastus, 256
Thierry, Jacques Nicolas Augustin, 376n.
Thouars, Guy de (also 'Guy de Tours'; third husband of Constance of Brittany), 66, 76, 81, 90
Thucydides, 375n.
Tieck, Dorothea, 54
Tieck, Ludwig, 54, 134, 378n., 379n.
Tillyard, E. M. W., 22, 29n., 390
Timber: or, Discoveries, see Jonson, Ben
Titian (Tiziano Vecellio), 77
Tonson, Jacob, 24n.
Tours, Guy de, *see* Thouars, Guy de
Tragicall Historye of Romeus and Juliet, The, see Brooke, Arthur
Traister, Barbara H., 30n.
Transactions (New Shakespeare Society), vii, 15, 301, 386n.
Trent, William P., 175
Troades, see Euripides
Troubled Waters, see Warner, Beverley, Ellison
Troublesome Raigne of King John, The (Anon.), 3-4, 7, 16, 19-20, 24n., 25n., 26n., 31-2, 34, 35, 50, 64-7, 86, 87, 88-9, 91, 93, 95, 97-8, 99, 100, 103, 108, 129, 134, 137-9, 140, 141, 144, 147, 163, 165, 176-8, 190, 193, 196, 198-9, 200, 201, 207-8, 224, 231, 236, 238-9, 241, 242-8, 251, 257-8, 262, 265, 268, 275-9, 284, 286, 287-9, 290, 291-2, 294, 296, 298-300, 302-5, 308-10, 311, 313-14, 315, 318, 319, 330-1, 332, 333, 334-5, 337, 338, 339, 340, 342, 344, 346, 347, 348, 352, 362-6, 367, 369, 370, 371, 374n., 375n., 376n., 377n., 378nn., 380n., 381n., 383n., 385nn., 385n., 386nn., 388
True Chronicle Historie of King Leir, The (Anon.), 362, 363, 364, 365, 386nn.
Tudor Myth, the, 22
Tuke, Daniel H., 168
Turner, J. M. W., 104, 377n.
Tyrwhitt, Thomas, 36, 44, 372n.

Ubaldini, Ruggiero degli, Archbishop, 76
Ugolino, Count of Donoratico, *see*, Gherardesca, Ugolino della
Ulrici, Hermann, ix, 10, 11, 13, 28n., 128-35, 266-7, 378, 378n., 379n., 381n., 383nn.
Under the Red Robe, see Rose, Edward
Upton, John, 3, 4, 5, 25n., 390
Ure, Peter, 384n.

Valpy, Richard, 26n., 388
Van de Water, Julia, 21, 390
Van Doren, Mark, 29n., 390
Vaughan, Virginia Mason, 29n., 30n., 390
Vecellio, Tiziano, *see* Titian
Velz, John W., 24n.
Verplanck, Gulian Crommelin., viii, 136-9, 378, 378n.
Verstegan, Richard (i.e., Robert Parsons), 209, 381n.; *A Declaration of the True Causes of the Great Troubles*, 381n.
Vice Versa, see Rose, Edward
Vickers, Brian, vii-x, xv, 24n., 25nn., 26nn., 45, 388
Vickery, Willis, 275
Victoria I, 101, 378n.
Victorianism, vii, ix, 13, 15, 17, 21, 28n., 270, 348
Videna, see Heraud, John Abraham
Virgil, 373n.; *The Aeneid*, 74, 373n.
Virgilius Restauratus, see Pope, Alexander
Voltaire, François Marie Arouet de, 194, 299, 375n.; *Merope*, 375n., 381n.

Wagner, Adolph, 64
Warburton, William, 2, 4, 42, 93, 101, 102, 209, 377n., 381n., 388
Warner, Beverly Ellison, 27n., 284-6, 384n.; *Troubled Waters*, 284
Watson, William, 210, 385n.; *Important Considerations*, 210, 385n.
Webster, John, 217; *The Duchess of Malfi*, 217; *The White Devil*, 217
Wedderburn, Alexander, 384n.
Weiss, John, 11, 15, 220-2, 382
Wells, Benjamin W., 175
Welsted, Leonard, 25n., 390
Wendell, Barrett, 11, 16, 287, 384
Wendover, Roger of, 21, 376n., 378n., 379n., 380n., 388; *Flowers of History*, 376n., 378n., 380n., 388
Wentersdorf, Karl, 19, 28n., 387
Westminster Review, The, 111
Weyman, Stanley, 242
White Devil, The, see Webster, John
White, Diana, 296
White, Edward J. 27n., 388
White, Richard Grant, viii, 10, 27n., 175-80, 380
Whitman, Walt, 265
Whole Contention betweene the Two Famous Houses, Lancaster and Yorke, The (1619), *see Henry VI* plays (II Shakespeare's Works)
Whyte, Edward, 34
Widomar (also 'Vidomar'), Viscount of Limoges, 7, 65, 89, 129, 144, 166, 375n.
Wilde, Oscar, 348
Wilkes, George, 27n., 233-7, 382
Wilkes' Spirit of the Times, 233
Wilson, John Dover, 388
Wilson, F. P., 387

Winkfield, Sir Edward, 33
Wiseman, Nicholas Patrick Stephen, Cardinal, 207
Wixson, Douglas C., 22, 390
Wolsey, Thomas, Cardinal, *see* Wolsey (historical figure) (II Shakespeare's Works)
Woodring, Carl, 26n., 380n., 388
Woodson, William C., 45
Wordsworth, William, 98, 101, 152, 198, 202, 212, 249, 379nn.; 'Rob Roy's Grave', 152, 379n.; 'It is not to be thought of that the Flood', 379n.; 'Milton! thou shouldst be living at this hour', 379n.; *Lyrical Ballads*, 377n.
Wright, William Aldis, viii, 175

Xantippe (also 'Xanthippe'), 7, 350
'Ye Mariners of England', *see* Campbell, Thomas
Year's Work in English Studies, The, 290

Zeno, Apostolo, 375n.; *Merope*, 375n.
Zimmern, Helen, 280